CAMBRIDGE:
PRESS OF JOHN WILSON AND SON.

TO THE

HON. ISAAC F. REDFIELD, LL.D.,

WHOSE LABORS HAVE ILLUSTRATED THE JURISPRUDENCE OF TWO COUNTRIES AND WHOSE KINDLY SYMPATHIES ENDEAR HIM TO THE YOUNG, EVEN MORE THAN HIS UNWEARIED PATIENCE AND INDUSTRY COMMAND THEIR RESPECT,

THIS WORK IS GRATEFULLY DEDICATED

BY JAMES SCHOULER.

PREFACE.

THE purpose of the writer, in the present treatise, is to furnish a clear, accurate, and comprehensive analysis of the law of the domestic relations, as administered in England and the United States at the present day.

To accomplish this purpose, and at the same time not to transcend the limits of a single volume, was not easy. It became necessary to treat of principles rather than details, and to avoid matters of local practice altogether. A few topics, such as curtesy and dower, which are fully discussed in other treatises, have been for the same reason touched upon lightly, and the work, on the whole, made elementary in its method of treatment, though at the same time practical. The lawyer who misses elaborate head-notes and subdivisions will yet find assistance in a full index and table of contents: and what has been lost in this respect is gained in subject-matter. Especial pains have been taken to present in this work such topics, pertaining to the general subject, as were not easily accessible elsewhere.

The writer has freely consulted the valuable law libraries of the Suffolk Bar, at Boston, and of Congress, at Washington, — the latter being the most extensive in this country. Among works which have afforded him the greatest assistance, are Macqueen on Husband and Wife, Peachey on Marriage Settlements, Macpherson on Infancy, and Smith on Master and Servant, — treatises of acknowledged merit in England, though little known in the United States. Other books, more familiar, which need not be enumerated at length, furnished valuable material in certain parts of this work, as the foot-notes sufficiently indicate. The writer deems it just to himself to add, that the time-honored treatise of Judge Reeve has been found of little service, — the radical changes of the last fifty years rendering new labor, new materials, and a new plan of treatment absolutely essential to meet the growing wants of the age.

If, on the whole, the present work is found to answer its purpose, in the judgment of his professional brethren, the writer will cheerfully acknowledge such errors and blemishes as the judicious critic may kindly point out.

JAMES SCHOULER.

WASHINGTON, D.C., April 30, 1870.

CONTENTS.

PART I.

INTRODUCTORY CHAPTER.

PART II.

HUSBAND AND WIFE.

CHAPTER I.

MARRIAGE.

CHAPTER II.

THE GENERAL DISABILITIES OF COVERTURE.

CHAPTER III.

THE EFFECT OF COVERTURE UPON THE WIFE'S DEBTS AND CONTRACTS.

CHAPTER IV.

THE EFFECT OF COVERTURE UPON THE WIFE'S INJURIES AND FRAUDS.

CHAPTER V.

THE EFFECT OF COVERTURE UPON THE WIFE'S PERSONAL PROPERTY.

CHAPTER VI.

THE EFFECT OF COVERTURE UPON THE WIFE'S CHATTELS REAL AND REAL ESTATE.

CHAPTER VII.

COMMON-LAW RIGHTS AND DISABILITIES OF THE HUSBAND ON HIS WIFE'S DECEASE.

CHAPTER VIII.

COMMON-LAW RIGHTS AND DISABILITIES OF THE WIFE ON HER HUSBAND'S DECEASE.

CHAPTER IX.

THE WIFE'S DOWER AND HOMESTEAD RIGHTS.

CHAPTER X.

THE WIFE'S SEPARATE ESTATE: ENGLISH DOCTRINE.

CHAPTER XI.

THE WIFE'S SEPARATE ESTATE: AMERICAN DOCTRINE.

CHAPTER XII.

THE WIFE'S DOMINION OVER HER SEPARATE ESTATE.

English Doctrine.

American Doctrine.

CHAPTER XIII.

THE WIFE'S PIN-MONEY, SEPARATE EARNINGS, AND POWER TO TRADE.

CHAPTER XIV.

THE WILLS OF MARRIED WOMEN.

CHAPTER XV.

ANTENUPTIAL SETTLEMENTS.

CHAPTER XVI.

POSTNUPTIAL SETTLEMENTS, AND GIFTS BETWEEN HUSBAND AND WIFE.

CHAPTER XVII.

SEPARATION AND DIVORCE.

PART III.

PARENT AND CHILD.

CHAPTER I.

OF LEGITIMATE CHILDREN IN GENERAL.

CHAPTER II.

THE DUTIES OF PARENTS.

CHAPTER III.

THE RIGHTS OF PARENTS.

CHAPTER IV.

THE PARENT'S RIGHT OF ACTION FOR THE CHILD'S INJURIES.

CHAPTER V.

DUTIES AND RIGHTS OF CHILDREN, WITH REFERENCE TO THEIR PARENTS.

CHAPTER VI.

ILLEGITIMATE CHILDREN.

PART IV.

GUARDIAN AND WARD.

CHAPTER I.

OF GUARDIANS IN GENERAL.

CHAPTER II.

APPOINTMENT OF GUARDIANS.

CHAPTER III.

TERMINATION OF THE GUARDIAN'S AUTHORITY.

CHAPTER IV.

NATURE OF THE GUARDIAN'S OFFICE.

CHAPTER V.

RIGHTS AND DUTIES OF GUARDIANS CONCERNING THE WARD'S PERSON.

CHAPTER VI.

RIGHTS AND DUTIES OF THE GUARDIAN AS TO THE WARD'S ESTATE.

CHAPTER VII.

SALES OF THE WARD'S REAL ESTATE.

CHAPTER VIII.

THE GUARDIAN'S BOND, INVENTORY, AND ACCOUNTS.

CHAPTER IX.

RIGHTS AND LIABILITIES OF THE WARD.

PART V.

INFANCY.

CHAPTER I.

THE GENERAL DISABILITIES OF INFANTS.

CHAPTER II.

ACTS VOID AND VOIDABLE.

CHAPTER III.

ACTS BINDING UPON THE INFANT.

CHAPTER IV.

THE INJURIES AND FRAUDS OF INFANTS.

CHAPTER V.

RATIFICATION AND AVOIDANCE OF CONTRACTS.

CHAPTER VI.

ACTIONS BY AND AGAINST INFANTS.

PART VI.

MASTER AND SERVANT.

CHAPTER I.

NATURE OF THE RELATION; HOW CREATED AND HOW TERMINATED.

CHAPTER II.

MUTUAL OBLIGATIONS OF MASTER AND SERVANT.

CHAPTER III.

RIGHTS AND LIABILITIES OF THE SERVANT AS TO THIRD PERSONS.

CHAPTER IV.

RIGHTS AND LIABILITIES OF THE MASTER AS TO THIRD PERSONS.

TABLE OF CASES CITED.

A.

D.

G.

I.

J.

K.

L.

O.

P.

Q.

R.

S.

U.

DOMESTIC RELATIONS.

THE DOMESTIC RELATIONS.

PART I.

INTRODUCTORY CHAPTER.

THE law of the domestic relations is the law of the household or family, as distinguished from that of individuals in the external concerns of life. Five leading topics are embraced under this head: *First*, husband and wife. *Second*, parent and child. *Third*, guardian and ward. *Fourth*, infancy. *Fifth*, master and servant. These will be successively considered in the present treatise.

Our general rule of classification is borrowed from Kent.[1] But other writers on the domestic relations have analyzed their subject differently. Blackstone omits infancy as a topic distinct from parent and child, and hence makes but four divisions.[2] The same is true of Reeve.[3] Such a method of treatment answered the purpose of these writers sufficiently; but since their day the topic of guardian and ward has grown into importance, giving occasion to the discussion of many principles which apply as well to parent and child, for which reason it is found better to draw off from both what is peculiar to neither d make the new heading of infancy. Bingham, on the other hand, wrote a treatise in which the only divisions observed were those of infancy and coverture.[4] This plan would be found defective for a work like the present; for, in the first place, the subject of master and servant must be ignored

1 2 Kent Com. Lec. 26–32.
2 1 Bl. Com. Lec. 14–17.
3 Reeve's Dom. Rel.
4 Bing. Inf. & Cov.

altogether; and, secondly, that of guardian and ward cannot receive the distinctive treatment it deserves. Besides, the very juxtaposition of two such words as infancy and coverture suggests a similitude neither flattering to woman, nor in accordance with the present law of husband and wife; as will fully appear hereafter. Fraser, who wrote for readers of the civil, or rather the Scotch law, while otherwise classifying like Blackstone, adds the relation of master and apprentice to that of master and servant,[1] in which respect his example is not to be imitated by common-law writers. Upon the whole, therefore, the rule of Kent seems to us the preferable one, as being concise, comprehensive, and well adapted to the present state of English and American law.

It is curious to notice that all of these writers — and there are none else of standard authority who profess to occupy the whole subject — plunge at once into the law of their leading topics with nothing by way of general introduction; nothing to indicate to the reader whither he proposes leading him. Not one has attempted to draw the chart which shall determine his legal bearings. Nor is a definition of the term domestic relations to be found in the books above specified. Indeed were it not for the title-page of Reeve's work, and a few casual passages, in Kent's Commentaries, where the same words occur, one might ask how the expression domestic relations crept into general use among lawyers. Blackstone uses the terms "private economical relations," and "relations in private life;" words which of themselves would seem to give a much wider scope to our subject.[2] But Blackstone, at all times, manifests a strong predilection for independent analysis, with special reference moreover to the arrangement of his course of lectures, and in this particular instance the context as well as the classification seems to show that "domestic relations" was the topic in his mind. Fraser's complete title is

[1] Fras. Dom. Rel. (Scotch). 2 vols.

[2] 1 Bl. Com. Lec. 14. The writer had just finished discussing at length the rights and duties of persons as standing in the public relations of magistrates and people; and the word private marks the desired contrast.

"personal and domestic relations." Notwithstanding all this it is certain that "domestic relations" is now the well-sanctioned title of that law which embraces the topics specified by us at the outset; as those who examine the digests of reported cases, and the codes of our leading States, can testify. To legal precision in this respect, Reeve certainly contributed not a little by the choice of a suitable title for his volume, so long the standard text-book for English and American students.

Starting then with a definition simple, natural, and well adapted to the materials in hand, we next ask what are the proper limitations of our subject; what should a text-book on the English and American law of the domestic relations comprise. As to three of our topics, — husband and wife, parent and child, and infancy, — the question is easily answered. Their very names convey a distinct significance even to the mind of the unprofessional reader. Except it be in the meaning of the word infancy, which the law applies to all persons not arrived at majority, but popular usage restricts to the period of helplessness, all intelligent persons agree in the general use of the terms we have employed. And so strong are the moral obligations which attend marriage and the training of offspring, so intimately blended with the welfare and happiness of mankind are the ties of wife and child, that scarcely any one grows up without some knowledge of the general principles of law applicable to these topics, and particularly of such of the rights and duties as concern the person rather than the property. For positive law but enforces the mandates of the law of nature, and develops rather than creates a system.

Yet even here it should be observed by the professional reader, that the term husband and wife is acquiring at law a more limited and technical sense than formerly. The idea of marriage involves both the entrance to the relation and the relation itself; and akin to marriage celebration is the dissolution of marriage by divorce, or what we may term the exit to the relation. Hence marriage and divorce constitute an important topic by themselves; and we find treatises which profess to deal with these alone. The rights and duties which grow out of the marriage relation, on the other hand, still remain for separate discussion; the consequence of the celebration; the effect of marriage upon the property of each; the personal status of the parties; in short, what new legal responsibilities are assumed and what legal privileges are gained by the two persons who have once voluntarily united as husband and wife. It is to this latter subdivision rather than the former that the title of husband and wife seems at the present day to apply. Reeve devotes but a brief chapter to marriage and divorce. Kent separates the subdivisions completely, applying the title husband and wife as above. Yet Blackstone, writing before either, had devoted two-thirds of his lecture on husband and wife to the treatment of marriage and divorce alone, and very briefly disposed of the rights and disabilities of the marriage union under the same general heading. The many and rapid changes to which the entire law of husband and wife has been latterly subjected; the growth of divorce legislation on the one hand, and of property legislation for married women on the other, fully justifies a subdivision so important. We shall subordinate, then, the topic of marriage and divorce to that of the marriage status, following in this respect the modern legal usage; at the same time noting that if some special term could be coined to distinguish the subdivision husband and wife from that general division which bears the same name, our analysis would be more exact.

As to guardian and ward, the limitations of our treatise are not so easily marked out. In respect of the domestic relations, the guardian is a sort of temporary parent, created by the law, to supply to young children the place of a natural protector. But the term guardian is used rather indiscriminately in these days with reference to all who need protection at the law. Thus we have guardians of insane persons; guardians of spendthrifts; and even guardians of the poor. Blackstone treats of such guardians under the head of public relations; and certainly they do not fall within the clear scope of private or domestic relations. Yet the legal principles applicable to one class of guardians frequently extend as well to all others; and we shall hardly expect in these pages to trace with distinctness that shadowy line which separates the temporary parent from the town officer; nor would the consulting lawyer expect us to do so. Again, a guardian's duties are chiefly with respect to property; and herein they so nearly resemble those of testamentary trustees that one frequently finds himself gliding unconsciously from the law of the family into the law of trusts.

With the last topic of the domestic relations — that of master and servant — the rule of classification becomes even more uncertain. If servants connected with the household were alone to be considered in a treatise upon the domestic relations, the modern cases would be simple and few; but no writer has presumed to limit himself to such narrow bounds. In former centuries, this relation had a marked significance. In these days, we dislike to call any man master. The recent abolition of slavery in the United States has wellnigh removed all traces of an institution known to the ancient Roman empire, elsewhere recognized as the common barbarian accompaniment of barbarian triumphs; and in spirit, if not in the letter, once fastened upon the common law, while the feudal system lasted. As one of the domestic relations, this topic of master and servant is of little present importance in England or America; although it has doubtless an existence. In its analogies, however, or as a relation *sub modo*, master and servant has features which the courts constantly regard. Apprentices are, without much violation of principle, included under this head; they are generally bound out during minority and brought up in families. Clerks are not so readily confined within the circle of domestic relations as formerly; and the same is to be said of factors, bailiffs, and stewards. The *em-*

ployés of a corporation are frequently designated as servants; so are laborers generally. But it cannot be denied that master and servant is rather a repulsive title, and fast losing favor in this republican country; that as one of the purely domestic relations it rarely attracts attention; and that in sounding its legal depths one often loses sight of his landmarks, and finds himself drifting out into the more general subject of principal and agent.

Whether we consult the facts of history or the inspirations of human reason, the family may be justly pronounced the earliest of all social institutions. Man, in a state of nature and alone, was subject to no civil restrictions. He was independent of all laws, except those of God. But when man united with woman, both were brought under certain restraints for their mutual well-being. The propagation of offspring afforded the only means whereby society could hope to grow into a permanent and compact system. Hence the sexual cravings of nature were speedily brought under wholesome regulations; as otherwise the human race must have perished in the cradle. Natural law, or the teachings of a divine providence, supplied these regulations. Families preceded nations. These families at first lived under the paternal government of the person who was their patriarch or chief. But as they increased, they likewise divided; their interests became conflicting, and hostilities arose. Hence when men came afterwards to unite for their common defence, they composed a national body, and agreed to be governed by the will of him, or those on whom they had conferred authority. Thus did government originate. And government, for its legitimate purposes, placed restrictions upon the governed; which restrictions thenceforth were to apply to individuals in both their family and social relations.[1] But the law of the domestic relations is nevertheless older than that of civil society. In fact nations themselves are often regarded as so many families; and the very name which is

[1] See Burlamaqui Nat. Law, ch. iv. §§ 6, 9.

placed at the head of this work, the legislator constantly applies to the public concerns of his own country as contrasted with those of foreign governments.

The supremacy of the law of family should not be forgotten. We come under the dominion of this law at the very moment of birth; we thus continue for a certain period, whether we will or no. Long after infancy has ceased the general obligations of parent and child may continue; for these last through life. Again we subject ourselves by marriage to the law of family; this time to find our responsibilities still further enlarged. And although the voluntary act of two parties brings them within the law, they cannot voluntarily retreat when so minded. To an unusual extent, therefore, is the law of family above and independent of the individual. Society provides the home; public policy fashions the system: and it remains for each one of us to place himself under rules which are, and must be, arbitrary.

So is the law of family universal in its adaptation. It deals directly with the individual. Its provisions are for man and woman; not for corporations or business firms. The ties of wife and child are for all classes and conditions; neither rank, wealth, nor social influence weighs heavily in the scales. To every one public law assigns a home or domicile; and this domicile determines not only the status, capacities, and rights of the person, but also his title to personal property. There is the political domicile, which limits the exercise of political rights. There is the forensic domicile, upon which is founded the jurisdiction of the courts. There is the civil domicile, which is acquired by residence and continuance in a certain place. The place of birth determines the domicile in the first instance; and one continues until another is properly chosen. The domicile of the wife follows that of the husband; the domicile of the infant may be changed by the parent.[1] Thus does the law of domicile conform to the law of nature.

[1] See 1 Burge Col. & For. Laws 32, 33.

The most interesting and important of the domestic relations is that of husband and wife. The law of England and America, on this topic, is now undergoing a remarkable change; and so unsettled are its principles at the present time, that the writer has felt constrained to depart somewhat from the usual plan of law treatises, adopting what might be termed a consecutive or historical arrangement of his materials; since otherwise the subject would furnish to the reader's mind little else than a series of unreconciled contradictions. To show clearly why the later cases conflict with the earlier, will at least aid the future legislator and jurist in their efforts to place the law of husband and wife upon a firm and just basis; and meanwhile afford to the practising lawyer all the assistance which he can reasonably expect.

This confused state of the law of husband and wife results from a contest still going on between two opposing schemes, for adjusting the property rights of the married parties. The one is the common-law scheme; the other that of the civil law. The former is at the basis of our jurisprudence, English and American. The latter has had a powerful influence in modern times, moulding the doctrines of the equity tribunals and shaping recent legislation. Let us examine these schemes separately.

The common-law scheme makes unity in the marriage relation its cardinal point. But to secure this unity the law starts with the assumption that the wife's legal existence becomes suspended or extinguished during the marriage state; it sacrifices her property interests, and places her almost absolutely within her husband's keeping, so far as her civil rights are concerned. Her fortunes pass by marriage into her husband's hands, for temporary or permanent enjoyment, as the case may be; she cannot earn for herself, nor, in general, contract, sue, or be sued in her own right; and this because she is not in legal contemplation a person. The husband loses little or nothing of his own independence by marriage; but in order to distribute the matrimonial burdens with some approach to equality, the law compels him to pay debts on his wife's account, which he never in fact contracted, not only where she is held to be his agent by legal implication, but whenever it happens that she has brought him by marriage outstanding debts without the corresponding means of paying them. Husband and wife take certain interests in one another's lands, such as curtesy and dower, which become consummate upon survivorship. In general, their property rights are summarily adjusted by the law with reference rather to precision than principle. On the whole, however, the advantages are with the husband; and he is permitted to lord it over the wife with a somewhat despotic sway: as the old title of this subject — *baron and feme* — plainly indicates. Yet marriage stood well at the common law, and the Anglo-Saxon home has long been proverbial for peace and purity. This is partly because of the liberal tendencies of the race, that love of justice and personal independence which always characterized it, and the steadfast disposition of the courts both to administer the unwritten law impartially, and to extend and adapt its provisions to the ever-changing wants of society. Even in feudal times woman was the object of reverent esteem, if not of idolatry; her weakness made men all the more zealous to cherish and defend her; and elevated to the pedestal of honor, the wife stood perhaps as securely as she ever can upon the prosaic ground of legal equality.

The civil-law scheme pays little regard to the theoretic unity of a married pair. It looks rather to the personal independence of both husband and wife. Each is to be protected in the enjoyment of property rights. In the most polished ages of Roman jurisprudence, we find therefore that husband and wife were regarded as distinct persons, with separate rights, and capable of holding distinct and separate estates. The wife was comparatively free from all civil disabilities. She was alone responsible for her own debts; she was competent to sue and be sued on her own contracts; nor could the husband subject her or her property to any liability for his debts or engagements.[1] Whether in setting at naught that identity of interests which is essential to domestic happiness, such a scheme is fatally defective, need not here be discussed. Certain it is, however, that the policy of the Roman empire in respect of the marriage institution furnishes by no means an example of marked success, whether we regard its effect upon either husband or wife. Wide-spread incestuous intercourse, licentiousness, most loathsome and unnatural, followed in the wake of marital independence; and as the interests of husband and wife began to diverge the bonds of family affection became weakened. When Rome sank into utter dissolution, woman possessed a large share of cultivation and personal freedom; yet she had touched the lowest depths of social degradation.

The more minute details of the common-law scheme of husband and wife belong to the main portion of this volume, and need not here be anticipated. Not so however with the civil-law scheme; and we proceed to elaborate it somewhat further. In the earlier period of Roman law the marital power of the husband was as absolute as the *patria potestas*. But before the time of the Emperor Justinian it had assumed the aspect already noticed; in which it is to be distinguished from all other codes. The *communio bonorum*, which is to be found in so many modern systems of jurisprudence, might have been part of the Roman law, but it had long before the compilation of the digest fallen into disuse. The peculiarities of the civil law in this respect may be referred to the disuse into which formal rites of marriage had fallen. Formal marriage gave to husband and wife a community of interest in each other's property. But marriage *per usum*, or by cohabitation as man and wife, which became universally prevalent in later times, did not alter the status of the female: she still remained subject to her father's power. Hence

[1] See 1 Burge Col. & For. Laws, 202, 263.

parties united in a marriage *per usum* acquired no general interest in one another's property, but only an incidental interest in certain parts of it. The wife brought her *dos;* the husband his *anti-dos;* in all other property each retained the rights of owners unaffected by their relation of husband and wife. The *dos* and *anti-dos* were somewhat in the nature of mutual gifts in consideration of marriage. Every species of property which might be subsequently acquired as well as that owned at the time of marriage might be the subject of dotal gift. The father, or other paternal ancestor of the bride, was bound to furnish the *dos*, and the husband could compel them afterwards, if they failed to do so; the amount or value being regulated according to the means of the ancestor and the dignity of the husband. This pecuniary consideration appears to have influenced the later marriages to a very considerable extent. And while the husband had no concern with the wife's extra-dotal property, — since this she could manage and alienate free from all control or interference, — over her dotal property he acquired a dominion which was determinable on the dissolution of the marriage, unless he had become the purchaser at an estimated value. As incidental to this dominion he had the usufruct to himself, he might sue his wife or any one else who obstructed his free enjoyment, and he could alienate the personal property at pleasure. But he could not charge the real estate unless a purchaser; and upon his death the wife's dotal property belonged to her, or if she had not been emancipated, to her father; and to secure its restitution after the dissolution of marriage the wife had a tacit lien upon her husband's property. Of the *anti-dos*, or *donatio propter nuptias*, not so much is known; but this appears to have generally corresponded with the *dos;* it was restored by the wife upon the dissolution of marriage; and was regarded as her usufructuary property in like manner. It was not necessarily of the same value or amount with the wife's *dos*. Over his general property the husband retained the sole and absolute power of alienation, and his wife had no interest in it, nor could she interfere with his right of management.[1]

But the civil law allowed agreements to be made by which these rights might be regulated and varied at pleasure. And by their stipulations the married parties might so enlarge their respective interests as to provide for rights to the survivor.[2] These agreements were not unlike the antenuptial settlements so well known to modern equity courts.

The *communio bonorum*, or community system, occupies an intermediate position between the civil and common law schemes, The *communio bonorum* may have been part of the Roman law at an earlier period of its history, but it had ceased to exist long before the compilation of the digest; though parties might by their nuptial agreement adopt it.[3] This constitutes so prominent a feature of the codes of France, Spain, and other countries of modern Europe, whence it has likewise found its way to Louisiana, Florida, Texas, California, and other adjacent States, once subject to French and Spanish dominion, that it deserves a passing notice. The relation of husband and wife is regarded by these codes as a species of partnership, the property of which, like that of any other partnership, is primarily liable for the payment of debts. This partnership or community applies to all property acquired during marriage; and it is the well-settled rule that the debts of the partnership have priority of claim to satisfaction out of the community estate. Sometimes the community is universal, comprising not only property acquired during coverture, but all which belonged to the husband and wife before or at their marriage.[4] It is evident therefore that the provisions of such codes may differ widely in different States or countries. The principle which distinguishes the community from both the civil and common law schemes is however clear; namely, that husband and wife can have no property apart from one another. This law embraces profits,

[1] 1 Burge Col. & For. Laws, 202; ib. 263, *et seq.*

[2] Ib. 273.

[3] 1 Burge Col. & For. Laws, 263.

[4] Ib. 277 *et seq.*

income, earnings, and all property which, from its nature and the interest of the owner, is the subject of his uncontrolled and absolute alienation; but certain gifts made between husband and wife in contemplation of marriage are of course properly excluded.[1] Whether antenuptial debts are to be paid from the common property, as well as debts contracted while the relation of husband and wife continues, would seem to depend upon the extent of the *communio bonorum*, as including property brought by each as capital stock to the marriage, or only such property as they acquire afterwards.[2] The codes of modern Europe recognize no general capacity of the wife to contract, sue and be sued, as at the later civil law. On the contrary, the husband becomes by his marriage the curator of his wife. He has therefore the sole administration and management of her property and that of the community; and she is entirely excluded in every case, in which her acts cannot be referred to an authority, express or implied, from her husband.[3] Hence, too, all debts and charges are incurred by the husband. The community ceases on the termination of marriage by mutual separation or the death of either spouse.[4] And the various codes provide for the rights of the survivor on the legal dissolution of the community by death.

The reader may readily trace the influence of the community system upon the jurisprudence of Louisiana and the other States to which we have referred by examining their judicial reports. The civil code of Louisiana, as amended and promulgated in 1824, pronounced that the partnership or community of acquêts or gains arising during coverture should exist in every marriage where there was no stipulation to the contrary. This was a legal consequence of marriage under the Spanish

[1] 1 Burge Col. & For. Laws, 281, 282. By the French law only the personal estate entered into the community; but the Spanish law included both real and personal estate. Childress *v.* Cutter, 16 Mis. 24.

[2] Ib. 294.

[3] Ib. 296, 301.

[4] Ib. 303, 305.

law.[1] The statutes of Texas, Florida, Missouri, California, and other States are characterized by similar features. But all of these laws have been modified by settlers bringing with them the principles of the common law. So the doctrines of separate estate, revived in modern jurisprudence, are introduced into the legislation of these, as other American States. The chief controversies in the courts, regarding community property, appear to be as concerning the method of its disposal after dissolution by death.[2] On the whole, there is in the doctrines of community much that is fair and reasonable; but in the practical workings of this system it is found rather complicated and perplexing, and hence unsatisfactory.

What are familiarly known as the "married women's acts," the product of American legislation during the last quarter of a century, aim to secure to the wife the independent control of her own property, and the right to contract, sue and be sued, without her husband, under reasonable limitations. These acts therefore substitute in a great measure the civil for the common law. Three propositions may be laid down at this transition period. *First.* That the common law, in denying to the wife the rights of ownership in property acquired by gift, purchase, bequest, or otherwise, did her injustice; and that a radical change became necessary. This is shown, not only in the legislation of our States, but by the fact that the equity tribunals have gradually moulded the unwritten law of England so as to secure like results. *Second.* That the courts of England and the American States (with scarcely an important exception) agree in regarding the wife's separate property rights as contrary to rule: in other words, that they require her in each case to rebut the presumption that whatever she acquires vests in the husband and to establish a distinct ownership. *Third.* That as to rights of the person, or what are sometimes

1 Art. 2312, 2369, 2370. 2 Kent Com. 183 *n.*

2 See Packard *v.* Arellanes, 17 Cal. 525; Waul *v.* Kirkman, 25 Miss. 609; Succession of McLean, 12 La. Ann. 222; Jones *v.* Jones, 15 Tex. 143; 1 Burge Col. & For. Laws, 277 *et seq.*, where the law of community is fully set forth; and the learned note to 2 Kent Com. 183.

contrasted with civil as moral rights, no essential changes are wanted; the property rights of married women coming alone within the scope of a sweeping reform. In this respect the peculiarities of the civil code are regarded; for as to the conjugal duties of adherence, obedience, protection, maintenance and support, power of correction, and the like, it furnished little that the common law has not either recognized from the earliest times or else gradually improved upon.[1]

The danger to be apprehended from all legislation of this sort is that it will weaken the ties of marriage by forcing both sexes into an unnatural antagonism; teaching them to be independent of one another, and to earn their own living apart; whereas God's law points to family and the mutual intercourse of man and woman as among the strongest safeguards of human happiness. Where one pursues the objects of personal ambition the intellect must soon predominate over the affections; wandering out of her sphere of action, woman soon finds herself the object of affront instead of admiration; for, whatever triumphs Art may achieve, Nature to the last remains the stronger. Trials we all have; we may make them subservient to high purposes, yet they remain to gall us to the last; and if it be wrong to murmur at the impediments of physical infirmity, it is supreme folly to chafe and fret and struggle continually against the fetters of sex. In England, the rights of married women have been gradually enlarged, and that, too, by judicial construction rather than statute, the law still holding fast to the stability of the marriage relation. With us, each Gordian knot is cut in twain by legislative enactment, and the courts have only to look on in bewilderment. When husband and wife can once be made to understand their respective bounds, they will doubtless regard them; but so long as their rights remain in confusion and perplexity, collisions must constantly occur, and domestic peace remain in constant jeopardy.

[1] See as to civil law, 1 Burge Col. & For. Laws, 202.

Add to this loose divorce laws, loosely administered, and can it be said that the marriage relation is encouraged and fostered by the State? That it should be admits of no question.

Our legislation regarding the rights of married women should then be harmonized and simplified as soon as practicable. This is not easy with so many independent States, each carving out its own career. Our difficulty is aggravated from the fact that the married women's acts had no common origin; there was no model found to work from, English or American, and the results were necessarily discordant. Yet should public sentiment once set in the right direction, much might be accomplished at no distant day.

If, too, the married women's codes of this country are to serve as a guide to other nations they should bear the impress of a clear and well-defined purpose. Either the ultimate object should be to place the wife on an independent footing and enable her to maintain herself against the world, or else providing honorably, faithfully, and generously against all possible misfortune, to teach her still to lean upon the stronger arm of her husband, and look to man for guidance. But our legislators sometimes appear to attempt both systems together, as if goaded on by the gadfly of feminine persistency. Laws which invite married women to embark in separate trade, tend plainly to the wife's independence. Laws, on the other hand, which class widows and orphans together as subjects for special protection, preserve homestead exemptions, permit of settlements against the husband's creditors, are founded on the policy of the wife's dependence. It is not to be presumed that frank and straightforward discussion is inappropriate to any topic where radical changes are demanded; nor can the fundamental relation of the sexes and the balance of society be lightly disturbed. Equality and freedom are precious words; but if the respective spheres of man and woman are equally honorable, equally useful, equally free, need they be precisely identical? Does not inequality manifest itself when the two seek to run the same circuit? As a logical proposition, if woman in her pursuits has the right to become a man, man has no less the right to become a woman. Whether the change would be expedient and wise, however, is another question. Certain it is that woman cannot claim the privileges of the two sexes; if she would grasp at civil honors she must surrender her time-honored tribute of chivalrous homage. Our people can afford to wait; and, leaving the burden of proof upon those who would falsify all the teachings of human experience, and gain for woman a foothold in an untried sphere of action, the legislator need not feel called upon to press forward with new-fashioned privileges in the spirit of old-fashioned politeness, before he is assured that they are either desired or desirable.

A calm and dispassionate investigation of many acts shows that the common-law disabilities of the wife have been more carefully pruned than those of the husband. Some legislative changes in favor of the latter are desirable. Thus the common law obliged the husband to pay his wife's antenuptial debts, because he might have received a fortune by her; if then she retains her property, notwithstanding the marriage, this liability on his part should not continue. Again, it is possible that the husband, in some States, has lost his tenancy by the curtesy in his wife's lands; if so, is there any reason why the wife should retain a dower interest in her husband's lands? So, too, compensation was formerly recoverable by the husband for injuries sustained by the wife, while on the other hand he was compelled to respond in damages for her misconduct; many statutes now give compensation to the injured wife for her injuries; yet the husband must respond for her ill-behavior as before. Nor is it clear that where a married woman being of ample means retains her property independently of her husband, while his income continues slender, he ought to be held as strictly liable for her necessaries as in the days when the beneficial enjoyment of her property would have vested absolutely in him.[1]

But perhaps the worst that can be said of the married women's acts in their present state, is the constant temptation they hold out to fraud and perjury. If the wife can ever be made a willing party to dishonorable transactions, it is when the husband seeks her protection against his own creditors. A large proportion of the cases which have arisen under the married women's acts involve secret transfers of property between husband and wife, made for the purpose of defeating the payment of just debts; and in not a few of these cases the courts seem to have connived at what they probably considered a sort of pious fraud. Every American lawyer of moderate professional experience knows that it is now quite common for men when straitened to turn their property over to their wives, and thus, if not avoiding justice altogether, at least hoping to bring creditors to their own terms. Where solemn instruments are dispensed with, and the ownership of property as between husband and wife is a mere matter of circumstantial evidence, such transfers are easily effected, and the capital of one may furnish credit for the other. Let us not forget that the marriage relation is a close one, and in pecuniary matters places two persons before the world somewhat in the light of partners. Under the common law no serious difficulty could arise. The community system recognizes the partnership liability distinctly. And under the civil law, which our statutes profess to follow, while husband and wife could contract with each other for a valuable consideration, and could buy and borrow, sell and lend, between themselves, they were absolutely prohibited from making gifts without consideration; and so strict was the law in this respect that all persons to whose power they were subject came within the terms of the prohibition; nor did it matter that the gifts were made through the intervention of third persons.[2] A

[1] In some States, particularly as to antenuptial debts, the desired legislation is supplied, in others it is wanting.

[2] 1 Burge Col. & For. Laws, 274. Gifts *causa mortis* stood upon a different footing.

strict system of registry, applied to the wife's separate property, might check the frauds now justly complained of under our present statutes.

Of the remaining topics to be discussed in the present treatise, little need be said by way of general preface. These have felt the softening influences of modern civilization. The common-law doctrine of parent and child finds its most important modifications in the gradual admission of the mother to something like an equal share of parental authority; in the growth of popular systems of education for the young; in the enlarged opportunities of earning a livelihood afforded to the children of idle and dissolute parents; and in the lessened misfortunes of bastard offspring. Guardian and ward, a relation of little importance up to Blackstone's day, has rapidly developed since into a permanent and well-regulated system under the supervision of the chancery courts, and in this country the tribunals with probate jurisdiction; and much of the old learning on this branch of the law has become rubbish for the antiquary. The law of infancy remains comparatively unchanged. Of master and servant, we have spoken.

We are now to investigate in detail the law of these several topics. But first the reader is reminded that the office of the text-writer is to inform rather than invent; to be accurate rather than original; to chronicle the decisions of others, not his own desires; to illumine paths already trodden; to criticise, if need be, yet always fairly and in furtherance of the ends of justice; to analyze, classify, and arrange; from a mass of discordant material to extract all that is useful, separating the good from the bad, rejecting whatever is obsolete, searching at all times for guiding principles; and, in fine, to emblazon that long list of judicial precedents through which our Anglo-Saxon freedom "broadens slowly down."

PART II.

HUSBAND AND WIFE.

CHAPTER I.

MARRIAGE.

THE word marriage signifies, in the first instance, that act by which a man and woman unite for life, with the intent to discharge towards society and one another those duties which result from the relation of husband and wife. The act of union having been once accomplished, the word comes afterwards to denote the relation itself.

It is frequently said in the courts of this country that marriage is nothing more than a civil contract. That it is a contract is doubtless true, to a certain extent, since the law always presumes two parties of competent understanding who enter into a mutual agreement, which becomes executed, as it were, by the act of marriage. But this agreement differs essentially from all others. This contract of the parties is simply to enter into a certain status or relation. The rights and obligations of that status are fixed by society, in accordance with principles of natural law, and are beyond and above the parties themselves. They may make settlements and regulate the property rights of each other; but they cannot modify the terms upon which they are to live together, nor superadd to the relation a single condition. Being once bound they are bound for ever. Mutual consent, as in all contracts, brings them together; but mutual consent cannot part them. Death alone dissolves the tie,— unless the legislature, in the exercise of a rightful authority, interposes by general or special ordinance to pronounce a solemn divorce; and this it should only do when the grossly immoral conduct of one contracting party brings unmerited shame upon the other, disgraces an innocent offspring, and inflicts a wound upon the community. So in other respects the law of marriage differs from that of ordinary contracts. For as concerns the parties themselves, mental capacity is not the only test of fitness, but physical capacity likewise; a new element for consideration no less important than the other. Again the encumbrance of an existing union operates here as a special disqualification. Blood relationship is another. So too an infant's capacity is treated on peculiar principles, as far as the marriage contract is concerned, for he can marry young and be bound by his marriage. International law relaxes its usual requirements in favor of marriage. And finally the formal celebration now prevalent, both in England and America, is something peculiar to the marriage contract; and in its performance we see but the faintest analogy to the execution and delivery of a sealed instrument.

We are then to consider marriage, not as a contract in the ordinary acceptation of the term; but as a contract *sui generis*, if indeed it be a contract at all; as an agreement to enter into a solemn relation which imposes its own terms. On the one hand discarding the unwarranted dogmas of the Church of Rome by which marriage is elevated to the character of a sacrament, on the other we repudiate that dry definition with which the law-giver or jurist sometimes seeks to impose upon the natural instincts of mankind. We adopt such views as the distinguished Lord Robertson held.[1] And Judge Story observes of marriage: "It appears to me something more than a mere contract. It is rather to be deemed an institution of society, founded upon the consent and contract of the parties; and in this view it has some peculiarities in its nature, character, operation, and extent of obligation, different from what belongs to

[1] Duntze *v.* Levett, Ferg. 68, 385, 397; 3 Eng. Ec. 360, 495, 502.

ordinary contracts."[1] So Fraser, while defining marriage as a contract, adds in forcible language: "Unlike other contracts, it is one instituted by God himself, and has its foundation in the law of nature. It is the parent, not the child, of civil society."[2] And we may add that a recent American text-writer, of high repute, not only pronounces for this doctrine, after a careful examination of all the authorities, but ascribes the chief embarrassment of American tribunals in questions arising under the conflict of marriage and divorce laws, to the custom of applying the rules of ordinary contracts to the marriage relation.[3]

A distinction is made at law between void and voidable marriages. This distinction, which appears to have originated in a conflict between the English ecclesiastical and common-law courts, is first announced in a statute passed during the reign of Henry VIII.; and it is also to be found in succeeding marriage and divorce acts down to the present day. The distinction of void and voidable applies not to the legal consequences of an imperfect marriage, once formally dissolved, but to the status of the parties and their offspring before such dissolution. A void marriage is a mere nullity and its validity may be impeached in any court, whether the question arises directly or collaterally, and whether the parties be living or dead. But a voidable marriage is valid for all civil purposes until a competent tribunal has pronounced the sentence of nullity, upon direct proceedings instituted for the purpose of setting the marriage aside. When once set aside, the marriage is treated as void *ab initio;* but unless the suit for nullity reaches its conclusion during the life-time of both parties, all proceedings fall to the ground, and both survivor and offspring stand as well as though the union had been lawful from its inception.[4] Hence we see that while a void marriage makes cohabitation at all times

[1] Story Confl. Laws, § 108 *n.*
[2] 1 Fras. Dom. Rel. 87. [3] 1 Bish. Mar. & Div. 4th ed. § 18.
[4] Stat. 32 Hen. 8, c. 38. See 1 Bish. Mar. & Div. 4th ed. § 108, *et seq.*

unlawful, and bastardizes the issue, a voidable marriage protects intercourse between the parties for the time being, furnishes the usual incidents of survivorship, such as curtesy and dower, and encourages the propagation of children. But the moment the sentence of nullity is pronounced the shield of the law falls, the incidents vanish, and innocent offspring are exposed to the world as bastards; and herein is the greatest hardship of a voidable marriage.

The old rule is that civil disabilities, such as idiocy and fraud, render a marriage void; while the canonical impediments, such as consanguinity and impotence, make it voidable only. This test was never a clear one, and it has become of little practical consequence at the present day. Statutes both in England and America have greatly modified the ancient law of valid marriages, and it can only be affirmed in general terms that the legislative tendency is to make marriages voidable rather than void, wherever the impediment is such as might not have been readily known to both parties before marriage; and where public policy does not rise superior to all considerations of private utility. Modern civilization strongly condemns the harsh doctrine of *ab initio* sentences of nullity; and such sentences have now in general a prospective force only, in order that rights already vested may remain unimpaired, and, still more, that children may not suffer for the follies of their parents.[1]

We shall briefly consider in this chapter that act by which parties unite in matrimony, — for to this the term marriage is most frequently applied. It may be stated generally that, in order to constitute a perfect union, the contracting parties should be two persons of the opposite sexes, without disqualification of blood or condition, both mentally competent and physically fit to discharge the duties of the relation, neither of

[1] Shelf. Mar. & Div. 154; ib. 479–484; 1 Bl. Com. 434; 1 Bish. Mar. & Div. 4th ed. §§ 105–120. See Stat. 5 & 6 Will. 4, c. 54; 2 N. Y. Rev. Sts. 139, § 6; Mass Gen. Sts. c. 106, § 4.

them being bound by a previous nuptial tie, neither of them withholding a free assent; and the expression of their mutual assent should be substantially in accordance with the prescribed forms of law. These are the essentials of marriage. Hence we are to treat of the following topics in connection with the essentials of a valid marriage: first, the disqualification of blood; second, the disqualification of social condition; third, mental capacity; fourth, physical capacity; fifth, the disqualification of infancy, which in reality is based upon united considerations of mental and physical unfitness; sixth, prior marriage undissolved; seventh, fraud, force, and error; eighth, the formal celebration of a marriage, under which last head may be also included the consent of parents or guardians, not to be deemed an essential, except in conformity with the requirements of the marriage celebration acts. These essentials all have reference solely to the time, place, and circumstances of entering into the marriage relation, and not to any subsequent incapacity of either party.

And, first, as to the disqualification of blood. On no point have writers of all ages and countries been more united than in the conviction that nature abhors, as vile and unclean, all sexual intercourse between persons of near relationship. But on few subjects have they differed so widely as in the application of this conviction. Among Eastern nations, since the days of the patriarchs, practices have prevailed which to Christian nations and in days of civilized refinement seem shocking and strange. The difficulty then is not in discovering that there is some prohibition by God's law, but in ascertaining how far that prohibition extends. This difficulty is manifested in our language by the use of two terms: consanguinity and affinity; one of which covers the *terra firma* of incestuous marriages, the other offers debatable ground. The disqualification of consanguinity applies to marriages between blood relations in the lineal or ascending and descending lines. There can be but one opinion concerning the union of relations as near as brother and sister. The limit of prohibition among remote collateral kindred has however been differently assigned in different countries. The English canonical rule is that of the Jewish law. The Greeks and Romans recognized like principles, though with various modifications and alterations of opinion. But the church of the Middle Ages found in the institution of marriage, once placed among the sacraments, a most powerful lever of social influence. The English ecclesiastical courts made use of this disqualification, extending it to the seventh degree of canonical reckoning in some cases, and beyond all reasonable bounds. So intolerable became this oppression, that statutes passed in the time of Henry VIII., forbade these courts thenceforth to draw in question marriages without the Levitical degree, "not prohibited by God's law."[1] Under these statutes, which are still essentially in force in England, the impediment has been treated as extending to the third degree of the civil reckoning inclusive; or in other words so as to prohibit all marriages nearer than first cousins. Archbishop Parker's table of degrees, which recognizes this limit, has been since 1563, the standard adopted in the English ecclesiastical courts.[2] The statute prohibition includes legitimate as well as illegitimate children, and half-blood kindred equally with those of the whole blood.

But the English law goes even further, and places affinity on the same footing as consanguinity as an impediment. Affinity is the relationship which arises from marriage between a husband and his wife's kindred, and *vice versa*. It is shown that while the marriage of persons allied by blood produces offspring feeble in body and tending to insanity, that of persons connected by affinity leads to no such result; and further, that consanguinity has been everywhere recognized as an impediment, but not affinity. The worst that can probably be said of the latter

[1] Stat. 32 Hen. 8, c. 38; see Bish. Mar. & Div. 4th ed. §§ 106, 107; 2 Kent Com. 82, 83; Shelf. Mar. & Div. 163 *et seq.*; Wing *v.* Taylor, 2 Swab. & T. 278, 295.

[2] 1 Bish. Mar. & Div. 4th ed. § 318; Butler *v.* Gastrill, Gilb. Ch. 156.

is, that it leads to confusion of domestic rights and duties. No question has been discussed with more earnestness in both England and America, with less positive result, than one which turns upon this very distinction; namely, whether a man may marry his deceased wife's sister. This question has received a favorable response in Vermont.[1] But in England such marriages are still deemed incestuous, and within the prohibition of God's law.[2]

Marriages within the forbidden degrees of consanguinity were formerly voidable only in English law; but by modern statutes they have been made null and void. In this country they are generally pronounced void by statute, and the offending parties are liable to imprisonment. But with regard to marriages among relatives by affinity, the rule is not so stringent as in England.[3]

Second, as to the disqualification of social condition. Race, color, and social rank do not appear to constitute an impediment to marriage at the common law, nor is any such impediment now recognized in England.[4] But by local statutes in some of the United States, intermarriage has been discouraged between persons of the negro, Indian, and white races.[5] With the recent extinction of slavery, many of these laws have passed into oblivion, together with such as refused to allow to persons held in bondage the rights of husband and wife. The thir-

[1] Blodget *v.* Brinsmaid, 9 Vt. 27; and see 1 Bish. Mar. & Div. 4th ed. § 314; Paddock *v.* Wells, 2 Barb. Ch. 331.

[2] Hill *v.* Good, Vaugh. 302; Harris *v.* Hicks, 2 Salk. 548; Shelf. Mar. & Div. pp. 172, 178; 2 Kent Com. 84, note, and authorities cited; Reg. *v.* Chadwick, 12 Jur. 174, 11 Q. B. 173.

[3] 2 Kent Com. 83, 84, and notes; 1 Bish. Mar. & Div. 4th ed. §§ 312–320; Regina *v.* Chadwick, 12 Jur. 174; Sutton *v.* Warren, 10 Met. 451; Bonham *v.* Badgley, 2 Gilm. 622; Wightman *v.* Wightman, 4 Johns. Ch. 343; Butler *v.* Gastrill, Gilb. Ch. 156; Burgess *v.* Burgess, 1 Hag. Con. 384; Blackmore *v.* Brider, 2 Phillim. 359.

[4] 1 Bish. Mar. & Div. 4th ed. §§ 308–311; 1 Burge Col. & For. Laws, 138.

[5] See Bailey *v.* Fiske, 34 Me. 77; The State *v.* Hooper, 5 Ire. 201; The State *v.* Brady, 9 Humph. 74; Barkshire *v.* The State, 7 Ind. 389; 1 Bish. Mar. & Div. 4th ed. §§ 154–163.

teenth article of amendment to the constitution gives Congress power to enforce the abolition of slavery "by appropriate legislation." As to persons formerly slaves, there are now acts of Congress which legitimate their past cohabitation, and enable them to drop the fetters of concubinage. And the manifest tendency of the day is towards removing all legal impediments of rank and condition, leaving individual tastes and social manners to impose the only restrictions of this nature.[1]

Third, as to mental capacity. No one can contract a valid marriage unless capable at the time of giving an intelligent consent. Hence the marriages of idiots, lunatics, and all others who have not the use of their understanding, are now treated as null; though the rule was formerly otherwise. What degree of insanity will amount to disqualification is not easily determined; so varied are the manifestations of mental disorder at the present day, and so gradually does mere feebleness of intellect shade off into hopeless idiocy. Certain it is that a person may enter into a valid marriage, notwithstanding he has a mental delusion on certain subjects, is eccentric in his habits, or is possessed of a morbid temperament, provided he displays soundness in other respects, and can manage his own affairs with ordinary prudence and skill.[2] Every case stands on its own merits; but the usual test applied in the courts is that of fitness for the general transactions of life; for, it is argued, if a man is incapable of entering into other contracts, neither can he contract marriage.[3] This test is sufficiently precise for most purposes. Yet we apprehend the real issue is whether the man is capable of entering understandingly into

[1] Act July 25, 1866, ch. 240; Act June 6, 1866, ch. 106, § 14. See Stewart *v.* Munchandler, 2 Bush, (Ky.) 278.

[2] 2 Kent Com. 76; Browning *v.* Reane, 2 Phillim. 69; 1 Bish. Mar. & Div. 4th ed. §§ 124–142; Turner *v.* Meyers, 1 Hag. Con. 414; 4 Eng. Ec. 440; 1 Bl. Com. 438, 439.

[3] Mudway *v.* Croft, 3 Curt. Ec. 671; Anon. 4 Pick. 32; Cole *v.* Cole, 5 Sneed, 57; Atkinson *v.* Medford, 46 Maine, 510; Ward *v.* Dulaney, 23 Miss. 410; McElroy's Case, 6 W. & S. 451. See 1 Bish. Mar. & Div. § 128; Ex parte Glen, 4 Des. 546.

the relation of marriage; for natural impulses are so strong that a man may know well the contract he assumes by the act of marriage, while he is not equally fit to enter into other engagements. There are two questions, however: first, whether the party understands the marriage contract; second, whether he is fit to perform afterwards the obligations which that contract imposes.

Marriage contracted during a lucid interval is at law deemed valid;[1] but the English statute provides that such marriages are void when a commission of lunacy has once been taken out and remains unrevoked.[2] Similar provisions are to be found in some of our States. On the other hand, marriage contracted by a person habitually sane, during temporary insanity, is unquestionably void.[3] And upon the principle of temporary insanity, drunkenness incapacitates, if carried to the excess of *delirium tremens;* though not, it would appear, if the party intoxicated retains sufficient reason to know what he is doing.[4] Drunkenness was formerly held a bad plea; for the common law permitted no one to stultify himself; but the modern rule is more reasonable. Some cases require that fraud or unfair advantage should be shown; yet the better opinion is that even this is unnecessary.[5] Deaf and dumb persons were formerly classed as idiots; this notion, however, is exploded. They may now contract marriage by signs.[6] Total blindness, or mere deafness, of course constitutes no incapacity. Suits of nullity, brought to ascertain the facts of insanity, are favored by law both in England and America; and modern legislation discountenances all collateral disputes involving questions so painful

1 Shelf. Mar. & Div. 197; 1 Bish. Mar. & Div. § 130.

2 Stat. 15 Geo. 2, c. 30, 1742.

3 Legeyt *v.* O'Brien, Milward, 325; Parker *v.* Parker, 2 Lee, 382; 6 Eng. Ec. 165.

4 Clement *v.* Mattison, 3 Rich. 93; 1 Bish. Mar. & Div. 4th ed. § 131; Gore *v.* Gibson, 13 M. & W. 623; 2 Kent Com. 451 and authorities cited; Lord Ellenborough in Pitt *v.* Smith, 3 Camp. 33.

5 See 1 Bish. Mar. & Div. 4th ed. §§ 131, 132, and conflicting cases cited.

6 1 Bish. Mar. & Div. 4th ed. § 133 and cases cited; 1 Fras. Dom. Rel. 48; Dickenson *v.* Blisset, 1 Dickens, 268; Harrod *v.* Harrod, 1 Kay & Johns. 4.

and perplexing. "Though marriage with an idiot or lunatic be absolutely void, and no sentence of avoidance be absolutely necessary," says Chancellor Kent, "yet, as well for the sake of the good order of society, as for the peace of mind of all persons concerned, it is expedient that the nullity of the marriage should be ascertained and declared by the decree of a court of competent jurisdiction."[1] In many States this is now the only course to be pursued, such marriages being treated as voidable and not void.

Fourth. The question of physical capacity involves an investigation of facts even more painful and humiliating than that of mental capacity. Yet as marriage is instituted, in part at least, for the indulgence of natural cravings and with a view to propagate the human family, sound morality demands that the proper means shall not be wanting. Where impotence exists, there can be no valid marriage. By this is meant simply that the sexual organization of both parties shall be complete. But mere barrenness constitutes no legal incapacity, nor can a physical defect which does not interfere with copulation; nor indeed any disability which is curable, even though not actually cured.[2] The necessity of judicial sentence, before such marriage can be considered null, is too obvious for argument.[3] The reader will find Dr. Lushington's opinion, in the leading case of *Deane* v. *Aveling*,[4] sufficiently suggestive as to the extent of malformation which invalidates a marriage on the ground of physical incapacity. We shall only add, that with the rapid progress of medical science during the present century, cases

[1] 2 Kent Com. 76. See 1 Bish. Mar. & Div. 4th ed. §§ 136–142; Crump *v.* Morgan, 3 Ire. Eq. 91; Goshen *v.* Richmond, 4 Allen, 458; Hamaker *v.* Hamaker, 18 Ill. 137; Williamson *v.* Williams, 3 Jones Eq. 446. See recent English case of Hancock (falsely called Peaty) *v.* Peaty, Law Rep. 1 P. & D. 335.

[2] 1 Bish. Mar. & Div. §§ 321–340, and cases cited; 1 Fras. Dom. Rel. 53; B. *v.* B. 28 E. L. & Eq. 95; 1 Bl. Com. 440, *n.* by Chitty and others; Ayl. Parer. 227; Devanbagh *v.* Devanbagh, 5 Paige, 554; Essex *v.* Essex, 2 Howell St. Tr. 786; Briggs *v.* Morgan, 3 Phillim. 325.

[3] See A. *v.* B. Law Rep. 1 P. & D. 559.

[4] 1 Robertson, 279. And see recent case of U. *v.* J. Law Rep. 1 P. & D. 460.

of absolute and incurable impotence are happily diminishing in number.[1]

Fifth. Infancy may be an impediment to marriage; but only so far, on principle, as the marrying party, by reason of imperfect mental and physical development, may be brought within the reason of the last two rules. Hence we find that infancy is not a bar to marriage to the same extent as in ordinary contracts; since minors cannot repudiate their choice on reaching majority. Not that marriage calls for less discrimination; for it carries with it consequences far beyond all other contracts, involving property rights of the gravest import; but because public policy must protect the marriage institution against reckless imprudence. A certain period is established called the age of consent, which in England is fixed at fourteen for males and twelve for females, a rule adopted from the Roman law, but which, in this country, varies all the way from fourteen to eighteen for males, and twelve to fourteen for females, according to local statutes; differences of climate and physical temperament contributing doubtless to make the rule of nature in this respect a fluctuating one.[2] Marriages without the age of consent are as binding as those of adults; marriages within such age may be avoided by either party on reaching the period fixed by law. And even though one of the parties was of suitable age and the other too young, at the time of marriage, yet the former may disaffirm as well as the latter.[3] Herein is observed a departure from that principle of law, that an infant

[1] See recent cases: W. *v.* H. 2 Swab. & T. 240; T. *v.* M. Law Rep. 1 P. & D. 31; T. *v.* D. Law Rep. 1 P. & D. 127; Carll *v.* Prince, Law Rep. 1 Ex. 246.

[2] See 2 Kent Com. 79, notes, showing the periods fixed in different States as the age of consent. In the old States the common-law rule generally prevails. In Ohio, Indiana, and other Western States, the age of consent is raised to eighteen for males, and fourteen for females. See also Bennett *v.* Smith, 21 Barb. 439, as to the power of the New York courts to annul marriages with persons under age.

[3] Co. Lit. 79 and Harg. *n.* 45; 1 East P. C. 468; 1 Bish. Mar. & Div. 4th ed. § 149.

may avoid his contract while the adult remains bound: it is a concession which the law makes in favor of mutuality in the marriage compacts. Marriages celebrated before both parties have reached the age of consent may be disaffirmed in season, either with or without a judicial sentence. When the age of consent is reached, no new ceremony is requisite to complete the marriage at the common law; but election to affirm will then be inferred from circumstances, such as continued intercourse, and even slight acts may suffice to show the intention of the parties. If they then choose to remain husband and wife they are bound for ever. Marriage within the age of consent seems therefore to be neither strictly void nor strictly voidable, but rather inchoate and imperfect.[1]

Sixth, as to the impediment of prior marriage undissolved. It is a well established rule in civilized countries that marriage between parties, one of whom is bound by an existing marriage tie, is not only void, but subjects the offenders to criminal prosecution.[2] Polygamy, or bigamy as it is often termed,— since the common law of England could scarcely conceive of such conjunctions carried beyond a double marriage,— is discarded by all Christian communities. It is tolerated, though not sanctioned, in certain territory of the United States. The fundamental doctrine of Christian marriage is that no length of separation can dissolve the union, so long as both parties are actually living, even though lapse of time should raise a reasonable supposition of death. But to render the second marriage void at law, the first should have been valid in all respects.[3] Some of the harsher features of the old law have been

[1] Co. Lit. 33 *a.*; 2 Kent Com. 78, 79; 1 Bish. Mar. & Div. 4th ed. §§ 143–153 and cases cited; 1 Bl. Com. 436; 1 Fras. Dom. Rel. 42; Parton *v.* Hervey, 1 Gray, 119. See Shafher *v.* State, 20 Ohio, 1; *contra*, Goodwin *v.* Thompson, 2 Iowa, 329, as to the invalidity of such marriages, unless confirmed by cohabitation after reaching the statutory age.

[2] Cro. Eliz. 858; 1 Salk. 121; 2 Kent Com. 79 and notes; 1 Bish. Mar. & Div. §§ 296–303 and authorities cited; Shelf. Mar. & Div. 224.

[3] Bruce *v.* Burke, 2 Add. Ec. 471; 2 Eng. Ec. 381; Reg. *v.* Chadwick, 12 Jur. 174; Patterson *v.* Gaines, 6 How. (U. S.) 550.

softened in our own legislation; and statutes are not uncommon which extend facilities for divorce, and in any event protect the offspring of a new marriage contracted erroneously but in good faith by parties who had reason to believe a former spouse dead.[1] So too polygamy in fact is relieved of its penal consequences as concerns parties not guilty of polygamy in intention; but a certain period must elapse — usually seven years — before death can be presumed from continuous absence alone. Such was one of the provisions in the English statute passed in the reign of James I.,[2] which also exempted from punishment for bigamy persons during the lifetime of the former spouse re-married after a divorce, sentence of nullity, or disaffirmance on reaching age of consent. Similar statutes are enacted in this country.[3] Polygamy, with such exceptions, remains an indictable offence. One of its less obvious evils — though not the least important when polygamy is regarded as a legalized institution, in a free country — is that the patriarchal principle which it introduces is thoroughly hostile to free institutions; this fact was pointed out many years ago by one of our best writers on political ethics.[4]

Under this same head may be considered a disqualification introduced into some parts of this country by legislative enactments; namely, the impediment which follows divorce.[5] A divorce *a vinculo* should on general principles, leave both parties free to marry again. But such is not always the case. Thus in Kentucky the person injured may not marry again be-

[1] See N. Y. Rev. Stat. vol. 2, p. 139, §§ 6, 7.

[2] Stat. 1 Jac. 1, c. 11, 1604. See Queen *v.* Lumley, L. R. 1 C. C. 196.

[3] In New York, the period of absence is five years; in Ohio, three years; in Massachusetts, seven years, but with a special relaxation of the penalty. Still further, see 2 Kent Com. 79 and notes. Parties are not free to marry again, but only relieved of penal consequences. Miles *v.* Chilton, 1 Robertson, 684; Williamson *v.* Parisian, 1 Johns. Ch. 389; and other authorities cited in 1 Bish. Mar. & Div. 4th ed. § 299.

[4] 2 Lieber Pol. Ethics, 9, cited in note to 2 Kent Com. 81. See Hyde *v.* Woodmansee, Law Rep. 1 P. & D. 130.

[5] 1 Bish. Mar. & Div. 4th ed. §§ 304–307.

fore the expiration of two years from the decree of dissolution.[1] And in several States, the guilty party is prohibited from marrying again during the lifetime of the innocent spouse divorced; a provision of law seemingly more judicious to apply *in terrorem* by way of prevention than as a suitable method of punishment.[2] In Scotland there is a peculiar law which forbids the guilty party after divorce from marrying the *particeps criminis;* this was framed evidently to defeat collusive practices between persons desiring to put away an outstanding obstacle to their own union.[3]

Seventh. All marriages procured by force or fraud, or involving palpable error, are void; for here the element of mutual consent is wanting, so essential to every contract.[4] The law treats a matrimonial union of this kind as absolutely void *ab initio*, and permits its validity to be questioned in any court; at the option however of the injured party, who may elect to abide by the consequences when left free to give or withhold assent. Force implies a physical constraint of the will; fraud, some deception practised, whereby an unnatural state of the will is brought about.[5] Cases of palpable error, which are very rare, usually contain one or both of these ingredients. What amount of force is sufficient to invalidate a marriage is a question of circumstances. Evidently the same test could not apply to the mature and the immature, to the strong and the weak, to man and to woman. The general rule is that such amount of force as might naturally serve to overcome one's free volition and inspire terror will render the marriage null.[6] And where

[1] Cox *v.* Combs, 8 B. Monr. 231.

[2] See Parke *v.* Barron, 20 Ga. 702, where it is intimated that such marriages would not be void.

[3] 1 Fras. Dom. Rel. 82.

[4] 2 Kent Com. 76, 77; 1 Bish. Mar. & Div. 4th ed. §§ 164–215; Harford *v.* Morris, 2 Hag. Con. 423, 4 Eng. Ec. 575; Countess of Portsmouth *v.* Earl of Portsmouth, 1 Hag. Ec. 355, 3 Eng. Ec. 154; Scott *v.* Shufeldt, 5 Paige, 43; Dalrymple *v.* Dalrymple, 2 Hag. Con. 54, 104, 4 Eng. Ec. 485; Keyes *v.* Keyes, 2 Fost. N. H. 553.

[5] 1 Fras. Dom. Rel. 234.

[6] Shelf. Mar. & Div. 213; 1 Bish. Mar. & Div. 4th ed. § 211.

the party employing force sustains a superior relation of influence, which he chooses to abuse, this circumstance carries great weight. Thus in *Harford* v. *Morris*, where one of the guardians of a young and timid school-girl, having great influence and authority over her, took her to a foreign country, hurried her from place to place, and then married her without her free consent, the marriage was set aside.[1] So marriage by compulsion is procured when one under illegal arrest is forced to marry; and so probably, though the arrest was legal, if malicious circumstances are manifest.[2] But if a man under some slight duress marries a woman whom he had seduced, in order to avoid criminal prosecution, the law will favor a presumption of honest repentance on his part and hold him bound.[3] As to fraud, in order to vitiate a marriage, it should go to the very essence of the contract. But what constitutes this essence? The marriage relation is not to be disturbed for trifles, nor can the cumbrous machinery of the courts be brought to bear upon impalpable things. The law, it has been well observed, makes no provision for the relief of a blind credulity, however it may have been produced.[4] Fraudulent misrepresentations of one party, as to birth, social position, fortune, good health, and temperament, cannot therefore vitiate the contract. *Caveat emptor* is the harsh but necessary maxim of the law. Love, however indispensable in an æsthetic sense, is by no means a legal essential to marriage; simply because it cannot be weighed in the scales of justice. So too all such matters are peculiarly within the knowledge of the parties themselves, and they are put upon reasonable inquiry. Not even does the concealment of previous unchaste and immoral

[1] 2 Hag. Con. 423, 4 Eng. Ec. 575.

[2] Reg. *v.* Orgill, 9 Car. & P. 80; Soule *v.* Bonney, 37 Maine, 128; Barton *v.* Morris, 15 Ohio, 408; Benton *v.* Benton, 1 Day, 111. See 1 Bish. Mar. & Div. 4th ed. § 212.

[3] Jackson *v.* Winne, 7 Wend. 47.

[4] Lord Stowell, in Wakefield *v.* Mackay, 1 Phillim. 137; 2 Kent Com. 77; 1 Bish. Mar. & Div. 4th ed. §§ 166–168.

behavior in general vitiate a marriage; for although this seems to strike into the essence of the contract, yet public policy pronounces otherwise, and opens marriage as the gateway to repentance and virtue.[1] If the profligate continue a profligate after marriage the divorce laws afford an easy escape to the deluded victim. Still as this doctrine seems to bear hard upon innocent persons marrying in good faith and with misplaced confidence, it is applied not without some limitations: thus where a woman pregnant by another man at the time of the nuptials, bears a child soon after to an innocent husband, the marriage may be avoided by him, for she has thereby not only inflicted upon him the grossest possible injury, but subjected them both to scandal and ill-repute.[2] As to error, it may be said as in fraud that the error should reach the essentials; thus where one is actually substituted for another. Chancellor Kent justly observes, however, that it would be difficult to find a case where simple error, without some other element, would be permitted to vacate a marriage.[3]

There is an English case in point where a man courted and afterwards married a young lady, believing her to be a certain rich widow whom he had known only by reputation. She and her friends had countenanced the deception. It was held nevertheless that the marriage must stand.[4]

In most of the reported cases of fraud, force, and error, two or more of these elements are united; and frequently another impediment appears, such as tender years on the part of the injured party; or with regard to the offender, the suppression

[1] 1 Bish. Mar. & Div. §§ 170, 179; Rogers Ec. Law, 2d ed. 644; 1 Fras. Dom. Rel. 231; Ayl. Parer. 362, 363; Swinb. Spousals, 2d ed. 152; Best *v.* Best, 1 Add. Ec. 411, 2 Eng. Ec. 158.

[2] Reynolds *v.* Reynolds, 3 Allen, 605. See Foss *v.* Foss, 12 Allen, 26; Baker *v.* Baker, 13 Cal. 87; Montgomery *v.* Montgomery, 3 Barb. Ch. 132.

[3] 2 Kent Com. 77. But see Lord Campbell, in Reg. *v.* Millis, 10 Cl. & F. 534, 785; 1 Bish. Mar. & Div. 4th ed. § 207; Clowes *v.* Clowes, 3 Curt. Ec. 185, 191.

[4] Fielding's Case, cited in Burke's Celebrated Trials, 63, 78, and in 1 Bish. Mar. & Div. 4th ed. § 204.

of material facts relative to some former marriage, or to his own mental or physical incapacity, or some other cause of nullity is shown by the evidence. In the reported cases where the complainant was successful, some unprincipled man has generally sought to gain undue advantages from the person and fortunes of one whose feebler will rendered her an easy prey; it rarely if ever appears that force or fraud led to a reasonable and well-assorted match. Such unequal alliances need find favor from no tribunal.[1]

All marriages of this sort are binding without further ceremony, provided the injured party sees fit to affirm it after all constraint is removed; but no such freedom of choice seems to be left to the offending party. Hence, this sort of marriage seems neither void nor voidable in the legal acceptation; but rather inchoate or incomplete until ratified, though void, if the injured choose so to treat it. Where consummation never followed the nuptials, the courts are the more readily disposed to set aside the match; but in any event copulation, with knowledge of the fraud, and after removal of all constraint, is an effectual bar to relief.[2] The issue is between the offender and the injured party, and third persons have no right to interfere, although it be alleged that there was intent to defraud them in their own property interests.[3] We may add that where such marriages are effected through the fraudulent conspiracy of third persons, the rule is that unless one of the contracting parties is cognizant of the fraud, the marriage is perfect; but if cognizant, it is to be deemed the fraud of such party.[4]

[1] See Heffer *v.* Heffer, 3 M. & S. 265; Rex *v.* Burton-upon-Trent, 3 M. & S. 537; Swift *v.* Kelly, 3 Knapp, 257; Nace *v.* Boyer, 6 Casey, 99; Powell *v.* Cobb, 3 Jones Eq. 456. If a person is unwittingly entrapped into a marriage ceremony, not meaning that it shall be binding, the marriage is void. Clark *v.* Field, 13 Vt. 460.

[2] 1 Bish. Mar. & Div. 4th ed. §§ 214, 215; 1 Burge Col. & For. Laws, 137; 1 Fras. Dom. Rel. 229; Scott *v.* Shufeldt, 5 Paige, 43.

[3] McKinney *v.* Clarke, 2 Swan, 321.

[4] Sullivan *v.* Sullivan, 2 Hag. Con. 238, 246; Rex *v.* Minshull, 1 Nev. & M. 277; 1 Bish. Mar. & Div. § 173 *et seq.*

Eighth. We are now brought to the important subject of the formal marriage celebration. Here there is a wide difference noticeable between general principles and established practice. We are to consider this topic, then, in two separate aspects: first, as to marriage observance in the absence of civil requirements; second, as to marriage observance under the statutes now in force in England and America.

It is to be premised, however, that some form of marriage promise, some ceremony however slight, has always been deemed essential to its validity. The common language of the books is that, in the absence of civil regulations to the contrary, nothing but mutual consent is required. And the old maxim of the Roman law is quoted to support this view: *Nuptias non concubitus, sed consensus facit.*[1] But is there not an ambiguity in the use of such language? For it is material to ask whether *consensus* or *consent* is used in the sense of simple volition or an expression of volition. We maintain that the latter is the correct legal view; and that it should be said that the law requires in such cases *a simple expression of mutual consent*, and no more. For the very definition of marriage, implies that there should be not only the consenting mind, but an expression of the consenting mind, by words or signs, which expression in proper form constitutes in fact the marriage agreement. It is in this sense that we shall apply the terms *formal* and *informal* to marriage in the following sections.

To constitute a marriage, then, where there are no civil requirements, — or, in other words, to constitute an informal marriage, — words clearly expressing mutual consent are sufficient, without other solemnities. Two forms of consent are mentioned in the books: the one consent *per verba de præsenti*, with or without consummation; the other, consent *per verba de futuro*, followed by consummation.[2] Some writers have added

[1] See 2 Kent Com. 86, 87; Co. Litt. 33 *a*; 1 Bish. Mar. & Div. §§ 218–267.

[2] Swinb. Spousals, 2d ed. 8; 2 Burn. Ec. Law, Phillim. ed. 455 *e*; Lord Cottenham in Stewart *v.* Menzies, 2 Rob. Ap. Cas. 547; 1 Bish. Mar. & Div. 4th ed. § 227.

a third form of consent, — by habit and repute; but this is, very clearly, nothing more than evidence of consummated marriage amounting to a conclusive presumption. So, too, there is reason to suppose that the marriage *per verba de futuro* is of the same sort; marriage *per verba de præsenti* constituting the only real marriage promise, while consummation following *de futuro* words of promise, raises a legal presumption, perhaps conclusive, that words *de præsenti* afterwards passed between the parties. The copula is no part of the marriage; it only serves to some extent as evidence of marriage.[1] *Consensus, non concubitus*, is the maxim of the civil, ecclesiastical, and common law alike.[2]

Informal celebration constitutes marriage as known to natural and public law. The English canon law as it stood previous to the Council of Trent, the law of Scotland, the law of some of the United States, and perhaps the common law of England, all dispense with the ceremonial observances of formal marriage. But, as we shall see, the marriage acts now in force in England and most of the United States render certain solemnities, religious or secular, indispensable. Most of the decisions relating to informal marriages are therefore to be found in the Scotch reports, where the general doctrine has been pretty fully discussed. And the great, almost insuperable, difficulty which presents itself at the outset in such cases is thus clearly indicated by Lord Stowell, in *Lindo* v. *Belisario:* "A marriage is not every carnal commerce; nor would it be so even in the law of nature. A mere carnal commerce, without the intention of cohabitation and bringing up of children, would not constitute marriage under any supposition. But when two persons agree to have that commerce for the procreation and bringing up of children, and for such lasting

[1] 1 Bish. Mar. & Div. 4th ed. § 228; Jackson *v.* Winne, 7 Wend. 47; Dumaresly *v.* Fishly, 3 A. K. Mar. 368, 372.

[2] Dalrymple *v.* Dalrymple, 2 Hag. Con. 54, 4 Eng. Ec. 485, 489; Shelf. Mar. Div. 5–7.

cohabitation,—that, in a state of nature, would be a marriage, and, in the absence of all civil and religious institutions, might safely be presumed to be, as it is popularly called, a *marriage in the sight of God*."[1] Did parties coming thus together mean fornication or did they mean marriage?

Here it is seen that there should not only be words of promise, but that they should be uttered with matrimonial intent. To ascertain the purpose of the parties in each case, the courts will look at all the circumstances; and even admit parol evidence to contradict the terms of a written contract; in this respect modifying the ordinary rules of evidence. For writings of matrimonial acknowledgment may have been interchanged as a blind or cover for some scheme well understood between the parties.[2] Or again by way of jest.[3] But in cases of doubt the rule is to sustain the marriage as lawful and binding. If there has been continued intercourse between the parties, this presumption becomes of course still stronger. And if promises were exchanged, while one acted in good faith and in earnest, the other is not permitted to plead a mental reservation.[4]

Words of present promise, in order to constitute a marriage, must contemplate a present, not a future, assumption of the status. And herein lies a difficulty: that of discriminating between actual marriage and what we now commonly term an engagement. If the agreement be by words of present promise,—as if the parties should say, "We agree to be henceforth man and wife,"—the marriage is perfect. The form of expression is not material.[5] And Swinburne says that though the words should not of themselves conclude matrimony, yet the marriage would be good if it appeared that such was the in-

[1] 1 Hag. Con. 216, 4 Eng. Ec. 367, 374. See 1 Bish. Mar. & Div. 4th ed. §§ 216-267 and cases cited; 2 Kent Com. 86 and *n.*; 1 Fras. Dom. Rel. 149, 184, 187, 212.

[2] Dalrymple *v.* Dalrymple, 2 Hag. Con. 54, 105, 4 Eng. Ec. 485, 508, 509, cited in 1 Bish. Mar. & Div. 4th ed. §§ 239-241.

[3] Ib.

[4] Ib. And see 1 Fras. Dom. Rel. 213; Lockyer *v.* Sinclair, 8 Scotch Sess. Cas. N. S. 582.

[5] 1 Bish. Mar. & Div. 4th ed. §§ 227, 229; 1 Fras. Dom. Rel. 145-149.

tent.[1] The proposal of one must be actually accepted by the other; though such acceptance may be indicated by acts, such as a nod or courtesy. Written promises are of course unnecessary; though the reported cases show frequently letters or other writings interchanged, from which the intent was gathered. And in the celebrated Scotch case of *Dalrymple* v. *Dalrymple*, a marriage promise was established from the successive united acknowledgments of the parties as man and wife, the writings having been preserved by the lady and produced by her at the trial. In this case the principle was sustained, that words importing secrecy or alluding to some future act or public acknowledgment, when superadded to words of present promise, do not invalidate the agreement.[2] More uncertainty arises in matrimonial contracts where a condition inconsistent with marriage is superadded; as if parties should agree to live together as man and wife for ten years; but *bona fide* intent may be fairly presumed where there are no special circumstances to throw light upon the conduct of the parties.[3]

Marriage by words of future promise is consummated when two persons agree to marry at some future period and afterwards actually do cohabit. But in this class of cases it is requisite that the promise *de futuro* should be absolute and mutual. Mere courtship does not suffice, though followed by carnal intercourse.[4] Nor in general do words of promise with immoral conditions annexed. It is not clear whether cohabitation after *verba de futuro* raises a conclusive presumption of marriage at law or not: the more reasonable doctrine, however, is that it

[1] Swinb. Spousals, 2d ed. 87.

[2] Dalrymple *v.* Dalrymple, 2 Hag. Con. 54, 4 Eng. Ec. 485; McInnes *v.* More, Ferg. Consist. Law Rep. 33; Hoggan *v.* Cragie, Maclean & Rob. 942.

[3] See 1 Bish. Mar. & Div. 4th ed. §§ 245–250; Currie *v.* Turnbull, Hume, 373; 1 Fras. Dom. Rel. 154. See Hamilton *v.* Hamilton, 9 Cl. & F. 327; Hantz *v.* Sealy, 6 Binn. 405; Robertson *v.* Cowdry, 2 West. Law Jour. 191, and in Bish. supra.

[4] Reid *v.* Laing, 1 Shaw Ap. Cas. 440; Stewart *v.* Menzies, 2 Rob. Ap. Cas. 547, 591; 1 Fras. Dom. Rel. 188; Reg. *v.* Millis, 10 Cl. & F. 534, 780; Dumaresly *v.* Fishly, 3 A. K. Mar. 368; 1 Bish. Mar. & Div. 4th ed. §§ 253–265 and other cases cited.

does not, and that the intent of the parties may be shown as in other cases. But innocence will be inferred, if possible, rather than guilt.[1] So it has been said that where a legal impediment exists to a marriage between persons living in licentious intercourse, as the impediment sinks the status rises.[2] In New York, this doctrine of marriage by words *de futuro* is utterly repudiated, and it is maintained that informal marriages were unknown to the English common law.[3] This last has been long a mooted point in the courts, and will ever remain so; but whatever may have been the historical fact, certain it is that the necessity of a more formal observance of marriage has been almost universally recognized; and the very words, "marriage in the sight of God," so familiar to the readers of the Scotch matrimonial law, not only import the peculiar embarrassments which attend the justification of such loosely contracted alliances before the world, but attests the solemn character of this institution.

All the learning of informal marriages was swept out of the English courts when formal religious celebration was prescribed by positive statute. Ceremonials had long been required by those canons upon which the ecclesiastical law was based. Lord Hardwicke's Act, passed in the reign of George II.,[4] is the most famous of these statutes. This act required all marriages to be solemnized in due form in a parish church or public chapel, with previous publication of the bans; and marriages not so solemnized were pronounced void, unless dispensation should be granted by special license. Some harsh

[1] See Cheney *v.* Arnold, 15 N. Y. 345; Duncan *v.* Duncan, 10 Ohio, St. 181; and comments of Mr. Bishop, supra, §§ 255–258; Reg. *v.* Millis, 10 Cl. & F. 534; Swinb. Spousals, 2d ed. 225, 226.

[2] 1 Bish. Mar. & Div. 4th ed. § 248. See Breadalbane Case, Law Rep. 1 H. L. (Scotch) 182.

[3] Cheney *v.* Arnold, 15 N. Y. 345. The opinion of Lord Stowell in the case of Dalrymple *v.* Dalrymple, to which we have alluded, is an admirable exposition of the law of informal marriages. It is a masterpiece of judicial eloquence and careful research.

[4] 26 Geo. 2, c. 33 (1753).

provisions of this act were relaxed in the reign of George IV., but soon re-enacted.[1] More recent legislation permits of a civil ceremonial before a register, to satisfy such as may have conscientious scruples against marriage in church.[2] Such, too, is the general tenor of legislation in this country; the law justly regarding civil observances and public registration sufficient for its own purposes, while human nature clings to the religious ceremonial.[3]

Either celebration before a clergyman or in presence of such civil officers as the statute may designate is therefore at the option of parties choosing at the present day to marry. This is the law of England and America. And the only controversies ever likely to occur in our courts would be where the language of the statutes in some particular State left it doubtful whether marriages celebrated informally were to be considered absolutely null. It is to be borne in mind that Lord Hardwicke's Act is of too recent a date to be considered as part of our common law. Was, then, marriage *in facie ecclesiæ* essential in England before the passage of this act? It is admitted that the religious marriage celebration was customary previous to the Reformation. It is further allowed that the church, centuries ago, created an impediment, now obsolete, called precontract, the effect of which was that parties engaged to be married were bound by an indissoluble tie, so that either one could compel the other to submit at any time to the ceremonial marriage. But whether precontract rendered children legitimate, and carried dower, curtesy, and the other incidents of a valid marriage, is not clear. In 1844, the question whether at the common law a marriage without religious ceremony was valid went to the English House of Lords, and resulted in an equal division.[4] And, curiously enough, such was the fate of a

1 3 Geo. 4; 4 Geo. 4, c. 76.

2 See 6 & 7 Wm. 4, c. 85 & c. 88; 7 Wm. 4, and 1 Vict. c. 22, and 3 & 4 Vict. c. 92.

3 See 2 Kent Com. 88–90; 1 Bish. Mar. & Div. 4th ed. § 279.

4 Reg. *v.* Millis, 10 Cl. & F. 534.

similar case in this country before the highest tribunal in the land.[1] So that we may fairly consider the law on this point as for ever unsettled.[2]

Among most nations and in all ages has the celebration of marriage been attended with peculiar forms and ceremonies, which have partaken more or less of the religious character. Even the most barbarous tribes so treat it where they hold to the institution at all. The Greeks offered up a solemn sacrifice, and the bride was led in great pomp to her new home. In Rome, similar customs prevailed down to the time of Tiberius. Marriage, it is true, degenerated afterwards into a mere civil contract of the loosest description; parties being permitted to cohabit and separate with almost equal freedom.[3] The early Christians, there is reason to suppose, treated marriage as a civil contract; yielding perhaps to the prevailing Roman law. Yet the teachings of the New Testament and church discipline gave peculiar solemnity to the relation. And religious observances must have prevailed at an early date; for in process of time marriage became a sacrament. In England, centuries later, it needed only Lord Hardwicke's Act to apply statute law to a universal practice; and although, in the time of Cromwell, justices of the peace were permitted to perform the ceremony, popular usage by no means sanctioned the change. Informal marriages are uncommon even in Scotland where the civil law prevails. In our own country, it is not surprising that local jurisprudence should have exhibited some signs of reaction

[1] Jewell *v.* Jewell, 1 How. (U. S.) 219.

[2] See full discussion of this question with authorities in note to 2 Kent Com. 87; also in 1 Bish. Mar. & Div. 269–282. The American doctrine is, that the intervention of one *in holy orders* was not essential at common law. This is the view of Chancellor Kent, Judge Reeve, and Professor Greenleaf, as expressed in their respective text-books; also the general current of American decisions. Mr. Bishop confirms these conclusions while suggesting new reasons. Such a rule however is not in conflict with the statement of the text. See 1 Bish. Mar. & Div. 4th ed., §§ 279–282, and decisions collated; 2 Kent Com. 87; Reeve Dom. Rel. 195 *et seq.*; 2 Greenl. Ev. § 460.

[3] Smith's Dict. Antiq. "Marriage."

against ancient canon and kingly ordinance. Yet even with us, the almost universal custom repudiates informal and civil observances; and, secured in the privilege of choosing prosaic and business-like methods of procedure, Christian America yields its testimony in favor of marriage *in facie ecclesiæ.*[1]

The consent of parents or guardians was not necessary to perfect a marriage at the common law. But Lord Hardwicke's Act made the marriage of minors void without such consent first obtained.[2] This proved intolerable. A *bona fide* and apparently regular marriage was in one instance set aside, after important rights had intervened, for no other cause than that an absent father, supposed to be dead, but turning up unexpectedly, had failed to bestow his permission, and the mother had acted in his stead.[3] Gretna Green marriages, on Scotch soil, became the usual recourse for children with unwilling protectors. The law was afterwards modified so that without the requisite consent, marriages, although forbidden, might remain valid.[4] And these features are found to characterize the marriage acts in the different States of this country.[5]

[1] See 2 Kent Com. 89 and authorities cited.

We do not mean to imply that marriage is a sacrament, or that religious ceremonies are essential to its due observance. We are speaking only of the universal testimony as to the fitness of peculiar and in general religious observances. Judge Reeve, exhibiting his contempt for "Popish" practices, says, "There is nothing in the nature of a marriage contract that is more sacred than that of other contracts that requires the interposition of a person in holy orders, or that it should be solemnized in church." Reeve Dom. Rel. 196. At the time he wrote was not the practice prevailing in New England contrary to his theory, as it was before and as it remains still? And who has ever proposed in modern times to perform a business contract in church?

[2] 26 Geo. 2, c. 33. See 2 Kent Com. 85; Rex *v.* Hodnett, 1 T. R. 96; 1 Bish. Mar. & Div. 4th ed. §§ 293–295 and cases cited.

[3] Hayes *v.* Watts, 2 Phillim. 43.

[4] Rex *v.* Birmingham, 8 B. & C. 29; Shelf. Mar. & Div. 309–322; Stat. 4 Geo. 4, c. 76.

[5] 1 Bish. Mar. & Div. §§ 341–347 and cases cited; Smyth *v.* the State, 13 Ark. 696; Wyckoff *v.* Boggs, 2 Halst. 138; Bollin *v.* Shiner, 2 Jones Pa. 205; and see Wood *v.* Adams, 35 N. H. 32; Kent *v.* The State, 8 Blackf. 163. The language of some statutes leaves the point in doubt as to whether marriages without the consent of parents renders the marriage void or only subjects offending parties to a penalty.

Clandestine marriages are doubtless to be discouraged, and the law will willingly inflict penalties upon clergymen, magistrates, and all others who aid the parties in their unwise conduct; but experience shows that legislation cannot safely interpose much farther.

Defective marriages have in some instances been legalized by statute; as where parties within the prohibited degrees of consanguinity or affinity have united. So with marriages before a person professing to be a clergyman or justice of the peace, but without actual authority. On principle, there seems no reason to doubt that any government, through its legislative branch, may unite a willing pair in matrimony, as well as pass general laws for that purpose.[1] But though legislative divorces are not unfrequent, a legislative marriage is something unknown, not to say uncalled for.

A few words may be added concerning the conflict of laws relating to marriage. In England, such cases do not often come before the courts; but with us they are very common, the more so as each State adopts its own system concerning marriage and divorce. Marriage is favored beyond ordinary contracts in all nations. It is a well-recognized rule that a marriage lawful where celebrated is lawful everywhere; and that a marriage unlawful where celebrated is unlawful everywhere.[2] This rule, public policy, common morality, and the comity of nations demands, shall be enforced. Even when parties leave their own State or country, for the express purpose of evading the legal requirements, marry abroad, and then return, the marriage is to be sustained. This doctrine was very liberally applied in England, when the famous Gretna Green method of union were pronounced indissoluble.[3] So in this country,

[1] Brunswick *v.* Litchfield, 2 Greenl. 28; Moore *v.* Whitaker, 2 Harring. 50; Goshen *v.* Richmond, 4 Allen, 458; 1 Bish. Mar. & Div. 4th ed. §§ 657–659.

[2] Story Confl. Laws, §§ 79–81; 2 Kent Com. 91; Scrimshire *v.* Scrimshire, 2 Hag. Consist. Rep. 395; Harford *v.* Morris, 2 Hag. Consist. Rep. 423. Lord Tenterden in Lacon *v.* Higgins, 3 Starkie's N. P. Cases, 178; Simonin *v.* Mallac, 2 Swab. & T. 67.

[3] Compton *v.* Bearcroft, Bul. N. P. 114, 2 Hag. Consist. Rep. 443.

where persons disqualified by the laws of their own State, cross over into another.[1] In all such cases, the principle of ordinary contracts is disregarded, and the *lex loci contractûs* is permitted to prevail over the *lex domicilii.* But this doctrine, although favored by most writers on public law, has not received their unanimous support. Huberus, a continental jurist, maintained contrary to the view afterwards expressed in *Compton* v. *Bearcroft*, by the English courts, — that where parties go to a foreign country, in order to evade their own laws which require the assent of parent or guardian, their marriage should be deemed invalid; for, he observes, such acts tend *ad eversionem juris*, and should not be encouraged.[2] This opinion finds favor in France and Holland. And there is a statute in Massachusetts to the same purport.[3] But *Compton* v. *Bearcroft* is good law in England and most parts of the United States.[4]

There are exceptions to the rule of comity. Among them are to be classed immoral marriages, — or such as may be considered prohibited by the law of God. No Christian nation would tolerate polygamy within its borders on the plea that the marriage took place in some Asiatic country. Nor would incest be permitted.[5] Nor, we apprehend, would the marriages of such as are mentally and physically incapable. In *Conway* v. *Beazley*, the English courts refused to recognize a Scotch divorce, and set aside a second marriage; but the facts showed

[1] Stevenson *v.* Gray, 17 B. Monr. 193; 1 Bish. Mar. & Div. 4th ed. § 355 and American cases cited.

[2] De Conflictu Legum, § 8. See other authorities cited to the same conclusion in Story Confl. Laws, § 123. Chancellor Kent intimates his disapproval of the doctrine of Compton *v.* Bearcroft. Note 6 to 2 Kent Com. 91. Burge, in 1 Col. & For. Laws, 194, attempts to reconcile the views of Huberus with the English rule.

[3] See Commonwealth *v.* Hunt, 4 Cush. 49.

[4] Swift *v.* Kelly, 3 Knapp, 257; Morgan *v.* McGhee, 5 Humph. 13; Wall *v.* Williamson, 8 Ala. 48; Patterson *v.* Gaines, 6 How. (U. S.) 550; Phillips *v.* Gregg, 10 Watts, 158; Fornstill *v.* Murray, 1 Bland, 479; and 1 Bish. Mar. & Div. 4th ed. § 356.

[5] Hyde *v.* Woodmansee, Law Rep. 1 P. & D. 130; Story Confl. Laws, § 114; 1 Burge Col. & For. Laws, 188; 1 Bish. Mar. & Div. 4th ed. §§ 372–376.

a clear case of bigamy.[1] Some difficulties must doubtless arise under the conflict of American local statutes relative to the impediments which follow a complete divorce.[2] The reasoning of Lord Chancellor Campbell and other peers in the recent English case of *Brook* v. *Brook*, which went on appeal to the House of Lords, would seem to carry the exception to the rule of comity so far as to include not only immoral marriages but marriages in violation of the law of domicile, which absolutely forbids such unions everywhere.[3] The point actually sustained however in this case was the invalidity of a marriage by affinity in a foreign country, where such marriages are lawful; but which have always been regarded as within the prohibition of God's law in England. The doctrine claimed, therefore, seems in reality that each nation shall define God's law for itself. The *lex loci contractûs*, we may remark in passing, does not seem of necessity to determine such legal consequences of a foreign marriage as the legitimation of antenuptial offspring.[4]

A marriage invalid where celebrated is as a rule invalid everywhere. But this principle being unfavorable to marriage, is applied with more hesitation than its converse.[5] Citizens sojourning abroad, parties made amenable to the general laws of another country, and yet retaining customs of their own, *quasi* foreigners who do not forfeit their original allegiance, often have special privileges shown them by the comity of nations. Thus, Protestants in a Roman Catholic country have been allowed

[1] 3 Hag. Ec. 639, 5 Eng. Ec. 242. See also recent cases of Shaw *v.* Gould, Law Rep. 3 H. L. 55; Wilson's Trusts, Law Rep. 1 Eq. 247.

[2] See Williams *v.* Oates, 5 Ire. 535; Dickson *v.* Dickson, 1 Yerg. 110; Ponsford *v.* Johnson, 2 Blatch. 51.

[3] 3 Smale & G. 481; s. c. 9 H. L. Cas. 193. See Sutton *v.* Warren, 10 Met. 451; Stevenson *v.* Gray, 17 B. Monr. 193.

[4] Putnam *v.* Putnam, 8 Pick. 433. See on this general subject Lord Brougham in Warrender *v.* Warrender, 2 Cl. & F. 488; cases cited in note to 2 Kent Com. 93; references *supra* to treatises of Story, Burge *v.* Bishop. The marriage abroad of one attainted of treason is lawful. Kynnaird *v.* Leslie, Law Rep. 1 C. P. 389.

[5] Lord Stowell in Ruding *v.* Smith, 2 Hag. Con. 371, 4 Eng. Ec. 551, 560.

to marry after their own forms.[1] Settlers from foreign parts are often permitted to take their national customs with them.[2] There are statutes, both in Great Britain and the United States, which permit citizens to marry abroad in presence of certain accredited representatives of their government, as ministers and consuls; and such marriages are considered lawful, though one of the parties is a foreigner.[3] Whatever may be pronounced by the courts in the adopted country of an emigrant, a marriage lawful by the laws of his native land would in his native land generally be upheld, if he had not forfeited his allegiance.

[1] But this seems permitted only on the assumption that the local law disqualifies. See 1 Bish. Mar. & Div. 4th ed. with authorities cited, § 390 *et seq.*; Kent *v.* Burgess, 11 Sim. 361; Lord Eldon in Lord Cloncurry's case, Cruise on Dignities, 276.

[2] See Ruding *v.* Smith, and 1 Bish. Mar. & Div. *supra;* Story Confl. Laws, § 2*a*.

[3] Lloyd *v.* Petigean, 2 Curt. Ec. 251, 7 Eng. Ec. 105; Loring *v.* Thorndike, 5 Allen, 257; 12 U. S. Stats. at Large, 79; 1860, c. 179, § 31. Invading armies carry the matrimonial law of their domicile with them. See 1 Bish. Mar. & Div. 4th ed. §§ 399, 400; Ruding *v.* Smith, *supra;* Lord Ellenborough in Rex *v.* Brampton, 10 East, 282.

CHAPTER II.

THE GENERAL DISABILITIES OF COVERTURE.

WHEN the parties to a lawful marriage have once completed the ceremony, or as it is said, have executed the contract of marriage, they are admitted into the marriage relation, and their mutual rights and obligations become at once limited, protected, and enforced by the general law of husband and wife. What that law is, will constitute the topic of discussion in this and the succeeding chapters. We have already alluded to the confusion and uncertainty which exist at the present day, and particularly in many of the United States, in the law of husband and wife, owing to the transition period through which we seem to be passing from the marriage relation of the common law to that known to the civil law.[1]

Our subject will be most conveniently treated by taking up the common-law doctrine first and thoroughly examining its principles; then passing to the modern or civil law doctrine, for discussion in like manner. First, then the rights and disabilities of marriage on the coverture scheme; secondly, the rights and disabilities of marriage on the separate existence scheme. But since these rights and disabilities have varied little, except as to the wife's property, we may here investigate those general principles of the common law which concern the person, once and for all.

The general principle of coverture, as defined by Blackstone, and other writers, is this: that by marriage, the husband and wife become one person in law; that is to say, the very being or legal existence of the woman, is suspended during the

[1] See chapter on "Domestic Relations."

marriage, or, at least, is incorporated and consolidated into that of the husband, under whose wing, protection, and *cover* she performs every thing; and is therefore called in the law-French a *feme-covert*, *fœmina viro co-operta;* is said to be *covert-baron*, or under the protection and influence of her *baron* or lord; and her condition during her marriage is called her *coverture*.[1] For this reason the term applied to the relation of husband and wife in the old books is *baron and feme*. Upon this fundamental principle depend at the common law, the general rights, duties, and disabilities of marriage. But this very definition shows inaccuracy, to say nothing of unfairness of application. Here are two conflicting notions: one that the existence of the wife is actually lost or suspended; the other that there is still an existence, which is held in subordination to the will of her lord and master, which last the word *coverture* fitly expresses. It will appear in fact that while some of the wife's disabilities seem based upon the one notion, others are based upon the latter, and probably more correct one. The wife's disabilities are deemed by Blackstone, "for the most part, intended for her protection and benefit." And he adds, by way of rhetorical period, "so great a favorite is the female sex of the laws of England!" a proposition which his commentators have gravely proceeded to dispute and dissect, and, it must be added, not without good success.[2]

The husband's right of dominion is therefore fully recognized at the common law. And never was the English doctrine, despite its failings, set forth in more terse and forcible language than in the words of Sir Thomas Smith: "The naturalest and first conjunction of two towards the making a further society of continuance, is of the husband and wife, each having care of the family: the man to get, to travel abroad, and to defend; the wife to save, to stay at home, and to distribute

1 1 Bl. Com. 442; Co. Litt. 112; 2 Kent Com. 129.

2 1 Bl. Com. 445; notes by Christian, Hargrave and others. It is probable that Blackstone used this expression in a strain of playful gallantry, not uncommon with lecturers. Even Chancellor Kent's observations are not free from suspicion. See 2 Kent Com. 182, closing sentence at foot of the page.

that which is gotten, for the nurture of the children and family; which to maintain, God has given the man greater wit, better strength, better courage, to compel the woman to obey, by reason or force; and to the woman, beauty, fair countenance, and sweet words, to make the man obey her again for love. Thus each obeyeth, and commandeth the other; and they two together rule the house, so long as they remain in one."[1]

In accordance with these principles, and perhaps too the laws of nature and divine revelation, the husband is the head of the family and the *dignior persona.* As to the more strictly personal consequences of the marriage union, his rights and duties have suffered no violent change at our modern law. It is for the wife to love, honor, and obey; it is for the husband to love, cherish, and protect. The husband is bound to furnish his wife with a suitable home; to provide according to his means and condition of life, for her maintenance and support; to defend her from personal insult and wrong; to be kind to her; to see that the offspring of their union are brought up with tenderness and care; and generally to conduct himself, not according to the strict letter of the matrimonial contract, but in its spirit. So long as he does this, his authority is acknowledged with common law, and if the wife's wishes and interests clash with his own, she must yield.

Marriage necessarily supposes a home and mutual cohabitation. Each party has therefore a right to the society of the other. They married to secure such society. And the obligation rests upon both to live together — or as the expression sometimes goes *to adhere.* This is the universal law.[2] Its observance is essential to the mutual comfort of husband and wife, and the well-being, if not the existence, of their children. But to this rule there are obvious exceptions. The wife is not bound to live with her husband, where he is imprisoned, or

[1] Commonwealth of England, Book 1, ch. 2, quoted in Bing. Inf. & Cov. p. 184.

[2] 1 Fras. Dom. Rel. 447, 452

has otherwise ceased to be a voluntary agent, and to perform the duties of a husband. So if he is banished, for marriage does not force the parties to share the punishment of one another's crimes. This was the rule of the civil as it is that of the common law.[1] And in general such causes as would justify divorce *a mensa et thoro* or divorce *a vinculo* in any state justify the innocent party in breaking off matrimonial cohabitation. Partial and temporary separation for purposes connected with the husband's profession or trade, — as for instance, where he is an army officer — constitutes no breach of the marriage relation, unless continued beyond necessary and reasonable bounds, or accompanied by negligence to provide while absent for the maintenance of wife and family. And under some other circumstances cohabitation may be properly allowed to cease for a time, without involving the breach of marital obligations.[2]

As there must be a home, so there is also a matrimonial domicile of the parties recognized by universal law. And the husband, as the *dignior persona*, has the right to fix it where he pleases. Grotius says: "*De domicilio constituere jus est marito.*"[2] But this applies only to the real domicile of the husband; not to a fictitious place of residence which he may take up for a special purpose, or as an involuntary agent. In a genuine sense the domicile of the husband becomes that of the wife, and wherever he goes she is bound to go likewise; not, however, unless his intent be *bona fide* and without fraud upon her property rights.[3]

Any contract, therefore, which the husband may make with his wife or her friends, before marriage, not to take her away from the neighborhood of her parents, is void. Public policy repudiates all contracts in restraint of such marital rights. There might be circumstances under which such a promise would be reasonable, but at best it can create a moral obliga-

1 Co. Litt. 133; 1 Bl. Com. 443; 1 Fras. Dom. Rel. 448; 2 Kent Com. 154.

2 See 2 Kent Com. 181; 1 Fras. Dom. Rel. 240 *et seq.*, ib. 447; Chretien *v.* Her Husband, 17 Martin, La. 60.

3 1 Fras. Dom. Rel. 447, 448; 1 Burge Col. & For. Laws, 260.

tion only. The husband has the right to establish his domicile at any time, wherever he pleases, and the wife must follow him through the world.[1]

But the courts of our day hesitate to apply a rule so apparently harsh as that announced in the last sentence. With the increasing regard for female privileges has grown up a strong disposition to reduce the husband's right over the matrimonial domicile to a sort of *divisum imperium*. The question is not new, whether reasonable exceptions to this rule may not exist; as, for instance, where the husband proposed to take the wife into an enemy's country, *flagrante bello*, or on a journey perilous to her life.[2] Such exceptions may be justified, it is generally admitted, on the ground that the wife would be thereby exposed to bodily harm. But, whether the apprehension be that of personal violence, or ill health from the fatigue of a journey or the change of climate, little favor seems to have been shown to the wife either at the English or Scotch law, unless the circumstances rendered a change of domicile on her part equivalent to a moral suicide.[2] At the present day, a rule less stringent would doubtless be applied. Nay more, there are several recent decisions in this country which point to an obligation on the husband's part to show reasonable cause why his wife should follow him when he changes his abode.[3]

This later uncertainty in the law is unfortunate. Where a pair disagree in the choice of a home, either the right of decision must belong to one of them or the court should sit as umpire. No one has suggested that the wife should choose the domicile, nor can judicial interference be well called in except to divorce the parties. Yet, without a home in common, of what avail is matrimony? We cannot but regret that any of our courts should seem to legalize domestic discord; that there should be good American authority to sanction the wife's refusal

1 Hair *v.* Hair, 10 Rich. Eq. 163.

2 See 1 Fras. Dom. Rel. 448.

3 Bishop *v.* Bishop, 30 Penn. St. 412; Gleason *v.* Gleason, 4 Wis. 64; Powell *v.* Powell, 29 Vt. 148. See Moffatt *v.* Moffatt, 5 Cal. 280.

to accompany her husband on any such trivial pretext as "the dislike to be near his relatives."[1] Perhaps, however, the harsh remedy usually sought to be applied in modern cases—divorce for wilful desertion—may tempt our tribunals to relax the old doctrine of conjugal obedience for the wife's benefit. For, after all, the decision is in favor of prolonging the marriage relation.

The English rule as to the wife's duty of adherence still continues strict. A wife recently petitioned for divorce, on the ground of her husband's desertion. The facts showed that shortly after her marriage she went with her husband to Jamaica, where he held an appointment from which he derived not more than £100 a year, and in consequence of his slender income she had to put up with some hardship. Her health suffered, and in less than a year, namely, in 1846, she returned to England. Her husband continued abroad, during the greater part of the time at Jamaica, where he succeeded in getting a more lucrative appointment. When she left him for England, he acted kindly to her, promised to allow her £30 a year, but made no arrangement for a permanent separation. Their correspondence continued until 1851, when the husband asked her to return, and provided funds for her passage, but she wrote that her health would not permit her to do so. Here all the correspondence and intercourse ceased until 1856, when an allowance was again effected through the intervention of a relative; this the husband continued until 1860, and then stopped it. He appears to have led a loose life after his wife's refusal to return. The court held that these circumstances did not constitute desertion on the husband's part nor entitle her to divorce.[2]

As no legal process can safely be enforced to compel husband and wife to live together, against the will of either, so the peace

[1] Powell *v.* Powell, *supra.*

[2] Keech *v.* Keech, Law Rep. 1 P. & D. 641 (1868). Adultery being proved, however, divorce was granted on that ground.

of society forbids that they should sue one another for damages for breach of the marital obligations. Here again is marriage *sui generis*, and not like other contracts. But the failure of the one to perform recognized duties may sometimes absolve the other from certain corresponding obligations. Thus, if the wife leaves her home without justifiable cause, the husband may refuse to support her.[1] If the husband is cruel, or makes his home unfit for a chaste woman to live in, the wife may leave and compel him to support her elsewhere.[2] This is well recognized law. In general, however, the violation of marital obligations is effectually punishable, not by enforcing them, but by putting an end to the relation altogether.[3]

Inasmuch as the husband is entitled to his wife's society, he may recover her from any person who would withhold or withdraw her from him. This is a well-understood principle the world over.[4] And the common law gives him the right to sue for damages all persons who seek to entice her away.[5] But in such cases malice and improper motives are always to be considered; and parents and near relatives stand on a different footing from strangers. So is the previous conduct of the husband towards his wife a material element to be considered; since this, and not the interference of others, may have occasioned the separation. It is one thing to actively promote domestic discord, but quite another to harbor from motives of kindness and humanity one who seeks shelter from the oppression of her own lawful protector.

But such conduct, whatever the motives, is exceedingly perilous on the part of strangers, generally open to misconstruction, and never to be encouraged. They should leave the parties to

[1] 2 Kent Com. 147; Manby *v.* Scott, 1 Mod. Rep. 124; 1 Bl. Com. 443.

[2] Houliston *v.* Smyth, 3 Bing. 127. And see *infra*, as to wife's necessaries.

[3] See 1 Bish. Mar. & Div. § 771; 1 Fras. Dom. Rel. 452.

[4] 1 Fras. Dom. Rel. 240, 241.

[5] 1 Chitty Plead. 91; Hutcheson *v.* Peck, 5 Johns. 196; Friend *v.* Thompson, Wright, 636; Rabe *v.* Hanna, 5 Ham. 530; Bennett *v.* Smith, 21 Barb. 439; Barnes *v.* Allen, 30 Barb. 663.

their legal remedies against one another. With parents it is different. There are several cases in the American reports where a father is not only held to be absolved from liability for sheltering his daughter who has fled from a drunken and profligate husband, but even stimulated to do so. "A father's house," says Chancellor Kent, "is always open to his children; and whether they be married or unmarried, it is still to them a refuge from evil and a consolation in distress. Natural affection establishes and consecrates this asylum."[1] But this does not justify even a parent in hostile interference against the husband; for the latter's rights are still superior; and the father must give up his daughter, and the marriage-offspring, whenever she wishes to return, unless the proper tribunal has decreed otherwise; though he might, we suppose, by fair arguments, urged to promote her true good, seek to dissuade her from returning. The legal doctrine seems to be this, that honest motives may shield a parent from the consequences of indiscretion, while adding nothing to his right of actual control; that a husband forfeits his right to sue others for enticement, where his own misconduct justified and actually caused the separation, and so long as it continues voluntary on the wife's part; but that otherwise his remedy is complete against all persons whomsoever who have lent their countenance to any scheme for breaking up his household.

A curious case of this sort came before the Supreme Court of North Carolina in 1849. The defendant had enticed away the wife of the plaintiff. The two afterwards entered into an agreement that the defendant should keep the plaintiff's wife and child at his own home, and should raise, educate, and provide for the child by appropriating the portion of property formerly intended for the mother's provision; that he should not be liable for having enticed the wife away; and that the plaintiff might visit his wife and child not exceeding four or

[1] Hutcheson *v.* Peck, *supra.* See also Friend *v.* Friend, Wright, 639; Friend *v.* Thompson; Bennett *v.* Smith, *supra.*

five days at a time. The wife was not made a party to the contract, though it appeared to have been made with her approval. The plaintiff afterwards rescinded the agreement, demanded his wife, and, upon refusal of the defendant to give her up, sued him in damages. The court sustained him; pronouncing the contract to be "neither in form or substance a contract for a separation, but simply a license to harbor the wife and child, securing the defendant against any legal responsibility for so doing until withdrawn." And it was further intimated that such a contract was absolutely void as against public policy.[1]

In a ruder state of society the husband frequently maintained his authority by force. The old common law recognized the right of moderate correction, which, according to Blackstone, was deemed a privilege by the lower orders in his day.[2] The civil law went still further, permitting, in certain gross misdemeanors, violent flogging with whips and rods.[3] But since the time of Charles II. the wife has been regarded more as the companion of her husband; and this right of chastisement may be regarded as exceedingly questionable at the present day. The rule of love has superseded the rule of force. Few cases of importance are to be found on this subject. In England, not many years ago, where a wife sought divorce from bed and board for cruelty, it was shown that the husband had spit upon her, pushed and dragged her about the room, and once slapped her face; and upon this proof the divorce was granted.[4] The right to inflict corporal punishment upon the wife seems not to have been favored in this country, and its exercise would now generally justify proceedings for a divorce.[5]

[1] Barbee *v.* Armstead, 10 Ired. 530. See also 1 Burge Col. & For. Laws, 238, for a like doctrine at the civil law.

[2] 1 Bl. Com. 444, 445.

[3] *Flagellis et fustibus acriter verberare uxorem.* See 1 Bl. Com. 445.

[4] Saunders *v.* Saunders, 1 Rob. Ec. Rep. 549. And see 1 Bish. Mar. & Div. 4th ed. §§ 748, 754.

[5] But see recent case of State *v.* Rhodes, 1 Phill. (N.C.) 453, where the right of moderate correction is sustained.

But either spouse may use force in self-defence. And the husband may restrain his wife from acts of violence against others as well as himself; certainly wherever the law makes him answerable in damages for her misbehavior.[1]

The right of gentle restraint over the wife's person rests upon better authority than that of chastisement. This right, however, depends upon the proposition that the husband is *dignior persona*. And its exercise is often to be justified in the courts on the same grounds; namely, that he must answer to others for his wife's conduct. Blackstone says that in case of any gross misbehavior the husband can restrain his wife of her liberty. The later expression of Kent is, that he may resort to "gentle restraint."[2] Strong instances for the exercise of this right occur where the wife has eloped with a libertine and the husband wishes to bring her home, or where she purposes an elopement and he seeks to prevent it.[3] So restraint may be justified where she becomes insane, threatens him with danger, or wantonly destroys his property. And by virtue of the husband's authority over his own household, he might be allowed, if not by physical force, at least by moral coercion, to regulate her movements so as to prevent her from going to places, associating with people, or engaging in pursuits disapproved by himself on rational grounds. This doctrine has been asserted in England; and Mr. Fraser carries it to the extent of forbidding her relatives to visit her; "for," he adds, "though the wife may be very amiable, her connections may not be so."[4] But this rule is to be laid down with great caution, and it is especially unpopular in America. Mr. Justice Coleridge, in an English case, observes, that the husband's right must not be

[1] 2 Kent Com. 181; People *v.* Winters, 2 Parker (N. Y. Cr.), 10; 1 Bl. Com. 445; Richards *v.* Richards, 1 Grant, 389.

[2] 2 Kent Com. 181; 1 Bl. Com. 445. See 1 Bish. *supra*, § 756.

[3] So strongly does the common law detest conjugal unfaithfulness, that the husband who kills his wife or her paramour in the act of adultery is only guilty of manslaughter. See Regina *v.* Kelly, 2 Car. & K. 814.

[4] 1 Fras. Dom. Rel. 459.

exercised unnecessarily or with undue severity; and that the moment the wife, by her return to conjugal duties, makes the restraint of her person unnecessary, such restraint becomes unlawful.[1] For unreasonable and improper checks upon her liberties, the wife may have relief on *habeas corpus*. But the writ is not available for the husband to secure the person of his wife, voluntarily absenting herself from his house.[2]

Husband and wife may be indicted for assault and battery upon each other.[3] This is a means of redress not unfrequently sought against cruel husbands.

The custody of children belonged at common law to the father. Blackstone observes, "A mother, as such, is entitled to no power, but only to reverence and respect."[4] But by an English statute, passed in 1839, the Court of Chancery is permitted to interfere and award the custody of children to such parent as may be deemed most suitable. Its special object was to enable married women who should be ill-treated by their husbands to assert their rights without the fear of being separated from their offspring.[5] In this country, as we shall see hereafter, the tendency of legislation is to place the wife upon an equal footing with her husband in this respect.

When we come to the property rights of married women, the inequalities of the common law are plainly seen. The husband yields to his wife no participation whatever in his own property, whether acquired before or during the continuance of the marriage relation, except a certain right of inheritance to his goods and chattels, of which he can generally deprive her by his will and testament, and also dower in his real estate, which is her only substantial privilege. In return for this, she parts with all control, for the time being, over her own property, whensoever and howsoever obtained, by gift, grant, purchase, devise, or in-

[1] *In re* Cochrane, 8 Dowl. P. C. 631.
[2] Sandiland *Ex parte*, 12 E. L. & Eq. 463.
[3] Bradley *v*. The State, Walker, 156.
[4] 1 Bl. Com. 453.
[5] 2 & 3 Vict. c. 54; Warde *v*. Warde, 2 Ph. 786. See *infra*, Parent and Child.

heritance; gives him outright her personals in possession; allows him to appropriate to himself all outstanding demands, known in law as her *choses in action;* parts with the usufruct of her real estate, creating likewise a possible encumbrance upon it in the shape of tenancy by the curtesy; and finally takes, if she survives him, only her real estate, such of her personal property as remains undisposed of and unappropriated, with a few articles of wearing apparel and trinkets called *paraphernalia.* She cannot restrain his rights by will. She is not allowed to administer on his personal estate in preference to his own kindred, though the whole of it were once hers; while he can administer on her estate for his own benefit and exclude her kindred altogether, even from participation in the assets. Thus unequal are the property rights of husband and wife by the strict rule of coverture. We speak not here of recent statutory benefits conferred upon the wife; nor of that relief which equity affords in permitting property to be held to the wife's separate use, and giving her a provision from her *choses in action*, when the husband seeks its aid in appropriating them to his own use; but of what is to be properly termed the common law of husband and wife.[1]

Some recompense is afforded to the wife for the loss of her fortune, in the rule that her husband shall pay her debts contracted while a *feme sole;* that is, unmarried. And while coverture lasts he is liable for all just debts incurred in her support. He has even been held guilty of murder in the second degree when he has suffered her to die for want of proper supplies.[2] The wife cannot make a contract so as to bind herself; but in this, and other cases of express or implied authority, she can bind her husband, and so secure a maintenance. That which cannot be enforced by the wife as a matter of obligation is often attained at the common law in some indirect way.[3]

[1] See 1 Bl. Com. 442–445 and notes, by Christian, Hargrave, and others; 2 Kent Com. 130–143; and chapters *infra.*

[2] Reg. *v.* Plummer, 1 Car. & K. 600.

[3] Ch. 3 *infra.* See 1 Bl. Com. 442; 2 Kent Com. 143–149.

So too the husband is liable for the frauds and injuries of the wife, committed during coverture; being sued either alone or jointly with her, in accordance with the legal presumption of coercion in such cases. And he must respond in damages, whether she brought him a fortune by marriage or not. But this rule does not apply to crimes, except that the law shows the wife a certain indulgence where a similar presumption can be alleged on her behalf. On the other hand, the husband takes the benefit of such injuries as she may suffer, by suing with her and appropriating the compensation by way of damages to himself.[1]

We may add that the wife is relieved of the disabilities of coverture and placed upon the footing of a *feme sole*, with the privilege to contract, sue and be sued, on her own behalf, in one instance, namely, where her husband has abjured the realm or is banished; for he is then said to be dead at the law.[2] And the necessity of the case furnishes the strongest argument for this exception.

Some of the disabilities of the marriage relation are placed upon both parties at the common law; partly because of the want of mutuality where coverture exists; partly from considerations of public policy. Thus husband and wife cannot make gifts or sales to one another during coverture, though the same parties might have done so before and in contemplation of marriage. Nor can they in other respects contract or enter into covenants with one another.[3] Nor can one sue the other. But, as we shall hereafter see, equity introduces a different principle.

One of the most important of the mutual disabilities of the marriage state is the disqualification of husband and wife to testify as witnesses in the courts for or against one another. Blackstone places this prohibition on a technical ground,—unity

[1] Bl. Com. 443; 2 Kent Com. 149, 150. See ch. 4.

[2] 1 Bl. Com. 443; 2 Kent Com. 154.

[3] Lord Hardwicke in Lannoy *v.* Duke of Athol, 2 Atk. 448; 1 Bl. Com. 442; 2 Kent Com. 129.

of the person; for, he says, if they testify in behalf of one another they contradict the maxim "*Nemo propriâ causâ testis esse debet;*" and, if against one another, that other maxim, "*Nemo tenetur se ipsum accusare.*"[1] He also suggests interest as another ground for the rule. But a more solid reason than either is that of public policy. "The happiness of the married state," says Mr. Greenleaf, "requires that there should be the most unlimited confidence between husband and wife; and this confidence the law secures, by providing that it shall be kept for ever inviolable; that nothing shall be extracted from the bosom of the wife which was confided there by the husband."[2]

So unyielding is this rule, that mutual consent will not authorize the breach of it.[3] Whether the suit be civil or criminal, in law or at equity, it matters not. And after coverture has terminated by death or divorce, still the prohibition lasts as to all which took place while the relation existed.[4] The disability of the husband is in this respect as great as that of the wife.[5] So far, indeed, has the prohibition been carried, that in one case, where the defendant married a witness after she had been summoned into court, she was forbidden to testify.[6] The rule applies alike to evidence of declarations made by husband and wife for or against one another as to their testimony in person.[7]

This rule of exclusion applies only to persons occupying the

[1] 1 Bl. Com. 443.

[2] 1 Greenl. Evid. § 254. See also 2 Kent Com. 178–180, to the same effect.

[3] 1 Greenl. Evid. § 340 and cases cited; Lord Hardwicke in Barker *v.* Dixie cas. temp. Hardw. 264; Davis *v.* Dinwoody, 4 T. R. 679, per Lord Kenyon; *contra*, Pedley *v.* Wellesley, 3 Car. &. P. 558; 2 Kent Com. 179.

[4] Monroe *v.* Twistleton, cited in Averson *v.* Lord Kinnaird, 6 East, 192; Doker *v.* Hasler, Ry. & M. 198; Stein *v.* Bowman, 13 Pet. 223; 1 Greenl. Evid. § 337. See also Terry *v.* Belcher, 1 Bailey, 568; State *v.* Jolly, 3 Dev. & Bat. 110; Barnes *v.* Camack, 1 Barb. 392. But see Dickerman *v.* Graves, 6 Cush. 308.

[5] See cases cited in 1 Greenl. Evid. § 334.

[6] Pedley *v.* Wellesley, 3 Car. & P. 558. The authority of this case seems questionable.

[7] 1 Greenl. Evid. § 341; Alban *v.* Pritchett, 6 T. R. 680; Denn *v.* White, 7 T. R. 112; Kelly *v.* Small, 2 Esp. 716.

bona fide relation of husband and wife; not, of course, to parties in immoral cohabitation. But at the same time the courts lean kindly towards *prima facie* marriages, and make no rigid investigation.[1] The policy of the rule is evidently to treat as privileged communications all that passes between persons supposing themselves lawfully married, and at all events not to prejudice the rights of the innocent party to an invalid marriage; but the rule has not always been carried to such an extent.

Some exceptions exist to the rule, founded mainly on considerations of public policy. Thus the wife may testify as to her forcible abduction and marriage; but in such cases she is hardly to be considered the wife.[2] In general, husband and wife can make criminal complaints and testify against one another as to personal injuries; for this the rule of self-preservation requires.[3] High treason also was formerly held an exception to the rule; for the allegiance due to the crown was said to be paramount to all private considerations; but this is not probably good law at the present day.[4] The wife's testimony has been admitted as to some peculiar secret facts.[5] Dying declarations of one are admissible to charge the other with murder. And in collateral proceedings, only remotely affecting their mutual interests, their evidence is admissible though it may tend to criminate or contradict or subject the other to a legal demand; as in a suit relating to a pauper settlement, where the wife's testimony tends to convict her husband of bigamy.[6] To this we may add, that the wife's declarations

[1] 1 Greenl. Evid. § 339 and cases cited; 2 Stark. Evid. 400; Bull. N. P. 287; Campbell *v.* Twemlow, 1 Price, 81.

[2] 2 Russ. on Crimes, 605, 606; 1 Bl. Com. 443; 1 Greenl. Evid. § 343, and cases cited in note.

[3] See ibid.; and Ld. Mansfield in Bentley *v.* Cooke, 3 Doug. 422; 1 East. P. C. 455. But see Lord Thurlow in Sedgwick *v.* Walkins, 1 Ves. 49.

[4] 1 Greenl. Evid. § 345 and authorities cited; *contra*, 4 Bl. Com. 29.

[5] Rex *v.* Reading, cas. temp. Hardw. 79, 82; Ratcliff *v.* Wales, 1 Hill, 63; 1 Greenl. Evid. § 344.

[6] 1 Greenl. Evid. § 342; Fitch *v.* Hill, 11 Mass. 286; Griffin *v.* Brown, 2 Pick. 308; 2 Stark. Evid. 401.

may be given in evidence for or against her husband, where material, as part of the *res gestæ;* as in a suit regarding an insurance policy where she is the party insured; in an action against the husband for her board, he having turned her out of doors; and, in general, wherever she acts as his agent.[1] Where several are tried together for a joint offence, the wife of one is not a good witness against the others, so long as her testimony might affect her husband's case; but if he has already been convicted or acquitted, or the grounds of defence for each are entirely distinct, the rule is otherwise.[2] Both husband and wife may testify, after the relation has terminated, as to facts which came to each other's knowledge by means equally accessible to any person not standing in that relation; for here the same principle applies as in the case of privileged communications between attorney and client.[3]

There have been some important changes introduced into the law of evidence in some parts of this country by statute; such as permitting interested persons to testify in their own suits. Where the old doctrine prevails, the exclusion of the husband, by reason of direct interest, operates to exclude his wife likewise.[4] So the husband cannot be a witness in a controversy respecting his wife's separate estate, though in respect to other parties concerned he might be competent.[5] The English Evidence Act of 1853, 16 & 17 Vict. ch. 83 (which has been substantially enacted in some parts of this country), renders husbands and their wives competent and compellable witnesses for each other, except in criminal cases and in cases of adul-

1 See Averson *v.* Lord Kinnaird, 6 East, 188; Walton *v.* Green, 1 Car. & P. 621; Thomas *v.* Hargrave, Wright, 595; and other cases cited in note to 1 Greenl. Evid. § 342. But see Brown *v.* Laselle, 6 Blackf. 147.

2 Hall P. C. 301; Dalt. Just. c. 111; 1 Greenl. Evid. § 335 and notes; 1 Phil. Evid. 75 *n.*; Regina *v.* Williams, 3 Car. & P. 558; Rex *v.* Locker, 5 Esp. 107.

3 1 Greenl. Evid. § 338; Coffin *v.* Jones, 13 Pick. 445; Williams *v.* Baldwin, Vt. 506; Cornell *v.* Vanartsdalen, 4 Barr, 364.

4 1 Greenl. Evid. § 341; *Ex parte* Jones, 1 P. Wms. 610; and cf. Stat. 6 Geo. 4, ch. 16, § 37.

5 1 Burr. 424, per Lord Mansfield; 12 Vin. Abr. Evidence B. And see note to 1 Greenl. Evid. § 341, with authorities cited.

tery; but neither shall be compelled to disclose communications made during marriage.[1]

Story, in his Conflict of Laws,[2] after an extended discussion of the great diversity of laws existing in different countries, as to the incidents of marriage, lays down the following general rules, which are of general application. *First.* Where parties are married in a foreign country, and there is an express contract respecting their rights and property, present and future, it will be held equally valid everywhere, unless under the circumstances it stands prohibited by the laws of the country where it is sought to be enforced. It will act directly on movable property everywhere. But as to immovable property in a foreign territory, it will, at most, confer only a right of action, to be enforced according to the jurisdiction *rei sitæ*. *Second.* Where such an express contract applies in terms or intent only to present property, and there is a change of domicile, the law of the actual domicile will govern the rights of the parties as to all future acquisitions. *Third.* Where there is no express contract, the law of the matrimonial domicile will govern as to all the rights of the parties to their present property in that place, and as to all personal property everywhere, upon the principle that movables have no *situs*, or, rather, that they accompany the person everywhere. As to immovable property, the law *rei sitæ* will prevail. *Fourth.* Where there is no change of domicile, the same rule will apply to future acquisitions as to present property. *Fifth.* But where there is a change of domicile, the law of the actual domicile, and not of the matrimonial domicile, will govern as to all future acquisitions of movable property; and, as to all immovable property, the law *rei sitæ*.[3] He further adds, that although in a general sense the law of the matrimonial domicile is to govern in rela-

[1] See Ed. note to 10th ed. 2 Kent Com. 181; Stapleton *v.* Croft, 10 E. L. & Eq. 455; Barbat *v.* Allen, ib. 596; Alcock *v.* Alcock, 12 ib. 354. And see State *v.* Wilson, 30 N. J. 77; Farrell *v.* Ledwell, 21 Wis. 182.

[2] §§ 125–183.

[3] Story Confl. Laws, §§ 184–187.

tion to the incidents and effects of marriage, yet the doctrine must be received with many qualifications and exceptions, inasmuch as no nation will recognize such incidents and effects when incompatible with its own policy or injurious to its own interests. So, too, perplexing questions will sometimes arise in determining upon the real matrimonial domicile of parties who marry *in transitu*, during a temporary residence abroad, or on a journey made for that purpose with the intention of returning. But the true principle in such cases is to consider as the real matrimonial domicile the place where, at the time of marriage, the parties intended to fix their abode, and not the place where the ceremony was in fact performed.[1]

[1] Story Confl. Laws, §§ 189–199, and cases cited. See also 1 Burge Col. & For. Laws, 244–639.

CHAPTER III.

THE EFFECT OF COVERTURE UPON THE WIFE'S DEBTS AND CONTRACTS.

One of the immediate effects of marriage at the common law is that the husband at once becomes bound to pay all outstanding debts of his wife — her debts *dum sola*, as they are called, — of whatever amount. This is a sort of recompense he makes for taking her property into his hands. But whether she brings him a fortune or not, his liability is not affected. She may owe large sums at the time of marriage and have nothing to offset them. She may have studiously concealed the existence of the debts from her affianced husband. But none of these considerations can avail to shield him. When married, she is married with her debts as well as her fortunes. As Blackstone observes, her husband must be considered to have "adopted her and her circumstances together." [1]

This rule is moreover applied without discrimination as to individuals. An infant who marries is bound equally with an adult husband.[2] A second husband is liable for the debts of his wife outstanding at the close of her widowhood, whether contracted prior to the first marriage, or while living separate and from her first husband upon a separate maintenance, or after the termination of her first coverture and subsequent to the second.[3]

On the other hand, the husband remains liable for the debts of his wife *dum sola* only so long as coverture lasts. As his

[1] 1 Bl. Com. 443; 3 Mod. 186; 2 Kent Com. 143–146; Macq. Hus. & Wife, 39–41; Heard *v.* Stamford, 3 P. Wms. 409; cases temp. Talb. 173.

[2] Roach *v.* Quick, 9 Wend. 238; Butler *v.* Breck, 7 Met. 164.

[3] 1 T. R. 5; 7 T. R. 348; Prescott *v.* Fisher, 22 Ill. 390; Angel *v.* Felton, 8 Johns. 149.

liability originated in the marriage so it ceases with it. Hence if the obligation be not enforced in the lifetime of the wife, the surviving husband retains her fortune (if any) in his hands and cannot be charged further with her debts either at law or in equity.[1] The wife's *choses in action* still unreduced to possession at the time of her death may however be reached by her creditors where he has received them as her administrator; but only to the actual amount of such assets; so that this would afford them but partial relief.[2] Nor can the husband's estate after his death be made liable for the wife's debts contracted while sole.[3]

The injustice of the rule in certain cases is obvious. Supposing a *feme sole* is worth fifty thousand dollars and owes at the time of her marriage five thousand dollars. She marries and dies before her creditors have had time to sue her husband. Thereupon the husband retains for himself the fifty thousand dollars and the creditors are without a remedy. Such was the character of the argument pressed upon the distinguished Lord Talbot more than a century ago, in the case of *Heard* v. *Stamford*.[4] But his reply was as follows: "The question is, whether the husband, as such, be chargeable for a debt of his wife's, after her death, in a court of equity? As, on the one hand, the husband is by law liable to all his wife's debts during the coverture, although he did not get one shilling portion with her, and although her debts should amount to any sum whatever; so, on the other hand, it is as certain that if the debt be not recovered during the coverture, the husband is no longer chargeable as such, let the fortune he received be ever so great. The case perhaps may be hard, but the law hath made it so; and the alteration of it is the proper work of the legislature only."

[1] 2 Kent Com. 144.

[2] Heard *v.* Stamford, 3 P. Wms. 409; cases temp. Talb. 173; Morrow *v.* Whitesides, 10 B. Mon. 411.

[3] Woodman *v.* Chapman, 1 Camp. 189; Curtton *v.* Moore, 2 Jones Eq. 204.

[4] See *supra*.

Lord Macclesfield still later encountered a different objection to the common-law rule, arising from an opposite state of facts. This he endeavored to answer. It may be hard, he observes, that the husband should be answerable for the wife's debts, when he receives nothing from her; but we are to set off against that hardship the rule, that if the husband has received a personal estate with the wife, and happens not to be sued during the coverture, he is not liable. He runs a hazard in being liable to the debts, much beyond the personal estate of the wife; and in recompense for that hazard, he is entitled to the whole of her personal estate, though far exceeding the debts, and is discharged from the debts as soon as the coverture ceases.[1] Constituting a right by balancing off two wrongs may seem unsatisfactory to the modern reader. Still the court decided aright: for the difficulty was in the common law itself.

If the wife survives her husband, she becomes liable once more on her debts while sole. And this too, though the means for extinguishing them may have already been squandered by her husband or placed beyond her reach.[2] Here is a third hardship. Coverture, therefore, seems to operate as a temporary disability and not so as to utterly merge the wife's identity. The husband becomes liable by marriage not as the debtor but as the husband; the remedy being suspended, or rather shifted, during coverture.

The English common-law courts hold that if the husband, during coverture, obtains a certificate of discharge in bankruptcy the wife's debts *dum sola* are wiped out as well as his own.[3] We apprehend the equity doctrine to be that though the husband be discharged, the wife's suspended liability yet remains; and this has been announced in New York.[4] And

[1] Earl of Thomond *v.* Earl of Suffolk, 1 P. Wms. 469, cited in 2 Kent Com. 144.

[2] Woodman *v.* Chapman, 1 Camp. N. P. 189, per Lord Ellenborough.

[3] Miles *v.* Williams, 1 P. Wms. 249; Lockwood *v.* Salter, 5 B. & Ad. 303.

[4] Mallory *v.* Vanderheyden, 3 Barb. Ch. 9; S. C. 1 Comst. 453.

in Maine the wife's creditors *dum sola* may have a fraudulent conveyance of her property set aside notwithstanding her husband's bankruptcy.[1] The national bankruptcy system recently established by statute will affect materially the future consideration of this subject in our courts.[2]

The liability of the husband for his wife's debts while sole, is limited strictly to legal demands; that is to such as she was bound to pay at the time of her marriage.[3] And if a demand would not be enforceable against her remaining sole, neither is it enforceable against her husband. But the promise or part-payment of the wife cannot take a debt out of the statute of limitations as against her husband, nor can the promise or part-payment of the husband as against his wife. Nor can their admissions charge one another.[4] Their rights in this respect are separately regarded. All actions for the wife's debts while sole must be brought against husband and wife jointly, and not against either separately; and judgment obtained by disregarding this rule will be reversed on error.[5] The object is to retain the remedy in hand so that execution may be taken out against the proper party according to circumstances; for, if the husband should die pending the suit, the wife on her survivorship would become liable.

If judgment be recovered against a *feme sole* on her debt before she marries, and she dies before execution is taken out, having married in the mean time, her husband will be discharged from liability. But if judgment be recovered against both during coverture, and the wife dies before execution, the

1 Hamlin *v.* Bridge, 24 Maine, 145.

2 See Act Congress March 2, 1867, ch. 176.

3 Cowley *v.* Robertson, 3 Camp. 438; Caldwell *v.* Drake, 4 J. J. Marsh. 246.

4 Ross *v.* Winners, 1 Halst. 366; Sheppard *v.* Starke, 3 Munf. 29; Brown *v.* Lasselle, 6 Blackf. 147; Moore *v.* Leseur, 18 Ala. 606; Farrar *v.* Bessey, 24 Vt. 89. But see Lord Tenterden in Humphreys *v.* Boyce, 1 Mood. & Rob. 140, as to admissions of the wife allowable in evidence after her death.

5 Robinson *v.* Hardy, 1 Keb. 281; Drue *v.* Thorn, Alleyn, 72; Angel *v.* Felton, 8 Johns. 149; 7 T. R. 348; Gage *v.* Reed, 15 Johns. 403; Gray *v.* Thacker, 4 Ala. 136.

husband is still charged, because by the judgment the nature of the debt was altered and it became his own debt.[1] So, too, when judgment was obtained before coverture and *scire facias* brought upon it against husband and wife afterwards.[2] When judgment has been obtained for a debt of the wife while sole, and she afterwards marries, execution must in strictness be taken out against her alone, because execution must always follow the judgment.[3] But if the creditor desires to charge a person who was not a party to the record, as the husband in this instance, *scire facias* should be issued so as to make him a party.[4] This rule applies likewise where the wife marries pending the suit. The death of the wife, after action has been commenced against husband and wife and before judgment, puts an end to the suit.[5]

The rule as laid down in England concerning the wife's personal liability on her debts *dum sola* is that coverture does not wholly relieve her from the consequences of judgment for the time being; for that both may be taken on execution; and when the wife is taken, she shall not be discharged unless it appear that she has no separate property out of which the demand can be satisfied.[6] This rule does not seem to have been recognized with such strictness in this country.[7] But where the wife after marriage pays a portion of her debt contracted while sole from funds derived from her separate property, it is said that the husband will be bound by the act unless he disaffirms it within a reasonable time.[8]

[1] 2 Bright Hus. & Wife, 3; Burton *v.* Burton, 5 Harring. 441; O'Brien *v.* Ram, 3 Mod. 186; Sid. 337; Treviband *v.* Lawrence, 2 Ld. Raym. 1050.

[2] O'Brien *v.* Ram, *supra.* Mr. Bright seems to have stated this point incorrectly. See 2 Bright Hus. & Wife, 3.

[3] Doyley *v.* White, Cro. Jac. 323; Bull. Ch. P. 23; Benyon *v.* Jones, 15 M. & W. 566; and see Haines *v.* Corliss, 4 Mass. 659; Commonwealth *v.* Phillipsburgh, 10 ib. 78; Triggs *v.* Triggs, 2 M. & Ry. 126 *n.*

[4] 2 Bright Hus. & Wife, 3, 4; Cooper *v.* Hunchin, 4 East, 521.

[5] Williams *v.* Kent, 15 Wend. 360.

[6] Tidd Pract. 9th ed. 1026; Sparkes *v.* Bell, 8 B. & C. 1; Newton *v.* Roe, 7 Man. & Gr. 329; Evans *v.* Chester, 2 M. & W. 847.

[7] Mallory *v.* Vanderheyden, 3 Barb. Ch. 9; s. c. 1 Comst. 453.

[8] Hall *v.* Eaton, 12 Vt. 510.

On general principles, the husband is bound for the debt of his infant wife while sole, just as much as though she were an adult, though only to the same extent as she would have been bound. Hence, where the demand is for necessaries furnished her while an infant, the husband after marriage becomes bound to pay it, since she would have been liable if she had not married. And the infancy of the husband himself cannot be pleaded against this obligation.[1]

So far is this doctrine carried that the agreement of a widow after her husband's death, to pay a debt which she had contracted during coverture, and which consequently was not binding upon herself, but upon her husband, has been treated as void, on the ground that the promise was without consideration and only morally binding.[2] But in another case it was held a sufficient consideration to support a widow's promissory note that it had been given by her, out of respect for her late husband's memory, to secure a debt due by him.[3]

In respect to her disability to contract, the wife may be considered, as Mr. Bingham has remarked, worse off at the common law than infants; for the contracts of an infant are for the most part voidable only, while those of married women are, with few exceptions, absolutely void. But the disabilities incident to these two conditions rest upon different grounds. For the disabilities attached to infancy are designed as a protection for the inexperienced against the fraudulent; while those incident to coverture are the simple consequence of that sole or paramount authority which the law vests in the husband.[4] Common sense teaches that married women have sufficient discretion to act for themselves, and stand on a different footing from young children; this the English law fully recognizes,

[1] Cole *v.* Seeley, 25 Vt. 220.

[2] Meyer *v.* Hawworth, 8 Ad. & El. 467.

[3] Ridout *v.* Bristow, 1 Cr. & J. 231; Tyr. 84. See also Nelson *v.* Searle, 3 Jur. 290 (1839); Waul *v.* Kirkman, 25 Miss. 609; Brunner's Appeal, 47 Penn. St. 67.

[4] See Bing. Inf. & Cov. 181, 182, Am. ed.; 2 Kent Com. 150.

irrespective of equity rules, by empowering all women to contract up to the very moment of their marriage and from the time when coverture ceases.

Lord Nottingham, in a case mentioned in the old reports, once refused to absolve a husband after his wife's death from payment for goods which she had purchased while single but never paid for, there being proof that he had actually received the goods. His lordship declared with warmth that he would change the law on that point.[1] But in this case it appears that the goods did not actually come to the husband's hands until after the wife's death. And the authority of this decision has since been greatly impaired.[2] In equity the creditors of the first husband may, where his wife was administratrix, follow the assets in the hands of a second husband, although the wife be dead; and at law during her life.[3]

The husband may make in his own right such contracts as he pleases, as well during coverture as before. He is never presumed to act under the wife's influence.[4] But the wife by coverture becomes disqualified, except in the single instance where her husband is *civiliter mortuus*, as we have already stated.[5] And another exception prevailed in certain parts of England by local custom — as that of London, — where she might carry on a trade and sue and be sued in reference thereto as though single.[6] But otherwise her incapacity at the common law is total. She cannot earn money for herself.[7] She cannot sign or indorse a promissory note so as to bind her estate;[8] nor execute a bond; nor otherwise make a valid contract.[9] She is permitted, as we shall hereafter see, to pass her real estate by joining in a deed with her husband; but when she does so she

1 Cha. Ca. 295.

2 Cha. Ca. 295, 1 Eq. Cas. Abr. 60.

3 Cha. Ca. 80; 1 Vern. 309; 2 Vern. 61, 118; 1 Eq. Cas. Abr. 60, 61; Cro. Car. 603, 1 Roll. Abr. 35. See Magruder *v.* Darnall, 6 Gill, 269.

4 City Council *v.* Van Roven, 2 McCord, 465.

5 *Supra*, p. 63.

6 1 Selw. N. P. 298; Bing. Inf. 261, 262.

7 Offley *v.* Clay, 2 Man. & Gr. 172.

8 Mason *v.* Morgan, 2 Ad. & El. 30; T. R. 616.

9 Avery *v.* Griffiths, Law Rep. 6 Eq. 606; Goulding *v.* Davidson, 28 Barb. 438.

is not bound by her covenants, nor was her separate conveyance (except by some matter of record) of any effect whatsoever.[1] In all these cases the wife is under the husband's dominion and unable to act for herself.[2]

But although the wife, as such, has no power to make a contract, she is allowed at the common law to bind her husband in certain cases as his agent. Her authority may be general or special, express or implied. On this principle rests the liability of the husband in contracts made by his wife for necessaries. Blackstone says that the power of the wife to act as attorney for her husband, implies no separation from, but is rather a representation of, her lord.[3] Whenever the husband expressly empowers his wife to make a contract for him, he will be bound as in the case of any other principal. And he may bind himself in like manner for any unauthorized contract proceeding from his wife as agent, by subsequent conduct on his part amounting to ratification. But greater difficulty arises in determining his liability upon contracts where the authority is not express, but only implied. How far does the law go in presuming against the husband, and what are the proper limits of an implied authority in the wife to bind him by her contracts?

It is a clear obligation which rests upon every husband to support his wife; that is, to supply her with necessaries suitable to her situation, and his own circumstances and condition in life. But though this obligation rests on the foundation of natural justice, the common law assigns, as the true legal reason, that she may not become a burden to the community. So long as that calamity is averted, the wife has no direct claim upon her husband under any circumstances whatever; for even

[1] 2 Bl. Com. 293, 351, 364, and *n.* by Chitty and others; 2 Kent Com. 150–154; ib. 167, 168.

[2] Marshall *v.* Rutter, 8 T. R. 545; 11 East, 301; 2 B. & P. 226; 3 B. & C. 291; Jackson *v.* Vanderheyden, 17 Johns. 167; Benjamin *v.* Benjamin, 15 Conn. 347; Ayer *v.* Warren, 47 Maine, 217; Young *v.* Paul, 2 Stockt. 401; Savage *v.* Davis, 18 Wis. 608; Williams *v.* Coward, 1 Grant, Cas. 21.

Aliter as to separate estate.

[3] 1 Bl. Com. 442; 2 Man. & Gr. 172; Mizen *v.* Peck, 3 M. & W. 481.

in the case of positive starvation she can only come upon the parish for relief; in which case the parish authorities will insist that the husband shall provide for her to the extent of sustaining life.[1] If a husband fail in this respect, so that his wife becomes chargeable to any parish, the statute 4 Geo. IV. ch. 83, § 3, says that "he shall be deemed an idle and disorderly person, and shall be punishable with imprisonment and hard labor."[2]

And this obligation extends to the whole family, with such modifications as will be more properly noticed under the topic of parent and child. If a man marry a widow he is not bound to maintain her children; unless he holds them out to the world as part of his own family.[3] But by the statute 4 and 5 Will. IV. ch. 76, § 57, the husband is required to maintain as part of his family, any child or children, till the age of sixteen, legitimate or illegitimate, that his wife may have at the time of entering into the contract.

To enforce these marital obligations the law takes a circuitous course: and the wife may secure herself and the family from want against a cruel and miserly husband, of ample means to support them, by pledging his credit and making such purchases as are needful, on the strength of an implied authority for that purpose. Here, all other things being equal, it is presumed that she was her husband's agent; and no direct permission need be shown. Indeed, wherever the facts are clear that those articles were actually needed, and that the husband failed to supply them, this presumption is carried so far as to control even the express orders of the husband himself.

The wife's necessaries are such articles as the law deems essential to her health and comfort; chiefly food, drink, lodging, fuel, washing, clothing, and medical attendance. They are to be determined, both in kind and amount, by the means and social position of the married pair, and must therefore vary

[1] Rex *v.* Flintan, 1 B. & Ad. 227; Reg. *v.* Inhabitants of Wendron, 7 Ad. & El. 819.

[2] See Macphers. Inf. 42, 43.

[3] 4 T. R. 118; Cooper *v.* Martin, 4 East, 76; Stone *v.* Carr, 3 Esp. N. P. 1. See Parent and Child, *infra.*

greatly among different grades and at different stages of society.[1] Thus a large milliner's bill might not be deemed necessaries for the wife of a laborer, while a wealthy merchant would be bound to pay it. So too necessaries to-day are not what they were fifty years ago. Nor is the ordinary test to be found in the real situation and means of the married parties; for this a tradesman cannot be expected to investigate; but in their apparent situation, the style they assume, and the establishment they maintain before the world; which every husband is supposed to regulate with sufficient prudence.[2] The decisions in the books, relating to necessaries, are therefore somewhat confusing, as might be expected; the more so since the dividing line between law and fact, in such cases, is not marked with distinctness. Sometimes the court decides whether articles are necessary, sometimes a jury. The ordinary rule is that the court shall decide whether certain articles are to be classed as necessaries; while the jury may determine the question of amount, and apply this classification to the facts;[3] but this rule, though seemingly precise, is found difficult in its practical application.

Among the cases we find the following articles classed as necessaries for the wife: Board and lodging. Medicines, medical attendance, and reasonable expenses during illness.[4] Furniture of a house for a wife to whom the court had decreed £380 a year as alimony.[5] Silver fringes to a petticoat and side-saddle (value £94) furnished to the wife of a sergeant-at-law.[6] Legal expenses incurred by a wife who had been deserted by her husband, preliminary and incidental to a suit for

[1] 2 Bright Hus. & Wife, 7, 8; Ozard *v.* Durnford, Sel. N. P. 260; Dennys *v.* Sargeant, 6 Car. & P. 419; Berreblock *v.* Michael, Cro. Jac. 257, 258. Note to 2 Kent Com. 10th ed. 146; ib. 138, 139; 1 Bl. Com. 442.

[2] Waithman *v.* Wakefield, 1 Campb. 120.

[3] Renaux *v.* Teakle, 20 E. L. & Eq. 345; 1 Pars. Contr. 241; Hall *v.* Weir, 1 Allen, 261; Parke *v.* Kleeber, 37 Penn. St. 251.

[4] Harris *v.* Lee, 1 P. Wms. 438; Mayhew *v.* Thayer, 8 Gray, 172; Cothran *v.* Lee, 24 Ala. 380.

[5] Hunt *v.* De Blaquiere, 5 Bing. 550.

[6] Skin. 349.

restitution of her conjugal rights, and in obtaining professional advice as to the proper method of dealing with tradesmen who were pressing their bills.[1] A horse worth $45 for the invalid wife of a miller earning $30 per month, in order that she might take exercise as advised by a physician ; the question of suitableness however being left to the jury.[2] The cost of divorce proceedings, including fees of a proctor, where the wife had reasonable ground for instituting them, but not otherwise.[3] A set of false teeth.[4] Household supplies reasonable and proper for the ordinary use of a family, although the wife receives the earnings of two daughters living with her.[5] Perhaps a piano.[6]

But, on the other hand, the following articles have been held not to be necessaries: Articles of jewelry for the wife of a special pleader.[7] A deed of separation.[8] The expense of an indictment by the wife for assault.[9] Counsel fees in a suit for divorce and to enforce a marriage settlement, whether the wife be plaintiff or defendant.[10] Money lent the wife for the purchase of necessaries, unless at the husband's request.[11] And on the same principle money lent for the purchase of a passage ticket to enable the wife to join her husband.[12] Medical attendance rendered without the husband's assent, by a quack doctor;[13] though when a husband disputes a bill for medical attendance

1 Wilson *v.* Ford, Law Rep. 3 Ex. 63.

2 Cornelia *v.* Ellis, 11 Ill. 584.

3 Brown *v.* Ackroyd, 34 E. L. & Eq. 214.

4 Gilman *v.* Andrus, 28 Vt. 241.

5 Hall *v.* Weir, 1 Allen, 261.

6 Parke *v.* Kleeber, 37 Penn. St. 251.

7 Montague *v.* Benedict, 3 B. & C. 631.

8 Ladd *v.* Lynn, 2 M. & W. 265.

9 Grindall *v.* Godmond, 5 Ad. & El. 755.

10 Pearson *v.* Darrington, 32 Ala. 227; Morrison *v.* Holt, 42 N. H. 478; Coffin *v.* Dunham, 8 Cush. 404; Shelton *v.* Pendleton, 18 Conn. 417; Johnson *v.* Williams, 3 Iowa, 97; Williams *v.* Monroe, 18 B. Mon. 514.

11 Walker *v.* Simpson, 7 W. & S. 83; Stone *v.* McNair, 7 Taunt. 432; Stevenson *v.* Hardy, 3 Wils. 388. But in equity, the person lending the money stands in the stead of the tradesman, and is allowed to recover if the money was used for necessaries. Harris *v.* Lee, 1 P. Wms. 482; Walker *v.* Simpson, 7 W. & S. 83.

12 Knox *v.* Bushell, 3 C. B. (N. S.) 334.

13 Wood *v.* O'Kelly, 8 Cush. 406.

on the ground of malpractice, or an unneccessary surgical operation, the burden is on him to show it.[1] Articles in short which are extravagant and altogether beyond the husband's circumstances and degree in life.[2]

In the leading English case of *Montague* v. *Benedict*, the rule as to the husband's liability for his wife's necessaries was thus laid down: "If a man without any justifiable cause turn away his wife, he is bound by any contract she may make for necessaries suitable to her degree and estate. If the husband and wife live together, and the husband will not supply her with necessaries, or the means of obtaining them, then, although she has her remedy in the Ecclesiastical Court, yet she is still at liberty to pledge the credit of her husband for what is strictly necessary for her own support. But whenever the husband and wife are living together, and he provides her with necessaries, the husband is not bound by contracts of the wife, except where there is reasonable evidence to show that the wife has made the contract with his assent. Cohabitation is presumptive evidence of the assent of the husband, but it may be rebutted by contrary evidence; and when such assent is proved the wife is the agent of the husband duly authorized."[3] Hence the husband's liability for necessaries may arise in two classes of cases: first, where the wife lives with him; secondly, where she lives separate from him. And where the wife lives with him, the husband's assent to her contract for necessaries is inferred from circumstances which show authority actually conferred, or else the law supplies an assent for her benefit where he has improperly refused or neglected to provide for her wants. Where they live apart separation is either voluntary or involuntary.

Let us consider these two classes of cases separately. Here we are met at the outset by the broad presumption of assent

[1] M'Clallan *v.* Adams, 19 Pick. 333.
[2] Caney *v.* Patton, 2 Ashm. 140.
[3] B. & C. 631.

which cohabitation of itself furnishes. The simple circumstance that husband and wife are living together is held sufficient, when nothing to the contrary intervenes, to raise a presumption that the wife is rightfully making such purchases of necessaries as she may deem proper.[1] Whoever then supplies her in good faith need inquire no further, but may send his bill to her husband. This rule is a fair one; for it is not to be supposed that a husband will go in person to buy every little article of dress or household provision which may be needful for his family. As Lord Abinger observed, a wife would be of little use to her husband in their domestic arrangements, if his interference was always to be deemed necessary.[2] Accordingly if an action be brought against the husband for the price of goods furnished under such circumstances, it must be taken *prima facie* that these goods were supplied by his authority, and he must show that he is not responsible.[3]

The wife's contract for necessaries will bind the husband to a still greater extent if the evidence warrants the inference that a more extensive authority has in fact been given.[4] Thus the presumption which cohabitation furnishes is strengthened by proof that the wife has been permitted by the husband to purchase other articles of the same sort for the use of the household.[5]

But the question is, after all, one of evidence; it turns upon the question of authority from the husband; and this presumption in the wife's favor may be rebutted by contrary testimony on the husband's behalf.[6] Lord Holt says, "His assent shall

1 2 Bright Hus. & Wife, 6, 7; Bull. N. P. 134; Langfort *v.* Tyler, Salk. 113; Atkins *v.* Curwood, 7 Car. & P. 756. See also Dyer *v.* East, 1 Ventr. 42; Beaumont *v.* Weldon, 2 Bent. 155; Manby *v.* Scott, 1 Mod. 124; 1 Sid. 109; 1 Roll. Abr. 351, pl. 5; Freestone *v.* Butcher, 9 Car. & P. 643.

2 Emmett *v.* Norton, 8 Car. & P. 506.

3 Clifford *v.* Laton, 3 Car. & P. 15, per Lord Tenterden.

4 2 Bright Hus. & Wife, 9; cases cited in *n.* to Filmer *v.* Lynn, 4 Nev. & Man. 559; M'George *v.* Egan, 7 Scott Cases, 112.

5 1 Sid. 128; Jewsbury *v.* Newbold, 40 E. L. & Eq. 518.

6 Lane *v.* Ironmonger, 13 M. & W. 368.

be presumed to all necessary contracts, upon the account of cohabiting, *unless the contrary appear.*" [1]

Not only is the husband permitted to show that the articles in controversy are not such as can be considered necessaries, but he may show that he supplied his wife himself or by other agents, or that he gave her ready money to make the purchases.[2] This is on the principle that so long as the husband has provided necessaries in some way his marital obligation is discharged, whatever may be the method he chooses to adopt. And in the class of cases which we are now considering, so long as the husband is willing to provide necessaries at his own home he is not liable to provide them elsewhere.[3] In general, a husband who supplies his wife with necessaries suitable to her position and his own is not liable to others for debts contracted by her without his previous authority or subsequent sanction.[4] But in all such cases the burden of proof is on the husband.[5]

This last rule suggests another point of which the tradesman may avail himself, as against the husband, on the general principles of agency; namely, that subsequent ratification is as good as a previous authority. So then if it can be shown that the husband knew his wife had ordered certain necessaries, and yet failed to rescind the purchase; or if there be proof that he saw her wearing the articles and yet expressed no disapprobation; the law presumes approval of her contract and binds him.[6] To this principle perhaps may be referred the rule which

[1] Etherington *v.* Parrott, 1 Salk. 118. See also to the same effect, Holt *v.* Brien, 4 B. & Ald. 252; McCutchen *v.* McGahay, 11 Johns. 281; and *n.* by Am. editor to Bing. Inf. 187. The position assumed by Mr. Story, in his work on Contracts, that, as to the wife's necessaries, "the law raises an *uncontrollable* presumption of assent on the part of the husband," is therefore incorrect. Story Contr. 2d ed. § 97.

[2] Manby *v.* Scott, 1 Sid. 109; 2 Smith's Lead. Cas. (6th Am. ed.) 469; Etherington *v.* Parrott, 2 Ld. Raym. 1006.

[3] Morgan *v.* Hughes, 20 Tex. 141.

[4] Seaton *v.* Benedict, 5 Bing. 28.

[5] Tebbets *v.* Hapgood, 34 N. H. 420.

[6] Seaton *v.* Benedict, 5 Bing. 28; 2 Moo. & P. 74; Parke B. in Lane *v.* Ironmonger, 13 M. & W. 368; Ogden *v.* Prentice, 33 Barb. 160.

Mr. Roper further states (without, however, citing any authorities), that the husband is liable whenever the goods purchased by his wife come to her or his use with his knowledge and permission, or when he allows her to retain and enjoy them; in other words, that a legal liability becomes fixed from the fact that the husband and his household take the benefit of the purchase.[1] But the mere fact that a husband sees his wife wearing articles purchased without authority will not charge him; the question is one of approval or disapproval, assent or dissent.[2]

As a rule, a husband who furnishes his wife and family with necessaries, in any reasonable manner, has the right to prohibit particular persons from trusting or dealing with her on his account. Notice to this effect, properly given, will be effectual as against any presumption which cohabitation raises.[3] And notice given to a tradesman's servant has been held sufficient notice to the master. But notice given in the newspapers not to trust a wife is held to be of no effect against such as have not had actual notice.[4] Nor is a successful defence against one bill sufficient notice of prohibition against subsequent bills.[5]

In all cases the husband will be discharged from liability where it appears that the goods were not supplied on his credit, but that the party furnishing them trusted the wife individually.[6] She might have separate property, independently of her husband, to which the tradesman looked for payment, or a special allowance of sufficient amount might have been made her by her husband.[7] Thus, where the husband during a tem-

1 2 Rop. Hus. & Wife, 112; 2 Bright Hus. & Wife, 9. Mr. Macqueen (Hus. & Wife, *n.* to p. 132) points out this statement of Mr. Roper with a doubt as to the authority, although he admits the justice of such a rule, on the civil-law maxim, that "no one should enrich himself at another's loss."

2 Atkins *v.* Curwood, 7 Car. & P. 756.

3 McCutchen *v.* McGahay, 11 Johns. 281.

4 Walker *v.* Laighton, 11 Fost. (N. H.), 111.

5 Ogden *v.* Prentice, 33 Barb. 160.

6 Metcalfe *v.* Shaw, 3 Camp. 22; Bentley *v.* Griffin, 5 Taunt. 356; Pearson *v.* Darrington, 32 Ala. 227; Stammers *v.* Macomb, 2 Wend. 454; Moses *v.* Forgartie, 2 Hill (S. C.), 335; Carter *v.* Howard, 39 Vt. 106.

7 Levett *v.* Penrice, 24 Miss. 416; Simmons *v.* McElwain, 26 Barb. 420.

porary absence made an allowance to his wife, he was held not to be liable for necessaries supplied to her, the tradesman having trusted to payment from her allowance.[1] So if credit be given to a third party, the husband is not liable.[2] And of course, if the tradesman has agreed not to charge him, there is no liability incurred by the husband.[3] Though the wife be without property, the rule is the same; and it would appear that the husband may give permission to trust his wife on her separate credit without incurring liability.[4]

That the wife has a separate income, that the invoices are made out to her, that the plaintiff has drawn bills of exchange upon her for part-payment of the amount due, and that she has accepted such bills in her own name, payable at her own banker's from her separate funds, — all these are circumstances which go to repel the presumption of agency and show that the wife was purchasing on her own credit with the tradesman's assent.[5] So is the studious concealment of the purchases from the husband's knowledge, by the tradesman and the wife, and the attempt of the latter to secure the debt by her own promissory note.[6] All these are facts for the jury.[7] The husband is not relieved by the single circumstance that the goods were charged on the shop books to the wife; since *prima facie* the actual credit is always supposed to be given to the husband.[8] His dissent to his wife's purchase of necessaries should be expressed in an effectual and suitable manner. Mere objection on his part is insufficient. Thus a bill for medical attendance

[1] Holt *v.* Brien, 4 B. & Ald. 252; Montague *v.* Benedict, 3 B. & Cr. 631; Harshaw *v.* Merryman, 18 Miss. 106; Renaux *v.* Teakle, 20 E. L. & Eq. 345.

[2] Harvey *v.* Norton, 4 Jur. 42.

[3] Dixon *v.* Harwell, 8 Car. & P. 717.

[4] Taylor *v.* Shelton, 30 Conn. 122.

[5] Freestone *v.* Butcher, 9 Car. & P. 643; Macq. Hus. & Wife, 135.

[6] Mitchell *v.* Treanor, 11 Geo. 324. But see Day *v.* Burnham, 36 Vt. 37.

[7] Attorney General *v.* Riddle, 2 Cr. & Jer. 493; 2 Tyr. 523; Barnes *v.* Jarrett, 2 Jur. 988.

[8] Jewsbury *v.* Newbold, 40 E. L. & Eq. 518; Godfrey *v.* Brooks, 5 Harring. 396; Furlong *v.* Hysom, 35 Maine, 332.

must be paid by him, even though he objected to the visits, as long as he was present and gave no notice to the physician that the latter must look elsewhere for payment.[1] And private arrangements between husband and wife as to the method of payment cannot affect the rights of third parties.[2] If he means, when sued in assumpsit for necessaries, to defend the action as to part only, it would appear that his proper plea will be that he is not liable beyond a certain amount, and he should pay that amount into court.[3] But if he means to dispute the charge altogether, common honesty dictates that the articles unwarrantably purchased should be restored without delay.[4] He may introduce evidence at the trial to show that the commodities in question were not necessaries, inasmuch as the wife had incurred other similar debts with other parties.[5] In a word, the question is (in the absence of such evidence of necessity as may show an agency in law) whether there was an agency and authority in fact.[6]

Wherever the husband neglects to supply his wife with necessaries, she may obtain them, although it be against his wishes, on the pledge of his credit. And the person furnishing the articles may sue the husband notwithstanding he has been expressly forbidden to trust her.[7] But here the law raises a presumption of agency only for the purpose of enforcing a marital obligation. And the tradesman or other party furnishing supplies in this case is bound to show affirmatively and clearly that the husband did not provide necessaries for his wife suitable to her condition in life.[7] It is held in Massachusetts, that a town may supply a wife who is in need of relief, through the neglect of her husband, and then sue him for

1 Cothran *v.* Lee, 24 Ala. 380.
2 Ib.; Johnson *v.* Sumner, 3 Hurl. & Nor. 261.
3 Emmet *v.* Norton, 8 Car. & P. 506.
4 Macq. Hus. & Wife, 136; Gilman *v.* Andrus, 28 Vt. 241.
5 Renaux *v.* Teakle, 20 E. L. & Eq. 345.
6 Read *v.* Teakle, 24 E. L. & Eq. 332.
7 Keller *v.* Phillips, 40 Barb. 390; Cromwell *v.* Benjamin, 41 ib. 558.

necessaries suitable to the condition of a pauper, and no more.[1] In New York, if the husband be of sufficient ability to support his wife, it would appear that she cannot be supported by the public as a pauper at all.[2] And so in Indiana.[3]

Marriage *de facto* is always sufficient to charge the husband with his wife's necessaries. There seem to be two reasons why this should be so: one, that a tradesman cannot be expected to inquire into such matters; the other, that it is just that any man who holds out a woman to society as his wife should maintain her as such. Hence an agency is to be inferred wherever there is cohabitation of parties as husband and wife; though not, it would appear, where the cohabitation is irregular and calculated to raise a different impression. Lord Kenyon used very strong language to this effect in *Watson* v. *Threlkeld*, where it appeared that the tradesman knew that there had been no marriage: "It is certain that if a man has permitted a woman to whom he was not married to use his name and pass for his wife, and in that character to contract debts, he is liable for her debts; and I am of opinion that he is liable whether the tradesman who furnished the goods knew the circumstances to be so or not. He gives her a credit from his name and cohabitation; and it is not be supposed that the tradesman could look to the credit of a woman of that description and not to that of the man by whom she was supported."[4] The *dictum* of Lord Ellenborough in *Robinson* v. *Nahon* would seem to narrow this rule so as to exclude tradesmen having actual knowledge of the illicit relation of the parties.[5] And the death of the *quasi* husband is held to revoke his authority altogether, so that a sub-

[1] Monson *v.* Williams, 6 Gray, 416. And see Rumney *v.* Keyes, 7 N. H. 571.

[2] Norton *v.* Rhodes, 18 Barb. 100.

[3] Commissioners *v.* Hildebrand, 1 Carter, 555.

[4] 2 Esp. 637. And see 1 Greenl. Ev. § 207.

[5] 1 Camp. 245. But reference to the case shows that this doubt is suggested more strongly in the reporter's head-note than his lordship's opinion. See Jewsbury *v.* Newbold, 40 E. L. & Eq. 518; Munroe *v.* De Chemant, 4 Camp. 215.

sequent contract is void against his estate, under all circumstances.[1]

An adult husband is bound on the contracts of his minor wife for necessaries.[2] And a minor husband is liable for necessaries furnished his wife, whether she be minor or adult.[3] The ordinary rules of husband and wife therefore apply so far as family necessaries are concerned. If old enough to contract marriage, an infant is presumed old enough to pay for his wife's board and lodging as well as his own. And such claims may be enforced against his estate though he die under age.[4] But with regard to his wife's general contracts it would seem that infancy, which incapacitates him from making contracts in person, also disqualifies him from employing an attorney.

The common-law courts include articles of the peace under the head of necessaries, though by stretching very considerably the doctrine of agency. Since this proceeding generally assumes the husband and wife to be living together, we may here allude to the doctrine. A husband is at common law held liable to an attorney who acts for his wife in exhibiting such articles against him. But the proceeding must have been justified by the circumstances. This is the English rule;[5] followed likewise in New Hampshire.[6] Even if the husband and wife dwelt apart the English courts will not inquire whether she might not have paid her counsel fees and costs from her maintenance; for, as Lord Denman observes, "she has her maintenance for other purposes."[7] But the wife cannot carry her privilege so far as to indict her husband; and here the English courts seem to have stopped short in their perplexity, and placed a final limit to this fiction of agency. "It cannot be maintained," says

[1] Blades *v.* Free, 9 B. & C. 167. But see Ginochio *v.* Porcella, 3 Bradf. Sur. 277. See reference to *ib.*, *infra.*

[2] Nicholson *v.* Wilborn, 13 Geo. 467.

[3] Cantine *v.* Phillips, 5 Harring. 428. And see Bush *v.* Lindsey, 14 Geo. 687.

[4] Ibid.

[5] Shepherd *v.* Mackoul, 3 Camp. 326; Macq. Hus. & Wife, 136, 137.

[6] Morris *v.* Palmer, 39 N. H. 123.

[7] Turner *v.* Rookes, 10 Ad. & El. 47.

Patteson, J., in *Grindell* v. *Godmond*, "that an indictment against the husband for assaulting his wife is a necessary."[1]

The law will not imply a contract as against a son-in-law, to pay his wife's board while staying at her father's house. "Persons in such a near connection as father and children do not usually live together upon a footing of obligation to account with and pay for attentions and services, or board and lodging. When the parties intend to live in that way, it is but reasonable to require that there should be an express understanding between them to that effect."[2] And this principle is extended to the husband's own board; the law implying no contract by which the relation of debtor and creditor arises between father in-law and son-in-law, either for support on the one hand or services on the other.[3]

Some of the old books raise a curious distinction: namely, that if the wife takes up goods, as silk, and before they are made into clothes, pawns them, the husband shall not pay for them; but that it is otherwise if they are made up and worn, and then pawned; for in the former case they never came to the husband's use, while in the latter they did.[4] We apprehend that the real question in such cases would be whether the articles were or were not in fact necessaries; while at the same time purchases of cloth in quantities, it might be admitted, are not so clearly necessaries as clothing made up for wear and worn. The practical application of this rule is in cases where the wife (being, as we have said, forbidden to borrow money for the purchase, real or ostensible, of necessaries) undertakes to raise funds for her own purposes by purchasing goods and then selling or pawning them. We do not find a modern decision on this point.

In the second class of cases which we are to consider, the

[1] 5 Ad. & El. 755. See *supra* as to "necessaries."

[2] Per Court, in Cantine *v.* Phillips, 5 Harring. 428.

[3] Sprague *v.* Waldo, 38 Vt. 139. See Parent and Child, *infra*.

[4] Holt, C. J. in Etherington *v.* Parrott, 1 Salk. 118. See also Reeve Dom. Rel. 84.

husband's liability for his wife's necessaries arises where they are living apart. The rule is that where the husband abandons his wife, turns her away without reasonable cause, or compels her by ill usage to leave him, he is liable for her necessaries, and sends credit with her to that extent.[1] The wife's faithfulness on the one hand to her marriage obligations; on the other, the husband's disregard of his own; these afford the reason of the above rule and suggest its proper limitation. The wife in such cases has an authority; but what may be called an authority of necessity.[2] The law by a fiction infers an agency without asking evidence which should show authority in fact.

This rule suggests then three cases where the wife may pledge her husband's credit when they are living apart: the first, where he abandons her; the second, where he turns her out of doors without reasonable cause; the third, where his misconduct compels her to leave him. In the first two cases his own acts impose the necessity, and her conduct is involuntary. But in the third her conduct is voluntary, though induced by his misconduct; and the rule here becomes perplexing. The doctrine of *Horwood* v. *Heffer*, an old case, is that the wife is not justified in leaving her husband unless she has been driven from the house by actual violence or apprehension for her personal safety; and in this case the husband was held not to be liable, since she had quitted his house because he had placed a profligate woman at the head of the table.[3] This doctrine has been strongly condemned in later times, and the modern cases justly regard such studied insults as capable of legal redress. If therefore the husband, by his indecent conduct, renders his house unfit for a modest

[1] 2 Kent Com. 146, 147; 2 Bright Hus. & Wife, 10–12; Snover *v.* Blair, 1 Dutch. 94; Mayhew *v.* Thayer, 8 Gray, 172.

[2] See Pollock C. B. in Johnston *v.* Sumner, 3 Hurl. & Nor. 261.

[3] 3 Taunt. 421.

woman to share it, the rule now is that she may leave him, and pledge his credit elsewhere for her necessaries.[1] This subject will be considered further under the head of divorce for cruelty and desertion.

Where the wife is justified on any of the above grounds in living apart from her husband, he is not discharged from liability by showing that her contract was in fact made without his authority and contrary to his wishes. Nor will his general advertisement or particular notice to individuals not to give credit to his wife affect the case.[2] The legal presumption must prevail for the wife's protection.

Nor, in such cases, can the husband terminate his liability for necessaries supplied his wife during the separation by a simple request on his part that she shall return.[3] And it is clear that if he only offers to take her back upon conditions which are unreasonable and improper, his liability continues.[4] It is the husband's duty by some positive act to determine his liability; though if the wife voluntarily returns, his liability for necessaries furnished abroad is discontinued. But in default of any amicable arrangement, he must institute proceedings in the courts with divorce jurisdiction. And until some such unequivocal act is done, a person making a claim in a court of law for necessaries supplied to the wife is entitled to recover against him.[5]

But the wife should have weighty and sufficient cause for leaving her husband in order to be permitted to pledge his credit abroad. In general the same facts suffice as justify

[1] Per Lord Ellenborough, Liddlow *v.* Wilmot, 2 Stark. 77; 1 Selw. N. P. 298, 11th ed.; Per Best C. J., Houliston *v.* Smyth, 3 Bing. 127; 10 Moo. 482; 2 Car. & P. 22; Descelles *v.* Kadmus, 8 Clarke, 51.

[2] Harris *v.* Morris, 4 Esp. 41; 1 Selw. N. P. 298, 11th ed.; 2 Strange, 1214. See Black *v.* Bryan, 18 Tex. 453.

[3] Emery *v.* Emery, 1 You. & Jer. 501.

[4] Reed *v.* Moore, 5 Car. & P. 200. See Flanagan *v.* Bishop Wearmouth, 8 El. & B. 451.

[5] Reed *v.* Moore, *supra.* See Atkyns *v.* Pearce, 2 C. B. (N. S.) 763.

divorce from bed and board.[1] But where she leaves her husband without sufficient cause and against his will she cannot bind him elsewhere; especially if the person furnishing goods knows that cohabitation has ceased and makes no further inquiries.[2]

Supposing the wife leaves voluntarily and without sufficient cause, against her husband's wishes, and she afterwards returns to her husband, is he bound to receive her; and, if he refuse to receive her, can she make him liable for debts contracted thenceforth for necessaries? The current of authorities is in favor of such a position, provided she has conducted herself properly in her absence.[3] Some however have suggested doubts as to this doctrine; for, they say, since the wife by her own voluntary act, discharged the husband from his obligation to maintain her, by unnecessarily quitting his house without his consent, it is but reasonable to say that his liability to support her afterwards should not be revived by implication without his express concurrence in consenting to his wife's return to his protection, or until cohabitation was restored by mutual agreement or by the sentence of a court with matrimonial and divorce jurisdiction.[4] This is fair reasoning on general grounds, and applies a mutual doctrine to husband and wife, but the courts appear to have thought otherwise.

But, as the reader may have inferred, if the wife elopes and commits adultery, or if her adultery causes separation, the husband is relieved from her support. Her crime ought

[1] Brown *v.* Patton, 3 Humph. 135; Hancock *v.* Merrick, 10 Cush. 41; Caney *v.* Patton, 2 Ashm. 140; Rea *v.* Durkee, 25 Ill. 503; Schindel *v.* Schindel, 12 Md. 294.

[2] Brown *v.* Midgett, 40 Vt. 68; Etherington *v.* Parrott, 2 Ld. Raym. 1006; Manby *v.* Scott, 1 Sid. 130; Bailey *v.* Calcott, 4 Jur. 699; Collins *v.* Mitchell, 5 Harring. 369.

[3] Manby *v.* Scott, 1 Sid. 129; 1 Mod. 131; Child *v.* Hardyman, 2 Stra. 875; Rawlins *v.* Vandyke, 3 Esp. 251; Edwards *v.* Towels, 5 Man. & Gr. 624; Hindley *v.* Westmeath, 6 B. & C. 200; Howard *v.* Whetstone, 10 Ohio, 365; McCutchen *v.* McGahay, 11 Johns. 281.

[4] See 2 Bright Hus. & Wife, 13. But see 2 Bish. Mar. & Div. 4th ed. § 33. The husband should not be deprived of his divorce remedies.

to put an end to her authority to bind the injured spouse, and it does.[1] In such case his refusal to take her back again will not revive his obligation to maintain her. But as forgiveness always interposes a bar to legal remedies on behalf of the injured one, he becomes once more liable for her necessaries, where he voluntarily receives her again and forgives her.[2]

There are cases where the marital rights and duties become more confused. Supposing the wife be turned out of doors, or, what amounts to the same thing, be forced by her husband's misconduct to leave; and she afterwards, being beyond that shelter which every wife needs, commit adultery: is he then relieved from supporting her? In *Govier* v. *Hancock* it was held that he was, even though his own adultery caused her departure.[3] This was a very harsh decision. The court however admitted that necessaries furnished before her own adultery could be recovered from her husband. And in a subsequent case it was held that adulterous conduct of the wife, with the connivance of the husband, or at least without such a separation of the married pair as to make her misconduct notorious, would not, *per se*, operate as a defence and protect the husband from liability.[4] And more to the point is a case decided only a short time ago, where the husband was held liable, even though the wife had been found guilty of adultery in the divorce court; since it appeared that he also had been found guilty of adultery, so that no divorce was decreed.[5]

There is a *dictum* of Lord Holt to be found in an old case, (or rather in the reporter's note) which sometimes finds its way to the text-books; namely, that if a husband receives back

[1] Morris *v.* Martin, 1 Stra. 647; Manwaring *v.* Sands, 2 Stra. 707; Hardie *v.* Grant, 8 Car. & P. 512. And see Rex *v.* Flintan, 1 B. & Ad. 227; Hunter *v.* Boucher, 3 Pick. 289; Gill *v.* Read, 5 R. I. 343; Cooper *v.* Lloyd, 6 C. B. (N. S.) 519.

[2] Harris *v.* Morris, 4 Esp. 41; Robison *v.* Gosnold, 6 Mod. 171; Holt *v.* Brien, 4 B. & Ald. 252; Quincy *v.* Quincy, 10 N. H. 272; Hall *v.* Hall, 4 ib. 462.

[3] 6 T. R. 603.

[4] Norton *v.* Fazan, 1 Bos. & Pull. 226.

[5] Needham *v.* Bremner, Law Rep. 1 C. P. 582.

his wife, he becomes liable for her debts contracted during the whole period of her unauthorized absence.[1] This seems very unreasonable. The true doctrine is, doubtless, that after reconciliation the husband is liable upon her subsequent contracts only. And this is the rule expressly asserted in some American cases.[2]

How far the wife can contract liability for necessaries in her own person, when the husband is discharged by her delinquency, was considered in the case of *Marshall* v. *Rutton.*[3] Lord Kenyon observed, that it was not a necessary consequence of the determination of the husband's responsibility that the wife should be at liberty to act as a *feme sole;* but that the contrary was the truth; and that any persons knowing her condition who chose to trust her could not complain if they found themselves unable to sue her. But these remarks are very cautiously put; and it seems reasonable to suppose, as Justice Buller expresses himself in the case upon which Lord Kenyon commented, that the wife would become liable therefor; certainly if she represents herself as a single woman.[4]

It is to be carefully observed that whenever husband and wife separate, under circumstances showing misconduct on the part of either, the presumption of agency changes sides. While they cohabit it is for the husband to show a want of authority; when they cease to cohabit the tradesman must prove authority; that is to say, he must prove that the wife was in need of the goods, that the husband failed to supply her, and that the husband and not the wife was at fault. *Prima facie*, therefore, a woman living apart from her husband, upon involuntary separation, has no authority to bind him.[5]

1 Robison *v.* Gosnold, 6 Mod. 171. See Bing. Inf. 190, *n.*, Am. ed.

2 Williams *v.* Prince, 3 Strobh. 490; Reese *v.* Chilton, 26 Mis. 598. See also Chitty Contr. 168; Williams *v.* McGahay, 12 Johns. 293.

3 8 T. R. 547.

4 Cox *v.* Kitchin, 1 Bos. & Pull. 339. See Childress *v.* Mann, 33 Ala. 206; and separate estate rights, *infra.*

5 Etherington *v.* Parrott, 2 Ld. Raym. 1006; Mainwaring *v.* Leslie, 1 Mood. & Malk. 18; Montague *v.* Benedict, 3 B. & C. 631; Per Lord Tenter-

The wife of a lunatic living separate from her in an asylum, may yet pledge his credit for necessaries.[1] But not, it would seem, where he is in prison; for then the law recognizes her as *feme sole*.[2] If the wife be in an insane asylum, the husband is not the less liable for her support.[3] But not where she is in prison.[4] And it seems that under circumstances of misconduct on the wife's part the husband may compel her to assent, after her release from confinement, to live separate on an allowance, without being chargeable for her support, as one who has turned his wife out of doors.[5]

But besides involuntary separation, there is the case of voluntary separation to be considered. This last, now so frequent, the law tolerates, but does not favor. The rule is, that where a husband and wife part by mutual consent, and a suitable allowance is furnished the wife, the husband is not bound to pay any bills which she may have contracted as his agent.[6] It is enough that the separation be a matter of common reputation where he resides. But to this allowance two things are requisite: first, that it shall be really sufficient for the wife; second, that it shall be regularly paid. If either requirement be wanting, the wife is not confined to her remedy on the deed of separation, if any, but may pledge her husband's credit.

den, Clifford *v.* Laton, Mood. & Malk. 101; 3 Car. & P. 16; Bird *v.* Jones, 3 M. & R. 121; Walker *v.* Simpson, 7 W. & S. 83; Mitchell *v.* Treanor, 11 Geo. 324; Rea *v.* Durkee, 25 Ill. 503; Pool *v.* Everton, 5 Jones, 241; Porter *v.* Bobb, 25 Mis. 36. But see Frost *v.* Willis, 13 Vt. 202.

[1] Reed *v.* Legard, 4 E. L. & Eq. 523; Shaw *v.* Thompson, 16 Pick. 198.

[2] Reeve Dom. Rel. 86.

[3] Wray *v* Wray, 33 Ala. 187. And see Alna *v.* Plummer, 4 Greenl. 258; Wray *v.* Cox, 24 Ala. 337. See Brookfield *v.* Allen, 6 Allen, 585.

[4] Fowler *v.* Sir John Dineley, 2 Str. 1122. See Bates *v.* Enright, 42 Me. 105.

[5] See *n.* 3, *supra.*

[6] Dixon *v.* Harrell, 8 Car. & P. 717; Todd *v.* Stokes, 1 Salk. 116; 1 Ld. Raym. 444; Hindley *v.* Westmeath, 6 B. & C. 200; Migen *v.* Peck, 3 M. & W. 481; Reeve *v.* Marquis of Conyngham, 2 Car. & K. 444; Calkins *v.* Long, 22 Barb. 97; Kemp *v.* Downham, 5 Harring. 417; Caney *v.* Patton, 2 Ashm. 140; Baker *v.* Barney, 8 Johns. 72; Mott *v.* Comstock, 8 Wend. 544; Willson *v.* Smith, 1 B. & Ald. 801.

As to the first requirement, the question is not whether the wife consented to accept a certain allowance as sufficient for her support, but whether it be actually sufficient in the opinion of the jury.[1] As to the second, the mere covenant or contract of the husband to pay separate maintenance will not discharge him from liability for necessaries; for, as was observed in a leading case, "the common law does not relieve any man from an obligation on the mere ground of an agreement to do something else in the place, unless that agreement be performed."[2] But perhaps it would be held otherwise where articles of separation provide that the wife shall be paid through a trustee, and the trustee squanders or misapplies the allowance which is properly paid into his hands.[3] Allowance of a separate maintenance will not exempt the husband from liabilities caused by his own misconduct.[4]

The payment of alimony, although insufficient, will discharge the husband from liability for his wife's necessaries.[5] But the husband is liable for necessaries supplied to the wife before alimony is decreed, although the decree afterwards direct the alimony to commence from a day preceding the supply of the necessaries.[6] It is immaterial whether the wife's allowance be secured by deed or not, since it is the payment which discharges him.[7] And of course, where the fact of separation is not commonly known, or where by occasional visits the husband keeps up the appearance of cohabitation with his wife, he is *prima*

[1] Thompson *v.* Harvey, 4 Burr. 2177; Hodgkinson *v.* Fletcher, 4 Camp. N. P. 70; Pearson *v.* Darrington, 32 Ala. 227; Lidlow *v.* Wilmot, 2 Starkie, 77; Emmett *v.* Norton, 8 Car. & P. 506.

[2] Nurse *v.* Craig, 5 B. & P. 148, per Heath J.; Hindley *v.* Westmeath, 6 B. & C. 200; Lockwood *v.* Thomas, 12 Johns. 248; Kimball *v.* Keyes, 11 Wend. 33.

[3] Calkins *v.* Long, 22 Barb. 97. But see Burrett *v.* Booty, 8 Taunt. 343.

[4] Turner *v.* Rookes, 10 Ad. &. El. 47.

[5] Willson *v.* Smith, 1 B. & Ad. 801.

[6] Keegan *v.* Smith, 5 B. & C. 375; Mitchell *v.* Treanor, 11 Geo. 324. See Dowe *v.* Smith, 11 Allen, 107; and chapter on Divorce, *infra.*

[7] Hodgkinson *v.* Fletcher, 4 Camp. 70; Emery *v.* Neighbor, 2 Halst. 142; Holden *v.* Cope, 2 Car. & K. 437. But see Ewers *v.* Hutton, 3 Esp. 255.

facie liable as before;[1] though notice of an allowance is notice of his dissent to the wife's contracts.[2] He may agree with the wife's tradesman, while living apart from her, that the goods supplied shall not be charged to him; and to such special agreement the tradesman will be held.[3]

Courts will always regard the rule of good faith in matters relative to the wife's necessaries. Thus if the husband and wife be living apart without the husband's fault, and he wishes to terminate his liability by requesting her to return home, his conduct must show sincerity; though, if his intentions are *bona fide*, and he makes suitable provision at his own home, the wife forfeits all claim to further support by refusing to return.[4] So where a husband expels his wife and afterwards designedly misleads her into the belief that he is dead, whereupon she marries another with honest motives, and leaves him at once on learning that her husband is alive, her husband cannot set up her bigamy as a defence to an action against him for her subsequent necessaries.[5]

The case of *Johnston* v. *Sumner* came before the English Exchequer Court in 1858.[6] A married pair had separated by mutual consent, with the understanding that the wife should receive £200 a year, for her maintenance, from a fund settled on her at the time of marriage. A third person, who afterwards supplied her with necessaries, sued the husband to recover payment. The court ruled that the latter was not liable unless the plaintiff could show that the wife's allowance was insufficient; that the burden of proof was upon him and not upon the husband. In this case the law of agency for necessaries was very fully discussed, and the principle laid down that whether separation be voluntary or involuntary, so

1 Rawlins *v.* Vandyke, 3 Esp. 250, per Lord Eldon.

2 Hinton *v.* Hudson, Freem. 248; Kimball *v.* Keyes, 11 Wend. 33.

3 Dixon *v.* Harrell, 8 Car. & P. 717.

4 Walker *v.* Laighton, 11 Foster, 111.

5 Cartwright *v.* Bate. 1 Allen, 514. See Pidgin *v.* Cram, 8 N.H. 350.

6 3 Hurl. & Nor. 261.

long as the parties live apart the burden of proof is upon the person who supplies the commodities. Chief Baron Pollock, after stating that the only ground of the husband's liability for his wife's necessaries, in any case, is that of agency, observes, that this agency may be either express or implied, arising sometimes from conduct which induces others to believe that an agency in fact exists; or that there may be an agency of necessity, such as the captain of a ship sometimes exercises. If a man and his wife live together, it matters not what private agreement they may make, the wife, as such, has authority to bind him. If the husband turns her away, it is not unreasonable to say that she has an authority of necessity; for she by law has no property, and cannot earn her own living. If, however, she leaves against his will and without misconduct on his part, she has none of the ordinary authorities of a wife, for she is not in the ordinary case of a wife, namely, living with her husband; nor has she authority of necessity, because she has brought the condition on herself. She has no express or implied authority. Now suppose she leaves with his consent, but without misconduct on his part, she has not the ordinary authority of a wife living with her husband, nor any authority of necessity. Her authority must therefore be express or implied. It is admitted that in this case there was no express authority. But was there an implied authority? Now, where they part by mutual consent, and nothing is said of an allowance, and she has no means of support, a jury might infer that the husband meant that his credit should be pledged,—perhaps even though he said otherwise. But upon what principle can an authority be implied where they part upon terms negativing any authority in her, and making a provision for her not shown to be insufficient for her maintenance? The case is not essentially different from that of a wife leaving against her husband's will; nor can the line be readily drawn so as to distinguish the two. "We think the more convenient rule is that which we have suggested; namely, an authority must be shown, and shown in one or the other of the ways we have mentioned."[1] Such, in brief, is the law of the wife's agency in procuring necessaries, as expounded by the most recent English authority. This decision is chiefly as to the burden of proof; the requirements being usually as we have stated.

The wife may bind her husband for other contracts than those for necessaries, where an agency, express or implied, can be shown. The natural incapacities of her sex superadded to those of the marriage state, the practical difficulties which persons dealing through such an agent must encounter, particularly where they find she has exceeded her authority, and yet cannot hold her liable in person, her own exposure to fraud, deceit, and coercion,— all these combine to render the wife an undesirable business representative; and cases of this sort come rarely before the courts. But the wife may be delegated an attorney, even under a sealed instrument.[2] And on principle there is little reason to doubt her capacity to bind her husband in all general transactions where he has given an express authority. So too her agency may be inferred from his acts and conduct respecting her; and the general rule applies that such agency is to be measured by the scope of the usual employment.[3]

The usual cases in which a wife binds the husband on con-

[1] Per Pollock C. B., Johnston *v.* Sumner, ib. See also Ozard *v.* Darnford, 2 Sel. N. P. 275, 10th ed.; Hodgkinson *v.* Fletcher, 4 Camp. 70; Liddlaw *v.* Wilmot, 2 Stark. N. P. 77; Emmett *v.* Norton, 8 Car. & P. 506; Nurse *v.* Craig, 5 Bos. & Pul. 148; Willson *v.* Smith, 1 B. & Ad. 801; Holden *v.* Cope, 2 Car. & K. 437; 2 Roper Hus. & Wife, 108, are all commented upon in this case, and doctrine of 2 Smith's Lead. Cas. 389 denied. The court considered it doubtful whether, if a laboring man turns his wife away, she being capable of earning, and earning as much as he did; or if a man turn his wife away, she having a settlement double his income in amount, the wife in such cases could bind the husband. The drift of the law where wives own separate property, is in this case plainly indicated.

[2] Goodwin *v.* Kelly, 42 Barb. 194.

[3] Cox *v.* Hoffman, 4 Dev. & Batt. 180; Mackinley *v.* McGregor, 3 Whart. 369; Camelin *v.* Palmer Co., 10 Allen, 539; Ruddock *v.* Marsh, 38 E. L. & Eq. 515; Pickering *v.* Pickering, 6 N. H. 124; Abbott *v.* Mackinley, 2 Miles, 220; Gray *v.* Otis, 11 Vt. 628; Miller *v.* Delamater, 12 Wend. 433; Hughes *v.* Stokes, 21 Hayw. 372.

tracts not for necessaries may be reduced to two classes: the one where the nature of his employment is such that the wife is expected to share in it; the other where he is absent from home, and some one must carry on the household and small business matters. Instances of the first class are those of farmers, victuallers, and small shop-keepers.[1] While, on behalf of married women, extended authority is to be implied from the fact of a husband's absence, as in our second class, every wife will readily be regarded as her husband's representative in the ordinary household purchases, such as provisions and furniture, although the articles may not be strictly included among her personal necessaries. They might be called household necessaries. But where the husband is a laboring man, or otherwise obliged to be absent from his home much of the time, the presumption of the wife's agency would be stronger and extend further. If the occupation be that of carrying on a farm, or if small bills are to be collected, such as he and his wife have always attended to, her powers in his absence take a still wider scope; and this too seems reasonable. Usage will go far in determining such questions. But since persons carrying on a large business, totally distinct from their household occupation, are not in the habit of employing their wives to manage it for them, strong proof of agency for such transactions would be required to warrant a wife's interference during her husband's absence; the more so if he has left other competent agents of his own to manage the business for him. So too in large pecuniary affairs of whatever nature her agency is not readily inferred; while it often is in collecting rents and paying tradesman's bills; her payments and receipts being permitted to bind her husband. And although a wife may, by actual authority from her husband, indorse his notes, mortgage and dispose of his personal property, conduct his business as a trader, and even borrow money for carrying on his business on the pledge of his credit, signing the notes and securities in his behalf,—for all this is some-

[1] See Webster *v.* McGinnis, 5 Binn. 235; Rotch *v.* Miles, 2 Conn. 638.

times done,—such authority requires strict proof; or at least conduct on the part of the husband showing his own approval of such hazardous proceedings on her part.[1]

The difficulty of laying down a more positive rule on this subject is shown by two cases which came before the courts of two of our neighboring States, not many years since, on a presentation of facts almost identical, but where the respective decisions were precisely opposite. A farmer was absent from home. His wife had been left in charge of the farm, but without express authority from him. A creditor attached the real estate and crops; and she permitted the hay after attachment to be used by the officer; to the advantage of the creditor, or at least to her husband's detriment. In the Vermont case, it was held that the wife had a *prima facie* authority to bind her husband; in the Connecticut case, it was held that she had not. Neither of these tribunals erred in their statement of leading principles, but their duty here being rather an application of broad rules to facts, than a clearly legal deduction, they differed just as two men would have done, sitting upon a jury.[2]

[1] Church *v.* Landers, 10 Wend. 79; Gates *v.* Brower, 5 Seld. 205; Leeds *v.* Vail, 15 Penn. St. 185; Alexander *v.* Miller, 16 Penn. St. 215; Burk *v.* Howard, 13 Mis. 241; Godfrey *v.* Brooks, 5 Harring. 396; Savage *v.* Davis, 18 Wis. 608; Krebs *v.* O'Grady, 23 Ala. 726; Sawyer *v.* Cutting, 23 Vt. 486; Shaw *v.* Emery, 38 Me. 484; Spencer *v.* Tisue, Addis. 316; Green *v.* Sperry, 16 Vt. 390; Reakert *v.* Sandford, 5 Watts & Serg. 164; Abbott *v.* M'Kinley, 2 Miles, 220; Shoemaker *v.* Kunkle, 5 Watts, 107; Gilbert *v.* Plant, 18 Ind. 308. See subsequent chapters as to wife's power to bind real estate by her contracts. It seems that contracts made by the wife as agent, including promissory notes, should show such authority on the face. Minard *v.* Mead, 7 Wend. 68; Galusha *v.* Hitchcock, 29 Barb. 193; 2 Man. & Gr. 172.

[2] Felker *v.* Emerson, 16 Vt. 653; Benjamin *v.* Benjamin, 15 Conn. 347. A third person may be sued on a contract made with a married woman after she has performed her part, although she had no right to make it. Ham *v.* Boody, 20 N. H. 411. See 1 Greenl. Evid. § 185; Plimmer *v.* Sells, 3 N. & M. 422; Dodd *v.* Acklom, 6 M. & Gr. 673; Thrasher *v.* Tuttle, 22 Me. 335; Hopkins *v.* Mollineux, 4 Wend. 465; Filmer *v.* Lynn, 4 N. & M. 559; Taylor *v.* Green, 8 Car. & P. 316, as to the rule of evidence sufficient to show the wife's authority to manage her husband's business. The principles of ordinary agency generally apply in such cases. See also Wharton *v.* Wright, 1 Car. & K. 585; Clifford *v.* Burton, 1 Bing. 199; Petty *v.* Anderson, 3 Bing. 170; Emerson *v.* Blounden, 1 Esp. 142.

CHAPTER IV.

THE EFFECT OF COVERTURE UPON THE WIFE'S INJURIES AND FRAUDS.

Frauds and injuries may have been committed upon the wife; or they may have been committed by the wife. Again they may have been committed before coverture; or they may have been committed during coverture. Once more, they may have reference to the person; constituting a bodily injury, such as assault and battery, or an injury to the character, such as slander; or they may have reference to property. But in any event, so far as the fraud or injury is made the subject of a civil suit, the general principle of the wife's disability remains the same; namely, that the husband compensates or receives the compensation.

This principle does not of course extend to criminal prosecutions. For, as Blackstone observes, the union is only a civil union.[1] Or, to come more to the point, it would be cruel and unjust to punish one person for the crime of another, or even to compel the two to bear the penalty together; while it would be impolitic as well as unjust, to allow any relation which human beings, morally responsible, may sustain with one another to absolve either from legal accountability. Here coverture as a theory, contradicts itself, by leaving the wife answerable alone for her crimes, just as a single woman. The utmost the law can do is to furnish a presumption of innocence in her favor in cases where the coercion of her husband may be reasonably inferred. This indulgence, it is said, is carried so far as to excuse her from punishment for theft, burglary, or other civil offences "against the laws of society," when committed in the presence or by the

[1] 1 Bl. Com. 443.

command of her husband; but not so as to exculpate the wife for moral offences. For *mala prohibita* she is not punished, for *mala in se* she is. Such a distinction is variable and somewhat shadowy; the line seems to be drawn more wisely between such heinous crimes as murder and manslaughter, and the lighter offences.[1] And the better opinion is that in all cases coercion is only a legal presumption, which may be rebutted by evidence to the contrary.[2]

As to private wrongs the question occurs, why should the husband be made to stand in the wife's place where the offence is considered against an individual, any more than when it is between herself and the State. This seems to be the true answer, as in case of her debts *dum sola;* namely, that the husband adopts her and her circumstances together; that he takes her fortune, if she has one, and assumes all possible liabilities therefrom.

We must however notice one important distinction made between the wife's general contracts and her frauds and injuries. In the one case the husband is held liable to third parties for her acts as agent, even though never married to her; and simple cohabitation is sufficient to charge him. But simple cohabitation will not be enough to make him responsible for her civil injuries. Marriage in fact must appear. And this last principle applies likewise where he seeks indemnity for her injuries.[3] The facility with which an agency is created at law may serve to explain the difference between the two cases.

The general rule of law is that the husband is liable for the frauds and injuries of the wife, whether committed before or

1 2 Kent Com. 11th ed. 150; 4 Bl. Com. 28, 29, and Christian's notes; 1 Hawk. P. C. b. 1, ch. 1, § 9; 1 Russ. Crimes, 18–24.

2 2 Kent Com. 11th ed. 150; State *v.* Parkerson, 1 Strobh. 169; 1 Russ. Crimes, 22; Rex *v.* Martha Hughes, *coram* Thomson B., 2 Lew. C. C. 229; Uhl *v.* Commonwealth, 6 Gratt. 706; Wagener *v.* Bill, 19 Barb. 321. But a wife cannot be convicted of feloniously receiving stolen goods from her husband. Regina *v.* Brooks, 14 E. L. & Eq. 580. See also on the general subject of coercion, 8 Car. & P. 19, 541; Anon., 2 East P. C. 559; 1 Greenl. Evid. 10th ed. § 28.

3 Overholt *v.* Ellswell, 1 Ashm. 200. See Norwood *v.* Stevenson, Andr. 227.

during coverture; if committed in his company or by his order, he, and he alone is liable; otherwise, both are liable.[1] For where the fraud or injury is committed in his company or by his order, coercion is presumed, and the husband becomes the only wrong-doer; and where committed without his order and in his absence, the wife is, in reality, the offending party, while the husband has become responsible for her acts by reason of her coverture. In the latter class of cases the husband is properly joined with his wife in the suit; for if the wife alone were sued, his property might be seized without giving him an opportunity for defence; and if the husband alone were sued, he would become chargeable absolutely. In the former class of cases the husband is sued alone.[2]

The last statement suggests that the husband's liability is after all a limited one, where he, in the first instance, was free from wrong; that is to say that the death of the wife before the recovery of damages, puts an end to his liability altogether. This is correct, not only on the principle announced in the case of the wife's debts, *dum sola*, but because wrongs being personal, die with the person, which last is the common explanation of this rule. If the husband dies before damages are recovered in the suit, the wife alone remains liable.[3] So it would seem that the common law recognizes a liability on her part which continues through the marriage relation, coverture operating, however, so as to suspend the remedy against the married woman, and to bring in as a joint party the custodian of her fortune.

This presumption of coercion is much the same in civil as in criminal offences. A wrong committed by the wife in company

1 2 Kent Com. 149; Bing. Inf. 256, 257; Angel *v.* Felton, 8 Johns. 149; Gage *v.* Reed, 15 Ill. 403; Carl *v.* Wonder, 5 Watts, 97; Whitman *v.* Delano, 6 N. H. 543; Gray *v.* Thacker, 4 Ala. 136; McKeown *v.* Johnson, 1 McCord, 578; Benjamin *v.* Bartlett, 3 Miss. 86; Wright *v.* Kerr, Addis. 13; 7 T. R. 348; 2 Roll. 53; 3 T. R. 631; Ball *v.* Bennett, 21 Ind. 427.

2 Park *v.* Hopkins, 2 Bailey, 411; Matthews *v.* Fiestel, 2 E. D. Smith, 90.

3 2 Bright Hus. & Wife, 22 *n.*; and see Stroop *v.* Swarts, 12 S. & R. 76.

with her husband or by his order, is presumed to have been involuntary on her part and compelled by her husband; and we have supposed that this presumption may be, in either instance, controlled by evidence to the contrary. The legal definition "in company with" the husband should, however, receive a liberal interpretation, so as to include all cases of constructive presence. It is said that the privilege of presumptive coercion extends to no other person than a wife, not even to a servant.[1]

Hence husband and wife are sued together for the libel or slander of the wife.[2] So too for assault and battery.[3] The fact that the husband is made responsible by the fact of coverture, and did not commit the wrong in person, cannot go in mitigation of damages.[4] The husband has full management of the defence. And we need hardly add that he may compromise without his wife's assent.[5] His liability lasts so long as the relation lasts, even though the married pair be permanently separated; but not perhaps if the wife be living in adultery at the time the wrong was committed.[6]

There are however not only *torts simpliciter*, or simple wrongs at law, but wrongs where the substantive basis of the fraud is the wife's contract. The common law has been supposed to apply with the same force in both cases, partly because in the latter instance the person injured would be otherwise without a remedy.[7]

This point came directly before the Court of Exchequer in 1854, for decision. The circumstances of the case were as follows: A man applied for a loan of £30 to a loan association, upon the security of a promissory note, to be signed by himself

1 Reeve Dom. Rel. 72; Barnes *v.* Harris, Busbee, 15; Griffin *v.* Reynolds, 17 How. (U. S.) 609.

2 Austin *v.* Wilson, 4 Cush. 273.

3 Griffin *v.* Reynolds, 17 How. (U. S.) 609; Roadcap *v.* Sipe, 6 Gratt. 213.

4 Austin *v.* Wilson, 4 Cush. 273.

5 Coolidge *v.* Parris, 8 Ohio St. 594.

6 Head *v.* Briscoe, 5 Car. & P. 484.

7 Macq. Hus. & Wife, 130, 131; Head *v.* Briscoe, 5 Car. & P. 484, per C. J. Tindal; Reeve Dom. Rel. 72, 73.

and sureties. One of the sureties was a married woman who falsely represented herself to the association as single. The security was accepted and the loan made. Afterwards the loan association, recurring to the sureties for payment of the note, sought to make her husband liable on the note, alleging her fraud. The court decided that the action was not maintainable; on the ground that though the husband is liable for the wife's general frauds, yet when the fraud is directly connected with her contract, and is the means of effecting it and part and parcel of the same transaction, the wife cannot be responsible, nor can the husband be sued for the fraud together with the wife.[1]

But there are cases where the wife will bind her husband by her fraudulent representations on the ground of her agency. Thus in *Taylor* v. *Green* an advertisement appeared in a newspaper offering for sale a baker's shop with the good-will of the business, and misrepresenting the extent of the business. It did not appear that the baker took any part in the transaction, further than to receive the purchase-money and pay the broker his commission. The court held nevertheless that he was bound by the fraudulent representations of his wife, inasmuch as she was his agent in managing the shop and finding a purchaser, and that he must respond in damages.[2] Nor is the doctrine of the loan association case as yet broadly applied.[3]

The husband of an administratrix or executrix is liable for her devastavit, or other wrongful act committed before or during coverture, if his liability be fixed before the death of the wife.[4] And if she survive him, her appointment having been complete in all respects, she becomes liable once more; even

[1] Liverpool Adelphi Loan Association *v.* Fairhurst, 9 Exch. 422. See also Cooper *v.* Witham, 1 Lev. 247; Keen *v.* Hartman, 48 Penn. St. 497; Barnes *v.* Harris, Busbee, 15.

[2] 8 Car. & P. 316; Macq. Hus. & Wife, 127. And see as to the wife's *quasi* criminal act, in violation of the excise laws, Attorney General *v.* Riddle, 2 Cromp. & Jer. 493.

[3] See Wright *v.* Leonard, 11 C. B. N. S. (1861) 258.

[4] 2 Bright Hus. & Wife, 22–36, and cases cited; Bobe *v.* Frowner, 18 Ala. 89.

for a *devastavit* committed by him when alive.[1] But the husband cannot be sued as an executor *de son tort* for acts of his wife done without his knowledge; though it is otherwise where he advises or aids her in the commission of the wrongful acts; for every one so participating becomes a principal.[2]

Where there is no collusion apparent a husband will not be committed for his wife's breach of injunction.[3]

For injuries to the person or character of the wife, the husband and wife at the common law should sue together.[4] But where the right of action for damages is founded on the prior possession of personal property, the husband must sue alone; since his possession is the possession of both.[5] And the joinder of the wife in actions relating to personal property, where the injury was committed after marriage, is good ground of demurrer, or motion to arrest, or even of error after judgment.[6] Whether the same principle applies to property of the wife parted with before marriage is not so clear. This is the rule, however, when the action is for a wrong, which before the marriage was committed in respect to such property.[7] But where the trover is laid before the marriage and the conversion afterwards, there has been some controversy, the result of which seems to be that the action is well brought, either with or without joining the wife.[8] The principle sought is whether such a suit amounts to a disaffirmance of the husband's constructive title to the goods on the marriage.[9]

1 Soady *v.* Turnbull, Law Rep. 1 Ch. 494.

2 Hinds *v.* Jones, 48 Me. 348. The wife cannot hold such offices during coverture independently of her husband's control, as we shall see hereafter.

3 Hope *v.* Carmegie, Law Rep. 7 Eq. 254.

4 Bing. Inf. & Cov. 247, Am. ed. and cases cited.

5 Bing. Inf. & Cov. 253, and cases cited; Cro. Eliz. 133; 1 Chit. Pl. 93; 1 Salk. 114.

6 Rawlins *v.* Rounds, 27 Vt. 17.

7 3 Rob. Pract. 188; Milner *v.* Milnes, 3 T. R. 627; Fewell *v.* Collins, 1 Const. 207.

8 Powes *v.* Marshal, 1 Sid. 172; Ayling *v.* Whicher, 6 Ad. & El. 259; Blackborne *v.* Haigh, 2 Lev. 107; 3 Rob. Pract. *supra.* There is some uncertainty on this point, however. See Bac. Abr. Baron & Feme (K.); *contra,* Brown *v.* Fifield, 4 Mich. 322; Wellborn *v.* Weaver, 17 Geo. 267. The better course is doubtless to join the wife.

9 As to injuries to the wife's real estate, see *infra,* ch. 6.

On these principles it is held that husband and wife must sue together for slanderous words spoken against the latter.[1] Also for battery of the wife.[2] Also for injuries sustained by her through the negligence of a common carrier.[3] Also for the malpractice of a physician.[4] Also for frauds upon the wife; as in case of an action *qui tam* to recover penalties for a fraudulent conveyance.[5] And the rule is the same in all these cases, whether the fraud or injury was committed before or during coverture. But if the wife be a privy to the wrong, or knowingly suffers an injury to be committed upon her, the husband cannot maintain his action; for his right to damages cannot be greater than hers would have been, had she remained single.[6] Nor can an action be maintained where the husband instigates the wrong.[7] In a joint action for personal wrong to the wife, the declaration should conclude "to their damage."[8] And it is a well recognized principle, both in England and America, that whenever the wife is the meritorious cause of action, her interest must appear on the face of the pleadings or the omission will be considered fatal.[9]

The damages allowed as compensation for the frauds and injuries sustained by the wife, go to the husband, as well as the rest of her personal property, if recovered during his lifetime. But such suits survive to her; and on the death of the hus-

[1] Smalley *v.* Anderson, 2 Monr. 56; Throgmorton *v.* Davis, 3 Blackf. 383. These words must be actionable *per se.* See Beach *v.* Ranney, 2 Hill, 309; Saville *v.* Sweeney, 4 B. & Ad. 514; Ryan *v.* Madden, 12 Vt. 51.

[2] Pillow *v.* Bushnell, 5 Barb. 156.

[3] Heirn *v.* McCaughan, 32 Miss. 17.

[4] Even though it afterwards cause her death; Cross *v.* Guthery, 2 Root, 90; Hyatt *v.* Adams, 16 Mich. 180.

[5] Fowler *v.* Frisbie, 3 Conn. 320. But see Crump *v.* McKay, 8 Jones, 32, as to negligence "sounding in contract," not admitted to be cause of action.

[6] Pillow *v.* Bushnell, 5 Barb. 156.

[7] Tibbs *v.* Brown, 2 Grant's Cases, 39. Nor in slander where the words are not actionable, though the wife become ill in consequence of the slanders. Wilson *v.* Goit, 17 N. Y. 442.

[8] Horton *v.* Byles, 1 Sid. 387; Smalley *v.* Anderson, 2 Monr. 56.

[9] Bing. Inf. & Cov. 248; Staley *v.* Barhite, 2 Caines, 221; Serres *v.* Dodd, 5 B. & P. 405; Thorne *v.* Dillingham, 1 Denio, 254.

band, pending legal proceedings, the wife may proceed to judgment and collect the damages for herself; or if her husband had never brought an action, she may then do so in her own right.[1] The husband on the other hand has no such interest in the suit at common law that he may prosecute it in his own name after his wife's death. His joinder in the first place was only because of the marriage relation. He may, however, under some statutes, be let in as her administrator, and in such capacity prosecute the suit to its conclusion.[2] If the wife dies after judgment, the husband surviving may take the benefits of the suit: for a judgment debt takes the place of the original cause of action. The death of the wife pending suit for her personal tort put an end to the action altogether by the old law.[3]

Since the husband is at the common law entitled to the society and services of his wife, two separate causes of action may arise from injuries inflicted upon her person. One, in the name of both for her own injuries, we have just considered; the other is in the name of the husband alone *per quod consortium amisit*.[4] Thus, if the wife be wantonly bruised and maltreated, her husband may bring his special action *per quod* for the loss of her society and his medical expenses. But there can be no special damage recovered by the husband by way of aggravation in the joint suit for his wife's injuries. Thus, if the action be for an assault on the wife, the surgeon's bill cannot be recovered; if for slander of the wife, the loss of wages cannot be claimed; there the sole right of the husband should be sued for in his name.[5] It would appear that the husband may release the damages for

1 Bing. Inf. & Cov. 247, 248; Newton *v.* Hutter, 2 Ld. Raym. 1208.

2 Chitty Pl. 74; Norcross *v.* Stuart, 50 Me. 87; Pattee *v.* Harrington, 11 Pick. 221; Crozier *v.* Bryant, 4 Bibb, 174.

3 Bac. Abr. Baron & Feme (K).

4 3 Bl. Com. 140; Cro. Jac. 501; ib. 538. See also Brockbank *v.* Whitehaven Junction R. R. Co., 7 Hurl. & Nor. 834.

5 Dengate *v.* Gardiner, 4 M. & W. 6. See Lewis *v.* Babcock, 18 Johns. 443. An action cannot be in general maintained by the wife, there being no misfeasance towards her independently of a contract with the husband alone. Longmeid *v.* Holliday, 6 Exch. 761.

his wife's injuries, and then recover for the loss arising to himself alone.[1] Of the suits which the husband may bring for loss of his wife's society, that for enticing a wife away has already been considered.[2] Somewhat akin to this is his action for his wife's seduction, founded on the same general marital rights. But the common law still keeps up its legal fiction of the wife's civil incapacity, and treats the seducer as guilty of trespass by force of arms, whether the wife actually consent to the guilt or not.[3] The damages which the husband may here recover in his own right are not affected by the social rank or condition of the parties;[4] nor by his own character, save his character as a husband;[5] but they may be materially influenced by the wife's previous character for chastity;[6] while if the husband be privy to the crime or consenting thereto, the law treats him as the seducer, and gives him no damages.[7] But the earlier cases seem to have regarded this last circumstance as tending only to reduce his compensation.[8] A husband who lives apart from his wife, under articles of separation or a decree of divorce from bed and board, cannot maintain a suit for damages *per quod*, since he has suffered no loss of her society.[9]

1 Southworth *v.* Packard, 7 Mass. 95.

2 *Supra*, ch. 2.

3 3 Bl. Com. 139, 140. An action on the case is allowable, though not usual. Chamberlain *v.* Hazlewood, 5 M. & W. 517. See Morris *v.* Miller, 4 Burr. 2057; Birt *v.* Barlow, Doug. 171; Freelaconey *v.* Coleman, 1 B. & Ald. 90; Canefield *v.* Chamber, 6 East, 244; Tone *v.* Sumners, 2 Nott & McCord, 267; Forney *v.* Hallaker, 8 S. & R. 159.

4 Norton *v.* Warner, 9 Conn. 172; Per Cheves J. in Buford *v.* McLung, 1 Nott & McCord, 268, 277; otherwise, according to Blackstone. See 3 Com. 140.

5 Norton *v.* Warner, 9 Conn. 172. And see Bromley *v.* Wallace, 4 Esp. 237.

6 3 Bl. Com. 140; Bull. N. P. 296. Blackstone (ib.) adds the consideration of the husband's obligation, by settlement or otherwise, to provide for those children which he cannot but suspect to be spurious.

7 Greenl. Evid. § 578; Duberly *v* Gunning, 4 T. R. 651, per Lord Kenyon; Cibber *v.* Sloper, Bull. N. P. 27; Reeve Dom. Rel. 64; Train *v.* Bayer, 24 Barb. 614, and cases cited. See Lord Alvanley, in Bromley *v.* Wallace, 4 Esp. 237.

8 Selw. N. P., *Adultery*, Bull. N. P. 27.

9 Reeve Dom. Rel. 64; Fry *v.* Derstler, 2 Yeates, 278. The husband may discharge the cause of action, so as to bar the wife's remedy, even though they are living apart through his fault. Ballard *v.* Russell, 33 Me. 196.

Instantaneous death of the husband or wife at the common law gave no right of action to the survivor. Nor could the husband, whose wife was thus killed by another's carelessness, sue *per quod*, because he could not be said to have lost her society during any portion of her life.[1] The wife, of course, was never permitted to sue for the loss of her husband's society and services,[2] though on general principle it is hard to see why, save for her "coverture," she should not have been. Modern legislation has supplied many new remedies much needed in these classes of cases, particularly with reference to injuries and loss of life occasioned through the carelessness of railroad companies and other common carriers.[3] And wherever by special statute some right of action for damages is given (as against a town for a defective highway), our courts seem disposed to allow the husband's medical expenses by way of aggravation, in the joint suit of husband and wife, even though he may not be empowered to bring a suit in his own name to recover for them as damages *per quod*.[4]

It should be finally observed that wherever husband and wife are both injured they have two distinct and separate causes of action, which must not be confounded. Thus for libel against husband and wife, the husband must sue alone for the libel against him; and husband and wife jointly for the libel against her; they cannot sue together for the libel against both.[5]

1 Yelv. 89, 90; Baker *v.* Bolton, 1 Camp. 493; Green *v.* Hudson R. R. Co., 28 Barb. 9; Hallenbeck *v.* Berkshire R. R. Co., 9 Cush. 109.

2 2 Kent Com. 182; Carey *v.* Berkshire R. R. Co., 1 Cush. 475. See as to survivorship, Waldo *v.* Goodsell, 33 Conn. 432; Long *v.* Morrison, 14 Ind. 595.

3 Dickens *v.* N. Y. Central R. R. Co., 28 Barb. 41; Stat. 9 & 10 Vict. ch. 93; Mass. Gen. Stats. ch. 63, § 97.

4 Harwood *v.* Lowell, 4 Cush. 310; Sanford *v.* Augusta, 32 Me. 536; Fuller *v.* Naugatuck R. R. Co., 21 Conn. 557. See Carlisle *v.* Town of Sheldon, 38 Vt. 440, as to right defeated by husband's own carelessness.

5 Gazynski *v.* Colburn, 11 Cush. 10; Ebersoll *v.* King. 3 Binn. 555; Newton *v.* Hatter, 2 Ld. Raym. 1208.

CHAPTER V.

THE EFFECT OF COVERTURE UPON THE WIFE'S PERSONAL PROPERTY.

Personal property comprises things in possession, or goods and effects, such as money, furniture, and farm stock, which one holds as the property itself, and things in action, such as bonds and other outstanding debts, which, properly speaking, do not constitute property, but are only the evidence of property to be recovered.[1] The husband's title to his wife's personal property at the common law is either absolute or qualified, according as the particular property belongs to the one class or the other. We shall, therefore, in this chapter, treat of *first*, the wife's things or personal property in possession; *second*, her things or personals in action.

But in general it may be premised that the wife's personal property goes to the husband, whether belonging to her at the time of marriage, or acquired afterwards by gift, bequest, or purchase; whether actually or beneficially possessed; whether principal fund or income. So her earnings belong to her husband. Marriage, therefore, operates as a gift to the husband, and while the gift is only qualified, so far as things in action are concerned, it lies in his power to make the gift absolute during coverture.[2]

This privilege of the husband lasts as long as the marriage relation continues; even though he be living apart from his wife in adultery, and she acquire the property by her own labor.[3]

1 2 Bl. Com. 389, 396; 2 Kent Com. 351.

2 1 Bright Hus. & Wife, 34, 35; Co. Litt. 305 a, 351 b; 2 Kent Com. 130, &c.

3 Russell *v.* Brooks, 7 Pick. 65; Turtle *v.* Muncy, 2 J. J. Marsh. 82; Armstrong *v.* Armstrong, 32 Miss. 279.

Neither divorce from bed and board, nor separation, takes away his right.[1] But divorce from the bonds of matrimony, or the death of either party puts an end to the gifts of coverture, leaving open the adjustment of the rights of the respective parties with one another, or between the survivor and the representatives of the deceased on other principles to be hereafter explained.

And it is a matter of course that the wife's property should be hers in her own right in order that the husband's title may attach. For property may come to her with restrictions upon the husband's rights, such as the giver has seen fit to impose.[2] Her *paraphernalia* follow a rule somewhat peculiar.[3] And, as we shall see in other chapters, much of the common law bearing upon this subject is practically superseded.

First, then, as to the wife's *choses* or personals in possession. To these the husband's right at common law is immediate and absolute. He may dispose of them as he sees fit during his life, whether with or without his wife's consent; he may bequeath them by will; and after his death such property is regarded as assets of his estate, the title passing to his executors and administrators, to the exclusion of the wife, though she survive him.[4]

If the wife's interest in personal property be that of a tenant in common the husband becomes a tenant in common in her stead.[5] So money of a female ward, and in the hands of her guardian, being legally hers at the time of marriage, becomes

[1] Glover *v.* Proprietors of Drury Lane, 2 Chitty, 117; Washburn *v.* Hale, 10 Pick. 429; Prescott *v.* Brown, 23 Me. 305; 1 Roll. Abr. 343 But see Divorce, *infra*.

[2] Co. Litt. 351; 11 Mod. 178.

[3] See *infra*, ch. 8.

[4] Co. Litt. 300, 351 b; 2 Kent Com. 143; Legg *v.* Legg, 8 Mass. 99; Lampher *v.* Creed, 8 Ves. 599; Winslow *v.* Crocker, 17 Me. 29; Bing. Inf. & Cov. 208, cases cited by Am. ed.; Hoskins *v.* Miller, 2 Dev. 360; Hyde *v.* Stone, 9 Cow. 230; Morgan *v.* Thames Bank, 14 Conn. 99; Hawkins *v.* Craig, 6 Monr. 257; Caffee *v.* Kelly, 1 Busb. 48; Skillman *v.* Skillman, 2 Beasley, 403; Hopkins *v.* Carey, 23 Miss. 54; Cropsey *v.* McKinsey, 30 Barb. 47.

[5] Hopper *v.* McWhorter, 18 Ala. 2229.

her husband's and his marital rights attach at once, notwithstanding the guardian retains possession longer.[1] The wife's vested remainder in personal estate goes to the husband on termination of the particular estate; and where both husband and wife die during the continuance of the particular estate, the husband's representatives, and not the wife's, take such remainder.[2] But the husband cannot be considered a purchaser by marriage for a valuable consideration against a legal title admitted to be valid by his wife before marriage.[3]

Chattels bequeathed to the wife, without restriction, pass to the husband at once like her other things in possession.[4] So all her movables, such as jewels, household goods, and the like, also cash in her hands, go to him absolutely and at once, whether owned by the wife at the time of marriage or nominally vesting in her at some period of her coverture. Whether money at her banker's follows the same principle may depend upon a distinction first taken by Sir William Grant in *Carr* v. *Carr*.[5] He there says that a balance at a banker's is a debt and not a deposit. But if the money were delivered to the banker in a sealed bag, it would then be truly a *depositum*. It would then have what is called an ear-mark. In other words, it would be a specific chattel, and, as such, would vest by the marriage in the husband as his absolute property.[6] Therefore, should the husband die without recovering such specific chattels or goods, they would belong to his representatives, and not to the wife by right of survivorship.[7] The true test of the hus-

[1] Sallee *v.* Arnold, 32 Mis. 532; Chambers *v.* Perry, 17 Ala. 726; McDaniel *v.* Whitman, 16 Ala. 343; Miller *v.* Blackburn, 14 Ind. 62.

[2] Tune *v.* Cooper, 4 Sneed, 296.

[3] Willis *v.* Snelling, 6 Rich. 280.

[4] Shirley *v.* Shirley, 9 Paige, 363; Newland *v.* Paynter, 4 M. & C. 408; Crane *v.* Brice, 7 M. & W. 183; Rex *v.* French, R. & R. C. C. 491.

[5] 1 Mer. 543, *n.*

[6] Per Sir William Grant in Carr *v.* Carr, ib.; Hill *v.* Foley, 1 Phill. 404. See Pott *v.* Clegg, 11 Jur. 289.

[7] Powes *v.* Marshall, 1 Sid. 172; Macq. Hus. & Wife, 19, 20; 1 Bac. Abr. 700, Tit. Baron & Feme, V.; 1 Roper Hus. & Wife, 169; 1 Vent. 261. As to the husband's right to sue in his own name for his wife's specific chattels, in the hands of third parties, see last chapter.

band's title is this: whether the personal property in question was or was not a thing in possession.

Earnings of the wife belong to the husband. The rule of the common law is that he takes all the benefits of her industry.[1] He alone can give a discharge for any demand which may arise from her services. He may of course constitute her his agent for receiving the pay to herself; but, without evidence of some such authority, the person who employs her, as a nurse for instance, cannot protect himself by showing her separate receipts.[2]

Secondly. The husband's right to his wife's things in action — or *choses in action*, as they are commonly called — is qualified. Marriage operates, not as an absolute gift of such property, but rather as a conditional gift; the condition being that the husband shall do some act, while coverture lasts, to appropriate the *choses* to himself. If he happen to die before he has done so, such *choses*, not having been reduced to possession, remain the property of the wife, and his personal representatives have no title in it.[3] But this applies only to outstanding things in action; for some may have been reduced to possession by the husband during his lifetime, and some may not.

With respect to such *choses in action* as may accrue to the wife solely, or to the husband and wife jointly, during coverture, the same doctrine applies. The husband may disagree to his wife's interest and make his own absolute at any time during coverture, by recovering in suit in his own name or otherwise reducing them to possession. But until such dis-

[1] Macq. Hus. & Wife, 44, 45; Reeve Dom. Rel. 63.

[2] Offley *v.* Clay, 2 Man. & Gr. 172; and see Glover *v.* Drury Lane, 2 Chitt. 117; Russell *v.* Brooks, 7 Pick. 65; but see Starrett *v.* Wynn, 17 S. & R. 130. See chapter 13 on the wife's right to trade. We do not here speak of cases where articles of separation between husband and wife provide a different disposition of her earnings.

[3] Co. Litt. 351; 1 Bright Hus. & Wife, 36; 2 Kent Com. 135, *et seq.* and cases cited; Scawen *v.* Blunt, 7 Ves. 294; Langham *v.* Nenny, 3 Ves. 467; Tritt *v.* Colwell, 31 Penn. St. 228; Needles *v.* Needles, 7 Ohio St. 432; Burleigh *v.* Coffin, 2 Foster, 118.

agreement, such *choses in action* belong to the wife, and, if not reduced into possession by the husband, will likewise survive to her.[1]

It becomes important, therefore, to distinguish the wife's things in action from her things in possession. To the class of things in action belong such property as rests upon obligation, contract, or other security, for payment; and not only rights presently vested and capable of immediate reduction to possession, but those which are contingent upon some event or reversionary upon some prior interest.[2] Debts owing the wife, arrears of rents, of profits, and of income, also outstanding loans, are plainly *choses in action*.[3] Money due on mortgage is, before foreclosure, a *chose in action*, and even though lent before coverture with covenants running to the wife's heirs or executors, it must follow the usual rule.[4] So are bonds and certificates of stock. Income of a *chose in action* is as much a *chose* as the principal itself; and according to the ordinary rule the wife becomes entitled to it by survivorship.[5] A devise of land to be sold and proceeds to be divided among certain persons, gives to each a *chose in action*.[6] Bills of exchange and promissory notes, though unlike other *choses in action* in being legally transferable by simple indorsement, are now considered *choses in action* of a peculiar nature, though it was formerly thought that they vested absolutely in the husband by marriage;[7] and bank checks and public securities of a

[1] Coppin *v.* ——, 2 P. Wms. 497; Day *v.* Padrone, 2 M. & S. 396, *n.*; Howell *v.* Maine, 3 Lev. 403; Wildman *v.* Wildman, 9 Ves. 174; 1 Bright Hus. & Wife, 37; 2 Kent Com. 135, and cases cited; Wilkinson *v.* Charlesworth, 11 Jur. 644; Standeford *v.* Devol, 21 Ind. 404. The wife's survivorship will be considered in another chapter.

[2] See Bell Hus. & Wife, 52.

[3] 1 Bright Hus. & Wife, 36; Clapp *v.* Stoughton, 10 Pick. 463.

[4] Bell Hus. & Wife, 52; *contra*, Turner *v.* Crane, 1 Vern. 170; Rees *v.* Keith, 11 Sim. 388.

[5] Wilkinson *v.* Charlesworth, 11 Jur. 644.

[6] Smilie's Estate, 22 Penn. St. 130. And see Wells *v.* Tyler, 5 Fost. 340.

[7] Gaters *v.* Maddeley, 6 M. & W. 423; Nash *v.* Nash, 2 Madd. 133; 1 Roper Hus. & Wife, 211; 1 Bright Hus. & Wife, 37 *a*, 38; Richards *v.* Richards, 2 B. & Ad. 447; Scarpellini *v.* Acheson, 7 Q. B. 864; 9 Jur. 827; Phelps *v.* Phelps, 20 Pick 556; Hayward *v.* Hayward, ib. 525.

negotiable character may be placed in the same class. Legacies and distributive shares are sometimes treated as though they vested absolutely in the husband without reduction into possession; but unquestionably the better opinion is that they are *choses in action*, in which case the creditor of the husband ought not to be allowed to attach them before the latter has done some act disaffirming his wife's title.[1] The wife's *choses in action* must not be confounded with her goods or specific chattels in the hands of third parties, which, unlike her *choses in action*, vest in the husband absolutely by the marriage.[2]

What acts on the husband's part amount to an appropriation of his wife's *choses in action*, or in other words constitute reduction into possession so as to bar her rights by survivorship, may here be fitly considered. Mere intention on his part is not sufficient. The purpose must be followed by some positive act asserting an ownership.[3]

Nor is actual possession of the *chose in action* a sufficient reduction *per se*, for the husband's intention may be to hold it in the right of another. Thus he may take the property in trust for his wife; and if so he is accountable like any other trustee.[4] So he may receive it as a loan from his wife, in which case he shall refund it like any other borrower. That reduc-

[1] 2 Kent Com. 135; cases cited in Am. editor's notes to Bing. Inf. & Cov. 209; Carr *v.* Taylor, 10 Ves. Jr. 574, 578; Lamphire *v.* Creed, 8 ib. 599; Palmer *v.* Trevor, 1 Vern. 261. See Schuyler *v.* Hoyle, 5 Johns. Ch. 196; Curry *v.* Fulkinson, 14 Ohio, 100; Wheeler *v.* Moore, 13 N. H. 478; Harper *v.* Archer, 8 Sm. & M. 229; Probate Court *v.* Niles, 32 Vt. 775; Chappell *v.* Causey, 11 Geo. 25; Gillete *v.* Camp, 19 Mis. 404; Johnson *v.* Spaight, 14 Ala. 27; Gallego *v.* Gallego, 2 Brock. 285; Revel *v.* Revel, 2 Dev. & Batt. 272; Wallace *v.* Tallia-ferro, 2 Call, 447; Clifton *v.* Haig, 4 Des. 330. See *contra*, Albee *v.* Carpenter, 12 Cush. 382; Wheeler *v.* Bowen, 20 Pick. 563; Griswold *v.* Penniman, 2 Conn. 564; Holbrook *v.* Walters, 19 Pick. 354. But even in Massachusetts where the doctrine prevails which is disapproved in the text, it is held that if the husband die before judgment in the suit by creditors, his wife's survivorship is not barred. Strong *v.* Smith, 1 Met. 476. See also Parks *v.* Cushman, 9 Vt. 320.

[2] See last chapter.

[3] Blount *v.* Bestland, 5 Ves. Jr. 515.

[4] Baker *v.* Hall, 12 Ves. Jr. 497; Estate of Hinds, 5 Whart. 138; Mayfield *v.* Clifton, 3 Stew. 375; Resor *v.* Resor, 9 Ind. 347; Bell Hus. & Wife, 57.

tion into possession which makes the *chose* absolutely as well as potentially the husband's, is a reduction into possession, not of the thing itself, but of the title to it.[1] Constructive possessions are not favored in law when they tend to defeat the wife's survivorship. Yet reduction into possession of the wife's *chose in action*, unexplained by other circumstances, is *prima facie* evidence of conversion to the husband's use, and is therefore effectual.[2]

The receipt of the husband and wife jointly for the wife's *chose in action* does not constitute sufficient reduction by the husband, for this is the proper form of receipt given to third parties when the fund is placed in the wife's hands.[3] But the sole receipt of the husband with intent to appropriate constitutes a complete reduction, the property having been delivered to him instead of the wife.[4]

It is clear that the receipt of interest due on a bond or note is not a sufficient reduction of the latter, nor of future installments, although it constitutes a reduction of the particular interest installment itself.[5] The same principle applies to the conversion of stock dividends. Nothing short of the transfer of stock standing in the wife's name to the husband's name seems to be a sufficient reduction into possession.[6]

Since stock which stands in the wife's name does not belong to her husband until reduced to possession by him, it follows that he cannot be made personally liable in respect to the fund where he has failed to so reduce it.[7]

As to bills and notes, there is a conflict between the earlier

[1] Strong J. in Tritt's Admr. *v.* Caldwell's Admr., 31 Penn. St. 233.

[2] Johnston *v.* Johnston, 1 Grant Cas. 468. Lapse of time may raise a presumption of reduction in the husband's favor. Harper *v.* Archer, 28 Miss. 212.

[3] Timbers *v.* Katz, 6 W. & S. 290.

[4] Roll. Abr. 342, 350; 1 Bright Hus. & Wife 53; Lowe *v.* Cody, 29 Geo. 117.

[5] Howman *v.* Corrie, 2 Vern. 190; Hart *v.* Stephens, 6 Q. B. 937; Stanwood *v.* Stanwood, 17 Mass. 57; Burr *v.* Sherwood, 3 Bradf. Sur. 85.

[6] Arnold *v.* Ruggles, 1 R. I. 165; 2 Bright Hus. & Wife, 54.

[7] Dodgson *v.* Bell, 3 E. L. & Eq. 542. And see Matter of Reciprocity Bank, 22 N. Y. 9.

and later cases, from the fact that negotiable instruments were not formerly regarded as *choses in action* at all.[1] Assuming them to be such, however, the indorsement and transfer of the husband is a sufficient reduction into possession. Hence, if a note be made payable to the order of a *feme sole*, and she afterwards marries, her husband may transfer the note to himself or others by his own indorsement.[2] The receipt of partial payment, it would seem, is only a reduction *pro tanto*.[3] The wife cannot indorse over a note payable to her order, even with authority from her husband, where it does not appear that the indorsement was made for value received by the husband from the indorsee, or as a gift from the husband to the indorsee; if she does so, it does not bar her rights by survivorship.[4] Her indorsement without his assent is *prima facie* bad.[5] If a note be not negotiable, the husband alone can transfer it.[6] A note made payable to order of "A. B. (a married woman), or to A. B. and her husband" in the alternative, constitutes the husband the payee.[7] What evidence, irrespective of indorsement and transfer by the husband, suffices to show reduction into possession — as for instance where the note is payable to bearer—is not quite clear from the authorities. But reduction of the wife's notes into possession is not effected by the husband, merely because he keeps them for safety and at her request, with his own papers; nor does the fact that her whole prop-

[1] See Scarpellini *v.* Acheson, 7 Q. B. 864; 9 Jur. 827; Gaters *v.* Maddeley, 6 M. & W. 423; McNeilage *v.* Holloway, 1 B. & Ald. 218; Sherrington *v.* Yates, 12 M. & W. 855; 1 Pars. Bills and Notes, 87. If a note be payable to husband *and* wife, it would clearly survive to the latter. Richardson *v.* Daggett, 4 Vt. 336; Draper *v.* Jackson, 16 Mass. 480. See also *post*, as to gifts to husband and wife.

[2] Mason *v.* Morgan, 2 Ad. & El. 30; Evans *v.* Secrest, 3 Ind. 545. And the wife's signature is mere surplusage where both indorse the note. Ib.

[3] Nash *v.* Nash, 2 Madd. 133.

[4] Scarpellini *v.* Acheson, 7 Q. B. 864.

[5] Wall *v.* Tomlinson, 16 Ves. Jr. 413; Hemmingway *v.* Matthews, 10 Tex. 207; Tryon *v.* Sutton, 13 Cal. 490.

[6] Evans *v.* Secrest, 3 Ind. 545.

[7] Wildman *v.* Wildman, 9 Ves. Jr. 174; Twisden *v.* Wise, 1 Vern. 161; Ryland *v.* Smith, 1 M. & C. 53.

erty consisted of such notes, and that at her request and because they were not due, he provided the wedding dress and furnished the house, give the husband a lien upon them, or amount to a reduction.[1] A collection of the wife's notes would be a reduction into possession; and so perhaps would be transfer and delivery, with intent to pass the property.

Reduction into possession is not necessarily affected by delivery into the husband's hands of a *chose in action;* for the intent of the parties at the time of delivery is open to explanation. Thus where the makers of a promissory note, payable to the wife, or bearer, and given as the proceeds of sale of her real estate, hand the note to the husband who immediately delivers it to the wife, in whose separate possession it thereafter continues, no reduction takes place.[2] But it would be otherwise, we apprehend, if the husband had placed the note among his own effects, never given it to his wife, nor admitted a trust on his part, and in all other respects acted as the owner of the property.

An agreement to sell the fund is not a reduction into possession.[3] Nor is a fund reduced by being set off against the husband's debt, no money having passed nor releases having been interchanged. At least this is the doctrine of some cases. Thus in *Harrison* v. *Andrews*, a testator gave a legacy to the wife; the husband being indebted to the testator in an equal amount, the husband and wife agreed to set off the debt against the legacy, and signed a legacy receipt for the amount; but it was held that these acts constituted no reduction.[4]

If the husband pledges his wife's *chose in action* not already reduced to possession or assigns it as collateral security, it would appear that on the redemption of such pledge or security

[1] Holmes *v.* Holmes, 28 Vt. 765.

[2] Barber *v.* Slade, 30 Vt. 191; Hall *v.* Young, 37 N. H. 134; Barron *v.* Barron, 24 Vt. 375.

[3] Harwood *v.* Fisher, 1 Younge & Coll. Eq. Ex. 110; 1 Bright Hus. & Wife, 52.

[4] 13 Sim. 595. So Sir Wm. Grant in Carr *v.* Taylor, 10 Ves. Jr. 574. See other cases cited in *n.* to 1 Bright Hus. & Wife, 52.

the *chose* is placed in *statu quo*, and remains the property of the wife until further reduction.[1] Whether the same can be said of a chattel mortgage is not certain.[1] The language of the instrument in describing the parties might aid in determining the question of intention whenever it arises. Certainly, whatever may be the technical difference between a pledge and a chattel mortgage, the latter operates a defeasible title only in the mortgagee. As to money secured by a mortgage to the wife, it is held that if the debt has been once paid to the husband reduction is completed, even though he die before executing a reconveyance of the property. Under such circumstances equity will actually compel the wife to reconvey and perfect the title without allowing her any benefits from the property.[2]

Where real estate of the wife is sold, and notes are given, payable to her, the property changes its character and becomes personal property in the shape of a *chose in action.*[3] The husband may then reduce into possession as in other cases. And if the executor or other party making the sale pays the cash proceeds into the husband's hands, the money belongs to him absolutely, and his receipt extinguishes all claims of his wife.[4] So if the notes taken for the purchase-money are in the husband's own name the reduction is held complete.[5] Money paid by a married woman upon a bond to convey land to her is *prima facie* her husband's, and may be recovered by him.[6]

1 Latourette *v.* Williams, 1 Barb. 9; Hartman *v.* Dowdel, 1 Rawle, 279. There is a *dictum* of Chancellor Kent (2 Kent Com. 137; also in Schuyler *v.* Hoyle, 5 Johns. Ch. 196) to the effect that the mortgage of a *chose in action* is of itself a sufficient reduction into possession. We find no authorities to support this statement. But see Tritt *v.* Colwell, 31 Penn. St. 228, a recent case which recognizes a distinction in this respect between a pledge and a mortgage.

2 Rees *v.* Keith, 11 Sim. 388; Bosoil *v.* Brander, 1 P. Wms. 458; Bates *v.* Dandy, 2 Atk. 208.

3 Taggart *v.* Boldin, 10 Md. 104; McCrory *v.* Foster, 1 Iowa, 271. See Peacock *v.* Pembroke, 4 Md. 280; Ramsdale *v.* Craighill, 9 Ohio, 199.

4 Johnson *v.* Bennett, 39 Barb. 237.

5 Dixon *v.* Dixon, 18 Ohio, 113; Talbot *v.* Dennis, 1 Carter, 471; McCrory *v.* Foster, 1 Iowa, 271. But if secured by mortgage, the mortgage also ought to be in the husband's name.

6 Casey *v.* Wiggin, 8 Gray, 231.

And proceeds of the sale of a widow's dower vest in her second husband.[1]

Legacies and distributive shares in like manner vest absolutely in the husband by reduction into possession; but not before. And where a wife is entitled to a portion of the assets of her first husband's estate, and then re-marries, her second husband must reduce this portion into possession during coverture or it will survive to her.[2] The institution of a suit to recover a legacy accruing to the wife is not *sua vi* a reduction when brought in the name of both parties.[3] But payment to the husband or his attorney, after judgment, operates a reduction.[4] The husband may assign a legacy or distributive share like any other *chose.*[5] Reduction of a legacy has been considered complete where the husband takes a quitclaim deed from the testator's residuary devisee upon condition that he shall pay this and the other legacies.[6] But some distinct act of ownership on the husband's part is necessary; and it is doubtfnl whether his right is complete even after a decree of distribution; the decree itself effecting no reduction. The share or legacy should be actually severed from the bulk of the estate whence it was derived.[7]

Any act on the husband's part which amounts to a complete act of ownership over his wife's *chose in action* — such act of ownership extending to the whole fund in question — is an effectual reduction into his own possession. The rule is, that if he recovers her debt by a suit in his own name, or if he re-

[1] Ellsworth *v.* Hinds, 5 Wis. 613; Bartlett *v.* Janeway, 4 Sandf. Ch. 396 (N. Y. Stat.). But see Barber *v.* Slade, 30 Vt. 191.

[2] Harper *v.* Archer, 28 Miss. 212. See *Ex parte* Norton, 35 E. L. & Eq. 609; Montefiore *v.* Belireno, Law Rep. 1 Eq. 171.

[3] Knight *v.* Branner, 14 Md. 1; 3 Sneed, 536; Hall *v.* McLain, 11 Humph. 425.

[4] Alexander *v.* Crittenden, 4 Allen, 342.

[5] Bryan *v.* Spirill, 4 Jones Eq. 27; Weems *v.* Weems, 19 Md. 334.

[6] Howard *v.* Bryant, 9 Gray, 239.

[7] Short *v.* Moore, 10 Vt. 446; Probate Court *v.* Niles, 32 Vt. 775; Lewis *v.* Price, 3 Rich. Eq. 172. But see Walker *v.* Walker, 25 Mis. 367; Vanderveer *v.* Alston, 16 Ala. 494.

leases the debt, or novates the debt by taking a new security in his own and not in his wife's name; in all these cases, upon his death, the right of survivorship in the wife to the property ceases.[1] But the property must come under the actual control of the husband, *quasi* husband, and not as trustee or attorney for the wife.[2] And the cases show that there should always exist both the intent to appropriate to his own use and the act of appropriation.

Reduction into possession may be effected through the medium of a third person duly empowered to act for that purpose.[3] And the receipt of the wife's distributive share by an agent appointed under a power of attorney executed by the wife to her husband is a sufficient reduction by the husband, and enables the latter to sue the attorney for the proceeds.[4]

It is held in England that, where the husband was a lunatic, payment into court of the wife's *chose in action* to the credit of the lunacy amounted to a reduction into possession.[5] But in New Hampshire a singular doctrine is laid down; namely, that the husband's right of reduction is so far personal to him, that it cannot be exercised by his guardian, if he be insane.[6]

The husband's right to reduce his wife's *choses in action* into possession is one of election merely. He may therefore neglect or refuse to do so, and thus keep the property vested in his wife.[7] This becomes a very important principle in determining the rights of his creditors. For, supposing him to be embar-

[1] 2 Kent Com. 137, 138. See Hanson *v.* Miller, 14 Sim. 22; 8 Jur. 209, 352; Burnham *v.* Bennett, 2 Coll. C. C. 254. See Scott *v.* Hix, 2 Sneed, 192.

[2] Wall *v.* Tomlinson, 16 Ves. 413; Ryland *v.* Smith, 1 My. & Cr. 53; Burnham *v.* Bennett, 2 Coll. 254; Barron *v.* Barron, 24 Vt. 375; Savage *v.* Benham, 17 Ala. 119. But see Rees *v.* Keith, 11 Sim. 388.

[3] Roll. Abr. 342, 350; 1 Bright Hus. & Wife, 53; Golds. 160.

[4] Turton *v.* Turton, 6 Md. 375; Alexander *v.* Crittenden, 4 Allen, 342. See Hill *v.* Hunt, 9 Gray, 66.

[5] *In re* Jenkins, 5 Russ. 183.

[6] Andover *v.* Merrimack County, 37 N. H. 437.

[7] Coffin *v.* Morrill, 2 Fost. 352; Harris *v.* Taylor, 3 Sneed, 536; Gallego *v.* Gallego, 2 Brock. 287; Mellingen *v.* Bansmann, 45 Penn. St. 522; Stoner *v.* The Commonwealth, 16 Penn. St. 387. See Peacock *v.* Pembroke, 4 Md. 280.

rassed in his affairs, can they attach the unreduced *choses in action* of his wife as his property? It is settled that they cannot. But if he once makes the property his own they can reach it; and he cannot transfer it again to his wife in prejudice of their pre-existing rights, even though it vested in him but for a brief time. And of course his own expressions of regret cannot avail against the husband's actual appropriation of his wife's *choses in action*.[1]

This brings us to a very perplexing branch of the present subject; namely, that of the husband's reduction into possession by assignment. *Choses in possession* are capable of assignment. *Choses in action*, however, with the exception of bills of exchange, checks, and promissory notes (to which we may doubtless add coupon bonds[2]), cannot be assigned at law; but in equity they may.[3] The assignment, however, to be effectual, should be without reservation. And the husband's agreement to assign is likewise sustainable in equity, on the principle that what one agrees to do shall be considered as done.[4] But whether the assignment of itself will bar the rights of the wife by survivorship and constitute reduction into possession, is quite another thing.

If the assignment of the wife's *choses in action* be purely voluntary and without consideration, it does not bind the wife.[5] As, for instance, where a husband, pending divorce proceedings against him, makes a pretended transfer for the purpose of barring her rights to the property. Nor does a voluntary assignment for the benefit of creditors carry them.[6] A general assignment in bankruptcy or insolvency passes at law the wife's

[1] Nolen's Appeal, 23 Penn. St. 37.

[2] See Thomson *v.* Lee's County, 3 Wall. 327.

[3] Crouch *v.* Martin, 2 Vern. 595; Honner *v.* Morton, 3 Russ. 65.

[4] Druce *v.* Dennison, 6 Ves. 394; Steed *v.* Cragh, 9 Mod. 43.

[5] Wright *v.* Rutter, per Lord Alvanley, 2 Ves. Jr. 673; Burnett *v.* Kinnaston, 2 Vern. 401; Sir Wm. Grant in Mitford *v.* Mitford, 9 Ves. 87; Sir Thomas Plumer in Johnson *v.* Johnson, 1 Jac. & Walk. 472; Jewson *v.* Moulson, 2 Atk. 417; 2 Kent Com. 137; Hartman *v.* Dowdel, 1 Rawle, 279.

[6] Cases *supra;* Wright *v.* Rutter, 2 Ves. Jr. 673; 1 Bright Hus. & Wife, 81.

property, and by way of partial recompense, as it would appear, the husband's discharge has been allowed to operate upon the wife's debts *dum sola* as well as his own. But in equity the assignees are permitted to take the same interest in the wife's *choses in action* as the husband possessed, and no more; and unless they reduce them into possession during her husband's lifetime she will be entitled to them by survivorship.[1] Indeed, in Pennsylvania a voluntary assignment of the husband to trustees for wife and child, so as to defeat his creditors, has been upheld by a court of equity against such creditors on the ground that it was for the benefit of his wife and child.[2]

But the equity rule as to assignments of the wife's *choses in action* to individuals for valuable consideration is very capricious. It was formerly maintained that the husband's assignment of his wife's *chose in action* for a valuable consideration would bar not only a present interest of the wife, but also a contingent interest, or the possibility of a term or a specific possibility.[3] Sir William Grant threw doubt upon this doctrine by the objection that this would give the assignee a greater right than the husband himself.[4] It remained for Sir Thomas Plumer to break it down completely, and to place all assignments upon the same footing. This he attempted in the celebrated case of *Purdew* v. *Jackson*,[5] where the question arose as to the effect of an assignment by husband and wife of her vested interest in remainder. In an elaborate opinion he maintained

1 Sherrington *v.* Yates, 12 M. & W. 855; Miles *v.* Williams, 1 P. Wms. 249; Mitford *v.* Mitford, 9 Ves. 87; 2 Kent Com. 138; Van Epps *v.* Van Deusen, 4 Paige, 64; Outcalt *v.* Van Winkle, 1 Green Ch. 516; Moore *v.* Moore, 14 B. Monr. 259; 1 Bright Hus. & Wife, 79, 83, and cases cited; Hay *v.* Bowen, 5 Beav. 610; Poor *v.* Hazleton, 15 N. H. 564; Mann *v.* Higgins, 7 Gill, 265.

2 Siter *v.* Jordan, 4 Rawle, 468. See also Andrews *v.* Jones, 10 Ala. 400. See *contra*, Dold *v.* Geiger, 2 Gratt. 98.

3 See Chandos *v.* Talbot, 2 P. Wms. 601; Bates *v.* Dandy, 2 Atk. 207; Hawkins *v.* Obin, ib. 549; Note to 2 Kent Com. 138.

4 Mitford *v.* Mitford, 9 Ves. 87. And see Hornsby *v.* Lee, 2 Madd. Ch. 16.

5 1 Russ. 1–71 (1823). In Ashby *v.* Ashby, 1 Coll. 553, this rule was fully approved. See, too, Ellison *v.* Elwin, 13 Sim. 309.

that whatever the nature of the assignment, whether in bankruptcy, to trustees for payment of debts, or to a specific purchaser for value, it could pass the husband's interest and no more; that the assignee must afterwards reduce the property to possession during the husband's lifetime; and that no assignment was possible of the wife's reversionary interest, so as to bar her as survivor, provided the interest continued reversionary. Afterwards Lord Lyndhurst, while approving this doctrine to the extent of the actual decision, suggested a distinction between the cases where the husband can completely appropriate, at the time of assignment, and those where he cannot; and thought that the assignment might stand in the former instance as an agreement to appropriate or a sort of equitable reduction into possession.[1] The later English cases seem to follow this suggestion.[2] So that the present doctrine in England is understood to be that the husband's assignment for value to a specific purchaser will bar the wife's survivorship, provided the husband has during coverture the right of reducing into his own possession; but that he cannot assign, so as to bar the wife's survivorship, unless such reduction becomes possible before his death.[3]

In this country the rule is far from uniform. The Pennsylvania courts, repudiating this modern chancery doctrine altogether, maintain that the assignment to a specific purchaser for value bars the wife's right of survivorship.[4] For, it is said, the husband by marriage gains a full power of disposal over his wife's property, and any distinction between vested and contingent interests in respect to the marital dominion and power of transfer is unsound.[5] This doctrine has received approval

[1] Honner *v.* Morton, 3 Russ. 65.

[2] Per Lord Brougham, Stanton *v.* Hall, 2 Russ. & My. 175; Elliott *v.* Cordell, 5 Madd. Ch. 149.

[3] Tidd *v.* Lister, 17 E. L. & Eq. 567; s. c. on Appeal, 3 De G., M. & G. 857.

[4] Shuman *v.* Reigart, 7 W. & S. 169; Siter's case, 4 Rawle, 468; Webb's Appeal, 21 Penn. St. 248; Smilie's Estate, 22 Penn. St. 130.

[5] See Siter's case, ib., per Gibson Ch. J.

in some other States.[1] But the doctrine of *Purdew* v. *Jackson* has been more frequently approved by our courts; probably, if the question should now arise again, with the qualifications which Lord Lyndhurst introduced.[2]

There seems to be no reason for a distinction between releases and assignments from the husband, so far as the effect upon the wife's survivorship is concerned. But in one case it was observed that the husband's release might amount to reduction as against the wife.[3] A later decision, however, puts releases and assignments on the same footing.[4] And in this country no distinction is made between the two modes of transfer.[5]

The wife's outstanding *choses* may be recovered by a suit so as to prevent it from going back to her in case she be the survivor. The general rule is that for property accruing to the wife *before* marriage, the wife must be joined in the suit, although the husband during coverture may alter the debtor's liability, as by changing the security, or giving time on a promise to himself, and may then sue alone;[6] in which case, perhaps, the reduction into possession is effected by the alteration of the debt and not by the suit. Where, however, property accrues to the wife *after* marriage the husband may elect either

1 Manion *v.* Titsworth, 18 B. Monr. 582; Turtle *v.* Fowler, 22 Conn. 58; Hill *v.* Townsend, 24 Tex. 575.

2 Bugg *v.* Franklin, 4 Sneed, 129; George *v.* Goldsby, 23 Ala. 326; Arrington *v.* Yarborough, 1 Jones Eq. 72; Lynn *v.* Bradley, 1 Met. (Ky.) 232; Smith *v.* Atwood, 14 Geo. 402; State *v.* Robertson, 5 Harring. 201; Needles *v.* Needles, 7 Ohio St. 432; Bryan *v.* Spruill, 4 Jones Eq. 27. The husband's assignee may avail himself of fraud upon the husband's marital rights. Joyner *v.* Denny, Busbee Eq. 176. In Stiffe *v.* Everitt, 1 M. & C. 37, Lord Cottenham suggests what may be at the foundation of the present distinction in the English equity rule as to assignees for value, namely, that neither the husband alone, nor the husband and wife together, can dispose of the wife's life-interest in a fund, beyond the duration of the coverture. See Macq. Hus. & Wife, 58, 59.

3 Hore *v.* Becher, 12 Sim. 465, 6 Jur. 94, Shadwell V. C.

4 Rogers *v.* Acaster, 11 E. L. & Eq. 300; 14 Beav. 445.

5 Needles *v.* Needles, 7 Ohio St. 432; Kenny *v.* Udall, 5 Johns. Ch. 464.

6 Yard *v.* Ellard, 1 Salk. 117, pl. 8; Carth. 463; Sid. 299.

to sue alone or to join his wife as the meritorious cause.[1] Such being the state of the law, there is a distinction between suits brought in the husband's name alone, and suits in the name of both husband and wife. In the former case he elects to disaffirm his wife's title, and bringing the suit operates as a reduction.[2] In the latter he admits her possible title by survivorship and the reduction is ineffectual until the debt is collected on execution or otherwise.[3]

In chancery proceedings both husband and wife are made parties; and as we shall presently see, equity compels a settlement upon the wife before entering a decree in the husband's favor. It is said that decrees in chancery so far resemble judgments at law that until the money be ordered to be paid, or declared to belong to the husband, the wife's rights will remain undisturbed. But an order for payment of money to the husband, vests it in him free from the wife's right by survivorship.[4]

As to the submission to arbitration it is said that the original claim is extinguished by the award and a new duty thereby created.[5] If the money awarded be *to the husband*, and he dies before payment, it will go to his personal representatives, and not his wife.[6] So much has been decided. Some are of the impression that in other respects the wife's interest will depend upon the stage of proceedings reached at the time of the hus-

1 See Bright Hus. & Wife, 61–66; Chitty Pl. 32–38, 7th ed.

2 Oglander *v.* Baston, 1 Vern. 396; 2 Ves. Sen. 677; 12 Mod. 346. See Pierson *v.* Smith, 9 Ohio St. 554.

3 Bond *v.* Simmons, 3 Atk. 21. The exception formerly made in favor of bills of exchange and promissory notes does not now exist. See cases *supra*, p. 118. The husband must therefore follow the above rules of suit. Sherrington *v.* Yates, 12 M. & W. 855; 1 Dowl. & L. 1032. And see Pike *v.* Collins, 33 Maine, 43; Mason *v.* McNeill, 23 Ala. 201.

4 See Nanney *v.* Martin, Eq. Cas. Abr. 68; 3 Atk. 726; Macaulay *v.* Phillips, 4 Ves. 19; Heygate *v.* Annesley, 3 Bro. C. C. 362; 1 Bright Hus. & Wife, 67–69; Lowery *v.* Craig, 30 Miss. 19.

5 Reeve Dom. Rel. 21. But see Hunter *v.* Rice, 15 East, 100; Thorpe *v.* Eyre, 1 Ad. & El. 926; 3 Nev. & M. 214.

6 Oglander *v.* Baston, 1 Vern. 396.

band's death, and that neither the submission to arbitration, nor the award itself, unless in the husband's favor, operates as a reduction into possession.[1]

The result of the foregoing observations is that reduction into possession offers many very nice distinctions, involving conflicting rights of considerable magnitude. Courts of equity, which have taken this subject under their especial control, seem to lay down variable rules; and it must be confessed that the law of reduction is so built upon exceptions, that one may more readily determine what acts of the husband do *not*, than what acts *do*, bar the wife's survivorship.

The wife's equity to a settlement, which constitutes an important branch of the English chancery jurisprudence, is closely connected with the husband's right of reduction into possession. Whenever the husband or his representative has to seek the aid of a court of chancery in order to recover his wife's property, he must submit to its order of a suitable settlement from the fund. This settlement, which is made upon the wife for the separate benefit of herself and the children as a provision for their maintenance and comfort, is known as the wife's equity.[2] Thus chancery, by a stretch of power somewhat arbitrary, interferes to do an act of justice. The doctrine seems to rest upon two grounds: first, that whoever comes into equity must do equity; second, that chancery is the special champion of women and children.[3]

The rule is the same whether the thing to be reduced into possession, be a debt, legacy, or distributive share belonging

[1] See 1 Bright Hus. & Wife, 70; Macq. Hus. & Wife, 52. The wife will not be bound by her agreement pending suit. Macaulay *v.* Phillips, 4 Ves. 15. But why should not the husband be allowed to disaffirm his wife's title by submitting the *chose* to arbitration as his own as well as in suing alone?

[2] 2 Kent Com. 139–143 and cases cited; 1 Bright Hus. & Wife, 230–265; 2 Story Eq. Juris. 635.

[3] Meals *v.* Meals, 1 Dick. 373; Peachey Mar. Settl. 158, 159. This jurisdiction appears to have been exercised from the earliest period. Sturgis *v.* Champneys, 5 M. & C. 103, per Lord Chancellor Cottenham.

to the wife, or any other *chose in action.*[1] Chancery will also restrain the husband by injunction from proceeding to recover a fund in the ecclesiastical or probate courts, until a like provision is made; for the reason that it has a concurrent or appellate jurisdiction in the settlement of estates.[2] In this country a court of equity has sometimes gone so far as to lay hold of property for which recovery is sought in the courts of common law.[3] But the English cases do not warrant such an exercise of power.[4] The blending of equity and common-law functions in American tribunals may here justify a departure.

But the wife's equity does not attach to her property while in the hands of third persons. They may, if they choose, defeat it by placing the fund directly in the husband's hands without the intervention of a suit. Thus where an executor pays over a legacy accruing to the wife, taking a proper receipt from the husband, a court of equity will not call it back from the husband, to enable a settlement to be enforced;[5] but it is otherwise if the executor pays the legacy over after proceedings are commenced. For as soon as the bill is filed the court becomes the trustee of the fund.[6]

1 Kenney *v.* Udall, 5 Johns. Ch. 464; 3 Cow. 590; Durr *v.* Bowyer, 2 McCord, Ch. 368; Duvall *v.* Farmers' Bank of Maryland, 4 Gill & Johns. 282; Abernethy *v.* Abernethy, 8 Fla. 243; Haviland *v.* Bloom, 6 Jones Ch. 178; Smith *v.* Kane, 2 Paige, 303. But see Tobin *v.* Dixon, 2 Met. (Ky.) 422; *Ex parte* Gedder, 4 Rich. Eq. 301.

2 Jewson *v.* Moulson, 2 Atk. 419; Dumond *v.* Magee, 4 Johns. Ch. 318.

3 Van Epps *v.* Van Deusen, 4 Paige, 64; Note to 2 Kent Com. 140; 2 Kent Com. 141, 142; Corley *v.* Corley, 22 Geo. 178; Dearin *v.* Fitzpatrick, Meigs, 551. But see Matter of Miller, 1 Ashm. 323; Parsons *v.* Parsons, 9 N. H. 309–336; Allen *v.* Allen, 6 Ired. Eq. 293; Barron *v.* Barron, 24 Vt. 375, 391; Wiles *v.* Wiles, 3 Md. 1.

4 1 Roper Hus. & Wife, 263; Jacob's notes to 1 Roper Hus. & Wife, 257, 558; Oswell *v.* Probert, 2 Ves. Jr. 682; Sturgis *v.* Champneys, 5 M. & C. 105; Jewson *v.* Moulson, 2 Atk. 419. According to the latest English decisions the wife's equity does not extend to a reversionary interest. No settlement can be asked until the fund falls into possession; i. e., until the husband has a right to receive it. Osborn *v.* Morgan, 8 E. L. & Eq. 192.

5 Glaister *v.* Hewer, 8 Ves. 205; Murray *v.* Elibank, 10 Ves. 90; Bell Hus. & Wife, 115; Pool *v.* Morris, 29 Geo. 374.

6 Murray *v.* Elibank, 10 Ves. 90; Delagarde *v.* Lempriere, 6 Beav. 347; Wiles

As to assignees and legal representatives of the husband the rule is the same. Their application to the court is treated as the husband's would have been; especially if the assignment in question has not effected a complete reduction so as to bar the wife's survivorship: a topic which has already been sufficiently discussed.[1] The court disregards the party who asks equity, and fastens the obligation upon the property itself.[2]

But the wife's right of equity to a settlement is something distinct from her right of survivorship; that is, her right upon her husband's death to property not reduced by him.[3] And even if the husband has assigned the fund the court will protect such equity upon due application.[4] The husband's assignee for valuable consideration takes subject to the wife's equity, although her survivorship may have been barred by the assignment.[5] But the wife's antenuptial debts must first be provided for.[6]

A distinction seems to have been made, however, in the English chancery courts, between cases in which the wife takes an absolute interest, and those in which she takes a life-interest only. In cases where the wife takes an absolute interest the provision is for her and her children. But where her interest is only for life the provision is for her separate benefit alone; and it is impossible in such cases to make any provision for children; the question consequently is one between the husband and wife simply. So, too, where the wife's interest is absolute, her right

v. Wiles, 3 Md. 1; Crook *v.* Turpin, 10 B. Monr. 243. But see Dearin *v.* Fitzpatrick Meigs, 551.

1 Oswell *v.* Probert, 2 Ves. Jr. 679; Jacobson *v.* Williams, 1 P. Wms. 382; Jewson *v.* Moulson, 2 Atk. 417; Earl of Salisbury *v.* Newton, 1 Eden, 370; Bosvil *v.* Brander, 1 P. Wms. 458; Kenney *v.* Udall, 5 Johns. Ch. 464; 2 Bright Hus. & Wife, 236. See discussion of Purdew *v.* Jackson, and other cases *supra*; Carter *v.* Carter, 4 S. & M. 59.

2 Aguilar *v.* Aguilar, 5 Mad. 414; Osborne *v.* Edwards, 3 Stockt. 73. See 2 Story Eq. Juris. § 1414; Wiles *v.* Wiles, 3 Md. 1; Guild *v.* Guild, 16 Ala. 121.

3 Norris *v.* Lantz, 18 Md. 260; Hall *v.* Hall, 4 Md. Ch. 283.

4 Osborne *v.* Edwards, 3 Stockt. 73.

5 Moore *v.* Moore, 14 B. Monr. 259; 2 Story Eq. Juris. § 1412 and cases cited.

6 Barnard *v.* Ford, Law Rep. 4 Ch. 247.

to a provision for herself and children is independent of the conduct of her husband; but where she takes a mere life-interest, her right arises from the non-fulfillment of his obligations. Finally, where the wife has an absolute interest the purchaser takes subject to a settled equity; but where the wife takes for life only such equity may not exist.[1]

The wife's equity to a settlement does not extend to a reversionary interest. The settlement of such a fund cannot be asked for until it falls into possession; that is, until the husband has a right, subject to the wife's equity, to receive it.[2] But as to all vested interests, whether acquired by gift, devise, or inheritance, before or during coverture, the rule of equity is that the property is subject to the settlement of a suitable provision for her support, unless expressly waived by her, or forfeited through her misconduct; and this settlement will be protected equally against the husband, his creditors or his assignees, with or without value, so far as chancery can properly exercise jurisdiction in the premises.[3] Where part of a reversionary fund falls into possession, the wife's equity may be settled upon her from such part, with liberty to apply upon the remaining portion of the fund falling into possession.[4]

Where the interest claimed by the husband in right of his wife is merely equitable, or where, though in its nature legal, it becomes from collateral circumstances the subject of a suit in equity, the wife has a right to a provision out of the fund. As where for example it is vested in trustees who have the legal estate, the wife, or rather the husband in her right, having only the equitable or beneficial interest.[5] But the smallness of a fund is no bar to a settlement.[6]

[1] Tidd *v.* Lister, on Appeal, 3 De G., M. & G. 857; s. c. 10 Hare, 152; Peachey Mar. Settl. 162–164; Cases of Stanton *v.* Hall, 2 Russ. & M. 175, and other cases, commented upon in Tidd. *v.* Lister, ib.

[2] Osborn *v.* Morgan, 8 E. L. & Eq. 192; 9 Hare, 432.

[3] Barron *v.* Barron, 24 Vt. 375.

[4] Marshall *v.* Fowler, 15 E. L. & Eq. 430.

[5] Macq. Hus. & Wife, 69; *Ex parte* Blagden, 2 Rose, 251; Oswell *v.* Probert, 2 Ves. Jr. 680; Sturgis *v.* Champneys, 5 M. & C. 103.

[6] *In re* Kincaid's Trusts, 17 E. L. & Eq. 396. A strong instance of the

Equity courts will generally preserve the wife's portion from the capital of the fund which is made the subject of equity proceedings, and the husband is allowed to appropriate the income of the fund without hindrance.[1] But a liberal discretion will be exercised by the court; and where the husband received a large fortune through his wife, and has squandered nearly the whole of it, the remaining fund may be placed where it will accumulate for her benefit or the income paid for her support. So if he maltreats her or otherwise conducts himself shamefully. And if he becomes insolvent the wife may have a reasonable provision secured to her out of her life-estate.[2]

There is no definite rule fixed as to the proportion which the wife should receive for her equity. The amount is regulated at discretion and will depend upon a variety of circumstances, such as the husband's income from other sources, the funds he may have already received through his wife, the extent of former settlements, and the marital conduct of both parties.[3] Where the husband is shown to be cruel, dissolute, or improvident, or where he has abandoned his family and neglected to provide for their support, a court of chancery will not hesitate to set apart at least the greater part of the fund for the benefit of the wife and children.[4] So if he be insolvent, the wife is favored to the exclusion, if necessary, of his creditors. In one case it was observed by Alderson B. that the wife and children ought to have the whole fund as against the husband's assignee in insolvency,

liberality of the court of equity is afforded in Scott *v.* Spashett, 16 Jur. 157; 9 E. L. & Eq. 265.

[1] Bond *v.* Simmonds, 3 Atk. 20; Elliott *v.* Cordell, 5 Mad. 156; Vaughan *v.* Buck, 13 Sim. 404.

[2] Bond *v.* Simmonds, 3 Atk. 20. As to insolvency where husband has not taken benefit of bankrupt acts, see *Ex parte* Cosegayne, 1 Atk. 192; Pryor *v.* Hill, 4 Bro. C. C. 142; Oswell *v.* Probert, 2 Ves. 682; Bell Hus. & Wife, 121.

[3] 2 Bright Hus. & Wife, 240, 241, and cases cited; Freeman *v.* Fairlee, 11 Jur. 447; Gardner *v.* Marshall, 14 Sim. 575; Green *v.* Otte, per Sir J. Leach, 1 S. & S. 254; Farrar *v.* Bessly, 24 Vt. 89; Bagshaw *v.* Winter, 11 E. L. & Eq. 272; Cutler's Trust, 6 E. L. & Eq. 97; McVey *v.* Boggs, 3 Md. Ch. 94.

[4] Coster *v.* Coster, 9 Sim. 597.

and he said that if he was bound by the practice of the court to take out any part of it, he would take out one shilling.[1]

But though the wife's equity to a settlement is recognized as due herself and her children, the right is so far personal to herself that it cannot be exercised by any one else, and it expires if she die pending proceedings, though there may be children surviving her.[2] The husband in such case takes the proceeds as in other cases. So her adultery is a complete bar to the equity; and other misconduct would certainly reduce the amount if not extinguish the equity altogether.[3] But it does not follow that in case of the wife's adultery the fund would be decreed absolutely and at once to the husband; the court might wait until the anomalous relationship of the parties had been legally determined by divorce.[4]

The husband may become the purchaser of his wife's fortune where he has made a competent settlement upon her before marriage. Regarding him in this light, chancery will in such a case not only refuse to allow the wife a settlement from the fund in litigation, but will let in his representatives after his

1 Brett *v.* Greenwell, 3 Y. & C. Eq. Ex. 230. But see Pugh *ex parte*, 12 E. L. & Eq. 350. Most frequently one-half has been allowed the wife as her equity under ordinary circumstances. 2 Bright Hus. & Wife, 241 and cases cited ; Peachey Mar. Settl. 176, 177. Where the wife had been allowed a divorce for adultery, the whole fund was settled upon her, the court justly observing that if adultery of the wife barred her from receiving, adultery of the husband ought to bar him equally. Burrows *v.* Burrows, 12 E. L. & Eq. 268. For latest English rule see *In re* Suggitt's Trusts, Law Rep. 3 Ch. 215.

2 Delagarde *v.* Lempriere, 6 Beav. 344, per Lord Langdale; Baldwin *v.* Baldwin, 5 De G. & S. 319 ; *contra*, Steinmetz *v.* Halthin, 1 G. & J. 67. See Peachey Mar. Settl. 166, 167. But not, according to the English equity practice, if she die, after a certain advanced stage of the proceedings. See Rowe *v.* Jackson, 2 Dick. 604; Murray *v.* Elibanks, 10 Ves. 92; Lloyd *v.* Mason, 5 Hare, 149; Bell Hus. & Wife, 128, 129; Peachey Mar. Settl. 168 and cases cited ; Baldwin *v.* Baldwin, 15 E. L. & Eq. 158.

3 Ball *v.* Montgomery, 2 Ves. Jr. 191; Carr *v.* Eastabrooke, 4 Ves. 146; Peachey Mar. Settl. 174–176; *In re* Walker, Lloyd *v.* Goold, T. Sugd. 327 ; Carter *v.* Carter, 14 S. & M. 59 ; Fry *v.* Fry, 7 Paige, 462.

4 Barrow *v.* Barrow, 18 Beav. 529. This rule has been modified in extreme cases, however, so as to grant equity, even after adultery. *In re* Lewin's Trusts, 20 Beav. 378; Greedy *v.* Lavender, 13 Beav. 64; Ball *v.* Coults, 1 Ves. & B. 302. See also *In re* Walker, Lloyd *v.* Goold, T. Sugd. 327.

death to make the reduction complete.[1] Lord Eldon said, however, that in order to bar the wife's equity the articles of marriage settlement should expressly state that it was in consideration of the wife's fortune or else the contents must import it as clearly as if expressed.[2] A jointure is not an adequate settlement, for this is merely a bar of her possible dower. But any adequate settlement, *eo nomine*, seems to be an effectual bar to the wife's equity. A covenant to settle must be performed by the hsuband before he can be regarded as a purchaser.[3] And the cases admit that a marriage settlement is not presumed to cover property accruing during coverture, but is to be confined to such as belongs to the wife at the time of settlement, unless apt words are used to indicate a different intent of the parties thereto.[4]

The wife may waive her equity to a settlement; for, unlike her right of survivorship, it is the mere creature of equity. But her consent must be formally taken under the direction of the court, and apart from her husband.[5] The court will not receive the wife's consent until her share is ascertained,[6] and an order made with the wife's consent may afterwards be set aside if prejudicial to her interests.[7]

A married woman may also be precluded by her own fraud from claiming her equity against purchasers. Thus where a married woman wrote out an assignment of her reversionary interest in a trust fund, dating it before marriage and signing it in her maiden name, in order to enable her husband to borrow money upon it; and afterwards gave to the purchasers a letter

1 2 Kent Com. 143; Cleland *v.* Cleland, Prec. in Ch. 63; Poindexter *v.* Jeffries, 15 Gratt. 363.

2 Druce *v.* Dennison, 6 Ves. 395. See Salway *v.* Salway, Amb. 692; Carr *v.* Taylor, 10 Ves. 574; Doe *v.* Ford, 2 El. & B. 970.

3 Bell Hus. & Wife, 413, and cases cited; Holt *v.* Holt, 2 P. Wms. 647; Pyke *v.* Pyke, 1 Ves. Sen. 376.

4 Note to 2 Kent Com. 143. See chapter on Marriage Settlements, *post.*

5 1 Dan. Ch. Pract. 95; Set. on Decrees, 255, 256; Macq. Hus. & Wife, 75; Coppedge *v.* Threadgill, 3 Sneed, 577; Ward *v.* Amory, 1 Curt. Ct. Ct. 419. See Campbell *v.* French, 2 Ves. 321; May *v.* Roper, 4 Sim. 360. The consent of an infant will not be taken. Abraham *v.* Newcome, 12 Sim. 566; Phillips *v.* Hassell, 10 Humph. 197.

6 Jernegan *v.* Baxter, 6 Mad. 32; Peachey Mar. Settl. 181.

7 Watson *v.* Marshall, 19 E. L. & Eq. 569; 17 Jur. 651.

to one of the trustees of the fund, stating that she had before her marriage assigned her interest in the same to her husband; it was held, notwithstanding some evidence of coercion in the first instance, that she was debarred from claiming a settlement.[1]

Property held by the wife in a representative capacity at the time of marriage cannot vest in the husband; for here she has no beneficial interest which the law can transfer to her husband.[2] Any other rule would operate a fraud upon creditors and *cestuis que trust.* But if the wife be executrix or administratrix at the time of her marriage, the husband is entitled to administer in her right, by way of partial offset to his liability for her frauds and injuries in such capacity. As incidental to this authority, he may release and compound debts, and dispose of the effects, and reduce outstanding trust property into possession, as his wife might have done before coverture.[3] He is accountable for all property which came to her possession, whether actually received by him or not.[4] A married woman cannot become executrix or administratrix without her husband's concurrence; so long, at least, as he remains liable for her acts;[5] nor will payments made to her in such capacity without his assent be valid.[6] It is to be generally observed in cases of this kind that the right of disposition which the husband exercises is strictly the right of performing the trust vested in his wife, it being assumed that she cannot perform it consistently with her situation as a *feme covert.*

An administrator cannot sue in his representative character

[1] *In re* Lush's Trusts, Law Rep. 4 Ch. 591. And see Sharpe *v.* Foy, Law Rep. 4 Ch. 35.

[2] Co. Litt. 351; 11 Mod. 178; 1 Bright Hus. & Wife, 39, 40.

[3] Ib.; Jenk. Rep. 79; Woodruffe *v.* Cox, 2 Bradf. Sur. 153; Keister *v.* Howe, 3 Ind. 268; Claussen *v.* La Franz, 1 Iowa, 226.

[4] Scott *v.* Gamble, 1 Stockt. 218.

[5] For administration has been granted to a wife living apart from her husband under a deed of separation with apt provisions. Goods of Hardinge, 2 Curt. 640.

[6] 1 Salk. 282; Lover *v.* Lover, 6 Jur. 156; Bubbers *v.* Hardy, 3 Curt. 50; cases cited in 2 Redf. Wills, 78. As to the indorsement of a note payable to the wife as administratrix, see Roberts *v.* Place, 18 N. H. 183.

upon contracts made after the death of the intestate in the course of carrying on the intestate's business. Hence the husband must sue alone, for goods supplied by husband and wife, in carrying on the business of the wife's father, whose administratrix the wife was; and the joinder of the wife is improper.[1]

It is recently decided that a married woman cannot bind herself by her contract to convey estate which is devised to her in trust for sale.[2]

[1] Bolingbroke *v.* Kerr, Law Rep. 1 Ex. 222.

[2] Avery *v.* Griffin, Law Rep., 6 Eq. 606.

CHAPTER VI.

THE EFFECT OF COVERTURE UPON THE WIFE'S CHATTELS REAL AND REAL ESTATE.

CHATTELS real, such as leases and terms for years, have many of the incidents of personal property. But as between husband and wife they differ from personal chattels. The title acquired therein by the husband is of a somewhat anomalous nature, for upon them marriage operates an executory gift, as it were, the husband's title being imperfect unless he does some act to appropriate them before the wife's death. He may sell, assign, mortgage, or otherwise dispose of his wife's chattels real without her consent or concurrence;[1] excepting always such property as she may hold by way of settlement or otherwise as her separate estate.[2] Chattels real, unappropriated during coverture, vest in the wife absolutely, if she be the survivor. In all these respects they resemble *choses in action*. But if the husband be the survivor, such chattels will belong to him *jure mariti*, and not as representing his wife. And in this respect they resemble *choses in possession*.

As to the wife's chattels real, therefore, husband and wife are in possession during coverture by a kind of joint tenancy, with the right of survivorship each to the other: not, however, like joint-tenants in general, but rather under the title of husband and wife; since husband and wife are, in contemplation

[1] Co. Litt. 46 c.; 2 Kent Com. 134; Sir Edward Turner's Case, 1 Vern. 7; Whitmarsh *v.* Robertson, 1 Coll. New Cases, 570.

[2] Tullett *v.* Armstrong, 4 M. & C. 395; Draper's Case, 2 Freem. 29; Bullock *v.* Knight, Ch. Ca. 266.

of law, but one person and incapable of holding either as joint-tenants or tenants in common.[1]

The wife's chattels real may be taken on execution for the debts of the husband while coverture lasts, by which means the title becomes transferred by operation of law to the creditor, and the wife's right, even though she should survive her husband, is gone.[2] They may also be bequeathed by the husband by will executed during marriage, or by other instrument to take effect after his death; with, however, this result: that if the wife dies first the bequest will be effectual, not having been subsequently revoked by the husband: while, if the husband dies first, the wife will take the chattel in her own right, unaffected by any will which he may have made, or by any charge he may have created.[3]

It would appear that any assignment of a chattel real by the husband will completely appropriate it, even though made without consideration.[4] And if a single woman has a decree to hold and enjoy lands until a debt due her has been paid,—known at the old law as an estate by *elegit*,—and she afterwards marries, her husband may make a voluntary assignment so as to bind her.[5] The right of appropriating the wife's chattels real is, therefore, to be distinguished from the right of reducing things in action into possession. The husband's interest in his wife's chattels real may be called an interest in his wife's right, with a power of alienation during coverture; and an interest in possession, since such chattels are already in possession, but lying in action.[6]

As the husband is entitled to administer in his wife's right when she is executrix or administratrix, he may release or assign terms for years or other chattels real vested in her as

[1] 2 Kent Com. 135; Co. Litt. 351 *b*. Butler's note 304 to Co. Litt. lib. 3, 351 *a*.

[2] 2 Kent Com. 134; Miller *v.* Williams, 1 P. Wms. 258.

[3] Co. Litt. 466; 351 *a*; Roberts *v.* Polgrean, 1 H. Bl. 535.

[4] Cateret *v.* Paschall, 3 P. Wms. 200. But see *n.* to 1 P. Wms. 380.

[5] Merriweather *v.* Brooker, 5 Litt. 256; Paschall *v.* Thurston, 2 Bro. P. C. 10

[6] Mitford *v.* Mitford, 9 Ves. 98.

such.[1] But if he is entitled to a term of years in his wife's right as executrix or administratrix, and have the reversion in fee in himself, the term will not be merged; for to constitute a merger both the term and the freehold should vest in a person in one and the same right.[2]

An exception to the husband's right by survivorship to his wife's chattels real occurs in case of joint tenancy. If a single woman be joint-tenant with another, then marries and dies, the other joint-tenant takes to the exclusion of her husband surviving her: for the husband's title is the newer and inferior one.[3]

Where, during coverture, a lease for years is granted to the wife, adverse possession, which commences during coverture, may be treated as adverse either to the wife or to the husband.[4]

When the husband succeeds to his wife's chattel real upon surviving her, or appropriates it during coverture, he takes it subject to all the equities which would have attached against her. In other words, being not a purchaser for a valuable consideration, he can claim no greater interest than she had. Thus where the wife's chattel interest is subject to the payment of an annuity, the husband must continue to make payment so long as the encumbrance lasts. And though he may not in all cases be bound on her covenant to make new leases, yet if he does so the equity of the annuitant will attach upon them successively.[5]

The law enables the husband during coverture to defeat his wife's interest by survivorship by an absolute disposition of the whole term, either with or without consideration.[6] And the same rule applies to the wife's trust terms as to her legal

1 Arnold *v.* Bidwood, Cro. Jac. 318; Thrustout *v.* Coppin, W. Bl. 801.

2 Co. Litt. 338 *b.*; 1 Bright Hus. & Wife, 97, and cases cited.

3 Co. Litt. 185 *b.*

4 Doe *v.* Wilkins, 5 Nev. & M. 435.

5 Moody *v.* Matthews, 7 Ves. 183; Rowe *v.* Chichester, Amb. 719. On the question of contribution by annuitants, see Winslowe *v.* Tighe, 2 Ball & B. 204; Hubbs *v.* Rath, 2 ib. 553.

6 1 Bright Hus. & Wife, 98; Grute *v.* Locroft, Cro. Eliz. 287; Jackson *v.* McConnell, 19 Wend. 175.

terms.[1] In order to make it effectual, the right of the party in whose favor the disposition is made must commence *in interest* during the life of the husband; but it is not necessary that it should commence *in possession* during that period. Thus the husband, though he cannot bequeath these chattels by will, as against the wife's right by survivorship, may grant an underlease for a term not to commence until after his death; and this act will divest the right of the wife under the original lease so far as the underlease is prejudicial to such right.[2] Nor need his disposition cover the whole chattel, since the disposition necessarily operates *pro tanto*.[3] Nor need it be absolute, since a conditional disposition is good if the condition subsequently takes effect.[4] And the law enables the husband to dispose not only of the wife's interest in possession, but also of her possibility or contingent interest in a term, unless where the contingency is of such a nature that it cannot happen during his life.[5]

A distinction is, however, made between cases where the disposition is intended of the whole or of part of the property, and where it is intended as a collateral grant of something out of it. In the latter case the transaction will not bind the wife, for if she survive her husband, her right being paramount, and her interest in the chattel not having been displaced, she will be entitled to it absolutely free from such encumbrance.[6]

The husband may by other acts than express alienation divest his wife's title, and defeat her rights by survivorship in her chattels real. Thus, if the husband, holding a term in right of his wife, grant a lease of the lands covered by the

1 Tudor *v.* Samyne, 2 Vern. 270 (incorrectly reported, according to note, 1 Bright Hus. & Wife, 99). Sir Edward Turner's Case, 1 Ch. Ca. 307; Packer *v.* Windham, Prec. in Ch. 412.

2 Grute *v.* Locroft, Cro. Eliz. 287; Bell Hus. & Wife, 104, 105.

3 Sym's Case, Cro. Eliz. 33; Loftris's Case, ib. 276.

4 Co. Litt. 46 *b*. But see 4 Vin. Abr. 50 pl. 14.

5 Doe d. Shaw *v.* Steward, 1 Ad. & El. 300; 1 Bright Hus. & Wife, 100. And see Donne *v.* Hart, 2 Russ. & My. 360.

6 Co. Litt. 184 *b.*; 1 Bright Hus. & Wife, 103.

term, for the lives of himself and his wife, the wife's term would thereby merge, and her right in it be defeated.[1] Or if, while in possession, under a lease to himself and the wife, the husband should accept from the lessor a feoffment of the lands leased, the term would be extinguished and the wife's right along with it; for the livery would amount to a surrender of the term.[2] On the other hand, there are acts by the husband, which, although they amount to the exercise of an act of ownership, yet, as they do not pass the title, will not defeat the wife's right by survivorship.

An instance of the latter is that of the husband's mortgage of his wife's chattels real; or, what is the same thing in equity, a covenant to mortgage. This is in reality a disposition as security, and until breach of condition the mortgagee has no further title. But, in order to protect the mortgagee's rights, equity treats the mortgage or covenant as good against the wife to the extent of the money borrowed; that once paid the chattels will continue hers.[3] After breach of condition, the mortgagee's estate becomes absolute; or, at least, he can make it so by foreclosure; and the alienation of the term being then completed at law, the wife's legal right by survivorship is defeated; subject however, to the equity of redemption, where the husband has not otherwise disposed of that likewise.[4] So too transactions, not constituting mortgages, in the ordinary sense of the term, may yet be so construed in equity where such was their substantial purport. And while the intention of the husband to work a more complete appropriation, will be justly regarded by the court, the mere circumstance of a proviso in the conveyance for redemption, pointing to a mode of reconveyance not in conformity with the original title, will not,

1 2 Roll. Abr. 495, pl. 50.

2 Downing *v.* Seymour, Cro. Eliz. 912. And see Lawes *v.* Lumpkin, 18 Md. 334.

3 Bates *v.* Dandy, 2 Atk. 207; Bell Hus. & Wife, 107; 1 Bright Hus. & Wife, 106.

4 See Pitts *v.* Pitts, T. & R. 180; 1 Prest. on Estates, 345.

it seems, debar the wife from asserting her rights by survivorship.[1]

Among the miscellaneous acts of the husband, which will defeat the wife's survivorship to her chattels real, are the following: A disseverance of his wife's joint tenancy during coverture.[2] An award of the term to the husband, if carried into effect.[3] The husband's criminal acts; such as attainder.[4] So too his alienage.[5] Lord Coke considered that ejectment recovered by the husband in his own name, would work appropriation; but he was probably in error.[6] Waste operates as a forfeiture of a term.[7] And finally, the husband's creditors may sell the wife's chattels real on execution, and by their own act determine her interest altogether.[8]

By marriage, the husband becomes entitled to the usufruct of all real estate owned by the wife at the time of her marriage, and of all such as may come to her during coverture. He is entitled to the rents and profits during coverture. His estate is, therefore, a freehold. But it will depend upon the birth of a child alive during coverture, whether his estate shall last for a longer term than the joint lives of himself and wife, or not. In the event of such birth, his interest lasts for his own life, whether his wife dies before him or not. If there is no child born alive, his interest lasts only so long as his wife lives. In either case, he has not an absolute interest, but only an estate for life, and his right is that of beneficial enjoyment. When his estate has expired, the real estate vests absolutely in

1 Clark *v.* Burgh, 9 Jur. 679.

2 Co. Litt. 185 *b.*; Plow. Com. 418.

3 Oglander *v.* Baston, 1 Vern. 396; Note of Jacobs to 1 Roper Hus. & Wife, 185, and cases commented upon.

4 Co. Inst. 351 *a*; 4 Bl. Com. 387; Steed *v.* Cragh, 9 Mod. 43

5 2 Bl. Com. 421; 4 Bl. Com. 387. Attainder and alienage apply in general to real estate rights of the husband. See *post.*

6 See Jacob's note to 1 Roper Hus. & Wife, 185; Co. Litt. 46 *b.*; 4 Vin. Abr. 50, pl. 18.

7 Co. Litt. 351.

8 Miles *v.* Williams, 1 P. Wms. 258; Co. Litt. 351.

the wife or her heirs, and the husband's relatives have no further concern with it.[1]

While, therefore, the husband has the beneficial enjoyment of his wife's freehold property during coverture, at the common law, the ownership remains in the wife. Herein, her right becomes suspended, not *extinguished*, by her marriage. The inheritance is in her and her heirs. Consequently, the husband may sue in his own name for injury to the profits of his wife's real estate; as where growing crops are destroyed or carried off; for this relates to his usufructuary interest. But for injuries to the inheritance, such as trespass, by cutting trees, burning fences, and pulling down houses, and generally in actions for waste, the wife must be joined; and if the husband dies before recovering damages, the right of action survives to the wife. And if the wife survive her husband, she may commence such suits without joining her personal representatives.[2]

Besides the rents and profits during coverture, the husband, if the survivor, is entitled to all arrears accrued up to the time of his wife's death. Such property is not treated like the wife's *choses in action*, not reduced to possession. Accordingly, he may maintain suit after coverture to recover all rents and profits which had accrued while coverture lasted. And where the wife joins her husband in a lease, the covenant for payment of rent is for the husband's benefit alone while the usufruct continues.[3] But it would appear to be otherwise where rent is reserved to husband and wife, and *her* heirs and assigns.[4]

[1] Co. Litt. 351 *a*; 2 Kent Com. 130; 1 Bac. Abr. 286; Junction Railroad Co. *v.* Harris, 9 Ind. 184. The husband's rights and liabilities attach to property bought by himself and held in his name as trustee for his wife; Pharis *v.* Leachman, 20 Ala. 662. But not, as will be seen hereafter, to his wife's separate real estate.

[2] 2 Kent Com. 131; Weller *v.* Baker, 2 Wils. 423, 424; Beaver *v.* Lane, 2 Mod. 217; Bac. Abr. Title Baron & Feme, K.; 1 Chit. Pl. (6th Am. ed.) 85; 1 Bl. Com. 362; Thacher *v.* Phinney, 7 Allen, 146. The husband can sue alone for digging up the soil and carrying it away; Tallmadge *v.* Grannis, 20 Conn. 296.

[3] 1 Washb. Real Prop. 44; Co. Litt. 351 *b.*; Jones *v.* Patterson, 11 Barb. 572.

[4] Hill *v.* Saunders, 4 B. & C. 529. The wife need not be joined in such

In all cases, emblements or growing crops go to the husband or his representatives at the termination of his estate.[1] This rule was extended at the common law to cases of divorce *causa precontractus*.[2] But it does not apply to divorce for the husband's misconduct under modern statutes.[3] The husband's lease in right of his wife operates so far in the tenant's favor as to entitle the latter to emblements.[4] The rule is the same whether the husband be tenant by curtesy or not. No action, therefore, can be maintained by the wife in such cases.

The husband's interest in his wife's real estate is liable for his debts and may be taken on execution against him. But nothing more than the husband's usufruct is thereby affected; nor can the attachment or sale affect the wife's ultimate title.[5] The rule in Massachusetts is to allow the purchaser to take the rents and profits for a definite period, or the whole life-estate, at an appraisal of the value founded on a proper estimate of the probability of human life. But where the whole life-estate is of more value than the amount of the execution, the more proper, and perhaps the only mode, is the former.[6] It has been held that the husband, under a *bona fide* deed of separation, without trustees, executed before judgment, may relinquish to his wife all interest in her lands, and thus avoid the demands of his creditors upon the property, even though an annuity be

suits for rent, Clapp *v.* Houghton, 10 Pick. 463; Beaver *v.* Lane, 2 Mod. 217; Shaw *v.* Partridge, 17 Vt. 626; Edrington *v.* Harper, 3 J. J. Marsh. 360; Bailey *v.* Duncan, 4 Monr. 260.

[1] Reeve Dom. Rel. 28, and cases cited; Weems *v.* Bryan, 21 Ala. 302.

[2] Orland's Case, 5 Coke, 116 *a*.

[3] See Vincent *v.* Parker, 7 Paige Ch. 65, per Chancellor Walworth; Jenney *v.* Gray, 5 Ohio St. 45.

[4] Rowney's Case, 2 Vern. 322; Gould *v.* Webster, 1 Vt. 409.

[5] 2 Kent Com. 131; Babb *v.* Perley, 1 Me. 6; Mattocks *v.* Stearns, 9 Vt. 326; Perkins *v.* Cortrell, 15 Barb. 446; Brown *v.* Gale, 5 N. H. 416; Canby *v.* Porter, 12 Ohio, 79; Williams *v.* Morgan, 1 Litt. 168; Nichols *v.* O'Neill, 2 Stockt. 88; Montgomery *v.* Tate, 12 Ind. 615; Sale *v.* Saunders, 24 Miss. 24; Cheek *v.* Waldrum, 25 Ala. 152; Schneider *v.* Starke, 20 Mis. 269. But see Jackson *v.* Suffern, 19 Wend. 175.

[6] Litchfield *v.* Cadworth, 15 Pick. 23.

reserved to himself.[1] And it is certain that the sheriff's deed cannot convey a greater interest than the defendant has at the time of attachment or of levy and sale.[2] Therefore, where a statute allows the husband a distributive share in his wife's lands in the event of his survivorship, no such interest passes to the purchaser of lands sold on execution for his debts during her life.[3] Since the husband's life-interest is liable for his own debts, it is liable for the debts of the wife *dum sola*.[4] The creditors of the husband cannot attach mere contingencies of the wife which cannot happen before the death of either.[5] But it is held in Pennsylvania that where a husband has conveyed his life-estate in fraud of his creditors, they may levy upon the growing crops.[6]

Where the husband was an alien, he could not acquire an interest in his wife's real estate at the common law.[7] But the disability is now removed in great measure by statute.[8]

So at the common law, attainder of treason or other felony worked a forfeiture or escheat of real estate to the government. And corruption of blood affected the inheritance in such cases. But as regards the wife's real estate, nothing more can be taken than the husband's life-interest; the freehold continues in the wife as before. For the same reason, where the wife was at common law attainted of felony, the lord might enter to the lands by escheat, and eject the husband whenever the crown

[1] Bonslaugh *v.* Bonslaugh, 17 S. & R. 361. But see Bowyer's Appeal, 21 Penn. St. 210.

[2] Williams *v.* Amory, 14 Mass. 20; Johnson *v.* Payne, 1 Hill, 111; Rabb *v.* Aiken, 2 McC. Ch. 119.

[3] Starke *v.* Harrison, 5 Rich. 7.

[4] Moore *v.* Richardson, 37 Maine, 438.

[5] Hornsby *v.* Lee, 2 Madd. Ch. Cas. 16; Allen *v.* Scurry, 1 Yerg. 36; Sale *v.* Saunders, 24 Miss. 24. And see Osborne *v.* Edwards, 3 Stockt. 73.

[6] Stehman *v.* Huber, 21 Penn. St. 260.

[7] 1 Washb. Real Prop. 48 and cases cited; Bell Hus. & Wife, 151; Co. Litt. 31 *b*; Menvill's Case, 13 Co. 293; 2 Bl. Com. 293; 2 Kent Com. 39–75.

[8] See note to 1 Washb. Real Prop. 49, giving statutory changes. And see Bell Hus. & Wife, 151, 241. Stat. 7 & 8 Vict. ch. 66, removes disabilities as to dower for the most part.

had had its prerogative forfeiture of a year and day's waste.[1] The common law of attainder is of no force in this country so far as forfeiture and corruption of blood is concerned; but it probably applies to the husband's life-interest in his wife's lands.[2]

The husband alone has power at common law to bind or alienate the wife's real estate during coverture. This right lasts, at any rate, during their joint lives (provided the parties are not in the mean time divorced); and if the husband becomes a tenant by curtesy, it lasts during his whole life. But the husband's power is commensurate with his estate. He cannot encumber the property beyond the period of his life-interest, nor prevent his wife, if she survives him, or her heirs after his death, from enjoying the property free from all encumbrances which he may have created.[3] Under the ancient law of tenures, the husband could transfer the property so as to vest it in the grantee, subject to the wife's entry by writ *cui in vita;* for his act amounted to a discontinuance. Statute 32 Hen. VIII. ch. 28, was remedial in its effect, so far as to give the wife her writ of entry, notwithstanding her husband's conveyance. Copyhold lands followed a different rule, not being considered within the letter or the equity of this statute. But by the more recent statutes of 3 & 4 Will, IV. ch. 27, and ch. 74, and 8 & 9 Vict. ch. 106, fines and recoveries have been abolished and feoffments deprived of their tortious operation; and it is enacted that no discontinuance or warranty made after the 31st day of December, 1833, shall defeat any right of entry or action for the recovery of land. At the present day there is, therefore, no mode of conveyance in the English law by which the husband can convey more than his own estate in his wife's lands.[4]

These latter statutes are not, *per se*, of force in this country, for they were passed in England after the colonization of Amer-

[1] Bell Hus. & Wife, 149, 150; 2 Bl. Com. 253, 254. As to the wife's right of dower in such cases, see 2 Bl. Com. 253 and notes by Chitty and others.

[2] See Const. U. S. Art. III. § 3.

[3] 2 Kent Com. 133.

[4] 1 Bright Hus. & Wife, 162–168 and authorities cited; Bell Hus. & Wife, 195; Robertson *v.* Norris, 11 Q. B. 916.

ica. But the same result has been very generally reached in this country through a different process. In Massachusetts, the statute of 32 Hen. VIII. is still in force as a modification and amendment to the common law.[1] In other States, ejectment or other summary process may be resorted to.[2] The universal doctrine, whatever may be the form of remedy, prevails, that the husband can do no act or make any default to prejudice his wife's inheritance. And while his own alienation passes his life-estate, it can do no more; and the wife, notwithstanding, may enter after his death and hold possession.[3]

So far as the effect of the husband's lease was concerned, the statute 32 Hen. VIII. ch. 28, changed the old common law. By this statute, husband and wife are permitted to make a joint lease of the wife's real estate for a term not exceeding three lives or twenty-one years. There were, however, some restrictions placed upon the operation of this statute. Thus it was further declared that things which lie *in grant*, such as franchises, should be excepted; though tithes followed the general principle. And the old lease must have been surrendered either in writing or by operation of law within one year from making the new lease. Property in possession might be leased under the statute, but not property in reversion. The lease should not exempt the tenant from responsibility for waste. And the rent reserved should not be less than the average rent of the preceding twenty years. This statute has been strictly construed both in the common law and equity courts of England.[4]

But the husband's lease of the wife's lands, whether alone or jointly with her, may be good at the common law, though not made in compliance with the statute. In such case, the wife

[1] Bruce *v.* Wood, 1 Met. 542.

[2] Miller *v.* Shackleford, 4 Dana, 264; N. Y. Rev. Stats. 4th ed. vol. 2, p. 303; 2 Kent Com. 133 *note*.

[3] 2 Kent Com. 133 *note*; 1 Washb. Real Prop. 279; Butterfield *v.* Beall, 3 Ind. 203.

[4] Bell Hus. & Wife, 179–181; 1 Bright Hus. & Wife, 193–219; Darlington *v.* Pulteny, Cowp. 267.

may affirm or disaffirm the lease at the expiration of coverture. And the same right may be exercised by her issue, or by others claiming under her or in privity with her. So, too, where she marries again after her husband's death, her second husband has the privilege of election in her stead. But those who claim by paramount title to the wife, as for instance a joint-tenant surviving her, cannot exercise this right.[1]

Some acts of the wife, on being released from coverture, will amount to an affirmance of her husband's informal lease. Thus acceptance of rent from the tenant, after her husband's death, will confirm the lease.[2] But parol leases of the wife's real estate are affected by the statute of frauds; and not even acceptance of rent can bind the wife surviving: the lease will be treated as utterly void at the husband's death, and not voidable only.[3] Whether acceptance of rent by the wife after the husband's death would confirm a lease in writing, made by the husband alone, is a question on which the authorities are not agreed.[4]

A distinction, however, is sometimes made between leases for life and leases for terms of years, when made by the husband alone. The former it is said, being freehold estates and commencing by livery of seisin could only be avoided by entry; while the latter became void absolutely on the husband's death. But according to the better authority both kinds of leases follow the same principle, and are not void but voidable at the husband's death.[5]

[1] Bell Hus. & Wife, 175, 177; Jeffrey *v.* Guy, Yelv. 78; Smalman *v.* Agborow, Cro. Jac. 417; Anon. 2 Dyer, 159. See also Toler *v.* Slater, Law Rep. 3 Q. B. 42, a recent case on this subject.

[2] Doe *v.* Weller, 7 T. R. 478.

[3] Bell Hus. & Wife, 178.

[4] Bell Hus. & Wife, 177 and cases cited; Preamble to Stat. 32 Hen. 8, ch. 28; Jordan *v.* Wikes, Cro. Jac. 332; Bac. Abr. Leases C. 1. See Wolton *v.* Hele, 2 Saund. 180, *n.* 10; Bro. Abr. Acceptance, 1; Dixon *v.* Harrison, Vaugh. 40; Goodright *v.* Straphan, 1 Cowp. 201; Perry *v.* Hindle, 2 Taunt. 180; Hill *v.* Saunders, 2 Bing. 112.

[5] Bell Hus. & Wife, 177, 178 and cases cited; *contra*, notes to 2 Kent Com. 133 and authorities referred to, including note of Sergt. Williams to Wolton *v.* Hele, *supra*.

The husband's mortgage of his wife's real estate is effectual to the same extent as his absolute conveyance; that is to say, it will operate upon his life-estate or the joint life-estate of himself and his wife, as the case may be, and no further. And his lease of the wife's lands for a term of years for the purpose of creating an encumbrance in the nature of a mortgage, is treated in equity as a mortgage; and the wife's acceptance of rent after his death, cannot make such a lease other than void on the termination of his life-estate.[1]

If a husband mortgage the legal interest in a term of years, belonging to him in right of his wife, on a claim to foreclose this mortgage against the husband and wife as defendants, no equity for a settlement upon the wife arises.[2]

The wife's remedy for waste deserves a passing notice. Waste consists in such acts done by a tenant for life or years to the estate he holds, as injure or impair the inheritance. Since the husband holds his wife's real estate as a life-tenant only, it would seem on principle that he ought to be held liable for waste like other life-tenants. A difficulty occurs, however, in applying the remedy; and since the common-law action of waste is founded on the privity of parties competent to sue one another, no such suit can be technically maintained as between husband and wife.[3] But if the husband conveys to a third party, and such third party commits waste, the action will lie. So when waste is committed by the husband's creditor who has taken his freehold interest on execution.[4] So, also, the heir of the wife can sue the husband for waste; though it would seem that he cannot sue the husband's as-

[1] Bell Hus. & Wife, 193, 194; Goodright *v.* Straphan, 1 Cowp. 201; Drybutter *v.* Bartholomews, 2 P. Wms. 127. The husband's mortgage, in this country also, passes only his life-estate, under the like circumstances. Miller *v.* Shackleford, 3 Dana, 291; Barber *v.* Harris, 15 Wend. 615; Railroad Co. *v.* Harris, 9 Ind. 184.

[2] Hill *v.* Edmonds, 15 E. L. & Eq. 280.

[3] 2 Kent Com. 131, 132; 1 Washb. Real Prop. 118–124; 1 Bright Hus. & Wife, 110.

[4] Babb *v.* Perley, 1 Maine, 6; Mattocks *v.* Stearns, 9 Vt. 326, *supra.*

signee for want of privity.[1] The wife is not without remedy against her husband, however, for chancery will interfere on her behalf by injunction, and stop him from committing waste upon her land; and this is now the usual remedy against life-tenants.[2] And at the common law the husband was said to forfeit his term by such misconduct.[3]

The husband may dissent from a purchase, gift, or devise of real estate to his wife during coverture; since otherwise he might be made a life-tenant to his own disadvantage. But by such dissent he cannot and ought not to defeat her ultimate title as heir.[4] Nor on principle should he be permitted to dissent to any purchase, gift, or devise to the wife's separate use, by the terms of which his own interest as life-tenant is legally excluded. Subject to the husband's dissent and the wife's disagreement after her coverture ends, a conveyance to the wife in fee is always good.[5]

If the real estate of the wife be converted into personalty during her life by a voluntary act of the parties, the proceeds become personal estate, and the husband may reduce into his own possession or otherwise take the proceeds. This principle has already been noticed.[6] But where conversion takes place by act of law, independently of husband and wife, the rule is not so clear. In New York, however, it is held[7] that where the real estate of a married woman has been converted into personalty by operation of law during her lifetime, it will be disposed of by a court of equity after her death in the same

1 Walker's Case, 3 Coke, 59; Bates *v.* Shraeder, 13 Johns. 260.

2 See 1 Washb. Real Prop. 125; ib. 281.

3 Co. Litt. 351; 1 Bright Hus. & Wife, 110, 169. As to the husband's allowance for improvements on the wife's lands, see next chapter.

4 Co. Litt. 3 *a*; 1 Dane Abr. 388; 4 ib. 397; 1 Washb. Real Prop. 280.

5 Co. Litt. 3 *a*, 356 *b*; 2 Bl. Com. 292, 293; 2 Kent Com. 150. The wife's privilege of disagreement to purchase extended to her heirs, ib.

6 *Supra*, p. 120.

7 Graham *v.* Dickinson, 3 Barb. Ch. 170; In this case, Flanagan *v.* Flanagan, 1 Bro. C. C. 500, appears to have been disapproved.

manner as if she had herself converted it into personal property previous to her death.[1]

On the other hand, the rule is announced that where a married woman is entitled to a legacy, and land is given her in lieu thereof, the husband having effected no prior reduction of the legacy, it is to be held as hers and for her sole benefit. A case of this sort was lately decided in Pennsylvania.[2] And it is held that lands purchased by a married woman with the proceeds of a legacy which the husband has declined to reduce into possession, is not liable for the husband's debts.[3]

Where a husband is in possession of land with a claim of title, his title will not be affected by the act of a third person who pretends to put his wife into possession.[4] But the rule seems to be general that the husband's marital rights do not attach to property which is in the actual and rightful possession of another, and of which he cannot obtain possession during coverture without becoming a trespasser; notwithstanding the wife may have rights therein after his death.[5]

By the old law of England it appears that if a husband agreed to convey real estate belonging to his wife, he might be compelled to execute the contract by getting her to levy a fine.[6] This rule no longer holds good in that country.[7] Even where

[1] Graham *v.* Dickinson, 3 Barb. Ch. 170. See also Ellsworth *v.* Hinds, 5 Wis. 613; Jones *v.* Plummer, 20 Md. 416; Osborne *v.* Edwards, 3 Stockt. 73. But a husband may demand and reduce into possession his wife's legacy, even though it be made payable, by the terms of a will, from proceeds of the sale of the testator's real estate. Thomas *v.* Wood, 1 Md. Ch. 296. Conversion takes place where husband and wife convey to trustees to sell and dispose for payment of debts, balance to be paid them as they shall direct or appoint. Siter *v.* McClanachan, 2 Gratt. 80.

[2] Davis *v.* Davis, 46 Penn. St. 342. And see Shallenberger *v.* Ashworth, 25 Penn. St. 152; Kempe *v.* Pintard, 32 Miss. 324.

[3] Coffin *v.* Morrill, 2 Fost. 352.

[4] Powell *v.* Felton, 11 Ired. 469.

[5] Hair *v.* Avery, 28 Ala. 267.

[6] 2 Bright Hus. & Wife, 47; Macq. Hus. & Wife, 32.

[7] Frederick *v.* Coxwell, 3 Y. & J. 514; Emery *v.* Ware, 8 Ves. 505; Sug. V. P. 4th ed. 231; 2 Story Eq. Juris. 49–53; Martin *v.* Mitchell, 2 Jac. & W. 413; Thayer *v.* Gould, 1 Atk. 617; Daniel *v.* Adams, 1 Amb. 495. But see Davis *v.* Jones, 4 B. & P. 267.

the agreement has been made, not by the husband, but by the wife herself *before her marriage*, the agreement cannot now be enforced against the wife.[1] But it is nevertheless binding upon the husband.[2]

An agreement by a *feme covert* for the sale of her real estate, the same not being separate property, cannot be enforced at law or in equity against her.[3] And Sugden considers it doubtful whether a married woman, having a power of appointment, can thus bind herself.[4]

Under the modern statute of 3 & 4 Will. IV. ch. 74, which took effect in England from the end of the year 1833, married women are permitted to alienate or encumber their real estate by conveyances executed with their husbands pursuant to its provisions. This important law, with its later modifications, unfettered property which had long been fast bound.[5] The statute requires the concurrence of the husband in such conveyances: also that the wife shall make an acknowledgment before certain judicial officers designated by the act, apart from her husband, to the effect that her own consent is freely and voluntarily given.[6]

In this country the custom of a wife's joining her husband in a deed of conveyance of her lands has prevailed from a very

[1] Per Lord Ch. Cottenham, Jordan *v.* Jones, 2 Phill. 170. See Rowley *v.* Adams, 6 E. L. & Eq. 124.

[2] Griffin *v.* Taylor, Tothill, 106; Hall *v.* Hardy, 3 P. Wms. 187; Morris *v.* Stephenson, 7 Ves. 474.

[3] Macq. Hus. & Wife, 32; Emery *v.* Ware, 5 Ves. 846; Sug. V. & P. 11th ed. 230.

[4] Sug. V. & P. 11th ed. 231.

[5] See 8 & 9 Vict. ch. 106.

[6] See Macq. Hus. & Wife, 28–32; ib. Appendix 1–47; where the provisions of this act, the rules of court made in pursuance, and leading decisions on the construction of different sections are fully given. We have not thought it worth while to embody them in this work as they have only a local application. There are many cases constantly arising in the English courts as to the interpretation of this statute, with its amendments; but they seem chiefly confined to the effect of the wife's acknowledgment. Previous to the statute of 3 & 4 Wm. 4, ch. 74, the wife could convey her interest only by levying a fine, which, as well as recoveries, is abolished by that statute. 1 Washb. Real Prop. 280; 1 Wms. Real Prop. 88.

early period. In most, if not all, of the States, there are existing statutes as to the mode of execution, which contemplate the joinder of husband and wife in the conveyance, and an acknowledgment by one or both of the parties.[1] Some of the States require a separate acknowledgment by the wife apart from her husband; but in this respect the laws are not uniform. There is less formality in general than under the English statute. Thus does the wife's title pass.

And since in the tenure of lands and the mode of conveyance the law in this country has always varied considerably from that of England, the rights of married women, in other respects may be different. Thus it would seem that the joint assent of husband and wife in accepting a title should be as good as in granting one.[2] And in New Hampshire it is held that a deed to a *feme covert*, made with her own and her husband's assent, vested the title legally in her.[3] And in Vermont it has been held that a deed of gift to a wife during coverture, if accepted by her husband, is accepted by her, and that her refusal apart from him is of no consequence.[4]

But following the English doctrine, the wife's agreement to convey real estate is in this country held void, like her general contracts, though made with her husband's assent, and specific performance cannot be enforced against her.[5] So it has been held in Vermont that the wife cannot, either separately or jointly with her husband, execute a valid power of attorney to

[1] 1 Washb. Real Prop. 281 and cases cited; Davey *v.* Turner, 1 Dall. 15; Jackson *v.* Gilchrist, 15 Johns. 109; Page *v.* Page, 6 Cush. 196; 2 Kent Com. 151–155, and notes, showing custom in different States; Albany Fire Ins. Co. *v.* Bay; 4 Comst. 9.

[2] 1 Washb. Real Prop. 280.

[3] Gordon *v.* Haywood, 2 N. H. 402.

[4] Brackett *v.* Wait, 6 Vt. 411.

[5] 2 Kent Com. 168; Butler *v.* Buckingham, 5 Day, 492; Holmes *v.* Thorpe, 1 Halst. Ch. 415; Lane *v.* McKeen, 15 Me. 304. We make, of course, no reference here to the wife's *separate property*, or to her rights under what are known as the "married women's acts." See Blake *v.* Blake, 7 Iowa, 46. A contract to convey, made by husband and wife, may be good against the husband though void as to the wife. Steffey *v.* Steffey, 19 Md. 5; Johnston *v.* Jones, 12 B. Monr. 326; 2 Kent Com. 168.

convey her lands.[1] And a deed, in order to bind the wife's heirs, must have been delivered as well as executed, during her lifetime.[2] Nor can her husband, after her decease, as against such heirs, confirm a conveyance which was fatally irregular on her part.[3]

In some States the separate conveyance of a married woman or her execution jointly with her husband, but without observance of the statute formalities is void.[4] But in others such irregularities are not held fatal to the instrument, and she is bound on the usual principles.[5]

The deed of a married woman as trustee is good against her heirs, claiming adversely to the trust, even though given without the assent of her husband. And a like deed executed under a power of attorney, granted by her alone, is equally valid.[6]

So, too, in this country a married woman may mortgage as well as alienate her real estate by joining her husband in the conveyance and making due acknowledgment.[7] Where the wife joins her husband in a conveyance of the nature of a mortgage, she subjects her real estate to the risk of complete alienation by foreclosure for her husband's debt. She is estop-

[1] Sumner *v.* Conant, 10 Vt. 1. See Gillespie *v.* Worford, 2 Cold. 632.

[2] Thoenberger *v.* Zook, 34 Penn. St. 24. But see Ackert *v.* Pultz, 7 Barb. 386.

[3] Dow *v.* Jewell, 1 Fost. 470.

[4] Trimmer *v.* Heagy, 16 Penn. St. 484; Scarborough *v.* Watkins, 9 B. Monr. 540; Dow *v.* Jewell, 18 N. H. 340; Kerns *v.* Peeler, 4 Jones, 226; Cincinnati *v.* Newell, 7 Ohio St. 37; Pratt *v.* Battels, 28 Vt. 685; Boyle *v.* Chambers, 32 Mis. 46.

[5] Albany Fire Insurance Co. *v.* Bay, 4 Comst. 9; Card *v.* Patterson, 5 Ohio, 319; Smith *v.* Perry, 26 Vt. 279. The question in such cases is frequently one of statute construction. A deed of real estate executed by husband and wife while the latter is under age may be avoided by her afterwards, though thirty years have elapsed. Yourse *v.* Norcross, 12 Mis. 549. The wife's title to lands vested in her under an unrecorded deed cannot be divested by her parol consent to its cancellation and a new deed to her husband. Wilson *v.* Hill, 2 Beasl. 143.

[6] Gridley *v.* Wynant, 23 How. (U. S.) 500; Lew. Trusts and Trustees, 89, 90; Sug. Pow. 192, 196. See further, Galusha *v.* Hitchcock, 29 Barb. 193.

[7] Eaton *v.* Nason, 47 Me. 132; Swan *v.* Wiswall, 15 Pick. 126; Whiting *v.* Stevens, 4 Conn. 44; 1 Hill. Mort. 272; Demarest *v.* Wynkoop, 3 Johns. Ch. 144; 2 Kent Com. 167; Siter *v.* McClanachan, 2 Gratt. 280.

ped by her own acts from denying the validity of the mortgage.[1] She may covenant that *scire facias* may issue in default of payment.[2] She may create a valid power in the mortgage to sell in default of payment.[3] And in general she may convey upon condition and prescribe the terms.[4]

The rights of the wife are nevertheless in such cases treated with great consideration in our courts.[5] In all cases the wife, who joins her husband in a mortgage of her own property to secure his debts or the payment of money loaned to him, is the surety merely of her husband, and is entitled to all the rights and privileges of a surety. This rule is well settled.[6] And the fact that by the terms of a mortgage, the surplus is to be paid to the husband after satisfying the mortgage debt, and not to the wife, or to the mortgagors jointly, will not repel the idea that the wife was, or intended to be, a surety.[7]

A wife is not bound by her warranty in a deed which she executes. Nor by any covenants contained therein. This is the general common-law rule in England and America.[8] For this accords with the principle that married women are incapable of binding themselves by contract. In England, where the wife formerly passed her real estate by suffering a fine, it was

1 McCullough *v.* Wilson, 21 Penn. St. 436.

2 Black *v.* Galway, 24 Penn. St. 18.

3 2 Kent Com. 167; Vartie *v.* Underwood, 18 Barb. 561.

4 Demarest *v.* Wynkoop, 3 Johns. Ch. 129; 2 Kent Com. 167. So too in England. Pybus *v.* Smith, 1 Ves. Jr. 189; Essex *v.* Atkins, 14 ib. 542. See Gilbert *v.* Mayford, 1 Scam. 471; Ruscombe *v.* Hare, 2 Bligh, 192; Bird *v.* Davis, 1 McCart. 467.

5 See Bayler *v.* Commonwealth, 40 Penn. St. 37. "Will a court of equity interfere in favor of one who is an assignee or covenantee, but not for value, to enforce a wife's engagement to pay an old debt of her husband? The answer is plain. If it will not decree the performance of an ordinary agreement, not founded on a valuable consideration, much less will it enforce such a contract against a *feme covert.*" Per Strong, J.; ib. p. 44.

6 Neimcewicz *v.* Gahn, 3 Paige, 614; Hawley *v.* Bradford, 9 Paige, 200; Vartie *v.* Underwood, 18 Barb. 561.

7 Vartie *v.* Underwood, 18 Barb. 561. But see Dean *v.* Phillips, 17 Ind. 406.

8 2 Kent Com. 167, 168; Fowler *v.* Shearer, 7 Mass. 21, per Parsons C.J. Falmouth Bridge Co. *v.* Tibbetts, 16 B. Monr. 637; Den *v.* Demarest, 1 Zab. (N. J.) 525; Rawle Cov. 573, 574.

held long ago that if the grantee should be evicted by a paramount title, the wife could be sued on her covenant of warranty after her husband's death.[1] So, too, it was formerly said that the wife should be held bound on the covenants contained in a lease of her lands executed during coverture, with her husband and affirmed by herself after his death, by such acts as the acceptance of rent;[2] and this doctrine is certainly not unreasonable so far as a subsequent breach of covenant is concerned. But further than this courts would not probably go at this day. And in this country the wife's covenants in a conveyance executed jointly with her husband are considered binding upon her only by way of estoppel, and cannot subject her to suit for damages.[3] Indeed, in New York the wife's privilege in this respect is carried much further, for she is permitted to execute a conveyance of land with her husband, containing a covenant of warranty on her part, and then to defeat the title by acquiring an adverse interest afterwards.[4]

If the wife at the time of her marriage has a life-estate in lands, her husband becomes seised of such estate in the right of his wife, and he is entitled to the profits during coverture. So if it were granted to a trustee for her own use. And the same rule applies whether the estate be for the life of the wife or of some other person. If the estate be for the wife's own life it terminates at her death, and the husband has no further interest in it. But if it be an estate for the life of another person who survives her, the husband takes the profits during the remainder of such person's life as a special occupant of the land. The husband's representatives in either case

[1] Wotton *v.* Hele, 2 Saund. 177; 1 Mod. 290. Chancellor Kent justly observes that this was a very strong case to show that she might deal with her land by fine as a *feme sole*. 2 Kent Com. 167.

[2] 2 Saund. 80, note 9.

[3] Nash *v.* Spofford, 10 Met. 192; Jackson *v.* Vanderheyden, 17 Johns. 167.

[4] Jackson *v.* Vanderheyden, 17 Johns. 167; Carpenter *v.* Schermerhorn, 2 Barb. Ch. 314. *Contra*, Colcord *v.* Swan, 7 Mass. 291; Hill *v.* West, 8 Ohio, 225; Massie *v.* Sebastian, 4 Bibb, 436; Nash *v.* Spofford, 10 Met. 192. And see 4 Com. Dig. 79 b.

take crops growing on the land at the time of his death.[1] But the husband might at common law take a release or confirmation to enlarge his life-estate.[2]

As concerns the wife's life-estate in her real or personal property, the English chancery courts have followed out exceptions to the doctrines of equitable assignment.[3] Not only is the husband's assignment sufficient to bar the wife's survivorship; but a purchaser for value takes it free from the encumbrance of the wife's equity to a settlement. In this case, it it said, equity will follow the law, which gives to the husband the power of dealing with the income of his wife's property, and will not put in force the rule that he who comes into equity must do equity, whereby purchasers would be involved in inquiries into the relations between husband and wife, their property, and means of maintenance.[4]

A husband acquires by his marriage the right to use and occupy during coverture lands held by his wife in joint tenancy.[5]

[1] 2 Kent Com. 134; 1 Bright Hus. & Wife, 112, 113.

[2] Co. Litt. 299.

[3] See Purdew *v.* Jackson, 1 Russ. 1, and other cases commented upon, *supra.*

[4] Tidd *v.* Lister, 17 E. L. & Eq. 560; 10 Hare, 140; s. c. on appeal, 3 De G. M. & Gord, 868. And see Drew *v.* Long, 21 E. L. & Eq. 339; Hileman *v.* Bonslaugh, 13 Penn. St. 344.

[5] Bishop *v.* Blair, 36 Ala. 80; Royston *v.* Royston, 21 Geo. 161.

CHAPTER VII.

COMMON-LAW RIGHTS AND DISABILITIES OF THE HUSBAND ON HIS WIFE'S DECEASE.

On the death of the wife, the husband becomes entitled to administer on her estate. The court having jurisdiction in such matters must issue letters to him, and to him alone, unless he renounce or decline. The foundation of this claim has been variously stated; by some it is said to be derived from the statute 31 Edw. III., on the ground of the husband's being "the next and most lawful friend" of his wife; while there are other authorities which insist that the husband is entitled at common law, *jure mariti*, and independently of the statutes. But this right, however founded, is now regarded in England as unquestionable, and is expressly confirmed by the statute 29 Car. II. c. 3 (amendatory of statute 22 & 23 Car. II. c. 10), which enacts that the statute of distributions "shall not extend to the estates of *femes covert*, that shall die intestate, but that *their husbands may demand and have administration* of their rights, credits, and other personal estates, and recover and enjoy the same as they might have done before the making of the said act."[1] This same right of the husband is generally, though not universally, recognized in this country, and in the different States there are statutes which regulate the subject of administration, not only as to the wife dying intestate, but as to all others.[2]

To this rule some exceptions have been introduced in later years, owing chiefly to the modern facilities for separation and

[1] 1 Wms. Ex'rs. 4th Am. ed. 336, &c.

[2] 2 Kent Com. 135; ib. 410.

divorce, and the enlarged capacity given to the wife to act as a *feme sole*, and to dispose of her own property. Thus in a late English case where a married woman lived separate from her husband, after having obtained an order of protection, and then died leaving him and a minor son, administration was granted to a guardian elected by the son, upon proper security, without citing the father.[1] And in this country the marital rights of the husband over his wife's unadministered property, when her death occurred during a state of separation for his misconduct, has been sometimes denied.[2]

Since, as we have already seen, the husband takes absolutely his wife's personal *choses in possession* at the common law by virtue of the marriage, and, if he be the survivor, her chattels real likewise, there would generally appear to be no object gained in seeking letters of administration on her estate, unless she had *choses in action* unrecovered at the time of her death. But a case might arise where he has a just claim against her estate, and wishes to enforce it by a sale of her real estate as administrator. Or he might intend to prosecute a suit. Or letters of administration might be desirable for the purposes of creditors.

There is a distinction between property acquired by the husband absolutely by virtue of marriage, and property acquired in his representative capacity. The former is his own, free from all demands of his wife's creditors. But the latter comes to him only by way of distribution, after payment of all just debts against his wife's estate. A notable case in point is that of *Heard* v. *Stamford*, where a single woman contracted a debt for which she gave her promissory note of £50. She afterwards married, and brought to her husband a fortune of £700. On her death it appeared that the husband had acquired a portion of this fortune during coverture; the other portion was still

[1] Goods of Stephenson, Law Rep., 1 P. & D. 285.

[2] Cooper *v.* Maddox, 2 Sneed, 135. And see Moyer's Appeal, 16 Penn. St. 405.

outstanding at her death as a *chose in action*, and could only be recovered by the late husband as her administrator. Lord Chancellor Talbot decided that from the latter portion, after it had been recovered, the creditor should be satisfied; but that no claim could be enforced against the former portion.[1] Debts contracted by the wife during marriage follow a somewhat different rule at the common law; for either they are the debts of the husband or no legal debts at all.

By the English statutes of distribution (and perhaps by the common law), not only is the husband entitled to administer upon his wife's estate in preference to all others, but, subject to the payment of such debts as we have described, he recovers her outstanding property to his own use and enjoyment, including rights vested and contingent, and funds at her disposal during her lifetime or held in trust for her. Even if he does not take out letters of administration, he is equally entitled to the property.[2] He is therefore said to administer for his own benefit. And since husband and wife are not, properly speaking, next of kin to one another, the title the husband thus acquires may be designated as a title *jure mariti* under the statutes of distribution.[3]

The statutes of distribution in this country seem to have very generally adopted the English principle, and to have given the husband the sole title to the wife's outstanding personal property upon her death, to the exclusion of her kindred, even to the exclusion of her own children.[4] Hence if the husband, after

[1] Ca. Temp. Talb. 173; 3 P. Wms. 409; Macq. Hus. & Wife, 188. And see Hetrick *v.* Hetrick, 13 Ind. 44; Donnington *v.* Mitchell, 1 Green Ch. 243. The statute rule now introduced into many States, is that the husband is liable as administrator on the estate of his wife for her debts, only to the extent of the assets received by him. See N. Y. Rev. Stat. vol. 2, p. 75.

[2] Clough *v.* Bond, 6 Jur. 50.

[3] 2 Bl. Com. 515; Watt *v.* Watt, 3 Ves. 246, 247; 2 Kent Com. 136, and authorities cited.

[4] Ransom *v.* Nichols, 22 N.Y. 110; McCosker *v.* Golden, 1 Bradf. Sur. 64; 2 Kent Com. 136; Donnington *v.* Mitchell, 1 Green Ch. 243; Jones *v.* Brown, 34 N. H. 439; Hawley *v.* Burgess, 22 Conn. 284; Stockett *v.* Bird, 18 Md. 484; Rice *v.* Thompson, 14 B. Monr. 377; Williams *v.* Carle, 2 Stockt. 543; Walker

his wife's death, obtain possession of her personal property, without taking out letters of administration, he may retain it against her next of kin.[1] And if the wife's next of kin administer, he will be a trustee for the husband or his representatives, in accordance with the English rule.[2]

But the principle that the husband administers exclusively for his own benefit on his wife's estate is not recognized in Vermont, but on the contrary has been pronounced incompatible with the legislation of that State.[3] And the rule, as there declared, is that *choses in action* of the wife, not reduced to possession by her husband, during her life, nor as her administrator, by reason of his removal by the court, go to her heirs, according to the statute of descents and distribution. So in some other States the husband is entitled by law to a portion only of the balance in his hands as administrator, or is postponed to her next of kin altogether; and he cannot succeed to her estate by virtue of his marital right without taking out letters of administration; nor can he administer without accounting for his balances to the persons designated by statute as entitled to distributive shares.[4]

Where the husband himself dies before the wife's outstanding personal chattels are recovered, his next of kin will be entitled to them in equity. This is the rule in England; also in America, wherever the husband's right to administer for his own benefit is recognized. For it is the necessary consequence of that doctrine. But in England a somewhat circuitous course was usually taken in such cases. The wife's next of kin were held entitled to letters of administration *de bonis non* of her

v. Walker, 25 Mis. 367; Shumway *v.* Cooper, 16 Barb. 556; Clay *v.* Irvine, 4 W. & S. 232.

[1] Henden *v.* Colgin, 4 Munf. 231.

[2] Betts *v.* Kimpton, 2 B. & Ad. 273; Hunter *v.* Hallett, 1 Edw. Ch. 388; Whitaker *v.* Whitaker, 6 Johns. 112. See also statutes of the several States which generally regulate the subject of administration and distribution.

[3] Holmes *v.* Holmes, 28 Vt. 765.

[4] Cox *v.* Morrow, 14 Ark. 603; Welch *v.* Welch, 14 Ala. 76; Nelson *v.* Goree, 34 Ala. 565; Baldwin *v.* Carter, 17 Conn. 201; Curry *v.* Fulkinson, 14 Ohio, 100.

estate not received by her husband during his life. But they were accountable as trustees for the legatees or next of kin of the husband.[1] In this country, if the husband dies, leaving assets of his wife unadministered, the right of administration follows the right of estate, and devolves upon the husband's next of kin.[2] And this seems to have been finally adopted as the English practice in such cases.[3] Whenever administration *de bonis non* of the wife is granted to a third person, in either England or America (subject to such exceptions as were noted in the preceding section), this administrator is a trustee for the representatives of the husband in case he dies after his wife.[4]

In a late English case a female took administration of the estate of a deceased person as creditor, got in a large part of the estate, and paid some of the debts; she afterwards married and died. The husband had taken possession of leaseholds, part of the estate, but no fund had been set apart for the payment of the wife's debt. It was held that administration of the unadministered effects of the deceased could not be taken by the husband in his own right as a creditor, but only as representative of his wife.[5]

In another case the defendant received money for a married woman, and wrote to her that he held it at her disposal. The wife died, and then the husband, who had not interfered in the matter; and the wife's administratrix sued the defendant

[1] Bell Hus. & Wife, 52; Macq. Hus. & Wife, 53, *note;* Humphrey *v.* Bullen, 1 Atk. 458; Squib *v.* Wyn, 1 P. Wms. 378; Cart *v.* Rees, ib. 381; Elliot *v.* Collier, 3 Ark. 526.

[2] Roosevelt *v.* Ellithorp, 10 Paige, 415; Stewart *v.* Stewart, 7 Johns. Ch. 229; Bryan *v.* Rooks, 25 Geo. 622; Ward *v.* Thompson, 6 Gill & J. 349; Patterson *v.* High, 8 Ired. Eq. 52.

[3] Fielder *v.* Hanyer, 3 Hag. Eccl. 770; 2 Redf. Wills, 70; 1 Wms. Exrs. 360.

[4] English cases cited above; Whitaker *v.* Whitaker, 6 Johns. 112; Hendin *v.* Colgin, 4 Munf. 231; Clark *v.* Clark, 6 W. & S. 85; 2 Kent Com. 136, and cases cited; Betts *v.* Kimpton, 2 B. & Ad. 273; Bryan *v.* Rooks, 25 Geo. 622. By statute in New York the husband's executors and administrators take the property, and no administrator *de bonis non* need be appointed on the wife's estate. Lockwood *v.* Stockholm, 11 Paige, 87.

[5] Goods of Risdon, Law Rep. 1 P. & D. 637.

for money had and received to the use of the wife. It was held that he could maintain the action.[1]

An action for a legacy due to a wife, or for other *choses* not reduced into possession during coverture, is properly brought in the name of her administrator after her death.[2] And the rule would appear to be the same, though the consideration of the *chose* was the wife's real estate.[3] The true test is whether the property in question was in reality a *chose in action* or not. So it is held that where a legacy was given to a trustee for the use of a married woman, who died without having received it, and the husband afterwards died without having recovered it, the personal representative of the husband is entitled to a decree in equity, as against the personal representative of the wife, for such portion thereof as may have come to the hands of the latter, and against the trustee for the balance retained by him.[4]

But the husband as tenant by the curtesy may have, upon certain conditions, an enlarged life-interest in his wife's lands, extending beyond her life if he survives. Tenancy by the curtesy, or tenancy by curtesy, is a freehold estate in the husband for the term of his natural life. He acquires it by the fact that a child capable of inheritance is born of the marriage. The meaning of the term is somewhat obscure. Some have thought the word "curtesy" signifies the favor or courtesy with which the law regards the husband. Others that it comes from the Latin word *curtis*, and has reference to the feudal custom which permitted the husband, as soon as a son was born, to attend court as one of the *pares curiæ*, and do homage without his wife. But there is reason to believe that tenancy by the curtesy existed in the civil law during the reign of Constantine.[5] This privilege of the husband extends to all lands and tenements of which the wife was seised at any time

[1] Fleet *v.* Perrins, Law Rep. 4 Q. B. 500; s. c. Law Rep. 3 Q. B. 536.

[2] Willis *v.* Roberts, 48 Maine, 257; Allen *v.* Wilkins, 3 Allen, 321.

[3] Driggs *v.* Abbott, 27 Vt. 580.

[4] Coleman *v.* Hallowell, 1 Jones Eq. 204. But see Fleet *v.* Perrins, *supra.*

[5] 1 Washb. Real Prop. 128 and authorities cited; 2 Bl. Com. 126, and notes by Chitty and others; Wright Ten. 193, 194; 2 Bright Hus. & Wife, 116.

during coverture, whether legal or trust estate, whether in fee simple, or by way of remainder or reversion.[1] The law affords herein a rare but positive instance of public policy discriminating in favor of the propagation of children.

Four things are essential, at common law, to entitle a husband to curtesy. *First.* A lawful marriage. *Second.* Seisin of the wife at some time during coverture. *Third.* Birth alive of issue capable of inheritance. *Fourth.* Death of the wife. After the birth of the child the husband's title to curtesy becomes possible; and the curtesy is then initiate. After the death of the wife the title to curtesy becomes complete; and the curtesy is then consummate.[2]

Of late years tenancy by the curtesy has become practically infrequent in England by reason of the prevalence of marriage settlements excluding such right.[3] In this country it has existed in all of the older States, but is modified in many of them, expressly or by implication, by late statutes. In Iowa and Indiana, curtesy is expressly abolished, and a certain defined interest in the wife's real estate goes to her husband instead, by way of inheritance. In Texas, California, Louisiana, and other States where the tenure of real estate comes from the community or civil law, rather than the common law, curtesy is not recognized. In some of the States the right of curtesy appears to be denied to husbands who wilfully neglect and desert their wives. In certain New England States, as Massachusetts and Rhode Island, tenancy by the curtesy is expressly reserved by statute.[4] As to its present existence in New York there is some uncertainty.[5]

1 Ib.; Co. Litt. 30 *a*; ib. 29 *a*, *n*. 165; Watts *v.* Ball, 1 P.Wms. 109.

2 For a full description of curtesy with its incidents, see 1 Washb. Real Prop. 127; Wms. Real Prop. 8th ed. 218.

3 Wms. Real Prop. 187; 1 Washb. Real Prop. 129.

4 See statutes of different States cited in 1 Washb. Real Prop. 258 and note; and notes to 4 Kent Com. 34. Statute provisions as to curtesy and dower are frequently alike. And see Ross *v.* Adams, 4 Dutch. 160; Noble *v.* Noble, 19 Ind. 431.

5 Hurd *v.* Cass, 9 Barb. 366; Clark *v.* Clark, 24 Barb. 581; *contra*, Billings *v.* Baker, 28 Barb. 343.

For an injury to the wife's inheritance in lands the husband cannot sue alone, for the cause of action will not survive to him.[1] Consequently he cannot prosecute such an action after the death of the wife during the pendency of such a suit and before judgment.[2] If the husband should die first, however, the suit will not abate, as he is not the real plaintiff.[3]

Inasmuch as the husband's interest in his wife's lands is limited to the usufruct as a life-tenant, it follows that all claims presented by him against her estate, after her death, in relation to such property, will be closely scrutinized. Thus it has been held that he cannot claim reimbursement for moneys paid in settling controversies in regard to the title of his wife's real estate.[4] So where a husband was sued with his wife for her debt contracted before marriage and secured by a mortgage of her land, and after her death voluntarily suffered judgment to be rendered against him for the amount of the debt, when he knew that he was not legally liable to a judgment, and paid the debt on execution, taking to himself no assignment of the mortgage, but suffering it to be discharged altogether, it is held that he cannot seek indemnity from his wife's heirs either at law or in equity, even though he had misapprehended the legal effect of his consent to the judgment.[5]

So the general rule is strict as regards improvements made by the husband upon his wife's real estate. The English doctrine is that if the husband erects buildings upon his wife's lands, or otherwise makes permanent improvements thereon, expending his own money for such purpose, the presumption is

[1] Clapp *v.* Stoughton, 10 Pick. 463; Fuller *v.* Naugatuck R. R. Co., 21 Conn. 557; Com. Dig. Baron & Feme, V.

[2] 1 Bl. Com. 443; 1 Chitty Pl. 75; Ryder *v.* Robinson, 2 Greenl. 127; Buck *v.* Goodrich, 33 Conn. 37. And see Deadrich *v.* Armour, 10 Humph. 588.

[3] 1 Chitty Pl. 22; Little *v.* Downing, 37 N. H. 355; Jaques *v.* Short, 20 Barb. 269.

[4] Campbell *v.* Wallace, 12 N. H. 362; Burleigh *v.* Coffin, 2 Fost. 118.

[5] Warren *v.* Jennison, 6 Gray, 559. But see 2 Story Eq. Juris. § 1023; Pitt *v.* Pitt, 1 Turn. & Russ. 180; Shrewsbury *v.* Shrewsbury, 1 Ves. Jr. 233; Jenness *v.* Robinson, 10 N. H. 218.

that he intended the expense for his wife's benefit, and he cannot recover for it.[1] Several cases of this sort have come before our own courts quite recently, the claims being usually presented after the wife's death; and this principle has been rigidly applied, though doubtless occasioning in some instances positive hardship and wrong.[2] And since the husband has no interest in improvements upon his wife's real estate, neither, of course, have his creditors.[3] Agreements between husband and wife might vary the principle. But if a husband improves his wife's land without any agreement for compensation, he cannot bring in a claim after her death to be enforced, either against her estate or her heirs.[4]

The husband, too, is bound to bury his deceased wife in a suitable manner; that is to say, he is bound to defray all necessary funeral expenses.[5] Even when a wife dies who had been living separate from her husband, it is held that her surviving husband is bound to provide her with a funeral at a reasonable expense; and, if he neglects to do so, any person who voluntarily employs an undertaker for that purpose and pays him for his services, is entitled to recover the sum thus expended from the husband in an action at law.[6] So, too, where the wife died during the absence of her husband abroad, so that it was necessary for another to superintend the funeral.[7] And it is held that even an infant husband may contract for the interment of his deceased wife, or lawful children, so as to be bound by his contract. The contract will have validity, because it is a contract for the burial of those who are *personæ*

[1] 1 Roper Hus. & Wife, 54; Campion *v.* Colton, 17 Ves. 264; 1 Washb. Real Prop. 281.

[2] Burleigh *v.* Coffin, 2 Fost. 118; White *v.* Hildreth, 32 Vt. 265. And see Washburn *v.* Sproat, 16 Mass. 449.

[3] Lichty *v.* Hager, 13 Penn. St. 565; Robinson *v.* Huffman, 15 B. Monr. 80.

[4] Webster *v.* Hildreth, 33 Vt. 457.

[5] Macq. Hus. & Wife, 191.

[6] Ambrose *v.* Kenison, 4 E. L. & Eq. 361; Bradshaw *v.* Beard, 12 C. B. (N. S.) 344.

[7] Jenkins *v.* Tucker, 1 H. Bl. 90.

conjunctæ with him by reason of the marriage, and as such it is to be regarded as a contract for his own personal benefit.[1]

These points were decided in England; and the subject seems to have received little attention in the courts of this country. But it is believed that a similar rule prevails in most, if not all of the States, except so far as modified by the divorce laws. And in recognition of the husband's paramount right in matters relative to his wife's burial it is held in Massachusetts, that a husband who has interred his wife in a public burial-ground is not liable as a trespasser for removing a gravestone, since placed at her grave by her mother, without injuring the stone, and for the purpose of substituting another.[2]

The husband's liability for his wife's debts *dum sola*, ceases at her death. His liability for her necessaries, and upon contracts in general which she had made as his agent during her life, does not so terminate; for they are his contracts and not hers. And it is held that where the husband, during coverture, pays the debt of his wife, contracted *dum sola*, in a specific article, and the title to that article fails, he remains liable for its value, notwithstanding his wife died in the meantime, and the title failed by reason of her unexpected death.[3] But on the other hand, the husband of one who inherited personal property from a grantor who had conveyed land with covenants of warranty cannot be held liable after her death for a breach of the covenant.[4]

[1] Chapple *v.* Cooper, 13 M. & W. 252.
[2] Durell *v.* Hayward, 9 Gray, 248.
[3] Crawford *v.* Verry, 12 Ind. 427.
[4] Howes *v.* Bigelow, 13 Mass. 384. See remarks of Parker C. J. in ib.

CHAPTER VIII.

COMMON-LAW RIGHTS AND DISABILITIES OF THE WIFE ON HER HUSBAND'S DECEASE.

On the dissolution of a marriage by the death of the husband, the widow is usually selected to administer upon his estate, provided she is willing and competent to take the trust. But her right of administration on her husband's estate is not co-extensive with that of the husband on her estate. For in the one instance the husband is to be preferred to all others; whereas in the other, administration may be granted by the court at discretion, either to the widow alone, or to the next of kin, or to both together.[1] This is the law in England, and the same prevails generally in this country, under the statutes of the different States.[2]

Under the English statute of distributions, 22 & 23 Car. II. c. 10, the widow surviving her husband, who deceased intestate, is entitled to one-third of the personal property which remains after payment of the husband's debts, while the remaining two-thirds go to the children or their representatives.[3] The widow's share is not unfrequently termed her "thirds," or incorrectly her "thirds of personal estate at common law."[4] The statute further provides that when the husband dies intestate, leaving a widow only and no lineal descendant, the widow

[1] Fawtry *v.* Fawtry, 1 Salk. 36; 11 Vin. Abr. 92; Anon., Stra. 552; Lovelas, 3; Macq. Hus. & Wife, 145; Case of Williams, 3 Hag. Ecc. 217.

[2] 2 Kent Com. 410, 411, and notes. But by the New York statutes (vol. 2, p. 74, Rev. Stats.) the widow *and* next of kin are designated.

[3] 2 Bl. Com. 515, 516.

[4] See Lord Cottenham in Gurley *v.* Gurley, 8 Cl. & Fin. 741; Macq. Hus. & Wife, 146.

is entitled to *a moiety*, or *half* of his personal estate, and the other half goes to the husband's next of kin. When there are no next of kin, the widow is not entitled to the whole of her husband's personal estate; but one-half belongs to her, and the other half goes to the crown.[1] Here, too, the wife's right is not coequal with that of her husband; for he surviving her takes the whole of her personal estate, while she surviving him cannot in any event be entitled to more than one-half of his personal estate, even though the estate consisted wholly of property which belonged to her before marriage. It is held, that the widow of a deceased child cannot take as a representative of such child under the statutes of distributions.[2] The husband and wife, by a marriage settlement may exclude one another from all benefits by way of distribution in their respective estates, other provisions having been substituted by way of recompense.[3]

In this country the statute of Charles II. is at the basis of our legislation regarding the estates of intestates, though modifications are frequently to be met with. Thus in Vermont, if there be no issue, the widow takes the whole estate, if not exceeding two thousand dollars, and one-half of the residue above that sum. In Massachusetts, if there be no issue, the widow takes the residue to the amount of five thousand dollars, and one-half of the excess above ten thousand dollars. In New York, there are statute provisions on the general subject of distribution quite full and minute. If no descendant or parent survive the husband, the widow takes two thousand dollars and one-half of the surplus. But if there be no next of kin to the intestate, as near as nephew or niece, she takes the whole surplus.

[1] 2 Bl. Com. 515, 516; 2 Kent Com. 427; Cave *v.* Roberts, 8 Sim. 214. In certain localities of England a different rule prevails as to distribution of the estates of intestates, the statute of distributions permitting the local customs to continue in force; as in the city of London and Provinces of York. 2 Bl. Com. 518.

[2] Price *v.* Strange, 6 Madd. 161.

[3] Earl of Buckinghamshire *v.* Drury, 2 Eden, 60.

In Maryland, the widow takes, as under the common law at the time of its colonization, her "reasonable share," which is one-third or one-half, according to circumstances. In Pennsylvania, the law gives the same rights, so far as regards the widow and general kindred, as prevail in England under the statute of distributions. In Ohio, the widow takes the entire personal estate after the debts are paid, if there be no children; and if there are any, she takes one-half if the estate amounts only to $400; and if it exceeds that sum she takes one-third of the surplus. In Indiana, something like the community system has been lately adopted. In Georgia, the widow's share in her intestate husband's personal estate is affected by her election to take dower. Where there is no widow or kindred, the State generally claims the balance under the statutory provisions, as in England; but if there be a widow, it is common in this country to give her the whole surplus in default of the husband's kindred; while it is moreover apparent, from the foregoing statute provisions, that American legislation strongly favors the widow as against distant kindred of the intestate.[1]

It is held that a bequest to the wife by the husband, in full of her legal claims, is no bar to her right to a distributive share in a lapsed bequest.[2] So acts of the husband during his lifetime, committed for the purpose of defrauding the wife of her distributive share in his personal estate after his decease have been set aside in equity. Thus in Maryland, in a case where it appeared that the husband with such design had turned his personal into real estate, and had then executed conveyances of the real estate to other parties, while retaining the title deeds in his own hands and keeping in possession of the premises, the conveyances were set aside after his death as a fraud upon his wife's lawful rights.[3]

The wife's privilege is carried even farther in Massachusetts,

[1] See 2 Kent Com. 11th ed. 427, 428, and notes.

[2] Garthshore v. Chalie, 10 Ves. Jr. 1. But see Wright v. Fearis, 3 Swanst. 181.

[3] Hays v. Henry, 1 Md. Ch. 337.

by a statute which permits the widow to waive a provision made for her by her husband's will, and thereupon to take such portion as the law would have given her had he died intestate. But this privilege is accorded with some restrictions as to the full amount to be allowed her.[1] And it is to be inferred that the right of election is personal to herself, and cannot be exercised by her representatives after her death.

Another liberal provision made by the legislatures of some American States is that known as the widow's allowance. This is a reasonable sum, such as the court of probate may order, as necessaries to the widow for herself and the family, or, if there be no widow, to the minor children. The allowance is set apart as something superior to the claims of general creditors, and is even preferred to the expenses of administration, funeral and last illness of the husband. The amount is at the discretion of the court, and where the husband has died insolvent, leaving few assets, it is not uncommon for the whole of the personal property to be thus awarded to the widow, whereby is afforded an expeditious means of settling perplexing little estates. This right is treated as personal to the widow, provided she survive her husband; it does not pass to her representatives. Nor is it considered in the same light as a distributive share; but the amount, if allowed, is to be regulated according to the necessitous circumstances of the widow and her family.[2]

The widow's *paraphernalia* is a species of property recognized at the common law, though borrowed from the civilians. It consists of such articles of wearing apparel, personal ornament, and personal convenience as are suitable to a wife's rank and degree, and such as she continued to use during the marriage.[3] The term *paraphernalia* is derived from the Greeks, and transmitted to England through the civil law. But while the wife's

[1] Mass. Stats. 1861, ch. 164; Firth *v.* Denny, 2 Allen, 468.

[2] Mass. Gen. Sts. ch. 96, §§ 4, 5. See Hollenbeck *v.* Pixley, 3 Gray, 521; Brazer *v.* Dean, 15 Mass. 183; Adams *v.* Adams, 10 Met. 170; Smith's Prob. Pract. (Mass.) 106–109.

[3] 2 Bl. Com. 436; Macq. Hus. & Wife, 147.

paraphernalia at the çivil law resembled what we call the wife's separate property, the word itself has a more limited signification in England and America, being confined to personal necessaries or ornaments, and having no possible application to real estate. Blackstone says the word signified "something over and above her dower;" whereas, as a late English writer observes, it really meant something of her own, not surrendered by her at her marriage; something reserved and kept back from the *dos*, or fortune, which she brought her husband.[1]

The common-law doctrine of *paraphernalia* is this: that the suitable ornaments and wearing apparel of a married woman, which she had at the time of her marriage, or which come to her through her husband before or during coverture, remain his personal property during his life, and he may sell and dispose of them during his life; but such as may remain at the time of his death belong thenceforth to her absolutely as her *paraphernalia*.[2] It seems that he may even give them away while coverture lasts, in the exercise of his marital rights. But he certainly cannot bequeath them from his wife; nor on principle dispose of them as *donatio causa mortis*.[3]

Paraphernalia are therefore to be distinguished from the wife's separate property, as we shall presently see, inasmuch as her rights are perfected, only when she becomes a widow, and the property is alienable not by herself, but her husband, during his life.[4] Such gifts from the husband are further to be distinguished from gifts bestowed solely upon the wife by her father, or by a relative or even by a stranger. For in the latter instance they would be deemed gifts to her separate use; and

[1] Macq. Hus. & Wife, 152. Writers sometimes make confusion by citing maxims of Roman law in definition of English doctrines. See 2 Roper Hus. & Wife, 140; 1 Bright Hus. & Wife, 286 *n.*

[2] Tipping *v.* Tipping, 1 P. Wms. 730; 1 Rolle, 911, L. 35; Com. Dig. Baron & Feme, Paraphernalia; Macq. Hus. & Wife, 147, 148. The State *v.* Hays, 21 Ind. 288.

[3] 2 Bl. Com. 436; Noye's Max. ch. 49.

[4] Cro. Car. 344; Com. Dig. Baron & Feme, Paraphernalia.

then, if received with the husband's consent, neither he nor his creditors could afterwards dispose of them.[1]

Mere ornaments for a parlor are not to be treated as paraphernal property.[2] Nor can articles be claimed as such which are, in fact, heirlooms.[3] But a gold watch worn by the wife of one who maintains a fair social position may be treated as paraphernal.[4] A "necessary bed" is paraphernal.[5] Jewels purchased by the husband and worn by the wife with her other ornaments, it is said, become her *paraphernalia* in absence of evidence to the contrary; while family jewels by merely being worn by the wife do not.[6] Where a piece of jewelry, in possession of the husband at the time of marriage as an heirloom, is greatly enhanced in value by adding new diamonds, and is then given the wife to wear, though bequeathed to his heirs, the rule, as laid down by Lord Chancellor Macclesfield, is to separate the new diamonds after the husband's death, and bestow them upon the widow as her *paraphernalia*, leaving the heirs to enjoy the residue.[7] And the old books say that if the husband delivers cloth to his wife for her apparel, and dies before it is made up, she shall have the cloth.[8] The question of value is not material in setting off the widow's *paraphernalia*, so long as the articles are suitable to her degree.[9] And while the modern cases which turn on such questions, are rare, especially in this country, it cannot be doubted that a liberal rule will at this day be applied in the widow's favor.

As to personal ornaments, it seems to be an important element in the title, that the wife should be seen to wear them at intervals. Particularly is this true where the husband kept them in his own possession, for then it might be said

1 2 Story Eq. Juris. 555.

2 Graham *v.* Londonderry, 3 Atk. 393.

3 Calmady *v.* Calmady, 11 Vin. Abr. 181, 182.

4 Tllexan *v.* Wilson, 43 Me. 186.

5 See Com. Dig. Baron & Feme, Paraphernalia.

6 Jervoise *v.* Jervoise, 17 Beav. 566.

7 Calmady *v.* Calmady, 11 Vin. Abr. 181, 182.

8 1 Rolle, 911, L. 35; Com. Dig. Baron & Feme, Paraphernalia.

9 Ib.; Macq. Hus. & Wife, 148.

that he never gave them to her. But it is enough to establish her claim that he had allowed her to wear them on birthdays or other suitable occasions.[1]

Paraphernalia would seem to be so far personal to the widow, that if not claimed by her during her lifetime, they cannot after her death be demanded by her executor or administrator. Accordingly it is held that if the husband should bequeath them to her for life and then over, and she should make no election to have them as her paraphernal goods, her representative after her decease would be excluded.[2] But in a recent English case, not only was the committee of the widow, being a lunatic, permitted to elect in her stead while she remained alive; but upon her subsequent death, her next of kin were allowed to come in and choose whether to take the *paraphernalia* or the benefits given her under her husband's will; and, upon their choice of the former, an order in chancery was made accordingly.[3]

The wife's paraphernal property is subject to her husband's debts during his life; for in truth it is not then her property at all.[4] Nor can she maintain an indictment against any one who steals it, while her husband is alive.[5] So, too, it is liable for his debts after his death, when there is a deficiency of assets in the administrator's hands.[6] But even then her necessary clothing is protected; for, in the words of an ancient judicial resolution: "She ought not to be naked or exposed to shame and cold."[7] And in many of the United States there are at the present day statutes which justly reserve to the widow, in any event, necessaries in the house at the time of her

1 Graham *v.* Londonderry, 3 Atk. 393.

2 Macq. Hus. & Wife, 150; Clarges *v.* Albemarle, 2 Vern. 246; Com. Dig. Baron & Feme, Paraphernalia.

3 *In re* Hewson, 23 E. L. & Eq. 283.

4 Tllexan *v.* Wilson, 43 Me. 186; 1 Bright Hus. & Wife, 288.

5 The State *v.* Hays, 21 Ind. 288.

6 2 Bl. Com. 436; Macq. Hus. & Wife, 147, 149; Snelson *v.* Corbet, 3 Atk. 369; Howard *v.* Munifer, 5 Pike, 668; Ridout *v.* Earl of Plymouth, 2 Atk. 104.

7 1 Rolle, 911, L. 35, cited in Macq. Hus. & Wife, 147.

husband's death, and the ornaments and clothing of herself and children.[1]

If a husband pawn his wife's *paraphernalia* as collateral security for money borrowed, and give power to the lender to sell for a sum certain during his absence, this will not be deemed an absolute alienation, but shall stand as a pledge redeemable by the widow; and if the husband have left sufficient to redeem (after payment of all his debts) she is entitled to have the redemption money raised out of his personal estate.[2] But creditors must first be satisfied in all cases; though the widow's right in respect to such property, is superior to that of any legatee of the husband.[3]

Real estate is to be appropriated, in payment of the husband's debts after his death before the widow's paraphernal property can be held subject to the demands of his creditors. Such at least is the English practice; and where paraphernal property has been used up by the executor or administrator in satisfaction of specialty debts the widow is allowed, in equity, to stand in their stead to reimburse herself out of the real estate in possession of the heir.[4] In this country a summary sale of the husband's real estate, under direction of the probate court, is usually requisite, where the personal assets in the hands of his executor or administrator prove inadequate to meet the debts, whether by specialty or simple contract.

An English writer of excellent authority on this subject distinguishes between the case where the devised estate is subject to a charge or trust for the payment of debts from the case where the devised estate is *not* so subjected. In the

[1] See Mass. Gen. Sts. ch. 96, §§ 4, 5; Ginochio *v.* Porcella, 3 Bradf. Sur. 277.

[2] Graham *v.* Londonderry, 3 Atk. 393.

[3] Ib.; Tipping *v.* Tipping, 1 P. Wms. 729; Ridout *v.* Earl of Plymouth, 2 Atk. 104; Burton *v.* Pierpont, 2 P. Wms. 80. And even though contingent assets come to hand afterwards, the wife's claim is gone. Ib.

[4] Snelson *v.* Corbet, 3 Atk. 370; Aldrich *v.* Cooper, 8 Ves. 397; 2 Roper Hus. & Wife, 144; Macq. Hus. & Wife, 149. Probably in England, since the Statute 3 & 4 Will. 4, ch. 104, which makes lands of all kinds assets for the payment of debts, the lands are absolutely assets for satisfaction of the widow's claim. Bell Hus. & Wife, 215.

former case he holds the widow entitled to have the assets marshalled as against the devisee; but not in the latter case.[1] We find no authority to support this distinction. It would certainly trench closely upon her right to hold such property against all bequests of her husband to others; a right which is clearly admitted in the English courts.[2] A bequest from husband to wife of all the household goods, furniture, plate, jewels, and the like (including what in point of fact are *paraphernalia*) does not debar the widow from claiming her paraphernal property, as such, if she chooses to set up her lawful privilege as against her husband's bequest.[3]

Letters written to a wife by a former husband belong to her and not to his estate; and her own gift of them is valid as against the executor of such estate or her second husband.[4]

We have already observed that a wife may join with her husband in executing a mortgage of her real estate as security for his debts, and that, if this mortgage be properly foreclosed, and equities of redemption barred, her right to the real estate is gone.[5] Yet the courts have gone as far as they consistently could in upholding the wife's title under such circumstances. This is shown, in the first place, by favoring her right to the equity of redemption as against her husband; in the second place, by the allowance of exoneration or reimbursement from her husband's estate, after his death, where the assets prove sufficient for that purpose.

In general, therefore, it is construed in courts of equity, that the equity of redemption remains in the wife and her heirs. Accordingly, when the marriage is dissolved by the death of the husband, the widow, or her heirs after her, may put this equity in operation. It must therefore be quite manifest that a change of property was intended by the husband during his life before

[1] Note by Mr. Jacobs to 2 Roper Hus. & Wife, 145.

[2] 2 Bl. Com. 436, *supra*.

[3] Marshall *v.* Blew, 2 Atk. 217; *In re* Hewson, 23 E. L. & Eq. 283.

[4] Grigsby *v.* Breckenridge, 2 Bush, 480.

[5] See last chapter.

the widow can be excluded.[1] Thus, where an estate belonging to the wife was mortgaged, and the equity of redemption was in words reserved to the husband and his heirs, the court held that there was nevertheless a resulting trust for the wife and her heirs.[2] And the rule is general that where husband and wife mortgage the wife's estate, and the equity of redemption is reserved to the husband and his heirs, without recital of special circumstances to show an intention to make a new settlement of the estate, the husband has the equity of redemption only *jure uxoris*.[3] And in considering this question the mere form of the reservation of the equity of redemption will not of itself be held sufficient to alter the previous title. In such a case (where fraud is out of the question) it is supposed to arise from inaccuracy or mistake, which is to be explained and corrected by the state of the title as it was before the mortgage.[4]

But in the leading English case of *Jackson* v. *Innes*, which came before the House of Peers, on appeal from the decree of Lord Eldon in the Court of Chancery, the rule in the wife's favor was limited at this point. And it was decided after a full examination of the previous cases on the subject, that wherever the transaction, importing more than a mere mortgage security, gives satisfactory evidence of an intention to effect a change of the beneficial interest, the husband and his heirs, and not the widow or her heirs, will be entitled to the equity of redemption.[5] The learned opinion in this case was given by Lord Redesdale, and Lord Eldon subsequently admitted his own error in laying down a contrary doctrine. This case has since remained as the correct exposition of the English law on this subject. And it may be added, in the emphatic language of Lord Eldon on another occasion, "If it clearly appear to have

[1] Macq. Hus. & Wife, 172.
[2] Jackson *v.* Jones, 1 Bli. 115. And see Ruscombe *v.* Hare, 6 Dow, 1.
[3] Ruscombe *v.* Hare, 6 Dow, 1.
[4] Per Lord Redesdale, in Jackson *v.* Innes, 1 Bli. 115.
[5] Ib. See also Sir John Leach, in Reeve *v.* Hicks, 2 Sim. & Stu. 403.

been the intention of the wife that the husband should have the equity of redemption, he *must* have it."[1]

The wife has also the right in equity to have her estate exonerated out of her husband's personal and real assets. This is known as the wife's equity of exoneration. The principle is that the wife, when mortgaging her property for her husband's debt, stands in the position of a surety, and therefore may claim indemnity from the principal for whose benefit her security was interposed.[2] Lord Hardwicke has announced this rule with clearness and precision.[3] The husband's other creditors have no preference over the wife on marshalling the assets of her husband's estate; but she is entitled to the benefit of any securities, and to have satisfaction of her debt according to its rank. But the widow may waive her right of exoneration from the estate of her deceased husband, and her waiver will be inferred from circumstances.[4]

In this country, as we have seen, the wife is regarded as her husband's surety, and the presumptions are in her favor.[5] The rule as to her equity of redemption is doubtless quite as liberal as that laid down by Lord Redesdale in England. Perhaps it is more so, but authoritative cases on this point are wanting, and recent statutes affect the whole subject. In New York, the widow's right of exoneration is expressly admitted.[6]

[1] Ruscombe *v.* Hare, 6 Dow, 1. It is said that the case of Jackson *v.* Innes is the only marked instance in which a judgment of Lord Eldon's was ever reversed. And the generous candor with which the learned lawyer admitted his error serves as a memorable example to the courts of successive generations. To Lord Redesdale, whose politics kept him in comparative seclusion most of his life, though his professional reputation was great in his day, a most appropriate tribute is paid by Mr. Macqueen, in his excellent treatise, p. 180, note.

[2] Macq. Hus. & Wife, 181; Bell Hus. & Wife, 195; Wotton *v.* Hele, 2 Saund. 177; 1 Mod. 290.

[3] Robinson *v.* Gee, 1 Ves. Sen. 252, per Lord Hardwicke; Parteriche *v.* Powlet, 2 Atk. 384; and see Lord Thurlow in Clinton *v.* Hooper, 1 Ves. Jr. 186, to the same effect.

[4] Bell Hus. & Wife, 195; Clinton *v.* Hooper, 1 Ves. Jr. 188. But see Lancaster *v.* Evors, 10 Beav. 154.

[5] See as to husband's right of mortgage, *supra*.

[6] Vartie *v.* Underwood, 18 Barb. 561.

And in Indiana, the wife's rights as surety, are very strongly favored.[1]

The common-law obligation of the widow to bury her deceased husband rests upon weaker foundations than the corresponding obligation of the husband. In truth it seems somewhat inconsistent with the doctrine of coverture; for why, it may be asked, should a woman answer for the indigence of one whose lawful privilege it was to strip her of her own means of support? Where the husband leaves an estate, the funeral expenses are to be paid by his executor or administrator, and not by his widow. This is the rule both in England and America; and it is doubtless reasonable so far as it goes.[2] But in an English case, decided not many years ago, the court seemed to regard this subject somewhat differently, and intimated that husband and wife should stand upon a like footing, as regards the obligation of burying one another.[3] Here a widow, who was also an infant, was held bound by her contract for the expense of her husband's interment. The decision proceeded upon the ingenious doctrine, that, since a husband ought to bury his wife and lawful children, who are the *personæ conjunctæ* with him, as a matter of personal benefit to himself, the wife should do the same by her husband, as a benefit and comfort to herself; and therefore that the case came within the rule of law which makes a contract good where the infant is a gainer by it.[3]

Where a married woman contracts with authority from her husband and the husband dies suddenly, and in point of fact before certain purchases have been made on his credit, is his estate liable, or is his widow; or must the creditor bear the loss? The general rule undoubtedly is that the authority of an attorney or agent expires with the principal. A dead man can have no one acting by his name and authority. And since the wife contracts only as her husband's agent at the common

1 Philbrook *v.* McEwen, 29 Ind. 347.

2 2 Redf. Wills, 224; 2 Wms. Ex'rs, 871; Macq. Hus. & Wife, 183.

3 Chapple *v.* Cooper, 13 M. & W. 252.

law, her case would seem to fall within the general doctrine. Such in fact was the ruling of the court in *Blades* v. *Free*, where a man who had some years cohabited with a woman, who passed as his wife, left her and her family in England, and went into foreign parts where he died.[1] Here it was held that the executor was not bound to pay for necessaries supplied to her after his death, although before information of the event had reached her. In this case, however, there was only a *quasi* widow, and perhaps the court felt the stigma of an illicit cohabitation. But the precedent proved a stumbling-block in the next case of *Smout* v. *Ilberry*.[2] A man who has been in the habit of dealing with a butcher for meat supplied to his house, went abroad, and his wife who remained at home, continued the employment of the butcher. Here it was held that she was not personally liable for meat supplied after her husband's death, and purchased by her in good faith, supposing him to be still alive. The principle of the latter case seems to have been, that, although the authority had expired, yet the agent was not in fault, nor in the commission of any fraud; that the revocation occurred by act of God. But the loss had to fall somewhere; so the court put it upon the butcher. These seem to be the only cases of importance on this subject in England; and we find none in this country to shed further light. Yet questions of this sort must frequently arise in the dealings of people. The modern inclination is clearly to relax somewhat the rigid rule of the common law of agency, and to favor the Roman doctrine, which binds the principal or his estate in respect to acts done in good faith by his agent before notice of revocation.[3]

1 9 B. & Cr. 167; 4 Man. & Ry. 282.

2 10 M. & W. 1.

3 Story Agency, §§ 488, 497, and notes, in last edition. See Bradford, Surrogate of New York city, in Ginochio *v.* Porcella, 3 Bradf. Sur. 277, in which this subject is ably discussed, though the case in question, upon a close examination, appears to have decided little or nothing. This able lawyer evidently leans against the authority of Blades *v.* Free, though he expresses himself very guardedly. See also Macq. Hus. & Wife, 129, to the same purport.

It is held that where family necessaries are purchased and brought into the house during the last illness of the husband, and are used in part while he is sick and in part at his funeral, his estate is liable to the person who furnished them.[1]

[1] Sterling *v.* Potts, 2 South, 773.

CHAPTER IX.

THE WIFE'S DOWER AND HOMESTEAD RIGHTS.

WHILE marriage impresses at once the personal property of the wife with a new title, — namely, that of her husband, — the personal property of the husband remains unaffected thereby. He may buy, sell, and dispose of his own goods and chattels after marriage as before without let or hindrance from his wife. She cannot be said to acquire a title to his general personal property, actual or potential (independent of a gift or settlement), until her coverture has terminated. Then her rights are rather those of a widow than of a wife. But as to the husband's real estate, which in old times was the only property regarded at law as really of much consequence, the rule has always been otherwise. The husband's possible life-interest attached to the wife's lands whenever acquired by her; the wife's possible life-interest to the husband's lands whenever acquired by him. The husband's estate was known as curtesy, the wife's as dower. These estates had not, perhaps, the same origin: they certainly had not, in all respects, the same incidents; but both rights were known in England from a very early period, and both have remained with very little change down to a recent date in England and America. Each estate is in the nature of a possible encumbrance, and conveyancers seek to get rid of it whenever the owner of lands wishes to pass the title in fee to another. Dower, to be sure, gave the widow only a life-interest to the extent of one-third, while curtesy gave the surviving husband the full life-interest. But on the other hand, dower became absolute in the widow when she outlived her husband, while curtesy, as we have seen, never attached at all unless the husband outlived his wife and was fortunate enough to have had a child by her besides. So that in these respects the rights of husband and wife, if not equivalent, were nearly so.

Dower is to be defined as that provision which the law makes for a widow out of the lands or tenements of her husband.[1] It is said to be given for her support and the nurture of her children, but it applies, in fact, whenever she is the survivor, without reference to her actual circumstances. Dower extends to all estates of inheritance which the husband has held at any period of the coverture in his own right, and which any issue of hers might, if born, possibly inherit.

The word dower is of ancient origin, and seems to come from the word *dos* at the civil law, which, however, signified something quite different, more nearly approaching what we express by the term dowry. Whether the custom of dower was introduced into England by the Saxons, or came over with the Normans, is a disputed question; but it was clearly established at or before the reign of Henry III. An early writer remarks that "tenant in dower is so much favored as that it is the common byword of the law that the law favoreth three things: life, liberty, dower."[2] But these three things do not seem to have kept an equal pace in the march of civilization.

There were various kinds of dower at the English law, one only of which — namely, dower at common law — is in use in this country. Dower at common law extends to one-third of the husband's real estate, and is often known as the "widow's thirds," though of course inapplicable in this sense to her distributive share of personal property. Ancient customs varied the proportion somewhat in England; thus gavelkind gave one-half instead of one-third, and was limited to widowhood. The other species of dower were abolished by statute in Eng-

[1] Co. Litt. 30 *a*; 2 Bl. Com. 130; 1 Washb. Real Prop. 146.

[2] Bac. Law Tracts, 331. See 1 Washb. Real Prop. 147; Wright Ten. 191; Co. 2d Inst. 16; 2 Bl. Com. 129; 1 Cruise Dig. 152.

land, in the time of Charles II., after having previously fallen into general disuse.[1]

The magna charta of Henry III., which established and defined the rule of dower for future guidance, besides relieving the widow of certain burdens imposed upon heirs at the feudal law, distinctly set forth the proportion of which she should be endowed in her husband's lands, and further provided that she might tarry forty days after her husband's death in her husband's house.[2] This last privilege has been since known as the widow's *quarantine*, and has been recognized by statute law in some of the United States.[3] It was designed manifestly as something preliminary to the assignment of dower.

Dower attaches to all lands, tenements, or hereditaments, corporeal and incorporeal, of which the husband may have been seised in fee or in tail.[4] But the husband's estate must have been one of inheritance, since the wife's estate is said to be a mere continuance of the estate of her husband. Very nice questions have arisen as to what constitutes an estate of inheritance. Thus where a husband has a life-estate with fee-simple in the heirs of his body, his wife cannot claim dower.[5] Nor can she claim, even though he holds an estate for another's life and dies before the *cestui que vie*.[6]

The three essentials of dower nearly correspond with those of curtesy: though birth of issue is not requisite. They are marriage, seisin of the husband, and his death.[7] But a careful comparison of the two estates shows some inequalities: thus while the husband might have curtesy in the wife's trust

1 Stat. 12 Car. 2, c. 24. See 1 Washb. Real Prop. 149, and 2 Bl. Com. 133, as to these ancient kinds of dower; dower *ad ostium ecclesiæ*, dower *ex assensu patris*, and dower *de la plus belle*.

2 2 Bl. Com. 135.

3 Mass. Gen. Stats. ch. 96, §§ 4, 5.

4 2 Bl. Com. 131; 1 Washb. Real Prop. 152.

5 Burris *v.* Page, 12 Mis. 358; 1 Washb. Real Prop. 152.

6 1 Washb. Real Prop. 153; Park. Dower, 48; Gillis *v.* Brown, 5 Cow. 388; Fisher *v.* Grimes, 1 S. & M. Ch. 107; 2 Bl. Com. 129.

7 See 1 Washb. Real Prop. 162 *et seq.* and cases cited; Scrib. Dower; Park. Dower, for a full description of the nature and incidents of dower.

property, the wife could not claim dower from that of her husband. This injustice grew out of an apparent necessity: it was remedied in England by the late dower act, and apparently never had a firm foothold in the United States.[1]

Manifestly in ancient theory the widow's dower was an independent and valuable interest. But in England, through the medium of trusts and the operation of the doctrine just noticed, the conveyancers for generations have been enabled to defeat this estate. The late English Dower Act, 3 & 4 Will. IV. ch. 105, while it places dower and curtesy on a like favorable footing as to trust estates, provides further that no widow shall be entitled to dower "out of any land which shall have been absolutely disposed of by her husband in his lifetime or by his will." [2] Little, therefore, is left for the law to operate upon; for the husband, by his independent act, may now extinguish all dower encumbrances whatsoever.

Jointures, a species of provision in lieu of dower, are little known at the present day in England; nor were they ever of much importance in this country.[3]

While the law of dower has been gradually fading out of sight in England, it attains its fuller development in this country. Curiously enough, most of the modern cases on this subject are American.[4] Our local statutes have very generally favored the widow's rights, and unless she has joined her husband in his conveyances during his life, she may assert the privilege at his death. But dower is found a great inconvenience in an age when real estate passes from hand to hand as an article of commercial traffic; and legislatures show some disposition to get rid of it altogether, together with curtesy. In

[1] 1 Washb. Real Prop. 163 and cases cited; Stat. 3 & 4 Wm. 4, ch. 105.

[2] Wms. Real Prop. 194; 1 Washb. Real Prop. 219; Macq. Hus. & Wife, 165. The English dower act went into effect in 1834.

[3] See Wms. Real Prop. 217 notes; 1 Washb. Real Prop. 261–274.

[4] 1 Washb. Real Prop. 257, 258; 2 Crabb Real Prop. 154, 155; Hoffman *v.* Savage, 15 Mass. 130; Symmes *v.* Drew, 21 Pick. 278; Childs *v.* Smith, 1 Md. Ch. 483; Crockett *v.* Crockett, 2 Ohio St. 180; Park. Dower, 355; 1 Washb. Real Prop. 168.

New York, the widow can only claim her dower out of lands of which her husband died seised.[1] In some States her interest is treated as something for the benefit of herself and children jointly. In others, the "thirds" are dispensed with, and a different rate is fixed. And finally, the State of Indiana has set a good example by abolishing both curtesy and dower, and substituting in behalf of husband and wife an interest in one another's real estate, remaining at decease, on principles analogous to the distribution of personal property of intestates; thus placing both sexes on the mutual footing of justice, and treating lands and personal estate as subject to analogous rules.[2]

The homestead may properly be considered in connection with dower; for although this right is not strictly personal to married women, inasmuch as it exists for the benefit of both wife and children, it is an encumbrance upon the real estate of the husband which is generally released by the wife in connection with her dower. The homestead system is of recent origin, is peculiar to our American States, and exists for protection against the husband's creditors. The policy on which it rests, by no means a new one in our legislation, is that a householder with a family shall always have a place of shelter where legal process cannot reach him. While open to some serious objections, as concerns the rights of creditors, the homestead system is to be warmly commended in respect of the encouragement it affords to agriculture, and still more as offering rewards to domestic fidelity.[3]

[1] N. Y. Stats. 1860, March 20.

[2] 1 Ind. Sts. (1862) 291 *et seq.* And see 1 Washb. Real Prop. 219 and notes; 4 Kent Com. 36, and statutory changes in notes.

[3] See 1 Washb. Real Prop. 3d ed. 325 *et seq.*, where this system is detailed.

CHAPTER X.

THE WIFE'S SEPARATE ESTATE; ENGLISH DOCTRINE.

EMERGING from coverture and the common law, we come out into the light of equity; and here all things assume a new aspect. The married woman is no longer buried under legal fictions. She ceases to hold the strange position of a being without an existence, one whose identity is suspended or sunk in the *status* of her husband; she becomes a distinct person, with her own property rights and liabilities. Her condition is not as independent as before marriage; this the very idea of the marriage relation and the disabilities of her sex forbid. But she is dependent only so far as the several laws of nature and the forms of society make her so; while her comparative feebleness renders her the special object of chancery protection, whenever the interests of herself and her husband clash together. She may contract on her own behalf; she may sue and be sued in her own name; she may hold lands, goods, and chattels in her own right, and this property is known as the wife's separate estate, or estate limited to her separate use.

The doctrine of the wife's separate estate originated in the spreading conviction that it was expedient for the interests of society that means should exist by which, upon marriage, either the parties themselves by contract, or those who intended to give bounty to a family, might secure property without that property being subject to the control of the husband.[1] In England, this doctrine was established more than a century ago, and to the equity courts belong the credit of the invention.[2]

[1] Rennie *v.* Ritchie, 12 Cl. & Fin. 234; Peachey Mar. Settl. 259.

[2] Harvey *v.* Harvey, 1 P. Wms. 124; Woodmeston *v.* Walker, 2 R. & M. 205; Tullett *v.* Armstrong, 1 Beav. 21.

While at common law the separate existence of the wife was neither known nor contemplated, equity considered that a married woman was capable of possessing property to her own use, independently of her husband, and the courts gradually widened and developed this principle, until it became fully settled that, however the wife's property might be acquired, whether through contract with her husband before marriage, or by gift from him or from any stranger independently of such contract, equity would protect it, if duly set apart as her separate estate, no matter though the husband himself must be held as the trustee to support it.[1]

This great change in the jurisprudence of England was effected by a few great men without any help from the legislature. The Court of Chancery in this as in other respects recognized its true function of making the law work justice, by accommodating its operation to the altered circumstances of society.[2] Obscure and doubtful indications of the wife's separate estate are found as early as the reign of Queen Elizabeth. It seems to have been plainly recognized by Lord Nottingham, Lord Somers, and Lord Cowper. In Lord Hardwicke's time it was perfectly established; and Lord Thurlow, in sanctioning the clause against anticipation, prevented the wife herself from destroying the fabric which had been reared for her benefit.[3]

Where property comes to the wife's separate use, it is treated in equity as trust estate of which she is *cestui que trust*. But it is not actually necessary that the instrument constituting the separate use should itself make an appointment of trustees. Formerly the rule was otherwise; but at the present day equity makes the husband a trustee and thus supports the trust.[4] And where a trustee, regularly appointed, in breach of his duty, and

[1] Tullett *v.* Armstrong, 1 Beav. 21; Peachey Mar. Settl. 260 and cases cited.

[2] Macq. Hus. & Wife, 284.

[3] See Pybus *v.* Smith, 4 Bro. C. C. 485; Tullett *v.* Armstrong, per Lord Langdale, 1 Beav. 22; Macq. Hus. & Wife, 285.

[4] Bennett *v.* Davis, 2 P. Wms. 316; Davison *v.* Atkison, 5 T. R. 435; Messenger *v.* Clarke, 5 Exch. 393; Peachey Mar. Settl. 260; Macq. Hus. & Wife,

without the privity of the wife, pays the trust-money over to the husband, equity follows the money into the husband's hands, and makes him likewise accountable as his wife's trustee.[1] It impresses a trust upon the wife's separate estate wherever such estate may be found. But while the appointment of trustees is not essential to give the wife a separate estate, or a separate interest in any particular estate, it is certainly desirable on many accounts, and there is in it this marked advantage, that the property is made thereby more secure, because such influence of the husband over the wife is prevented as might induce her to abandon the property to him.[2]

Prima facie, the legal ownership of property which is in his wife at the time of marriage, or comes to her during coverture, vests in the husband, under his marital right. It is therefore necessary that the intention to establish a separate use be clearly manifested; else courts of equity will not interpose against him. No technical formalities or expressions are required; but the purpose must appear beyond the reach of reasonable controversy, in order to entitle the wife to claim the property as her own in derogation of the common law.[3]

As to the words which in themselves indicate the intention of creating a separate use, there have been numerous decisions. Among them the following are held sufficient. "For her full and sole use and benefit."[4] "For her own sole use and benefit."[5] "For her sole use."[6] "For her sole and separate use and benefit."[7] "For her sole and separate use."[8] "For her

[1] Rich *v.* Cockle, 9 Ves. 375. See also Izod *v.* Lamb, 1 Cr. & J. 35.

[2] Newland *v.* Paynter, 10 Sim. 377; s. c. on Appeal, 4 M. & Cr. 408; Humphrey *v.* Richards, 25 L. J. Eq. 444; s. c. 2 Jur. 433; Peachey Mar. Settl. 260; Macq. Hus. & Wife, 291.

[3] Macq. Hus. & Wife, 307; Tyler *v.* Lake, 2 Russ. & M. 183; Kensington *v.* Dollond, 2 M. & K. 184; Moore *v.* Morris, 4 Drew. 37; Peachey Mar. Settl. 279.

[4] Arthur *v.* Arthur, 11 Ir. Eq. 511.

[5] *Ex parte* Killick, 3 Mon. D. & De G. 480.

[6] Lindsell *v.* Thacker, 12 Sim. 178.

[7] Archer *v.* Rorke, 7 Ir. Eq. 478.

[8] Parker *v.* Brooke, 9 Ves. 583; Adamson *v.* Armitage, 19 Ves. 415.

sole use and benefit."[1] "For her own sole use, benefit, and disposition."[2] "For her sole and absolute use."[3] "For her own use, and at her own disposal."[4] "To be at her disposal, and to do therewith as she shall think fit."[5] "Solely and entirely for her own use and benefit."[6] "For her own use, independent of any husband."[7] "Not subjected to the control of her husband."[8] "For her own use and benefit, independent of any other person."[9] "For her livelihood."[10]

So, too, the intention of excluding the husband's marital rights, may be inferred from the nature of the provisions attached to the gift, as where, for example, the direction is that the property shall be at the wife's disposal, or there is some other clear indication that such was the donor's intention.[11] Lord Thurlow once decided that a direction "that the interest and profits be paid to her, and the principal to her or to her order by note, or writing under her hand," created a trust for the wife's separate use.[12] So in the judgment of Sir William Fortescue, Master of the Rolls, did the words "that she should enjoy and receive the issues and profits of the estate."[13] And Lord Loughborough gave a like effect to a direction that certain property should be delivered up to a married woman, "whenever she should demand or require the same."[14] A similar construction has also been applied to the words, "to be

[1] —— v. Lyne, Younge, 562.

[2] *Ex parte* Ray, 1 Mad. 199.

[3] Davis v. Prout, 7 Beav. 288.

[4] Prichard v. Ames, Turn. & Russ. 222.

[5] Kirk v. Paulin, 9 Vin. Abr. 96, pl. 43.

[6] Inglefield v. Coghlan, 2 Coll. 247.

[7] Wagstaff v. Smith, 9 Ves. 520.

[8] Bain v. Lescher, 11 Sim. 397.

[9] Margetts v. Barringer, 7 Sim. 482.

[10] Darley v. Darley, 3 Atk. 399. And see Peachey Mar. Settl. 279, 280; Macq. Hus. & Wife, 308, 309.

[11] Prichard v. Ames, Turn. & Russ. 223; Peachey Mar. Settl. 279.

[12] Hulme v. Tenant, 1 Br. C. C. 16.

[13] Tyrrell v. Hope, 2 Atk. 561. "For to what end should she receive it," says this judge, "if it is the property of the husband the next moment?"

[14] Dixon v. Olmius, 2 Cox, 414.

laid out in what she (the wife) shall think fit."[1] And in Lee *v.* Prieaux, a legacy to a married woman, "her receipt to be a sufficient discharge to the executors," was held sufficient.[2] A legacy added by a codicil to the legacy given by a will is subject to the incidents of the original legacy; and the separate use may be extended by construction from the will to the codicil.[3]

Yet, on the other hand, the form of expression will go far towards determining whether property is or is not limited to the wife's separate use. Vice-Chanceller Wigram, in a case before him not many years ago, was forced to admit that while ruling out certain property, from the wife's separate use, on account of the testator's insufficient language, he had a strong opinion that he decided against the real intention of the testator.[4] It is to be observed, then, that courts of equity will not deprive the husband of his rights at law, unless the words of themselves leave no doubt of the intention to exclude him.[5] A mere trust therefore to pay the income of a fund to a married woman, and her assigns, is not sufficient to prevent the marital rights from attaching.[6] Even a gift to a wife "for her use," has been held not a sufficiently unequivocal declaration of an intention to create a trust for the separate use of the wife.[7] Some words have greater efficacy than others. Thus it has been said that the word "enjoy" is very strong to imply a separate use.[8] And much controversy has arisen in the English chancery courts over the use of the word "own" as synonymous with "sole," the result of which is to establish that

1 Atcherley *v.* Vernon, 10 Mod. 518. See Blacklow *v.* Laws, 2 Hare, 52.

2 Warwick *v.* Hawkins, 13 E. L. & Eq. 174.

3 Day *v.* Croft, 4 Beav. 561.

4 Blacklow *v.* Laws, 2 Hare, 49.

5 Peachey Mar. Settl. 281; Tyler *v.* Lake, 2 Russ. & M. 188; Massey *v.* Parker, 2 M. & K. 181; Macq. Hus. & Wife, 309.

6 Lumb *v.* Milnes, 5 Ves. 517.

7 Jacobs *v.* Amyatt, 1 Mad. 376 *n.*; Wills *v.* Sayers, 4 Mad. 411; Roberts *v.* Spicer, 5 Mad. 491.

8 Sir Wm. Fortescue in Tyrrell *v.* Hope, 2 Atk. 558.

there is a substantial distinction between a gift to a wife, "for her sole use," and a gift "for her own use," or "for her own use and benefit."[1] And it having been decided that the word "own" had no exclusive meaning, it was next determined that a trust to pay the proceeds of real estate into the proper hands of a married woman for her own use and benefit was not a gift to the wife's separate use, the word "proper" being the Latin form of the word "own," and therefore payment into the wife's proper hands, signifying the same thing, as into her own hands.[2] Lord Brougham, thus in effect overruled a decision of Lord Alvanley, who had held that the use of the word "proper" would create a separate use.[3] This later construction, coming from a jurisdiction so conclusive, has since prevailed, though not without some expressions of dissatisfaction in the lower courts.[4] And again, language of the donor, expressive of his intent to limit property to the wife's separate use, may be controlled by other words or provisions so as to negative such a supposition. This principle was applied to the wife's disadvantage, in a case where others were made the objects of the bounty with her.[5] Yet it has been held that a gift to the wife's separate use was good, although the support and education of children was annexed as a charge upon it.[6]

Whether the word "sole" is of itself sufficient to create a separate use is doubtful. Different opinions have been expressed on this point. But in a recent case before Vice-Chancellor Kindersley, the word "sole" was deemed insufficient, in a devise of property to a female, her heirs, executors, ad-

1 See Lord Brougham's judgment in Tyler *v.* Lake, 2 Russ. & M. 187; Johnes *v.* Lockhart, 3 Br. C. C. 383 *n.*; Peachey Mar. Settl. 282.

2 Tyler *v.* Lake, 2 Russ. & M. 187.

3 Hartley *v.* Hurle, 5 Ves. 545.

4 See Vice-Chancellor Wigram, in Blacklow *v.* Laws, 2 Hare, 49; Macq. Hus. & Wife, 309; Peachey Mar. Settl. 282.

5 Wardle *v.* Claxton, 9 Sim. 524. And see Gilchrist *v.* Cator, 1 De G. & S. 188.

6 Cape *v.* Cape, 2 You. & Coll. Exch. 543. And see note to Macq. Hus. & Wife, 310.

ministrators, and assigns, "for her and their own sole and absolute use and benefit," to create a separate estate; since the word "sole," as here used, had reference not only to the female herself, but to her heirs, executors, administrators, and assigns, who certainly could not be considered beneficiaries under any such trust.[1]

A gift of the produce of a fund, is to be considered a gift of that produce in perpetuity; hence, it is a gift of the fund itself, nothing appearing to show a different intention. Therefore a bequest of a fund to a woman, with the interest thereon, to be vested in trustees, — the income arising therefrom to be for her separate use and benefit, — vests the capital for her separate use.[2] Where a testator simply directs the investment of a fund in trustees, for the benefit of a married woman, independent of the control of her husband, this is enough to carry the whole fund to her separate use.[3] So it is held that where stock was given to trustees upon trust, to pay the dividends to a married woman for her separate use, and there was no limitation of a life-interest, an absolute interest in the capital passed to her, of which she could dispose as a *feme sole*.[4]

It is fair to suppose that in equity, the wife's separate use binds the produce of the fund, as well as the fund itself. There are some cases decided in the courts of common law, where the contrary has been maintained, and to this effect, that, although a wife may be entitled to separate property, the dividends arising therefrom vest in her husband.[5] This is no reason, however, why the equity doctrine should not be as we have stated; indeed, if it were otherwise, as an English writer

[1] Lewis *v.* Mathews, Law Rep. 2 Eq. 177. And see Troutbeck *v.* Boughey, Law Rep. 2 Eq. 534. See also as to property to husband and another in trust, *Ex parte* Beilby, 1 Glyn & Jam. 167; note to Peachey Mar. Settl. 283.

[2] Adamson *v.* Armitage, 19 Ves. 416; Macq. Hus. & Wife, 311; Troutbeck *v.* Boughey, Law Rep. 2 Eq. 534.

[3] Simons *v.* Howard, 1 Keen, 7, per Lord Langdale.

[4] Elton *v.* Shephard, 1 Bro. C. C. 532; Haig *v.* Swiney, 1 Sim. & Stu. 487.

[5] Tugman *v.* Hopkins, 4 Man. & Gr. 389; Carne *v.* Brice, 7 M. & W. 183.

has observed, the object of separate use would be in many instances frustrated.[1]

The quality of separate estate ceases on the death of the wife; and if her husband survives her, he becomes entitled to the property as though it had never been settled to her separate use. For the separate use was created only for the marriage state, and was not designed to extend beyond the dissolution of marriage, or when the necessity of the trust should be no longer felt. Thus *choses in possession* settled to the wife's separate use vest in the husband absolutely upon his survivorship.[2] The wife's separate *choses in action* may be recovered by him in his right, as her administrator.[3] So, doubtless, her separate chattels real go to the husband as survivor. In short, the wife's separate property upon the wife's death is freed from its peculiar incidents, and becomes like any other estate of hers, which may remain at her decease.[4] And it seems clear that the husband may be tenant by the curtesy, as usual if not expressly excluded from all marital interest.[5]

Yet the wife may defeat her husband's claim after her death by exercising her power of disposition during her lifetime; a power which is recognized in a married woman so far as her separate property is concerned.[6] So too by the terms of the trust the husband's rights may be prevented from attaching. Thus, where a wife entitled to separate property for life, under a settlement which directed that all the trust property and all the

[1] See Macq. Hus. & Wife, 291 and note. And see *dictum* of Sir Lancelot Shadwell in Molony *v.* Kennedy, 10 Sim. 254 (quoted ib.), which intimates that this is the equity doctrine; per Lord Hardwicke, Churchill *v.* Dibbin, 9 Sim. 447, *note.* *Contra,* Peachey Mar. Settl. 263, where cases are cited which do not support the statement in the text.

[2] Molony *v.* Kennedy, 10 Sim. 254.

[3] Proudley *v.* Fielder, 2 Myl. & K. 57; Drury *v.* Scott, 4 You. & Coll. Ch. 264; Stead *v.* Clay, 1 Sim. 294.

[4] Macq. Hus. & Wife, 285; Peachey Mar. Settl. 278; Sloper *v.* Cottrell, 6 El. & Bl. 501; Bird *v.* Pegrum, 13 C. B. 650; s. c. 17 Jur. 579.

[5] Lushington *v.* Sewell, 1 Sim. 548; Roberts *v.* Dixwell, 1 Atk. 606, per Lord Hardwicke; Macq. Hus. & Wife, 287. See *infra* p. 196.

[6] Macq. Hus. & Wife, 285.

income thereof "remaining unapplied" at her death should go in a certain manner, left her husband some years before her death; and the trustees received the income regularly and paid it into a bank in their own names, with her privity, making remittances to her as she required money; and upon the wife's death the sum of £888 was found among her effects, and a balance of £2,049 accumulated income stood to the credit of the trustees in the bank; it was held by the Vice Chancellor of England that the former went to the surviving husband by virtue of his marital right, while the latter was bound by the trusts of the deed as the result of income "remaining unapplied" at her death.[1]

Since the separate use can exist only in the married state, it may sometimes have an ambulatory operation; so as to be effectual according as the woman happens at the time to be covert or sole. Supposing, then, a gift be made to the separate use of a woman who is single at the time the gift takes effect; it is clear that she shall enjoy the gift absolutely and without restraint. But if she afterwards marries will the separate use operate? It will, unless by the terms of her marriage settlement she expressly renounces it.[2] Supposing, however, she outlives her husband, the separate use ceases as in other cases; since it can only be effectual during coverture. But if she marries again the separate use revives once more; and so onwards, from time to time, ceasing and reviving alternately, upon each alteration of her personal condition.[3]

A single woman, having a gift expressed to be to her separate use, may renounce such separate use upon her marriage. This will be readily admitted. Yet the courts construe an act of this

[1] Johnstone *v.* Lumb, 15 Sim. 308. As to the wife's rights over money not the savings of her separate estate, see Barrack *v.* McCulloch, 3 Kay & Johns. 114; Brooke *v.* Brooke, 4 Jur. N. S. 472; Peachey Mar. Settl. 262. But see Messenger *v.* Clarke, 5 Exch. 388, for the doctrine at law.

[2] Tullett *v.* Armstrong, 1 Beav. 1; Anderson *v.* Anderson, 2 Myl. & K. 427; Macq. Hus. & Wife, 305.

[3] Macq. Hus. & Wife, 306; Tullett *v.* Armstrong, 1 Beav. 1, affirmed by Lord Cottenham, 4 Myl. & Cr. 377.

sort strictly.[1] The evidence must be clear in all cases, that a single woman marrying has renounced her separate use; for it will not be presumed that she means, by the mere fact of matrimony, to relinquish her control of the property. But antenuptial settlements may be made on reasonable terms by the parties contemplating marriage. And there is nothing to prevent the operation of a trust for separate use from being confined to a particular coverture, where all concerned are so minded. In such cases, however, the wife marrying again can always stipulate for her separate use.[2]

The husband is entitled to curtesy in an equitable fee settled to his wife's separate use.[3]

It would appear to be the English doctrine that the marital obligations of the husband are not essentially altered by her right to separate property. Thus, it is held that the wife is not bound to maintain her husband out of her separate fortune, nor to bring any part of it into contribution for family purposes.[4] And there seems to be no legal authority to support the notion that the husband's liabilities on her general debts are thereby altered during their joint lives.[5] But it is held that the separate estate of a married woman is after her death a trust for the payment of her debts.[6] The common-law liabilities of the husband, to be sure, rest in great measure upon his right to his wife's property; yet it would be difficult to adjust any new rule except upon partnership principles. If one marries a rich wife, therefore, who chooses to hoard her savings by herself, bequeath all to others, and compel him, a poor man, to pay for every thing she or the children need, all their lives; and her general debts besides, it is possible that even equity will deny him relief.

1 Johnson *v.* Johnson, 1 Keen, 648; Macq. Hus. & Wife, 306. See Marriage Settlements of Infants, *post.*

2 Macq. Hus. & Wife, 307. See Knight *v.* Knight, 6 Sim. 121; Bradley *v.* Hughes, 8 Sim. 149; Benson *v.* Benson, 6 Sim. 126.

3 Appleton *v.* Rowley, Law Rep. 8 Eq. 139. But see Moore *v.* Webster, Law Rep. 3 Eq. 267.

4 Lamb *v.* Milnes, 5 Ves. 520.

5 See Macq. Hus. & Wife, 288. But see as to antenuptial debts, *infra.*

6 2 Story Eq. Jur. § 1398, *n.*; Norton *v.* Turrill, 2 P. Wms. 144.

Moreover the wife is not bound to maintain, educate, or provide for her children out of her separate property; and even though she elope from her husband, equity will not lay hold of her estate for that purpose. This is a settled point in England, unless the legislature shall change the law hereafter; for the House of Lords so decided in *Hodgden* v. *Hodgden*, on appeal from the lower court of chancery, and under the advice of Lord-Chancellor Cottenham.[1] And yet whenever a settlement of the wife's equity is decreed, where the husband or his legal representative seeks to recover her *choses in action*, the children of the marriage are included within its benefits; though, to be sure, the wife may waive the claim altogether without reference to them.[2]

It is possible that a provision for the wife's separate use may fail, as against third parties purchasers, wherever the husband can dispose of the property without their having notice of the trust.[3]

The clause of restraint upon anticipation is an important element in the doctrine of the wife's separate use, as administered in England. This clause was sanctioned by Lord Thurlow;[4] is frequently to be met with in modern conveyances; and is pronounced by Mr. Macqueen, and such as he chooses to denominate "the wise," a salutary clause which takes from the wife the power of bringing ruin upon herself; though it is manifestly in form a fetter upon the trust estate, while the wisdom of its establishment in any case depends upon the folly of the beneficiary.[5] With a perfect liberty of disposal, the danger arose that the wife might be persuaded to part with, or charge her separate property, even against her better judgment, through

1 4 Cl. & Fin. 323, reversing the decree of the court below.

2 See *supra*, chapter 5, the wife's equity to a settlement.

3 Parker *v.* Brooke, 9 Ves. 583 ; Macq. Hus. & Wife, 291.

4 Miss Watson's Case. See Pybus *v.* Smith, 3 Br. C. C. 340 *n*. This doctrine was afterwards affirmed in Jackson *v.* Hobhouse, 2 Mer. 487, by Lord Eldon.

5 See Macq. Hus. & Wife, 312.

the secret and subtle influences which her husband might bring to bear upon her. But by the clause against anticipation, the wife's hands are tied up; she has not the power of alienating or encumbering the property; and the donor can place his gift beyond the possibility of matrimonial contention. The restraint upon anticipation extends even to landed property, notwithstanding the common-law methods by which the wife may ordinarily alienate and encumber such estate; so that a person may now devise lands to a married woman in fee-simple in such a manner as to disable her during coverture from making any sale, mortgage, charge, or encumbrance whatever to take effect against it.[1]

The name of this important clause originates in the circumstances under which it was first applied.[2] The general purport of this expression is that the wife shall be prohibited the anticipation of the income of her separate property or the anticipation of the capital of the fund. Yet the word "anticipation" need not be used in clauses of this sort, nor is any particular form of expression necessary.[3]

Like the separate use itself, this clause of restraint on anticipation exists only in the marriage state; and property vested in a single woman she may dispose of absolutely, despite such limitation, so long as she remains unmarried; but upon her coverture, while retaining such property, the separate use and the restraint upon anticipation attach and become effective

[1] Bagget *v.* Meux, 1 Phil. 627, per Lord Lyndhurst; 1 Coll. 138; Macq. Hus. & Wife, 312; Peachey Mar. Settl. 284.

[2] See Pybus *v.* Smith, 3 Br. C. C. 340; Jodrell *v.* Jodrell, 9 Beav. 59.

[3] Per Lord Cranworth, *In re* Ross's Trust, 1 Sim. 199; Doolan *v.* Blake, 3 Ir. Ch. 349; Peachey Mar. Settl. 287. See further, Moore *v.* Moore, 1 Coll. 57; Tullett *v.* Armstrong. 1 Beav. 1; Macq. Hus. & Wife, 314, note; Steedman *v.* Poole, 6 Hare, 193; Parkes *v.* White, 11 Ves. 222; Clark *v.* Pister, 3 Br. C. C. 346, cited in Pybus *v.* Smith; Barrymore *v.* Ellis, 8 Sim. 1; Brown *v.* Bamford, 1 Phil. 620; Field *v.* Evans, 15 Sim. 375; Baker *v.* Bradley, 2 Jur. N. S. 104; Peachey Mar. Settl. 287, 288, and cases cited; Harrop *v.* Howard, 3 Hare, 624; Harnett *v.* M'Dougall, 8 Beav. 187; Acton *v.* White, 1 Sim. & Stu. 429.

together, cease together upon her widowhood, and revive together upon her re-marriage.[1]

But the restraint on anticipation does not exempt a married woman from the ordinary consequences of lapse of time and acquiescence. That fetter upon alienation was imposed for her protection against her husband, but was not intended to exonerate her from the obligation of asserting her claim within a reasonable period. Indeed, it is but reasonable that, as a court of equity creates and models the separate estate, the estate so created and modelled should be subject to the ordinary rules of the court.[2] Nor can the court mould at will the fetter imposed upon alienation, though the language used by some of the earlier judges would seem to indicate otherwise; moreover, though the power to impose restraint on anticipation is a mere creature of the court, the restraint itself is always imposed by the author, the settlor of the gift.[3]

As a wife is only made a party to a suit instituted by her husband on the alleged ground of her having separate estate in regard to which she is a *feme sole*, the husband, by making her a party, admits it to be her separate estate.[4]

Although the wife's separate use is the creature of equity, and specially consigned to its watchful keeping, courts of law will sometimes afford it protection. This seems to be, however, only in cases where a trustee is interposed to hold the legal estate; for, since the common-law courts maintain their own maxims, there should be some person designated to hold the fund for the wife; and such person will be considered as the legal owner so as to save the property from attachment and sale for the husband's debts.[5]

1 Tullett *v.* Armstrong, 1 Beav. 1; 4 Myl. & Cr. 377; Macq. Hus. & Wife, 313; Clarke *v.* Jaques, 1 Beav. 36; Dixon *v.* Dixon, 1 Beav. 40.

2 Derbishire *v.* Home, 3 De G., M. & G. 113.

3 Robinson *v.* Wheelwright, 21 Beav. 220; S. C. on appeal, 6 De G., M. & G. 535; 2 Jur. N. S. 554. See Peachey Mar. Settl. 289; Fitzgibbon *v.* Blake, 3 Ir. Ch. 328.

4 Earl *v.* Ferris, 19 Beav. 69.

5 See Izod *v.* Lamb, 1 Cr. & J. 35; Davison *v.* Atkinson, 5 T. R. 434; Dean *v.* Brown, 2 Car. & P. 62; Macq. Hus. & Wife, 291.

CHAPTER XI.

THE WIFE'S SEPARATE ESTATE; AMERICAN DOCTRINE.

THE doctrine of the wife's separate estate is one of peculiar growth and development in this country, though doubtless originating in the maxims of the English Chancery, and deriving much of its strength from the splendid accomplishments of Langdale, Thurlow, and Eldon, in their own land. What such men and their successors effected by judicial policy, we have carried into our statutes; nay, we have gone further. In England, the equitable rights of married women are the triumph of the bench; with us the early efforts of the bench have been eclipsed by the later achievements of the legislature, and the judge follows the law-giver to restrain rather than enlarge.

When this country was first settled, the separate use was but little understood in England. Its development there was gradual, and its final establishment of a later date. Our ancestors brought over the common law with them; but for equity they had little respect. True, it cannot be said that by the jurisprudence of a single State, property bestowed upon a married woman to her separate use, free from the control and interference of her husband, would remain subject, notwithstanding, to his marital dominion; but prior to the late married women's acts there were, in many parts of this country, no judicial precedents to combat such a doctrine. That such trusts might be created was not denied; but whether there were courts with authority to enforce them appeared frequently doubtful.[1]

[1] It is true that the general recognition of the wife's separate use has been presumed by our text-writers. See 2 Kent Com. 162; Reeve Dom. Rel. 162; 2 Story Eq. Juris. § 1378 *et seq.* We confine our observation to judicial precedents. What Chancellor Kent has to say on the American equity doctrines

In the New-England States, scarcely a vestige of the separate use was to be found.[1] New York, with such eminent chancellors as Kent and Walworth, took the lead in building up an equity system parallel with that of England; and in the reports of this State are to be found most of the leading cases and the ablest discussions of what may be termed American chancery doctrines. New Jersey recognized the separate use, and her chancery court exercised liberal powers. In Pennsylvania, the doctrine was recognized to some extent. The courts of Maryland, Virginia and the Southern States generally, had frequent occasion to apply the separate-use doctrine; none more so than those of North and South Carolina. And it may be remarked that the aristocratic element of society in that section of the country, also the prevalent disposition for family entails, marriage settlements, and fetters upon the transmission of landed property, aided much in developing therein the English system. So was it in Kentucky and Tennessee, States founded upon like institutions. But as to Ohio, Indiana, Illinois, and the other states erected from what was formerly known as the North-west Territory, society was modelled more after New England, and we find no clear recognition of the wife's equitable separate use. Louisiana, and such contiguous States as were originally governed by French and Spanish laws, had more or less of the civil or community system; and to these States English equity maxims had at best only a limited application. Such, then, is the wife's separate use, viewed in the light of judicial precedents, as known in the United States up to a quarter of a century ago.[2]

in his work must be taken by the general student with some qualifications, inasmuch as the learned writer draws largely upon his judicial opinions, in a State which especially favored chancery jurisprudence. The want of a general recognition of the wife's separate use, as unfolded in England, explains the curious fact that our States were legislated into a system which the English chancery had felt competent to rear unaided.

[1] But see Pinney *v.* Fellows, 15 Vt. 525 (1843).

[2] See U. S. Eq. Dig. Husband & Wife, 12; Reade *v.* Livingston, 3 Johns. Ch. 481; Meth. Ep. Church *v.* Jaques, 1 Johns. Ch. 65; Rogers *v.* Rogers, 4 Paige,

But where recognized and enforced at all, the strict American rule was borrowed from that of England. Thus it has been frequently said that the wife's separate estate requires no trustee to sustain it.[1] For when no other trustee is interposed the courts of chancery are prepared to treat the husband as such.[2]

So, too, an intention clearly manifested to create a separate estate has always been deemed necessary in our courts, in order to exclude the husband's marital rights. The mere intervention of a trustee is insufficient.[3]

The language employed must be suitable. Thus in North Carolina, the words "for her use" have been held sufficient to exclude the husband's dominion.[4] So, too, the words for the "entire use, benefit, profit, and advantage."[5] But in South Carolina, the words for "the use of his wife," are held insufficient.[6] In Kentucky, the words "for her own proper use and benefit," are held sufficient.[7] Such, too, seems to have been the rule in Alabama.[8] The words "to the use and benefit," are held sufficient in Tennessee.[9] So in Alabama, words importing enjoyment, "without let, hindrance, or molestation whatever."[10] And where one clause of a will applies the

516; Vernon *v.* Marsh, 2 Green Ch. 502; Steel *v.* Steel, 1 Ired. Eq. 452; Jackson *v.* McAliley, Spears Eq. 303; Boykin *v.* Ciples, 2 Hill. Ch. 200, 204; Hunt *v.* Booth, 1 Freem. Ch. 215; Warren *v.* Haley, 1 S. & M. Ch. 647; Hamilton *v.* Bishop, 8 Yerg. 33; Griffith *v.* Griffith, 5 B. Monr. 113; McKennan *v.* Phillips, 6 Whart. 571; Gray *v.* Crook, 12 Gill & J. 236; Howard *v.* Menifee, 5 Pike, 668.

[1] McKennan *v.* Phillips, 6 Whart. 571; Thompson *v.* McKusick, 3 Humph. 631; Fellows *v.* Tann, 9 Ala. 999; Trenton Banking Co. *v.* Woodruff, 1 Green Ch. 117.

[2] Boykin *v.* Ciples, 2 Hill Ch. 200; Hamilton *v.* Bishop, 8 Yerg. 33; Wallingsford *v.* Allen, 10 Pet. 583; Porter *v.* Bank of Rutland, 19 Vt. 410; Harkins *v.* Coalter, 2 Port, 463; Franklin *v.* Creyon, 1 Harp. Ch. 243; Freeman *v.* Freeman, 9 Mis. 763.

[3] Hunt *v.* Booth, 1 Freem. Ch. 215; Graham *v.* Graham, Riley, 142; Taylor *v.* Stone, 13 S. & M. 653; Lenoir *v.* Binney, 15 Ala. 667.

[4] Steel *v.* Steel, 1 Ired. Eq. 452; Good *v.* Harris, 2 Ired. Eq. 630.

[5] Heathman *v.* Hall, 3 Ired. Eq. 414.

[6] Tennant *v.* Stoney, 1 Rich. Eq. 222; M'Donald *v.* Crockett, 2 McC. Ch. 130.

[7] Griffith *v.* Griffith, 5 B. Monr. 113. This is contrary to the present English rule. See last chapter.

[8] Warren *v.* Halsey, 1 S. & M. Ch. 647. [9] Hamilton *v.* Bishop, 8 Yerg. 33.

[10] Newman *v.* James, 12 Ala. 29. And see Clarke *v.* Windham, ib. 798.

words, "in trust for the separate use," to certain property, and another applies to certain property the words "in trust" only, the separate use may by construction embrace the whole.[1]

But the words "sole and separate use" are most commonly applied. A gift or bequest to "a married woman and her children, born and thereafter to be born," does not invest her with an estate to her sole and separate use, but makes her a tenant in common (joint-tenancy having been abolished), with her children.[2] And it would appear in general, that where property is given for the use and support of two or more together, one of them being a married woman, it cannot be considered as vesting a separate estate in the married woman; for exclusiveness of enjoyment is an important element in such estates.[3] This doctrine is not inconsistent with the well-established right of a donor to make a trust first to the wife's separate use, then over to some one else, provided the instrument uses apt language for that purpose.[4] And provisions for the sole and separate use, support, and maintenance of a wife and children are frequently sustained, though the trust does not vest their respective interests consecutively.[5] As in England, our courts permit an estate to be so settled on an unmarried female as to exclude the marital rights of any future husband.[6]

In Vermont, it is decided that a third person may create a parol trust for a married woman's exclusive benefit, except as to landed property, which falls within the statute of frauds. Thus in a case where it appeared that the father of a married woman had intimated to her and her husband, in conversation, that he was about to make her an advance in money, which he wished to have invested for the benefit of herself and her children, and that he had subsequently enclosed in a letter to her

[1] Davis *v.* Cain, 1 Ired. Eq. 304.

[2] Dunn *v.* Bank of Mobile, 2 Ala. 152.

[3] Harkins *v.* Coalter, 2 Port, 463; Clancy Hus. & Wife, 269; Inge *v.* Forrester, 6 Ala. 418.

[4] See Warren *v.* Hally, 1 S. & M. 647.

[5] Good *v.* Harris, 2 Ired. Eq. 630; Hamilton *v.* Bishop, 8 Yerg. 33; Anderson *v.* Brooks, 11 Ala. 953.

[6] Beaufort *v.* Collier, 6 Humph. 487.

husband, a check for $1000, payable to his daughter, or bearer, expressing in the letter a wish that the money might be invested for the mutual benefit of his daughter and her heirs, leaving the mode to be determined by her and her husband, on consultation between them; also, that she had at the time of the suit three children; the court considered that there had been a trust created for the exclusive benefit of the donor's daughter and her children; and the husband was taken to be the trustee, as against his own creditors who had attached certain bank stock which he purchased in his own name with such funds; the evidence showing that the creditors had received notice that the stock was held in trust.[1]

Our courts of equity will sometimes overlook informalities in order to give effect to the wife's separate use. As where a deed of trust to a commissioner has been ordered by the court, but never executed, and the commissioner gives possession to the husband in the mean time.[2] Or where a deed has not been recorded in compliance with the statute.[3] So a trust may be enforced, although the details of the arrangement cannot be ascertained by the most stringent proof; and it would appear that a person may by his acts make himself a trustee *sub modo* to support the wife's separate use.[4] The wife cannot be debarred of her separate estate through the fraud of others; it must be a fraud to which she is a party, that will bar her beneficial title.[5] Even a purchaser, still more a volunteer, taking possession of the trust property, with a notice of the trust, will be made a trustee in chancery.[6]

A married woman cannot by contract acquire any property

[1] Porter *v.* Bank of Rutland, 19 Vt. 410. Mr. Macqueen suggests the opinion that a parol trust would be good in England, though admitting that he finds no decision of the question. Marriage settlements, however, may be affected by the statute of frauds. Macq. Hus. & Wife, 293.

[2] Jackson *v.* McAlilly, Spears Ch. 303.

[3] Hamilton *v.* Bishop, 8 Yerg. 33.

[4] Sledge *v.* Clopton, 6 Ala. 589.

[5] Jackson *v.* McAliley, Speers Eq. 303.

[6] Ib. And see Fry *v.* Fry, 7 Paige Ch. 461.

to her separate use; but the benefit of her contract, if any, enures to her husband.[1] Where, however, a married woman, with her husband's consent, purchases lands which she was the meritorious cause of acquiring, and takes a deed to another, it is held in Vermont that a trust results in her favor.[2] On the other hand if a testator gives a legacy to trustees for the use of a daughter, and directs that it may be invested in real estate for her use, if she should desire it, and that the trustees should take the title in the name of the daughter only, though married, the trustees must follow his directions, and they cannot take a title in any other name, though by taking it in the name of the daughter, the property might be subjected to the husband's debts.[3]

The English doctrine that the wife's separate estate is not necessarily liable for her own debts is also admitted here. Thus it is held in New York that the only ground on which the wife's separate property can be reached for her antenuptial debts, is that of appointment; that is, some act of hers after marriage which indicates an intention to charge the property.[4] Nor can the bankruptcy of the husband, although it suspends the legal remedy against the wife during coverture, afford any ground for proceeding in equity to charge her separate estate.[5] Nor in the absence of an intention on the wife's part to make such estate liable can it be subjected to her general debts contracted during coverture.[6] But in Mississippi a disposition has been manifested to overturn this doctrine, and to establish a new and fairer rule in equity, and it is held that the wife's separate property, owned before marriage, may be thus subjected to

[1] Lansier *v.* Ross, 1 Dev. & Bat. Eq. 39.

[2] Pinney *v.* Fellows, 15 Vt. 525. And see Pulliam *v.* Pulliam, 1 Freem. Ch. 348.

[3] Vernon *v.* Marsh, 2 Green Ch. (N. J.) 502.

[4] Vanderheyden *v.* Mallory, 1 Comst. 452.

[5] Ib. See McKay *v.* Allen, 6 Yerg. 44; Pearce *v.* Spierin, 2 Desaus. 460.

[6] Dickson *v.* Miller, 11 S. & M. 594; Knox *v.* Picket, 4 Desaus. 92; Gee *v.* Gee, 2 Dev. & Bat. 103; Haygood *v.* Harris, 10 Ala. 291; Curtis *v.* Engel, 2 Sandf. Ch. 287.

the payment of necessaries furnished her while sole and a minor.[1]

In general the husband's obligation to maintain his wife and family remains unaffected by the fact that the wife holds separate property. This rule is fully asserted in New York. For it is declared that, though by a marriage settlement the wife's whole property is secured to her separate use, her husband is nevertheless bound to maintain her, and cannot make the expenses a charge on her separate estate. Nor can the admissions of the wife, during coverture, that the expenses were to be borne by her separate estate, be set up by the husband to impair her rights under the settlement.[2] "The utmost I can do in this case," observed Chancellor Kent, "is to allow the husband to be credited with any necessary reparations bestowed by him on any part of her estate; and with any particular specific appropriation of her property (not being for the ordinary maintenance of her or his family) which may have been made by her special assent and direction, in the given case, and apparently, for her benefit."[3]

Where a conveyance is made in trust for the separate use of a married woman, or for such person as she should direct, and she makes no appointment, it is held in Pennsylvania that the trustee after her death is entitled to recover the property for her representatives.[4] But if a married woman, having a sep-

[1] Dickson *v.* Miller, 11 S. & M. 594. "In marriage," observes Mr. Justice Thacher, "although a husband runs the hazard of becoming liable for his wife in an amount greater than the value of the estate he receives by her, he also has the chance of receiving by her an amount far exceeding her debts. But where the whole estate of a wife, notwithstanding coverture, continues separate to her, there is no such recompense to the husband for his obligation for his wife's debts, but on the contrary, there may be a certainty of his becoming indebted on behalf of his wife, with no possibility of his receiving an amount even equal to her debts." Ib. And see Cater *v.* Everleigh, 4 Desaus. 19.

[2] Meth. Ep. Church *v.* Jaques, 1 Johns. Ch. 450.

[3] Ib. It may be said that the above case arose out of an antenuptial contract between husband and wife, and that the court merely restrained the husband from setting aside his own bargain.

[4] Dinsmore *v.* Biggert, 9 Barr, 133.

arate estate, survives her husband, the restraints upon the disposal of the estate inconsistent with its general character, cease with the coverture.[1] Nor do they revive on her second marriage.[2] And where, by a will, personal estate was given to a trustee, in trust, to pay over the profits to a daughter of the testator, a married woman, semi-annually, for her sole benefit during her life, the will containing no provision for a second marriage of the daughter; it has been held in North Carolina that upon the death of the husband the separate use ends, and does not revive upon the remarriage of the beneficiary. On the contrary, the second husband's marital rights attach upon the property.[3] The husband surviving his wife has the same rights in her separate estate, as in her other property, even though another be appointed administrator.[4] This last is the English doctrine.

The savings of the interest arising from the separate estate of a married woman, are as much separate property as the principal, unless she has suffered it to pass under her husband's marital control. And property purchased with such savings belongs to her and continues subject to the same rules.[5] But furniture purchased by the wife, with the income of her separate estate, and mixed with the furniture of the husband, becomes the property of the husband, unless it was understood between them, at the time of the purchase, that the property should be kept by him as her trustee merely.[6]

Upon a bill by husband and wife to recover her separate property the court may decline to make the husband trustee, and order payment to be made to some third person as trustee

[1] Smith *v.* Starr, 3 Whart. 62. See O'Kill *v.* Campbell, 3 Green Ch. 13.

[2] Hamersley *v.* Smith, 4 Whart. 126.

[3] Miller *v.* Bingham, 1 Ired. Eq. 423.

[4] Spann *v.* Jennings, 1 Hill Ch. 325; Good *v.* Harris, 2 Ired. Eq. 630; McKay *v.* Allen, 6 Yerg. 44.

[5] Merritt *v.* Lyon, 3 Barb. 110; Hort *v.* Sorrell, 11 Ala. 386. See Kee *v.* Vasser, 2 Ired. Eq. 553. See English doctrine, last chapter.

[6] Shirley *v.* Shirley, 9 Paige, 363.

for her.[1] And where real estate is conveyed in trust for a married woman, and to such person as she shall appoint, it is not necessary that the husband should join in the appointment.[2] So on a suit, either by the husband or the wife, in relation to the wife's separate real and personal estate, a suitable maintenance will be provided for her, even as against the husband's execution creditor, and even though her equity extends to the whole estate.[3]

Where the wife's separate estate is sold for a debt of the ancestor from whom it descended, it has been held in New York that the surplus belongs to the husband.[4] And where a wife joins with her husband in the conveyance of her land, without any understanding or agreement that the proceeds are to be applied to her separate use, such proceeds vest absolutely in him discharged of all claims on her part.[5] For the presumption in such cases is that she voluntarily abandons her separate use in his favor; though the question after all is one of evidence.[6]

The wife's separate use was sustained in Connecticut, upon the comity of nations, in a case decided in 1842, prior to the married women's acts; a policy of insurance against fire having been issued by an office in that State, to a married woman residing in Canada, on her separate estate there situated. The court intimated that in Connecticut a married woman could not be the independent owner of property.[7]

The wife's separate use, as an American system, or rather as the system of certain American States, had thus far progressed when our local legislatures took the subject in hand. The American equity courts had followed the English precedents

1 Boykin *v.* Ciples, 2 Hill Ch. 200.

2 Thompson *v.* Murray, 2 Hill Ch. 204; 4 Kent Com. 318.

3 Haviland *v.* Myers, 6 Johns Ch. 25; Haviland *v.* Bloom, ib. 178; Barrett *v.* Oliver, 7 Gill & J. 191; Slowman *v.* Perryclear, Riley Ch. 47.

4 Wood *v.* Genet, 8 Paige, 137.

5 Chester *v.* Greer, 5 Humph. 26; Temple *v.* Williams, 4 Ired. Eq. 39.

6 SeeTemple *v.* Williams, *supra.*

7 Jones *v.* Ætna Ins. Co., 14 Conn. 501.

pretty closely, but without displaying the same vigor and boldness. None of the foregoing decisions had attracted popular attention or served to bring out the discussion of strong leading principles; though covering a period of sixty years down to the middle of the present century. During the preceding twenty-five years a change in public opinion had been gradually wrought in this country and in England,— though with us more rapidly than abroad. The married woman of America turned to the legislature rather than the courts of her State for a more complete marital independence, for the right to control her own property, for freedom from the burdens of coverture. In shaping popular sentiment, doubtless, the annexation of territory lately governed by the principles of Roman law had considerable influence, particularly in the States adjacent to Louisiana; still more in a national sense did our rapid advancement as a nation in principles of self-government, the spread of public education, of independence in life and manners, and of equal social intercourse of the sexes.

The year 1848 saw a wondrous revolution effected in the foremost States of this Union, as to the property rights of married women; and this revolution has since extended to every section of the country. The influence of these changes has also been felt abroad; and a like reform is now being pressed in the English Parliament.[1]

In 1821, the legislature of Maine authorized the wife, when deserted by her husband, to sue, make contracts, and convey real estate as if unmarried, prescribing the mode of procedure in such cases.[2] These appear to have been the earliest of the married women's acts, properly so called: the first fruits of the modern agitation on woman's rights. The example of Maine in this respect was soon imitated elsewhere. New Hampshire, Vermont, Tennessee, Kentucky, and Michigan all passed

[1] See 3 Juridical Society Papers (1870), part 17.

[2] See Rev. Sts. Maine (1840), p. 341. A like law had however existed in Massachusetts much earlier. See Rev. Sts. Mass. (1836) pp. 485, 487.

important laws before 1850. The independence of married women whose husbands were convicts, runaways, and profligates, became thus the first point gained in the new system. In Massachusetts and Rhode Island, the wife's separate use in life-insurance contracts for her benefit was an object of special solicitude; then, in 1845, the former State turned its attention further to a public recognition of marriage settlements and trusts for the wife's separate benefit, extending the equity jurisdiction of its courts for that purpose. The right of a married woman to dispose of her property by will was legalized in Illinois, Pennsylvania, Michigan, and Connecticut about the same time. In Connecticut, Ohio, Indiana, and Missouri its first reforms appear to have been directed towards exempting the wife's property from liability for her husband's debts rather than giving her complete dominion over it.[1]

The Roman principle of an independent estate prevailed in Louisiana at the time of its admission into the Union; and like traces appear in the legislation of Florida, Arkansas, Texas, and other adjacent States. So was the doctrine of separate estate promulgated by Mississippi statute as early as 1839.[2] So in other Southern States, as Alabama and North Carolina, where chancery jurisprudence was well established, appeared laws investing the courts with larger powers in matters of this sort.[3] Alabama and Mississippi appear to have first postponed the husband's liability for his wife's antenuptial debts to her separate estate.[4]

But the sweeping changes effected by the legislature of New York, in 1848, deserve more than a passing notice. The debates of the constitutional convention of that State in 1846 evinced the growing desire for a radical reform in the property rights of

[1] See 2 Bright Hus. & Wife, Am. ed. 1850, p. 627 *et seq.*, where married women's acts are cited by Mr. Lockwood; 2 Kent Com. 130, note.

[2] See 2 Bright, ib. The influence of a large commercial city, like New Orleans, was doubtless felt in the sparsely settled territory surrounding it. The codes of these States were all disfigured by "chattel" provisions, which detracted much from the merits of a policy otherwise humane to the wife.

[3] 2 Bright, ib.

[4] Ib. (1846).

married women; and the advocates of the movement, failing in their attempt to secure an article of amendment to the State constitution on their behalf, next addressed themselves to the legislature; and with success. On the 7th of April, 1848, was enacted a law "for the more effectual protection of married women," which provided that the real and personal property of any female already married or who may hereafter marry, which she shall own at the time of marriage, and the rents, issues, and profits thereof shall not be subject to the disposal of her husband, nor be liable for his debts, and shall continue her sole and separate property as if she were a single female; and that any married female may lawfully receive and hold property in like manner from any person other than her husband, — whether by gift, grant, devise, or bequest. This statute passed at such a time by the foremost State in the Union: a State thoroughly Northern in its institutions, while the recognized champion of chancery principles, could not fail to make a deep national impression.[1]

A parallel movement had meanwhile progressed in Pennsylvania; and in that State an act of the legislature, dated only four days later, conferred substantially the same rights of property upon married women, though expressed in different language. This act, still more remarkable in its general provisions than that of New York, not only recognized the wife's separate use in her own property as a legal right, but at the same time gave her the power to dispose of such estate by will, made it liable for family necessaries in failure of attachable property belonging to the husband, admitted children to the inheritance of separate personal estate in common with the surviving husband, and exempted the husband from all liability for his wife's antenuptial debts. It further provided that the wife's separate property should be absolutely liable for her general contracts

[1] We give the substance rather than the language of this statute. See 2 Bright Hus. & Wife, Am. ed. 1850, Lockwood's note, 581 *et seq.* This statute was afterwards considerably modified by acts of 1849, ch. 375, and 1860, ch. 90, § 1.

and torts, and that only her formal consent, given as therein specified, could bring the property under subjection for the husband's debts, or effect a lawful transfer.[1] It should be said that Michigan had enacted laws in 1844, giving enlarged powers to the wife to hold and dispose of separate property; thus anticipating some of the statutory changes both in New York and Pennsylvania.[2]

From this time forth the revolution became rapid, and extended to nearly all the States: Virginia and Delaware constituting exceptions. Scarcely a year has passed within the last fifteen years without some new married women's acts added to the local statute books.[3]

[1] Bright, ib. p. 648; Laws Penn. 1848, pp. 536, 537, 538.

[2] Rev. Stat. Mich. (1846) p. 340.

[3] The acts now in force, many of them perplexing, which need not here be detailed, may be briefly summed up as presenting this day the following American system of positive law. In Maine, a liberal right in married women of holding property to separate use independently of the husband's control, which the wife may relax by a revocable instrument enabling her husband to manage it. In New Hampshire, the right to hold from strangers, from her husband where not in fraud of creditors, and to acquire her own earnings when deserted. In Vermont, less explicit legislation (chancery powers in this State being ample); but earnings under like circumstances, and money damages in any case, secured to her separate use; rents, issues, and profits of her property being exempt from attachment for her husband's debts. In Massachusetts (the language of whose statutes has been closely followed in many of the Western States), a liberal right to hold, acquire, and control separate property, including compensation for release of dower and property under settlements from her husband; also her own earnings. In Rhode Island, exemption of the wife's sole and separate property from liability for the husband's debts, but favor shown to the husband's general control. In Connecticut, a somewhat limited recognition of separate estate in the wife; but a clear right given to her earnings and the proceeds of real estate; also personal estate, coming during coverture, made subject to her antenuptial debts; the husband's control being favored. In New York, the most liberal provisions on the wife's behalf as to property held before marriage and acquisitions during coverture through her husband or third persons; also her earnings; a complete emancipation from marital dominion. In New Jersey, a similar policy, but more guarded. In Pennsylvania, large privileges, as already detailed; which however the courts are disposed to restrict. In Maryland, a liberal policy, yet the disposition shown rather to secure against the husband's debts by chancery protection, than to give the wife a statutory marital dominion. In Ohio, no sweeping statutes, but general exemption of the wife's separate estate from her husband's debts, even to his life-interest in her real estate. In Michigan, a liberal

In general, it may be remarked that the American statutes relating to married women are designed for her benefit, and that they do not limit, but rather extend, her right to hold separate property. Thus it is held that the wife's equity to a settlement from her *choses in action* remains as before; for the legislature intended to offer her what was supposed to be a more valuable right, leaving it to her election to claim the benefit of the act or to assert her equity to a settlement without regard to its provisions.[1] So property purchased with funds held to her separate use, or with the proceeds or income thereof, is her separate property, even though her husband was the agent in making the purchase.[2] And a liberal rule is laid down in Connecticut

policy. In Indiana, a peculiar policy, somewhat on the community plan, tending to place all of the wife's real and personal property under the same marital rules, giving the wife a separate ownership in both, but restricting her power of transfer. In Illinois, laws similar to those of Massachusetts, but which, so far as the wife's control is concerned, the courts seem more disposed to enlarge. So in Wisconsin, Minnesota, and Kansas. In Iowa, rather more limited legislation on behalf of separate estate; including a wholesome registry provision. In California, a policy savoring strongly of the Spanish community system, formerly prevalent there; property of both husband and wife at the date of marriage, or acquired from others during coverture, being regarded as the separate property of each; property otherwise acquired during coverture, as the common property of both. In Nevada, similar laws. In Oregon, the exemption of the wife's property from liability for her husband's debts, a principle engrafted upon the fundamental law of that State. In Nebraska, liberal rights vested in married women. In Missouri, exemption of the wife's property from liability for her husband's debts, the legislation being directed rather to lands than personal estate. In Kentucky (where the wife's separate estate has been fully recognized in equity), a somewhat peculiar restraint placed upon the husband's marital rights so as to protect the wife's property, *prima facie*, from liability for his debts, while limiting the husband's liability for her antenuptial debts. Marital rights of the wife are favored in Tennessee so far as to shield her property from the husband's debts; but not so as to vest the control in her. In Arkansas, a liberal policy prevails, with apparently reasonable bounds. In view of the important changes now going on in the legislation of the Southern States, it is not deemed important to allude to the statutory rights of married women in that part of the country; but it appears likely that their laws will be brought into conformity with the general American system in this respect. See latest statutes of the different States above referred to; and see Cartwright *v.* Hollis, 5 Tex. 152; Childers *v.* Cutter, 16 Mis. 24; Panaud *v.* Jones, 1 Cal. 488; Cutter *v.* Waddingham, 22 Mis. 206.

[1] Blevins *v.* Buck, 26 Ala. 292.

[2] Hutchins *v.* Colby, 43 N. H. 159; Kirkpatrick *v.* Bauford, 21 Ark. 268. And see Teller *v.* Bishop, 8 Minn. 226.

with respect to the proceeds of real estate (which by statute are secured to the wife), while they lie in the bank for safety or remain in cash in the wife's possession awaiting an opportunity for investment.[1]

Yet broad as they may often appear these statutes are yet somewhat restrained by judicial construction. In Massachusetts, Maine, California, Wisconsin, and other States, the presumption is still, in absence of suitable words, or circumstances manifesting an intent on the part of those interested to claim the benefits of the statute, that a married woman's property belongs to her husband as at the common law; and his possession of the property undisputed and unexplained, gives him the marital dominion.[2] In Pennsylvania, the courts were at first disposed to rule otherwise, but they too have finally settled upon the same presumption.[3] On the other hand, the New York courts approve the new system to its widest extent, thus far; and it would appear that married women in that State are wellnigh emancipated altogether from marital restraints, so far as concerns their property, while the husband's own rights are exceedingly precarious.[4]

In New York and Mississippi it is held that the married women's act does not oust the original jurisdiction of courts of equity in cases affecting the separate estates of married women.[5] Speaking of the legislation in the former State, the court observes that the statutes of 1848 and 1849 are but the legislative adoption of the equitable rules, and their application to all property of the wife whether legal or equitable. "The evil complained of

[1] Jennings *v.* Davis, 31 Conn. 134.

[2] Eldridge *v.* Preble, 34 Me. 148; Smith *v.* Henry, 35 Miss. 369; Alverson *v.* Jones, 10 Cal. 9; Stanton *v.* Kirsch, 6 Wis. 338; Smith *v.* Hewett, 13 Iowa, 94. *Contra*, Johnson *v.* Runyan, 21 Ind. 115; Stewart *v.* Ball, 33 Mis. 154.

[3] Cf. Gamber *v.* Gamber, 18 Penn St. 363; Winter *v.* Walter, 37 Penn. St. 157; Bear's Administrator *v.* Bear, 33 Penn. St. 525; Gault *v.* Saffin, 44 Penn. St. 307; with Goodyear *v.* Rumbaugh, 13 Penn. St. 480.

[4] Peters *v.* Fowler, 41 Barb. 467; Knapp *v.* Smith, 27 N. Y. 277.

[5] Mitchell *v* Otey, 23 Miss. 236; Colvin *v.* Currier, 22 Barb. 371 [Strong J. dissenting].

was the too great subjection of the property of the wife, at common law, to the control of the husband and his creditors. The remedy was to apply the rule of this court, in respect to the separate property of married women, to all property belonging to the wife. It is true the property is thus converted into a legal estate, but it is none the less a *separate estate, independent of the husband.*"[1]

Some of the married women's acts charge the wife's separate estate with articles of "family supply;" though not unless she contracted for the articles, or unless at least her husband was destitute of the means of payment.[2] So it is now found in many of the States that the husband's liability for his wife's antenuptial debts is either modified to the extent of property received through her or else abolished altogether.[3] In Ohio and some other States, the husband's life-interest is protected from attachment during marriage; and it is generally preserved, as well as his tenancy by the curtesy.[4]

Some married women's statutes have either taken away the husband's liability for his wife's misconduct, and very properly fastened it upon her separate estate; or else limited his liability for her frauds and injuries to that of a surety.[5] So, too, the tendency of modern legislation is to secure to the wife's separate use all compensation in the nature of damages for injuries sustained by her through the negligence or misconduct of others.[6] And in Ohio it is held that where the wife's separate property is destroyed by the wrongful acts of a third party; as where her baggage is lost on a railroad; any judg-

[1] Ib. 382, per E. D. Smith, J.

[2] Cunningham *v.* Fontaine, 25 Ala. 644; Rogers *v.* Boyd, 33 Ala. 175; Finn *v.* Rose, 12 Iowa, 565. See Sharp *v.* Burns, 35 Ala. 653; Callahan *v.* Patterson, 4 Tex. 61.

[3] Bailey *v.* Pearson, 9 Fost. 77; Reunecker *v.* Scott, 4 Greene (Iowa), 185; Curry *v.* Shrader, 19 Ala. 831; Callahan *v.* Patterson, 4 Tex. 61.

[4] Bachman *v.* Chrisman, 23 Penn. St. 162; Van Note *v.* Downey, 4 Dutch. 219. See Ohio Stats. Montgomery *v.* Tate, 12 Ind. 615.

[5] Brown *v.* Kemper, 27 Md. 666.

[6] Waldo *v.* Goodsell, 33 Conn. 432; Moody *v.* Osgood, 50 Barb. 628; Knapp *v.* Smith, 27 N. Y. 277. See Moody *v.* Osgood, 50 Barb. 628.

ment she may recover therefor, becomes likewise her separate property.[1]

A married woman, in order to preserve her separate property, should keep it distinct from that of her husband; especially in States where the presumption is against her exclusive right. Thus it is held that if a married woman willingly allows her separate property to be so mixed into a common mass with that of the husband as to be undistinguishable, or acquiesces in leaving it so, it must as to her husband's creditors be treated as relinquished to him.[2] And, under the most favorable circumstances, she can only be treated in equity as a preferred creditor.[3] Nor can a title to separate estate be vested in the wife on her husband's credit, where the statutes only recognize her right to acquire from third persons, any more than it can by his money; and, if certain property be purchased in part from her own funds and in part from her husband's, whatever the form of the investment, her title extends only to the amount of her investment.[4]

How far the acts relating to the property of married women are qualified by constitutional restraints has been frequently discussed in late years. The Constitution of the United States expressly forbids the States to pass any *ex post facto* law, or law impairing the obligation of contracts.[5] The decisions are uniform to the effect that the late statutes cannot affect rights of the husband already vested under a prior marriage.[6] But they go no

[1] Pierson *v.* Smith, 9 Ohio St. 554.

[2] Glover *v.* Alcott, 11 Mich. 470; Gross *v.* Reddy, 45 Penn. St. 406; Kelly *v.* Drew, 12 Allen, 107.

[3] Glidden *v.* Taylor, 16 Ohio St. 509.

[4] Hopkins *v.* Carey, 23 Miss. 54; Worth *v.* York, 13 Ired. 206; 2 Story Eq. Jur. § 1201, note. See Barron *v.* Barron, 26 Vt. 375.

[5] Const. United States, Art. 1, § 10.

[6] Carter *v.* Carter, 14 S. & M. 59; Eldridge *v.* Preble, 34 Me. 148; Maynard *v.* Williams, 17 Ala. 676; Snyder *v.* Snyder, 3 Barb. 621; Perkins *v.* Cottrell, 15 Barb. 446; Ratcliffe *v.* Dougherty, 24 Miss. 181; Jenney *v.* Gray, 5 Ohio St. 45; Roby *v.* Boswell, 23 Ga. 51; Burson's Appeal, 22 Penn. St. 164; Tally *v.* Thompson, 20 Mis. 277; Peck *v.* Walton, 26 Vt. 82; Tyrson *v.* Mattair, 8 Fla. 107. See Love *v.* Robertson, 7 Tex. 6.

further; for, as it has been observed, the marriage contract does not imply that the husband shall have the same interest in the future acquisitions of the wife that the law gives him in the property she possesses at the time of the marriage, but that she shall have whatever interest, if any, the legislature, before she is invested with them, may think proper to prescribe.[1] As to whether the married women's acts can affect the wife's property in action not already reduced into possession authorities are divided.[2]

In Mississippi it is held that property purchased by the husband after the passage of the act with money acquired by the wife by gift or labor before it, even though bought expressly for the wife's benefit and in her name, belongs to the husband.[3] In Alabama separate estates created by deed before the statute went into effect remain unaffected thereby, though the marriage took place subsequently.[4] In New York, judgments recovered against a husband prior to the married women's act are not a lien upon the wife's subsequently acquired property.[5] In Missouri, the act exempting property of the wife from liability for the husband's debts does not affect debts contracted prior to the passage of the act and after the wife came into possession of the property.[6]

In New York, it is held that the legislature may fasten upon the wife's separate bank stock a personal liability to the extent of such stock.[7] Also that interest, accruing subsequently to the married women's act, on property previously vested in the husband continues his.[8] The California statutes embrace

1 Sleight *v.* Read, 18 Barb. 159; Southard *v.* Plumer, 36 Me. 64.

2 Goodyear *v.* Rumbaugh, 13 Penn. St. 480; Mellinger *v.* Bausman, 45 Penn. St. 522; Henry *v.* Dilley, 1 Dutch. 302, maintain the affirmative. Westervelt *v.* Gregg, 2 Kern. 202; Ryder *v.* Hulse, 24 N. Y. 372; Stearns *v.* Weathers, 30 Ala. 712, maintain the negative.

3 Sharp *v.* Maxwell, 30 Miss. 442.

4 Willis *v.* Cadenhead, 28 Ala. 472. And see Hardy *v.* Boaz, 29 Ala. 168.

5 Sleight *v.* Read, 18 Barb. 159.

6 Cunningham *v.* Gray, 20 Mis. 170.

7 Matter of Reciprocity Bank, 29 Barb. 369.

8 Rider *v.* Hulse, 33 Barb. 264; s. c. on appeal, 24 N. Y. 372. See Savage *v.* O'Neil, 42 Barb. 374.

property held as separate by women married after the passage of the act without reference to the time when it was acquired.[1]

There are later American decisions which rest upon strictly equitable rules; and increasing liberality toward the wife is manifested therein.[2] Thus it is held in Alabama that delivery of property to the husband by the donor with parol declarations of trust may suffice, though the deed of conveyance be technically defective.[3] In Massachusetts a separate use is created where the husband deposits money in a savings bank in the name and to the credit of his wife, declares that the money is hers and that he wishes it put in her name, and delivers the deposit book to her; so, too, when he keeps one bank account there in his own name and another in his wife's name.[4]

[1] Maclay *v.* Love, 25 Cal. 367.

[2] See as to words which constitute a separate estate, Wilson *v.* Bailer, 3 Strobh. Eq. 258; Clark *v.* Maguire, 16 Mis. 302; Goodrum *v.* Goodrum, 8 Ired. Eq. 313; Denson *v.* Patton, 19 Geo. 577; Bradford *v.* Greenway, 17 Ala. 797.

[3] Betts *v.* Betts, 18 Ala. 787.

[4] Fisk *v.* Cushman, 6 Cush. 20. But *contra*, where a deposit is made without the husband's privity. McCubbin *v.* Patterson, 16 Md. 179. And see Rider *v.* Hulse, 33 Barb. 264; Richardson *v.* Merrill, 32 Vt. 27; Hobensack *v.* Hallman, 17 Penn. St 154; Gaines *v.* Poor, 3 Met. (Ky.) 503.

CHAPTER XII.

THE WIFE'S DOMINION OVER HER SEPARATE ESTATE.

THE right to enjoy property carries with it, as a necessary incident, the right of free disposal. All other things then being equal, we shall expect to find that married women, when allowed to hold estate to their separate use, are permitted to sell, convey, give, grant, bargain, or otherwise dispose of it; and further, to encumber it as they please. Public policy may, however, restrain their dominion. We shall treat in this chapter, first, of the English, and second of the American, rule on this subject.

In England, it is the general rule, so far at least as concerns personal property, that from the moment the wife takes the property to her sole and separate use, from the same moment she has the sole and separate right to dispose of it; for upon being once permitted to take personal property to her separate use, as a *feme sole*, she takes it with all its privileges and incidents, including the *jus disponendi*.[1] And while she may be restrained by the language of the instrument under which her title is acquired, yet the intention to restrain her must be clearly expressed; or else she may deal with the property as she pleases, either by acts *inter vivos* or by will.[2] Her power of disposition is not confined to interests vested in possession, but extends to reversionary interests settled to her separate use.[3]

[1] Fettiplace *v.* Gorges, 1 Ves. Jr. 48; 3 Br. C. C. 9; Peachey Mar. Settl. 261, 262. See 20 & 21 Vict. ch. 57, the "reversionary act."

[2] Rich *v.* Cockell, 9 Ves. 369; Moore *v.* Morris, 4 Drew. 38; Darkin *v.* Darkin, 17 Beav. 581; Caton *v.* Rideout, 1 Mac. & Gord. 601.

[3] 2 Bright Hus. & Wife, 222; Macq. Hus. & Wife, 295; Sturgis *v.* Corp, 13 Ves. 192; Headen *v.* Rosher, 1 M'Cl. & Y. 89; Donne *v.* Hart, 2 Russ. & M. 360.

The same principle applies to the income and profits of the wife's separate property. The wife has the same control over her savings out of her separate estate, as over the separate estate itself; "for," to use the somewhat involved metaphor of Lord Keeper Cowper, so often quoted, "the sprout is to savor of the root, and to go the same way."[1]

Where the wife's separate property consists of real estate, her power of disposition is affected by technical difficulties, as to the method of executing conveyances.[2] But it has been suggested that, according to the principle of modern equity cases, the heir ought to be treated as a trustee, in case the wife had conveyed her beneficial interest by deed executed by herself alone, and that thus her sole conveyance would be allowed to operate.[3]

The wife may enter into contracts with reference to her separate property in like manner, and with the same effect as a *feme sole*. Formerly it was otherwise; and for a long period the English courts of equity refused to married women, having separate estate, the power to contract debts.[4] But the unfairness of permitting a wife to hold and enjoy her separate property after she had incurred debts upon the faith of it, soon became evident; as well as the inconvenience she suffered in

[1] Gore *v.* Knight, 2 Vern. 535; s. c. Prec. in Ch. 255. See also Messenger *v.* Clarke, 5 Exch. 392; Peachey Mar. Settl. 262; Newlands *v.* Paynter, 10 Sim. 377; s. c. on appeal, 4 M. & Cr. 408; Humphery *v.* Richards, 2 Jur. (N. S.) 432.

[2] 2 Roper Hus. & Wife, 182; 1 Bright Hus. & Wife, 224. See *Ex parte* Ann Shirley, 5 Bing. 226, cited in Macq. Hus. & Wife, 296. See also Peachey Mar. Settl. 267; Harris *v.* Mott, 14 Beav. 169. The reasoning of the court, in a recent case before the Lord Chancellor (which arose under the statute of wills), would indicate that a married woman may alienate her separate real property by her sole deed without the consent of her husband. Taylor *v.* Minds, 10 Jur. (N. S.) 166.

[3] Macq. Hus. & Wife, 296, 297; 2 Story Eq. Juris. § 1390 and cases cited; 3 Sugd. V. & P. App. 62; Newcomen *v.* Hassard, 4 Ir. Ch. 274; Burnaby *v.* Griffin, 3 Ves. 266; Peachey Mar. Settl. 268. The statute referred to as raising technical difficulties in real estate is 3 & 4 Wm. 4, ch. 74.

[4] Vaughan *v.* Vanderstegen, 2 Drew. 180; Peachey Mar. Settl. 269; Newcomen *v.* Hassard, 4 Ir. Ch. 274.

being unable to find credit where she meant to deal fairly. So the courts felt compelled after awhile, to admit that she might in equity charge her separate estate by a written instrument, executed with a certain degree of formality, such as a bond under her hand and seal.[1] One precedent in the right direction leads to another, and soon less formal instruments were brought one after another under this rule; promissory notes, bills of exchange, and lastly written instruments in general.[2] Even here the court could not safely intrench itself; for the inconsistency of drawing distinctions between the different sorts of engagements of a married woman having separate estate, could be readily shown; but it made a halt. The doctrine of an equitable appointment was alleged to support the new distinction.[3] Sound reasoning at last proved too strong an antagonist; this position was abandoned; and it may now be considered the settled doctrine of the equity courts of England that the engagements and contracts of a married woman are to be regarded as debts, and that her property so held is liable to the payment of them, whether the contract be expressed in writing or not.[4] "Inasmuch as her creditors have not the means at law of compelling payment of those debts," says Lord Cottenham, "a court of equity takes upon itself to give effect to them, not as personal liabilities, but by laying hold of the separate property, as the only means by which they can be satisfied."[5]

But while the contract for payment of money, made by a married woman having separate estate, is called a debt, it is only a debt *sub modo*, when compared with the debt of a man

[1] Biscoe *v.* Kennedy, 1 Br. C. C. 17; Hulme *v.* Tenant, 1 Br. C. C. 16.

[2] See Murray *v.* Barlee, per Lord Brougham, 3 Myl. & K. 210; Bullpin *v.* Clarke, 17 Ves. 365; Stuart *v.* Lord Kirkwall, 3 Mad. 387; Master *v.* Fuller. 1 Ves. Jr. 513; Gaston *v.* Frankum, 2 De G. & Sm. 561; s. c. on appeal, 16 Jur, 507; Peachey Mar. Settl. 270 and cases cited.

[3] Field *v.* Sowle, 4 Russ. 112.

[4] Peachey Mar. Settl. 271, 272 and cases cited; Vaughan *v.* Vanderstegen, 2 Drew. 184; Owens *v.* Dickenson, Craig & Phil. 48; Macq. Hus. & Wife, 303. But see Newcomen *v.* Hassard, 4 Ir. Ch. 274; 1 Sugd. Pow. 206, 7th ed.

[5] Owens *v.* Dickenson, Craig & Phil. 48.

or an unmarried female. It cannot be enforced against her at law; and Lord Cottenham's language indicates that it is enforceable in equity, not on the ground that she incurred a personal obligation, but because there is property upon which the obligation may be fastened. Hence it is said that there can in no càse be a decree against a married woman *in personam;* the proceedings are simply against her separate property *in rem.*[1] And though she is a necessary party to a suit to enforce payment against her separate estate, yet, if that estate be held in trust for her separate use, the suit must be against the trustees in whom that property is vested; the decree in such case being rendered, not against her, but against the trustees, to compel payment from her separate estate. Moreover, if the wife survive her husband, although the creditors may still enforce their demand in equity against her separate estate, yet her person and her general property remain as completely exempted from liability at law and in equity, as in other cases of debts contracted by her during coverture.[2]

Here, however, the fictions of equity create a new practical difficulty. For if the wife be a *feme sole* at all, with reference to her separate property, must she not have power to bind herself personally? In *Stead* v. *Nelson*, a husband and wife undertook, for valuable consideration, by writing under their hands, to execute a mortgage of her separate estate. The husband died. Lord Langdale held that the surviving wife was bound by the agreement, and ordered a specific performance.[3] Certainly the ground of this decision must have been that the obligation was not upon her property alone, but upon her person. At the same time, it is readily admitted that there are reasons of policy why the wife should be exempted from personal execu-

[1] Hulme *v.* Tenant, 1 Br. C. C. 16; Ashton *v.* Aylett, 1 Myl. & Cr. 111; Macq. Hus. & Wife, 304; Peachey Mar. Settl. 273. But see Keogh *v.* Cathcart, 11 Ir. Ch. 285.

[2] Vaughan *v.* Vanderstegen, 2 Drew. 184; Peachey Mar. Settl. 273; Macq. Hus. & Wife, 304.

[3] 2 Beav. 245; Macq. Hus. & Wife, 304.

tion during coverture. This latter view accords with the common-law practice in analogous cases.[1] Perhaps, then, the more consistent view of the subject would be that the wife incurs a personal obligation, morally and legally, on her contracts, express or implied, made during coverture with reference to her separate property; but that the general disabilities of coverture interpose obstacles to the enforcement of remedies by a creditor, which obstacles the courts of equity feel bound to regard; and hence they confine the remedies to her separate estate, upon the faith of which, it may reasonably be presumed, the creditor chose to rely.

Property limited to such uses as a married woman shall appoint is not separate estate. There is a difference between a mere power of appointment, and property settled to her sole and separate use. In the former instance she may dispose of the estate by executing an instrument according to the strict letter of her authority. In the latter, she is invested with a beneficial interest and enjoyment, however restricted may be the dominion allowed her by the donee. A power of appointment is much the same as any other special power, and on such a principle, not upon the ground that she is a *feme sole* as to the property, the courts both of equity and of law recognize her right to execute without joining her husband. She cannot charge the property with her debts or affect it by her general contracts, any more than she can other property which is not hers.[2] On the other hand, the wife's disposition of her separate estate does not arise from the exercise of a power, but it is the exercise of a dominion over that estate, unknown to the common law and created by a court of equity, whose rules provide not only for her dominion over it, but also for the rights of those in favor of whom that dominion shall be exercised.[3] A

[1] Sparkes *v.* Bell, 8 B. & C. 1.

[2] Vaughan *v.* Vanderstegen, 2 Drew. 378.

[3] Digby *v.* Irvine, 6 Ir. Ch. 149. See Peachey Mar. Settl. 276; Brown *v.* Bamford, 1 Ph. 620; Shattock *v.* Shattock, Law Rep. 2 Eq. 182; Hanchett *v.* Briscoe, 22 Beav. 496.

power of appointment given to a married woman and a trust for her separate use are then perfectly distinct, even when they affect succeeding interests in the same property.

The separate estate of married women may be affected, and their rights barred, by active participation in breaches of trust.[1] But on the other hand, to preclude the wife from the right to relief simply because she has improperly permitted her husband to receive the trust funds, would be to defeat the very purpose for which the trust was created; namely, the protection of the wife against her husband. Hence, according to the latest and best authorities, the court must be satisfied that the husband has not in any degree influenced her acts and conduct, before it holds her separate estate to be affected; and this upon the most jealous investigation.[2]

As a general rule, it may be laid down that wherever a married woman, having property settled to her separate use, enters into any contract by which it clearly appears that she intends to create a debt as against herself personally, it will be assumed that she intended that the money should be paid out of the only property by which she could fulfil the engagement.[3] Thus, in a case before Lord Brougham, the question came up for the first time, whether a married woman could bind her separate estate for legal expenses incurred by her, upon her retainer and promise to pay, there having been no reference to her separate estate in the agreement; and it was held that she could, and that the bill must be paid from her separate estate.[4] But on the other hand, in contracts where the husband is the interested party, the court will not make the wife's separate property

[1] Peachey Mar. Settl. 276; Ryder *v.* Bickerton, 3 Swanst. 80 *n.*; Lord Montford *v.* Lord Cadogan, 19 Ves. 635.

[2] Per Sir Geo. Turner, Hughes *v.* Wells, 9 Hare, 773. And see authorities, *supra;* Kellaway *v.* Johnson, 5 Beav. 319; Cocker *v.* Quayle, 1 Russ. & M. 535; Brewer *v.* Swirles, 2 Sm. & Gif. 219. *Contra,* Whistler *v.* Newman, 4 Ves. 129, doubted in Parkes *v.* White, 11 Ves. 223.

[3] Earl *v.* Ferris, 19 Beav. 69.

[4] Murray *v.* Barlee, 3 Myl. & K. 209. And see Waugh *v.* Waddell, 16 Beav. 521; Bolden *v.* Nicholay, 3 Jur. (N. S.) 884.

liable, if that fact be made plain; notwithstanding she may have had some agency in the transaction.[1] Nor is her separate estate liable for the expenses of litigation incurred for the children as her husband's agent.[2]

We need hardly add, that a married woman, having separate estate, without a clause restraining her right of disposition, may charge and encumber it in any manner she chooses, either as security for her husband's debts, her own, or those of a stranger; provided she does not appear to have been imposed upon in the transaction. And if her property is in the hands of trustees, they are bound to fulfil her engagement.[3] And where she mortgages it, the court will regard the true nature of the transaction.[4]

A married woman may bind the corpus of her separate property by her compromise of a suit which she has instituted by her next friend.[5] She may also contract for the purchase of an estate, and even though the contract makes no reference to her separate property it will be bound by her agreement.[6] So her contract to sell or mortgage her life-interest in her separate estate will be specifically enforced against her.[7] Both she and her husband must be parties to a suit concerning her separate property.[8] And it is held that the husband, by making her a party in respect of her separate estate, admits it to be such.[9]

The rule as to the wife's power to charge her separate estate for her debts is briefly and clearly stated in a very recent case, to this effect: If a married woman, having separate property, enters into a pecuniary engagement, whether by ordering goods,

[1] Tullett *v.* Armstrong, 4 Beav. 319.

[2] *In re* Pugh, 17 Beav. 336.

[3] Clerk *v.* Laurie, 2 Hurl. & Nor. 199; Peachey Mar. Settl. 292. See Horner *v.* Wheelwright, 2 Jur. N. S. 367.

[4] Gray *v.* Dowman, 6 W. R. 571.

[5] Wilton *v.* Hill, 25 L. J. Eq. 156.

[6] Dowling *v.* Maguire; Lloyd & Goold, t. Plunket, 1; Crofts *v.* Middleton, 2 Kay & Johns. 194; reversed on appeal.

[7] Wainwright *v.* Hardisty, 2 Beav. 363.

[8] Holmes *v.* Penney, 3 Kay & Johns. 91. And see Peachey Mar. Settl. 293–296 and cases cited; Macq. Hus. & Wife, 297.

[9] Earl *v.* Ferris, 19 Beav. 69.

or otherwise, which (if she were a *feme sole*) would constitute her a debtor, and in entering into such engagement she purports to contract, not for her husband, but for herself, and on the credit of her separate estate, and it was so intended by her, and so understood by the person with whom she is contracting, that constitutes an obligation for which the person with whom she contracts has the right to make her separate estate liable; and the question whether the obligation was contracted in this manner must depend upon the facts and circumstances of each particular case.[1]

A married woman may bestow her separate property upon her husband by virtue of her right of disposal; although at common law no such thing is known as a gift between husband and wife. She may likewise transfer it to him for a valuable consideration.[2] But acts of this sort are very closely scrutinized; and undue influence on the part of the husband, or the fraud of both upon creditors of either, will often explain the motive of such transactions, and suffice for setting them aside in equity. When the wife has made a gift to her husband she will be precluded, after his death, from charging his estate with what he so received.[3] If she allows him to take her separate property, without making a claim to it, or permits him to receive her separate income and apply it to the wants of the family, she will in general be presumed to have assented to the arrangement.[4] But if the circumstances do not warrant the inference that the wife has assented to, or acquiesced in, the husband's receiving her income, or in his mode of applying it, she will be entitled to reimbursement out of his estate.[5]

1 Per Kindersley V. C., Mrs. Matthewman's Case, Law Rep. 3 Eq. 787. In this case the wife's corporation shares were held liable to assessment. And see Johnson *v.* Gallagher, 3 D., F. & J. 494.

2 Lyn *v.* Ashton, 1 Russ. & M. 190; Macq. Hus. & Wife, 297.

3 Paulet *v.* Delavel, 2 Ves. Sen. 663; 2 Roper Hus. & Wife, 220; 1 Mad. Ch. 472.

4 Square *v.* Dean, 4 Br. C. C. 326; Beresford *v.* Archbishop of Armagh, 13 Sim. 643; Bartlett *v.* Gillard, 3 Russ. 149; Carter *v.* Anderson, 3 Sim. 370.

5 Parker *v.* Brooke, 9 Ves. 583; Macq. Hus. & Wife, 298.

So by the ordinary rule of the English chancery courts a wife is precluded from recovering the arrears of income on her separate estate for more than a year, upon the ground of a supposed gift to her husband.[1]

In this country whenever the wife's separate use has been admitted as a doctrine of equity, independently of statute, her right of dominion has also been recognized. The celebrated New York case of *Jaques* v. *The Methodist Episcopal Church*, which may justly be placed foremost among the very few important American chancery decisions of this class, established not only that a *feme covert*, with respect to her separate estate, was to be regarded in equity as a *feme sole*, so that she might dispose of it without the assent and concurrence of her trustee, unless specially restrained by the instrument under which it had been acquired — a position not likely to be disputed at this day; but, furthermore, that though a particular mode of disposition was specifically pointed out in the instrument, it would not preclude the wife from adopting any other mode of disposition unless she was by express language specially restrained to that particular mode.[2] In this latter doctrine Chancellor Kent (whose judgment in the lower court had been reversed) did not concur: adopting the more conservative view with reference to such restrictions. The distinction is rather a nice one, and successive American decisions in other States have generally sustained the Chancellor's views: but the cases are, on the whole, conflicting.[3]

[1] Peachey Mar. Settl. 291, and cases cited; Rowley *v.* Unwin, 2 Kay & Johns. 142; Arthur *v.* Arthur, 11 Ir. Ch. 513. And see Dalbiac *v.* Dalbiac, 16 Ves. 116; Fleet *v.* Perrins, Law Rep. 3 Q. B. 536; Parker *v.* Brooke, 9 Ves. 583; Caton *v.* Rideout, 1 Mac. & Gord. 599; Beresford *v.* Archbishop of Armagh, 13 Sim. 643; Howard *v.* Digby, 2 Cl. & Fin. 634; Symes *v.* Lee, 26 L. J. Eq. 665.

[2] 17 Johns. 548; Methodist Episcopal Church *v.* Jaques, 1 Johns. Ch. 450; 3 ib. 77.

[3] See Tullett *v.* Armstrong, referred to *supra*, for the English doctrine. For American authorities, see 2 Kent Com. 165, 166, and cases cited in last edition; Shipp *v.* Bowman, 5 B. Monr. 163; Tarr *v.* Williams, 4 Md. Ch. 68; Nix *v.* Bradley, 6 Rich. Eq. 53; Wylly *v.* Collins, 9 Geo. 233; Doty *v.* Mitchell, 9 Sm. & M. 435; Morgan *v.* Elam, 4 Yerg. 375; Ewing *v.* Smith, 3 Desaus. 417; Lancaster

In the exercise of her right of dominion the wife may also bestow her separate property upon her husband, give him the use and income thereof, or bind it for his debts.[1] It is also well settled, both under our married women's acts and independently of them, that a married woman may execute a mortgage jointly with her husband to secure his debts: in which case she is to be regarded as his surety; and this applies to lands held in her right, whether conveyed to her separate use or not.[2] And her separate estate will be bound by any debt properly contracted by her, even though her husband should be the creditor.[3]

So, too, she may bind her separate estate in person or by her agent, without the assent of her trustee, if the instrument creating the trust contains no restriction upon her power: and the trustee will be bound by her exercise of dominion, so far as concerns the estate in his hands.[4]

A married woman may, by her contracts, bind her separate property, and it is sufficient in such cases that there was an intention to charge her separate estate. By contracting a debt during coverture, she furnishes a presumption of that intention.[5] But where the debt is contracted before marriage the

v. Dolan, 1 Rawle, 231; Harris *v.* Harris, 7 Ired. Eq. 111; Hume *v.* Hord, 5 Gratt. 374; Hicks *v.* Johnston, 24 Geo. 194; Andrews *v.* Jones, 32 Miss. 274; Leaycraft *v.* Hedden, 3 Green Ch. 512; Penn. Co. *v.* Foster, 35 Penn. St. 134; Chew *v.* Beall, 13 Md. 348. The clause of restraint upon anticipation does not seem to have been applied much in American cases of this sort.

1 2 Kent Com. 111, and cases cited; 2 U. S. Eq. Dig. Husband and Wife, 18; Dallam *v.* Walpole, Pet. C. C. 116.

2 Demarest *v.* Wynkoop, 3 Johns. Ch. 129; Van Horne *v.* Everson, 13 Barb. 526; Vartie *v.* Underwood, 18 Barb. 561; Bartlett *v.* Bartlett, 4 Allen, 440; Young *v.* Graff, 28 Ill. 20; Watson *v.* Thurber, 11 Mich. 457; Eaton *v.* Nason, 47 Me. 132; Spear *v.* Ward, 20 Cal. 659; Ellis *v.* Kenyon, 25 Ind. 134; Green *v.* Scranage, 19 Iowa, 461; Wolff *v.* Van Meter, 19 Iowa, 134. And see Leavitt *v.* Peel, 25 N. Y. 474.

3 Gardner *v.* Gardner, 7 Paige, 112.

4 North American Coal Co. *v.* Dyett, 7 Paige, 1; Gibson *v.* Walker, 20 N. Y. 476. And see Lewis *v.* Harris, 4 Met. (Ky.) 353. But see Noyes *v.* Blakeman, 2 Seld. 567; s. c. 3 Sandf. 531, as to the effect of New-York statute relative to the declaration of trusts.

5 2 Kent Com. 164, and cases cited; Fire Ins. Co. *v.* Bay, 4 Comst. 9; Vanderheyden *v.* Mallory, 1 Comst. 452; 2 U. S. Eq. Dig. Husband and Wife, 19.

remedy against the separate estate of the wife is suspended during marriage.[1] In general, it is to be observed that the American equity doctrine of the wife's power to charge her separate estate, independently of the married women's acts, has fluctuated somewhat, as have likewise the English cases.

But the doctrine of the wife's dominion over her separate estate is at this day more generally asserted with reference to the married women's acts: and some of the later cases show important variations from the equity rule, as we shall proceed to notice.

The late case of *Yale* v. *Dederer* is an important one, as establishing in a leading American State, under cover of legislative policy, a new doctrine, utterly at variance with that of the modern English equity courts, and contrary to its own precedents.[2] It appeared that the husband had offered his promissory note to the plaintiff in payment of certain cows which he wished to purchase; that the plaintiff, doubting his solvency, required him to procure his wife to unite in a note with him. This he did. The note was subsequently renewed. At the time of signing the note Mrs. Dederer remarked that if her husband was not able to pay it she was. It was established that she had sufficient real estate, held in her own right, to satisfy the claim; and the judge, who heard the evidence, stated in his finding, that "the defendant, Mrs. Dederer, intended to charge, and did expressly charge, her separate estate for the payment of the note." The court of appeals nevertheless held that Mrs. Dederer was a mere surety for her husband; and that though it was her intention to charge her separate estate, such intention did not take effect. The principle of the decision was this: that, in order to create a charge upon the separate estate of a married woman, the intention to do so must be declared in the very contract which is the foundation of the charge, or the consideration must be obtained for the

[1] Vanderheyden *v.* Mallory, 1 Comst. 452. But see Dickson *v.* Miller, 11 S. & M. 594.

[2] Yale *v.* Dederer, 18 N. Y. 265; s. c. 22 N. Y. 450. The principle in these two cases differs.

direct benefit of the estate itself. The later New York decisions follow the rule of this case, and require a distinct written obligation to bind the wife where the debt is not contracted for the direct benefit of the estate.[1]

But it does not appear that this new doctrine has found favor in other States. In Wisconsin the decision of *Yale* v. *Dederer* is unsparingly condemned.[2] The general rule in this country still seems to be that the wife's separate estate will be held liable for all debts which she by implication or expressly, by writing or parol, charges thereon.[3] For the wife's debts are charged in equity upon her separate estate, not because of her power to make a valid written or verbal contract, but because it is right that her debts should be paid.[4]

The later American decisions under the married women's acts often manifest a disposition to charge the wife's engagements upon her separate estate rather than against the husband. Thus in Connecticut, while it is admitted that the wife's contracts can only bind her property and not her person, it is held that a promissory note, signed by her husband in her name, and as her trustee, and with full authority to act in the premises, being negotiated on the faith of her credit and not her husband's, cannot be enforced against him personally, though she should afterwards be found irresponsible.[5] And if

[1] White *v.* McNett, 33 N. Y. 371; Ledlie *v.* Vrooman, 41 Barb. 109; White *v.* Story, 43 Barb. 124. See Barnett *v.* Lichtenstein, 39 Barb. 194.

[2] Todd *v.* Lee, 15 Wis. 365.

[3] Pentz *v.* Simonson, 2 Beasl. 232; Grapengether *v.* Fejervary, 9 Iowa, 163; Rogers *v.* Ward, 8 Allen, 387; Major *v.* Symmes, 19 Ind. 117; Oakley *v.* Pound, 1 McCart. 178; Miller *v.* Newton, 23 Cal. 554; 2 Kent Com. 164; 2 Story Eq. Jur. §§ 1398, 1401. See Koontz *v.* Nabb, 16 Md. 549; Knox *v.* Jordan, 5 Jones Eq. 175; McFaddin *v.* Crumpler, 20 Tex. 374. In Rhode Island, a narrow rule is adopted. Cozzens *v.* Whitney, 3 R. I. 79.

[4] Cummins *v.* Sharpe, 21 Ind. 331; Pentz *v.* Simonson, 2 Beasl. 232; Glass *v.* Warwick, 40 Penn. St. 140. But see Maclay *v.* Love, 25 Cal. 367; Hanly *v.* Downing, 4 Met. (Ky.) 95.

[5] Taylor *v.* Shelton, 30 Conn. 122. And see Gilbert *v.* Plant, 18 Ind. 308; Baker *v.* Gregory, 28 Ala. 544; Gunn *v.* Samuel, 33 Ala. 201; Mayer *v.* Galluchat, 6 Rich. Eq. 1; Wyley *v.* Collins, 9 Geo. 223. See Black *v.* Bryan, 18 Tex. 453.

there be any good sense in the rule that where credit is once given to the wife, the husband will not be liable, though the articles purchased be a necessary, it is in cases where the wife has a separate income or separate property of her own and under her own control.

The undoubted right of the wife on general principles to treat her husband as the trustee of her separate property, has given rise, under the married women's acts, to perplexing questions as between herself and his creditors. In New York her privileges in this respect are carried very far; for she may employ her husband as her managing agent to control her property, without subjecting it to the claim of his creditors; the application of an indefinite portion of the income to his support does not impair her title to the property; and neither he nor his creditors acquire an interest in the property through his services thus rendered.[1] It seems to be the well settled American doctrine that by working upon the wife's lands the husband acquires no beneficial interest therein which can be enforced in equity on behalf either of himself or his creditors, in absence of a definite agreement for compensation.[2] The crops cannot be attached by his creditors.[3] Nor the betterments, buildings, and rents.[4] In some States the husband cannot dispose of his life-interest in his wife's lands at all, without the wife's assent.[5]

Where the question arises whether the husband is enjoying the wife's property by way of gift from her, or as her managing attorney, it must be determined by evidence. In either case the advantage seems to be with husband and wife in all controversies with the creditor. The general rule still prevails

[1] Buckley *v.* Wells, 33 N, Y. 518; Knapp *v.* Smith, 27 N. Y. 277.

[2] Buckley *v.* Wells, ib.; Welston *v.* Hildreth, 33 Vt. 457; Cheuvete *v.* Mason, 4 Greene (Iowa), 231; Betts *v.* Betts, 18 Ala. 787.

[3] McIntyre *v.* Knowlton, 6 Allen, 565; Lewis *v.* Johns, 24 Cal. 98; Allen *v.* Hightower, 21 Ark. 316.

[4] White *v.* Hildreth, 32 Vt. 265; Goss *v.* Cahill, 42 Barb. 310; Wilkinson *v.* Wilkinson, 1 Head, 305; Robinson *v.* Huffman, 15 B. Monr. 80.

[5] Coleman *v.* Satterfield, 2 Head, 259; Jenney *v.* Grey, 5 Ohio St. 45.

however that money transactions between husband and wife should be free from fraud, and not prejudicial to pre-existing creditors of the husband. The presumptions are not equally balanced in the different States. But presumptions of a gift from the wife are not to be strongly favored where the husband is held out to others as her agent.[1] So gifts of income would be more readily presumed than gifts of capital. In New Hampshire, it is held that the wife may lease her separate property to her husband.[2] And the rule is recognized under the statutes of many States, that she may bestow her separate estate upon him either by way of loan or gift.[3]

With the assent of the husband and father the labor of the wife and children may be bestowed upon the separate property of the wife and thus enure to their benefit. There is no known rule of law which requires the husband and father to compel his wife and children to work in the service of his creditors.[4] And it is held that the husband may stipulate, though insolvent, that the product of his own labor shall be appropriated to his wife's separate use.[5]

But a married woman's promissory note does not, as a rule, secure her husband's debts, nor does she bind herself lawfully as his surety on a contract not relating to her separate estate.[6] The same may be said of her undertakings for the benefit of third parties.[7] The tendency of some of the late cases is to exempt promissory notes which are drawn payable to a married

[1] See Wales *v.* Newbould, 9 Mich. 45; Elijah *v.* Taylor, 37 Ill. 247.

[2] Albin *v.* Lord, 39 N. H. 196.

[3] Hinney *v.* Phillips, 50 Penn. St. 382; Fox *v.* Jones, 1 West Va. 205; White *v.* Callinan, 19 Ind. 43; 2 Kent Com. 111, and cases cited, last ed.; Johnston *v.* Johnston, 1 Grant, 468; Gage *v.* Dauchy, 28 Barb. 622; Roper *v.* Roper, 29 Ala. 247. See chapter on Post-nuptial Settlements.

[4] Johnson *v.* Vail, 1 McCart. 423.

[5] Hodges *v.* Cobb, 8 Rich. 50. But see Penn *v.* Whitehead, 12 Gratt. 74.

[6] Parker *v.* Simonds, 1 Allen, 258; Shannon *v.* Canney, 44 N. H. 592; Keaton *v.* Scott, 25 Geo. 652; Yale *v.* Dederer, 18 N. Y. 265; Wolff *v.* Van Meter, 19 Iowa, 134; Sweeney *v.* Smith, 15 B. Monr. 325.

[7] Shannon *v.* Canney, 44 N. H. 592; Crane *v.* Kelley, 7 Allen, 250; Bailey *v.* Pearson, 9 Fost. 77; Lytle's Appeal, 36 Penn. St. 131.

woman or order from all liability for the husband's engagements.[1]

It is held in New Hampshire that a wife, owning a right of dower in her husband's lands, may properly convey it and take a promissory note of equal value payable to herself; or, owning a promissory note in her own right, secured by mortgage on the husband's estate, may sell and release her interest in such estate, and take a new note payable to herself.[2] Even promissory notes taken in the husband's name are open to explanation.[3] As to the wife's gratuitous undertaking to subject her property to her husband's debts, the Pennsylvania rule is that equity will not enforce it, but leave the parties to their legal remedies.[4]

There are many late decisions as to the husband's dominion over his wife's separate property. Thus in Wisconsin he may execute in her name a valid conveyance of her land under a power of attorney.[5] In Maine, he may sue for damages to his wife's separate estate while managing it for her.[6] And the wife may employ other agents, who will not be held answerable to him for executing her orders.[7] In New York, the marriage of the mortgagee to the mortgagor does not extinguish her right of foreclosure.[8]

In a case free from fraud or undue influence the wife may mortgage her separate property to secure a third person's debt.[9] But it is the declared rule of many States that the hus-

[1] See Cowles *v.* Morgan, 34 Ala. 535; Lewis *v.* Harris, 4 Met. (Ky.) 353; Chapman *v.* Williams, 13 Gray, 416; Paine *v.* Hunt, 40 Barb. 75.

[2] Nims *v.* Bigelow, 45 N. H. 343.

[3] Buck *v.* Gilson, 37 Vt. 653; Conrad *v.* Shomo, 44 Penn. St. 193. See Baker *v.* Gregory, 28 Ala. 544.

[4] White's Appeal, 36 Penn. St. 134.

[5] Weisbrod *v.* Chicago, &c., R. R. Co. 18 Wis. 35; Peck *v.* Hendershott, 14 Iowa, 40.

[6] Woodman *v.* Neal, 48 Me. 266. But only in her name, in accordance with statute.

[7] Southard *v.* Plummer, 36 Me. 64.

[8] Power *v.* Lester, 23 N. Y. 527.

[9] Bartlett *v.* Bartlett, 4 Allen, 440.

band cannot of his own act subject his wife's land to a mechanic's lien.[1] Nor mortgage it for his individual debt.[2] For it is a general principle that the wife's separate property cannot be made liable for the debts of her husband or others without her assent.[3]

While the wife may avoid a fraud upon her as against all who participated therein, it is held that a creditor's rights cannot be prejudiced by any misbehavior of the husband, which procured them the wife's security, if it was without his instigation, knowledge, or consent.[4] But when the husband makes a void transfer as his wife's trustee, it is held that she can follow the investment into other hands.[5] Or she may have him removed from his trusteeship for suitable cause.[6] In all controversies of this kind, the late observation of a Pennsylvania court is worth remembering, that a married woman cannot possibly enjoy her property as freely as before marriage; for the nature of her relation with her husband forbids it.[7]

The rule in many States, under the married women's acts, is that the husband must join the wife in contracts and conveyances relating to her separate property. Particularly is this true of transactions concerning the wife's real estate. Contracts and conveyances otherwise made are not binding.[8] But in

[1] Briggs *v.* Titus, 7 R. I. 441; Spinning *v.* Blackburn, 13 Ohio St. 131; Pell *v.* Cole, 2 Met. (Ky.) 252; Selph *v.* Howland, 23 Miss. 264.

[2] See Patterson *v.* Flanagan, 1 Ala. s. c. 427.

[3] Hutchins *v.* Colby, 43 N. H. 159; Hatz's Appeal, 40 Penn. St. 209; George *v.* Ransom, 15 Cal. 322; Cheuvete *v.* Mason, 4 Greene, (Iowa), 231; Yale *v.* Dederer, 18 N. Y. 265; Sharp *v.* Wickliffe, 3 Litt. 10; Johnson *v.* Runyon, 21 Ind. 115. And see Mgan *v.* Stevenson, 1 Grant, 402.

[4] Childs *v.* McChesney, 20 Iowa, 431; Edgerton *v.* Jones, 10 Minn. 427.

[5] George *v.* Ransom, 14 Cal. 658.

[6] Raney *v.* Rainey, 35 Ala. 282. So with any other trustee of her separate property. Johnson *v.* Snow, 5 R. I. 72. See Scott *v.* Scott, 13 Ind. 225; Ritter *v.* Ritter, 31 Penn. St. 390.

[7] Walker *v.* Reamy, 36 Penn. St. 410.

[8] Wright *v.* Brown, 44 Penn. St. 224; James *v.* Everly, 3 Grant, 150; Camden *v.* Vail, 23 Cal. 633; Murphy *v.* Bright, 3 Grant, 296; Alexander *v.* Saulsbury, 1 Ala. 436; Maclay *v.* Love, 25 Cal. 367; Pentz *v.* Simonson, 2 Beasl. 232; Major *v.* Symmes, 19 Ind. 117; Miller *v.* Hine, 13 Ohio St. 565; Haugh *v.* Blythe, 20 Ind. 24; Dodge *v.* Hollinshead, 6 Minn. 25; Eaton *v.* George, 42 N. H. 375; Miller *v.* Wetherby, 12 Iowa, 415. But see Stacker *v.* Whitlock, 3 Met. (Ky.) 244.

North Carolina it has been decided, on equity principles, that where a wife after marriage, supposing the whole interest in her land was in her, made a conveyance to a trustee for her sole and separate use, which her husband signed as a party, and by various clauses manifested a concurrence in her act, but did not profess directly to convey any estate, the recital in the deed that ten dollars was paid by the trustee to the wife raised a use, and in that way passed the husband's interest to the trustee.[1] The language of the married women's acts in many States authorizes the inference that nothing further than the written concurrence of the husband is requisite to complete the validity of the wife's transfer of separate personal property. And in some States the wife's sole deed of her separate real estate is sufficient to pass her entire interest.[2] But it has been held that the wife's execution of a conveyance in blank is void, though the deed be afterwards filled up according to her directions.[3]

Following the spirit of recent legislation, some American courts now hold the wife liable on her covenants contained in a conveyance of her separate lands.[4] So specific performance is decreed against her on her written promise to convey; provided the contract be executed with the formalities requisite in her conveyance.[5] And equity will not permit the wife to avoid a sale without refunding the purchase-money.[6] So it is held, under the married women's acts, that where a wife purchased goods giving her sole notes for them, and after her husband's death she promised to pay the notes and settle for other goods furnished, for which she gave no notes, the promise was founded on good consideration, and she might be sued by the vendors.[7]

1 Barnes *v.* Haybarger, 8 Jones, 76.

2 Springer *v.* Berry, 47 Me. 330; Farr *v.* Sherman, 11 Mich. 33; Beal *v.* Warren, 2 Gray, 447. And see Collier *v.* Connelly, 15 Ind. 141, as to indorsement of notes.

3 Burns *v.* Lynde, 6 Allen, 305.

4 Basford *v.* Peirson, 7 Allen, 524.

5 Woodward *v.* Seaver, 38 N. H. 29; Baker *v.* Hathaway, 5 Allen, 103. But see Rumfelt *v.* Clemens, 46 Penn. St. 455.

6 Kolls *v.* De Leyer, 41 Barb. 208.

7 Goulding *v.* Davidson, 26 N. Y. 604. But see Felton *v.* Reid, 7 Jones, 269.

But the fact that a husband allows his wife to treat and deal with, as her own, property acquired by her independently of the married women's acts is not inconsistent with his intention to assert his marital rights to it if he survive; neither if he allows her to dispose of the income and loan it on promissory notes running in her own name, would such income become thereby converted into her separate estate.[1] The married women's acts, in the absence of unequivocal language, do not change the common-law rule with reference to separate personal property of a married woman, not disposed of in her life nor by will; it goes to her surviving husband by his marital right in the same manner as before.[2] And a wife who has appropriated her separate property to her husband's use, during his life, cannot charge his assets with it after his death.[3]

The Supreme Court of Pennsylvania, commenting upon the recent married women's code in that State, observes that its purpose was to secure a wife in the use and enjoyment of her property, not to enable her to make contracts she could not have made before;[4] they consequently have treated as void her judgment for a debt contracted for the improvement of her real estate;[5] her bond, accompanied by a mortgage of her separate estate;[6] and her debt, contracted jointly with her husband, though for family necessaries.[7] And the manifest tendency in that State is plainly to limit the wife's general privileges to the statutory grant of power.[8] Nor is the New York doctrine of the husband's employment as "managing agent" favored to the injury of creditors.[9]

1 Ryder *v.* Hulse, 24 N. Y. 372; s. c. 33 Barb. 264.

2 Ranson *v.* Nichols, 22 N. Y. 110; Wilkinson *v.* Wright, 6 B. Monr. 576; Brown *v.* Brown, 6 Humph. 127.

3 Edelen *v.* Edelen, 11 Md. 415.

4 Brunner's Appeal, per Strong J., 47 Penn. St. 67.

5 Ib. And see Patton *v.* Stewart, 19 Ind. 233.

6 Steinman *v.* Ewing, 43 Penn. St. 63. See Ramborger *v.* Ingram, 38 Penn. St. 146.

7 Cummings *v.* Miller, 3 Grant, 146.

8 See Rumfelt *v.* Clemens, 46 Penn. St. 455; Parke *v.* Kleebor, 37 Penn. St. 251.

9 Keeney *v.* Good, 21 Penn. St. 349.

In Massachusetts the principle upon which the wife may charge her separate estate is stated to be that where by her contract the debt created is made expressly a charge on her separate estate, or is expressly contracted on its credit, or where the consideration goes to the benefit of such estate, or to enhance its value, equity will decree that it shall be paid from such estate or its income, to the extent to which the power of disposal by the married woman may go.[1] And the equitable relief which is afforded to enforce payment of such a debt out of her separate property is founded on the reason that the contract is entered into in such form as to indicate an intent by the wife to create a personal liability. Equity will give effect to this intention by assisting the creditor to reach and apply her separate estate, so far as the *jus disponendi* is vested in her. This intent and the facts on which it rests are in no degree affected by the giving of collateral security.[2] Hence payment may be enforced out of a married woman's separate estate upon a bond given by her for the price of land conveyed to her sole and separate use.[3]

Upon the ground that the wife's separate estate should be bound by contracts for its benefit, her debts for improvements upon lands conveyed to her sole and separate use have been enforced in several late instances.[4] So, too, the joint note of herself and husband for lumber and materials to be used thereon.[5]

There is some difficulty in the purchase by a married woman of property, whether real or personal, on credit, arising out of the circumstance that she cannot make a contract for payment which will be personally binding. In New Hampshire,

[1] Willard *v.* Eastham, 15 Gray, 328; Rogers *v.* Ward, per Bigelow C. J., 8 Allen, 387.

[2] Rogers *v.* Ward, ib.

[3] Ib. See Davenport *v.* Davenport, 5 Allen, 464.

[4] Conway *v.* Smith, 13 Wis. 125; Marshall *v.* Miller, 3 Met. (Ky.) 333; Carpenter *v.* Leonard, 5 Minn. 155; Britter *v.* Robertson, 11 Tex. 142. In Heugh *v.* Jones, 32 Penn. St. 432, it is held that unless the materials are *actually* so used the debt cannot be enforced against the estate.

[5] Parker *v.* Kane, 4 Allen, 346. And see Major *v.* Symmes, 19 Ind. 117.

it is held that a married woman cannot, under the statutes, make a contract for money or property in anticipation of the purchase of separate estate; and hence that her note given for money borrowed wherewith to make such purchase is void.[1] But, on the other hand, the New York doctrine is that she may purchase property on credit; and if the vendor will run the risk of being able to obtain payment of the consideration of the sale, the transfer will be valid, and no estate will pass to the husband, whether the wife had previously any separate estate or not.[2] And her separate estate is in fact charged by her purchase on credit.[3] A like rule seems to prevail in Massachusetts.[4]

In Maine it is held that a married woman may, under the statutes, hold an estate in trust and make contracts accordingly.[5] And in Maine, New York, Illinois, Indiana, and other States, a wife may now sue at law in matters relating to her separate property without joining her husband.[6] So she may bind herself by a submission to arbitration.[7] But she cannot confess judgment, though for a debt incurred for the benefit of her separate estate.[8] Under the married women's acts of some States the wife may sue her husband at law like any stranger.[9] But in other States she cannot.[10]

To attempt a minute analysis of the married women's acts would require more space than our plan will permit. Nor would it profit the reader. The independent legislation of some

1 Ames *v.* Foster, 42 N. H. 381. And see Johnson *v.* Chisson, 14 Ind. 415; Dunning *v.* Pike, 46 Me. 461.

2 Darby *v.* Calligan, 16 N. Y. 21; Knapp *v.* Smith, 27 N. Y. 277.

3 Bullin *v.* Dillage, 37 N. Y. 35.

4 Chapman *v.* Foster, 6 Allen, 136.

5 Spinger *v.* Berry, 47 Me. 330.

6 Walker *v.* Gilman, 45 Me. 28; Ackly *v.* Tarbox, 31 N. Y. 565; Peters *v.* Fowler, 41 Barb. 467; Emerson *v.* Clayton, 32 Ill. 493; Leonard *v.* Townsend, 26 Cal. 435; Weymouth *v.* Chicago, &c., R. R. Co., 17 Wis. 550; Jordan *v.* Cummings, 43 N. H. 134; Gee *v.* Lewis, 20 Ind. 149.

7 Palmer *v.* Davis, 28 N. Y. 242.

8 Watkins *v.* Abrahams, 24 N. J. 72. And see Patton *v.* Stewart, 19 Ind. 233.

9 Scott *v.* Scott, 13 Ind. 225.

10 Ritter *v.* Ritter, 31 Penn. St. 390.

thirty distinct communities, without uniformity of plan or principle, involving, as it does, the most interesting and yet the most perplexing of social problems, must necessarily produce results which cannot be reconciled. Even though the hand of innovation should be stayed for a while, and public attention centre in the work of blending these results into harmony, it would be many years before our courts, applying civil codes and the traditions of the English common law and equity jurisprudence to the discordant mass of material before them could hope to set up a consistent and thorough American system. As one of our own jurists remarks,[1] wherever the line may be drawn, it will be long before the public will understand and recognize the point where the power of a married woman to bind herself by her bargains ceases, and frauds upon the thoughtless and inconsiderate must often occur.

[1] Per Bell C. J. in Ames *v.* Foster, 42 N. H. 381.

CHAPTER XIII.

THE WIFE'S PIN-MONEY, SEPARATE EARNINGS AND POWER TO TRADE.

THE wife's pin-money constitutes a feature of English marriage settlements at the present day. Pin-money may be defined as a certain provision for the wife's dress and pocket, to which there is annexed the duty of expending it in her "personal apparel, decoration, or ornament." [1] It differs from the wife's separate estate in being a gift subject to conditions and not at her absolute disposal. It differs from her *paraphernalia* in being subject to her control during marriage, and not awaiting the husband's death.[2]

Upon a somewhat enlarged construction pin-money is in the nature of an annuity to pay the wife's ordinary personal expenses; and is rather the privilege of the wealthy than the poor. A person in an humble station of life pays his wife's bills as he pays his own. A person in a station rather higher is accustomed to make, for common convenience, an allowance to his wife of so much for house-keeping expenses, if she takes charge of them, and so much over for her own dress and the dress of her children. A person in a still higher station makes a general arrangement, which probably extends over years, if not over the whole coverture. But a person in a yet more elevated station makes a special stipulation by the marriage settlement, which is, as it were, saying, "You, the wife, shall not be reduced to the somewhat humiliating necessity of dis-

[1] Per Lord Langdale, Joddrell *v.* Joddrell, 9 Beav. 45; Howard *v.* Digby, 2 Cl. & Fin. 654.

[2] Macq. Hus. & Wife, 318; Peachey Mar. Settl. 298.

closing to me every want of a pound to keep in your pocket; or of taking my pleasure and obtaining my consent every time you want to go to the milliner's shop to order your dress; but you shall have so much, consistent with my estate and my income, which you shall retain apart from me and exempt from my control." And this supply, as Lord Brougham remarks, is the wife's pin-money.[1]

The exact period when pin-money was first introduced into England is not known. Lord Brougham inclines to ascribe it to the feudal times.[2] But there is equally good authority for fixing the date at the Restoration; and the lawyers resort to Addison's Spectator in proof of this latter position.[3] The popular name of this provision scarcely suggests its real significance; for, so far from being a petty allowance, it is often of the most liberal amount imaginable.[4]

The subject of the wife's pin-money seems to have received little attention in this country.[5] And in England few cases of the sort have ever arisen. It is found more convenient in marriage contracts to settle a certain allowance upon the wife by way of separate estate, which allowance is subject to the usual incidents of separate property. Decisions as to pin-money and separate estate are frequently confounded.[6]

The leading English case on this subject is *Howard* v. *Digby*, which went to the House of Lords in 1834. The main decision was to the effect that the personal representatives of the wife could not recover arrears.[7] The correctness of its principle has been questioned by some writers.[8] In general, the usual

1 Howard *v.* Digby, 2 Cl. & Fin. 654.

2 Ib. 676.

3 Spectator, 295. See Peachey Mar. Settl. 300; Sugd. Law Prop. 165.

4 In one reported English case, by no means recent, £13,000 a year was secured to the wife as her pin-money. See 2 Russ. 1, and *n.* to Macq. Hus. & Wife, 318.

5 But see Miller *v.* Williamson, 5 Md. 219.

6 See Lord Brougham, in Howard *v.* Digby, 2 Cl. & Fin. 670, commenting upon 2 Roper Hus. & Wife, 133. In this case the whole subject receives ample discussion.

7 2 Cl. & Fin. 670.

8 Sugd. Law Prop. 170. See Peachey Mar. Settl. 307; Macq. Hus. & Wife, 319 *n.*

equity rule against claiming more than one year's arrears appears to apply to separate estate and pin-money alike.[1] In other ways the wife's claim may be barred.[2]

The wife was formerly supposed also to gain a title to savings out of her house-keeping allowance.[3] So where the husband allowed the wife to make profit of butter, eggs, poultry, and other farm produce, which allowance he called her pin-money, it was held that she acquired a separate ownership therein.[4] But these cases rest upon questionable authority.[5] And more recently it has been decided that where the wife of a farmer, with his knowledge and sanction, deposited the produce of the surplus butter, eggs, and poultry, with a firm in her own name, and he called it "her money," and on his death-bed gave his executor directions to remove the money, and do the best he could with it for his wife, such evidence was insufficient to establish a gift between them, and that the husband had made neither the firm nor himself trustee for his wife.[6]

Indeed, the well settled principle both of law and equity is that, in absence of a distinct gift from the husband, all the wife's earnings belong to him and not to herself. But by recent statutes enacted in many of the United States married women are allowed the benefits of their own labor and services, when performed on their sole and separate account.[7] These statutes vary somewhat in their terms. Thus by a Maryland statute the amount she may so acquire is limited to one thousand dollars over and above her debts. The presumptions concerning the wife's title to her earnings seem to be the same as

1 See Peachey Mar. Settl. 303, and cases cited.

2 Arthur *v.* Arthur, 11 Ir. Eq. 511.

3 Paul Neal's Case, Prec. in Ch. 44, 297. But see Tyrrell's Case, Freem. 304.

4 Slanning *v.* Style, 3 P. Wms. 337.

5 See Macq. Hus. & Wife, 320.

6 Mews *v.* Mews, 15 Beav. 529. See McLean *v.* Longlands, 5 Ves. 78, cited herein with approval. And see Rider *v.* Hulse, 33 Barb. 264, for a similar American decision.

7 See latest statutes of New York, Massachusetts, Rhode Island, Maryland and California.

in other separate property purporting to belong to her.[1] And it may be generally observed that statutes which authorize married women to hold property acquired by gift, grant, or purchase, from any person other than the husband, do not carry the wife's earnings by implication.[2]

Independently therefore of statutes which plainly secure to married women their separate earnings, it is held that an agreement between the wife, with the knowledge and consent of her husband, and a third person, for nursing and attention, the stipulation being that she shall be paid what her services are reasonably worth, gives to the wife no title as against her husband.[3] Nor does equity raise a resulting trust in the wife's favor, where she contracted, with the consent of her husband, for the purchase of a lot of land, conveyed to him, though she paid off the mortgage, given for part of the purchase-money, from her own earnings.[4]

But where a statute provides that property acquired by a married woman by her personal services shall be her separate property, and exempt from liability for her husband's debts, money due for her services is protected in the same manner as if the money had been received.[5] And even on general principles of equity, the husband may in this country, as in England, create in his wife a separate estate in the proceeds of her own toil; the validity of such gifts, as against creditors, being subject to the same rules which apply to other voluntary conveyances.[6] So where a married woman by her industry, made money as a basket-maker, — thus supplying her family with

[1] Raybold *v.* Raybold, 20 Penn. St. 308; Elliott *v.* Bentley, 17 Wis. 591; Laing *v.* Cunningham, 17 Iowa, 510.

[2] Rider *v.* Hulse, 33 Barb. 264; Hoyt *v.* White, 46 N. H. 45; Merrill *v.* Smith, 37 Me. 394; Grover *v.* Alcott, 11 Mich. 470.

[3] Woodbeck *v.* Havens, 42 Barb. 66. And see Elliott *v.* Bentley, 17 Wis. 591; Duncan *v.* Roselle, 15 Iowa, 501; McKarlin *v.* Bresslin, 8 Gray, 177.

[4] Skillman *v.* Skillman, 15 N. J. Ch. 478.

[5] Whitney *v.* Beckwith, 31 Conn. 596.

[6] Pinkston *v.* McLemore, 31 Ala. 308; Neufville *v.* Thompson, 3 Edw. Ch. 92; Barron *v.* Barron, 24 Vt. 375; Smart *v.* Comstock, 24 Barb. 411.

necessaries; and was in the habit of lending out the surplus money, and collecting it when due, with her husband's knowledge; even a court of law has liberally stretched its authority to protect her acts, on the ground of an implied agency from her husband.[1]

The wife's power to carry on a separate trade is another topic, known long ago to the law of England; and in this respect our American legislation of the present day seems to have been somewhat anticipated. The wife's lawful power to carry on a trade on her own account, independently of her husband, like most of her other separate privileges, is founded upon contracts made with her in derogation of the husband's marital rights. It appears that a wife, desiring to go into business on her own account, makes an agreement with her husband. When the agreement is made before marriage it will bind the husband and his creditors; when made during the coverture, it binds the husband only, and is void against creditors.[2] This species of contract seems to have been recognized in the common-law tribunals.

If, for the purpose of enabling a married woman to carry on her separate trade, property be vested in trustees before the marriage, the wife will at law be considered their agent, and in that character will have the benefit of the property, and enjoy its increase and profits independently of her husband, and free from liability in respect of his debts.[3] The law considers the wife as the agent of her own trustee, and her possession is his possession.

The question whether the trade be carried on solely by the wife, or jointly with her husband, is a question of fact for the jury. If they find that it is a joint business, the stock in trade

[1] White *v.* Oeland, 12 Rich. 308.

[2] Macq. Hus. & Wife, 321; 2 Bright Hus. & Wife, 292; Lavie *v.* Phillips, 3 Burr. 1783; 2 Roper Hus. & Wife, 165, 175, and cases cited. See antenuptial and postnuptial settlements *infra*.

[3] Jarman *v.* Wooloton, 3 T. R. 618; Macq. Hus. & Wife, 321; 2 Bright Hus. & Wife, 297.

will be subject to the husband's obligations.[1] So the husband will be liable for the debts, if it appear that he participated with the wife in the benefits.[2]

Separate trading was also permitted the wife by the "custom of London;" and herein she was regarded as liable to arrest and imprisonment for debt without her husband, and, moreover, might be declared a bankrupt.[3]

Notwithstanding these provisions of the law, it does not appear that separate trading in England was ever very common. No modern equity cases are to be found on this subject.[4] The difficulties in the way of establishing credit, and negotiating securities on the wife's sole behalf, were probably found insurmountable, even though married women were found anxious to assume the responsibilities of trade.

This doctrine comes up anew in this country of late years with our recent policy in favor of the independence of married women. And the rule seems to be well established in the United States that the husband, in pursuance of a marriage contract, antenuptial or postnuptial, may confer upon his wife the right to trade for her exclusive benefit.[5] Nor have the American cases uniformly insisted upon formal contracts between husband and wife; seemingly regarding the question as one of mutual intention merely. Thus the equity rule in Vermont is that the wife shall hold the result of her earnings, in every case, against the husband and his heirs, and generally against his creditors, so long as he allows her to keep the property separate from the general mass of his own estate; although his own name may be used in the formal conduct of the busi-

[1] Barlow v. Bishop, 1 East, 432; Macq. Hus. & Wife, 322; 2 Bright Hus. & Wife, 297.

[2] Petty v. Anderson, 2 Car. & P. 38; Macq. Hus. & Wife, 322.

[3] Beard v. Webb, 2 Bos. & Pul. 97. See 2 Roper Hus. & Wife, 124.

[4] See comments in Macq. Hus. & Wife, 323, on the cases cited in 2 Roper Hus. & Wife, 172, 173.

[5] Richardson v. Estate of Merrill, 32 Vt. 27; Tillman v. Shackleton, 15 Mich. 447; Wieman v. Anderson, 42 Penn. St. 311; Duress v. Horneffer, 15 Wis. 195; James v. Taylor, 43 Barb. 530; Wilthaus v. Ludicus, 5 Rich. 326.

ness; unless in the case of creditors, this may lead to a false credit on the part of the husband.[1] And in a recent case the stock in a millinery shop, resulting from the wife's credit and her earnings, under the sanction of her husband, was treated as her separate property, and held liable for demands affecting it.[2]

So in Michigan the wife is now permitted on equity principles to keep a boarding-house as her own separate business, and upon her own account; and the same is said of other pursuits, though the courts seem disposed to restrict her to the exercise of such business as is usually carried on by females and consists largely and almost necessarily of female labor.[3] In Pennsylvania it is decided, that a wife may trade with merchandise acquired in her own right, and with the proceeds of sales buy other goods to be held and traded with, exempt from seizure for her husband's debts, though she may not be a *feme sole* trader.[4] In Wisconsin, where a married woman, with the assent of her husband, engages in business as a sole trader, and contracts a debt for goods to carry it on, verbally pledging the faith of separate estate, her whole separate estate must answer for it.[5] And in Indiana it is said that while, as an abstract proposition, the law may not authorize a married woman to enter into a contract of partnership, yet if she does make such contract, and in pursuance thereof places her separate funds in the firm of which she is by contract a partner, such funds cannot while there be made subject to her husband's debts.[6]

The husband's assent is in general necessary. It is held in New York that the husband's assent does not carry with it an implied authority to make an assignment for the benefit of creditors of that business.[7] But in New Jersey a wife, who has been permitted by her husband to trade, may transfer her stock

[1] Per Redfield C. J. in Richardson *v.* Estate of Merrill, 32 Vt. 27.

[2] Partridge *v.* Stocker, 36 Vt. 108.

[3] Tillman *v.* Shackleton, 15 Mich. 447; Glover *v.* Alcott, 11 Mich. 471.

[4] Wieman *v.* Anderson, 42 Penn. St. 311; Manderbach *v.* Mock, 29 Penn. St. 43. But see Hoffman *v.* Toner, 49 Penn. St. 231.

[5] Todd *v.* Lee, 16 Wis. 480.

[6] Mayhew *v.* Baker, 15 Ind. 254.

[7] Cropsey *v.* McKinney, 30 Barb. 47.

in payment of notes given for the purchase-money.[1] And in South Carolina a *feme sole* trader is bound to a third person by her indorsement to him of a note drawn by her husband payable to herself.[2]

The conclusion to be drawn from this class of cases is that, modern policy having once conferred upon the wife large powers both as to the acquisition and enjoyment of separate property, as well as the right to invest and re-invest the same, married women naturally sought business opportunities with their capital; and thus the courts were drawn into the practical concession of trading privileges, while professing to deny to the wife on general principles the right to engage in mercantile pursuits without more explicit statute provisions to that effect.[3] Where it is clearly for the wife's advantage to reap the benefits of her business, the disposition of the law to yield them must be strong; but where, as must often be the case, she speculates imprudently and becomes deeply involved, the court is perplexed while anxious to relieve her.

On the other hand the earlier American cases seem to have regarded with very little favor the doctrine that the wife, while living with her husband, could carry on a business of her own, without rendering her husband liable and subjecting her stock in trade to his debts.[4] And the same may be said, at this day, of States whose legislatures have practically ignored the rights of married women.[5] In North Carolina the whole doctrine of separate trading is expressly repudiated.[6]

The recent married women's acts in many of the United States have enlarged and more fully established the wife's power to trade on her own account; and the profits of her business are thus secured to her sole and separate use.[7] She

[1] Green *v.* Pallas, 1 Beasl. 267.

[2] Wilthaus *v.* Ludicus, 5 Rich. 326.

[3] The Vermont equity rule, indicated in a former section, though not an unreasonable one, goes far beyond all the English precedents cited to support it.

[4] McKinley *v.* McGregor, 3 Whart. 378, and cases cited.

[5] Godfrey *v.* Brooks, 5 Harring. 396; Penn *v.* Whiteheads, 12 Gratt. 74.

[6] McKinnon *v.* McDonald, 4 Jones Eq. 1.

[7] Such statutes are to be found in New York, Maine, New Hampshire, Massachusetts, Kansas, New Jersey, and other States.

may even enter, in some States, into general partnership for this purpose. But the statutes of Massachusetts require her to first register her partnership intention.[1] In general, what the wife acquires under the statutes is declared to be exempt from liability for the husband's debts, and not subject to his control or interference.

In Massachusetts, where the statutory doctrine of the wife's power to trade and acquire separate earnings has thus far received its most complete exposition in the courts, it is made a rule that the wife's contracts regarding her separate business are binding on her separate property, and that the husband is not answerable for her solvency. And where a married woman carries on the business of keeping boarders on her sole and separate account, and has purchased goods to be used in her business on her sole credit, she alone is liable, although her husband lived with her when the goods were purchased; and her own acts and admissions in reference to the business, are competent evidence against her.[2] But the earnings of the wife are still, *prima facie*, the property of her husband; and where she buys articles of family furniture partly from her own earnings and partly with means furnished by her husband, it is to be supposed, in the absence of further proof to the contrary, that she has no exclusive title to any portion of the property.[3] The statutes permit a married woman to form a copartnership in business with third parties, though not with her husband; and this exception the court has so strictly enforced, that her transactions as a member of any firm in which her husband is interested as a partner are utterly void, whether to her advantage or injury, inasmuch as she cannot contract with her husband singly or jointly.[4]

The New York doctrine is that where the husband permits

[1] Mass. Stats. 1862, 198.

[2] Parker *v.* Simonds, 1 Allen, 258. See language of the statute herein cited, to the effect that she shall be treated as a *feme sole*, in respect to such property.

[3] Kelly *v.* Drew, 12 Allen, 107. See Woodcock *v.* Reed, 5 Allen, 207.

[4] Lord *v.* Parker, 3 Allen, 127; Edwards *v.* Stevens, ib. 315; Plumer *v.* Lord, 7 Allen, 481.

his wife, without objection, to hold herself out before the world as transacting business on her sole and separate account, though he may advance money to her in her business, the title to property purchased therewith, as against the husband, vests in the wife.[1] And as against her husband's creditors, she may make him managing agent, let him conduct the business in her name, while she furnishes the capital from her own means and takes the profits to herself; paying the managing agent what she thinks best without subjecting the stock in trade to his debts.[2] So it is held that a wife by allowing chattels belonging to her, and which remain *in specie*, to be employed by her husband in carrying on a business for their common benefit, does not devote them to her husband, so as to render them liable for his debts.[3] The courts of that State intimate, however, that there should be no fraud in such transactions; which otherwise the reader might doubt.

Under statutes which permit the wife to trade separately, it is held in New Jersey that her debts can be collected from her in equity.[4]

In Maine the husband cannot be sued for goods and chattels furnished his wife by third persons in the course of her business, even though such purchases were made by her with his knowledge and consent, and although she appropriated part of the proceeds to the support of her husband and family.[5] But where the purchase and sales are made with his knowledge and consent, and he participates in the profits of the business, knowing them to be such, and that she professed to act for him, it may be inferred that the purchases were made on the husband's credit.[6]

[1] Sammis *v.* McLaughlin, 35 N. Y. 647.

[2] Buckley *v.* Wells, 33 N. Y. 518.

[3] Sherman *v.* Elder, 24 N. Y. 381. And see Abbey *v.* Deyo, 44 Barb. 374; Barton *v.* Beer, 35 Barb. 78.

[4] Wheaton *v.* Phillips, 1 Beasl. 221.

[5] Colby *v.* Lamson, 39 Me. 119.

[6] Oxnard *v.* Swanton, 39 Me. 125.

By the civil code of France, the wife may carry on a trade independently of her husband.[1] So the wife may be a separate trader under the custom of Paris.[2] And a similar right is recognized by the laws of Spain and other European countries.[3]

From the civil, rather than the common law, are derived those property rights of married women which are recognized in Louisiana, California, and others of the South-western States, originally colonized by the Spanish and French. Thus the Louisiana code recognizes the capacity of the wife to carry on separate trade, or, as it is said, to constitute herself a public merchant, provided she act *bona fide*, and has an active agency in the concern.[4] And in California there are recent statutes, under which it is held that married women, as sole traders, may buy on credit, and execute all necessary instruments of purchase.[5] Not only is the husband not forbidden to become a partner, but the plain intention of the law is, that he may furnish part of the capital stock. The wife may sue alone in such business, and may employ her husband to manage it; and even though the trade be unsuitable to her sex, fraud upon the husband's creditors will not be conclusively presumed.[6] In other South-western States separate trading seems to be permitted on similar principles.[7]

[1] Code Civil, Art. 220; 1 Burg. Col. & For. Laws, 219.
[2] 1 Burge Col. & For. Laws, 218.
[3] Ib. 226, 420, 698.
[4] La. Code, Art. 128; Christensen *v.* Stumpf, 16 La. Ann. 50.
[5] Camden *v.* Mullen, 29 Cal. 564.
[6] Guttman *v.* Scannell, 7 Cal. 455.
[7] See Atwood *v.* Meredith, 37 Miss. 635; Oglesby *v.* Hall, 30 Ga. 386.

CHAPTER XIV.

THE WILLS OF MARRIED WOMEN.

MARRIED women cannot at the common law make a valid will. Their incapacity in this respect results partly from the general disabilities of coverture, and partly from the common-law policy of preserving unimpaired the husband's marital control and right of succession.

So, too, the marriage of a *feme sole* is such an entire change in her condition and relations, that it is generally held to work a revocation of her will executed before that event.[1] And the effect was the same, even where she survived her husband, and was thus restored to her former condition.[2]

On the other hand, the marriage of a man has at the common law no such effect upon his right of testamentary disposition. He can make a will of his own property, whether married or single. Nor is marriage of itself a revocation of his will previously executed. But marriage and the birth of a child is regarded as having such an effect upon his condition and relations in life, that a prior will is thereby revoked.[3] Even this implied revocation, so far as concerned his real estate, was not conceded in the English courts without a struggle.[4]

To the wife's testamentary incapacity there are some exceptions. Thus by the English law she may make a valid will of

[1] Forse & Hembling's Case, 30 & 31 Eliz., 4 Co. Rep. 60, 61; Hodsden *v.* Lloyd, 2 Br. C. C. 534.

[2] 1 Jarm. Wills, Eng. ed. 1861, 114; Cotter *v.* Layer, 2 P. Wms. 623, 624; 1 Redf. Wills, 293.

[3] 1 Redf. Wills 293–302 and authorities cited; 1 Jarm. Eng. ed. 1861, 115.

[4] Johnston *v* Johnston, 1 Phillim. 447; Marston *v.* Fox, 8 Ad. & El. 14.

personalty, with the consent of her husband. But this is upon the condition that he survives her, and does not elect, after her death, to disaffirm his consent already given. The will of a married woman, when presented for probate, is treated as a mere nullity.[1] But where it is alleged to have been made with the assent of the husband the court assumes jurisdiction. Hence, the wife's right in such cases is founded upon the husband's gift, or, as it is said, the waiver of his own right to administer for his own benefit.[2] And if the husband die before his wife, her will is void, so far as it could have derived any validity from his consent.[3] And his consent to the particular will, it would appear, does not pass subsequently acquired property.[4]

In order to establish a will by the husband's consent, it should be shown that the husband has consented to the particular will that his wife has made. His general assent, that she may make a will is not deemed sufficient.[5] But his consent to a particular will may be inferred from circumstances; and if after his wife's death he acts upon the will, or once agrees to it, he is not considered at liberty to retract his assent afterwards, and oppose the probate.[6] Such acts as expressing gratification at his wife's selection of an executor, or recommending him to particular places to procure suitable preparations for the burial, may constitute a conclusive presumption of assent after the wife's death; at least, if the executor has been thereby induced to act under the instrument.[7] And recently it has been decided that he cannot withdraw his assent before probate, after giving the sole legatee a written memorandum containing his

[1] Tucker *v.* Inman, 4 M. & G. 1049; Fane *ex parte,* 16 Sim. 406.

[2] 1 Wms. Ex'rs, 45, 49; 1 Redf. Wills, 25; Stevens *v.* Bagwell, 15 Ves. 156.

[3] 1 Redf. Wills, 25.

[4] Ib.; 1 Wms. Ex'rs, 49.

[5] 1 Wms. Ex'rs, 44; Rex *v.* Betlesworth, 2 Stra. 891. And see Kurtz *v.* Saylor, 20 Penn. St. 215.

[6] 1 Wms. Ex'rs, 44; Brook *v.* Turner, 2 Mod. 170; Maas *v.* Sheffield, 10 Jur. 417; 1 Rob. Ecc. 364.

[7] Ib.; 1 Redf. Wills, 24.

sanction of the will, in order to borrow it for an alleged particlar purpose.[1]

The rule is general in this country that the husband may allow his wife to make a valid will of her personal estate, and that his assent cannot be revoked after probate of the will.[2]

Another class of so-called exceptions to the wife's incapacity is, when she takes property in character of executrix, and her will is confined to matters and things which she takes in that character; in which case she may make a will without the husband's assent, and the ecclesiastical or corresponding court assumes jurisdiction.[3] But if the wife had before marriage reduced to possession personal chattels, to which she was entitled as executrix, the right of the husband attaches, and the wife cannot dispose of them by will.[4] Since this exception does not concern property, to which the wife takes a beneficial title it can hardly be called an exception at all.

A third class of exceptions, recognized in England, is where personal property is given or settled, or is agreed to be given or settled to the wife's separate use. In such a case the wife may dispose of such property to the full extent of her interest, although no particular form is prescribed in the instrument creating the trust. This follows as an incident to the right of beneficial enjoyment. It makes her right of disposition complete.[5] "I have always taken this ground," says Lord Thurlow,

[1] Maas *v.* Sheffield, 10 Jur. 417; 1 Rob. Ecc. 364. But see Van Winkle *v.* Schoonmaker, 15 N. J. Ch. 384, where the doctrine is asserted that the husband may withdraw his assent at any time before probate.

[2] Cutter *v.* Butler, 5 Fost. 343; Fisher *v.* Kimball, 17 Vt. 323; George *v.* Bussing, 15 B. Monr. 558; Wagner *v.* Ellis, 7 Penn. St. 413; Lee *v.* Bennett, 31 Miss. 119; Newlin *v.* Freeman, 1 Ired. Law, 514. As to the method of expressing assent, see Grimke *v.* Grimke, 1 Desaus. 366; Cutter *v.* Butler, 5 Fost. 343; 1 Redf. Wills, 29; Kurtz *v.* Saylor, 20 Penn. St. 205. The husband's covenant in a marriage settlement will repel his right of administration. Newlin *v.* Freeman, 1 Ired. 514.

[3] Tucker *v.* Inman, 4 M. & G. 1076.

[4] Scammel *v.* Wilkinson, 2 East, 552; 1 Wms. Ex'rs, 44; 1 Redf. Wills, 23; Hodsden *v.* Lloyd, 2 Br. C. C. 534.

[5] Fettiplace *v.* Gorges, 1 Ves. Jr. 46; Lord Eldon in Rich *v.* Cockell, 9 Ves. 375; 1 Redf. Wills, 23; 1 Wms. Ex'rs, 48, and English cases cited.

of this class of cases, "that personal property, the moment it can be enjoyed, must be enjoyed with all its incidents."[1] And as to the wife's separate estate savings out of allowance may be bequeathed by will as well as the capital; for this, too, is separate estate.[2] But it should be borne in mind that as to her right of disposition, a married woman is a *feme sole sub modo* only, and is limited by the terms of the gift or settlement from which her estate is derived.[3] There is no reason for distinguishing between real and personal estate settled to the wife's separate use; the exception ought to embrace both kinds of property.[4] But the English cases for some time manifested a doubt on this point, and the testamentary *jus disponendi* was thought not so clear in the case of separate real estate, as of separate personalty.[5]

The recent case of *Taylor* v. *Mead* would appear to set this doubt at rest.[6] In this case the wife had lands conveyed in trust to her separate use, with a power given her to appoint it by any instrument in writing, "to be by her signed, sealed, and delivered" after a certain manner; the formalities prescribed being greater than the statute of wills prescribed for testamentary dispositions. The property was limited over to others in default of such appointment. She made an instrument in writing, which conformed to the statute of wills, but which, not being under seal, was not in accordance with the power given her. It was decided that the instrument was defective as the execution of a power of appointment; but that it was a valid devise, such as she had the right to make, of estate settled to her sole and separate use.[7]

1 Fettiplace *v.* Gorges, 1 Ves. Jr. 46.

2 Brooke *v.* Brooke, 25 Beav. 342. But as to pin-money see Barrack *v.* M'Culloch, 3 Kay & Johns. 114, and last chapter.

3 See ch. 12, *supra.*

4 1 Jarm. Wills, ed. 1861, 34, 35; Per Lord Lyndhurst, Baggett *v.* Meux, 1 Ph. 628.

5 Harris *v.* Mott, 14 Beav. 169; Churchill *v.* Dibben, 9 Sim. 447 *n.*

6 10 Jur. (N. S.) 127; overruling Buckell *v.* Blenthorne, 5 Hare, 131.

7 Ib. And the Vice Chancellor has decided that her devise is equally valid,

A married woman's right to make a will is recognized in cases where her husband is dead at the law. As where he has been banished for life.[1] Or is transported for life.[2] Or is an alien enemy.[3] For in such cases she is no longer regarded as under the disabilities of coverture. And some writers have thought that while a husband's marital rights are suspended, as by his temporary banishment, his wife ought to be able to make a valid will of property acquired by her in the meantime.[4]

If a wife acquires any property after her husband's death, it cannot pass by a will made during her coverture, though by the consent of her husband; for at the time of making the will she was intestable as to that property.[5]

Married women were expressly excepted from the statute of wills, 34 & 35 Hen. VIII. ch. 5; though no new disability was thereby created, since they had been regarded as incapable of executing a will at a much earlier date. The present English statute of wills, 1 Vict. ch. 26, § 8, provides that "no will made by any married woman shall be valid, except such will as might have been made by a married woman before the passage of this act." But the exceptions have so multiplied upon the prohibition of late years as to constitute of themselves a new rule.

So by the recent English statute, wills are held to be absolutely revoked by the subsequent marriage of the testator, whether made by a man or woman, unless such will be made in execution of certain specified powers; and it is further provided that no will shall be revoked, by any presumption of in-

though the property was given to her separate use, without the intervention of trustees. Hall *v.* Waterhouse, 11 Jur. (N. S.) 361.

[1] Countess of Portland *v.* Progers, 2 Vern. 104; Compton *v.* Collinson, 2 Br. C. C. 377.

[2] Newsome *v.* Bowyer, 3 P. Wms. 37; Goods of Martin, 15 Jur. 686; Atlee *v.* Hook, 23 L. J. Ch. 776.

[3] Deerly *v.* Mazarine, 1 Salk 116.

[4] 1 Jarm. Wills, ed. 1861, 35; *Ex parte* Franks, 1 Moore & Sc. 11. But see Coombs *v.* The Queen's Proctor, 16 Jur. 820.

[5] Scammell *v.* Wilkinson, 2 East, 556.

tention on the ground of an alteration of circumstances.[1] Thus again is a mass of legal learning swept away and another opening made towards the equality of the sexes.

In this country, the great revolution which has been effected in the property rights of married women leaves its traces upon their testamentary privileges. The principles indicated in the married women's acts, though not uniformly expressed in clear and unambiguous language, is that the wife may devise or bequeath, by her sole will, whatever separate property the statutes secure to her; and that such will is valid without the joinder or assent of her husband.[2]

In some States the capacity of married women to execute a valid will seems to have been conferred by implication. The statutes of Vermont give them the power to devise their real estate by last will and testament; and since equity has given so liberal a scope to their powers over separate property, it would appear that they may make a valid bequest of separate chattels likewise, without the concurrence of their husbands, and as part of the *jus disponendi*.[3] But in States which draw the doctrine of separate use from their own local legislation a more stringent

[1] 1 Redf. Wills, 297. Wills in execution of a power are excepted from the statute.

[2] Such express provisions are to be found in the laws of Maine, New Hampshire, Massachusetts, Rhode Island, New York, Pennsylvania, Ohio, Indiana, Wisconsin, and other States. The language of these statutes is sometimes restricted to the wife's "separate" property; in other States, the word "separate" is not employed. Some States employ the word "devise," and omit the word "bequeath;" thus suggesting the inquiry whether the legislature meant that the wife could dispose of her lands, but not her chattels. Certain rights of the husband are found to be expressly reserved in many of these acts; and in Massachusetts it is provided that the wife cannot deprive her husband of more than one-half her personal estate without his consent in writing. In Ohio, it is declared that the will of a *feme sole* is not revoked by her subsequent marriage. Some legislatures have manifested special opposition to the husband's influence over the wife's disposition. The laws of Pennsylvania, for instance, expressly forbid him from executing the will as a witness. And it would appear that under the New Hampshire statute the husband cannot receive any benefit under his wife's devise of her separate real estate.

[3] See Caldwell *v.* Renfrew, 33 Vt. 213; Heirs of Holmes *v.* Adm'rs of Holmes, 27 Vt. 765.

rule might be enforced. The whole subject has as yet received little attention in the courts.[1]

It is well understood that, by the Roman civil law, a married woman possessed the same testamentary capacity in all respects as a *feme sole*.[2] And such is the law in France, Holland, Spain, and the European countries generally.[3] In Scotland, the wife may bequeath her share of the common goods, even without the husband's assent.[4] The early policy of England in this respect seems in truth peculiar to itself. For Voet and other publicists have declared that, although the wife should not be allowed to make a contract without the consent of her husband, yet she should be permitted to make a will, because it did not take effect until the marital authority had ceased.[5]

In Mississippi, it is held that the wife's testamentary disposition of her personal chattels, with the assent of her husband,

[1] In Virginia, and the Southern Atlantic States generally, as well as Alabama, the doctrine of the wife's testamentary capacity seems to be founded upon the earlier English cases. But in these and some other States which borrow largely from the chancery jurisprudence of England, perhaps the wife at this day would be allowed to devise and bequeath property duly settled to her separate use, should such cases occur. See Burton *v.* Holley, 18 Ala. 408; Porcher *v.* Daniel, 13 Rich. 349; Michael *v.* Baker, 12 Md. 158. It has been perceived that this right of testamentary disposition, as incidental to the wife's beneficial enjoyment of her separate property, has been but gradually conceded in England, and that the beneficial rule for a long time was supposed to apply to her personal estate simply.

[2] 2 Bl. Com. 497; 1 Redf. Wills, 22.

[3] 4 Burge Col. & For. Laws, 326.

[4] Ib. 328.

[5] Voet, Sande, and Rodenb., cited 4 Burge Col. & For. Laws, 326. We may understand, therefore, why the Louisiana Code permits the wife to make her testament without the authority of her husband. La. Code, Art. 132. And in other South-western States, under the community system, the wife's right of testamentary disposition is likewise to be found. In Mississippi this right has been long favored, nor is it abridged by construction of the married women's acts. Lee *v.* Bennett, 31 Miss. 119. In California the statute gives the wife power to dispose of all her separate estate without the concurrence of her husband, but her will must be attested, witnessed, and proven after the ordinary manner of wills. It cannot be said in any of these States that the doctrine of the wife's testamentary capacity was borrowed entirely from the English common law, or underwent corresponding modifications; though the final results at this day are quite similar.

is entitled to all the effect of a will made by a person *sui juris.* But whether the paper be regarded as a will, or as an instrument in the nature of a last will and testament, it must be regularly admitted to probate before it can have any force whatever.[1] And marriage operates as a revocation of her will made while single; nor can it revive on her husband's death.[2]

Independently of late statutes conferring a special power, the older States agree that a married woman cannot devise lands not held in her sole right.[3] But the Ohio courts, many years ago, decided that under its own statutes, giving "every male person aged twenty-one years or upward, and every female aged eighteen years or upward," the power to devise property, a married woman could make a valid will to pass her real estate.[4] In Massachusetts, it is held that under the statutes now in force a married woman may, by will duly executed with her husband's assent, dispose of all interest in her real estate, so as to cut off his rights as a tenant by the curtesy.[5]

In New York, a married woman might formerly make a valid will under the written authority of her husband; but the right was afterwards taken away; for by the Revised Statutes, married women were expressly excepted from the provision conferring general testamentary power.[6] By the married women's statutes now in force, however, it would appear that the wife has all the powers of a *feme sole* over her own property.[7]

Under the present English statute, the will of a married woman is not rendered void, if executed during coverture, by sole reason of her surviving her husband. There must be a

1 Lee *v.* Bennett, 31 Miss. 119.

2 Garrett *v.* Dabney, 27 Miss. 335.

3 Osgood *v.* Breed, 12 Mass. 525; Taber *v.* Packwood, 2 Day, 63; West *v.* West, 10 S. & R. 446; Marston *v.* Norton, 5 N. H. 205; Newlin *v.* Freeman, 1 Ired. Law, 514.

4 Allen *v.* Little, 5 Ohio, 65.

5 Silsby *v.* Bullock, 10 Allen, 94.

6 Moehring *v.* Thayer, 1 Barb. Ch. 264; Wadhaus *v.* Am. Home Missionary Society, 12 N. Y. 415.

7 See White *v.* Wager, 25 N. Y. 328.

confirmation or republication of the will after coverture ceases. And it must be in the particular mode pointed out by the statute, and not by parol.[1] Hence a mere signature by herself, and other parties as witnesses, the testatrix saying nothing about the reason of her signing, and making no request for the others to sign as witnesses, is held not to amount to a republication of the will.[2]

Where property of the wife is, by marriage settlement, surrendered by the husband to the wife's "full and free disposal," she "to have, and to hold the sole discretion and guidance thereof," it is held that she has the power during coverture, to dispose of the same absolutely by will.[3]

There can be little doubt of the reluctance with which courts of equity sustain devises from the wife to her husband. And there are cases to the effect that the husband cannot become the gainer, or have his marital rights extended by his wife's testamentary disposition of her lands. But they generally turn rather upon statutory construction than principle.[4] In New York, the married women's act of 1849 gave the wife power "to convey and devise real and personal property," "as if she were unmarried," and it was held that, notwithstanding these words, a deed executed by a wife, in contemplation of death, to her husband, in good faith and voluntarily, was wholly ineffectual.[5]

Wills of married women unduly obtained, through the marital influence and authority of their husbands, are of course invalid, though the case should fall within one of the exceptions to her general incapacity.[6] So if a wife having power to dispose of

[1] 1 Redf. Wills, 377; Dickinson *v.* Swatman, 6 Jur. (N. S.) 831; Wollaston *In re*, 12 W. 18.

[2] Dunn *v.* Dunn, Law Rep. 1 P. & D. 277.

[3] Porcher *v.* Daniel, 13 Rich. 349. But see Hood *v.* Archer, 1 M'Cord, 225.

[4] White *v.* Wager, 25 N. Y. 328; Morse *v.* Thompson, 4 Cush. 562; Wakefield *v.* Phelps, 37 N. H. 295. See Hood *v.* Archer, *supra*.

[5] White *v.* Wager, 25 N. Y. 328. But see Caldwell, Adm'r *v.* Renfrew, 33 Vt. 213; Noble *v.* Enos, 19 Ind. 72.

[6] Marsh *v.* Tyrrell, 2 Hag. 84; Wms. Ex'rs, 47.

property by her will, makes her will, and afterwards destroys it, by the compulsion of her husband, it may be established afterwards on due proof of his misconduct, and of its contents and execution.[1]

But in the analogous instance of the wife's appointment to her husband, it is held that the circumstances that the deed had been prepared by her husband's solicitor, that it had not been read over at the time of the execution, and the evidence of one of the attesting witnesses that she was agitated and distressed at the time of the execution, and signed it in a reluctant manner, will not be sufficient to invalidate the deed.[2]

A married woman, being desirous of making a disposition of her real estate, to take effect after her decease, united with her husband in the execution of a deed of the same to a trustee, authorizing him to make a sale thereof, and out of the proceeds to pay certain sums to particular individuals, and the remainder to her legal representatives. The husband received the deed after its execution, upon his express promise to deliver it to the grantee, at his wife's decease, if that should occur before his own. Upon her death before the husband, a court of equity decreed the delivery of the deed to the grantee, on the ground that the title to such estate had vested in him.[3] Dispositions of the wife in the nature of a will may be admitted to probate.[4]

The same principles which regulate the wife's testamentary disposition of her personal chattels regulate her *donatio causa mortis* likewise. Therefore, it is held that the wife's gift of any of her property during her last illness, and in expectation of death, is, like her will, valid only by the assent of her husband.[5] Where the wife held notes to her separate use, it was

[1] 1 Wms. Ex'rs, 47.

[2] Nedby *v.* Nedby, 11 E. L. & Eq. 106. See Noble *v.* Enos, 19 Ind. 72.

[3] Woodward *v.* Camp, 22 Conn. 457.

[4] Emery *v.* Neighbor, 2 Halst. 142. And see Chapman *v.* Gray, 8 Geo. 341; White *v.* Hart, 1 Yeates, 221.

[5] Jones *v.* Brown, 34 N. H. 439.

decided in Vermont that she might make them the subject of a *donatio causa mortis* to her husband as trustee for other persons, and thereby vest in him a good legal title as against her administrator. "In this view alone," added the court, "it seems to be needless to discuss whether the husband could be a donee *causa mortis* of the wife; and yet on principle it is quite difficult to assign a cogent or plausible reason why he might not be."[1] But of course the husband may set up his antenuptial contract with his wife in reference to certain property, so as to prevent her *donatio causa mortis* to others from taking effect to his prejudice.[2]

Finally, it may be observed that, both in England and America, a married woman may make a testamentary disposition of real or personal estate under a power, even where her general testamentary capacity is by law denied or restricted. There are many decisions found to this effect.[3] And in some cases, particularly those involving property rights in the wife's lands, the courts seem to have been misled by the similarity between separate estates and estates with a power of appointment given to the wife; and therefore to have applied the terms "devise," "will," and "appointment," somewhat indiscriminately.

1 Caldwell *v.* Renfrew, 33 Vt. 213.

2 Lawrence *v.* Bartlett, 2 Allen, 36.

3 4 Kent Com. 506; Heath *v.* Withington, 6 Cush. 497; West *v.* West, 10 S. & R. 446; 1 Redf. Wills, 28, and cases cited; Dominick *v.* Michael, 4 Sandf. 374; Hughes *v.* Wells, 13 E. L. & Eq. 389; Shattock *v.* Shattock, Law Rep. 2 Eq. 182; Rogers *v.* Hinton, 1 Phill. (N. C.) Eq. 101. In cases of doubt a limited probate of the instrument may be granted. Raylon *v.* Tongue, Law Rep. 1 P. & D. 158; Goods *v.* Richards, Law Rep. 1 P. & D. 156.

CHAPTER XV.

ANTENUPTIAL SETTLEMENTS.

Settlements are a useful contrivance for preserving estates intact in a family. As between husband and wife, the word settlement is applied to their mutual contracts in reference to the property of one another, by means of which they change and control the general rules of the marriage state. They cannot vary the terms of the conjugal relation itself; they cannot add to or take from the personal rights and duties of husband and wife; but they may essentially alter the interest which each takes in the property of the other, if they choose to enter into special stipulations for that purpose. These special stipulations may be either antenuptial or postnuptial; while, as we shall soon perceive, the two classes are more alike in name than substance, and the term marriage settlements is frequently applied to antenuptial settlements only.

A distinction meets us at the outset, between promises to marry and promises in consideration of marriage. The Statute of Frauds, section four, requires that promises and agreements in consideration of marriage, shall be "in writing, and signed by the party to be charged therewith, or some other person thereunto by him lawfully authorized." Yet a promise to marry is binding, although verbal.[1] It would strike any one (except perhaps a lawyer) that a promise by a woman to marry a man in consideration of his promising to marry her was an agreement made in consideration of marriage, but it is not.[2] Per-

[1] Macq. Hus. & Wife, 220; Cook *v.* Baker, 1 Str. 34; Harrison *v.* Cage, 1 Ld. Raym. 386. See chapter 1, *supra.*

[2] See Smith on Contracts, 57.

haps it is public policy which sustains the latter, rather than the former contract. Perhaps too this carries weight, that a promise to marry is merely a promise to enter into a certain relation, and so clearly interpreted by any court without the aid of written evidence, provided the promise be once proved; while the Statute of Frauds is found most convenient for fixing mutual stipulations which might be varied in a thousand ways and so affect the property rights of contracting parties accordingly. At all events, a promise to marry, whether verbal or written, affords a singular remedy; namely, no right of specific performance, but always damages to the injured party.[1]

In marriage settlements, the marriage affords a sufficient consideration. Hence a man cannot set aside an agreement in contemplation of marriage, on the plea that his wife's fortune fell short of his expectations, for, as Lord Hardwicke observed, it would be extremely mischievous to set aside marriage settlements upon such grounds.[2] It is the consideration of marriage, not the consideration of a corresponding fortune, which runs through the whole settlement or agreement, and supports every part of it; thus making marriage not only a high but the highest consideration, in fact, known to the law.[3]

In this country, the validity of marriage settlements is generally recognized; and it is well understood that almost any *bona fide* and reasonable agreement, made before marriage, to secure the wife either in the enjoyment of her own property, or a portion of that of her husband, whether during coverture or after his death, will be carried into execution in chancery.[4] "These marriage settlements," observes Chancellor Kent, "are be-

[1] For further discussion of this topic, see Macq. Hus. & Wife, 220, *et seq.*; and see chap. 1, *supra.*

[2] *Ex parte* Marsh, 1 Atk. 159.

[3] Ford *v.* Stuart, 15 Beav. 499; Nairn *v.* Prouse, 6 Ves. 752; Peachey Mar. Settl. 56.

[4] Stilley *v.* Folger, 14 Ohio, 610; 2 Kent Com. 163; 2 U. S. Eq. Dig. Hus. & Wife, 22–30; English *v.* Foxall, 2 Pet. 595; Hunter *v.* Bryant, 2 Wheat. 32; Tarbell *v.* Tarbell, 10 Allen, 278; Skillman *v.* Skillman, 2 Beasl. 403; Cartledge *v.* Cutliff, 29 Geo. 758; Albert *v.* Winn, 5 Md. 66; Snyder *v.* Webb, 3 Cal. 83; Smith *v.* Chappell, 31 Conn. 589.

nignly intended to secure to the wife a certain support in every event, and to guard her against being overwhelmed by the misfortunes, or unkindness, or vices of her husband. They usually proceed from the prudence and foresight of friends, or the warm and anxious affection of parents; and if fairly made, they ought to be supported according to the true intent and meaning of the instrument by which they are created."[1] And marriage is of itself pronounced in the supreme court of this land to be not only a valuable consideration to support a marriage settlement, but "a consideration of the highest value."[2]

But this rule must be taken with some caution. The marriage consideration supports every provision with regard to the husband, the wife, and the issue. It does not, however, in all cases, as to collaterals;[3] though Sir Matthew Hale and others held formerly that it would, maintaining that the influence of the marriage consideration extended to purchasers generally.[4] Nor are covenants in favor of strangers supported by the marriage consideration unless specially provided for.[5] The consideration of marriage will support a settlement against creditors; this too it would appear, though the parties both knew of the husband's indebtedness, so long as the provisions of the settlement were not grossly out of proportion to his station and circumstances.[6] But if it appear that the celebration of marriage is part of a scheme to defraud and delay creditors, such settlement will not be allowed to protect the property.[7]

Yet in *Neves* v. *Scott*, which came up on appeal before

[1] 2 Kent Com. 165.

[2] Per Story J., Magniac *v.* Thompson, 7 Pet. 348. And see Armfield *v.* Armfield, 1 Freem. Ch. 311.

[3] Peachey Mar. Settl. 58, 60, and cases cited; Davenport *v.* Bishop, 1 Phil. 701; Barham *v.* Earl of Clarendon, 10 Hare, 133; Ford *v.* Stuart, 15 Beav. 505; Cotterell *v.* Homer, 13 Sim. 506.

[4] Jenkins *v.* Kemis, 1 Ch. Cas. 103, 1 Lev. 152.

[5] Sutton *v.* Chetwynd, 3 Mer. 249, per Sir Wm. Grant; Sugden Law Prop. 153; Peachey Mar. Settl. 61.

[6] Campion *v.* Cotton, 17 Ves. 272; *Ex parte* McBurnie, 1 De G., M. & G. 446; Ramsay *v.* Richardson, Riley Ch. 271; Armfield *v.* Armfield, 1 Freem. Ch. 311.

[7] Columbine *v.* Penhall, 1 Sm. & Gif. 228; Goldsmith *v.* Russell, 5 De G. M. & G. 555; Peachey Mar. Settl. 63; Simpson *v.* Graves, Riley Ch. 232.

the Supreme Court of the United States, the rights of collaterals under a marriage agreement received consideration. And it is declared as the result of the authorities, English and American, that if, from the circumstances under which the marriage articles were entered into by the parties, or as collected from the face of the instrument itself, it appears to have been intended that the collateral relatives, in a given event, should take the estate, and a proper limitation to that effect is contained in them, a court of equity will enforce the trust for their benefit. They will not be regarded as volunteers outside of the deed, but as coming fairly within the influence of the considerations on which it is founded; the consideration extending, in fact, through all the limitations for the benefit of the remotest persons provided for consistent with law.[1]

If an agreement be made in writing before marriage, for the settlement of an estate, the settlement, although made after marriage, will be deemed valuable.[2] This is a well settled rule, and should be constantly borne in mind. There are *dicta* to the effect that a settlement after marriage, reciting a parol agreement before marriage, is not fraudulent against creditors, provided the agreement had actual existence; but this point has never been distinctly decided in England; and some late authorities appear to doubt its correctness.[3] The payment of money would, however, make a good consideration for such a settlement as against subsequent creditors.[4] The language of the Statute of Frauds has a material bearing upon all such

[1] Neves *v.* Scott, 9 How. 196, ib. 13 How. 268. And see Eaton *v.* Tillinghast, 4 R. I. 276; Buchanan *v.* Deshon, 1 Har. & G. 280; De Barranti *v.* Gott, 6 Barb. 492; Tabb *v.* Archer, 3 Hen. & M. 399; Wallace *v.* McCullough, 1 Rich. Eq. 426.

[2] Reade *v.* Livingston, 3 Johns. Ch. 481; Finch *v.* Finch, 10 Ohio St. 501; Izard *v.* Izard, 1 Bailey Ch. 228; Davidson *v.* Graves, Riley Ch. 219; Satterthwaite *v.* Emley, 3 Green Ch. 489; Rogers *v.* Brightman, 10 Wis. 55; Peachey Mar. Settl. 63; Sugd. Vend. & Purch. 13th ed. 590; Macq. Hus. & Wife, 257.

[3] See Peachey Mar. Settl. 63; Lassence *v.* Tierney, 1 Mac. & Gor. 571; Warden *v.* Jones, 5 W. R. 447. And see Babcock *v.* Smith, 22 Pick. 61; Simpson *v.* Graves, Riley Ch. 232.

[4] Stillman *v.* Ashdown, 2 Atk. 478; Brown *v.* Jones, 1 Atk. 189. And see Butterfield *v.* Heath, 15 Beav. 414.

cases. Yet very informal agreements are often sustained, rather on liberal than technical construction, the court taking into consideration the fact, that marriage had taken place, or other acts been performed, on the strength of the promise.[1]

With respect to the form of marriage settlements it may be generally observed that equity pays no regard to the externals, but considers only the substantial intention of the parties; and hence articles or an agreement will be binding between husband and wife without the intervention of trustees.[2] A strong instance of the liberality of the equity courts in this respect was afforded in an early decision by Lord Keeper Wright. The intended husband gave the intended wife a bond conditioned to leave her £1000 if she should survive him. They married, and of course the bond became void at law. But it was held that in equity this should subsist as an antenuptial agreement.[3] Even in law a bond with conditions properly expressed, may be enforced against the husband to the extent of the penalty therein named; yet equity, regarding the contract as one for specific performance, will not confine the remedy of the injured party to the penal sum named in the bond; but, enforcing the real obligations of the bond, will give, if need be, thirty times that sum to her who married on the strength of it. Such is the advantage of equity over the law.[4] Letters also,

[1] The disposition in this country is rather favorable to settlements after marriage in pursuance of informal prior agreements. See Livingston *v.* Livingston, 2 Johns. Ch. 481; Resor *v.* Resor, 9 Ind. 347; Brooks *v.* Dent, 1 Md. Ch. 523; West *v.* Howard, 20 Conn. 581. Other considerations, such as forbearance to sue, may intervene. Riley *v.* Riley, 25 Conn. 154 (1856). And see Miller *v.* Goodwin, 8 Gray, 542. See as to the like English practice Peachey Mar. Settl. 74, 87; Macq. Hus. & Wife, 234; Hammersley *v.* De Biel, 12 Cl. & Fin. 45; Lassence *v.* Tierney, 1 Mac. & Gor. 571. The numerous *dicta* in these cases serve rather to obscure than illustrate the principle.

[2] Peachey Mar. Settl. 65; Macq. Hus. & Wife, 242.

[3] Acton *v.* Pierce, 2 Vern. 480; Crostwaight *v.* Hutchinson, 2 Bibb. 407; Siles *v.* Fleming, 1 Dev. Eq. 185; Kenly *v.* Kenly, 2 How. Miss. 751.

[4] See Prebble *v.* Boghurst, 1 Swan. 309, before Lord Eldon; cited in Macq. Hus. & Wife, 243, *et seq.;* Cannel *v.* Buckle, 2 P. Wms. 242; Rippon *v.* Dawding, Ambl. 565; Peachey Mar. Settl. 65. Bonds have been frequently enforced in this country as constituting a marriage settlement. Aucker *v.* Levy, 3 Strobh.

if they sufficiently furnish the terms of the agreement, have been held good marriage contracts.[1] And it is now clearly settled that a letter which contains the terms of an agreement, or refers to another paper which specifies the terms, is sufficient to take the contract out of the Statute of Frauds.[2]

In this connection the use of the term "marriage articles" is properly to be noticed. "When promises and agreements in consideration of marriage," says Mr. Macqueen, "are meant to become the groundwork of settlements, they are called marriage articles. They are often drawn up hastily, and signed on the eve of the nuptial ceremony from want of time to prepare a final deed; which, however, when ultimately executed, if it be in strict conformity with the articles, will supersede them."[3] The American rule is favorable to marriage articles, although unskillfully drawn, so long as they are *bona fide* articles.[4]

While promises made in consideration of the marriage by a third party, such as the wife's father, may afterwards be enforced against him by the husband, it must appear that the latter knew of the promise, and that it entered as an ingredient into the marriage; and the husband cannot, upon finding after marriage, that his wife, while single, had received a letter from her father promising a certain allowance, hold the latter to specific performance.[5] And courts of equity have frequently refused to enforce marriage agreements on the ground of their being inconsistent, uncertain, and unintelligible.[6] Particularly

Eq. 197; Hunter *v.* Bryant, 2 Wheat. 32; Freeman *v.* Hill, 1 Dev. & Bat. Eq. 389; Baldwin *v.* Carter, 17 Conn. 201.

[1] Logan *v.* Wienholt, 1 Cl. & Fin. 611.

[2] Hammersley *v.* De Biel, 12 Cl. & Fin. 45; Moorhouse *v.* Colvin, 15 Beav. 349; Peachey Mar. Settl. 67.

[3] Macq. Hus. & Wife, 246.

[4] Neves *v.* Scott, 9 How. 196; Hooks *v.* Lee, 8 Ired. Eq. 157; Rivers *v.* Thayer, 7 Rich. Eq. 136. See Kinnard *v.* Daniel, 13 B. Monr. 496; Montgomery *v.* Henderson, 3 Jones Eq. 113; Smith *v.* Moore, 3 Green Ch. 485; Potts *v.* Cogdell, 1 Desaus. 456.

[5] Ayliffe *v.* Tracy, 2 P. Wms. 66; Madox *v.* Nowlan, Beatty, 632.

[6] Franks *v.* Martin, 1 Eden, 309; Kay *v.* Crook, 3 Jur. (N. S.) 107; Peachey Mar. Settl. 68; Quinlan *v.* Quinlan, Hayes & Jones Ir. Rep. 785; Maunsell *v.* White, 1 Jo. & Lat. 539.

is this found true of loose expressions contained in letters written by relatives of the married parties upon which the attempt is made to render them chargeable.

Lord Thurlow, once considering the question whether a letter written by the defendant, which referred to an unsigned agreement, would take the agreement out of the Statute of Frauds, remarked, "If he had said he never would sign it, he could not have been bound; but if he said he never would sign it, but would make it as good as if he did, it would be a promise to perform it. If he said he never would sign, because he would not hamper himself by an agreement, it would be too perverse to be admitted."[1] And on this last ground Lord Thurlow suffered the defendant in the case to go clear.

The result of a long array of diffuse, but exceedingly interesting English equity decisions under this head is to establish the following propositions. First, that if any one make a representation to another on which he would reasonably act, the party making the representation is bound thereby, and cannot recede from it; in other words, that a man who, by his deliberate assertion, induces another to enter into obligations, cannot afterwards by his acts negative the truth of that assertion.[2] Secondly, that moral obligations in matters of this description are treated in courts of equity as co-extensive with legal obligations; and that while vague and ambiguous representations may be made to persons on marriage, which are only morally binding upon the person making them, though creating reasonable expectation and belief of advantage in the minds of the marrying parties; yet, where the matter is clearly and distinctly expressed, then the legal obligation follows the moral obligation, and the contract will be enforced by the courts.[3]

A secret settlement made by a woman upon third persons, while engaged, and contemplating marriage, is liable to be set

[1] Tawney *v.* Crowther, 3 Br. C. C. 318, cited in Jorden *v.* Money, 5 Ho. of Lords, 253.

[2] Money *v.* Jorden, 15 Beav. 377; Pulsford *v.* Richards, 17 Beav. 94.

[3] Bold *v.* Hutchinson, 20 Beav. 259; Peachey Mar. Settl. 87.

aside in equity as a fraud upon the marital rights of her intended husband. *Prima facie*, her transactions as *a feme sole* with reference to her own property are valid both at law and in equity; it is only because of the fraud that her husband can afterwards obtain relief against them; yet the English courts have gone far in discountenancing all conveyances made by the intended wife in derogation of the property rights of her intended husband, where made without notice to him.[1] The secrecy of the proceeding is a material element from which fraud will be inferred.[2] The husband must have been kept in ignorance of the transaction up to the moment of marriage. For, as Lord Chancellor Brougham once observed, if a man, knowing what has been done, still thinks fit to marry the lady, he cannot be permitted to allege afterwards that he has been deceived.[3] Actual concurrence on the part of the intended husband in his wife's settlement will be even more conclusive against him; and, even though he were a minor, will preclude all subsequent allegations of fraud on the marital right.[4] It is the usual practice with English conveyancers at the present day to make the intended husband a party to all instruments executed by the intended wife in contemplation of or during a treaty of marriage.[5]

The same general doctrine has been repeatedly declared in the courts of this country; and secret and voluntary conveyances, made by a woman contemplating marriage, may be set aside on the husband's subsequent application as a fraud upon his marital rights.[6] Nor need she have formally settled her

1 Peachey Mar. Settl. 142, and cases cited; Doe d. Richards *v.* Lewis, 11 C. B. 1035; St. George *v.* Wake, 1 Myl. & K. 618; Countess of Strathmore *v.* Bowes, 1 Ves. Jr. 28; Macq. Hus. & Wife, 36; England *v.* Downes, 2 Beav. 522; Howard *v.* Hooker, 2 Ch. Rep. 81; 1 Eq. Cas. Ab. 59, pl. 1; Lance *v.* Norman, 2 Cas. in Ch. Rep. 79; 1 Eq. Cas. Ab. 59, pl. 2; Carleton *v.* Earl of Dorset, 2 Vern. 17; St. George *v.* Wake, 1 Myl. & K. 629; Goddard *v.* Snow, 1 Russ. 485.

2 England *v.* Downes, 2 Beav. 522; Macq. Hus. & Wife, 36.

3 St. George *v.* Wake, 1 Myl. & K. 610; Peachey Mar. Settl. 145, and cases cited.

4 Slowcombe *v.* Glubb, 2 Br. C. C. 545.

5 Peachey Mar. Settl. 155.

6 2 Kent Com. 174, 175, and notes, last ed.; Spencer *v.* Spencer, 3 Jones Eq.

whole property in order to come within the prohibition; any voluntary transfer, under fraudulent circumstances, is void, so far as that particular property is concerned.[1] But if the husband received notice of the transfer before marriage and chose to marry her notwithstanding, he is without a remedy.[2] Though not where he merely heard a vague rumor after he had married.[3] And the wife's antenuptial deed purporting to convey her property in trust for her separate use has been treated as fraudulent.[4]

Lord Thurlow says the question in all such cases is whether the evidence is sufficient to raise fraud.[5] And from the decisions it would appear that some alienations of the wife's property without her intended husband's knowledge will be allowed to stand.[6] The facts are always open to inquiry; and it seems settled that the court is warranted in considering such circumstances as the meritorious object of the conveyance and the situation of the husband in point of pecuniary means.[7]

From what has been said, it may readily be gathered that a secret settlement by the intended wife, made before she was courted, is not likely to be set aside, on proof that the complainant commenced courting her afterwards.[8] And the husband must show, not only that the wife contemplated marriage

404; Tucker *v.* Andrews, 13 Maine, 124, 128; Linker *v.* Smith, 4 W. C. C. 224; Williams *v.* Carle, 2 Stockt. 543.

1 Fletcher *v.* Ashley, 6 Gratt. 332.

2 Cheshire *v.* Payne, 16 B. Monr. 618; Terry *v.* Hopkins, 1 Hill Ch. 1. See 1 Story Eq. Juris. § 403. And see Cole *v.* O'Neill, 3 Md. Ch. 174; O'Neill *v.* Cole, 4 Md. 107.

3 Spencer *v.* Spencer, 3 Jones Eq. 404. But see as to registration, *infra;* and Peachey Mar. Settl. 155.

4 Belt *v.* Ferguson, 3 Grant, 289. And see Duncan's Appeal, 43 Penn. St. 67.

5 Strathmore *v.* Bowes, 1 Ves. Jr. 28.

6 Taylor *v.* Pugh, 1 Hare, 613; 2 Roper Hus. & Wife, 162; Peachey Mar. Settl. 147.

7 St. George *v.* Wake, 1 Myl. & K. 610; King *v.* Cotton, 2 P. Wms. 674. And see Thomas *v.* Williams, Mosely, 177; Blanchet *v.* Foster, 2 Ves. Sen. 264; Anonymous, 34 Ala. 430; Taylor *v.* Pugh, 1 Hare, 614; Lewellin *v.* Cobbold, 1 Sm. & Gifford, 376; Peachey Mar. Settl. 151.

8 King *v.* Cotton, 2 P. Wms. 674.

with some person at the time of the settlement, but that he was the person intended.[1]

There is this difference pointed out between promises and agreements, in consideration of marriage, and all other agreements; namely, that the contract, though broken by one of the parties, remains binding upon the other. The reason for this is, that such promises and agreements affect not only the rights of the married pair, but those of their offspring; the children being, in fact, regarded as purchasers.[2] But where the performance is sought by the defaulting party, the contract cannot be enforced against the person injured through such default.[3] The difference thus mentioned is, therefore, a difference which grows out of the peculiar nature of the contract, and the existence of parties, other than those contracting, who may be brought within the purview of the consideration. As Lord Eldon says, the issue have a right to say to the parents, "You shall, each of you, do what you can do, and we must not be disappointed."[4] Unquestionably, however, even in the case of a marriage settlement, the covenants may be so framed as to be mutually dependent; and if it be clear on the face of the settlement, that such was the intention, that intention must prevail, even against the offspring of the marriage.[5]

Marriage articles, to make a settlement of real property, should be drawn up only in extreme cases; though in the case of personalty, more latitude may be allowed; and when drawn

[1] England *v.* Downes, 2 Beav. 522; Peachey Mar. Settl. 15; Macq. Hus. & Wife, 37; Strathmore *v.* Bowes, 1 Ves. Jr. 22. And see Waters *v.* Tazewell, 9 Md. 291.

[2] Bale *v.* Coleman, 1 P. Wms. 145; Harvey *v.* Ashley, 3 Atk. 610.

[3] Crofton *v.* Ormsby, 2 Sch. & Lef. 583.

[4] Rancliffe *v.* Parkyns, 6 Dow, 209.

[5] Per Lord Cottenham, Lloyd *v.* Lloyd, 2 Myl. & Cr. 192; Pyke *v.* Pyke, 12 Ves. 67. See further *In re* Wilson's Estate, 2 Barr, 325; Bliss *v.* Sheldon, 7 Barb. 152; Mitchell *v.* Gates, 23 Ala. 438; Shock *v.* Shock's Executors, 19 Penn. St. 252; Jones *v.* Brown, 1 Md. Ch. 191; Charles *v.* Charles, 8 Gratt. 486; Saunders *v.* Saunders, 20 Ala. 710; Hamrico *v.* Laird, 10 Yerg. 222; Allen *v.* Rumph, 2 Hill Ch. 1; Gause *v.* Hale, 2 Ired. Ch. 241; Loftus *v.* Penn, 1 Swan, 445; Whitall *v.* Clark, 2 Edw. Ch. 149; Rutherford *v.* Craik, 2 Hay, 262.

up they should leave as little to construction as possible. Yet, marriage articles are frequently prepared in great haste, and many questions must necessarily arise, as to the intention of the parties; these the courts of equity endeavor to meet by adopting the intention of the parties as their true guide, and taking it for granted that the articles are merely minutes which the settlement may explain more at large, but which are not to be literally followed.[1]

The general rule as to reforming settlements framed upon antenuptial articles is thus laid down by Lord Chancellor Talbot:[2] "Where articles are entered into before marriage, and settlement made after marriage, differing from the articles, this court will set up the articles against the settlement." That is to say, the court will order the settlement to be reformed. Where both the articles and the settlement are prior to the marriage, at a time when all the parties are at liberty, the settlement differing from the articles will be taken as a new agreement between them, and the articles will be controlled accordingly.[3] For the discrepancy will be presumed to have arisen from some change of mutual intention, while matters remained open. But this rule is not invariable, according to the later authorities; for any clear and satisfactory evidence may be introduced to show that the discrepancy had arisen from a mistake.[4] Where the settlement expressly declares that it is made in terms of the articles, and yet differs from them, the settlement will be reformed, so as to correspond with the articles. This is no contradiction of the general rule; for where the settlement is expressly mentioned to be made in pursuance of the marriage articles, the intention of the parties is by writing shown to be the same as when the articles were

[1] Peachey Mar. Settl. 89–97; Macq. Hus. & Wife, 257; Trevor *v.* Trevor, P. Wms. 631; Blandford *v.* Marlborough, 2 Atk. 545; Rochfort *v.* Fitzmaurice, Dru. & War. 18. But see Breadalbane *v.* Chandos, 2 Myl. & Cr. 711.

[2] Legg *v.* Goldwire, Forrester, 20; Macq. Hus. & Wife, 259.

[3] Legg *v.* Goldwire, Forrester, 20; Peachey Mar. Settl. 134.

[4] See Peachey Mar. Settl. 135; Bold *v.* Hutchinson, 2 Jur. (N. S.) 97; 5 De G., M. & G. 567.

drawn, and must be construed accordingly. And curiously enough in an English case under this head, though the settlement followed the precise words of the marriage articles, the court reformed it, in order to carry out the actual intention of the parties.[1]

Mistakes in marriage settlements, either through error or fraud, will be corrected in equity; the principle being that the parties are to be placed in the same situation in which they would have stood, if the error to be corrected had not been committed.[2]

Many deeds of settlement provide what are called "portions." The word portion may be used to denote what the wife brings her husband in marriage, and in this sense it corresponds with the word *dos* at the civil law, or what we sometimes call her dowry. But in its more special acceptation, the word portion signifies that part of a person's estate which is given or left to a child. Marriage settlements usually contain some provision to secure portions for the children of the marriage.[3] Double portions may sometimes be created for children; as if a father should make a provision for a child by marriage settlement, and afterwards provide for the same child by will; but the presumption is always against such an intent, and in favor of regarding the latter as a substitute for the former.[4]

So, too, marriage settlements frequently contain a covenant on the husband's part, to settle all the after-acquired property of the wife. In most of the cases decided under this head, the courts have evidently sought to adapt the covenant to the

[1] West *v.* Errissey, 2 P. Wms. 350.

[2] Rooke *v.* Lord Kensington, 2 Kay & Johns. 770; Peachey Mar. Settl. 565, 576; Alexander *v.* Crosbie, Lloyd & Goold, temp. Sugd. 149; Sanderson *v.* Robinson, 6 Jones Eq. 155; Love *v.* Graham, 25 Ala. 187; Reade *v.* Armstrong, 7 Irish Eq. (N. S.) 381; Walker *v.* Armstrong, 2 Jur. (N. S.) 962; Brown *v.* Bonner, 8 Leigh, 1; Ball *v.* Storie, 1 Sim. & St. 210, 219.

[3] Wood *v.* Briant, 1 Atk. 522. For a full discussion of this topic, see Peachey Mar. Settl. 409 *et seq.* and cases cited.

[4] *Ex parte* Pye, 18 Ves. 147; Peachey Mar. Settl. 492 *et seq.* and cases cited; Earl of Durham *v.* Wharton, 3 Cl. & Fin. 155. But the Scotch rule of construction is otherwise. Kippen *v.* Darley, 3 Macq. 203.

presumed intention of the parties.[1] The question is, therefore, one of intention to be gathered from the contents of the instrument by which the parties have bound themselves.[1] And the rule of construction is the same, whether damages for breach of covenant be sought at law, or specific performance in equity.[2] Such covenants may be on the wife's part; or they may be conditional.[3]

In an early case, Lord Talbot is reported to have said that where marriage articles were pretty much in the nature of a jointure, they were not forfeitable by adultery or an elopement.[4] And upon the strength of this, it has been held that marriage articles will be enforced on behalf of the wife, although she be living in a state of adultery.[5] We find no late authority to support this doctrine, and it is doubtful whether such a rule would be enforced at this day.[6] The wife may, like all others, forfeit her rights to a trust for her benefit, by long acquiescence as well as active participation in the unlawful acts of the trustees under the marriage settlement.[7]

Property cannot be settled by the intended husband, so that in event of his future bankruptcy, or insolvency, the wife will be entitled to a provision.[8] But the wife's fortune may be settled on her husband till he fail, and then to her separate use.[9]

1 Ramsden *v.* Smith, 2 Drew. 302; Withers *v.* Weaver, 10 Barr, 391.

2 Smith *v.* Osborne, 6 Ho. Lords, 394; Blythe *v.* Granville, 13 Sim. 190; Tawney *v.* Ward, 1 Beav. 563; Young *v.* Smith, Law Rep. 1 Eq. 180; Peachey Mar. Settl. 523; Macq. Hus. & Wife, 268. As to the application of this covenant to separate property see Mainwaring's Settlements, Law Rep. 1 Eq. 180; Milford *v.* Peile, 17 Beav. 602.

3 Peachey Mar. Settl. 548.

4 Sidney *v.* Sidney, 3 P. Wms. 275; Seagrave *v.* Seagrave, 13 Ves. 443.

5 Macq. Hus. & Wife, 263; Buchanan *v.* Buchanan, 1 Ball & B. 206.

6 See Peachey Mar. Settl. 384; Legard *v.* Hodges, 4 Br. C. C. 421, cited by Lord Manners in Buchanan *v.* Buchanan, 1 Ball & B. 206. And see *supra*, p. 242, as to the wife's pin-money.

7 Jones *v.* Higgins, Law Rep. 2 Eq. 538. As to the settlements of infants, see *post*, Infancy.

8 Higginson *v.* Kelly, 1 Ball & B. 255; Peachey Mar. Settl. 219; *In re* Casey's Trusts, 4 Ir. Ch. (N. S.) 247.

9 Lester *v.* Garland, 5 Sim. 222; Sharp *v.* Cosserat, 20 Beav. 470; Lockyer *v.* Savage, 2 Str. 947; *Ex parte* Verner, 1 Ball & B. 260. And see Higginson *v.* Kelly, 1 Ball & B. 252.

Where fraud is committed by husband and wife, in reference to property embraced in the terms of a settlement, the rights of a subsequent mortgagee with insufficient notice, will, in some instances, be allowed preference over those who claim under the settlement.[1]

Marriage settlements are very common in England, among parties possessed of large means; not generally so in this country, although many are made in the Southern States and New York. The American policy is to dispense with trusts, and place a married woman's separate property in her own absolute keeping. Yet, marriage settlements might often be well resorted to in order to equalize the burdens, while local legislation remains in a crude condition. Our registry system raises questions of constructive notice, as to marriage settlements, often of great local importance.[2]

1 Sharpe *v.* Foy, Law Rep. 4 Ch. 35.

2 See particularly Ingham *v.* White, 4 Allen, 412. And see Gibbes *v.* Cobb, 7 Rich. Eq. 54; Logan *v.* Phillips, 18 Mis. 22; Levinz *v.* Will, 1 Dall. 430; O'Neill *v.* Cole, 4 Md. 107; 1 Story Eq. Juris. § 403; 2 Kent Com. 173*n.*; Reinhart *v.* Miller, 22 Geo. 402.

CHAPTER XVI.

POSTNUPTIAL SETTLEMENTS AND GIFTS BETWEEN HUSBAND AND WIFE.

THE important distinction between settlements before and settlements after marriage, is that, while the former are supported by the marriage consideration, the latter are without it.[1] The term postnuptial settlements, then, must not confuse the reader's mind. We use the language of the text-writers, without meaning to imply that it is appropriate, or that antenuptial and postnuptial settlements constitute two branches of one general subject. On the contrary, postnuptial settlements are usually nothing more nor less than gifts between husband and wife, which equity places, notwithstanding the disabilities of coverture, upon the footing of other gifts. Furthermore, it should be remembered that formal settlements made between parties in the marriage state, in pursuance of articles or memoranda signed before marriage, are not technically postnuptial settlements (as the name itself would seem to indicate), for the settlement relates back to the antenuptial stipulations, however loosely these may have been drawn up, and it is protected by the marriage consideration, like all other antenuptial contracts.

But though for want of consideration, postnuptial settlements are deemed voluntary, yet, like other voluntary transactions, they will be valid and binding, so far as the parties are concerned, and can only be impeached as fraudulent upon others. Postnuptial settlements, therefore, must be viewed in two dif-

1 Macq. Hus. & Wife, 273; Lannoy v. Duke of Athol, 2 Atk. 448.

ferent aspects: the one, as between the married parties and the creditor or purchasers of either; the other, as between husband and wife themselves.

There are two English statutes which control this subject, as concerns creditors and purchasers, to a great extent. The first is that of 13th Eliz. ch. 5, in favor of creditors; the second that of 27th Eliz. ch. 4, in favor of purchasers: the one being directed against fraudulent conveyances of all property, with intent to defeat or delay creditors, the other against fraudulent or voluntary conveyances of lands designed to defeat subsequent purchasers. These statutes, Lord Mansfield said, cannot receive too liberal a construction or be too much extended in suppression of fraud.[1]

As to the first of these statutes, it is held that, if a man who is indebted conveys property for the use of his wife and children, or in trust for their benefit, such a conveyance is subject to the statute prohibition, inasmuch as the consideration, although good between the parties themselves, is not *bona fide* as regards creditors.[2] But a voluntary deed is good as against subsequent creditors; and there can be nothing inequitable in a man's making a voluntary conveyance to a wife, child, or even a stranger, if it be not at the time prejudicial to the rights of third persons, or in furtherance of some design of future fraud or injury to them.[3] The question of fraudulent intent is the real point at issue. And as to fraud upon future creditors, it has been said that while an instrument might be executed with the purpose of defrauding them, it is not a thing very likely to happen.[4] But cases of this sort are not impossible. Thus a person might make a voluntary settlement upon his wife and children, raising enough cash to pay off existing creditors, and leaving those who advanced the cash without the

[1] Cadogan *v.* Kennett, Comp. 434; Peachey Mar. Settl. 189.
[2] Goldsmith *v.* Russell, 5 De G., M. & Gord. 547; Peachey Mar. Settl. 191.
[3] Holloway *v.* Millard, 1 Mad. 414; Peachey Mar. Settl. 192.
[4] Jenkyn *v.* Vaughan, 25 L. J. Eq. 339.

means of securing their reimbursement.[1] Doubtless such a transaction is to be set aside as fraudulent.[2]

The question of the husband's indebtedness, as affecting his postnuptial settlement, is not however as free from difficulty as it might appear at first sight. Concerning creditors existing at the time of the settlement, the settlement may be void under the statute; but not because the husband has creditors; for who goes through life without being indebted at all? It will be void when he is so far indebted, and his debts are so considerable in amount, as to render him likely to be insolvent. Probabilities are sufficient to meet this case; and if existing creditors wish to set the conveyance aside, they need only show that at the date of the instrument, he was indebted to such an extent that, having regard to his property, the effect might be to delay, hinder, and defraud them.[3] The question is not that of actual insolvency, but the intention to defraud.[4] But though the existence of debts then does not necessarily determine the validity of the settlement, it lays the foundation for inquiry, and is always material to the issue.

The property which may be recovered by creditors does not embrace property which is exempt from execution; for the creditors have no concern with any thing except assets, actual or possible, for the payment of their debts.[5] This was formerly a matter of dispute; but it is now apparently set at rest.

Voluntary settlements, in England, are likewise affected by

[1] Richardson *v.* Smallwood, Jac. 552; Holmes *v.* Penney, 3 Kay & Johns. 102.

[2] Ib.; Macq. Hus. & Wife, 275; Peachey Mar. Settl. 193.

[3] Jenkyn *v.* Vaughan, 3 Drew. 424; Turnley *v.* Hooper, 2 Jur. (N. S.) 1081.

[4] Peachey Mar. Settl. 195, and cases cited; Skarf *v.* Soulby, 1 M. & Gord. 375; French *v.* French, 6 De G., M. & Gord. 95; Wakefield *v.* Gibbon, 26 L. J. Eq. 508. As to the right of subsequent creditors to impeach a voluntary settlement, see Walker *v.* Burrowes, 1 Atk. 93; Richardson *v.* Smallwood, Jac. 552; Macq. Hus. & Wife, 275; Peachey Mar. Settl. 197. When the deed is once set aside, the property is thrown open to all creditors. Ede *v.* Knowles, 2 Y. & Col. C. C. 178; Kidney *v.* Coussmaker, 12 Ves. 136. Jenkyn *v.* Vaughan, 3 Drew. 419.

[5] Peachey Mar. Settl. 199 *et seq.*; 1 Story Eq. Juris. § 410. See 2 Kent Com. 443, note last ed.

the bankrupt acts, which are intimately connected with the statute of Elizabeth.[1] Here questions arise as to what acts amount to a contemplation of bankruptcy; and what constitutes a fraudulent preference; and these we need not here discuss. But it should be observed, that the husband cannot bestow his property upon his wife, conditional upon his future bankruptcy or insolvency; yet, that third persons may, by voluntary conveyance, settle property to the wife's separate use, free from all control of her husband; or in trust to pay the income to the husband for life, "or until he should become a bankrupt," and after that, to the wife's separate use.[2] In the former case the transaction would be simply an artifice of the husband to evade the bankrupt laws; in the latter, a third person parts with his own property, and makes his own terms as to its final disposition, as he has a right to do.

The Statute of 13 Eliz. ch. 5, is generally recognized throughout the United States; in some cases having been formally reenacted; in others claimed to be part of the common law transported hither by the first settlers; hence gifts of goods and chattels, as well as of lands, by writing or otherwise, are void when made with intent to delay, hinder, and defraud creditors, even though the gift be to wife and children.[3] For it is a maxim both at the civil and common law, that the claims of justice shall precede those of affection.[4] And in general the rule appears to be coextensive with the fraud, in this country as in England.

But the principle is not stated with equal precision in all the States, it must be admitted; and while some cases doubtless

[1] Peachey Mar. Settl. 210 *et seq.*

[2] Manning *v.* Chambers, 1 De G. & Sm. 282; Sharp *v.* Cosserat, 20 Beav. 473. A similar principle prevails in this country. See Levering *v.* Heighe, 2 Md. Ch. 81; Head *v.* Halford, 5 Rich. Eq. 128; Peigne *v.* Snowden, 1 Desaus. 591. And see *supra*, 274.

[3] 2 Kent Com. 440, 441 and cases cited; Bayard *v.* Hoffman, 4 Johns. Ch. 450; Montgomery *v.* Tilley, 1 B. Monr. 157; Reade *v.* Livingston, 3 Johns. Ch. 481; Pinney *v.* Fellows, 15 Vt. 525; Simpson *v.* Graves, Riley Ch. 232.

[4] Cicero, de Off. I. 14, cited in 2 Kent Com. 441.

proceed upon the doctrine that the voluntary gift fails because there is an intent to hinder and defraud, others again seem to rest upon the mere existence of actual creditors whose rights are thereby prejudiced. It is not within our province to treat of this subject in its general bearings, as in gifts between man and man, but so far as the American decisions concern gifts between husband and wife, we shall presently give the results somewhat at length.[1] The point of the distinction however is readily perceived to be this: that, whereas one class of cases establishes that the husband may never settle property upon his wife during coverture, if he owes debts at the time so as to be insolvent, but may otherwise do so absolutely without the fear of future creditors before his eyes, the other class of cases is to the purport that, no matter whether they be existing or subsequent creditors, his voluntary settlement will be voidable if with intent to prejudice their rights, and not otherwise. The latter we conceive to be the true rule; though the language of the statutes in some States contributes to the confusion. Furthermore, our registry system places the law on a somewhat different footing from that prevalent in England, in all settlements, as we noticed in the preceding chapter.

Settlements as concerns the right of creditors and purchasers are also affected by the statute of 27 Eliz. ch. 4. This statute too is to be considered as part of the common law brought to this country by our ancestors; though not generally adopted here to the full extent of the English equity decisions.[2] It provides that all conveyances of lands made with the intent to defraud and deceive purchasers, shall, as against them, be utterly void. The statute has no application whatever to personal estate.[3]

The English doctrine is that a voluntary conveyance, though

[1] See 2 Kent Com. 440 *et seq.*; 4 ib. 463 *et seq.*, where the subject is discussed at length, with citations from American cases.

[2] 4 Kent Com. 463.

[3] Sugden Vend. & Purch. 587, 13th ed.; Peachey Mar. Settl. 226; 4 Kent Com. 463.

for a meritorious purpose, shall be deemed to have been made with fraudulent views, and set aside in favor of a subsequent purchaser for a valuable consideration, even though he had notice of the prior deed.[1] In other words, while the statute of 13 Eliz. permits a voluntary conveyance to stand as against subsequent creditors, that of 27 Eliz. makes a voluntary conveyance of land void as against a subsequent purchaser for value. The principle on which the English cases rest appears to be that by selling the property over again for a valuable consideration the vendor so entirely repudiates the former transaction and shows his intention to sell, that the presumption against the prior gift becomes conclusive.[2] And while the correctness of this principle might well be doubted in its application to subsequent purchasers with notice, yet, as Lord Thurlow said, so many estates stand upon the rule that it cannot be now shaken.[3] This doctrine applies to postnuptial settlements in England.[4]

Fortunately, in this country we have been hampered by no such severe construction of this statute. And in a case before the Supreme Court of the United States it was held that the principle of construction which prevailed in England, at the commencement of the American Revolution, went no further than to hold the subsequent sale to be presumptiv e andnot conclusive evidence of a fraudulent intent in making the prior voluntary conveyance; and the court declined to follow the subsequently established construction of Westminster Hall.[5] And the better American doctrine seems to be that voluntary conveyances of land *bona fide* made, and not originally fraudulent, are valid as against subsequent purchasers.[6]

[1] Doe *v.* Manning, 9 East, 59.

[2] Doe *v.* Rusham, 17 Q. B. 724; 16 Jur. 359.

[3] Evelyn *v.* Templar, 2 Bro. C. C. 148; Peachey Mar. Settl. 228, and cases cited.

[4] See Bill *v.* Cureton, 2 Myl. & K. 510; Peachey Mar. Settl. 232, 240. And English conveyancers insert words importing certain valuable considerations in such deeds, in order to deter purchasers.

[5] Cathcart *v.* Robinson, 5 Pet. 280; 4 Kent Com. 463.

[6] 4 Kent Com. 464 *n.* and cases cited; Jackson *v.* Town, 4 Cow. 603; Ricker

In some States, the English statute is re-enacted with the language essentially changed; as in Connecticut and New York. And it is the settled American doctrine that a *bona fide* purchaser for value is protected, whether he purchases from a fraudulent grantor or a fraudulent grantee; and that there is no difference in this respect between a deed to defraud subsequent creditors, and one to defraud subsequent purchasers; both being voidable only and not absolutely void.[1] So where any marriage settlement is made for a valuable consideration, it cannot be avoided as fraudulent upon the creditors, unless both husband and wife were cognizant of the fraud.[2]

There are instances in which a postnuptial settlement has been sustained against creditors and purchasers on the ground that a valuable consideration is interposed. Thus, Lord Hardwicke has said, "If, after marriage, the father of the wife, or other person, in consideration of the husband making a settlement, advance a sum of money, such a settlement will be good and for a valuable consideration. And though the money be not paid at the time, yet if it be sufficiently secured, the settlement will stand."[3] So voluntary settlements, both in England and this country, may become valid by matter *ex post facto*.[4]

v. Ham, 14 Mass. 139; Atkinson *v.* Phillips, 1 Md. Ch. 507; Beal *v.* Warren, 2 Gray, 447. But *contra,* see Clanton *v.* Burges, 2 Dev. Ch. 13.

[1] 4 Kent Com. 464, and cases cited in notes; Anderson *v.* Roberts, 18 Johns. 515; Bean *v.* Smith, 2 Mason, 252; Oriental Bank *v.* Haskins, 3 Met. 332. So the English stat. 3 & 4 Wm. 4, ch. 27, § 26, protects *bona fide* purchasers for value.

[2] Magniac *v.* Thompson, 7 Pet. 348. And see Hawcott *v.* Collins, 23 Miss. 398.

[3] Wheeler *v.* Caryl, Ambl. 121. See further Macq. Hus. & Wife, 277; Cottle *v.* Tripp, 2 Vern. 220; Ward *v.* Shallet, 2 Ves. Sen. 17; Lavender *v.* Blackstone, 2 Lev. 147; Arundell *v.* Phipps, 10 Ves. 140. Very slight considerations are sometimes deemed sufficient in the English courts. Peachey Mar. Settl. 233, 238; Butterfield *v.* Heath, 15 Beav. 414; Fitzmaurice *v.* Sadlier, 9 Ir. Ch. 595; Hewison *v.* Negus, 16 Beav. 594.

[4] Peachey Mar. Settl. 236; Prodgers *v.* Langham, 1 Sid. 133; Brown *v.* Carter, 5 Ves. 877; 4 Kent Com. 463; Sterry *v.* Arden, 1 Johns. Ch. 261; Huston *v.* Cantril, 11 Leigh, 136. In numerous instances the equity courts of this country have sustained a postnuptial transaction in favor of the wife and against the husband's creditors, on the ground of a valid consideration. As where the husband has transferred property to his wife in consideration of payment from

The effect of postnuptial settlement, as between the parties themselves, claims our attention for the remainder of this chapter. In general, to constitute a voluntary gift between

her separate estate. Simmons *v.* McElwain, 26 Barb. 420; Bullard *v.* Briggs, 7 Pick. 533; Ready *v.* Bragg, 1 Head, 511. And see Teller *v.* Bishop, 8 Minn. 226. And where he conveys what her equity entitles her to claim. Poindexter *v.* Jeffries, 15 Gratt. 363. And where he has appropriated a like amount of his wife's property without her consent. Wiley *v.* Gray, 36 Miss. 510. So where the wife pays her husband's debts from her separate earnings. Dygert *v.* Remerschneider, 39 Barb. 417. Or releases her dower. Unger *v.* Price, 9 Md. 552; Garlick *v.* Strong, 3 Paige, 440; Hale *v.* Plummer, 6 Ind. 121; Andrews *v.* Andrews, 28 Ala. 432. Some of the later decisions speak of a "reasonable provision" made for the wife by the husband while in prosperous circumstances. Babcock *v.* Eckler, 24 N. Y. 628; Townsend *v.* Maynard, 45 Penn. St. 198. And the wife's relinquishment of her equity to a *chose in action* constitutes a valuable consideration, even perhaps for his settlement of the whole *chose* upon her. Bradford *v.* Goldsborough, 15 Ala. 311; Barron *v.* Barron, 24 Vt. 375. But where the consideration advanced by the wife is inadequate, equity will never sustain the settlement further than to secure the repayment thereof, and not always even to this extent; especially if she be privy, with her husband, to a fraud upon others. Herschfeldt *v.* George, 6 Mich. 456; Skillman *v.* Skillman, 2 Beasl. 403; Den *v.* York, 13 Ired. 206; Pusey *v.* Harper, 27 Penn. St. 469; 2 Kent Com. 174; William & Mary College *v.* Powell, 12 Gratt. 372; and see ch. 13, *supra.* And a settlement of all or the greater part of the husband's property upon his wife on the plea of a reasonable provision for her support is not sustainable in equity. Coates *v.* Gerlach, 44 Penn. St. 43. And see Lewis *v.* Caperton, 8 Gratt. 148.

The husband's possession of his wife's property is not a badge of fraud. Barncord *v.* Kuhn, 36 Penn. St. 383. Nor are his representations of ownership, as it would appear, sufficient to charge such property for his debts, unless deceitful and calculated to mislead the public. Lyman *v.* Cessford, 15 Iowa, 229. And in several States it is expressly held, that a voluntary transfer or conveyance from husband to wife is valid against all subsequent creditors and purchasers. United States Bank *v.* Ennis, Wright, 605; Beach *v.* White, Walk. Ch. 495; Davis *v.* Herrick, 37 Me. 397; Story *v.* Marshall, 24 Tex. 305. In New Jersey, however, the rule, as concisely stated, is that the husband's settlement, if voluntary, is fraudulent as to existing debts by an inference of law; and as to subsequent debts, fraud in fact must be proved. Belford *v.* Crane, 1 C. E. Green, 265. This is the doctrine in New York and many other States. Reade *v.* Livingston, 3 Johns. Ch. 481; Lyman *v.* Cessford, 15 Iowa, 229. And Chancellor Kent has ruled, in the leading American case on this subject, that if a settlement after marriage be set aside by the prior creditors, subsequent creditors are entitled to come in and be paid out of the proceeds of the settled estate. Reade *v.* Livingston, 3 Johns. Ch. 481. Subsequent creditors may probably impeach for fraud. See *supra* p. 278. As to the duty of one who is both assignee for husband and trustee for wife, see Borst *v.* Corey, 12 Barb. 136.

A settlement by a husband on his wife in consideration of her services, is voluntary merely. Belford *v.* Crane, 1 C. E. Green, 265. And see Keith *v.* Woombell, 8 Pick. 211.

parties, it must be complete or courts of equity will not enforce it; not only must the intention clearly appear, but that intention must have been executed.[1] But the rule is more favorable as to a *cestui que trust* claiming against his trustee;[2] and it is thus perceived why on general principles the intervention of a trustee is preferable to support the settlement. But in general all voluntary conveyances, though void against creditors and purchasers for value, are good against the grantor and those claiming under him.[3]

A voluntary promise does not constitute a perfect gift. Nor is a voluntary assignment, unaccompanied by other acts, more effectual to confer a title on the donee, than a mere agreement, as it has been repeatedly held in equity.[4] But there is some difficulty in reconciling the authorities on this latter subject; for it has been fully decided that the voluntary assignment of a *chose in action* is good, if the relation of *cestui que trust* and trustees be once established; while, on the other hand, if one assigns to trustees certain property immediately transferable, the gift is imperfect without the transfer.[5] The point of the distinction seems to be, that in the one case the donor, by the assignment, not only indicates the intention of making a gift, but executes his intention so far as it is possible for him to do so; while, in the other, by his failure to make the transfer, he does not execute his intention to the extent of his power, but leaves it incomplete. Whatever may be the real principle involved, the authorities proceed on the ground that a trust relation is in the former case created by the instrument.[5]

It has been repeatedly held, in our own courts, that gifts

[1] Cotteen *v.* Missing, 1 Mad. 176; Kekewich *v.* Manning, 1 De G., M. & G. 188.

[2] Ellison *v.* Ellison, 6 Ves. 662; Peachey Mar. Settl. 245, 246; Meek *v.* Kettlewell, 1 Hare, 470; Kekewich *v.* Manning, 1 De G., M. & G. 192; Beech *v.* Keep, 18 Beav. 289.

[3] Bill *v.* Cureton, 2 Myl. & K. 510; Doe *v.* Rusham, 17 Q. B. 724.

[4] Edwards *v.* Jones, 1 M. & Cr. 226; Holloway *v.* Headington, 8 Sim. 324.

[5] See Bridge *v.* Bridge, 16 Beav. 321; Donaldson *v.* Donaldson, Kay, 717; McFaddyn *v.* Jenkyns, 1 Hare, 462; Peachey Mar. Settl. 247, 248. See Scales *v.* Maude, 6 De G., M. & G. 52; Penfold *v.* Mould, Law Rep. 4 Eq. 562.

from husband to wife are as between themselves valid. But the evidence of intention should be clear and distinct in all such cases.[1] There should be either a clear irrevocable gift to a trustee for the wife, or some positive act by the husband, by which he divests himself of the property, and engages to hold it for the wife's separate use.[2]

If husband and wife may transfer property to one another without consideration, still more may they do so where the consideration is valuable. And their mutual contracts for a transfer, where there is a *bona fide* and valuable consideration, may be specifically enforced in equity, upon proof that the agreement has been executed by one party and not by the other. Thus a husband and wife agreed, by parol, that he should purchase a lot of land in her name, and build a house

[1] Borst *v.* Spelman, 4 Comst. 284; Coates *v.* Gerlach, 44 Penn. St. 43; Jennings *v.* Davis, 31 Conn. 134; George *v.* Spencer, 2 Md. Ch. 353; Deming *v.* Williams, 26 Conn. 226; Reynolds *v.* Lansford, 16 Tex. 286.

[2] The promissory note of a creditor may be thus transferred by the husband under some of the married women's acts. Motley *v.* Sawyer, 38 Me. 68; Dillage *v.* Parks, 31 Barb. 132; Slawson *v.* Loring, 5 Allen, 340; and, independently of such statutes, on equitable principles. Tullis *v.* Fridley, 9 Minn. 79. And it would appear to be the rule, that the gifts of a husband require less proof than the gifts of third persons. Deming *v.* Williams, 26 Conn. 226. In some States, however, the wife is put upon strict proof as to all implied gifts. Gannard *v.* Eslava, 20 Ala. 733; Paschall *v.* Hall, 5 Jones Eq. 108. The precise extent to which the rule of a gift without trustee will be enforced depends greatly upon the liberality of the married woman's legislation in any particular State; a subject which has already been discussed. But a familiar instance is that of a deposit by the husband in some savings bank, on his wife's separate account. Howard *v.* Windham County Savings Bank, 40 Vt. 597. And see Underhill *v.* Morgan, 33 Conn. 105; Brown *v.* Brown, 23 Barb. 565; Jennings *v.* Davis, 31 Conn. 134; Wilder *v.* Aldrich, 2 R. I. 518. A deed of property by the husband in trust for his wife, need not be formally accepted by her in writing in order to become binding. Hutchins *v.* Dixon, 11 Md. 29. And a gift with power to the wife to dispose thereof by will may be good against the husband's representatives. Churchill *v.* Corker, 25 Geo. 479. But it is said that a man cannot denude himself of his marital rights in property which the law vests in him by simply declaring that it belongs to his wife. Wade *v.* Cantrell, 1 Head, 346. See Johnston *v.* Johnston, 31 Penn. St. 450; Frierson *v.* Frierson, 21 Ala. 549. Gifts and voluntary transfers by the husband to third persons, if not with the actual intent of defeating the wife's rights, are held in Maryland to be sustainable, though leaving her without the means of subsistence; though here the statutes of Elizabeth would apply. Feigley *v.* Feigley, 7 Md. 537.

thereon, and be reimbursed from the proceeds of the sale of another house belonging to her. The husband having executed the agreement on his part, the wife died suddenly, before the sale of her former house could be effected. She left infant children. It was decreed in equity that the agreement should be carried into effect, the former house sold, a conveyance thereof executed by the infants, by their guardian *ad litem*, and the husband be reimbursed out of the proceeds of the sale.[1] But the mere fact, that the husband has received property in right of the wife, cannot constitute a valuable consideration by relation, to support a settlement upon her some years afterwards; and this on the general principle applicable to contracts.[2] Nor can an antenuptial settlement, once extinguished by the agreement of all parties concerned, be revived for such purpose.[3]

While instances of gifts from husband to wife are most commonly considered, gifts from wife to husband are by no means rare. But in the latter instance fraud or undue influence may be reasonably suspected; and transactions of this sort are scrutinized by the courts with great care.[4] Before the wife's separate use was established, little or no occasion could arise for the wife to bestow her personal property upon her husband, for the law sufficiently bestowed it without her aid.

In general, wherever a contract would be good at law, when made with trustees for the wife, that contract will be sustained in equity, when made between husband and wife, without the intervention of trustees.[5] A mutual agreement, by which the

[1] Livingston *v.* Livingston, 2 Johns. Ch. 537. And see Bowie *v.* Stonestreet, 6 Ind. 418; Jones *v.* Jones, 18 Md. 464; Steadman *v.* Wilbur, 7 R. I. 481.

[2] Lyne *v.* Bank of Kentucky, 5 J. J. Marsh. 545.

[3] Harper *v.* Scott, 12 Geo. 125.

[4] Cruger *v.* Douglas, 4 Edw. Ch. 433; Nedby *v.* Nedby, 11 E. L. & Eq. 106; Converse *v.* Converse, 9 Rich. Eq. 535; Stiles *v.* Stiles, 14 Mich. 72; Hollis *v.* Francois, 5 Tex. 195; Wales *v.* Newbould, 9 Mich. 45; Merriam *v.* Harsen, 4 Edw. Ch. 70. As to gifts and loans of the wife's separate property to her husband, including mortgages, see also ch. 13, *supra*.

[5] Wallingsford *v.* Allen, 10 Pet. 583; 2 Story Eq. Juris. § 1204; Slanning *v.* Style, 3 P. Wms. 334; Barron *v.* Barron, 24 Vt. 375; Resor *v.* Resor, 9 Ind.

wife renounces all further claim upon the husband for his services, or support for herself and children, and stipulates that she will contract no debts on his account, while the husband renounces all claim for her services or support, affords a strong illustration. This might not avail against creditors, but so far as the husband and his heirs, and in fact all who claim under him are concerned, it will be enforced.[1] But trustees are always desirable, and in some States it is a rule, that the wife can only contract with her husband through the intervention of third persons.[2] This passes a legal estate in any event and permits of suits relative to the property with more freedom. In no case can contracts in derogation of the husband's property rights rest upon slight proof; the relation of debtor and creditor must be distinctly shown.[3]

In Ohio, a note executed by a husband to his wife, acknowledging the receipt of one hundred dollars at her hands, and promising to allow her six per cent per annum interest thereon during her life, and, if she survived him, the same to be paid to her or her heirs, "extra of her thirds," was held to be a postnuptial contract, enforceable against the husband's estate after his death, even though there were not personal assets left sufficient to pay his debts.[4]

A conveyance by husband and wife of land belonging to the wife, to a third person, and a conveyance of the same land by such third person to the husband, vests the entire title in the husband.[5] But a conveyance of lands by the wife directly to

347; Coates *v.* Gerlach, 44 Penn. St. 43; Wright *v.* Wright, 16 Iowa, 496; Williams *v.* Maull, 20 Ala. 721; Schaffer *v.* Reuter, 37 Barb. 44; Hutton *v.* Duey, 3 Barr, 100.

[1] Barron *v.* Barron, 24 Vt. 375.

[2] McMullen *v.* McMullen, 10 Iowa, 412; Johnston *v.* Johnston, 1 Grant, 468.

[3] See Steadman *v.* Webber, 7 R. I. 481; Tripner *v.* Abrahams, 47 Penn. St. 220; Wales *v.* Newbould, 9 Mich. 45.

[4] Wood *v.* Warden, 20 Ohio, 518. This carries the doctrine very far. See Parham *v.* Parham, 6 Humph. 287. For cases of alleged fraud on the part of husband or wife, see Birdsong *v.* Birdsong, 2 Head, 289; Wells *v.* Wells, 35 Miss. 638; M'Clellan *v.* Kennedy, 3 Md. Ch. 234.

[5] Merriam *v.* Harsen, 4 Edw. Ch. 70; Durant *v.* Ritchie, 4 Mason, 45; Dempsey *v.* Tyler, 3 Duer, 73; Garvin *v.* Ingram, 10 Rich. Eq. 130.

her husband, especially if it be voluntary, has been considered ineffectual and void. And even under the late married women's acts, her right to make such a conveyance is still generally denied.[1] So it is the older rule that the husband cannot convey real estate to his wife directly, and without the intervention of a trustee.[2] But the husband may make a valid conveyance to his wife through the medium of a third person; and the deed (supposing it to have been properly recorded) will be good against all but injured creditors.[3]

The reason of this rule was the legal unity of husband and wife at the common law;[4] while the statute of uses furnished a mode of conveyance through trustees.[5]

It may here be added that a conveyance of land to husband and wife and their heirs, vests the entirety in each of them; and upon the death of one the survivor takes the whole estate.[6] They do not take by moieties; nor can either alienate the property alone so as to bind the other. The theoretic unity of husband and wife occasioned this rule likewise. It applies only to conveyances made to them during coverture. In the same way a conveyance to husband and wife, and a third person, gives only a moiety to husband and wife.[7] A judgment against a husband does not affect the joint estate of the husband and wife, and a decree in equity in favor of such a judg-

[1] White *v.* Wager, 32 Barb. 250; Winans *v.* Peebles, 32 N. Y. 423; Graham *v.* Van Wyck, 14 Barb. 531.

[2] Voorhees *v.* Presbyterian Church, &c., 17 Barb. 103.

[3] Jewell *v.* Porter, 11 Fost. 34.

[4] 1 Washb. Real Prop. 279.

[5] 1 Roper Hus. & Wife, 53; Thatcher *v.* Omans, 3 Pick. 521; 1 Washb. Real Prop. 279; Wms. Real Prop. 185. The later American cases are disposed to sustain all such conveyances, when with valuable consideration, upon equitable grounds. Winans *v.* Peebles, 32 N. Y. 423; Putnam *v.* Bicknell, 18 Wis. 333; 2 Story Eq. Juris. § 1204; Wallingsford *v.* Allen, 10 Pet. 583. In Maine, the trustee is now dispensed with altogether. Allen *v.* Hooper, 50 Maine, 371. And see Albin *v.* Lord, 39 N. H. 196.

[6] Wright *v.* Sadler, 20 N. Y. 320; Stuckey *v.* Keefe's Ex'or, 26 Penn. St. 397; Woodford *v.* Higby, 1 Wins. (N. C.) 237; Banton *v.* Campbell, 9 B. Monr. 587; Gilson *v.* Zimmerman, 12 Mis. 385; Bates *v.* Seely, 46 Penn. St. 248.

[7] See 1 Washb. Real Prop. 278; Wms. Real Prop. 184.

ment creditor can confer no better title than a sale of the premises under the judgment at law.[1] Nor can the wife maintain ejectment alone as to such premises.[2] Where the wife has an estate for life, and husband and wife are seised of the remainder in entirety, the estate for life does not merge in the estate in remainder.[3] And if the equitable title to land is in the wife, it cannot, of course, be conveyed to husband and wife so as to bar her rights.[4]

But if lands descend to A., B., and C., they each take a third part, though A. and B. happen to be husband and wife.[5] And it is said that by express words husband and wife may be made tenants in common by a gift to them during coverture.[6] In Connecticut, husband and wife are joint-tenants, and the husband may convey his interest.[7]

[1] Thomas *v.* De Baum, 1 McCart. 37; Tupper *v.* Fuller, 7 Rich. Eq. 170.

[2] Allie *v.* Schmetz, 17 Wis. 169. And see Torrey *v.* Torrey, 4 Kern. 430; Clark *v.* Thompson, 12 Penn. St. 274.

[3] Bomar *v.* Mullins, 4 Rich. Eq. 80. And see Brinton *v.* Hook, 3 Md. Ch. 477.

[4] Moore *v.* Moore, 12 B. Monr. 651. And see Hicks *v.* Cochran, 4 Edw. Ch. 107; Barncad *v.* Kuhn, 36 Penn. St. 383; Wright *v.* Sadler, 20 N. Y. 320; Wales *v.* Coffin, 13 Allen, 213; 1 Washb. Real Prop. 278, and cases cited.

[5] Knapp *v.* Windsor, 6 Cush. 156.

[6] Prest. Abst. 41; 1 Washb. Real Prop. 278.

[7] Whittlesey *v.* Fuller, 11 Conn. 337.

CHAPTER XVII.

SEPARATION AND DIVORCE.

SEPARATION is that anomalous condition of a married pair which involves a cessation of domestic intercourse, while the impediments of marriage continue. Either from choice or necessity, as the case may be, they throw aside the strong safeguards of a home and mutual companionship; they forfeit their most solemn obligations to protect, love, and cherish through life; they continue united in form and divided in fact. The spirit of the contract, all that dignifies and ennobles it, is gone; but the letter remains. Both parties submit in some degree, at least, to the degradation of public scandal; they are cast loose upon the world without the right to love and be loved again; the thought of kindling fresh flames at the altar of domestic happiness is criminal; and deprived of the comfort and support of one another, finding in society at best but timid sympathy and consolation, the moral character must be strong, and doubly so must be that of the wife, that each may buffet with success the tide which bears onward to destruction. Such a state of things no public policy can safely favor; but the law sometimes permits it, if for no other reason than that an adequate remedy is wanting to check or to prevent the evil; and hence it may be thought more expedient for the courts to enforce such mutual contracts of the unhappy pair as mitigate their troubles, than to dabble in a domestic quarrel and try to compel unwilling companionships.

This we conceive to be the rightful position of the English and American equity courts whenever they see fit to enforce separation agreements. Some, to be sure, are disposed to carry the argument further. Thus, recent English writers of much repute refer to the fact that divorces from bed and board are often granted in that country, and hence conclude that it is reasonable for the married parties themselves to compromise litigation, save court fees and avoid public notoriety, hence agree to live apart, just as though the court had entered a decree for that purpose.[1] But this argument proves too much; for if marriage and divorce are matters for private compromise, like ordinary contracts, why may not the discontented pair, upon just cause, agree to unloose the yoke altogether? Why may they not sometimes obtain divorce *a vinculo*, by collusion and default, and thus take the readiest means of avoiding scandalous and expensive suits? One shrinks from such conclusions. In fact, divorce laws do not belong to the parties themselves, but to the public; government guards the sanctity of marriage, just as it demands the duty of allegiance; though perhaps its policy cannot be enforced in the one case as well as the other. It is because marriage is *not* on the footing of ordinary contracts, that husband and wife cannot, on principle, compromise, arbitrate, or modify their relationship at pleasure. Furthermore, the above argument suggests that where a complete divorce, instead of divorce from bed and board, is attainable, deeds of separation do not hold good; nor, again, where parties separate for causes which do not even justify divorce from bed and board; neither of which positions is sustained by the actual decisions.

Lord Eldon was of the opinion that a settlement by way of separate maintenance, on a voluntary separation of husband and wife, was against the policy of the law and void. The ground of his opinion was that such settlements, creating a separate maintenance by voluntary agreement between husband and wife, were in their consequences destructive to the indissoluble nature and the sanctity of the marriage contract; and

[1] Macq. Hus. & Wife, 324 *et seq.* See also Jacob *n.* to 2 Roper Hus. & Wife, 277; Peachey Mar. Settl. 647.

he considered the question to be the gravest and most momentous to the public interest that could fall under discussion in a court of justice.[1] And Chancellor Kent sums up his authorities, which show that a private separation is an illegal contract, a renunciation of moral duties, in the emphatic words: "Nothing can be clearer or more sound than this conjugal doctrine."[2]

But in England final and complete dissolution of marriage is attainable only by act of Parliament. And this method of procedure was found so difficult, expensive, and uncertain, that parties who could not live peaceably together were led to consider some lesser means of mitigating their misfortune. To be sure the ecclesiastical courts awarded sentences of divorce *a mensa et thoro;* but these merely discharged the parties from the duty of cohabitation, permitting them to come together afterwards if they should so choose; and therefore, as a writer observes, these sentences "did not often, it must be owned, repay the pains bestowed in obtaining them."[3] The policy of the ecclesiastical courts in this respect seems however to have turned husband and wife to their own devices for effecting the same result, with less delay and annoyance, and in order to adjust more completely those property arrangements which never could be forgotten in their misery. Deeds of settlement, trusts, and the intervention of the equity courts, readily furnished a plan of operations; and the ubiquitous conveyancer appeared once more upon the stage to open the way, through subtle refinements, to freedom for discontented couples, and emolument for himself.

After a prolonged struggle, and in spite of public policy, it is therefore fully established at length, as a doctrine of equity, that deeds of separation may and must, if properly framed, be

[1] St. John *v.* St. John, 11 Ves. 530. See Mortimer *v.* Mortimer, 2 Hag. Consist. Rep. 318; Legard *v.* Johnson, 3 Ves. 352; Mercein *v.* The People, 25 Wend. 77.

[2] 2 Kent Com. 177 *n.*, where other cases are cited.

[3] Macq. Hus. & Wife, 326. See Hope *v.* Hope, 3 Jur. N. S. 456; S. C. 26 L. J. Eq. 425; Peachey Mar. Settl. 620; H. *v.* W., 3 Kay & Johns. 386, 387.

carried into execution by the courts.[1] They may be enforced in the common-law courts indirectly through the medium of covenants which are entered into between the husband and trustees, and in equity specific performance will be decreed where the stipulations are not contrary to law nor in contravention of public policy.[2] An agreement between husband and wife to live apart is still void as against public policy; but the husband's covenant with a third party is valid and binding, although it originates in this unauthorized state of separation and relates directly to it.[3]

It may seem strange that such an auxiliary agreement should be enforced, while the principal agreement is held contrary to the spirit and policy of the law. Lord Eldon, who strongly opposed the whole doctrine on principle, said that if the question were *res integra*, untouched by *dictum* or decision, he would not have permitted such a covenant to be the foundation of a suit in equity.[4] Sir William Grant appears to have been the first to call attention to the inconsistency of the courts in this respect; and his remark has come down through the later judges.[5] Lord Rosslyn, however, hit upon the explanation that an agreement for a separate provision between the husband and wife alone is void, merely from the general incapacity of the wife to contract:[6] an explanation which, we submit, is quite unsatisfactory.[7] The true reason for the anomalous distinction appears to be simply this: that contracts for separation are in general void as against public policy, but that the courts saw fit to let in exceptions so far as to enforce the covenants.[7]

[1] Wilson *v.* Wilson, 1 Ho. Lords Cas. 538; Peachey Mar. Settl. 620 and cases cited; Macq. Hus. & Wife, 329; Wilson *v.* Wilson, 5 Ho. Lords Cas. 59.

[2] Vansittart *v.* Vansittart, 2 De Gex & Jones, 249.

[3] Worrall *v.* Jacob, 3 Mer. 255; Peachey Mar. Settl. 621; Sanders *v.* Rodney, 16 Beav. 211; Warrender *v.* Warrender, 2 Cl. & Fin. 488.

[4] Westmeath *v.* Westmeath, Jac. 126; 2 Kent Com. 176.

[5] See Jones *v.* Waite, 5 Bing. 361; Frampton *v.* Frampton, 4 Beav. 293.

[6] Legard *v.* Johnson, 3 Ves. Jr. 352. See 2 Bright Hus. & Wife, 306, *n.* by Jacob.

[7] See Peachey Mar. Settl. closing chapter, for the details of the English doctrine.

Deeds of separation were never very common in the United States.[1] And there are at least three very good reasons why they should be less encouraged than in England. The first is that our legislation strongly favors the separate control of married women as to their own acquisitions, without the intervention of trustees and formal deeds of settlement, thus dispensing with the necessity of intricate property arrangements. The second is that equity, ecclesiastical, and common-law functions are usually blended in the same courts of final appeal, so that any State is at liberty to adopt the precedents of the ecclesiastical rather than the modern equity tribunals of England for its guidance; while an American court, on the other hand, cannot admit clearly the right of parties to declare terms of private separation, without bringing confusion and uncertainty upon its own divorce and matrimonial jurisdiction. The third is that sentences of divorce are procured in most American States with great ease, moderate expense, and little publicity. There are, however, individual American cases where separation deeds have been recognized so far as to permit parties to perform such marital duties as were incumbent upon them, notwithstanding separation.[2] The New England States do not in general seem to have sanctioned them at all.[3] And a recent North Carolina case distinctly maintains what ought to and may yet become the American doctrine: that separation deeds are void as against law and public policy.[4]

[1] 1 Bish. Mar. & Div. § 639 *et seq.;* Read *v.* Beazley, 1 Blackf. 97; Bettle *v.* Wilson, 1 Ohio, 257; Goodrich *v.* Bryant, 4 Sneed, 325; McCubbin *v.* Patterson, 16 Md. 179; Beach *v.* Beach, 2 Hill, 260.

[2] See 1 Bish. Mar. & Div. 4th ed. §§ 630–655 and cases cited. Our limits forbid an extended discussion of this subject. The English Ecclesiastical Courts steadily refused to recognize separate deeds. 1 Bish. ib. § 634.

[3] See Albee *v.* Wyman, 10 Gray, 222.

[4] Collins *v.* Collins, 1 Phill. N. C. Eq. 153. Under the new Divorce Acts, 20 & 21 Vict. ch. 85; 21 & 22 Vict. ch. 108, extending the facilities of legal separation, there may be a change effected in the English rule. That the public sentiment of England differs widely from that of America is evinced by the comments of a recent text-writer, who, after admitting that under the new statutes "*a more effectual separation can be obtained than under a simple deed or agreement to live apart,*"

As to the right of the wife, when abandoned by her husband, to earn, contract, sue, and be sued, to much the same effect as a *feme sole*, while such abandonment lasts: the current of American authority, legislative and judicial alike, decidedly favors so just a doctrine.[1] And in England recent statutes secure to a married woman privileges to a similar extent under like circumstances.[2]

A few words may be added on the topic of divorce. Divorce laws have constantly given rise to most interesting and earnest discussions; and men differ very widely in their conclusions, while all admit the subject to be of the most vital importance to the peace of families and the welfare of nations. Some favor a rigid divorce system as most conducive to moral health; others urge a lax system on the same grounds. On two points only do English and American jurists seem to agree: first, that the government has the right to dissolve a marriage during the lifetime of both parties, provided the reasons are weighty; second, that, unless those reasons are weighty, husband and wife should be divorced only by the hand of death.

The ancient nations, all recognizing the necessity of some divorce legislation, differed in their methods of treatment. Among the Greeks, despite their intellectual refinement, the

coolly proceeds to state that deeds of separation may yet be preferred, since they are available for purposes which do not justify a legal grant of separation, and that "even in those instances in which the court affords relief, many, if not most, persons *will prefer quietly arranging their differences by deed*, to painful discussions in a public court of justice." Peachey Mar. Settl. 647, 648.

1 See Shaw C. J. in Abbott *v.* Bayley, 6 Pick. 89; Benadum *v.* Pratt, 1 Ohio St. 403; Spier's Appeal, 2 Casey, 233; Mead *v.* Hughes, 15 Ala. 141; Rhea *v.* Rhenner, 1 Pet. 105; Moore *v.* Stevenson, 27 Conn. 14; Smith *v.* Silence, 4 Iowa, 321; Love *v.* Moynehan, 16 Ill. 277; Wilson *v.* Brown, 2 Beasl. 277. And see the numerous statutes in almost every State in the Union, enlarging the rights of married women in such cases. A careful examination of these and of the cases cited by Mr. Bishop, leads the writer to views entirely different from all those expressed by him. 1 Bish. Mar. & Div. 4th ed. § 610, *et seq.*

2 See Stat. 20 & 21 Vict. ch. 85; Midland R. R. Co. *v.* Pye, 10 C. B. N. S. 179. Chancery has long moulded its proceedings to secure a like privilege. See *In re* Lancaster, 23 E. L. & Eq. 127; Johnson *v.* Kirkwood, 4 Dru. & War. 379. See Wahl *v.* Braun, 38 E. L. & Eq. 300; Macq. Hus. & Wife, 99, 107, 108.

marriage institution was degraded, even in the palmiest days of Athens. The husband could send away his wife and the wife could leave her husband. The procedure in such cases was quite simple, being apparently nothing more than a formal notice filed with the judicial magistrate, unless the parties were disposed to contend; in which case they went to trial. If they agreed to be divorced, that would be enough; hence, the law was in their own hands; and, if divorced, they might marry again at pleasure.[1] In Rome, more of the moral and religious element prevailed; and so strict was the divorce law in the early days, that no divorce is supposed to have occurred for more than five hundred years from the foundation of the city: a tradition which those who pretend to fix the year of such foundation have not found difficulty in believing. The first recorded instance is, however, that of Spurius Canilius Ruga, B. C. 231; and even this was a case of barrenness, which hence fell possibly under the modern head of void and voidable marriages.[2] But Rome was built on family discipline, rather than domestic love; and the stately and somewhat severe Roman matron disappeared entirely in the later dissolute and corrupt years of the Roman republic.[3]

The ideal of marriage among the Hebrews was high: that husband and wife should cleave together and be one flesh; nevertheless, the usage of this nation, founded upon the Mosaic

[1] See p. 31 of Woolsey's Treatise on Divorce and Divorce Legislation: a little work recently published, which exhibits much careful research and scholarship, and which clearly presents the recent legislation of England and America affecting this subject. Any work from the President of Yale College is entitled to the respect of American lawyers, though not, in the strict sense, a legal text-book.

[2] See 1 Bish. Mar. & Div. 4th ed. § 23; Woolsey Div. 41.

[3] Horace divined the true cause of Rome's decay, when he wrote, —

"Fecunda culpæ secula nuptias
Primum inquinavere et genus et domos.
Hoc fonte derivata clades
In patriam populumque fluxit." — Carm. Lib. iii. 6.

See Woolsey Div. 44 *et seq.*, where some of the historical instances are cited.

code, permitted the husband, as it seems, to dismiss his wife at pleasure.[1]

It was this latter custom which called forth the merited rebuke of Christ, and occasioned him more than once to suggest a higher standard of marital indissolubility. These suggestions many have construed into an absolute prohibition of divorce except for the cause of adultery. Without accepting this construction of Scripture as the true one, or admitting all of the forced conclusions of commentators, which, whether correct or incorrect, must ever remain a matter for unsettled controversy,[2] we may clearly trace in the New Testament writings an intent to bring into prominence the moral obligations of the marriage state, to discountenance lax and immoral unions, and to warn the legislator that those whom God hath joined man may not with impunity put asunder.

The influence of Christianity has been felt in modern Europe; spreading to England, whence, too, it was brought to the wilds of America; the Christian rule ever shaping the policy of government. But the rule received different methods of interpretation.[3] The Church of Rome treats marriage as a sacrament, and indissoluble without a special dispensation,

[1] Deut. xxiv.; 1 Bish. Mar. & Div. 4th ed. § 25; Woolsey Div. 24.

[2] For the discussion of this question the reader is referred to Woolsey Div. 51 *et seq.* and authorities in 1 Bish. Mar. & Div. 4th ed. § 25 *n.*, where it will be perceived that writers on these New Testament texts are diametrically opposed to one another. The passages important to the issue are Matt. v. 31, 32; xix. 3–9; Mark x. 2–12; Luke xvi. 18. The writer merely reminds the strict constructionists of that well-known instance, where Christ refused to cast a stone at the adulterous woman, and bade her go and sin no more, as evincing that the great Christian Teacher had no design of ingrafting his code of morals, as a mere amendment, upon the Mosaic divorce law; which, as we understand it, would then have signified that a husband might "put away" his wife for adultery and have her stoned to death; that the wife could get no divorce at all; and that government was not concerned in the matter. Even Dr. Woolsey seems compelled to admit that St. Paul sanctioned divorce for desertion. See his comments (p. 70 *et seq.*) upon 1 Cor. vii. 15. See also 1 Bish. Mar. & Div. § 26, *n.* While it may well be doubted whether the New Testament prescribes an inflexible code to bind all legislators, it is clear that all approach to "free marriage" is therein discountenanced.

[3] 1 Bish. Mar. & Div. § 25; Woolsey Div. 87 *et seq.*

even for adultery. Protestants are divided, all regarding adultery as a sufficient cause of divorce, many considering desertion equally so, others cruelty; while a strong current of authority in this country tends to multiply the legal occasion for divorce even to such pretexts as incompatibility of temper.[1] So loose, indeed, and so confusing, is our local marriage and divorce legislation becoming, that it might be well to ask whether the cause of morality would not be promoted, if, by constitutional amendment, the whole subject were placed in the control of the national government; so that, at least, one uniform system could be applied, and the experiments of well-meaning reformers be subjected to an unerring and crucial test.

The leading ground of divorce is adultery; but besides this, desertion, cruelty, and kindred offences are frequently recognized as sufficient; and these kindred offences are greatly extended by statute in many of the United States. Divorce may be granted from bed and board, or from the bonds of matrimony; the former, which is a sort of judicial separation, being applied to the less heinous offences; while the latter, which alone is complete, is the remedy for the greater offences; or, according to the English policy, for adultery only. The one is partial divorce; the other final and full divorce.[2]

The principle of enforcing the specific performance of marriage vows, though perhaps theoretically commendable, proved in practice utterly futile; as was seen in the remedy for restitution of conjugal rights, which fell into disrepute and is now disused.[3] But some check being proper upon decrees so momentous as those of divorce, we find in the English system the principle of decrees *nisi*, which give delay for remedying error or affording to the parties a final opportunity for reconciliation. Decrees of divorce from bed and

[1] Conn. Laws, 1849; Woolsey Div. 205.
[2] See 1 Bish. Mar. & Div. 4th ed. § 38.
[3] See 1 Bish. Mar. & Div. 4th ed. § 31.

board subserve in the policy of some States a like wise purpose; otherwise, they are of very doubtful expediency, and apparently originated in the compromise of canonists between human necessities and scriptural misinterpretation.[1]

The effect of divorce from bonds of matrimony upon the property rights of married parties is substantially that of death, or rather annihilation. This is a topic upon which the common law, from the infrequency of divorce, furnishes no light, except by analogies. The settled usage of Parliament has been to introduce property clauses to such effect into the sentence of dissolution regulating the rights and liabilities of the respective parties.[2] Even in these cases the rights of divorced parties as to tenancy by the curtesy, chattels real, and rents of the wife's lands are still unsettled; and in general, as English writers observe, the consequence by act of Parliament "does not very clearly appear."[3]

But under the new English divorce act,[4] it is held in a very recent case that where the wife at the date of the decree of divorce *a vinculo* was entitled to a reversionary interest in a sum of stock which was not settled before her marriage and had been the subject of a postnuptial settlement; and after the decree the fund fell into possession; her divorced husband had no right to claim it. Says Vice-Chancellor Wood: "Here the contract has been determined by a mode unknown to the old law, namely, by a decree of dissolution; and as the

[1] See 1 Bish. Mar. & Div. 4th ed. § 29; 2 ib. §§ 754–764. As to the specific causes of divorce and procedure, see 1 Bish. Mar. & Div. 4th ed. § 703 *et seq.*; 1 Fraser Dom. Rel. 656; 2 Kent Com. 10 And see Woolsey Div. The leading causes of divorce as defined by statute, next to adultery, are desertion and cruelty; and the minor causes such as lengthened imprisonment, habits of intoxication, and neglect to support, generally involve these same elements.

[2] Macq. Hus. & Wife, 210, 214.

[3] 2 Bright Hus. & Wife, 366.

[4] Stats. 20 & 21 Vict. ch. 85; 21 & 22 Vict. ch. 108; 23 & 24 Vict. ch. 144. These important acts, which create a new court for divorce and matrimonial causes, in taking jurisdiction from the ecclesiastical courts, and extending legal facilities for divorce, date a new era in English jurisprudence. The first took effect in 1858.

husband was unable during the existence of the contract to reduce this chattel into possession, I must hold that the property remained the property of the wife."[1] The English doctrine as thus indicated is that the same consequences as to property must follow the decree of dissolution by the divorce court as if the marriage contract had been annihilated and the marriage tie severed on that date.

In this country, the effect of divorce *a vinculo* is frequently regulated by statute. And in general all transfers of property actually executed before divorce, whether in law or in fact, remain unaffected by the decree. For instance, personal *choses* of the wife already reduced to possession by the husband, remain his.[2] But as to rights dependent on marriage and not actually vested, divorce ends them. This applies to curtesy, dower, and the right to reduce *choses* into possession, and property rights under the statutes of distribution.[3] All this set forth in local codes, which frequently save certain rights — such as the wife's dower where divorce is occasioned by her husband's misconduct.

On the other hand, if the husband receives any property of the wife after divorce, she may recover it in a suit for money had and received.[4] How far on the divorce of the husband his assignee may claim against the wife does not clearly appear; but where the divorce is occasioned through his fault the wife's equitable provision, it seems, will be favorably regarded as against him.[5] Divorce takes away the husband's

[1] Wilkinson *v.* Gibson, Law Rep. 4 Eq. 162. And see Pratt *v.* Jenner, Law Rep. 1 Ch. 493.

[2] 2 Bish. Mar. & Div. 4th ed. § 705 *et seq.;* Lawson *v.* Shotwell, 27 Miss. 630.

[3] 2 Bish. ib.; Dobson *v.* Butler, 17 Mis. 87; 4 Kent Com. 53 *n.*, 54; Given *v.* Marr, 27 Maine, 212; Wheeler *v.* Hotchkiss, 10 Conn. 225; Rice *v.* Lumley, 10 Ohio St. 596. But see Wait *v.* Wait, 4 Comst. 95. See Ames *v.* Norman, 4 Sneed, 683.

[4] 2 Bish. ib. § 714; Legg *v.* Legg, 8 Mass. 99. See Kintzinger's Estate, 2 Ashm. 455.

[5] 2 Bish. ib. § 715, and conflicting cases compared; Woods *v.* Simmons, 20 Mis. 363; 2 Kent Com. 136 *et seq.; supra,* ch. 5.

right of administration, upon the estate of his divorced wife.[1] Such are some of the effects of divorce *a vinculo.*

Divorce from bed and board produces, however, no such definite results; the cardinal doctrine of such cases being that the marriage remains in full force, although the parties are allowed to live separate. Here we must consult the phraseology of local statutes with especial care, in order to determine the respective rights and duties of the parties. Thus the consequence of judicial separation under the present divorce acts of England, is to give to the wife, so long as separation lasts, all property of every description which she may acquire, or which may come to or devolve upon her, including estates in remainder or reversion; and such property may be disposed of by her in all respects as if she were a *feme sole;* and if she dies intestate it goes as if her husband had then been dead.[2]

In this country, independently of statutory aid, the property rights of the parties divorced from bed and board remain in general unchanged. For this divorce is only a legal separation, terminable at the will of the parties; the marriage continuing in regard to every thing not necessarily withdrawn from its operation by the divorce.[3] Thus, the husband still inherits from the wife and the wife from the husband; the one takes his curtesy, the other her dower; and even the right of reducing the wife's *choses in action* into possession still remains to the guilty husband.[4] But chancery, by virtue of its jurisdiction in awarding the wife her equity to a settlement, may, and

[1] 2 Bish. Mar. & Div. 4th ed. § 725; Altemus' Case, 1 Ashm. 49. See 2 Bish. ib. § 717; West Cambridge *v.* Lexington, 1 Pick. 506; Buffaloe *v.* Whitedeer, 3 Harr. Pa. 182; Babcock *v.* Smith, 22 Pick. 61; Blaker *v.* Cooper, 7 S. & R. 500; Miller *v.* Miller, 1 Sandf. Ch. 103, 2 Bish. ib. § 719; Clarke *v.* Lott, 11 Ill. 105. See ch. "Marriage Settlements," *supra.*

[2] Stats. 20 & 21 Vict. ch. 85, § 25; 21 & 22 Vict. ch. 108, § 8. See Romilly, M. R., *In re* Insole, Law Rep. 1 Eq. 470.

[3] Dean *v.* Richmond, 5 Pick. 461; 2 Bish. Mar. & Div. 4th ed. § 726 *et seq.*

[4] Clark *v.* Clark, 6 Watts & S. 85; Kriger *v.* Day, 2 Pick. 316; Smodt *v.* Lecatt, 1 Stew. 590; Ames *v.* Chew, 5 Met. 320.

doubtless will keep the property from his grasp, and do to both what justice demands.[1] The recent statutory changes affect this whole subject in most American States, either directly or by construction, so completely, that it is useless to follow this branch of our topic further.

The recent English statutes give the wife upon sentence of judicial separation the capacity to sue and be sued on somewhat the same footing as a *feme sole.* The rule in the United States is not uniform; but the tendency is clearly in the same direction.[2] On principle, the husband's right to administer on his wife's estate would seem not to be forfeited by his divorce from bed and board. Nor the wife's on the same principle. But it should be remembered that the wife's claim to administer, unlike the husband's, is never superior to that of the next of kin. So, too, in the case of both husband and wife, divorce from bed and board may be thought a good reason why the court should refuse to issue letters of administration to the guilty party, where others are interested in the estate, and the judge has discretion in the matter of appointment.[3]

[1] Holmes *v.* Holmes, 4 Barb. 295; *supra*, ch. 5.

[2] See 2 Bish. Mar. & Div. § 737, and cases cited; Lefevres *v.* Murdock, Wright, 205; Clark *v.* Clark, 6 Watts & S. 85.

[3] See 2 Bish. Mar. & Div. 4th ed. § 739; Clark *v.* Clark, 6 Watts & S. 85. The writer acknowledges his indebtedness to the justly valued treatise of Mr. Bishop. Yet he confesses his inability to follow those who argue that lax divorce laws will mend lax morals; not that either strict or lax divorce laws can fully subdue crime; but because history teaches that loose laws rather stimulate than check marital infidelity; while it is found otherwise with countries where stricter laws have prevailed. To say that crime causes the divorce, not divorce the crime, is illogical; the one acts upon the other. As one's familiarity with death tends to make him rather reckless than serious, ferocious than compassionate; and as contact with criminal courts inevitably corrupts the young; so the influence of divorces, when of common occurrence, is to deteriorate the national character. When parties united in such solemn responsibilities can coolly discuss and arrange the preliminaries of final dissolution, and haste to obtain judicial relief for the purpose of forming a new union, they are hardly fitted to discharge nature's highest obligations to one another; certainly they cannot do justice to their children nor to society. Thus may marriage lose half its significance by parting with all of its sanctity.

PART III.

PARENT AND CHILD.

CHAPTER I.

OF LEGITIMATE CHILDREN IN GENERAL.

The second of the domestic relations is that of parent and child; a relation which results from marriage, and is, as Blackstone terms it, the most universal relation in nature.[1] Both natural and politic law, morality and the precepts of revealed religion alike, demand the preservation of this relation in its full strength and purity. In the first period of their existence, children are a common object of affection to the parents, and draw closer the ties of their mutual affection; then comes the education of the child, in which the parents have a common care, which further identifies their sympathies and objects; the brothers and sisters of the child, when they come, bring with them new bonds of affection, new sympathies, new common objects; and the habits of a family take the place of the wishes of an individual. Thus do children give rise to affections which still further tend to bind together the community by links of iron.[2]

Children are divided into two classes, legitimate and illegitimate. The law prescribes different rights and duties for these classes.[3] It becomes proper, then, to consider them in order. First, then, as to legitimate children, to which alone the

[1] 1 Bl. Com. 447.
[2] 1 Whewell Elements of Morality, 100; 2 Kent Com. 189.
[3] 1 Bl. Com. 447.

relation of parent and child in strictness applies; this will occupy several chapters.

A legitimate child is one who is born in lawful wedlock or is properly brought within the influence of a valid marriage by reason of the time of birth. Legitimacy, as the word imports, will require that the child be born in a manner approved of by the law. If he is begotten during marriage and born afterwards, it is enough.[1]

The maxim of the civil law is *Pater est quem nuptiæ demonstrant;* a rule frequently cited with approval by common-law authorities, though, as we shall soon see, differently applied in some respects.[2] A distinguished Scotch jurist pronounces this "a plain and sensible maxim, which is the corner-stone, the very foundation, on which rests the whole fabric of human society."[3] Boullenois, a civil-law writer, likewise commends it as "a maxim recognized by all nations, which is the peace and tranquillity of States and families."[4] This maxim implies that it is always sufficient for a child to show that he is born during the marriage. The law draws from this circumstance the necessary presumption that he is legitimate.

Strong, however, as this presumption may be, it is not conclusive at law. For there may be other circumstances: such as long-continued separation of the parents; the impotence of the father; also, if the offspring be posthumous, the length of period which has elapsed since his death. Such circumstances would render it physically and morally impossible that the child was born and begotten in lawful wedlock. The civil law, therefore, admitted four exceptions to the general maxim: first, the absolute and permanent impotence of the husband; second, his accidental impotence or bodily disability; third, his absence

[1] 1 Bl. Com. 447; Fraser Parent & Child, 1; 1 Burge Col. & For. Laws, 59.

[2] 1 Bl. Com. ib; Stair III. 3, 42; 2 Kent Com. 212 *n.*; Fraser Parent & Child, 1, 2, and authorities cited; 1 Burge Col. & For. Laws, 59.

[3] Ld. Pres. Blair in Routledge *v.* Carruthers, 19 May, 1812, cited by Fraser, *supra.*

[4] Boullenois Traité des Statuts, tome 1, p. 62, also cited by Fraser, *supra.*

from his wife during that period of time in which, to have been the father of the child, he must have had sexual intercourse with her; fourth, the intervention of sickness, *vel alia causa.*[1] These concluding words admit the classification to be imperfect. The common-law rule, which subsisted from the time of the Year Books down to the early part of the last century, declared the issue of every married woman to be legitimate, except in the two special cases of the impotency of the husband and his absence from the realm.[2] But in *Pendrell* v. *Pendrell* the absurd doctrine of making legitimacy rest conclusively upon the fact of the husband being *infra quatuor maria*, was exploded.[3] Some Scotch jurists resolve the grounds upon which the presumption of legitimacy may be overthrown, into two: first, that the husband could not have had sexual intercourse with his wife by reason of his impotency; and second, that, having the power, he had in fact no sexual intercourse with her at the time of the conception.[4] This seems to mean, first, that the husband physically could not; second, that he actually did not; but does not the second exception swallow the first?

Perhaps the safer course is to abandon all attempts to classify; and to hold, with Chancellor Kent, that the question of the legitimacy or illegitimacy of the child of a married woman is one of fact, resting on decided proof as to the non-access of the husband, and that these facts must generally be left to a jury for determination.[5]

From the peculiarities attending the case of access or non-access, legitimacy or illegitimacy, great indulgence is to be shown by the courts. Said Lord Erskine: "The law of England has been more scrupulous upon the subject of legitimacy than any other; to the extent even of disturbing the rules of

[1] Dig. lib. 1, tit. 6, l. 6; 1 Burge Col. & For. Laws, 60.

[2] 2 Kent Com. 210; Co. Litt. 244 *a*; 1 Roll. Abr. 358.

[3] Str. Rep. 925; 2 Kent Com. 211, and cases cited; Shelley *v.* ——, (1806); 13 Ves. 56.

[4] Fraser Parent & Child, 4.

[5] 2 Kent Com. 211; 3 P. Wms. 275, 276; Harg. *n.* 193 to Co. Litt. lib. 2; Rex *v.* Luffe, 8 East, 193.

reason."[1] Still later was it asserted in English chancery that the ancient policy of the law remained unaltered; and that a child born of a married woman is to be presumed to be the child of the husband, unless there is evidence, beyond all doubt, that the husband could not be the father.[2] And it is at this day admitted that the presumption thus established by law is not to be rebutted by circumstances which only create doubt and suspicion; but the evidence against it ought to be strong, distinct, satisfactory, and conclusive.[3]

So far, indeed, is legitimacy favored at law, that neither husband nor wife can be a witness to prove access or non-access. This is clearly established in England;[4] and it is understood to be the law likewise in this country, though the decided cases seem to turn upon the admissibility of the wife's testimony.[5] Such evidence is treated as *contra bonos mores*. Yet the wife is an admissible witness to prove her own adultery, and in questions of pedigree; and husband and wife may prove facts, such as marriage and date of the child's birth; these may be conclusive as to illegitimacy.[6] Much testimony, extremely delicate, is also taken in divorce proceedings. When, therefore, the courts shut their eyes so tightly against such proof of access or non-access, perhaps it is not because they are shocked, but lest they should see illegitimacy established.

To carry this presumption of legitimacy so far as to disturb the rules of reason is unjust; for no man should be saddled with the obligations of children which clearly do not belong to him. And the rule of evidence in the English courts has been

1 Shelley *v.* ——, 13 Ves. 56.

2 Head *v.* Head, 1 Sim. & Stu. 150, (1823); Banbury Peerage Case, ib. 153; Pendrell *v.* Pendrell, 2 Str. 925.

3 Hargrave *v.* Hargrave, 9 Beav. 552; Archley *v.* Sprigg, 33 L. J. Ch. 345; Plowes *v.* Bossey, 8 Jur. (N. S.) 352, 10 W. R. 332.

4 Rex *v.* Inhabitants of Sourton, 5 Ad. & El. 188; Patchett *v.* Holgate, 3 E. L. & Eq. 100, 15 Jur. 308.

5 2 Stark. Evid. 404; 1 Greenl. Evid. § 344; Phillips *v.* Allen, 2 Allen, 453; People *v.* Overseers, &c., 15 Barb. 286; Parker *v.* Way, 15 N. H. 45; Dennison *v.* Page, 29 Penn. St. 420.

6 See 1 Greenl. Evid. § 343, 344; Canjolle *v.* Ferrié, 23 N. Y. 90.

severely and justly criticised, not without some good results.[1] The decision of the House of Lords, in the celebrated Banbury Peerage case, proceeded upon the reasonable assumption that moral as well as physical impossibilities may affect the rule of legitimacy. Here husband and wife occupied the same house at the very time the child must have been begotten, and no case of impotency was made out, and yet that child was held not to be the child of the husband; for the testimony as to a moral impossibility was sufficiently strong notwithstanding.[2] This case was confirmed by another, where husband and wife had voluntarily separated, but the husband resided at a distance of only fifteen miles, and sometimes visited his wife; and the wife was delivered of a child, which was pronounced a bastard, from evidence of the conduct of the wife and her paramour. Here it was said, "The case, therefore, comes back to the question of fact." [3] Impotency of the husband, and his absence from the realm, suggest then but two classes of cases, and those not the only ones, where children may now be pronounced bastards. "I apprehend," said Lord Langdale, "that evidence of every kind, direct or presumptive, may be adduced, for the purpose of showing the absence of sexual intercourse which, in cases where there has been some society, intercourse, or access, has been called non-generating access. We have, therefore, to attend to the conduct and the feelings, as evidenced by the conduct of the parties towards each other and the offspring, and even to the declarations accompanying acts, which are properly evidence. Such circumstances are of no avail against proper evidence of generating access; but they may have weight, when the effect of that evidence is doubtful. If the weight is not such as to convince the minds of those who

[1] 2 Kent Com. 211 *n.*; Fraser Parent & Child, 7.

[2] 1 Sim. & Stu. 153. See Nicolas on Adulterine Bastardy, 181, a volume written to show that this case overturns the old law of England.

[3] Morris *v.* Davies, 5 Cl. & Fin. 463. And see Barony of Saye & Sele, 1 Cl. & Fin. (N. S.) 507; Sibbett *v.* Ainsley, 3 L. T. (N. S.) 583 Q. B.; Fraser Parent & Child, 8; King *v.* Luffe, 8 East, 193.

have to determine the matter, the effect may only tend to shake, without removing, the presumption of legitimacy, which in such a case must prevail." [1]

In this country, cases have not unfrequently arisen which involve the legitimacy of offspring; and the more reasonable doctrine favors legitimacy to about the same extent as the later English decisions.[2] The presumption of legitimacy is strongly carried, as the cases below cited indicate.[3]

In respect of the legitimation of offspring by the subsequent marriage of their parents, the civil and common law systems widely differ. By the civil and canon laws, two persons who had a child as the fruit of their illicit intercourse, might afterwards marry, and thus place their child to all intents and purposes on the same footing as their subsequent offspring, born in lawful wedlock.[4] But the common law, though not so strict as to require that the child should be begotten of the marriage, rendered it indispensable that the birth should be after the ceremony.[5] Let us notice this point of difference at some length.

It appears that the law of legitimation *per subsequens matrimonium* is of Roman origin; introduced and promulgated by the first Christian Emperor, Constantine, as history alleges, at the instigation of the clergy. This was an innovation upon the earlier Roman system; and the object of its introduction was to put down that matrimonial concubinage which had become so universal in the empire.[6] Justinian afterwards made this law perpetual.[7] Its first appearance in the canon law is found in two re-

[1] Hargrave *v.* Hargrave, 9 Beav. 552.

[2] Patterson *v.* Gaines, 6 How. (U. S.) 582; 2 Kent Com. 211 and cases cited; Hemmenway *v.* Towner, 1 Allen, 209; Van Aernam *v.* Van Aernam, 1 Barb. Ch. 375; Wright *v.* Hicks, 15 Geo. 160.

[3] See Van Aernam *v.* Van Aernam, 1 Barb. Ch. 375. And see Kleinert *v.* Ehlers, 38 Penn. St. 439; Phillips *v.* Allen, 2 Allen, 453; Hemmenway *v.* Towner, 1 Allen, 209. See State *v.* Herman, 13 Ire. 502; Tate *v.* Pene, 19 Martin, 548; Cannon *v.* Cannon, 7 Humph. 410.

[4] 2 Kent Com. 208; 1 Burge Col & For. Laws, 92.

[5] 1 Bl. Com. 454.

[6] "Licita consuetudo semimatrimonium," Cod. lib. 6, tit. 57.

[7] Taylor's Civil Law, 272; Fraser Parent & Child, 32; 1 Burge Col. & For. Laws, 92, 93.

scripts of Pope Alexander III., preserved in the Decretals of Gregory, and issued in 1180 and 1172.[1] These extended the benefits of the marriage to the offspring of carnal love, and not merely to the issue of systematic concubinage. This law of legitimation was introduced into Scotland within the range of authentic history.[2] It is also admitted, with different modifications, into the codes of France, Spain, Germany, and most other countries in Europe.[3]

The principle to which the law of legitimation *per subsequens matrimonium* is to be referred, has been a subject of controversy. The canonists based the law not on general views of expediency and justice, but upon a fiction which they adopted in order to reconcile the new law with established rules; for, assuming that, as a general rule, children are not legitimate unless born in lawful wedlock, they declared that *fictione juris* the parents were married when the child was born. Such reasoning, by no means uncommon in days when the wise saw more clearly what was right, than why it was so, has not stood the test of modern logic; and the Scotch courts have placed the rule once more where its imperial founders left it; namely, on the ground of general policy and justice. "Legitimation is thought to be recommended by these considerations of equity and justice, that it tends to encourage what is at first irregular and injurious to society, into the honorable relation of lawful matrimony; and that it prevents those unseemly disorders in families which are produced where the elder born children of the same parents are left under the stain of bastardy, and the younger enjoy the status of legitimacy." [4]

This doctrine of the civil law has found great favor in the United States. It has prevailed for many years in the States

[1] Decr. IV. 17, 1; IV. 17, 6, cited in Fraser Parent & Child, 33. "Tanta est enim vis sacramenti (matrimonii) ut qui antea sunt geniti post contractum matrimonium habeantur legitimi."

[2] Fraser Parent & Child, 32, 33.

[3] 1 Burge. Col. & For. Laws, 101.

[4] Fraser Parent & Child, 35; Munro *v.* Munro, 1 Rob. H. L. Scotch App. 492.

of Vermont, Maryland, Virginia, Georgia, Alabama, Mississippi, Louisiana, Kentucky, Missouri, Indiana, and Ohio.[1] So in Massachusetts, bastards are to be considered legitimate after the intermarriage of their parents and recognition by the father.[2] And similar statutes are to be found in Maine, Pennsylvania, Vermont, Indiana, and elsewhere.[3]

On the other hand, the English law has very strongly opposed the whole doctrine of legitimation *per subsequens matrimonium.* Even so far back as the reign of Henry III., is found a memorable instance where the peers refused to change the law in this respect, when urged to do so by the English bishops ; declaring with one voice, *quod nolunt leges Angliæ mutare, quæ huc usque usitatæ sunt et approbatæ.*[4] Jealousy of canonical influence may partially account for this conduct, if not prejudice against the civil law generally. Certain it is that most English jurists have ever since stubbornly maintained the superiority of their own maxims, which place the immutability of the marriage relation above all the tender promptings of humanity towards innocent sufferers. Even Blackstone vigorously assails the civil-law doctrine, urging against it several rather artificial objections, in the apparent belief, that legal consistency is better than natural justice.[5] But on the other hand, Selden mentions that the children of John of Gaunt, Duke of Lancaster, were legitimated by an act of Parliament, in the reign of Richard II., founded on some obscure common-law custom.[6]

Upon such principles it has been decided by the House of Lords, that where a marriage is in its inception unlawful, being

[1] Griffith's Law Reg. *passim;* 1 Burge Col. & For. Laws, 101.

[2] Mass. Gen. Sts. 1860, ch. 91.

[3] Maine Laws, 1852, ch. 266 ; Penn. Laws, 1857, May 14 ; Vermont R. S. 1863, ch. 56 ; Ind. R. S. 1862, ch. 46. And see Graham *v.* Bennet, 2 Cal. 503 ; Starr *v.* Peck, 1 Hill (N. Y.), 270 ; Sleigh *v.* Strider, 5 Call. 439.

[4] Stat. of Merton, 20 Henry 3, ch. 9 ; 2 Kent Com. 209 ; 1 Bl. Com. 456.

[5] 1 Bl. Com. 454, 455.

[6] Selden on Fleta, ch. 9, § 2. And see Barrington p. 38 ; 2 Kent Com. 209.

at a time when the woman's first husband must have been alive, children born even after the time when it was presumed that the first husband had died, must be pronounced illegitimate; the mere continuance of the cohabitation after that event being insufficient without celebration to change the character of the connection.[1] Nor will an absolute presumption of law be raised as to the continuance of life to support such legitimacy; for in every instance the circumstances of the case must be considered.[2] And so strict is the rule that where a person, born a bastard, becomes, by the subsequent marriage of his parents, legitimate according to the laws of the country in which he was born, he is still a bastard, so far as regards the inheritance of lands in England.[3]

As to the status of children born after divorce, partial or complete, little can be stated from the books; for such divorces hardly existed at the common law.[4] They are probably illegitimate *prima facie*, if born within an unreasonable time after separation.[5]

The issue of marriages rendered null and void are on general principles necessarily illegitimate. Opposed to this is the civil-law doctrine of putative marriages, first introduced into the canon law by Pope Innocent III.; which upholds the legitimacy of the children in cases where the parties, or either of them, *bona fide* believing that they could marry, had entered into the contract, while there was an unknown impediment existing.[6] This subject is regulated by statute to a great extent in this country, and here again our system conforms to the civil rather than the common law.[7]

[1] Lapsley *v.* Grierson, (1848), 1 Cl. & Fin. (N. S.) 498; Cunningham *v.* Cunningham, 2 Dow, 482.

[2] Lapsley *v.* Grierson, ib. explaining Rex *v.* Twyning, 2 B. & A. 386.

[3] Doe d. Birtwhistle *v.* Vardill, 6 Bing. (N. C.) 385; 7 Cl. & Fin. 895. And see Husband & Wife, ch. 1, *supra*, p. 49.

[4] See Husband & Wife, *supra*, ch. 17; 2 Bish. Mar. & Div. 4th ed. § 559; Montgomery *v.* Montgomery, 3 Barb. Ch. 132.

[5] St George *v.* St. Margaret, 1 Salk, 123; 2 Bish. Mar. & Div. ib. § 740.

[6] Fraser Parent & Child, 22 *et seq.*; 1 Burge Col. & For. Laws, 96.

[7] See Husband & Wife, ch. 1, *supra*, p. 25. And see Graham *v.* Bennett, 2 Cal.

Legitimation by rescript of the Emperor appears in the Institutes of Justinian.[1] Still later did the Pope assume the power to grant the status of legitimacy; and in many of the canonical dispensations occur clauses of this sort.[2] The effect of these "high-sounding clauses" is now of little consequence.[3] The English Parliament, by virtue of its transcendent power, may render a bastard legitimate and capable of inheriting.[4] This same power has been claimed for the legislatures of the United States.[5] And except so far as legislative acts may come under constitutional restraints, against impairing the obligation of contracts, there seems no reason why they should not be uniformly upheld.

The domicile of a child's origin is to be determined by the domicile of his parents; or to speak more strictly, of his father. We speak at this time only of legitimate children. The domicile of origin remains until another is lawfully acquired. And since minors are not *sui juris* they may not change their domicile during their minority; hence they retain the domicile of their parents; if the parents change their domicile, that of the infant children follows it; and if the father dies, his last domicile is that of the infant children.[6] The surviving mother may change the domicile of her minor children, provided she do so without fraudulent views to the succession of their estate; though it would appear that she cannot change it after her re-marriage.[7]

503. Yet there is a case, that of Sir Ralph Sadlier, where Parliament gave relief. See Nicolas Adult. Bast. 61–63. Fraser Parent & Child, 24; Burnet's History, Book 1, ch. 19; Riddell Peer & Cons. Law, 421.

1 Nov. 74, ch. 1, 2; and 89, ch. 9.

2 See Fraser Parent & Child, 43.

3 Ib.

4 1 Bl. Com. 459. And see Stat. 6 Will. IV., ch. 22

5 Beall *v.* Beall, 8 Geo. 210; Vidal *v.* Commajere, 13 La. An. 516.

6 Story Confl. Laws, §§ 45, 46, and cases cited; 1 Burge Col. & For. Laws, 33; Abington *v.* North Bridgewater, 23 Pick. 170. But see Ishan *v.* Gibbons, 1 Bradf. Sur. 70; Somerville *v.* Somerville, 5 Ves. 750.

7 Potinger *v.* Wightman, 3 Merivale, 67; 1 Burge Col. & For. Laws, 39; Brown *v.* Lynch, 2 Bradf. Sur. 214; Carlisle *v.* Tuttle, 30 Ala. 613. And see Guardian & Ward, *infra*.

Some writers have said that when the laws of two countries are in conflict, the legitimacy or illegitimacy of children is to be determined by the domicile of origin.[1] Others again that it is dependent upon the *lex loci* of marriage.[2] Between these writers there is no real discrepancy; for in every such case two facts are involved, the one whether the marriage was in itself lawful, the other whether the child was legitimate by their marriage. Of the conflict of laws regarding marriage we have already spoken.[3] That involving the status of legitimacy is now under consideration.

A conflict manifestly arises between the laws of domicile of origin and subsequent marriage, and the laws of the actual domicile or situs of property, where those of the one country admit legitimation *per subsequens matrimonium*, and those of the other do not. As for instance, where children are born, and their parents afterwards intermarry in certain of the United States, or in Scotland, and then remove with their children to England; or where such children are deemed to have acquired property rights in the last-named country.

On this point there is much diversity of opinion. And the English courts have uniformly maintained their distinctive policy with considerable zeal in all doubtful cases. Thus particularly was this done in the case of *Birtwhistle* v. *Vardill*, where a child legitimate to all purposes in Scotland, was denied the full rights of a lawful child in England.[4] Yet the law of foreign countries as to legitimacy is so far respected in England that a person illegitimate by the law of his domicile of birth will be held illegitimate in England.[5]

[1] 1 Burge Col. & For. Laws. 111; Fraser Parent & Child, 45.

[2] Story Confl. Laws, § 105.

[3] See Husband & Wife, ch. 1, *supra*.

[4] 7 Cl. & Fin. 895, 4 Jur. 1076; ib. 5 B. & C. 438; Story Confl. Laws, § 93, *et seq.*, where the doctrine of Birtwhistle *v.* Vardill is strongly combated. See Boyes *v.* Bedale, 12 W. R. 232, before Wood V. C.; Story Confl. Laws, 6th ed. § 93, *w. n.* by Redfield. And see Goodman *v.* Goodman, 3 Gif. 643.

[5] Munro *v.* Saunders, 6 Bligh, 468; cases cited in Birtwhistle *v.* Vardill, 9 Bligh, 52.

The doctrine of general writers is, that the status of legitimacy or illegitimacy, or the capacity to become legitimate *per subsequens matrimonium*, is governed by the law of the domicile of the child's origin.[1] And, since the domicile of origin is that of the father, the great leading fact to be ascertained in such inquiries will be generally the domicile of the father.[2] A person born before wedlock, who, in the country of his birth is considered illegitimate, will not by a subsequent marriage of his parents in another country, by whose laws such a marriage would make him legitimate, cease to be illegitimate in the country of his birth.[3] On the other hand, without a subsequent marriage of his parents, lawful by the laws of the land where celebrated, it is clear that any child must remain illegitimate, whatever be the domicile of his origin.

By adoption a *quasi* parental relation was sometimes constituted at the civil law. Adoption is the taking or choosing of another's child as one's own.[4] The adoption of children is still regulated in Germany and France, but is not generally recognized in English or American law. But in Massachusetts it is recently provided that under a judicial decree, rendered upon due investigation, any person may adopt as his own the child of others ; and that the child so adopted shall be deemed, for the purposes of inheritance and all other legal consequences and incidents of the natural relation of parents and children, the child of the parents by adoption, the same as if he had been born to them in lawful wedlock.[5] In Louisiana, the laws once authorized adoption ; but this was changed by the code of 1808. Yet adoption by special act of the legislature is not unknown in that State.[6]

[1] 1 Burge Col. & For. Laws, 111.
[2] Fraser Parent & Child, 45.
[3] Story Confl. Laws, § 106.
[4] Inst. I. 11, 1. Burrill's Law Dict. "Adoption,"
[5] Mass. Gen. Sts. ch. 110.
[6] Vidal *v.* Commajere, 13 La. Ann. 516.

CHAPTER II.

THE DUTIES OF PARENTS.

THREE leading duties of parents, as to their legitimate children, are recognized at the common law: first, to protect; second, to educate; third, to maintain them. These duties are all enjoined by positive law; yet, the law of the natural affections is stronger in upholding such fundamental obligations of the parental state.[1]

First, as to protection: that cover or shield from evil and injury which is afforded by the parent. This duty the stronger owes to the weaker, and especially does the father owe it to his child, so long as the latter remains comparatively helpless. This obligation may be shifted in time, as age adds to the strength of the one, and the infirmities of the other.

It is to the credit of our civilization that the natural duty of protection is rather permitted than enjoined by any municipal laws; nature in this respect "working so strongly," to use the forcible words of Blackstone, "as to need rather a check than a spur."[2] The strongest illustration of protection at the common law which is furnished by this learned writer, — that of a father who revenged his son's injury by going near a mile and beating the offender to death with a cudgel, — though affording a questionable legal principle, as he puts it, at least shows what the verdicts of our juries are constantly confirming, that the sympathies of human tribunals are with him who defends his own offspring, even when his zeal outruns his discretion.[3]

[1] 1 Bl. Com. 447; 2 Kent Com. 189; Taylor's Civil Law, 383; Puff. b. 4, ch. 11, §§ 4, 5.

[2] 1 Bl. Com. 450.

[3] See 1 Hawk. P. C. 83, cited in 1 Bl. Com. 450; and *n.* by Coleridge, citing Fost. 294, and 2 Ld. Raym. 1498, in opposition to Blackstone's remark.

A parent may, by the common law of England, maintain and uphold his children in their lawsuits, without being guilty of the legal crime of maintaining quarrels.[1] He may also justify an assault and battery committed in defence of the persons of his children.[2] On the other hand, as we shall hereafter see, where he is cruel and devoid of natural affection, his children may be taken from his personal keeping. The doctrine of parental protection seems to have required little or no special judicial discussion in modern times.

The second duty of parents is that of education; a duty which Blackstone pronounces far the greatest of all these in importance.[3] This importance is enhanced by the consideration that the usefulness of each new member of the human family to society depends chiefly upon his character, as developed by the training he receives in early life. Not the increase of population, but the increase of a well-ordered, intelligent, and honorable population, is to determine the strength of a State; and, as a civil writer observes, the parent who suffers his child to grow up like a mere beast, to lead a life useless to others and shameful to himself, has conferred a very questionable benefit upon him by bringing him into the world.[4] Solon excused the children of Athens from maintaining their parents, if they had neglected to train them up in some art or profession.[5] So intimately is government concerned in the results of early training, that it interferes, and justly too, both to aid the parent in giving his children a good education, and in compelling that education, where the parent himself, and not the child, is delinquent in improving the opportunities offered.

Questions of parental education arise often in English law under the will of the father. It is laid down as the rule, that

[1] 2 Inst. 564. But a parent is not bound to employ counsel to defend the suits of his minor children. Hill *v.* Childress, 10 Yerg. 514.

[2] 1 Hawk. P. C. 131; 1 Bl. Com. 450.

[3] 1 Bl. Com. 450.

[4] Puff. Law of Nations, b. 6, ch. 2, § 12.

[5] Plutarch's Lives; 2 Kent Com. 195.

where one has left no direction in his will, as to the religion in which his children are to be educated, it will be presumed that his wishes were that they shall be educated in his own religion.[1] Further, the religious education of an infant of fifteen will not be changed unless he wishes it.[2] But no regard is paid to the wishes of a child ten years old.[3] The father is allowed to designate the plan of education, to be followed with respect to his children after his death. And while, as Lord Cottenham has observed, he has no power to prescribe a particular religion to his child, yet he has indirectly, the power of effecting his object by the choice of a guardian.[4]

The English courts of chancery have indeed exercised considerable jurisdiction over the education of minor wards: a topic which very seldom engages the attention of American tribunals. While the penal laws against Roman Catholics were in full force in England, it was considered the duty of the court of chancery, by analogy to the statute law, to see that all infants under its control should be brought up in the Protestant religion.[5] A case is reported in which Lord Cowper ordered a Roman Catholic girl to be sent to a Protestant school, evidently with a view to her conversion.[6] With the progress of religious toleration came a different rule of practice; and it is now a question whether, under any circumstances, the court would interfere with the testamentary guardian, and the infant's religion as decided by the former.[7] But schemes of education, in cases of disagreement among guardians, are still prescribed in chancery.[8] So the rights of the guardian as

[1] *In re* North, 11 Jur. 7, V. C. Bruce; Macphers. Inf. 555; Campbell *v.* Mackay, 2 Myl. & Cr. 34.

[2] Witty *v.* Marshall, 1 You. & C. N. C. 68.

[3] Regina *v.* Clarke, 7 El. & B. 186.

[4] Talbot *v.* Earl of Shrewsbury, 18 Law J. 125; Macph. Inf. 126. See also Hill *v.* Hill, 8 Jur. N. S. 609. And see Fraser Parent & Child, 82.

[5] Macphers. Inf. 123; Lady Teynham's Case, 9 Mod. 40.

[6] Hill *v.* Filkin, 2 P. Wms. 5. And see Blake *v.* Leigh, Ambl. 306; Jac. 264 *n.*; *In re* Bishop Reg. Lib. 1774, cited in Macphers. Inf. 124.

[7] Talbot *v.* Earl of Shrewsbury, 18 Law J. 125, per Lord Ch. Cottenham. And see Regina *v.* Clarke, 7 El. & B. 186.

[8] Campbell *v.* Mackay, 2 Myl. & Cr. 34; Macphers. Inf. 555.

judge of the place of his ward's education have been sometimes enforced in equity against the ward's own wishes.[1]

Courts of chancery, in short, have jurisdiction to superintend the education of infant children.[2] Yet the English courts seem to have acted rather for the purpose of securing the control of the child's education to the proper person, than to make independent regulations of their own according to the child's welfare. In this respect, as well as in enforcing the disabilities of the law against Roman Catholics and dissenters, chancery was manifestly influenced by considerations of national policy. Should such a subject come before the courts of this country, they might fairly take a different course, more in accordance with American legislation. Our municipal laws in general provide for the infant's educational wants; and this whole jurisdiction is one of great embarrassment and responsibility. We do not find a leading American case decided with direct and sole reference to the education of young children.[3]

The third parental duty is that of maintenance. It is a plain precept of universal law that young and tender beings should be nurtured and brought up by their parents; and this precept have all nations enforced. So well secured is the obligation of maintenance that it seldom requires to be enforced by human laws.[4] Are we brought into this world to perish at the threshold by suffering and starvation? No: but to live and to grow. Some one, then, must enable us to do so; and upon whom more justly rests that responsibility than upon those who brought us into being? Hence, as Puffendorf observes, the duty of maintenance is laid on the

[1] Tremain's Case, Stra. 168; Hall *v.* Hall, 3 Atk. 721. In Tremain's case, an "infant" went to Oxford contrary to the orders of his guardian, who wished him to study at Cambridge. The court sent a messenger to carry him from Oxford to Cambridge; and upon his repeated disobedience there went another *tam* to carry him to Cambridge, *quam* to keep him there. See Macphers. Inf. 121, 141.

[2] See 2 Story Eq. Juris. § 1342; Wellesley *v.* Wellesley, 2 Bligh N. S. 124.

[3] See the topic of Custody, *infra;* Jones *v.* Stockett, 2 Bland. 409.

[4] 2 Kent Com. 189.

parents, not only by nature herself, but by their own proper act in bringing the children into the world. By begetting them, they have entered into a voluntary obligation to endeavor, as far as in them lies, that the life which they have bestowed shall be supported and preserved.[1]

Maintenance is that support which one person gives to another for his living. This word, used by common-law writers, corresponds with the civil-law term aliment.[2]

The obligation on the parent's part to maintain the child continues until the latter is in a condition to provide for his own maintenance, and it extends no further, at common law, than to a necessary support.[3] The Roman system carried this obligation so far that it would not suffer a parent at his death to totally disinherit his child without expressly giving his reasons for so doing.[4] And the laws of Athens were to the same purport.[5] Blackstone does not appear to approve of carrying natural obligation so far. And he cites Grotius in support of a distinction which limits the child's natural right to *necessary* maintenance; what is more than that, depending solely upon the favor of parents, or the positive constitutions of the municipal law.[6] Coke observes that it is "nature's provision to assist, maintain, and console the child."[7]

The statute 43 Eliz. c. 2, slightly amended by 5 Geo. I. c. 8, points out the English policy in this respect. It is provided by this statute that the father and mother, grandfather and grandmother of poor, old, blind, lame, and impotent persons shall maintain them at their own charges, if of sufficient ability; and if a parent runs away and leaves his children, the municipal

[1] Puff. Law of Nations, I. 4, ch. 11; 1 Bl. Com. 447.

[2] Cf. Macphers. Inf. 210, and Fraser Parent & Child, 85.

[3] 2 Kent Com. 190; 1 Bl. Com. 448.

[4] Dig. 28, 230; Nov. 115, ch. 3. The statutes of some of the United States favor this doctrine to about the same extent. See Mass. Gen. Sts. ch. 92, §§ 26, 27.

[5] 2 Potter Greek Antiq. 351.

[6] Grot. De I. B. et P. I. 2, ch. 7, n. 3; 1 Bl. Com. 448.

[7] See 2 Kent Com. 190.

authorities, by summary judicial process, may seize upon his rents, goods and chattels, and dispose of them toward their relief.[1]

No person is bound to provide a maintenance for his issue, unless where the children are impotent and unable to act, through infancy, disease, or accident, and then is only obliged to furnish them with necessaries, the penalty on refusal being no more than twenty shillings a month. "For the policy of our laws, which are ever watchful to promote industry," says Blackstone, "did not mean to compel a father to maintain his idle and lazy children in ease and indolence; but thought it unjust to oblige the parent against his will to provide them with superfluities, and other indulgences of fortune; imagining they might trust to the impulse of nature, if the children were deserving of such favors."[2]

Lord Eldon, viewing the same subject afterwards in the light of equity principles, was differently impressed by these penal provisions, and founded the jurisdiction of chancery upon the very meagreness of the common-law remedies against keeping the child from starvation. "Is it," says he, "an eligible thing that children of all ranks should be placed in this situation, that they shall be in the custody of the father; although looking at the quantum of allowance which the law can compel the father to provide for them, they may be regarded as in a state little better than that of starvation? The courts of law can enforce the rights of the father, but they are not equal to the office of enforcing the duties of the father."[3]

The stat. 43 Eliz. may be considered as having been transported to the United States as part of our common law. Its provisions have also been re-enacted in many of our States,

[1] 1 Bl. Com. 448; Stubb *v.* Dixon, 6 East, 166; Macphers. Inf. 210. These statutes did not extend to illegitimates or step-children. Tubb *v.* Harrison, 4 T. R. 118; Cooper *v.* Martin, 4 East, 76. But this is changed by Stat. 4 & 5 Wm. IV., ch. 76.

[2] 1 Bl. Com. 449; Winston *v.* Newcomen, 6 Ad. & El. 301.

[3] Wellesley *v.* Duke of Beaufort, 2 Russ. 23 (1827).

as in New Hampshire, Connecticut, and South Carolina. In New York, Massachusetts, and other States, the provision as to grandparents is omitted.[1] This feeble and scanty provision of statute law was intended, as Kent observes, for the indemnity of the public against the maintenance of paupers.[2]

In absence of special statutes to the contrary, the father-in-law is not obliged in this country to maintain his step-children, and consequently is not entitled to their earnings.[3] Under the pauper acts, it is held that the father's obligation to support his vagabond son, who cannot support himself, does not accrue until after legal proceedings have been instituted; and the furnishing of previous supplies constitutes no legal consideration to support a new promise.[4] Nor is an insane mother, herself a pauper, under obligation to support a minor child, or entitled to his earnings.[5]

In general, the legal obligation of the father to maintain his child under the common law ceases as soon as the child is of age, however wealthy the father may be, unless the child becomes chargeable to the public as a pauper.[6] And as the language of stat. 43 Eliz. rendered it inapplicable to step-children, so does it apply to blood relations only; and the husband is not liable for the expense of maintaining his wife's mother,[7] nor the father for his daughter's husband.[8] But a *quasi* parental relation may sometimes be established; and one may stand *in loco parentis* to another, and thus become responsible for the maintenance and education of the latter on the

1 2 Kent Com. 191 and note; Dover *v.* McMurphy, 4 N. H. 162; Comm'rs of Poor *v.* Gansett, 2 Bail. 320. And see Haynes's Adm'r *v.* Waggoner, 25 Ind. 174.

2 2 Kent Com. 191.

3 Commonwealth *v.* Hamilton, 6 Mass. 273, 275; Freto *v.* Brown, 4 ib. 675; Worcester *v.* Marchant, 14 Pick. 510.

4 Mills *v.* Wyman, 3 Pick. 207; Loomis *v.* Newhall, 15 ib. 159.

5 Jenness *v.* Emerson, 15 N. H. 486. And see Sanford *v.* Lebanon, 31 Maine, 124; Farmington *v.* Jones, 36 N. H. 271.

6 2 Kent Com. 192; Parish of St. Andrew *v.* De Breta, 1 Ld. Raym. 699.

7 Rex *v.* Munden, 1 Str. 190.

8 Friend *v.* Thompson, Wright, 636.

principle that the child is held out to the world as part of his family.

In a state of voluntary separation, the husband *prima facie*, and not the wife, is liable for the support of children living with her.[1] But the wife carries no such agency with her when divorced, though it be for the husband's fault, and from bed and board only.[2] And while in case of either separation or divorce, without orders of custody, the obligation in general continues as before, it may be materially affected by the special circumstances of each case; and an award of children to the mother should be presumed to carry with it a transfer of parental duties, as well as of parental rights.[3]

We pass from maintenance under statute to chancery maintenance. Maintenance, as ordered by courts of equity, has grown into a topic of considerable magnitude, especially under the English system. The rule is, that where an infant has property of his own, and his father is dead, or is not able to support him, he may be maintained out of the income of property, absolutely his own, by the person in whose hands the property is held; and a court of equity will allow all payments made for this purpose, which appear upon investigation to have been reasonable and proper.[4]

As a general rule, the father must, if he can, maintain his infant children, whatever their circumstances may be; and no allowance will be made him for that purpose out of their property, while his own means are adequate for their support. This principle is clearly established, both in England and America.[5]

1 Rumney *v.* Keyes, 7 N. H. 571; Kimball *v.* Keyes, 11 Wend. 32; Walker *v.* Laighton, 11 Fost. 111; Gill *v.* Read, 5 R. I. 343.

2 Hancock *v.* Merritt, 10 Cush. 41; Fitler *v.* Fitler, 33 Penn. St. 50; Burritt *v.* Burritt, 29 Barb. 124. See Reynolds *v.* Sweetser, 15 Gray, 78.

3 Stanton *v.* Willson, 3 Day, 37, appears to carry the mother's right much farther; but its authority is questionable.

4 Macphers. Inf. 213: 2 Story Eq. Jur. § 1354.

5 Macphers. Inf. 145, 219; Wellesley *v.* Beaufort, 2 Russ. 28; Butler *v.* Butler, 3 Atk. 60; 2 Kent Com. 191; Jackson *v.* Jackson, West Ch. 31; Darley *v.*

But, if the father is unable to maintain his children, the court will order maintenance for them out of their own property.[1] And where the question turns upon the father's ability, maintenance is given, not only in case of his bankruptcy or insolvency, but whenever it appears that he is so straitened in his circumstances that he cannot give the child a maintenance and education suitable to the child's fortune and expectations.[2] The amount of such fortune, as well as the situation, ability, and circumstances of the father, will be taken into account by the court in all such cases.

Courts now look with great liberality to the state of facts in each particular case before them. Thus, there are precedents in the English courts where the father had a large income, and yet was allowed for the maintenance of his infant children, they having an income still larger;[3] though the increasing liberality of the courts is now chiefly exhibited in their construction of written directions for maintenance now common in deeds of settlement and other instruments, by which property is secured to the infant.[4] In this country there are many instances where the father has been allowed for his child's maintenance, though not destitute. As in a case where the father was guardian of his children, labored for their support, and had been put to increased expense by the death of their mother.[5] And again, where his resources were very moderate, and the two children, young ladies, had a comfortable income between them.[6] So

Darley, 3 Atk. 399; Cruger *v.* Heyward, 2 Desaus. 94; Dupont *v.* Johnson, 1 Bailey Ch. 274; Matter of Kane, 2 Barb. Ch. 375; Addison *v.* Bowie, 2 Bland. 606; Harland's Case, 5 Rawle, 323; Myers *v.* Myers, 2 McCord Ch. 255; 34 Ala. 15.

[1] 2 Kent Com. 191; Macphers. Inf. 220.

[2] Buckworth *v.* Buckworth, 1 Cox, 80; Macphers. Inf. 220; Newport *v.* Cook, 2 Ashm. 332; Matter of Kane, 2 Barb. Ch. 375.

[3] 2 Kent Com. 191; Jervois *v.* Silk, Coop. Eq. 52; 2 Story Eq. Jur. § 1354 *et seq.;* Greenwell *v.* Greenwell, 5 Ves. 194; Hoste *v.* Pratt, 3 Ves. 730; *Ex parte* Penleaze, 1 Bro. C. C. 387 *n.*

[4] See Macphers. Inf. 221–223; Heysham *v.* Heysham, 1 Cox, 179; Allen *v.* Coster, 1 Beas. 201.

[5] Harring *v.* Coles, 2 Bradf. Sur. 349.

[6] Matter of Burke, 4 Sandf. Ch. 617.

where the father was poor and disabled, and his daughter lived with him.[1]

Our courts in such cases endeavor to pursue the course which is best calculated to promote the permanent interest, welfare, and happiness of the children who come under its care. "And these," says Chancellor Walworth, "are not always promoted by a rigid economy in the application of their income, regardless of the habits and associations of their period of minority."[2] In the case before him, the father, who was also guardian of his daughters, had re-married since their mother's death, and his income was not more than sufficient to maintain himself and his second wife. The daughters were of ample means, and could afford to contribute towards the expenses of house-keeping, for the sake of living in the family. The Chancellor considered that a home suitable to their condition in life was much to their advantage; and, although it appeared that these daughters could have been boarded and educated at a female seminary at less expense, he felt warranted in allowing a liberal sum to the father for their support and education at his house.[3]

If special circumstances exist, the father may be allowed for the expenses of past maintenance; not otherwise, according to the English rule of the present day.[4] But the father's non-residence, and consequent inability to make a reasonable application for maintenance, is held a special circumstance to justify such allowance.[5] The rule in this country, as to restrospective allowances, does not appear, to be very strict as concerns the parent.[6]

[1] Watts *v.* Steele, 19 Ala. 656. And see Godard *v.* Wagner, 2 Strobh. Eq. 1; Newport *v.* Cook, 2 Ashm. 332.

[2] Matter of Burke, 4 Sandf. Ch. 619.

[3] See Haase *v.* Roerschild, 6 Ind. 67; Sparhawk *v.* Sparhawk's Exr. 9 Vt. 41.

[4] 2 Story Eq. Juris. Redf. ed. § 1354 *a*; Carmichael *v.* Hughes, 6 E. L. & Eq. 73, per Lord Cranworth; *Ex parte* Bond, 2 Myl. & K. 439. And see Presley *v.* Davis, 7 Rich. Eq. 105.

[5] Carmichael *v.* Hughes, 6 E. L. & Eq. 71. And see Stopford *v.* Lord Canterbury, 11 Sim. 82; Bruin *v.* Knott, 1 Phill. 572; 1 Tamlyn, 22.

[6] Matter of Kane, 2 Barb. Ch. 375; Matter of Burke, 4 Sandf. Ch. 619; Myers *v.* Myers, 2 McCord Ch. 214.

A father, though not in needy circumstances, may maintain his children out of any fund which is duly vested in him for that express purpose.[1] He may also contract that certain property shall be applied to the maintenance and education of his children, in which case also the contract may be enforced in his favor, without regard to the question of ability.[2] But it is clear from the cases, that where the fund is given, as a mere bounty, notwithstanding a provision for maintenance, the father, if of ability, must support the child.[3] This will not prevent a court from construing such provisions in his favor, where the facts show that the father ought, on general principles, to receive assistance.[4]

Where the trustee for an infant, in the exercise of rightful discretion, has paid over to the father, at his request, certain sums of money out of the income of the trust property, the father being a bankrupt, it is held that no promise can be implied under such circumstances, on the part of the father, to repay to the trustee the sums of money thus applied when he afterwards becomes able to do so; there should be something to show an express promise of repayment.[5]

The mother, after the death of the father, remains the head of the family. She has the like control over the minor children as he had when living; and she is then bound to support them, if of sufficient ability.[6] This we hold to be the rule most conformable to natural justice; though there are cases which would seem to exempt her from such obligations.[7] The

[1] Macphers. Inf. 220; Hawkins *v.* Watts, 7 Sim. 199; Andrews *v.* Partington, 2 Cox, 223.

[2] Mundy *v.* Earl Howe, 4 Br. C. C. 224; Stocken *v.* Stocken, 4 Sim. 152; Macphers. Inf. 220.

[3] Hoste *v.* Pratt, 3 Ves. 729; Hamley *v.* Gilbert, Jac. 354; Myers *v.* Myers, 2 McCord Ch. 255; Jones *v.* Stockett, 2 Bland. 409.

[4] See Andrews *v.* Partington, 2 Cox 223, commented upon in Hoste *v.* Pratt, 3 Ves. 729.

[5] Pearce *v.* Olney, 5 R. I. 269. See *In re* Stables, 13 E. L. & Eq. 61.

[6] Dedham *v.* Natick, 16 Mass. 140.

[7] Whipple *v.* Dow, 2 Mass. 415; Dawes *v.* Howard, 4 Mass. 97; 2 Kent Com. 191, and cases cited.

statute of Elizabeth, to which we have already referred, expressly includes the mother. And since the tendency of the day is to give the mother a more equal share in the parental rights, it follows that she should assume more of the parental burdens.

It is nevertheless clear that the courts show special favor to the mother, as they should; and, if the child has property, they will rather in any case charge the expenses of his education and maintenance upon such property than force her to contribute.[1]

Where the court takes away from the father the care and custody of the children, chancery does not call in aid of their own means the property of the father, and it directs maintenance out of their own fortunes whatever may be their father's circumstances.[2] But it is held in Illinois that where infants are taken from the custody of their father, and have no property of their own, the father is bound to support them at such rate as the court may order.[3] Local statutes sometimes affect the rule in this country.

If the father is alive and not able to maintain his child, maintenance will be allowed without considering the ability of the mother, though she may have a separate income.[4] And even the misconduct of the father will not always exclude him from participating in his child's fortune.[5]

Where a mother has maintained her infant child without the order of the court, upon his decease, she can claim for past maintenance only such sum as will effectually indemnify her for what she has spent, without reference to the amount of his fortune.[6] But in any case the widowed mother is entitled to a

[1] Ib.; Haley v. Bannister, 4 Mad. 275; Hughes v. Hughes, 1 Br. C. C. 388. And see Lanoy v. Duchess of Athol, 2 Atk. 447; *Ex parte* Petre, 7 Ves. 403; Macphers. Inf. 224; Beasley v. Magrath, 2 Sch. & Lef. 35; Anne Walker's Matter, ca. temp. Sug. 299.

[2] Wellesley v. Duke of Beaufort, 2 Russ. 1; Macphers. Inf. 224.

[3] Cowls v. Cowls, 3 Gilm. 435. And see *supra*, p. 322.

[4] Macphers. Inf. 224; Halley v. Bannister, 4 Mad. 275.

[5] Macphers. Inf. 251. See Allen v. Coster, 1 Beav. 202.

[6] Bruin v. Knott, 9 Jur. 979.

reasonable allowance out of her children's estate for their maintenance, where her own means are limited.[1]

Courts of chancery, following a well known principle, usually restrict the extent of a child's maintenance to the income of his property.[2] But where the property is small and the income insufficient for his support, the court will sometimes allow the capital to be broken.[3]

We have assumed in the cases already considered, that there was some fund in which the infants had an absolute right or interest. Where the interest is contingent merely the rule is necessarily strict.[4] Maintenance cannot be allowed to infants out of a fund which, upon the happening of the event contemplated by the testator in the bequest of the fund, will not belong to the infants but to some other person.[5]

Let us inquire how far the child may bind his father as agent. A father is not bound by the contracts or debts of his son, even for necessaries, as a rule, unless the circumstances show an authority actually given or to be legally inferred.[6] The principles of agency as between father and child might seem analogous to those which govern the relation of husband and wife; which last have already been considered at some length. On the one hand, the father should be compelled to discharge his legal and moral obligations as a parent, by providing suitable necessaries; on the other, he should not be prejudiced by the acts of his imprudent child.

[1] Wilkes *v.* Rogers, 6 Johns. 566; Heyward *v.* Cuthbert, 4 Desaus. 445; Osborne *v.* Van Horn, 2 Fla. 360; Bradshaw *v.* Bradshaw, 1 Russ. 528.

[2] 2 Story Eq. Jur. § 1355; Macphers. Inf. 252.

[3] Ib.; Barlow *v.* Grant, 1 Vern. 255; Bridge *v.* Brown, 2 You. & C. C. 181; *Ex parte* Green, 1 Jac. & W. 253; Osborne *v.* Van Horn, 2 Fla. 360; Newport *v.* Cook, 2 Ashm. 332. See *In re* Coe's Trust, 4 Kay & J. 199; Matter of Bostwick, 4 Johns. Ch. 100; Donovan *v.* Needham, 15 L. J. 193.

[4] *Ex parte* Kebble, 11 Ves. 604.

[5] Ib.; Errat *v.* Barlow, 14 Ves. 202; Turner *v.* Turner, 4 Sim. 430; Matter of Davison, 6 Paige, 136. As to rule of procedure in securing maintenance, see further Macphers. Inf. 214 *et seq.*

[6] 2 Kent Com. 192; Cromwell *v.* Benjamin, 41 Barb. 558; Gordon *v.* Potter, 17 Vt. 348; Pidgin *v.* Cram, 8 N. H. 350; Raymond *v.* Loyl, 10 Barb. 483; Tomkins *v.* Tomkins, 3 Stockt. 512; Van Valkenburg *v.* Watson, 13 Johns. 480; Mortimore *v.* Wright, 6 M. & W. 482.

If then the infant resides at home, it is to be presumed that the father furnishes whatever is necessary and proper for his maintenance; and a proper support being rendered, under such circumstances, a third person cannot supply necessaries and charge the father. So far, all is clear. Wherever the infant is *sub potestate parentis* in fact, there must be a clear and palpable omission of duty in this respect, on the part of the parent, to render him chargeable, unless he has conferred actual authority.[1]

The converse of this rule has more than once been suggested in our American courts; namely, that where the father abandons his duty, so that his infant child is forced to leave his house, he is liable for a suitable maintenance furnished the child elsewhere.[2] And upon this doctrine was a Connecticut case based many years ago, where an infant child had "eloped" from his father's house for fear of personal violence and abuse; and his necessary support and education were furnished by a stranger.[3]

It must be admitted that this doctrine of an implied agency, against the father's wishes, such as the common law raises for the wife's protection, ought hardly to be extended in an equal degree to persons too young to be *sui juris;* that the theory above advanced is supported rather by *dicta* than positive adjudication; and that whenever applied, such a rule is to be justified rather by public policy than the well-understood liabilities of the father, as defined by Blackstone. We look at the reports and find that in nearly every instance the father was held to be discharged from the obligation, or else was made liable on other grounds. There can be no doubt that a parent is under a natural obligation to provide necessaries for his minor children. But how that obligation is to be enforced is

1 Tomkins *v.* Tomkins, 3 Stockt. 512; Townsend *v.* Burnham, 33 N. H. 27; Clinton *v.* Rowland, 24 Barb. 634; Keaton *v.* Davis, 18 Geo. 457.

2 Owen *v.* White, 5 Port. 435, and cases cited in the two preceding notes.

3 Stanton *v.* Willson, 3 Day, 37. But the point decided was a different one.

not so clear.[1] In New York there is some confusion of opinion.[2] In Vermont this doctrine of implied agency, against the father's wishes, was disapproved in a case which discusses the subject fully; though the facts, it must be conceded, showed no clear omission of parental duty.[3] But in New Jersey, the rule seems to be enforceable.[4]

The latest English decisions are clearly against allowing the child to pledge his father's credit for necessaries to enforce a moral obligation. There must be some contract, express or implied, in order to charge him. If a child be turned upon the world by his father, he can only apply to the parish, and they will compel the father, if of ability, to pay for his support. Says Lord Abinger: "In point of law, a father who gives no authority, and enters into no contract, is no more liable for goods supplied to his son, than a brother, or an uncle, or a mere stranger would be. From the moral obligation a parent is under to provide for his children, a jury are, not unnaturally, disposed to infer against him an admission of a liability in respect of claims upon his son, on grounds which warrant no inference in point of law."[5]

But very slight evidence may sometimes warrant the inference that a contract for the infant's necessaries is sanctioned by the father; so zealous is the court to enforce a moral obligation wherever it can. English authority to the same effect is not equally pointed;[6] but the American rule is certainly humane and liberal in this respect. Thus, the father is held bound for necessaries, where he knows the circumstances, and makes no objection.[7] And for the expenses of education and maintenance

[1] 1 Bl. Com. 447; Edwards *v.* Davis, 16 Johns. 285; *In re* Ryder, 11 Paige, 188; 2 Kent Com. 190.

[2] Cf. Raymond *v.* Loyl, 10 Barb. 483, with cases, *supra.*

[3] Gordon *v.* Potter, 17 Vt. 348.

[4] Tomkins *v.* Tomkins, 3 Stockt. 517.

[5] Mortimore *v.* Wright, 6 M. & W. 482. And see Shelton *v.* Springett, 11 C. B. 452; 20 E. L. & Eq. 281; Seaborne *v.* Maddy, 9 Car. & P. 497.

[6] Blackburn *v.* Mackey, 1 Car. & P. 1; Law *v.* Wilkin, 6 Ad. & El. 781; cases of doubtful legal authority. See Macphers. Inf. 514, 515.

[7] Swain *v.* Tyler, 26 Vt. 9; Thayer *v.* White, 12 Met. 343.

furnished on his general consent, and in his negligence.[1] So too, being liable once, the father may be held liable afterwards by implication.[2]

The doctrine of agency is also extended to general transactions, on the principle of master and servant, in a Connecticut case, where certain articles had been delivered to, and work done for, a college student still in his minority; and the court held that the father was liable, although the goods were not necessaries; the evidence showing that the father had paid the plaintiff's former account of the same nature, without objection or giving notice not to trust his son further, and had then (without the plaintiff's knowledge) given positive orders to his son to contract no more debts, and had placed him under the care of a friend with instructions to furnish all that was necessary and suitable for him.[3]

Yet the rule of principal and agent is to be reasonably enforced, and in all cases where there appears neither palpable moral delinquency on the part of the parent, nor evidence of authority actually conferred upon his son, he cannot be held liable for the general contracts of the latter. A conditional offer to pay for goods ordered of a stranger by the child must have been clearly accepted in order to constitute such ratification as will bind the parent who makes it.[4] And in numerous instances have courts refused to make the father liable on the ground of agency.[5] So where a child has attained full age the presumption is that he will bind himself by his own contracts. Under the latter circumstances a mere request to furnish necessaries does not bind the father, though the son be living with him.[6] Whenever a minor son has left his father's home the

[1] Thompson *v.* Dorsey, 4 Md. Ch. 149.

[2] Plotts *v.* Rosebury, 4 Dutch. 146. And see Deane *v.* Annis, 14 Me. 26.

[3] Bryan *v.* Jackson, 4 Conn. 288. And see Brown *v.* Deloach, 28 Geo. 486; Deane *v.* Annis, 14 Me. 26.

[4] Andrews *v.* Garrett, 6 C. B. (N. S.) 262.

[5] Eitel *v.* Walter, 2 Bradf. Sur. 287; Raymond *v.* Loyl, 10 Barb. 483; Bushnell *v.* Bishop Hill Colony, 28 Ill. 204. See Loomis *v.* Newhall, 15 Pick. 159.

[6] Boyd *v.* Sappington, 4 Watts, 247. And see Mills *v.* Wyman, 3 Pick. 207; Wood *v.* Gills, Coxe, 449; Norris *v.* Dodge's Adm'r, 23 Ind. 190.

cause should be ascertained, for the disobedience of children is not to be encouraged in any event.[1] Under the most favorable aspect of the infant's right to bind his father as agent, a third person furnishing goods must take notice, at his peril, of what is necessary for the infant according to his precise situation.[2]

The parent's duty, according to some authorities, also extends to providing the children with a profession or trade along with a suitable education. How far the duty of competent provision extends, must depend upon the condition and circumstances of the father. Kent observes that this duty is not susceptible of municipal regulations, and it is usually left to the dictates of reason and natural affection.[3]

1 Raymond *v.* Loyl, 10 Barb. 483; Angel *v.* McLellan, 16 Mass. 28; Weeks *v.* Merrow, 40 Me. 151.

2 Van Valkenburgh *v.* Watson, 13 Johns. 480.

3 2 Kent Com. 202.

CHAPTER III.

THE RIGHTS OF PARENTS.

THE rights of parents result from their duties, being given them by law partly to aid in the fulfillment of their obligations, and partly by way of recompense.[1] As they are bound to maintain and educate, the law has given them certain authority over their children, and in the support of that authority a right to the exercise of such discipline as may be requisite for the discharge of their important trust. This is the true foundation of parental power.[2]

Some of the ancient nations carried the parental authority beyond all natural limits. The Persians, Egyptians, Greeks, Gauls, and Romans tolerated infanticide. Under the ancient Roman laws the father had the power of life and death over his children: on the principle that he who gave had also the power to take away;[3] and thus did law attribute to man those functions which belong only to the Supreme Being. This power of the father was toned down in subsequent constitutions, and in the time of the Emperor Hadrian the wiser maxim prevailed, "*Patria potestas in pietate debet, non in atrocitate consistere;*" for which reason a father was banished who had killed his son. The Emperor Constantine made the crime capital as to adult children; and infanticide was under Valentinian and Valens punishable by death. Thus was the doctrine of paternal supremacy gradually reduced, though at the civil law never wholly abandoned.[4]

[1] 1 Bl. Com. 452.

[2] 2 Kent Com. 203.

[3] Cod. 8, 47, 10; 2 Bl. Com. 452.

[4] 1 Bl. Com. 452; 2 Kent Com. 204; 1 Heinec. Antiq. Rom. Jur. 9; Dr. Taylor Civ. Law, pp. 403–406; Forsyth Custody, 3.

The common law, far more discreet, gives the parent only a moderate degree of authority over his child's person, which authority relaxes as the child grows older. With the progress of refinement parents have learned to enforce obedience by kindness rather than severity; and although the courts are reluctant to interfere in matters of family discipline, they will discountenance every species of cruelty which goes by the name of parental rule. The common law gives the right of moderate correction of the child in a reasonable manner: "for," it is said, "this is for the benefit of his education."[1] But at the same time the parent must not exceed the bounds of moderation, and inflict cruel and merciless punishment; for if he do, he is liable to be punished by indictment. And he may be found guilty of manslaughter, or even murder, under gross circumstances.[2] So may a parent at the common law be indicted for exposure and neglect of his children; and the heinousness of the offence depends in a great measure upon the proof of simple negligence or wilful cruelty. The parent who suffers his little child to starve to death commits murder, but when children grow up they are presumed to provide for their urgent wants.[3]

The topic of parental custody is one of absorbing importance in England and America; and its principles have received the most ample discussion in the courts of both countries. The fundamental principle of the common law is that the father has the paramount right to the custody and control of his minor children, and to superintend their education and nurture.[4] The mother, as such, had little or no authority in the premises.[5] So the Roman law enjoined upon children the duty of showing

[1] 1 Hawk. P. C. 130; 1 Bl. Com. 452.

[2] 1 Russ. Crimes, Grea. ed. 490; Regina *v.* Edwards, 8 Car. & P. 611; 2 Bish. Crim. Law, § 714.

[3] Johnson *v.* State, 2 Humph. 283; 4 Bl. Com. 182, 183; 2 Bish. Crim. Law, §§ 686, 712.

[4] *Ex parte* Hopkins, 3 P. Wms. 151; 2 Story Eq. Jur. §§ 1341, 1342; 2 Kent Com. 205; Forsyth Custody, 10; People *v.* Olmstead, 27 Barb. 9, and cases cited; *Ex parte* M'Clellan, 1 Dowl. P. C. 34.

[5] See 1 Bl. Com. 453.

due reverence and respect to the mother, and punished any flagrant instance of the want of it, but beyond this it seems to have recognized no claim on her part.[1] Indeed, the father is permitted by Anglo-Saxon policy to perpetuate his authority beyond his own life; for he may constitute a testamentary guardian of his infant children.[2]

In case there is no father, then the mother is entitled to the custody of the children; supposing, of course, the rights of no testamentary guardian intervene.[3] She has, as natural guardian, a right to the custody of the person and care of the education of her children; "and this in all countries," said Lord Hardwicke, "where the laws do not break in."[4] The priority of the surviving mother's right to custody is frequently a matter of statute regulation;[5] but her absolute right on re-marriage is not so clearly recognized. Her claims, as we shall see hereafter, may conflict with those of a guardian.

Were these invariable rules, uncontrolled by the courts, unchanged by statute, this common-law doctrine of custody would be as simple of application as unjust. It is neither. And the courts of chancery, in assuming a liberal jurisdiction over the persons and estates of infants, soon made the claims of justice override all considerations of parental or rather paternal dominion, at the common law.[6] Thus Lord Thurlow, in a case where it appeared that the father's affairs were embarrassed, that he was an outlaw and resided abroad, that his son, an infant, had considerable estate, and that the mother lived apart from her husband and principally directed the child's

[1] Cod. 8, tit. 47, § 4; Forsyth Custody, 5.

[2] Stat. 12 Car. 2, ch. 24, re-enacted in most of the United States. See Guardian and Ward, *infra*.

[3] See Guardian and Ward, *infra*.

[4] Villareal *v.* Mellish, 2 Swanst. 536; Forsyth Custody, 11, 109; 2 Kent Com. 506; People *v.* Wilcox, 22 Barb. 178; Osborn *v.* Allen, 2 Dutch. 388. So where the father is sentenced to transportation. *Ex parte* Bailey, 6 Dowl. P. C. 311.

[5] 2 & 3 Vict. ch. 54; Mass. Gen. Stats. ch. 109 § 4; State *v.* Scott, 10 Fost. 274; Striplin *v.* Ware, 36 Ala. 87. See Heyward *v.* Cuthbert, 4 Desaus. 445.

[6] 2 Story Eq. Jur. § 1341. And see Butler *v.* Freeman, Ambler, 302.

education, restrained the father from interfering without the consent of two persons nominated for that purpose; and with reference to the objection that the court had no jurisdiction, he added that he knew there was such a notion, but he was of opinion that the court had arms long enough to reach such a case and to prevent a father from prejudicing the health or future prospects of the child; and he signified that he should act accordingly.[1]

But the leading case on this subject is that of *Wellesley* v. *The Duke of Beaufort*, which went on appeal from Lord Eldon to the House of Lords; and in which the learned Lord Chancellor's judgment was unanimously affirmed.[2] There the children were taken from a father who was living in adultery. In the course of his elaborate judgment in this case, Lord Eldon cited with approbation a *dictum* of Lord Macclesfield, to the effect that where there is reasonable ground to believe that the children would not be properly treated, the court would interfere without waiting further, upon the principle that *preventing justice* was better than *punishing justice*.[3]

The evidence showed that the conduct of the father was of the most profligate and immoral description. It appeared that he had ill-treated his wife, continued his adulterous connection to the time of judicial proceedings, and in his letters to his young children had frequently encouraged them in habits of swearing and keeping low company. Lord Redesdale, in the course of his opinion before the House of Lords, repudiated emphatically the insinuation that paternal power is to be considered more than a trust. "Look at all the elementary writings on the subject," he adds; "they say that a father is intrusted with the care of his children; that he is intrusted with it for this reason, because it is supposed his natural affec-

[1] Creuze *v.* Hunter, 2 Br. C. C. 499, *n.*; 2 Cox, 242. And see Whitfield *v.* Hales, 12 Ves. 492.

[2] 2 Russ. 1; Wellesley *v.* Wellesley, 2 Bligh N. S. 124; Forsyth Custody, 23 *et seq.*

[3] Duke of Beaufort *v.* Perty, 1 P. Wms. 703, cited in Wellesley *v.* Duke of Beaufort, *supra.*

tion would make him the most proper person to discharge the trust."[1]

The result of the English authorities is to establish the principle, independently of statutory provisions, that the Court of Chancery will interfere to disturb the paternal rights only in cases of gross misconduct; though such misconduct seems to be regarded with reference rather to the interests of the child than the moral delinquency of the parent. If the father has so conducted himself that it will not be for the benefit of the infants that they should be delivered to him, or if their being with him will affect their happiness, or if they cannot associate with him without moral contamination, or if, because they associate with him, other persons will shun their society, the court will award the custody to another.[2] It is held that chancery has nothing to do with the fact of the father's adultery, unless he brings the child into contact with the woman.[3] But unnatural crime is otherwise regarded.[4] Atheism, blasphemy, irreligion call for interference, when the minds of young children may be thereby poisoned and corrupted; although in matters of purely religious belief there is of course much difficulty in defining that degree of latitude which should be allowed. Says Lord Eldon, "With the religious tenets of either party I have nothing to do, except so far as the law of the country calls upon me to look on some religious opinions as dangerous to society."[5]

Mere poverty or insolvency does not furnish an adequate ground for depriving the father of his children; not even though a fund is offered for their benefit, conditioned upon the

[1] Wellesley *v.* Wellesley, 2 Bligh N. S. 141 (1828).

[2] Anonymous, 11 E. L. & Eq. 281; S. C. 2 Sim. N. S. 54; Forsyth Custody, 52; De Manneville *v.* De Manneville, 10 Ves. 52; Warde *v.* Warde, 2 Phill. 786.

[3] Ball *v.* Ball, 2 Sim. 35; Lord Eldon, *n.* 6, to Lyons *v.* Blenkin, Jac. 254. The English divorce act indicates the peculiar views prevalent in that country as to adultery committed by a married man.

[4] Anonymous, 11 E. L. & Eq. 281; S. C. 2 Sim. N. S. 34.

[5] Lyons *v.* Blenkin, Jac. 256. See Shelley *v.* Westbrooke, Jac. 266.

surrender of their custody.[1] Yet so solicitous is chancery for the welfare of its wards, that it seems indisposed to sacrifice their large pecuniary opportunities to the caprice of the natural protector. Thus far has chancery carried its exception, that if property be settled upon an infant, upon condition that the father surrenders his right to the custody of its person, and he, by acquiescing for a time, and permitting the child to be educated in a manner conformably to the terms of the gift or bequest, encourages corresponding expectations, he will not be allowed to disappoint them afterwards by claiming possession of the infant. He has in such a case "waived his parental right."[2]

The English courts of common law likewise interfere in questions relating to the custody of infants by writ of *habeas corpus*, which, in general, lies to bring up persons who are in custody, and who are alleged to be subject to illegal restraint.[3] Lord Mansfield once said that the common-law court is not bound to deliver an infant, when set free from illegal restraint, over to anybody, nor to give it any privilege;[4] but the later English rule is, that where a clear right to the custody is shown to exist in any one, the court has no choice, but must order the infant to be delivered up to him.[5] This jurisdiction is less ample than that of the chancery courts, to whose authority it must be considered subservient.[6]

The English rule, up to the year 1839, was therefore that the

[1] *Ex parte* Hopkins, 3 P. Wms. 152; Colston *v.* Morris, Jac. 257, *n.* 11; Macphers. Inf. 142, 143; Forsyth Custody, 37; Earl & Countess of Westmeath, Jac. 251, *n. c.* But see *Ex parte* Mountfort, 15 Ves. 445.

[2] Per Lord Hardwicke, Blake *v.* Leigh, Amb. 307; Powell *v.* Cleaver, 2 Br. C. C. 499; Creuze *v.* Hunter, 2 Cox, 242. Forsyth Custody, 38, 53; Lyons *v.* Blenkin, Jac. 254, 262.

[3] Macphers. Inf. 152; *Ex parte* Glover, 4 Dowl. P. C. 293; Forsyth Custody, 17, 54; *In re* Pulbrook, 11 Jur. 185; *In re* Fynn, 2 De G. 457; s. c. 12 Jur. 713; Rex *v.* Greenhill, 4 Ad. & El. 624.

[4] Rex *v.* Delarel, 3 Burr. 1436; 1 W. Bl. 409.

[5] Rex *v.* Isley, 5 Ad. & El. 441.

[6] See Wellesley *v.* Wellesley, 2 Bligh N. S. 136, 142; *Ex parte* Skinner, 9 Moore, 278.

father is entitled to the sole custody of his infant child; controllable, in general, by the court only in case of very gross misconduct, injurious to the child. Such a state of things was unjust, since it took little account of the mother's claims or feelings in a matter which most deeply interested her. This finally led to the passage of stat. 2 & 3 Vict. ch. 54, known as Justice Talfourd's Act, which introduced important changes into the law of parental custody.[1]

This act does not appear to have interfered with the father's right of custody further than to introduce new elements and considerations under which that right is to be exercised. The act proceeds upon three grounds: First, it assumes and proceeds upon the existence of the paternal right. Secondly, it connects the paternal right with the marital duty, and imposes the marital duty as the condition of recognizing the paternal right. Thirdly, the act regards the interest of the child.[2] If the two considerations of marital duty to be observed towards the wife and of the interest of the child can be attained consistently with the father's retaining the custody of the child, his common-law paternal right will not be disturbed.[3]

In this country the doctrine is universal that the courts of justice may, in their sound discretion, and when the morals or safety or interests of the children strongly require it, withdraw their custody from the father and confer it upon the mother, or take the children from the parents and place the care and custody of them elsewhere.[4] The rule as to legal preference is essentially that of the common law, with, however, an increasing liberality in favor of the mother; strengthened, in no slight degree, by positive legislation. Our rule of procedure is somewhat different from that noticeable in the English system. Some-

[1] *Ex parte* Woodward, 17 Jur. 56; Forsyth Custody, 137. See Forsyth, ib. 139, 140.

[2] Per Turner V. C. in *Ex parte* Woodward, 17 E. & L. Eq. 77; 17 Jur. 56.

[3] Ib. See also Warde *v.* Warde, 2 Ph. 787. Stat. 3 & 4 Vict. ch. 90, empowers chancery to assign the care and custody of infants convicted of felony.

[4] 2 Kent. Com. 205, and cases cited; 1 Story Eq. Jur. § 1341.

times the right of custody is to be determined by *habeas corpus;* sometimes by proceedings in equity; very frequently it is incidental to divorce suits. In any case, the circumstances will be fully considered by the court, and a decision rendered on general equity principles.

The father has then, in America, the paramount right of custody independently of all statutes to the contrary.[1] But this paramount right may be forfeited by his misconduct.[1] Nor do the decisions in our courts go to the extent of the English rule in sustaining the husband against his wife, despite his immoral behavior or marital misconduct. "It is an entire mistake," says Judge Story, "to suppose that the court is bound to deliver over the infant to its father, or that the latter has an absolute vested right in the custody."[2] The cardinal principle relative to such matters is to regard the benefit of the infant; to make the welfare of the children paramount to the claims of either parent.[3] While States differ as to the extent of the father's claims in preference to the mother, in this latter principle they all agree; and judicial precedents, judicial *dicta*, and legislative enactments all lead to one and the same irresistible conclusion.

The primary object of the American decisions is then to secure the welfare of the child, and not the special claims of one or the other parent. The English case of *Rex* v. *Greenhill*,[4] which, in effect enabling the father to take his children from his blameless wife and place them in the charge of a woman with whom he cohabited, hastened the passage of Justice Talfourd's Act,[5] has been repeatedly condemned in the United States. Indeed, our courts have required no such statute

[1] 2 Kent Com. 205; People *v.* Mercein, 3 Hill, 399; People *v.* Olmstead, 27 Barb. 9; Miner *v.* Miner, 11 Ill. 43; Smith Pet'r, 13 Ill. 138. But see Gishwiler *v.* Dodez, 4 Ohio St. 615.

[2] United States *v.* Green, 3 Mason, 382.

[3] Case of Waldron, 13 Johns. 418; People *v.* Mercein, 3 Hill, 399; *Ex parte* Schumpert, 6 Rich. 344; Wood *v.* Wood, 3 Ala. 756; Gishwiler *v.* Dodez, 4 Ohio St. 615.

[4] 4 Ad. & El. 624.

[5] Forsyth Custody, 69, 137. Lord Denman, who had sat in this case, de-

to prevent them from taking the custody of any child from one whose parental influence is found to be injurious to the child's welfare; and if a father wrongs his wife, it is readily presumed that he will wrong his children likewise.[1]

The American rule is not, however, one of fixed and determined principles. Much must be left to the peculiar surroundings of each case. Thus it has been held, that a single act of adultery, if followed by repentance, will not, of itself, absolutely and forever, exclude the parent from the care of infant children.[2]

Proceedings, as to the custody of children, are usually in this country conducted by writ of *habeas corpus*. And the settled rule with us is that, while the court is bound to free the person from illegal restraint, it is not bound to decide who is entitled to the guardianship, or to deliver infants to the custody of any particular person; but this may be done whenever deemed proper. In other words, it is in the sound discretion of the court to alter the custody of the infants, or not.[3]

Our divorce jurisprudence being, until recently, quite different from that of England, further opportunity has been furnished for a departure from the common-law rules which favor the paternal right of custody. The same tribunal which hears the divorce cause has power to direct with whom of the parties, or what third person, the children shall be.[4] Like powers are

clared that there was not one of the court who had not felt ashamed at the state of the law. See ib. 69 *n.*

[1] Bedell *v.* Bedell, 1 Johns. Ch. 604; Barrere *v.* Barrere, 4 Johns. Ch. 187, 197; 2 Bish. Mar. & Div. 4th ed. § 532; *Ex parte* Schumpert, 6 Rich. 344; The People *v.* Chegaray, 18 Wend. 637. See Gishwiler *v.* Dodez, 4 Ohio St. 615.

[2] Cook *v.* Cook, 1 Barb. Ch. 639; Dailey *v.* Dailey, Wright, 514; Commonwealth *v.* Addicks, 2 S. & R. 174.

[3] Commonwealth *v.* Addicks, 5 Binn, 520; Armstrong *v.* Stone, 9 Gratt, 102; Case of Waldron, 13 Johns, 418; State *v.* Smith, 6 Me. 462; State *ex. rel.* State *v.* Paine, 4 Humph. 523; Commonwealth *v.* Briggs, 16 Pick. 203; Ward *v.* Roper, 7 Humph. 111; Foster *v.* Alston, 6 How. Miss. 406; Stigall *v.* Turney, 2 Zabr. 286; Mercein *v.* People, 25 Wend. 64; State *v.* King, 1 Geo. Dec. 93; State *v.* Banks, 25 Ind. 495; Bennet *v.* Bennet, 2 Beasl. 114; *Ex parte* Williams, 11 Rich. 452; State *v.* Richardson, 40 N. H. 272.

[4] 2 Bish. Mar. & Div. 4th ed. §§ 526, 530.

now conferred upon the English matrimonial court by recent statutes.[1]

Following the temper of the times, the New York legislature of 1860 enacted that "every married woman is hereby constituted and declared to be the joint guardian of her children, with her husband, with equal powers, rights, and duties in regard to them with her husband."[2] Such a statute, unexplained, might seem to do away altogether with the paramount claims of the husband. But the courts seemed disposed to regard the innovation with little favor; and the law was in 1862 repealed.[3] An earlier statute of New York provides that if the parents live in a state of separation, without being divorced, and without the fault of the wife, the courts may, on her application, award the custody of the child to the mother.[4] The discretion thus conferred upon the courts is a judicial one, however, and is to be exercised with due reference to the cause of separation, and the conduct and character of the parties. Legislative provisions of a like tendency are frequently to be met with in other States. Thus in Massachusetts, it is enacted that, pending divorce controversies, the respective rights of the parents shall, in the absence of misconduct, be regarded as equal, and that the happiness and welfare of the children shall determine the custody in which they shall be placed.[5] And under a still more recent statute in New Jersey, the court is to a certain extent deprived of its discretion in disposing of the

[1] Stats. 20 & 21 Vict. ch. 85, § 35; 22 & 23 Vict. ch. 61, § 4. See Ahrenfeldt *v.* Ahrenfeldt, 1 Hoff. Ch. 497; Spratt *v.* Spratt, 1 Swab. & T. 215; 2 Bish. Mar. & Div. 4th ed. §§ 532–544, and cases cited; Bedell *v.* Bedell, 1 Johns. Ch. 604; Bent *v.* Bent, 2 Swab. & T. 392.

[2] See Laws, p. 157.

[3] People *v.* Brooks, 35 Barb. 85; People *v.* Boice, 39 Barb. 307. In the former case a married woman, who lived apart from her husband, no misconduct on his part being shown, sought under the new statute to obtain custody of the children.

[4] 2 N. Y. Rev. Sts. p. 148; 2 Kent Com. 205 *n.*; People *v.* Mercein, 3 Hill, 399. And see People *v.* Brooks, *supra*. See N. Y. Act 1862, ch. 172, § 6, which restrains the father from binding his child as apprentice, or parting with his control, or creating a testamentary guardian, without the mother's written assent.

[5] Mass. Gen. Sts. ch. 107, § 37.

custody of children whose parents are separated, but not divorced; for by this statute the custody of the children under seven years of age is transferred from the father to the mother.[1]

The rights of parents in relation to the custody and services of their children may be enlarged, restrained and limited, as wisdom or policy may dictate, unless the legislative power is limited by some constitutional prohibition.[2]

Where the custody of an infant is the subject of chancery proceedings, the court is fully justified in making *interim* arrangements for his custody.[3]

It is sometimes a question, in proceedings relative to the custody of minors, how far the child's own wishes should be consulted. Where the object is simply that of custody, the rule, though not arbitrary, rests manifestly upon a principle elsewhere often applied; namely, that after a child has attained to years of discretion he may have, in case of controversy, a voice in the selection of his own custodian. The practice is to give the child the right to elect where he will go, if he be of proper age. If he be not of that age, and want of discretion would only expose him to dangers, the court must make an order for placing him in custody of the suitable person.[4]

It is held in England that an agreement by which the father surrenders custody of his child is not binding; and that he is at liberty to revoke his consent afterwards, and obtain the child by a writ of *habeas corpus*.[5] The policy of the rule is otherwise in some American States. Thus, there is a Massachusetts case

[1] Bennet *v.* Bennet, 2 Beasl. 114.

[2] United States *v.* Bainbridge, 1 Mason, 71, per Story J. And see Bennet *v.* Bennet, *supra.*

[3] Hutson *v.* Townsend, 6 Rich. Eq. 249.

[4] Forsyth Custody, 93, &c.; Rex *v.* Greenbill, 4 Ad. & El. 624. Nine or ten years of age has been considered too young; yet mental capacity appears the real test; and the wishes of children less than fourteen have been regarded. See Anon., 2 Ves. 274; *Ex parte* Hopkins, 2 P. Wms. 152; Curtis *v.* Curtis, 5 Gray, 535; People *v.* Mercein, 8 Paige, 47; *In re* Goodenough, 19 Wis. 274; Regina *v.* Clarke, 7 El. & B. 186; State *v.* Richardson, 40 N. H. 272.

[5] Regina *v.* Smith, 16 E. L. & Eq. 221.

where a child had been given up at its birth, the mother having then died, to its grandparents, who kept it for thirteen years, at their own expense, without any demand made by the father for its restoration; and, under these circumstances, the court refused afterwards to change the custody.[1]

The general doctrine appears to us, on the whole, to be this: that public policy is against the permanent transfer of the natural rights of a parent; and that such contracts are not to be specifically enforced, unless in the admitted exception of master and apprentice, to constitute which relation requires, both in England and America, certain formalities; and excepting in some parts of the United States, where the principles of legal adoption are part of the public policy. American courts hold fast, nevertheless, to the true interests and welfare of the child.[2]

If a father, after making an assignment of the services or society of his minor child, has retaken the child into his own keeping, the assignee's only remedy on his own behalf (if any he have) is by action on the contract.[3] An adjudication of the appropriate tribunal on the question of the custody of an infant child, brought up on *habeas corpus*, may be pleaded as *res adjudicata*.[4]

Nor can the father, under the common-law rule, divest himself even by contract with the mother, of the custody of his children, though he allows them to remain with her for several years.[5] Yet, the rule in some States is more

[1] Pool *v.* Gott, 14 Law Rep. 269, before Shaw C. J. And see *In re* Goodenough, 19 Wis. 274; Commonwealth *v.* Hamilton, 6 Mass. 273.

[2] Mayne *v.* Baldwin, 1 Halst. Ch. 454; People *v.* Mercein, 8 Paige Ch. 67; s. c. 3 Hill, 408; State *v.* Libbey, 44 N. H. 321; State *v.* Scott, 30 N. H. 274, establish that a parol transfer is insufficient. See 2 Kent Com. 205. As to the schoolmaster's power of inflicting chastisement, see State *v.* Pendergrass, 2 Dev. & Bat. 365; Lander *v.* Seaver, 32 N. H. 114.

[3] Farnsworth *v.* Richardson, 35 Maine, 267. And see Commonwealth *v.* M'Keagy, 1 Ashm. 248; Lowry *v.* Button, Wright, 330.

[4] Mercein *v.* The People, 25 Wend. 64.

[5] Torrington *v.* Norwich, 21 Conn. 543; People *v.* Mercein, 3 Hill, 408. And see Vansittart *v.* Vansittart, 4 Kay & J. 62; Johnson *v.* Terry, 34 Conn. 259.

flexible. In Massachusetts, it appears that the father may surrender the care and custody of a child to the mother.[1] He may, of course, emancipate the child, and give him a right to his own earnings, as will be seen hereafter. And in New Hampshire a father may surrender, by indenture, to strangers, his parental rights to the custody and services of his infant child, although the deed be not in form such as is essential between master and apprentice.[2]

Next to the right of custody of infants comes that of the value of their labor and services. The father, says Blackstone, has the benefit of his children's labor while they live with him and are maintained by him; and this is no more than he is entitled to from his apprentices or servants.[3] This right, like that of custody, rests upon the parental duty of maintenance, and furnishes some compensation to the father for his own services rendered the child.

Whether this right remains absolute in the father until the child has attained full age is apparently a matter of doubt. It is certainly perfect while the period of the child's nurture continues. But if this is all, it can be of little consequence, because the child's labor and services are for that period of little or no value; nor could compensation be thus afforded for the many years when the child was entirely helpless. All will admit that the father's right continues until the child reaches fourteen. And since the father's guardianship by nature extends through the full term of the child's minority; since, too, he may by will place a testamentary guardian of his own choice over the infant; since it is reasonable that the law should set off years of later usefulness against years of earlier helplessness; in short, since the age of majority is fixed as the period when an infant becomes legally emancipated from his father's control; we may fairly assume that, all other things

[1] Wodell *v.* Coggeshall, 2 Met. 89. And see State *v.* Smith, 6 Maine, 402.

[2] State *v.* Barrett, 45 N. H. 15.

[3] 1 Bl. Com. 453; 2 Kent Com. 193.

being equal, the father is actually entitled to the value of his child's labor and services until the latter becomes of age. This is the principle assumed by the elementary writers,[1] and in most of the judicial decisions;[2] though to this opinion Chancellor Kent appears to yield a somewhat doubtful assent.[3]

But the duties and rights of parents are limited, mutually dependent, and in a great degree resulting from one another. When the father has discharged himself of the obligation to support the child, or has obliged the child to support himself, our courts are reluctant to admit his right to the child's services. Under such circumstances, says a New Hampshire court, "there is no principle but that of slavery which continues his right to receive the earnings of his child's labor."[4] Thus if the father should refuse to support a son, deny him a home, force him to labor for his own living, or give him his time, as it is called, the law infers an emancipation, and gives the child the right to his own earnings. Of emancipation we shall speak hereafter.

If a father place his minor son to work for another, for no illegal purpose, and without knowledge and consent of his being illegally employed, he is still entitled to compensation for his son's services. As where a son is employed by another in unlawfully selling intoxicating liquors, the father being ignorant of the nature and character of the services while they were being performed.[5] Were the father privy to the offence he could not recover.

The right of action to recover for the services of a minor is

[1] 1 Bl. Com. 453; Reeve Dom. Rel. 290.

[2] Day *v.* Everett, 7 Mass. 145; Benson *v.* Remington, 2 Mass. 113; Plummer *v.* Webb, 4 Mason, 380; Gale *v.* Parrot, 1 N. H. 28; Nightingale *v.* Withington, 15 Mass. 272; The Etna, Ware, 462.

[3] 2 Kent Com. 193.

[4] Woods J. in Jenness *v.* Emerson, 15 N. H. 489. But in this case the principle seems to be assumed that the parent's obligation to support and his right to receive wages commence together, continue together, and ought always to terminate together.

[5] Emery *v.* Kempton, 2 Gray, 257.

then presumed to be in his father.[1] And it is held that the agreement of a father, merely in consideration of natural love and affection, to permit a minor son who lives under the paternal roof as a member of the family to cultivate a crop and receive its proceeds, is revocable by him at any time before the crop is gathered and disposed of by the son.[2] And the father may charge services rendered by his son, as a master for his apprentice or hired laborer, and consider it his own work.[3] The right to sue for services *quantum meruit* is likewise *prima facie* in the father.[4] And if a child being of full age chooses to remain with the father, or is imbecile and needs to be harbored at home, the relation may continue so as to entitle the parent, either as such or on the principle of master and servant, to recover for the child's wages in the same manner.[5] Female children will often thus remain in a family.

The parent may voluntarily relinquish the right to his child's earnings and may permit the child to earn for himself, receive his earnings, and appropriate them at pleasure. And if the parent authorize a third person to employ and pay the child, payment to the child and not to the parent will be a sufficient discharge. Such an agreement may be in express terms or it may be implied from circumstances.[6] An American court favorably regards contracts of this nature, for the child's benefit, as they are in conformity with the spirit of free institutions.[7] And a New York statute provides that unless the parent notifies the minor's employer within thirty days after the commencement of service that he claims the wages, payment to

[1] Dufield *v.* Cross, 12 Ill. 397; Shute *v.* Dorr, 5 Wend. 204. See Campbell *v.* Cooper, 34 N. H. 49.

[2] Stovall *v.* Johnson, 17 Ala. 14.

[3] Brown *v.* Ramsay, 5 Dutch. 117. But see Jones *v.* Buckley, 19 Ala. 604.

[4] Letts *v.* Brooks, Hill & Den. 36; Van Dorn *v.* Young, 13 Barb. 286.

[5] Brown *v.* Ramsay, 5 Dutch. 117; Overseers of Alexandria *v.* Overseers of Bethlehem, 1 Harr. 122.

[6] See Campbell *v.* Cooper, 34 N. H. 49; Jenness *v.* Emerson, 15 N. H. 489; Cloud *v.* Hamilton, 11 Humph. 104; Armstrong *v.* McDonald, 10 Barb. 300.

[7] Snediker *v.* Everingham, 3 Dutch. 143; Cloud *v.* Hamilton, 11 Humph. 104.

the minor will be good.[1] When the parent is a pauper and is maintained by a town, such town is held not entitled to the earnings of a minor child who is not himself a pauper.[2] The father may by his own delay forfeit the right of action for his son's wages; as where the minor agrees to work at certain monthly wages to be paid to himself, and the father, knowing of the agreement, gives no notice of his objection, but waits until the work has been done and payment is made to the child, before making a demand.[3] But if the father has given seasonable notice of his dissent and demand, to the stranger hiring his son, the fact that the son continues to work against his express dissent, and that the stranger notified him to come and take his son away and he neglected to do so, will not preclude him from recovering the wages.[4] Nor does the fact that the son has agreed with his father to buy out his time for the remainder of his minority by paying a certain sum therefor, which has not been paid, prevent the father from recovering his wages pending the payment of such sum.[5]

Whatever private arrangement may exist between the father and his son which is not brought to the employer's notice cannot be set up to justify payment to the minor himself. As for instance, where father and son had secretly agreed that the latter should have his own wages.[6] And the publication by a parent of a notice of his son's emancipation more liberal to the latter than the actual agreement between them, will not, as against one who has no knowledge of the publication, estop the father from insisting on such right to his son's wages as the contract between them actually gives.[7] But the usage of father and son may be alleged.[8]

[1] N. Y. Laws, 1850, p. 579. And see Everett *v.* Sherfey, 1 Iowa, 356.

[2] Jenness *v.* Emerson, 15 N. H. 486.

[3] Smith *v.* Smith, 30 Conn. 111.

[4] Ib.

[5] Cahill *v.* Patterson, 30 Vt. 592. And see Kauffelt *v.* Moderwell, 21 Penn. St. 222; Cloud *v.* Hamilton, 11 Humph. 104; Whiting *v.* Earle, 3 Pick. 201.

[6] Kauffelt *v.* Moderwell, 21 Penn. St. 222.

[7] Mason *v.* Hutchins & Co., 32 Vt. 780.

[8] Perlinau *v.* Phelps, 25 Vt. 478; Canovar *v.* Cooper, 3 Barb. 115.

One who employs the minor son of another cannot be liable to his father as for breach of contract, because of such minor's delinquencies. Hence, it is held, that where the father contracts that his son shall work for a specified time and price, and the son leaves his employer before the expiration of the time, against his father's will, the father can only recover for the time of actual employment, although the employer assented to the departure.[1]

Money entrusted to a minor son for a specific purpose and applied by him, without his father's assent, in compounding for his own crime, may be recovered by the father from the receiver. But if the payment was assented to by the father, or if the money was paid solely as civil damages in settlement of a trespass, whether with or without such assent, the father cannot afterward recover it from the receiver.[2]

The minor who is released from his father's service stands, as to his contracts for labor either with strangers or with him, upon the same footing as if he had arrived at full age.[3] After such release the father may contract to employ and pay the child for his services, and will be bound like any stranger to fulfil his agreement.[4]

Nor are the rights of a mother, in respect to the child's earnings, regarded as equivalent to those of a father, even though she be the only surviving parent.[5]

Wages due a minor seaman belong to his father. And payment of such wages to the son, although he was known by his employer to have been less than twenty-one at the time of making the contract, furnishes no defence to an action by the father, who had no knowledge of his hiring until after the wages

1 Hennessy *v.* Stewart, 31 Vt. 486.

2 Burnham *v.* Holt, 14 N. H. 367.

3 Steel *v.* Steel, 12 Penn. St. 64; Hall *v.* Hall, 44 N. H. 293.

4 Hall *v.* Hall, 44 N. H. 293.

5 1 Bl. Com. 453; Commonwealth *v.* Murray, 4 Binn. 487; Riley *v.* Jameson, 3 N. H. 29; People *v.* Mercein, 3 Hill, 400; Morris *v.* Law, 4 Stew. & Port. 123; Pray *v.* Gorham, 31 Me. 240; Snediker *v.* Everingham, 3 Dutch. 143. See Clapp *v.* Greene, 10 Met. 439. See Campbell *v.* Campbell, 3 Stockt. 268.

were earned.[1] Nor is the father in such case affected by the terms of the shipping articles, because it is an express contract which as against him the son has no right to make; he can claim under a *quantum meruit* for the value of the services. But mercantile custom may determine certain questions as to the remedy.[2] As to enlistments in the army or navy of the United States, the laws contemplate that the contract is personal and for the benefit of infants; and pay, bounties, and prize-money in general, though earned under State laws, are held to belong to the son, and not to the father.[3]

If a minor son abscond from his father's house, and enter the service of one who for his labor furnishes the infant a reasonable support, the parent cannot recover the son's wages without deducting the amount of the expense of such support.[4]

Where a father furnishes his son with clothing, such clothing is the property of the father, and he may maintain an action for the loss and injury thereof; but where he intrusts his son with a sum of money for general purposes, without specific directions as to its appropriation, and the son buys clothing with it, such clothing is not the property of the father.[5] The parent may give articles by parol to his child, and afterwards resume them, there being no consideration.[6]

A father has a pecuniary interest in the life of a minor child, and an insurance of the life of such child is not within the rule of law by which wager policies are declared void.[7]

As a rule, the parent has no rights over his child's general property. The law treats legacies, gifts, distributive shares, and the like, which may vest in a person during minority, as his own property; and the modern practice is to require the ap-

1 White *v.* Henry, 24 Me. 531. See Weeks *v.* Holmes, 12 Cush. 215.

2 Bishop *v.* Shepherd, 23 Pick. 492.

3 United States *v.* Bainbridge, 1 Mason, 84; Banks *v.* Conant, 14 Allen, 497; Mears *v.* Bickford, 55 Me. 528; Carson *v.* Watts, 3 Doug. 350.

4 Huntoon *v.* Hazelton, 20 N. H. 388.

5 Dickinson *v.* Winchester, 4 Cush. 114; Parmelee *v.* Smith, 21 Ill. 620.

6 Cranz *v.* Kroger, 22 Ill. 74; Stovall *v.* Johnson, 17 Ala. 14.

7 Mitchell *v.* Union, &c., Ins. Co. 45 Me. 104.

pointment of a guardian in such cases, to manage the estate until the child comes of age.[1] Under no pretext may the father appropriate such funds to himself, or use them to pay his own debts. The same may be said of the child's lands.

The parent has also a right of action in certain cases, where the infant child has suffered wrong. This subject will be discussed in the succeeding chapter.

[2] Keeler *v.* Fassett, 21 Vt. 539; Jackson *v.* Combs, 7 Cow. 36; Miles *v.* Boyden, 3 Pick. 213; Isaacs *v.* Boyd, 5 Port. 388; Kenningham *v.* M'Laughlin, 3 Monr. 30. And see Guardian and Ward, *infra*. But see Selden's Appeal, 31 Conn. 548.

CHAPTER IV.

THE PARENT'S RIGHT OF ACTION FOR THE CHILD'S INJURIES.

WHERE a child suffers wrong, he has his action for the personal injury. But besides this the parent may usually claim indemnity for loss of his child's services, to which should be added the incidental expenses incurred in consequence of the injury. Hence arises a cause of action in the parent *per quod*, the foundation of which is a loss of the child's services.

There are various tortious acts, by which a parent may be deprived of his child's services; and the law is liberal in securing compensation for the injury. But in this connection the parental relation is not strictly to be considered; the rule being that a parent has no remedy for an injury done to his child by the wrongful act of another, unless that child can be treated in law as his servant.[1]

This is laid down positively as the English rule. Thus, in a case where the plaintiff brought an action against the defendant for carelessly driving over and injuring the plaintiff's child, so that the plaintiff was obliged to expend a large sum of money in doctors and nurses, and it appeared that the child was only two years and a half old, and incapable of performing any act of service, it was held that the parent's action was not maintainable.[2] "The gist of the action is the loss of services, and therefore, though the relation of parent and child subsists, yet, if the child is incapable of performing any services the founda-

[1] 2 Hilliard Torts, 518–529; Addison Torts, 697; Grinnell *v.* Wells, 7 M. & Gr. 1041; Rogers *v.* Smith, 17 Ind. 323; Hatfield *v.* Roper, 21 Wend. 615; Dennis *v.* Clark, 2 Cush. 347.

[2] Hall *v.* Hollander, 7 Dowl. & Ry. 133; 4 Barn. & Cress. 660.

tion of the action fails."[1] And it is doubtful whether the father, as such, can even maintain a special action for expenses necessarily incurred by him in having so young a child cured of the injury.[2]

In this country, the rule appears to be more liberal towards the parent. A New York court observes, that it is quite questionable whether the father can be deprived of his right to sue for the loss of services, on account of the child's youth; though, of course, the right may be forfeited by the parent's culpable negligence.[3] And in Massachusetts it is decided that if an infant child, a member of his father's household, and too young to be capable of rendering any service to his father, is wounded or otherwise injured by a third person, or by a mischievous animal owned by a third person, under such circumstances as to give the child himself an action against such person, for the personal injury, and the father is thereby necessarily put to trouble and expense in the care and cure of the child, he may maintain an action against such person for indemnity. The court laid down the rule, however, with much caution.[4]

Statutes enlarging the rights of widows, dependent parents and others, in torts occasioned by the negligence of railroad corporations and other common carriers, are to be found in England and America. Under such statutes it is frequently provided that where a child is thus killed, the child's administrator may sue for the parent's benefit. The English statute, known as Lord Campbell's Act, 9 & 10 Vict. ch. 93, has given rise to suits of this kind; but the rule is laid down that such actions are not maintainable without some evidence of actual pecuniary damage, some loss of service.[5] But the damages are to be calculated in reference to a reasonable expectation of pecuniary benefit, as of

[1] Bayley J. in ib.

[2] See Addison Torts, 697; Grinnell *v.* Wells, 8 Scott N. R. 741. *Contra,* Hall *v.* Hollander, *supra.*

[3] Hartfield *v.* Roper, 21 Wend. 615.

[4] Dennis *v.* Clark, 2 Cush. 347.

[5] Duckworth *v.* Johnson, 4 Hurl. & Nor. 653.

right or otherwise, from the continuance of the life ; and where the father is old and infirm, and the son had been earning good wages, though not at the precise period of death, such circumstances are to be favorably considered in estimating the amount of damages.[1]

So statutes may affect the parent's right or remedy, in other respects. Thus, in Massachusetts, the owner of a vicious dog is made liable to the parent for double damages.[2]

Trespass lies *per quod* for loss of services occasioned by assault and battery of the child.[3] The true question seems to be, whether a loss of service was consequent upon the injury. For assault and battery on the high seas, there is likewise a remedy in admiralty.[4]

If the parent has finally relinquished his right to the services of his child, he cannot claim such damages ; they belong to the master, if any one ; but this question of relinquishment is for determination on the usual principles.[5] And where an injury is inflicted upon a child while living with and in the service of another, the proper remedy of the father is trespass on the case for the reversion, as it were, of the child's services ; as where a person who hired the son of another, put him upon a vicious horse, so that he was thrown and had his leg broken.[6]

The death of the child, after the injury, though it may, on familiar principles, terminate the right to sue for the child's tort, does not affect the parent's consequential right of action. The death occurring before the commencement of the suit, if in consequence of the injury, only aggravates the parent's remedy ; if the death is occasioned by other causes, it leaves the remedy as it stood before.[7]

1 Ib.; Franklin *v.* South-Eastern R. R. Co., 3 Hurl. & Nor. 211.

2 M'Carthy *v.* Guild, 12 Met. 291. And see Kennard *v.* Burton, 25 Me. 39.

3 Hammer *v.* Pierce, 5 Harring. 171; Hoover *v.* Heim, 7 Watts, 62; Plummer *v.* Webb, Ware, 75; Cowden *v.* Wright, 24 Wend. 429. But as to indictments it is different. See Hearst *v.* Sybert, Cheve. 177.

4 Plummer *v.* Webb, Ware, 75.

5 Arnold *v.* Norton, 25 Conn. 92.

6 Wilt *v.* Vickers, 8 Watts, 227.

7 Plummer *v.* Webb, Ware, 80; Winsmore *v.* Greenbank, Bull N. P. 78.

Every person who knowingly and designedly interrupts the relation subsisting between parent and child, by procuring the child to depart from the parent's service, or by harboring and keeping him after he has quitted his home, commits a wrongful act, for which he is responsible to the parent. The offence is known as enticement, and this applies to the relation of master and servant. In such cases, the parent sues on a principle analogous to that of the master: namely, on the ground of an alleged loss of service; or possibly in trespass *vi et armis* upon the more reasonable allegation of loss of the child's society.[1] And this action will lie on behalf of the mother after the father's death.[2] The *quo animo* of the defendant in such suits is always material. To afford shelter is one thing; to encourage filial disobedience another. The mere employment of a runaway child does not amount to enticement.[3] But where it appears that the defendant, knowing that the son had absconded from his father, boarded him in his family and allowed him to work on his farm as he pleased, doing this with the intention of aiding or encouraging, or with the knowledge that it aids and encourages the son to keep away from the father, he is liable to this action.[4]

A parent may maintain a libel in the admiralty for the wrongful abduction of his child, a minor, and carrying him beyond the seas.[5] Abduction is an offence similar to enticement, but implying the use of force rather than persuasion. Where father and mother live apart, the mother's assent to the child's enlistment as a sailor may sometimes affect the father's remedies.[6]

1 Lumley *v.* Gye, 2 El. & Bl. 224; Kirkpatrick *v.* Lockhart, 2 Brev. 276; 1 Woodes, Lec. 451; Sargent *v.* Mathewson, 38 N. H. 54; 3 Bl. Com. 140.

2 Jones *v.* Tevis, 4 Litt. 25.

3 Keane *v.* Boycott, 2 H. Bl. 511; Butterfield *v.* Ashley, 6 Cush. 249.

4 Sargent *v.* Mathewson, 38 N. H. 54; Everett *v.* Sherfey, 1 Iowa, 356.

5 Steele *v.* Thacher, Ware, 91; Plummer *v.* Webb, 4 Mason, 380. See Cutting *v.* Seabury, Sprague, 522; Weeks *v.* Holmes, 12 Cush. 215.

6 Wodell *v.* Coggeshall, 2 Met. 89. And see Worcester *v.* Marchant, 14 Pick. 510.

There must be a reasonable limit to suits by the parent for loss of his child's society and services. Hence it is now well settled in this country that the parent cannot sue for enticing his child into a marriage against the parent's consent.[1] For a forcible abduction, resulting in an imperfect marriage, and aggravated cases of a like nature, where, in fact, there is not a valid union, there might be a remedy. So the marriage statutes not unfrequently provide penalties to be meted out to offenders, who aid and encourage infants in evading statutes requiring the consent of parents or guardians. But for drawing children of suitable age into a marriage which pleases themselves, the law affords no redress; nor can it punish for the sake of parental discipline. And though the match be unhappy, yet marriage must supersede the filial relation.[2] Nor can a parent sue a school teacher, school trustees, or others, for excluding his children from school; the right of action, if any, being in the child;[3] and there being no real loss of services consequent upon the affront. In short, the general rule is to place all actions by the parent on the sole ground of value of the lost services of the child, who is regarded as a servant for the purpose of the suit; not to punish, for the sake of the father, those who wrong the child.[4] And the most liberal view of the subject indicated by American courts, is to regard the parent as in a measure entitled to the society and solace of his own children; though this reasonable position is not clearly supported by authority.

Even in seduction suits the same technical principle is rather

1 Jones *v.* Tevis, 4 Litt. 25; Hervey *v.* Moseley, 7 Gray, 479; Goodwin *v.* Thompson, 2 Greene (Iowa), 329. But see Hills *v.* Hobert, 2 Root, 48.

2 Marrying a parent's son and heir was a civil injury at common law during the continuance of the military tenures, for thereby the parent lost the value of his child's marriage; but this injury ceased long ago, with the right on which it was founded. See 3 Bl. Com. 140, with notes.

3 Spear *v.* Cummings, 23 Pick. 224; Donahoe *v.* Richards, 38 Me. 376; Boyd *v.* Blaisdell, 15 Ind. 73; Stephenson *v.* Hall, 14 Barb. 222.

4 Hall *v.* Hollander, 4 B. & C. 660; Grinnell *v.* Wells, 7 M. & Gr. 1033; Eager *v.* Grimwood, 1 Exch. 61. But see *dictum* in Stephenson *v.* Hall, 14 Barb. 222.

absurdly, though not always unkindly, applied. The foundation of the action by a father to recover damages against the wrongdoer for the seduction of his daughter, has been uniformly placed, from the earliest times, not upon the seduction itself, which is the wrongful act of the defendant, but upon the loss of service of the daughter, in which he is supposed to have a legal right or interest.[1] And without some allegation and proof of loss of service the action is not maintainable.

Thus where it was alleged by the father that his daughter was a poor person, maintaining herself by her labor and personal services, and not of sufficient ability to maintain herself otherwise; and that by being debauched she became unable to work, and had to be maintained by her father at considerable expense; all this was held insufficient allegation of loss of service.[2] So it is not enough to show that the father had apprenticed his daughter to the defendant to learn millinery, and had paid him a large sum of money to instruct her in a trade, but that the defendant seduced her and rendered her unable, by reason of pregnancy, to learn the trade.[3] The evidence of service may be very slight; and the making tea, milking cows, or doing any household work at the command of the parent, is esteemed quite sufficient to constitute the relationship of master and servant, when the girl is residing with her father and mother;[4] and the right of action once clear, damages far in excess of the loss of service are recoverable. Thus will justice, seeing the goal clearly, drive straight towards it, regardless of obstructions; either finding an avenue or making one.

But to render this action maintainable the parent must have

[1] Grinnell *v.* Wells, 7 M. & Gr. 1033; Eager *v.* Grimwood, 1 Exch. 61; Van Horn *v.* Freeman, 1 Halst. 322; McDaniel *v.* Edward, 7 Ired. 408; Sutton *v.* Huffman, 32 N. J. 58; Knight *v.* Wilcox, 14 N. Y. 413; Bartley *v.* Richtmeyer, 4 Comst. 38.

[2] Grinnell *v.* Wells, ib.

[3] Harris *v.* Butler, 2 M. & W. 539.

[4] 1 Addison Torts, 698, 701; Bennett *v.* Allcott, 2 T. R. 166; Thompson *v.* Ross, 5 Hurl. & Nor. 16; Manvell *v.* Thomson, 2 Car. & P. 303; Vossel *v.* Cole, 10 Mis. 634; 2 Kent Com. 205, last ed., and cases cited.

a genuine right to his daughter's services ; however slight the services which may be exacted. If therefore the daughter, at the time she was seduced, was at the head of an establishment of her own, and her father was living with her as a visitor in her own house, she cannot be treated as holding the subordinate position of a servant, and the action will not lie.[1] Nor can a parent sue, where the child is really in the service of another, and, by permission of her mistress, comes home to render slight assistance from time to time.[2] Nor where the child is seduced while in the service of another and then returns home and remains there in a state of pregnancy.[3] But if she is away only on a temporary visit, and still forms part of her father's family, and makes herself serviceable to him while she is at home, such temporary absence constitutes no impediment to an action by the father for damages.[4] In a word, the question is whether there was at the time the injury was committed a *bona fide* relation of constructive service between parent and child, which suffered by the wrongful act of the defendant.

There is a late New Jersey case where it appeared in evidence that the daughter was about twenty-two years of age when seduced, and was living a part of the time with her brother, who occupied a farm about a mile from her father, and part of the time with her father. While the rule was fully approved that the father and daughter must have stood in the relation of master and servant at the time the injury was committed, it was further held that it was not necessary that the daughter should be in the *actual service* of the father at the time of the seduction, if the relation of master and servant then existed between them; in other words, that the service rendered need not be house service, nor service from day to day, but that any accustomed service lost by the injury would sustain the action.[5]

1 Manley *v.* Field, 7 C. B. (N. S.) 96.

2 Thompson *v.* Ross, 5 Hurl. & Nor. 16. And see Blaymire *v.* Haley, 6 M. & W. 55.

3 Davies *v.* Williams, 10 Q. B. 725.

4 Griffiths *v.* Teetgen, 15 C. B. 344; 28 E. L. & Eq. 371. See, further, 1 Addison Torts, 698.

5 Sutton *v.* Huffman, 32 N. J. 58. And see Greenwood *v.* Greenwood, 28 Md.

In a very recent English case the plaintiff's daughter, being under age, left his house and went into service. After nearly a month the master dismissed her at a day's notice, and the next day, on her way home to her father's house, the defendant seduced her. It was held that as soon as the real service was terminated by the master, whether rightfully or wrongfully, the girl intending to return home, the right of the father to her services revived, and there was, therefore, sufficient evidence of service to maintain an action for the seduction.[1] This, the court admitted, was carrying the doctrine of constructive service very far. "The action, no doubt, is founded on the special ground of loss of service (this is not very creditable, perhaps, to our law), but the action is substantially for the aggravated injury that the father has sustained in the seduction of the child."[2]

It is not necessary that the daughter should be under age in order that the parent may maintain the action for seduction. The important question is, whether emancipation in fact had taken place at the time of the injury; for if the relation of master and servant exists between the father and his grown-up daughter, however this relation may have been created, the right of action is complete.[3] And even where a married woman, separated from her husband, returned to her father's house and lived with him, performing various acts of service, it was held that as against a wrong-doer it was sufficient to prove that there was the relationship of master and servant *de*

370; Emery *v.* Gowen, 4 Me. 33. In these and some other cases, there is a manifest tendency to exclude presumption of emancipation, so as to leave the parent's remedy unimpaired. The rule in Virginia is more strict. Lee *v.* Hodges, 13 Gratt. 726. In New York the doctrine of Martin *v.* Payne, 9 Johns. 387, and other cases, led to much confusion, by permitting suits to be brought where there was in reality no loss of service sustained. But in the later cases the courts have returned to the strictness of the English rule. Bartley *v.* Richtmeyer, 4 Comst. 38. And c. f. earlier and later notes to 2 Kent Com. 205.

1 Terry *v.* Hutchinson, Law Rep. 3 Q. B. 599 (1868).

2 Per Cockburn C. J. ib.

3 1 Addison Torts, 700; Sutton *v.* Huffman, 32 N. J. 58; Greenwood *v.* Greenwood, 28 Md. 370; Stevenson *v.* Belknap, 6 Iowa, 97.

facto.[1] So where one stands *in loco parentis*, he may recover damages, as an actual parent would; as in the case of an orphan living with a relation, or a friend and benefactor, and rendering such domestic attendance and obedience as is usually rendered by a daughter to her father.[2] But the parent cannot maintain an action for the seduction of a daughter over twenty-one and working out on her own account.[3] And it is held that a mother cannot maintain an action for the seduction of her daughter during the life of the father, though the illicit offspring be not born until after the father's death.[4]

The wrongful act for which the parent sues must be the natural and direct cause of the injury for which damages are sought, and the damages recoverable its necessary and proximate consequence. To this principle is to be referred a curious case in New York.[5] But mental illness directly resulting from the injury is, of itself, sufficient to support an action for loss of services.[6]

Where a person hires a girl as a servant for the purpose of withdrawing her from her family and seducing her, this is fraud, and the parent's right of action is not thereby forfeited; for in such a case the new relation of master and servant is not *bona fide* created, and the former relation may be held to have continued.[7]

As to the amount of damages, cases of seduction stand on a peculiar footing. The ground of action is the loss of services; yet the rule is well established that neither this nor the

[1] Harper *v.* Luffkin, 7 B. & C. 387.

[2] 1 Addison Torts, 700; Irwin *v.* Dearman, 11 East, 23; Edmondson *v.* Machell, 2 T. R. 4; Williams *v.* Hutchinson, 3 Comst. 312; Maguinay *v.* Saudek, 5 Sneed, 146; Ball *v.* Bruce, 21 Ill. 161.

[3] George *v.* Van Horn, 9 Barb. 533.

[4] Vossel *v.* Cole, 10 Mis. 634. And see George *v.* Van Horn, 9 Barb. 523.

[5] Knight *v.* Wilcox, 14 N. Y. 413. See Eager *v.* Grimwood, 1 Exch. 61; Boyle *v.* Brandon, 13 M. & W. 738; Reddie *v.* Scoolt, Peake, 240; 1 Addison Torts, 701, as to the various grounds of defence in seduction suits.

[6] Manvell *v.* Thompson, 2 Car. & P. 303; Seager *v.* Sligerland, 2 Caines, 219.

[7] Speight *v.* Oliviera, 2 Stark. 435; 2 Kent Com. 205; 1 Addison Torts, 699; Dain *v.* Wyckoff, 18 N. Y. 45.

medical expenses are all that the parent can recover. Lord Ellenborough, in his day, declared the principle inveterate, and not to be shaken, that, in estimating damages, the jury might go beyond the mere loss of service, and give damages for the distress and anxiety of mind which the parent has sustained in being deprived of the society and comfort of his child.[1] So must the situation in life and circumstances of the parties be taken into consideration.[2] "In point of form," observes Lord Eldon, "the action only purports to give a recompense for loss of service; but we cannot shut our eyes to the fact that it is an action brought by a parent for an injury to her child, and the jury may take into their consideration all that she can feel from the nature of the loss. They may look upon her as a parent losing the comfort, as well as the service, of her daughter, in whose virtue she can feel no consolation; and as the parent of other children whose morals may be corrupted by her example." [3] These principles are applied both in England and America.

In other suits, such as for enticement, the measure of damages applied is liberal, though the rule is somewhat conflicting in different States. It is a general principle, that where servants are enticed away, or forcibly abducted, the jury may award ample compensation for all the damage resulting from the wrongful act.[4] A parent can recover damages for the prospective value of the services of a young child injured or killed by an act of negligence.[5] Medical expenses for the care

[1] Irwin *v.* Dearman, 11 East, 23. [2] Andrews *v.* Askey, 8 Car. & P. 9.

[3] Bedford *v.* M'Kowl, 3 Esp. 120; Robinson *v.* Burton, 5 Harring. 335; Dain *v.* Wyckoff, 18 N. Y. 45. See further on this subject, Tullidge *v.* Wade, 3 Wils. 18; Dodd *v.* Norris, 3 Campb. 520; White *v.* Campbell, 13 Gratt. 573; Sellars *v.* Kinder, 1 Head. 134; Bracy *v.* Kibbe, 31 Barb. 273. Seduction may be a statutory misdemeanor. State *v.* Bierce, 27 Conn. 319. See 1 Addison Torts, 703; Eager *v.* Grimwood, 1 Exch. 61; Verry *v.* Watkins, 7 Car. & P. 308; Richardson *v.* Fouts, 11 Ind. 466; Reed *v.* Williams, 5 Sneed, 580; Bolton *v.* Miller, 6 Ind. 262; Zerfing *v.* Mourer, 2 Greene (Iowa), 520; Vossel *v.* Cole, 10 (Mis.) 634; *n.* 2 Kent Com. 205, last ed.

[4] Gunter *v.* Astor, 4 Moore, 15; 1 Addison Torts, 704; Lumley *v.* Gye, 2 El. & Bl. 216; Magee *v.* Holland, 3 Dutch. 86.

[5] Drew *v.* Sixth Avenue R. R. Co., 26 N. Y. 49; Ford *v.* Monroe, 20 Wend.

and cure of the child are, of course, recoverable. And even the expense of the mother's sickness which was caused, in an extreme case, by the shock to her feelings, is held to be a proper item of special damage.[1] So, it would seem, are the costs of prosecuting the suit.[2] But the negligence of parents, having the care of a young child, will defeat their right of action, if not that on the child's own behalf.[3] Nor can the parent recover for lacerated feelings, as well as for other injuries to the child, as in seduction suits.[4]

The question may sometimes be asked, how far a father is responsible, in damages, for the torts and frauds of his infant child. We have already seen that the husband's responsibility for his wife's injuries at the common law is founded upon his right, by marriage, to her entire property. Very different is the relation of parent and child, where, it is now plain, the father has little more than the right to claim his child's wages, so far as the infant's property is concerned. Yet some have been misled into the belief that the two cases are entirely analogous; and they would hold the father liable for his son's wrongful acts, as a husband for the wife. It is held in Pennsylvania, that the father may be sued in trespass for an injury committed by his son, when they ride together in the father's team, and the act is committed in the latter's presence.[5] Whether the principle can be safely carried farther, is extremely doubtful. In Missouri, it is decided that a father is not responsible for an assault committed by his infant son.[6] The same rule, with more caution, has been applied in New York,

210; Hoover *v.* Heim, 7 Watts, 62; Franklin *v.* South-Eastern R. R. Co., 3 Hurl. & Nor. 211. And see *supra*, p. 353. But see Williams *v.* Hutchinson, 3 Comst. 314.

[1] Ford *v.* Monroe, 20 Wend. 210.

[2] Wilt *v.* Vickers, 8 Watts, 227.

[3] Kreig *v.* Wells, 1 E. D. Smith, 74; Glassey *v.* Hestonville, &c. R. R. Co., 57 Penn. St. 172.

[4] Penn. R. R. Co. *v.* Kelly, 31 Penn. St. 372; Cowden *v.* Wright, 24 Wend. 429.

[5] Strohl *v.* Levan, 39 Penn. St. 177. And see Lashbrook *v.* Patten, 1 Duvall, 316.

[6] Baker *v.* Haldeman, 24 Mis. 219.

in a case where it was shown that a minor daughter, in her father's absence, and without his authority or approval, wilfully set his dog, not ordinarily a vicious animal, upon the plaintiff's hog, which was thereby bitten and killed.[1]

For such injuries an infant is answerable at law, out of his own estate; at least, if he is old enough to have known better.[2] But how as to the parent's liability? The principles of the Roman law cannot be cited to much advantage, in support of such liability, on the score of agency, or otherwise; since under that system, the child was little better than the slave of his father; and even as to slaves, it was considered at the time of the Institutes, that it would be very unjust, when a servant does a wrongful act, to make the master lose any thing more than the servant himself.[3] The modern rule of the civil law, in European countries, is to make every person responsible for injuries caused by the act of persons and things under his dominion; but a father incurs no responsibility for the act of his minor child, if he can prove that he was not able to prevent the act which gives rise to the liability.[4]

This point received some attention in a late English case, where the father of a young man, about seventeen or eighteen, was sued for trespass and false imprisonment. The plaintiff was "property-man" at a theatre, of which the defendant was lessee. The young man, minor son of the defendant, acted as his father's treasurer. The plaintiff, in his character of property-man, presented to the treasurer an account, containing some wrongful items of disbursement. The defendant, conceiving this to be an intentional fraud on the part of the plaintiff, dismissed him from his employment. His son, thereupon, without consulting the father, indiscreetly caused the plaintiff

[1] Tifft *v.* Tifft, 4 Denio, 175. And see McManus *v.* Crickett, 1 East, 106; Foster *v.* Essex Bank, 17 Mass. 479.

[2] Campbell *v.* Stakes, 2 Wend. 137; Bullock *v.* Babcock, 3 ib. 391.

[3] Smith's Dict. Greek & Roman Antiq. "Noxalis Actio." Inst. lib. 4, tit. 8, by Saunders.

[4] Civil Code France, Art. 1384; Cleaveland *v.* Mayo, 19 La. 414. See Baker *v.* Haldeman, 24 Mis. 219.

to be apprehended by a policeman, and taken to the station on a charge of obtaining money by false pretences. The plaintiff went before a magistrate, and was remanded, but was ultimately discharged. After the remand, the son told his father what he had done; the latter did not prohibit him from proceeding in the matter, but said that as the son had begun it, he would not interfere. The court decided that these facts showed neither a previous authority nor subsequent ratification by the father, sufficient to render him liable for his son's conduct, and on that ground dismissed the suit.[1]

The opinions of the several judges in this case, though expressed by way of *dicta*, exhibit considerable reluctance to hold the father liable, as a trespasser for his son's torts. Says Willes J., "The tendency of juries, where persons under age have incurred debts, or committed wrongs, to make their relatives pay, should, in my opinion, be checked by the courts. No man ought, as a general rule, to be responsible for acts not his own."[2] And says the chief justice: "Suppose the son had knocked the plaintiff down, and the father had said, 'I think it served him right,' would that be such a ratification of the son's act as to make the father liable as a trespasser?"[3]

[1] Moon *v.* Towers, 8 C. B. (N. S.) 611.

[2] Per Willis J., approved by Byles J. ib. Williams J. *dub.*

[3] Per Erle C. J. ib. As to the injuries of a servant, and his master's liability, see "Master and Servant," *infra.*

CHAPTER V.

DUTIES AND RIGHTS OF CHILDREN, WITH REFERENCE TO THEIR PARENTS.

"The duties of children to their parents," says Blackstone, "arise from a principle of natural justice and retribution. For to those who gave us existence we naturally owe subjection and obedience during our minority, and honor and reverence ever after; they who protected the weakness of our infancy are entitled to our protection in the infirmity of their age; they who by sustenance and education have enabled their offspring to prosper, ought in return to be supported by that offspring in case they stand in need of assistance."[1] Upon this principle rest whatever duties are enjoined upon children to their parents by positive law. The Athenians compelled children to provide for their father when fallen into poverty.[2] And Kent, enforcing the same precept, cites several other historical precedents less to the purpose.[3]

Perhaps this principle could not have been better expressed than in these words of Blackstone; but it is to be observed that the obligation, as a legal one, is somewhat vague and indefinite, extending little farther than the succor of parents in distress. Gratitude, certainly, is what all parents true to their trust have the right to expect; but whether it is due to those who were negligent and unfaithful to their offspring may admit at this day of much doubt. In other words, honor and reverence must be awarded somewhat according to one's deserts. The child, when full grown, naturally marries and assumes parental liabilities of his own; and in the usual course of

[1] 1 Bl. Com. 453. [2] 2 Potter's Antiq. 347–351 [3] 2 Kent Com. 207.

things adults, whether fathers or sons, should prudently provide for their future as well as their present wants. Some have thought it the duty of fathers to leave property to their children at their death, — a principle somewhat at conflict with this right to lean upon their children for their own maintenance. Yet exceptional cases must occur where a father, faithful to his own obligations, is yet left, through misfortune, penniless in his old age; and here the voice of nature bids the children aid, comfort, and relieve. Municipal law quickens the child, and says, "If your parent, however vagabond and worthless, becomes unable to maintain himself, the public shall not relieve him as a pauper; you, his children, being of sufficient means, must assume the burden." We speak not here of the mother, whose moral claims upon her children, if her own husband prove incapable, are much stronger; yet the municipal law makes no great distinction on her behalf.

Thus is explained what appears now a well-settled rule at the common law: namely, that there is no legal obligation resting upon a child to support a parent; that, while the parent is bound to supply necessaries to an infant child, an adult child, in the absence of positive statute, is not bound to supply necessaries to his aged parent.[1]

Statutes have been enacted, both in England and most parts of the United States, to enforce this imperfect legal obligation, usually to the extent of relieving cities and towns from the support of paupers. Such is the tenor of the English statutes of 43 Eliz. and 5 Geo. I., to which allusion has already been made; which declare in effect that the children, being of sufficient ability, of poor, old, lame, or impotent persons, not able to maintain themselves, must relieve and maintain them.[2] Ingratitude, to use the word in a more general sense, the parent may punish still further, as other statutes prescribe, by disin-

[1] Reeve Dom. Rel. 284; Rex *v.* Munden, 1 Stra. 190; Edwards *v.* Davis, 16 Johns. 281; Lebanon *v.* Griffin, 45 N. H. 558; Stone *v.* Stone, 32 Conn. 142.

[2] *Supra*, ch. 2; 2 Kent Com. 208.

heriting the undutiful children by will:[1] a punishment found by no means terrible in cases which arise under the statute of Elizabeth. The moral obligation of honor and reverence still remains clear and unquestioned, so far as parental faithfulness has earned it; doubtful in its more extended application; yet always a favorite theme of the poet and dramatist; and never to be lightly esteemed among men.[2]

The law does not imply, then, a promise from the child to pay for necessaries, furnished without his request to an indigent parent; and the natural obligation can only be enforced in the mode pointed out by statute.[3] The promise of a son to pay for past expenditures in relief of an indigent parent is not binding in law.[4] But for necessaries furnished to his parent at his request he is chargeable, as any one else would be.[5] And it is held, further, that where one of several children renders support at the request of the others, they will be liable on an implied promise to contribute.[6] So much, then, for the duties of children.

The rights of children may be considered more at length. We have already had occasion to observe, that the child may to a certain extent bind the parent as agent, not only for necessaries, but in some other transactions, where the child acts within the scope of authority properly conferred. But general transactions require proof of actual authority; and a son has

[1] N. Y. Rev. Sts. p. 614; 2 Kent Com. 208; and see *Ex parte* Hunt, 5 Cow. 284.

[2] No one can read "King Lear" without recognizing the sublimity of an unquestioning faith in this moral duty. Kent (2 Com. 207) quotes the speech of Euryalus in the Æneid; but the instance of *pius Æneas* himself is still stronger, perhaps the strongest, to be found in the classics; devotion to his aged father rendering him more illustrious in song than his heroic achievements, and atoning somewhat for the sin of conjugal unfaithfulness.

[3] Rex *v.* Munden, 1 Stra. 190; Edwards *v.* Davis, 16 Johns. 281; Dawson *v.* Dawson, 12 Iowa, 512. See Johnson *v.* Ballard, 11 Rich. 178.

[4] Mills *v.* Wyman, 3 Pick. 207; Cook *v.* Bradley, 7 Conn. 57. It is otherwise by the Civil Code of Louisiana, art. 245.

[5] Lebanon *v.* Griffin, 45 N. H. 558.

[6] See Stone *v.* Stone, 32 Conn. 142.

ordinarily no more right, as such, to lend his father's goods than a stranger.[1] And proof that in one instance the use by a son of his father's name upon negotiable paper discounted at a bank was known and acquiesced in by the father, is not proof that the son was authorized to sign subsequent notes in the same manner.[2] The principles of agency here applied.

A father may emancipate his child and thus give him a right to his own earnings. What then is emancipation, as used with reference to the child? Plainly, the term emancipation is borrowed from the Roman law; and may be referred to the ancient formality of enfranchisement by the father. This in ancient times was done by an imaginary sale, but Justinian substituted the simpler proceeding of manumission before a magistrate.[3] In Louisiana, the emancipation of minors is expressly recognized and regulated by law.[4] At the English law, the term emancipation is generally used with reference to matters of parochial settlement and the support of paupers.[5] But in American cases it often has a significance more nearly approaching that of the civil law; though the word is used without much regard to precision.

We find in the English books little said as to the emancipation of minor children by their fathers. In fact, the English municipal system is so different from ours, that the paternal authority during the period of minority, except as to custody, gives rise to little controversy. But there is a case where an infant was held not to have been emancipated by his enlistment.[6] And in this and some other instances the principle of emancipation was somewhat discussed; and the doctrine is maintained by Lord Kenyon and others, that during the minority of the child he will remain, under almost any circumstances,

[1] Johnson *v.* Stone, 40 N. H. 197. But see Bennett *v.* Gillett, 3 Min. 423.

[2] Greenfield Bank *v.* Crafts, 2 Allen, 269.

[3] Burrill Law Dict. "Emancipation;" Inst. 1, 12.

[4] Code, art. 367 *et seq.*

[5] See 7 Q. B. 574 *n.*

[6] Rex *v.* Rotherfield Grays, 1 B. & C. 347.

unemancipated; that in fact there can be no emancipation of an infant unless he marries, and so becomes himself the head of a family, or contracts some other relation so as to wholly and permanently exclude the parental control.[1]

Emancipation is not so strictly construed in this country. The American doctrine, as frequently stated, is that a father may "emancipate" his child for the whole remaining period of minority, or for a shorter term; that this emancipation may be by an instrument in writing, by verbal agreement or license, or by implication from his conduct; and that emancipation is valid against creditors, and to some extent against the father.[2] Let us see then, first, how emancipation may in this country be legally brought about; secondly, what is its legal effect.

And first, emancipation may be either by instrument in writing or by parol agreement, or it may be inferred from the conduct of the parent. As to instruments in writing, usually known as indentures, the statutes of the different States are quite explicit; and the same general doctrines apply to children who are bound out as to apprentices generally.[3] But such deeds, so far as they derogate from the child's personal independence and welfare, are not greatly favored; they are usually construed with great strictness as between the minor and his parent, guardian, or master; and the policy of American law is to require the consent of the child himself to the instrument, where he has passed the period of nurture.[4]

Next as to emancipation by parol agreement or license of the parent. In a well-considered Massachusetts case, it is decided

[1] Rex *v.* Roach, 6 T. R. 247; Rex *v.* Wilmington, 5 B. & Ad. 525.

[2] Abbott *v.* Converse, 4 Allen, 530, per Chapman J. See 2 Kent Com. 194 *n.*; Jenney *v.* Alden, 12 Mass. 375; Whiting *v.* Earle, 3 Pick. 201; Burlingame *v.* Burlingame, 7 Cow. 92; Varney *v.* Young, 11 Vt. 258.

[3] 4 Com. Dig. 579; State *v.* Taylor, 2 Penning. 467; Bolton *v.* Miller, 6 Ind. 262. See "Master and Servant," *infra;* Nickerson *v.* Easton, 12 Pick. 110.

[4] The minor child of pauper parents is not emancipated so as to gain a settlement by the indenture of the selectmen. Frankfort *v.* New Vineyard, 48 Maine, 565. Children may be bound out to the Shakers. Curtis *v.* Curtis, 5 Gray, 535; People *v.* Pillow, 1 Sandf. 672.

that the emancipation of a minor child by parol agreement and without consideration is revocable, until acted upon.[1] Yet, there can be little doubt at the present day that a father can verbally sell or give his minor son his time; and that after payment or performance the son is entitled to his earnings.[2] A special contract with a third person, authorizing him to employ and pay the child himself, will bind the parent, and payment to the child will be a defence against any action brought by his father against the employer.[2] Parol agreements are, however, within the Statute of Frauds.[3]

But emancipation, strictly so called, is not to be presumed; it must be proved. Where it appears that the father, by parol, places his daughter in a certain family, that by the terms of the agreement the employer may turn her away when dissatisfied, that the father may rescind the contract at pleasure and reclaim his daughter; these, and similar circumstances may be sufficient to entitle the child to her own wages for the time being, but they cannot constitute emancipation as against the father.[4] We are to distinguish, in fact, between a license for the child to go out and work temporarily, and the more formal renunciation of parental rights. Thus, if the father agrees to pay his son so much for every day he would labor for another, but without intending to give him his time, and merely as an incentive to industry, this is not to be construed into a contract of emancipation, but rather as a mere gratuity to encourage the son in the formation of industrious and useful habits.[5]

But other circumstances may raise a special contract on the minor's behalf, or indeed be held to emancipate him altogether.

[1] Abbott *v.* Converse, 4 Allen, 530. See Morris *v.* Low, 4 Stew. & Port. 123. But see Chase *v.* Smith, 5 Vt. 556.

[2] Shute *v.* Dorr, 5 Wend. 204; Snediker *v.* Everingham, 3 Dutch. 143; Gale *v.* Parrott, 1 N. H. 28; United States *v.* Metz, 2 Watts, 406; Corey *v.* Corey, 19 Pick. 29.

[3] Shute *v.* Dorr, 5 Wend. 204.

[4] Sumner *v.* Sebec, 3 Maine, 223. See Clark *v.* Fitch, 2 Wend. 459; Clinton *v.* York, 26 Maine, 167.

[5] Arnold *v.* Norton, 25 Conn. 92.

It is a well settled rule in this country that if the parent absconds, turns his child out of doors, or leaves him to shift for himself, the son is entitled to his own wages; and our courts are very liberal in allowing children to avail themselves of any breach of parental obligation so as to earn an honest livelihood by their own toil.[1] The presumption raised in such cases may be termed a presumption of necessity. So where the husband abandons his child to the care of his mother, his subsequent claims for the earnings of either are to be regarded with very little favor.[2] Even slighter circumstances, which impute no misconduct to the father, but evince a consent for his son to leave the parental roof and go into the world to seek his own fortune, are often construed into emancipation.[3] But the desertion of a minor from his father's home, with vagrancy and crime, does not of itself constitute emancipation.[4] And there may be complete emancipation, though the minor continue to reside with his father.[5]

The marriage of an infant, with his parents' consent, removes him from parental control, and, we may presume, gives him a right as against the father, to apply all his earnings to the support of his family; but whether all the consequences of legal emancipation necessarily follow is doubtful.[6] Marriage, without the consent of the parent, ought to confer the same right upon an infant, inasmuch as the claims of wife and child in either case are paramount, and the consequences of all marriages are much the same; but in Maine it has been decided

1 Clinton *v.* York, 26 Maine, 167; Cloud *v.* Hamilton, 11 Humph. 104; Nightingale *v.* Withington, 15 Mass. 275; Stansbury *v.* Bertron, 7 W. & S. 362; Everett *v.* Sherfey, 1 Iowa, 356; The Etna, Ware, 462; Gary *v.* James, 4 Desaus. 185; Conovar *v.* Cooper, 3 Barb. 115; Jenison *v.* Graves, 2 Blackf. 440; Lyon *v.* Bolling, 14 Ala. 753; Ream *v.* Watkins, 27 Mis. 516.

2 Wodell *v.* Coggeshall, 2 Met. 89. See Dennysville *v.* Trescott, 30 Maine, 470.

3 Campbell *v.* Campbell, 3 Stockt. 268; Johnson *v.* Gibson, 4 E. D. Smith, 231; Dicks *v.* Grissom, 1 Freem. Ch. 428; Boobier *v.* Boobier, 39 Maine, 406. But see Stiles *v.* Granville, 6 Cush. 458.

4 Bangor *v.* Readfield, 32 Maine, 66.

5 M'Closkey *v.* Cyphert, 27 Penn. St. 220.

6 Taunton *v.* Plymouth, 15 Mass. 203; Dicks *v.* Grissom, 1 Freem. Ch. 428.

otherwise, and the disobedient infant is punishable by being compelled to pay his father his earnings; though what is to become of the wife meantime does not clearly appear.[1]

Secondly. As to the effect of emancipation. The consequence is on the one hand to give the child the right to his own wages, the disposal of his own time, and, in a great measure, the control of his own person; on the other hand to relieve the parent of all legal obligation to support.[2]

Where a minor is emancipated, his earnings go to his administrator upon his decease, to be distributed according to law.[3]

A father may give to his son a part as well as the whole period of his minority, in which case the rights of the latter are limited accordingly.[4] If the father receives his son's earnings after giving the son his time, it will be a good consideration for any promise from the father.[5] And he cannot sue for the services of such son performed within the period embraced by the agreement, although he has given notice to the party employing the son not to pay his wages to him.[6] Nor can the father's creditors attach such earnings or property which was purchased therewith for the infant's benefit.[7] But the child sues in such case for his own wages.[8] And if he is actually emancipated by his father and an express promise is made to pay him for his labor, with the consent of his father, no other notice of his emancipation is necessary to charge the defendant and enable the minor to sue.[9]

[1] White *v.* Henry, 24 Maine, 531. See Burr *v.* Wilson, 18 Tex. 367.

[2] Nightingale *v.* Withington, 15 Mass. 272; Corey *v.* Corey, 19 Pick. 29; Varney *v.* Young, 11 Vt. 258; Johnson *v.* Gibson, 4 E. D. Smith, 231.

[3] Smith *v.* Knowlton, 11 N. H. 191.

[4] Tillotson *v.* M'Crillis, 11 Vt. 477. And see Winn *v.* Sprague, 35 Vt. 243.

[5] Jenney *v.* Alden, 12 Mass. 375.

[6] Morse *v.* Welton, 6 Conn. 547; Wodell *v.* Coggeshall, 2 Met. 89; Bray *v.* Wheeler, 29 Vt. 514.

[7] Chase *v.* Elkins, 2 Vt. 290; Weeks *v.* Leighton, 5 N. H. 343; M'Closkey *v.* Cyphert, 27 Penn. St. 220; Bobo *v.* Bryson, 21 Ark. 387; Lord *v.* Poor, 23 Me. 569; Lyon *v.* Bolling, 14 Ala. 753.

[8] Ream *v.* Watkins, 27 Mis. 516.

[9] Wood *v.* Corcoran, 1 Allen, 405. The earnings of an emancipated child

A child, on arriving at full age, becomes emancipated.[1] But, whether son or daughter, the child, by continuing with the parent and living at the same home, may still be legally in the service of the parent. On this point there is no dispute; but in settling the presumptions of law there is apparently some conflict of authorities. Thus, where the parent sues for loss of services because of the seduction of a grown-up daughter, a strong disposition is frequently manifested to rule against complete emancipation so as to give damages. Where the conflict is between parent and child, over work done for a stranger, the tendency is in favor of complete emancipation, and to allow the child, attained to full age, the right to control his own wages; this being for his benefit.

If a child, after arriving at the age of twenty-one years, continues to live, labor, and render service in the father's family, with his knowledge and consent, but without any agreement or understanding as to compensation, the law raises no presumption of a promise to enable the child to maintain an action to recover compensation.[2] The presumption is, that the parties do not contemplate payment of wages for services. For where the relation of parent and child exists, the law will not presume any other. But this presumption may be overthrown, and the reverse established, by proof of an express or implied contract; an implied contract being proven by facts and circumstances which show that both parties, at the time the services were performed, contemplated or intended pecuniary recompense.[3] The declarations of parents, if somewhat vague, are not apt to be construed in the child's favor.

cannot be attached by trustee process for the father's debts. Manchester *v.* Smith, 12 Pick. 113. And see Bray *v.* Wheeler, 29 Vt. 514.

[1] 2 Kent Com. 206; Poultney *v.* Glover, 23 Vt. 328; Hardwick *v.* Paulet, 36 Vt. 320.

[2] Dye *v.* Kerr, 15 Barb. 444; Munger *v.* Munger, 33 N. H. 581; Willis *v.* Dun, Wright, 134; Lipe *v.* Eisenlerd, 32 N. Y. 229; Mosteller's Appeal, 30 Penn. St. 473; Ridgway *v.* English, 2 N. J. 409; Andover *v.* Merrimack County, 37 N. H. 437; Reser *v.* Johnson, 1 Smith (Md.) 81; Williams *v.* Barnes, 3 Dev. 348.

[3] Miller *v.* Miller, 16 Ill. 296; Fitch *v.* Peckham, 16 Vt. 150; Swartz *v.* Haz-

But circumstances which show an unusual burden assumed by the son, or special advantages reaped by the father, are sometimes favorably construed in the child's favor. Thus, it is held that where a grown-up son purchases his father's farm and continues to support the father and an adult idiot brother upon it, not only may the father's board be recovered against his estate, on due proof, but also that of the helpless brother; for the moral obligation of a father to support an adult idiot son is greater than that of a brother, where the parties are equally able.[1] So where the adult son assumes entire control and management of the business, works the farm, and adds largely to the family profits by his extraordinary skill.[2] Such cases are by no means uncommon among the enterprising settlers of our Western country, who cultivate the soil and live in little colonies; and American courts cannot be insensible to the merits of young persons who adorn the filial relation. As to use and occupation of real estate, where the occupant is the son of the owner, it is held that while payment of rent may be presumed, slight evidence is sufficient to show the contrary.[3]

But the rule in some of the old States is rather strict. As in Vermont, where the plaintiff was brought up in her grandfather's family, and had gone abroad after becoming of age to work for herself, but returned at the defendant's request, upon the assurance she should be paid "as well as she was then doing." Notwithstanding repeated assurances of future payment, it was held that no definite expectation was thus shown that either the support or service would create a debt.[4] And in New Hampshire, the presumption of compensation is not favored,

lett, 8 Cal. 118. See Tremont *v.* Mount Desert, 36 Maine, 390; Leidig *v.* Coover's Ex'rs, 47 Penn. St. 534. But see Putnam *v.* Town, 34 Vt. 429.

[1] House *v.* House, 6 Ind. 60.

[2] Adams *v.* Adams, 23 Ind. 50. And see Fisher *v.* Fisher, 5 Wis. 472.

[3] See Oakes *v.* Oakes, 16 Ill. 106; Hays *v.* Seward, 24 Ind. 352. And see Whipple *v.* Dow, 2 Mass. 415.

[4] Davis *v.* Goodenow, 27 Vt. 717. And see Hall *v.* Hall, 44 N. H. 293. But see Steel *v.* Steel, 12 Penn. St. 66.

where children, residing with parents, carry on in common the farms they respectively own, the proceeds of the whole property being applied to the common benefit of the family, or to the improvement of the common property.[1]

But to support a general contract between parent and child, as against strangers, a slight consideration is held sufficient. And a deed of personal property from parent to child, the parent not being indebted at the time, by which it is agreed that the parent shall keep possession during life, is not considered void.[2] So it is held that a bond executed by a son to his parent for $500, with interest semi-annually, *if demanded*, is a valuable consideration, sufficient to sustain a conveyance of land as a purchase.[3] And even a deed from a parent to a child for the consideration of love and affection, is not absolutely void as against creditors. The want of a valuable consideration may be a badge of fraud, but it is only presumptive, not conclusive evidence of it, and may be met and rebutted by opposing evidence.[4] This is the American rule; but as we have seen the statutes of Elizabeth receive in England an interpretation more favorable to creditors.[5]

Where a son purchases and stocks a farm as a home for an indigent father, who resides and labors thereon, the products are not subject to attachment as the son's property.[6] On the other hand, where a parent permits the child to receive and invest his earnings, the benefit of the investment belongs to the child.[7] And in Pennsylvania, a minor child who improves and settles a tract of land with the father's permission, may acquire a title by making improvements as effectually as if he were of age.[8]

1 Seavey *v.* Seavey, 37 N. H. 125.

2 Bohn *v.* Headley, 7 Har. & J. 257; Shepherd *v.* Bevin, 9 Gill, 32. See Haines *v.* Haines, 6 Md. 435.

3 Jackson *v.* Peek, 4 Wend. 300.

4 Hinde's Lessee *v.* Longworth, 11 Wheat. 213; Seward *v.* Jackson, 8 Cow. 406; Haines *v.* Haines, 6 Md. 435.

5 See *supra*. "Postnuptial Settlements."

6 Brown & Scott, 7 Vt. 57.

7 Campbell *v.* Campbell, 3 Stockt. 268.

8 Galbraith *v.* Black, 4 S. & R. 207. See Jenison *v.* Graves, 2 Blackf. 441.

The English cases are few as to transactions between parent and child; and these turn chiefly upon trusts and family settlements. There are recent cases where the transactions of children with fortunes have been set aside in equity, for undue influence exerted over them by their parents. Thus a mortgage and subsequent sale by a son just arrived at full age, effected under the father's influence, and to his own injury, has been annulled.[1] So with a gift from child to parent, though not unless a suit to set the gift aside be instituted in due time.[2] The principle of equity is, that if there be a pecuniary transaction between parent and child, just after the child attains the age of twenty-one years, and prior to what may be called a complete emancipation, without any benefit moving to the child, the presumption is, that an undue influence has been exercised to procure that liability on the part of the child; and that it is the business and the duty of the party who endeavors to maintain such a transaction, to show that such presumption is adequately rebutted; but that the presumption may always be removed.[3] On the other hand, in transactions between members of the same family, even though that relation subsists between them, from whence the court will infer the moral certainty of the existence of considerable influence, and the probability of its having been exercised, yet if the transaction be one that tends to the peace or security of the family, to the avoiding of family disputes and litigation, or to the preservation of the family property, the principles by which such transactions must be tried are not those applicable to dealings between strangers, but such as on the most comprehensive experience have been found to be most for the interest of families.[4]

But see Bell *v.* Hallenback, Wright, 751; Fonda *v.* Van Horne, 15 Wend. 631; Brown *v.* M'Donald, 1 Hill Ch. 297.

[1] Savery *v.* King, 35 E. L. &. Eq. 100. And see Baker *v.* Bradley, ib. 449.

[2] Wright *v.* Vanderplank, 39 E. L. &. Eq. 147.

[3] Archer *v.* Hudson, 7 Beav. 551, per Lord Langdale. See Houghton *v.* Houghton, 11 E. L. & Eq. 134, s. c. 15 Beav. 278, where this subject is fully discussed. See also American case of Bergen *v.* Udall, 31 Barb. 9.

[4] Master of Rolls in Hoghton *v.* Hoghton, ib. and see cases cited.

If the father, during his lifetime, makes an advancement to any of his children, towards their distributive share in his estate, the rule is to reckon this in making the distribution.[1] In England, it would appear that acts of the father have often been so construed, with less reference to intention of the parties than the requirements of equal justice. Thus annuities are reckoned an advancement; contingent provisions; large premiums, it seems, for a trade or profession; and loans of considerable importance to a son.[2] But small and inconsiderable sums for current expenses, ornaments, and the education of children are not so reckoned.[3] Nor is the payment to the daughter's husband of £1,000, jocularly stated by the father to be in exchange for his snuffbox, to be considered an advancement to the daughter.[4]

In a modern English case a father lent the sum of £10,000 to his son, to assist him in forming a partnership in the business of a sugar-refiner, and took his promissory note for the repayment of that sum on demand. It appeared that the son engaged in business at the urgent desire of his father, that finding it was a losing concern he became desirous of retiring, but remained at the urgent request of his father; and continued the business with reluctance, sustaining heavy losses. The father on his death-bed caused the promissory note to be burned, and died intestate. It was held that although the circumstances under which the note had been destroyed amounted to an equitable release of the debt; yet, that the sum which remained due on it must be considered an advancement to the son.[5]

But the rule in this country does not appear to be so strict; and in Massachusetts and some other States the statutes of

[1] 2 Redf. Wills, 908 *et seq.*; Edwards *v.* Freeman, 2 P. Wms. 435.

[2] Smith *v.* Smith, 3 Gif. 263; 2 Wms. Ex'rs, 1385; Edward *v.* Freeman, 2 P. Wms. 435; 2 Redf. Wills, 908, 909.

[3] 2 Wms. Ex'rs, 1391. And see Miller's Appeal, 40 Penn. St. 57.

[4] McClure *v.* Evans, 29 Beav. 422.

[5] Gilbert *v.* Wetherell, 2 Sim. & Stu. 254, per Sir John Leach, M. R. But see Auster *v.* Powell, 31 Beav. 583 and *n.*

distributions, unlike those of England, permit nothing to be reckoned as an advancement to a child by the father, unless proved to have been so intended and chargeable on the child's share by certain evidence prescribed.[1] And it is laid down that whether a provision of the deceased in his lifetime be a gift or an advancement is a question of intention; but if it was originally intended by both as a gift, it cannot subsequently be treated by the father as an advancement, at least without the son's knowledge or consent.[2] Advancements do not bear interest.[3]

Where the child of a father dying intestate has received an advancement, in real or personal estate, and wishes to come into the general partition or distribution of the estate, he may bring his advancement into *hotchpot* with the whole estate of the intestate, real and personal; and shall thereupon be entitled to his just proportion of the estate. This is the English rule, and it prevails likewise in many of the United States.[4] In such case the value of the property at the time of advancement governs in the distribution.[5] The principle of this rule is equality of distribution of the ancestor's personal estate among his children and their descendants.

The sale of expectant estates by heirs is not to be encouraged; one reason being that it opens the door to taking undue advantage of an heir in distressed and necessitous circumstances; the other that public policy should prevent an heir from shak-

[1] Osgood *v.* Breed's Heirs, 17 Mass. 356; 2 Redf. Wills, 908, 909.

[2] Lawson's Appeal, 23 Penn. St. 85; Sherwood *v.* Smith, 23 Conn. 516. See Black *v.* Whitall, 1 Stockt. 572.

[3] Osgood *v.* Breed's Heirs, 17 Mass. 356; Nelson *v.* Wyan, 21 Mis. 347. As to proof of an advancement, see Bulkley *v.* Noble, 2 Pick. 337; and see Hartwell *v.* Rice, 1 Gray, 587; Miller's Appeal, 40 Penn. St. 57; Quarles *v.* Quarles, 4 Mass. 680; Kenney *v.* Tucker, 8 ib. 143; Vanzant *v.* Davies, 6 Ohio N. S. 52; 2 Story Eq. Jur. § 1202; Brown *v.* Burk, 22 Geo. 574; Cleaver *v.* Kirk, 3 Met. (Ky.) 270; Hodgson *v.* Macy, 8 Ind. 121. And see Vaden *v.* Hance, 1 Head, 300; Fulton *v.* Smith, 27 Geo. 413; Montgomery *v.* Chaney, 13 La. Ann. 207.

[4] 2 Bl. Com. 516; 2 Wms. Ex'rs, 1386; 2 Kent Com. 421; Grattan *v.* Grattan, 18 Ill. 167; Jackson *v.* Jackson, 28 Miss. 674.

[5] See Jenkins *v.* Mitchell, 4 Jones Eq. 207. For the New York rule, see Terry *v.* Dayton, 31 Barb. 519.

ing off his father's authority and feeding his extravagance by disposing of the family estate.[1] The principle was formerly laid down with much emphasis in Massachusetts.[2] But the present rule of chancery is to support such sales to others, if made *bona fide*, and for valuable consideration; and in case of an heir apparent, if the instrument be made with the knowledge and consent of the father.[3] Whether, however, the son can release to the father himself, so as to operate further than as a receipt for property advanced to him is more doubtful.[4]

It is well settled that in the absence of statutes a person is not entitled to the custody and earnings of step-children, nor bound by law to maintain them.[5] Yet, if a step-father voluntarily assumes the care and support of a step-child, he stands *in loco parentis;* and the presumption is, that they deal with each other as parent and child, and not as master and servant; in which case the ordinary rules of parent and child will be held to apply; and neither compensation for board is presumed on the one hand, nor for services on the other.[6] So may this *quasi* relation exist between the child and some other person; such as a grandfather.[7]

1 Per Lord Thurlow, 1 Br. C. C. 10; Co. Litt. 265 *a*; Sugd. Vendors, 314, and cases cited; 1 Story Eq. Juris. §§ 336–339.

2 But see Trull *v.* Eastman, 3 Met. 121; *contra*, Boynton *v.* Hubbard, 7 Mass. 112. See Varick *v.* Edwards, 1 Hoff. Ch. 383; 2 Kent Com. 475 and cases cited.

3 Curtis *v.* Curtis, 40 Me. 24.

4 See Robinson *v.* Robinson, Brayt. 59.

5 Tubb *v.* Harrison, 4 T. R. 118; 2 Kent Com. 192; Freto *v.* Brown, 4 Mass. 675; Worcester *v.* Marchant, 14 Pick. 510; Gay *v.* Ballou, 4 Ward, 403. See Eng. Stat. *n.* 2 Kent, ib.

6 Cooper *v.* Martin, 4 East, 77; Williams *v.* Hutchinson, 3 Comst. 312; Sharp *v.* Cropsey, 11 Barb. 224; Murdock *v.* Murdock, 7 Cal. 511; Gillett *v.* Camp. 27 Mis. 541; Hussee *v.* Roundtree, Busbee, 110; Lantz *v.* Frey, 14 Penn. St. 201; Davis *v.* Goodenow, 27 Vt. 715; Brush *v.* Blanchard, 18 Ill. 46.

7 Hudson *v.* Lutz, 5 Jones, 217.

CHAPTER VI.

ILLEGITIMATE CHILDREN.

ILLEGITIMATE children, or bastards, stand upon a different footing from legitimate children. We have already seen that bastards may be legitimated in many of the United States, by the subsequent marriage of their parents. The rights and disabilities of bastards, as such, and while continuing illegitimate, require our present attention.

The rights of a bastard are very few at the common law; children born out of a legal marriage having been from the earliest times stigmatized with shame, and made to suffer through life the reproach which was rightfully visited upon those who brought them into being. The dramatist depicts the bastard as a social Ishmaelite, ever bent upon schemes for the ruin of others, fully determined to prove a villain; thus fitly indicating the public estimate of such characters centuries ago in England. The law-writers, too, pronounce the bastard to be one whose only rights are such as he can acquire; going so far as to demonstrate, by cruelly irresistible logic, that an illegitimate child cannot possibly inherit, because he is the son of nobody; sometimes called *filius nullius*, and sometimes *filius populi*.[1] But Coke admitted that the bastard might gain a surname by reputation, though none by inheritance.[2]

The most important disability of an illegitimate child, then, at the common law, is that he has no inheritable blood; that he is incapable of becoming heir, either to his putative father or

[1] Fort de Ll. ch. 40; 1 Bl. Com. 458.

[2] Co. Litt. 3. The very term "bastard," said to be derived from the Saxon words "base start," expresses contempt. See Fraser Parent & Child, 119.

his mother, or to any one else; that he can have no heirs but those of his own body.[1] This was likewise the doctrine of the civil law; though the language of the Institutes as to spurious offspring, *patrem habere non intelliguntur*, deals more gently with a fact so extremely delicate and painful.[2] At the old canon law a bastard was also disqualified from holding dignities in the church; but this doctrine became exploded long ago. "And really," adds Blackstone, with warmth, as if to atone for a long and fallacious argument against legitimation by a subsequent marriage, "any other distinction but that of not inheriting, which civil policy renders necessary, would, with regard to the innocent offspring of his parents' crimes, be odious, unjust, and cruel to the last degree."[3] And so may the commentator of the commentaries stigmatize the efforts of those who have nothing better to urge against human rights, than the importance of preserving the symmetry of the law unimpaired.

The civil law, while offering in certain cases a hope of legitimation, made a distinction between spurious offspring born of promiscuous intercourse, and such as were conceived or born during the marriage of one of the natural parents; presuming that while the former might be rendered legitimate, the latter never could become so.[4] And the rule was more severe with the one class than the other. This principle is to be traced in the provisions of the Louisiana Code; children whose father is unknown and adulterous or incestuous children having no right of inheritance, while other natural or illegitimate children succeed to the estate of their mother in default of lawful children or descendants, and under certain conditions to the estate of the father who has acknowledged them.[5]

The well settled American rule, however, differs considera-

[1] 2 Kent Com. 212; 1 Bl. Com. 459.
[2] Inst. 1, 10, 12; 2 Kent Com. ib.
[3] 1 Bl. Com. 459.
[4] 1 Dig. 5, 23; Fraser Parent & Child, 119.
[5] See 2 Kent Com. 213.

bly from that of both civil and common law. We have already noticed that legitimation by subsequent marriage is a principle admitted very generally in the legislation of the different States. So, too, there are various statutes which permit even bastard children to inherit under certain restrictions; while the generally recognized doctrine is *partus sequitur ventrem*, and that the illegitimate child and his mother shall mutually inherit from each other. Thus, by recent statutes in Maine, the mother of an illegitimate child can inherit. In Massachusetts the illegitimate is an heir to his mother. In New York, in default of lawful issue of the mother, her illegitimate children may inherit her real and personal estate. In Pennsylvania bastards shall bear the name of the mother, and she and they shall inherit from each other. Certain kindred of the bastard's mother, in Georgia and Alabama, had rights of distribution under still earlier statutes. In Ohio, a very liberal rule is applied.[1] In Maryland, illegitimates may inherit from the mother and from illegitimate brothers and sisters; though illegitimates cannot take from the legitimate, neither legitimates from the illegitimate.[2] And, forty years ago, Kent instanced twelve States where bastards could inherit from, and transmit to, their mothers, real and personal estate, under some modifications; while in New York, the mother and her kindred could inherit from her bastard offspring.[3] There is scarcely a State in the Union which has not departed widely from the policy of the English common law; and statutes, which happily have required as yet very little judicial interpretation, perpetuate the record of our liberal and generous public policy towards a class of beings who were once compelled to bear the iniquities of the parent.

The doctrine that a natural tie connects the illegitimate child peculiarly with his mother was recognized at the civil law;

[1] Lewis *v.* Eutsler, 4 Ohio St. 354.

[2] Miller *v.* Stewart, 8 Gill, 128; Earle *v.* Dawes, 3 Md. Ch. 230.

[3] See 2 Kent Com. 11th ed. 212, 213, and notes.

for under the ordinance of Justinian, the bastard might to a certain extent inherit from his mother.[1] So at the common law have the obligations of consanguinity between the mother and her illegitimate offspring been applied in several instances. But as concerns any exclusive privileges on behalf of the mother, this does not seem very clear; for in a case which was decided in 1786, the rights of the putative father seemed to be placed on much the same footing as in other cases; and his consent was deemed *prima facie* essential under the marriage act of 26 Geo. I.; so was his right apparently admitted to take his illegitimate child out of the parish.[2]

There are, to be sure, occasional *dicta* to the effect that the putative father has no common-law right to the custody of the child as against the mother, and that certainly within the age of nurture, that is, under the age of seven, the mother has the exclusive right to the custody. The more correct statement, however, is that pauper children, whether legitimate or not, are under the English system made inseparable from the mother within the years of nurture; and that at common law neither the putative father nor the mother of an illegitimate child has any exclusive right of guardianship.[3] The common-law cases cited in the mother's favor, are only to the effect that where a bastard child within the period of nurture is in the peaceable possession of the mother, and the putative father gets possession of the child by force or fraud, the court will interfere to put matters in the same situation as before.[4] Both Lord Kenyon and Lord Ellenborough — the latter as late as 1806 — expressed doubts as to whether the court would take away the custody of an illegitimate child from the father who had fairly obtained possession, and award it to the mother.[5]

[1] Code, lib. 6, 57. See 2 Kent Com. 214.

[2] King *v.* Hodnett, 1 T. R. 96, and cases cited *passim;* Macphers. Inf. 67.

[3] Macphers. Inf. 67.

[4] Rex *v.* Soper, 5 T. R. 278; Rex *v.* Hopkins, 7 East, 579; Rex *v.* Moseley, 5 East, 223.

[5] Per Lord Kenyon, Rex *v.* Moseley, *supra* (1798); Per Lord Ellenborough, Rex *v.* Hopkins, *supra.*

Nor do the later English cases aid greatly in clearing up the doubt on this point. Lord Mansfield regarded the point as doubtful in his day, though inclining strongly to the opinion that the putative father had no right to his child's custody.[1] In 1841, a case came before the court of common pleas, on a writ of *habeas corpus*, applied for by the mother, the child being then between eleven and twelve years of age, and in the custody of her putative father. But the child was deemed old enough to exercise her own discretion as to where she would go; and as she appeared unwilling to go with her mother, the court would not permit the mother to take her by force.[2]

The chancery courts have in several instances favored the father of an illegitimate child to the exclusion of his mother. Thus, while the practice is not to appoint the putative father guardian of his illegitimate child having no property, unless he makes a settlement upon him; yet, if he does so, his appointment is favorably regarded. No special regard seems to have been paid to the mother of such children.[3] And while the committee of a lunatic might petition for an allowance for his bastard offspring, their mother might not.[4]

But the language of the new poor laws of England (after many changes), is favorable to the mother's special claims; being to the effect that the mother is in any case bound to maintain her bastard child under sixteen, unless such child meantime marries or acquires a settlement of its own; and that such child shall follow the settlement of the mother.[5] And if being of ability, she neglects to support such child, whereby it becomes chargeable to the parish, she may be punished under the vagrant acts.[6] Another section of the act

[1] Strangeways *v.* Robinson, 4 Taunt. 498. And see Pope *v.* Sale, 7 Bing. 477.

[2] *In re* Lloyd, 3 Man. & Gr. 547. Comparing all the *dicta* in the foregoing cases carefully together, it will be seen that they are not decidedly against the putative father's right of custody.

[3] Macphers. Inf. 110.

[4] *Re* Jones, 5 Russ. 154.

[5] 4 & 5 Will. 4, ch. 76, § 71.

[6] 7 & 8 Vict. ch. 101; 8 & 9 Vict. ch. 10.

of 4 & 5 Will. IV., which provides that the husband shall support step-children of his wife, includes in its terms illegitimate as well as legitimate children, and so far favors a husband's right of custody.[1] But unless a woman having illegitimate children re-marries, the obligation to maintain such children rests upon her.

The rights of the parents of bastards are regulated to a great extent in the United States by statute; and our policy is in general more favorable than that of England, as to the mother's rights. An illegitimate child follows the settlement of his mother in New York and some other States.[2] But in Connecticut the rule is that a bastard is settled where born, like any other child, and that his settlement follows that of the putative father.[3] In New York again, ever zealous in guarding the interests of women and children, it is broadly ruled that, as against the mother of a bastard child, the putative father has no legal right of custody; that the mother as its natural guardian, is bound to maintain it; and that she is entitled to control it.[4] Stratagem and force on the part of the putative father always furnish good grounds for restoration of the child to the mother.[5] And the Roman, Spanish, and French laws all deny the power of the putative father over the illegitimate child; this principle being likewise transferred to Louisiana and other States, once under the civil law.[6]

The common-law rule, in absence of statutes, is that the putative father is under no legal liability to support his illegitimate offspring. But upon the strength of the natural or moral obligation arising out of the relation of the putative father to his child, an action at common law lies for its main-

[1] 4 & 5 Will. 4, ch. 76, § 51. See comment of Maule J., *In re* Ann Lloyd, 3 Man. & Gr. 547.

[2] See 2 Kent Com. 214; Canajoharrie *v.* Johnson, 17 Johns. 41; Petersham *v.* Dana, 12 Mass. 429.

[3] Bethlem *v.* Roxbury, 20 Conn. 298.

[4] People *v.* Kling, 6 Barb. 366; Robalina *v.* Armstrong, 15 Barb. 247.

[5] Commonwealth *v.* Fee, 6 S. & R. 255.

[6] Acosta *v.* Robin, 19 Martin, 387.

tenance and support upon an express promise; and where one admits himself to be the father and adopts the child, while such adoption continues, a promise may be implied in favor of the party providing for it. He may renounce the adoption, and terminate this implied assumpsit, in which case there is no remedy to be pursued, unless under a statute. The father can only be charged then upon his contract.[1] But upon his promise to third persons, he may be held liable; and a promise by the putative father to pay the step-father for the child's support, past and future, if he will continue to support it, is binding.[2]

But the statutes which relate to the maintenance of bastard children, supply the want of adequate common-law remedies; the main element in such legislation being public indemnity against the support of such persons. Under the old poor laws of England, the mother had a compulsory remedy against the putative father; but this was taken away by the act of 4 & 5 Will. IV. ch. 76. By the statute of 7 & 8 Vict. ch. 101, however, the mother is afforded relief once more, and the father may be summoned before the petty sessions and ordered to pay a weekly sum for the child's maintenance, and the costs of obtaining the order; maintenance to last until the child is thirteen years of age. The money is to be paid to the mother, and may be recovered by distress and imprisonment.[3] The provisions of law in force in most of the United States are borrowed from the older English statutes, and our courts are very generally invested with plenary jurisdiction over such matters; and at the instance of the mother the father may be coerced by arrest and imprisonment, if need be, into giving bonds and furnishing

[1] Hesketh *v.* Gowing, 5 Esp. 131; Nichols *v.* Allen, 3 Car. & P. 36; Furillio *v.* Crowther, 7 Dowl. & Ry. 612; Cameron *v.* Baker, 1 Car. & P. 268; Moncrief *v.* Ely, 19 Wend. 405.

[2] Wiggins *v.* Keizer, 6 Ind. 252.

[3] And see 2 & 3 Vict. ch. 85; 8 & 9 Vict. ch. 101. The order may be obtained by a married woman, mother of the bastard. Regina *v.* Collingwood, 12 Q. B. 681. And see Follit *v.* Koetzow, 24 Jur. 651. In case of death or incapacity of the mother, and the child becomes chargeable to the parish, the order may be enforced by the guardians or overseers of the parish.

maintenance for his illegitimate child; thus relieving the mother to some extent of the burden to which his criminal misconduct has chiefly contributed, and indemnifying the public against the support of the penniless and unfortunate.[1]

Past seduction has been held sufficient to support a deed. There is an old English case, where equity compelled the specific performance of a deed poll, made by a man who had seduced a woman and had a child by her; the writing promising to pay £2,000 after his death for the purchase of an annuity for the mother and her child for their lives. Both the man and the child had died before the suit was brought.[2] In Pennsylvania, the same principle is pushed even farther; for it is ruled that seduction of a female and begetting a bastard is sufficient consideration to support a man's promise to give bonds for a sum of money.[3] But there must be nothing oppressive or unfair in such transactions, and if the promise be solely in consideration of stopping a criminal prosecution, it is void.[4] Nor ought agreements as to the wages of sin to be favored.[5]

A person standing *in loco parentis* may sue *per quod servitium* for the abduction of his daughter's illegitimate child.[6] And in some States, the rights of the mother in binding out her illegitimate son are favorably regarded.[7] But a parent is not bound to support the illegitimate offspring of his children.[8]

Bequests to illegitimate children, since they are not considered as relatives, are not favored in English law.[9] There have been, it is true, certain *dicta* to the contrary; but Lord Eldon

[1] 2 Kent Com. 215, and cases cited.

[2] Marchioness of Annandale *v.* Harris, 2 P. Wms. 433. And see Turner *v.* Vaughan, 2 Wils. 339.

[3] Shenk *v.* Mingle, 13 S. & R. 29. And see Phillipi *v.* Commonwealth, 18 Penn. St. 116; Knye *v.* Moore, 1 Sim. & Stu. 161.

[4] Ib.

[5] See Binnington *v.* Wallis, 4 B. & Ald. 650.

[6] Moritz *v.* Garnhart, 7 Watts, 302.

[7] McGunigal *v.* Mong, 5 Penn. St. 269.

[8] Hillsborough *v.* Deering, 4 N. H. 86.

[9] Macphers. Inf. 238.

was of the opinion that there must be something to show that the testator put himself *in loco parentis;* and it has since been decided that an illegitimate child is not merely, as such, within the rule, for he is "a stranger to the testator."[1] On the ground of uncertainty in the person, a bequest to an unborn legitimate child was long considered objectionable; but Lord Eldon and others maintained that legacies given to the unborn illegitimate child of a particular woman then pregnant, would be good, because the uncertainty of description could here be obviated.[2] But it is now well settled that a devise or bequest in favor of other future illegitimate children is void.[3]

Illegitimate children may, undoubtedly, take by purchase as persons designated, if sufficiently described.[4] The question in cases of this sort is really one of intention. *Prima facie*, the term children in a will, however, is intended to mean legitimate children; and if there are legitimate children, or if it be possible that there should be legitimate children of the person named, the English rule is that no illegitimate child can take under the description of children.[5] Yet, if they have acquired the reputation of being the children of a particular person, they are capable of taking under the description of "children," or "daughters."[6]

In *Medworth* v. *Pope*, the rule was concisely stated to be, that an illegitimate child *in esse* or *en ventre sa mere* may, if properly described, take the benefit of a devise or bequest, and

1 Lowndes *v.* Lowndes, 15 Ves. 304; Perry *v.* Whitehead, 6 Ves. 547; *contra*, per Lord Alvanley, Cricket *v.* Dolby, 3 Ves. 30.

2 Macphers. Inf. 570, and cases cited; Gordon *v.* Gordon, 1 Mer. 141; Dawson *v.* Dawson, 6 Mad. 292.

3 Beachcroft *v.* Beachcroft, 1 Mad. 430; Knye *v.* Moore, 1 Sim. & Stu. 61; Wilkinson *v.* Wilkinson, 1 You. & Coll. 657; Medworth *v.* Pope, 27 Beav. 71.

4 Blodwell *v.* Edwards, Cro. Eliz. 509; Co. Litt. 36; Peachey Mar. Settl. 885 *n.*

5 Gill *v.* Shelley, 2 Russ. & My. 336. See *In re* Wells's Estate, Law Rep. 6 Eq. 599.

6 Peachey Mar. Settl. 885, *n.*, and cases cited; Evans *v.* Davies, 7 Hare, 501; Owen *v.* Bryant, 2 De G., M. & G. 697; Hartley *v.* Tribber, 16 Beav. 510; Leigh *v.* Byron, 1 Sm. & Gif. 486; Tugwell *v.* Scott, 24 Beav. 141; Worts *v.* Cubitt, 19 Beav. 421. And see Williamson *v.* Codrington, 1 Ves. Sen. 511.

the court will not inquire as to his parentage or origin; but in respect of future illegitimate children, the law will not let them take under any description whatever. "The reason why the English law so holds is, that it considers such a provision for future illegitimate children as *contra bonos mores*."[1]

In this country, the tendency seems to be so far favorable to illegitimate children as to regard wills made in their favor with the same, or nearly the same, consideration as all others. And our courts regard bastards as having strong claims to equitable protection, notwithstanding the criminal indulgence of their parents. In several important cases, specific performance of voluntary settlements, made by the father in their favor, have been decreed.[2] And a devise, in specific terms, to an unborn natural child of a woman then pregnant, is sustained here as in England.[3] But whether our tribunals would sanction a bequest to other unborn illegitimate children, may admit of doubt; provided such child were never legitimated by subsequent marriage. For, after all, there must be some discrimination made against criminal intercourse.

1 Per M. R., in Medworth *v.* Pope, 27 Beav. 71. Further important illustrations of the equity doctrine may be seen in the recent cases of Clifton *v.* Goodbun, Law Rep. 6 Eq. 278; Savage *v.* Robinson, Law Rep. 7 Eq. 176; Hall *v.* Sindrey, Law Rep. 7 Eq. 170. And as to the application of 27 Eliz. ch. 4 to marriage settlements for bastards, see Clarke *v.* Wright, 6 Hurl. & Nor. 849. As to legacies and devises see Beachcroft *v.* Beachcroft, 1 Mad. 430, and cases cited; Durrant *v.* Friend, 11 E. L. & Eq. 2; Owen *v.* Bryant, 13 E. L. & Eq. 217; 4 Kent Com. 10th ed. 414; Bagley *v.* Mollard, 1 Russ. & My. 581. See *In re* Wells's Estate, Law Rep. 6 Eq. 599.

2 Gardner *v.* Heyer, 2 Paige, 11; Bunn *v.* Winthrop, 1 Johns. Ch. 338; Harten *v.* Gibson, 4 Desaus. 139; 2 Kent Com. 216; Shearman *v.* Angel, Bail. Eq. 351; Collins *v.* Hoxie, 9 Paige, 88.

3 Knye *v.* Moore, 5 Harr. & Johns. 10. As to legacies and devises to illegitimate children under American laws, see 4 Kent Com. 413, 414, 10th ed. and cases cited.

PART IV.

GUARDIAN AND WARD.

CHAPTER I.

OF GUARDIANS IN GENERAL.

THE guardian is a person entrusted by law with the interests of another, whose youth, inexperience, mental weakness, and feebleness of will disqualify him from acting for himself in the ordinary affairs of life, and who is hence known as the *ward.*

Guardianship usually applies to minor children; and in this sense the guardian may be either their natural protector, whose authority is founded upon universal law, or some person duly chosen to act on their behalf. Thus, the father (and sometimes the mother), exercises the right of custody and nurture as the child's natural guardian; but, if the parents are dead, some one must be selected to supply their place. And since the parental control does not extend to the estate of a minor, the appointment of a guardian may be both necessary and proper, when property becomes vested in a child under age. Guardianship applies also at the present day to idiots, lunatics, spendthrifts, and the like; and the guardian of such person derives his authority from statute law and a special appointment. This guardian is sometimes designated as the *committee.*

The law of guardianship is most naturally divided into guardianship of the person, and guardianship of the estate.

Guardianship of the person is a relation essentially the same as that of parent and child, though not without some important differences, as we shall see hereafter. Hence the guardian has been called "a temporary parent."[1] Guardianship of the estate bears a closer resemblance to trusteeship, guardians and trustees being alike bound to manage estates with fidelity and care, under the supervision and direction of the chancery courts. The same person is often guardian of both the person and estate of the ward; but not necessarily, for these may be kept distinct. So, too, there may be joint guardians, as in other trusts.

The law of guardianship, in England, is one of irregular growth. Guardians, until chancery jurisprudence became fully developed, were recognized only for certain limited purposes. Their powers were restricted, and new classes were created from time to time, as the exigency arose. One species of guardianship would fall into disuse and another spring up in its place. Hence it is found difficult to attempt a classification, or reduce the general authority of guardians to a definite system. The latest English text-writer enumerates no less than eleven different kinds of guardians, many of which are obsolete, and others of merely local application.[2] Among them may be mentioned *guardianship in chivalry*, an incident of the feudal tenure, more in the nature of a hardship than a privilege so far as the ward was concerned, which was finally abolished in the time of Charles II.; *guardianship by special custom*, which was confined to London and certain other localities, and appears to exist no longer; *guardianship by appointment of the spiritual courts*, traces of which still exist in the appointment of administrators *durante minore ætate; guardianship by prerogative*, applicable only to the royal family; and *guardianship by*

[1] 1 Bl. Com. 460; 2 Kent Com. 220.

[2] Macphers. Inf. 2 *et seq.* to which the reader is referred for a full account of these kinds of guardianship, including Guardianship under Stat. 4 & 5 P. & M. ch. 8, alluded to in 1 Bl. Com. 461, and repealed by 9 Geo. 4, ch. 31. See also 1 Bl. Com. 461, and Harg. notes.

election of the infant, which appears to us more properly considered at this day in connection with the appointment of chancery guardians. But *guardianship by nature and nurture*, *guardianship in socage*, *testamentary guardianship*, and *chancery guardianship* require special consideration, and these will be taken up in order.

Guardianship by nature and nurture denotes hardly more or less than the natural right of parents to the care and custody of their children. It has been usual to treat of guardians by nature as distinct from guardians by nurture ; but in reality the latter constitute, for practical purposes, only a species of the former. Mr. Macpherson considers them together and doubts whether guardianship by nature, as known in the old law, has existed since the time of Charles II., when feudal tenures were abolished ; for it appears to have originated in the practice of selling the marriage of the heir.[1]

Guardianship by nature and nurture belongs exclusively to the parents : first, to the father, and, on his death, to the mother. The father's right was formerly preferred to the mother's in all cases ; but the modern tendency is otherwise.[2] The office of natural guardian lasted during the minority of the child ; but guardianship by nurture ceased when he attained the age of fourteen. So guardianship by nature applied to the heir apparent or presumptive, and guardianship by nurture to the other children. Guardianship by nature was something higher than guardianship by nurture.[3] But it is, nevertheless, clear that the father has a right, recognized by general law, to the custody of all his children, not only during the period of nurture, but until the age of twenty-one. So, too, the mother, if not superseded by the infant's election at fourteen, or by the appointment of a new guardian, has, in absence of the father, the legitimate care of the child for the same period.[4]

[1] Macphers. Inf. 52, 58. See also 1 Bl. Com. 461 and Harg. notes 1 & 3 ; 2 Kent Com. 220, 221.

[2] See *ante*, Hus. & Wife, ch. 2.

[3] 1 Bl. Com. 461, and Harg. notes ; 2 Kent Com. 220, 221.

[4] Macphers. Inf. 61, 65.

The authority of such guardians extends only to the ward's person. They have no right to intermeddle with his property.[1] Blackstone says, that if an estate be left to an infant, the father is, by common law, the guardian, and must account to his child for the profits. But this is only because the law holds him and all others responsible as a *quasi* guardian; and it is well settled at the present day, that if a child becomes vested with property during his father's lifetime, there is no one strictly authorized to take it until a guardian has been duly appointed.

Guardianship by nature and nurture is inferior to guardianship in socage; and it yields to every kind of guardianship which exists by strict appointment, so far as the ward's property is concerned, though not necessarily as to his person.

Guardianship in socage arises, at common law, whenever an infant under fourteen acquires title to real estate; the chief object of the trust being the protection of such property and the instruction of the young heir in the pursuit of agriculture.[2] It applies only when the infant has land by descent, and cannot exist if his estate be merely personal. His title, too, must be *legal* and not merely *equitable;* hence it would seem that there cannot be a guardian in socage where the interest of the ward is only reversionary.[3] This species of guardianship was anciently assignable, so far at least as the custody of the infant was concerned; but by the doctrine and practice of later times it became regarded as a strictly personal trust, neither transmissible by succession, nor devisable, nor assignable.[4]

The duty of the guardian in socage is to take possession of the heir's person and real estate, to receive the rents and profits until the heir reaches the age of fourteen, to keep his evidences

[1] 1 Bl. Com. 461, and Harg. notes; 2 Kent Com. 220, 221; Hyde *v.* Stone, 7 Wend. 354; Kline *v.* Beebe, 6 Conn. 494; Fonda *v.* Van Horne, 15 Wend. 631.

[2] 1 Bl. Com. 461, and Harg. *n.*; 2 Kent Com. 220; Dagley *v.* Tolferry, 1 P. Wms. 285.

[3] Macphers. Inf. 19; 2 Bl. Com. 88.

[4] Macphers. Inf. 20 *et seq.;* 2 Bl. Com. 461, and Harg. *n.*; 2 Kent Com. 223.

of title safely, and to bring him up well.[1] His powers are commensurate with his duties. He acquires by virtue of his office an actual estate in the ward's land, though not to his own use;[2] he may gain a settlement by actual residence upon it;[3] and he can grant leases terminable and perhaps even void, when the ward reaches the age of fourteen.[4] A guardian in socage cannot be removed from office, but the ward may supersede him, at this age, by a guardian of his own choice.[5]

Guardianship in socage has been said to extend to the heir's personal property; but there is insufficient legal authority for such a supposition, though it is likely that the farm-stock, and household chattels of the ward were included; and when this guardianship was common, personal property consisted of little else.[6]

One peculiarity of this guardianship was, that the trust belonged only to such next of blood to the child as could not possibly inherit, and it devolved upon him without appointment; the common law, with a characteristic distrust of human nature, deeming it imprudent to confide the child's interests to one who expected the succession. For, as Fortescue and Sir Edward Coke affirmed, to commit the custody of the infant to such a person, was like giving up a lamb to a wolf to be devoured.[7] Guardianship in socage has passed into disuse, though it cannot be said to have been actually abolished.

Testamentary guardianship was instituted by the statute of 12 Car. II. ch. 24, and for this reason testamentary guardians are sometimes called *statute* guardians.[8] This statute provided

[1] Co. Litt. 89; Macphers. Inf. 28.

[2] Plowd. ch. 293; Macphers. Inf. 28; Rex *v.* Sutton, 3 Ad. & El. 597.

[3] Rex *v.* Oakley, 10 East, 491; Macphers. Inf. 28.

[4] Bac. Ab. Leases, i. 9; 1 Ld. Raym. 131; Rex *v.* Sutton, 5 Nev. & M. 353; Macphers. Inf. 35, 36.

[5] Co. Litt. 89 *a.*; Macphers. Inf. 41.

[6] Macphers. Inf. 31; Bedell *v.* Constable, Vaugh. 185. But see Harg. *n.* 67 to Co. Litt. 89.

[7] Co. Litt. 88 *b.*; 1 Bl. Com. 462.

[8] 1 Bl. Com. 462.

that any father, whether an infant or of full age, might, by deed executed in his lifetime, or by his last will and testament, dispose of the custody and tuition of his child, either born or unborn, to any person or persons in possession or remainder, other than popish recusants; such custody to last till the child attained the age of twenty-one, or for any less period, and to comprehend, meantime, the entire management of his estate, both real and personal. So far as popish recusants are concerned, this statute has since been modified; and all religious disabilities as to the office are now removed;[1] and since the statute of 1 Vict. ch. 26, an infant, though the father, cannot exercise the right of testamentary appointment; otherwise, the statute remains in force. Under this English law it matters not what are the father's religious opinions.[2] But a mother cannot appoint, nor a putative father, nor a person *in loco parentis*.[3] One testamentary guardian cannot appoint another, for his office is personal and not assignable.[4]

The important question arises, under this statute, whether the words "by deed executed in his lifetime" permits the father to dispose of his children by any instrument not testamentary, he may see fit to make. Lord Eldon was of the opinion that he could not, but was confined to a testamentary instrument in the form of a deed, which cannot operate during life and may be revoked at pleasure.[5] Such is doubtless the English law at the present day.[6]

Testamentary guardianship gives the custody of the ward's person, and of all his real and personal estate; and it embraces not only such property as comes to the ward through descent,

[1] 31 Geo. 3, ch. 32; 4 Mont. & C. 687; Corbet *v.* Tottenham, 1 Ba. & Be. 59.

[2] Villareal *v.* Mellish, 2 Swanst. 538.

[3] Macphers. Inf. 83; 1 Bl. Com. 462, Harg. *n.*; Vaugh. 180; 3 Atk. 519.

[4] Macphers. Inf. 82; Vaugh. 177; 2 P. W. 121; Gilb. Eq. Rep. 172; 2 Atk. 14.

[5] *Ex parte* Earl of Ilchester, 7 Ves. 367; Earl of Shaftesbury *v.* Lady Hannam, Finch Rep. 323.

[6] Macpherson intimates a different opinion. See Macphers. Inf. 84; Lecone *v.* Sheires, 1 Vern. 442.

devise, bequest, or inheritance from the father, but all that he may acquire from any person whomsoever, whether real or personal. This shows that the guardian's interest is derived not from the father, but from the law itself, for the father could give him no interest over that which was never his.[1]

Besides having the advantage of full control over the ward's entire estate, the testamentary guardian stands better than the guardian in socage, inasmuch as his power lasts until the ward reaches his majority, unless the father has seen fit to limit his trust to a less period.

Testamentary guardianship, as now understood, was unknown to the common law. Lord Alvanley said in *Ex parte* Ilchester: "It is clear, by the common law, a man could not, by any testamentary disposition, affect either his land or the guardianship of his children. The latter appears never to have been made the subject of testamentary disposition till the statute 12 Charles II."[2] But it seems probable, from some expressions of Lord Coke, that, so far as the custody of the ward's person was concerned, though not as to his lands, testamentary dispositions were not unknown to the old common law, and that this testamentary guardian, sometimes confounded with the guardian for nurture, had the care of the child until he reached the age of fourteen, with power to dispose of his chattels.[3]

Guardians by appointment of a court of equity, or *chancery* guardians, as they are termed, have, within the last century, assumed such importance, as almost to supersede in the English practice the other kinds. The earliest known instance of such an appointment occurred in 1696.[4] Blackstone speaks of the practice in his day as applicable chiefly to guardians with large estates, who sought to indemnify themselves and to avoid disagreeable contests with their wards, by placing them-

[1] Macphers. Inf. 91. See also Gilliat *v.* Gilliat, 3 Phillim. 222.

[2] 7 Ves. 370.

[3] Co. Litt. 87 *b.*; Co. Cop. § 23; Macphers. Inf. 68.

[4] Case of Hampden. See Co. Litt. 88 *b.*, Harg. *n.*

selves under the direction of the court of chancery.[1] The origin of this guardianship is obscure. Mr. Hargrave considered it an act of usurpation by the Lord Chancellor, but admitted the jurisdiction to have been fully established in his time.[2] Fonblanque warmly controverts the charge of usurpation, claiming that the jurisdiction exercised by the court of chancery over infants flows from its general authority, as delegated by the crown.[3] This latter view has met with the best judicial approval; for, as Lord Hardwicke and others have expressed it, the State must place somewhere a superintending power over those who cannot take care of themselves: and hence chancery necessarily acts, representing the sovereign as *parens patriæ*.[4] From the peculiar nature and restrictions of the other kinds of guardianship, many orphans, whose fathers had failed to appoint a testamentary guardian for them, would be otherwise without protection either of person or property. Whatever may be the origin of the jurisdiction by virtue of which courts of chancery appoint guardians in such cases, the right of making such appointments, and in general of controlling the persons and estates of minors has long been firmly established, and cannot at this day be shaken.

An infant is constituted a ward in chancery whenever any one brings him in as party plaintiff or defendant, by a bill asking the directions of the court concerning his person or estate, or the administration of property in which he is interested.[5] In this character he is treated as under its special protection. Again, a petition may be presented for the appointment of a chancery guardian, alleging that the infant has estate, real or personal. But the mere appointment of a guardian, in this instance, will not make him a ward in chan-

[1] 1 Bl. Com. 463.

[2] Co. Litt. 89 *a*, Harg. *n*. 70.

[3] 2 Fonb. Eq. 228, *n*. 5th ed.; 2 Story Eq. Jur. § 1333.

[4] Butler *v*. Freeman, Ambl. 301. See Lord Thurlow in Powell *v*. Cleaver, Br. C. C. 499; Lord Eldon in De Manneville *v*. De Manneville, 10 Ves. 52.

[5] Macphers. Inf. 103; Ambl. 302 *n*.

cery.[1] Where a suit is pending the court appoints a guardian of *the person* only; in other cases a guardian of *the person and estate*.[2] So chancery will appoint a guardian on petition, where testamentary guardians decline to act; and if necessary, determine on petition the right of a guardian already appointed.[3]

As to the general jurisdiction of chancery over infants, it may be observed that in the appointment and removal of guardians, in providing suitable maintenance, in awarding custody of the person, and in superintending the management and disposition of estates, the chancery court wields large powers for the benefit of the young and helpless. This jurisdiction, being clear of technical rules and dependent upon the discretion of the chancellor, adapts itself far more readily to the various grades of society, the intention of testators, the wants and wishes of the infants themselves, and the different varieties of property than all the other guardianships combined.[4] By compelling trust officers to give security to invest under its direction, and to keep regular accounts, the court exerts a wholesome restraint on the ward's behalf, while at the same time it arms the guardian against all attacks of a capricious heir, by affording its sanction to his official acts.

Chancery guardians are, in general, only appointed where there is property; but this is because guardianship can scarcely be necessary otherwise. Chancery, as Lord Eldon observed, cannot take on itself the maintenance of all the children in the kingdom.[5] Hence persons desiring to call in the authority of the court for the protection of an infant sometimes resort to the expedient of settling a sum of money upon him.[6] The great objection to chancery guardianship is its expense, and

1 Macphers. Inf. 104.
2 Ib. 105.
3 Ib. 104.
4 1 Bl. Com. 463, Harg. *n*.
5 Wellesley *v*. Duke of Beaufort, 2 Russ. 21.
6 Macphers. Inf. 103.

the lavish outlay of money which becomes requisite at every step renders the practical benefit to the minor often doubtful. Less cumbrous machinery would remedy this evil. There are some English statutes relating to the poor, the employment of apprentices, and the like, which, in connection with the writ of *habeas corpus*, are designed to supersede, in a measure, the necessity of personal guardianship, for those who are without property and need protection.[1]

Guardianship by election of the infant deserves a passing notice. We have seen that the infant in socage had the right of choosing a guardian at the age of fourteen. This age was recognized also as the limit to guardianship for nurture; the law choosing to yield somewhat to the ward's discretion thenceforth.[2] The socage ward might therefore, if he had no testamentary guardian, choose one to act on his behalf until majority, by executing a deed for that purpose. But little is really known on this subject, and the instances mentioned in the books are exceedingly rare.[3] Blackstone again, speaking of guardians for nurture, adds that in default of father or mother, the ordinary usually assigns some discreet person to take care of the infant's personal estate and to provide for his maintenance and education.[4] The practice in the spiritual court was to permit the minor, when of suitable age, to nominate his guardian subject to its approval. This was but a limited privilege after all, though it seems to have been granted to all children between seven and twenty-one.[5] It is manifestly different from the right of election allowed the socage ward. The authority of spiritual courts to appoint a guardian of the person and estate was emphatically denied by Lord Hardwicke, and chancery afterwards took this guardianship completely into its own keeping. The infant, above the age of fourteen, is

1 1 Bl. Com. 463, Harg. *n.* and acts there enumerated.

2 *Supra*, p. 393.

3 Co. Litt. 88 *b*. Harg. *n.* 16; Macphers. Inf. 77.

4 1 Bl. Com. 461.

5 Fitzgib. 164; Co. Litt. 88 *b*. Harg. *n.* 16.

still permitted to nominate his guardian before the court of chancery; but his nomination does not supersede the authority of the court, whether he be a socage ward or not.[1] Guardianship by election of the infant has thus become a misnomer, for he does not absolutely elect.

Guardianship in the United States differs considerably from guardianship in England. Here the whole subject is controlled in a great measure by local statutes. There are fewer kinds of guardians in American law, though some of the more important classes are recognized to a limited extent. Thus guardianship by nature and nurture, or the parental right of custody, prevails in most of the States. But as all children, male and female, inherit alike with us, guardianship by nurture is not even so clearly distinguished from guardianship by nature, as in the English practice.[2]

Guardianship in socage was never common in the United States. But traces of its existence are to be found. Thus in 1809, a guardian in socage, in New York, was permitted to bring trespass and ejectment.[3] This species of guardianship is now wholly superseded. In fact it could seldom have arisen, since half-blood and whole-blood relatives in this country inherit alike; so that a blood relation who cannot possibly inherit could rarely be found.[4]

We have testamentary guardians, with essentially the same powers and duties as in England. The statute of 12 Charles II. has been enacted in most of the United States, with the language somewhat changed. No religious disabilities are imposed in our law. But while some States follow the words of the ancient statute as to minor fathers, the right is elsewhere restricted to such as are competent to make a will, and this is

[1] Co. Litt. 88 *b.* Harg. *n.* 16; Hughes *v.* Science, 3 Atk. 631; Macphers. Inf. 74, 78.

[2] 2 Kent Com. 221; Reeve Dom. Rel. 315.

[3] Byrne *v.* Van Hoesen, 5 Johns. 66. See also Jackson *v.* De Walts, 7 ib. 157.

[4] 2 Kent Com. 222, 223; Reeve Dom. Rel. 315, 316.

a preferable expression. For precise modifications the student should consult the laws of his own State. Some statutes use the words "deed or will." The Ohio statute drops the word "deed" altogether.[1]

The right of testamentary appointment is still confined to the father in most States. But an Illinois statute permits the mother, if not re-married, to appoint such a guardian, provided no appointment was previously made by the father.[1] In New York, the consent of the mother is required to a testamentary appointment by the father.[2] So, too, the English principle prevails, that the testator can appoint a guardian over his own children only; although the right extends to posthumous offspring. He cannot appoint guardians for other children, though he give them his property.[3] But where a statute provides that a child may be adopted by one with the same rights as if the offspring were his own, it seems just that the father, thus constituted, should have the right of appointing a testamentary guardian for his adopted child.

Chancery guardianship may be considered as adopted to some extent in this country. The supreme courts in many States have now full chancery powers, as in England, over the persons and estate of infants; they may order investments, decree care and custody of the person, take children under their protection as wards of the court in certain cases, regulate the conduct of guardians, and otherwise exercise the important functions which vest in the English equity courts. But English chancery jurisprudence is one thing, and that of the United States another. While in one country the appointment, removal and general supervision of guardians, immediately belong to the equity courts, in the other a special tribunal is created for such matters. It is this special tribunal — somewhat resembling the English ecclesiastical court—which alone issues letters

[1] See 2 Kent Com. 225, 226. Hoyt *v.* Hellen, 2 Edw. Ch. 202; Matter of Pierce, 12 How. Pr. 532; Vanartsdalen *v.* Vanartsdalen, 14 Penn. St. 384.

[2] N. Y. Stat. 1862, ch. 172.

[3] Brigham *v.* Wheeler, 8 Met. 127; 2 Kent Com.

of guardianship, revokes them, and superintends trust accounts in the first instance. The guardians thus chosen have, in general, the rights and duties of chancery guardians of the person and estate.

The propriety of distinguishing between chancery guardians and those appointed by the special courts of this country — whether known as the probate, orphans', ordinary's, or surrogate's courts — is obvious when the origin of our probate jurisdiction is considered. At the time America was colonized, chancery guardianship was unknown in England. The ecclesiastical or spiritual courts, independent of all temporal authority, controlled the estates of orphans and their deceased parents. The necessity of some tribunal with probate jurisdiction was soon apparent to our ancestors; but, rejecting the idea of a church establishment, they distributed probate and equity powers among the common-law courts. Their judicial system was at first simple: that of local county courts with a supreme tribunal of appeal. With the growth of population came a division of these powers in the inferior courts. New county tribunals were erected for business appertaining to estates of the dead, testamentary trusts, and the care of orphans: a blending, as it were, of ecclesiastical and equity functions. The old county courts were left to their common-law jurisdiction, while the supreme tribunal retained control over them all, exercising appellate powers in common law, equity, and ecclesiastical suits. Such, in a word, is the origin of guardianship by judicial appointment in this country.[1] While the English chancery court was slowly extending its rights over the persons and estates of infants, another system was in process of growth on this side of the water, borrowing from English law as occasion offered, and adapting itself to the increasing wants of the community. This system, fostered doubtless by a strong prejudice against chancery practice, with its expensiveness and prolixity of pleadings, a prejudice widely

[1] See Smith (Mass.) Prob. Pract. 1–5.

prevalent during the last century, especially in New England, spread gradually into the new States and territories, the creature of statute law wherever it went.

Much confusion has arisen in our courts wherever this distinction has not been kept in view. The law of guardianship is often discussed as though we inherited the English chancery system, when in truth our usual practice is without its counterpart abroad. The only American text-writers of authority on this subject, Reeve and Kent, have contributed to this perplexity. The former was not precise in his classification.[1] The latter unwisely confused American and English appointments, applying the term *chancery guardians* to both.[2] But the courts have sometimes perceived the necessity of a separate name for guardians appointed by courts of probate jurisdiction. Accordingly, they have been called *guardians of the person and estate;*[3] but this name is quite as appropriate to others. So, too, they are designated as *statute guardians;* but there are statute modifications applied to all kinds of guardians, and besides, this name was long ago bestowed by English writers upon *testamentary guardians.*[4] We shall apply then in these pages, for want of something better, the distinguishing term *probate guardians;* this being sufficiently precise and suggestive; though it is admitted that the appointing power is not lodged in tribunals styled probate courts in every State, nor necessarily separated from courts exercising common-law functions.

By the civil law, minority was divided into two distinct periods: the first lasting until the age of puberty, fourteen in males, and twelve in females; the second continuing from that time until majority. During the first period, the guardian was called *tutor*, and the children *pupils*. During the second period, the guardian was called *curator*, and the children

[1] Reeve Dom. Rel. 311.
[2] 2 Kent Com. 226.
[3] See Arthurs' Appeal, 1 Grant (Penn.) 55.
[4] See *supra*, p. 393.

minors.[1] The same general divisions are to be found in the law of continental Europe at the present day, though modified somewhat by custom; also in Scotland;[2] also in Louisiana, and such other parts of this country, as were formerly under French and Spanish dominion.[3] So, the civil law recognized three kinds of guardianship: *tutela testamentaria*, conferred by testament; *legitima*, by the law itself; *dativa*, by the authority of the judge.[4] These divisions have their corresponding analogies in English and American law; since we may place testamentary guardians in the first class, socage and natural guardians in the second, and chancery and probate guardians in the third.

The different kinds of guardianship for minors having been considered, we proceed to speak briefly of guardians for idiots, lunatics, and spendthrifts. Under the king's sign manual, the Lord Chancellor was invested with jurisdiction over the persons and estates of insane persons. For this reason did chancery claim authority; not by virtue of the king's prerogative as *parens patriæ*, for idiots and lunatics, it is said, were not under the protection of the sovereign until the time of Edward II.[5] Lunatic asylums are provided by law and regulated from time to time. For legally determining the question of insanity in any case, chancery grants a commission in the nature of a writ, directed to masters in lunacy; and if the subject be found *non compos*, the court commits his person, together with a suitable allowance for his maintenance, to some person who is then called his committee.[6] Blackstone states that the rule in his day was to refuse this guardianship to the lunatic's next of kin, "because it is his interest that the party should die;"

[1] Story Confl. Laws, § 493; 3 Burge Col. & For. Laws, Pt. 2, ch. 23, § 5, p. 1001 to 1014.

[2] Fraser Parent & Child, 145.

[3] 2 Kent Com. 224.

[4] Co. Cop. § 23; Macphers. Inf. 573; 3 Burge, ib. 931.

[5] 2 Story Eq. Jur. §§ 1335, 1336; 1 Bl. Com. 303; 3 P. Wms. 108.

[6] 1 Bl. Com. 306. See Lunacy Regulation Act 1853, 16 & 17 Vict. ch. 70.

but this rule has long been disregarded in practice.[1] The committee manages his ward's estate, much the same as other guardians, being held to a strict account to the court of chancery, and to the ward, if he recovers, or otherwise to his personal representatives after his death. There are receivers appointed, with a salary, in case others refuse to act, but such officer is considered as committee and gives proper security.[2] Guardians of insane persons are appointed in this country; but in general by the courts exercising jurisdiction in case of minors, which derive also their authority from local statutes.[3] The civil law likewise assigned tutors and curators to such persons.[4]

Guardianship for spendthrifts was something recognized by the civil law. Where a man, by notorious prodigality, was in danger of wasting his estate, he was looked upon as *non compos*, and committed to the care of curators or tutors by the prætor.[5] And by the laws of Solon, such persons were branded with perpetual infamy.[6] Such guardianship is, however, unknown in England, and Blackstone considered it unsuitable to the genius of a free nation.[7] It has nevertheless been introduced into several of the United States.[8] Being the creature of statute law, the rights and powers of such guardians, and the method of their appointment are strictly construed.

The recent statutes relating to married women in this country have rendered some special provisions necessary for their benefit. While their husbands had the full enjoyment of their property, no guardian was necessary, and the only object of these statutes seems to be to provide a suitable trustee of the estate, in case a minor or insane wife is abandoned by her hus-

[1] *Ex parte* Cockayne, 7 Ves. 591.
[2] 1 Bl. Com. 306. See *Ex parte* Warren, 10 Ves. 622.
[3] See U. S. Dig. "Idiots and Lunatics."
[4] 1 Bl. Com. 306.
[5] Ff. 27, 10, 6, 16.
[6] Potter Antiq. b. 1, c. 26.
[7] 1 Bl. Com. 306.
[8] See Mass. Gen. Stats. c. 109, §§ 8, 9.

band, or he is likewise mentally unfitted for the trust. Such statutes are to be strictly construed, as in derogation of the common law.[1]

Besides guardians with general powers, there are guardians created by law for special purposes. Such are guardians under the English marriage act appointed for giving formal consent to the marriage of a minor, and guardians to release dower and homestead rights of insane married women. All such guardians derive their sole authority from statutes, and having performed the duty prescribed, they have no further concern with the ward. Nor do they act except in default of a general guardian. There are also public officers appointed for charitable purposes on behalf of the State, sometimes known as guardians; such as guardians of the poor; but, except for this appellation, they have no connection whatever with our subject.[2]

Finally, there is the guardian *ad litem*, who is simply a guardian for a special purpose; being one chosen to represent the ward in legal proceedings to which he is a party defendant. Where the ward is plaintiff he appears by next friend. The powers and duties of guardians *ad litem* are similar in England and the United States.[3]

1 Smith Prob. Pract. 87.
2 See Macphers. Inf. 164; Smith Prob. Pract. 87.
3 Macphers. Inf. 358; 2 Kent Com. 229. See Infants, *post*.

CHAPTER II.

APPOINTMENT OF GUARDIANS.

GUARDIANS derive their authority either from the law or a special appointment. And all guardians specially appointed must be appointed by the infant's parent; or by the infant himself; or by a court of competent jurisdiction.

Guardians by nature and nurture act under authority of the law; which designates, first, the father; and, after his death, the mother. These are the only natural guardians possible.[1] It has been said that the infant's next of kin succeed to the natural guardianship when both parents are dead.[2] This cannot be correct according to the sense of the term as used at this day. The mother is considered the natural guardian of a bastard, in this country, as against its putative father;[3] though the common law regarded such children as without a natural guardian.[4] On principle, it would seem that the natural guardianship of a child is shifted to the mother when custody is awarded her because of her husband's personal unfitness. And the modern tendency is to regard both husband and wife as guardians, by nature, of their own children.[5]

Socage guardians also derived their authority from the law, and not from a special appointment.[6]

Testamentary guardianship is the only recognized instance of

[1] Co. Litt. 88 *b.*; 1 Bl. Com. 461; 2 Kent Com. 220; Macphers. Inf. 52; Jarrett *v.* State, 5 Gill and Johns. 27; Eldridge *v.* Lippincott, Coxe, 397; Fields *v.* Law, 2 Root, 320.

[2] See Reeve Dom. Rel. 315.

[3] Wright *v.* Wright, 2 Mass. 109; Hudson *v.* Hills, 8 N. H. 417; People *v.* Kling, 6 Barb. 366; Dalton *v.* The State, 6 Blackf. 357.

[4] Macphers. Inf. 67; Rex *v.* Felton, 1 Bott. P. L. by Const. p. 478, pl. 629.

[5] See *supra*, p. 333; People *v.* Boice, 39 Barb. 307.

[6] 2 Kent Com. 223; see *supra*, p. 392.

authority derived from parental appointment. Guardians thus appointed require no further qualification; not even the probate of the will which appoints them.[1] But testamentary guardianship exists in this country chiefly by force of local statutes. And we find many modifications of the English rule; none more important than those of several States which render a probate of the will necessary before a testamentary guardian can act; while it is not unfrequently found that the appointment remains subject to the approval of the court, and presentation of due security by the person appointed.

The parol appointment of a testamentary guardian is insufficient.[2] But the instrument which designates him need not be executed with the same formality as a will; for the father, as the statute intimates, may appoint by testamentary deed. It has been held that the appointment of guardians by a will not duly attested was made good by a codicil duly attested, written on the same paper, making certain alterations in the will, and confirming it in other respects.[3]

It is sometimes difficult to determine what language will constitute testamentary guardianship. The statute uses the words "custody and tuition" in reference to the children; and such assignment of the children as confers, expressly or by implication, a power thus extensive, ought to suffice. Thus, where a testator gives the "care and custody" of his children, further directing that the person so entrusted shall be guided by the advice of his executors, as to the children's education, this is held to be a good appointment.[4] So it is held that testamentary guardianship was constituted, where a testator directed the trustees of his will to procure a suitable house for the residence of his children, who were infants, and to engage a proper

[1] Brigham *v.* Wheeler, 8 Met. 127; Hoyt's Case, 2 Edw. Ch. 113; *In re* Hart, 2 Con. & L. 375; Lady Chester's Case, Vent. 207. See 7 Ves. 365; Gilliat *v.* Gilliat, 3 Phillim. 222.

[2] Macphers. Inf. 84. See Johnstone *v.* Beattie, 10 Cl. & Fin. 42.

[3] De Bathe *v.* Lord Fingal, 16 Ves. 167. But see Marshall C. J. in Gaines *v.* Spann, 2 Brock. 81.

[4] See Corrigan *v.* Kiernan, 1 Bradf. 208.

person for the purpose of taking the management and care of the house and of his children during their minority; and requested his late wife's sister, if she should be alive at his decease, to take such management and care on herself.[1] And in general testamentary guardians need not be expressly designated as such; though in order to constitute them by implication, the powers essential to the office must be conferred.[2]

The devise of certain property *in trust* for infants is not a devise of guardianship. Thus, it was said by Lord Vaughan that, where a testator devised land to a trustee, to be held in trust for his heir, and for his maintenance and education until he should be of age, this was no devise of the custody within the statute, for he might have done this before the statute.[3] The same may be said generally of legacies and bequests in trust.[4]

Testamentary guardians, to use the statute expression, may be appointed "either in possession or remainder;" that is, successors may be designated. So they may be authorized to act during the full term of the infant's minority or for a less period. In other words, the testator is allowed a liberal discretion in his selection and in limiting authority. The paper which creates a person testamentary guardian, becomes thus the test of his official powers and responsibility. Letters of guardianship from the chancery or probate court give his appointment no additional force, unless required by statute. In fact such letters, however regarded in his dealings with strangers, are without jurisdiction.[5]

1 Miller *v.* Harris, 14 Sim. 540. See Mendes *v.* Mendes, 1 Ves. 89; s. c. 3 Atk. 619.

2 Gaines *v.* Spann, 2 Brock, 81; Peyton *v.* Smith, 2 Dev. & Batt. Eq. 325; Johnstone *v.* Beattie, 10 Cl. & Fin. 42; Balch *v.* Smith, 12 N H. 437.

3 Bedell *v.* Constable, Vaugh. 177.

4 Kevan *v.* Waller, 11 Leigh, 414; Dunham *v.* Hatcher, 31 Ala. 483.

5 Robinson *v.* Gollinger, 9 Watts, 169; Morris *v.* Harris, 15 Cal. 226; Holmes *v.* Field, 12 Ill. 424; Copp *v.* Copp, 20 N. H. 284. See Macphers. Inf. 84, 86; Stone *v.* Dorrett, 18 Tex. 700. If the testator's will prescribes that the wife shall be testamentary guardian of the children, "as long as she shall remain his widow," her authority ceases on her re-marriage and a new appointment becomes necessary. Corrigan *v.* Kiernan, 1 Bradf. Sur. 208; Holmes *v.* Field, 12 Ill. 424.

In a late New York case, it was held, on appeal from the surrogate, that no probate guardian could be appointed after the father's decease, where the father, being a man of indigent circumstances, had surrendered his children to a charitable institution by an instrument in writing, executed during his lifetime, and not long before his death, in presence of two witnesses, and purporting to "commit and surrender" the children to the said institution pursuant to its charter. There were no testamentary expressions used, nor did the instrument appear to have been executed in contemplation of death. The decision of the court appears to rest on statutory interpretation.[1] In general, a firm cannot be made guardian of an infant; nor probably can a corporation.[2]

The testator's power of appointment extends to all his lawful children surviving at his decease, being still minors and unmarried. Posthumous children are, likewise, included. And the testator's appointment of his wife as testamentary guardian, is not revoked by the birth of such issue, subsequent to the execution of the will or testamentary deed appointing her; the analogy of distribution of his property failing to affect this case.[3]

Guardianship by sole appointment of the infant cannot now be said to exist. But at the common law there was one instance where it arose; namely, when the heir above the age of fourteen chose to supersede his guardian in socage, by one of his own choice, under a deed of appointment.[4] Infants have still the privilege of nominating, though not appointing, a guardian in court, after arriving at this age; and, if judicially sanctioned, their choice is good. In the appointment of chancery guardians, the custom is for the court to approve such nomination without the usual reference to a master.[5] But this is not an

[1] The People *v.* Kearney, 31 Barb. 430.

[2] See Macphers. Inf. 109; De Mazar *v.* Pybus, 4 Ves. 644.

[3] Hollingsworth's Appeal, 51 Penn. St. 518; 2 Br. C. C. 538; Macphers. Inf. 87.

[4] *Supra*, pp. 393, 398; Co. Litt. 89 *a*.

[5] *Ex parte* Edwards, 3 Atk. 519; Macphers. Inf. 78, 109.

invariable rule.[1] Testamentary guardians cannot be superseded in this way, nor chancery guardians.[2] Statutes giving the right of selecting probate guardians to infants above fourteen have been enacted throughout the United States; though the extent of this privilege is not uniformly prescribed.[3] But the ward cannot set aside a testamentary or chancery guardian in this country; nor, on principle, should he be allowed to supersede a probate guardian properly appointed, unless authorized by a positive statute.[4] Having once exercised his right of choice, he is bound by the appointment, and cannot nominate again, as his fancy pleases.[5] In any event, the court must sanction the infant's selection, and issue letters before the guardian can act; so that this is guardianship rather by appointment of the court than of the infant.

Chancery and probate guardians, subject to the above qualification, are created in strictness by the special appointment of a court exercising competent jurisdiction. And in discussing the subject of judicial appointment we shall consider, first, the tribunal which appoints; second, the persons properly appointed; third, the method of appointment; and fourth, the effect of the appointment.

As to the first point, it may be premised that in England all guardians are appointed by the court of chancery in the exercise of inferior or appellate powers. Chancery guardians have been appointed in this country, but not frequently; and county courts of probate jurisdiction at the present day act in the first instance, issuing letters of guardianship as well as of administration, under their official seal. Thus, in New England and most of the Western States, probate guardians are ap-

1 *Ex parte* Watkins, 2 Ves. 470; Curtis *v.* Rippon, 4 Mad. 462; Coham *v.* Coham, 13 Sim. 639.

2 Palmer, 22; Andrew, 313; Matter of Dyer, 5 Paige Ch. 534; Matter of Nicoll, 1 Johns. Ch. 25.

3 See Ham *v.* Ham, 15 Gratt. 74; Dibble *v.* Dibble, 8 Ind. 307; Pitts *v.* Cherry, 14 Geo. 594; Arthurs' Appeal, 1 Grant, 55; Sessions *v.* Kell, 30 Miss. 458; Montgomery *v.* Smith, 3 Dana, 599; Palmer *v.* Oakley, 2 Doug. 433.

4 Dyer's Case, 5 Paige, Ch. 534.

5 Lee's Appeal, 27 Penn. St. 229. See also E. B. *v.* E. C. B., 28 Barb. 299.

pointed by the judge of probate; in New York, by the surrogate; in New Jersey, by the orphans' court or the ordinary; in Pennsylvania and Maryland, by the orphans' court; in Ohio, by the court of common pleas with chancery powers; in California, by the district courts possessing a similar jurisdiction. In Virginia, North and South Carolina, the chancery and county courts exercised a sort of concurrent jurisdiction; in others of the Southern States, as Alabama, there were orphans' courts; in Louisiana, the civil law prevailed.[1]

Two important elements enter into this jurisdiction over the ward: possession of property and actual residence within the judicial limits. Property in the infant has usually been deemed essential in chancery practice.[2] But in a case which came before Lord-Chancellor Cottenham, in 1847, it was held that the court should interfere on behalf of infants without property, so as to award custody of the person. "I have no doubt about the jurisdiction," was his emphatic language.[3] What may be called guardians of the person and estate in chancery are still appointed, however, on the allegation of property. In the United States, letters issue to probate guardians, whenever there is occasion for their appointment, the statute rarely prescribing narrower limits to the judge's authority; and, as our practice is simple and attended with little expense, the same necessity for inquiry into the means of the infant does not manifestly arise as in the case of chancery guardianship. But statute and practice generally have reference to cases of property.[4] Where the ward is a non-resident, guardianship is frequently recognized for the collection and preservation of his estate in the jurisdiction; and in such cases the court, where the property is situated, appoints some friend of the minor on his behalf, requiring proper security;

[1] See 2 Kent Com. 226, 227, and notes.
[2] See Macphers. Inf. 103; *supra*, p. 397.
[3] *In re* Spence, 2 Ph. 247.
[4] The People *v.* Kearney, 31 Barb. 430.

the existence of the property determining the right of jurisdiction.[1]

Far more important is the requirement of an actual residence within the jurisdiction; especially in States where the authority of courts with probate jurisdiction is strictly limited to their respective counties. Letters of guardianship obtained in the wrong county are null and void, and may be collaterally impeached in any court.[2] Where the courts of two or more counties have concurrent jurisdiction, as if a non-resident has property lying in different places, the general principle is that the court, where proceedings are first commenced, retains jurisdiction. And letters once properly issued are not revoked by the ward's removal to another county within the same general jurisdiction. And where a new appointment becomes necessary, next to the inquiry whether the party is a minor or otherwise legally subject to guardianship at all, is the determination of his actual residence. And, as just observed, property may give jurisdiction in some cases where the ward resides abroad.

Prima facie, the infant's residence, or domicile is that of his parent, and such it will remain during minority, in spite of his temporary absence at school or elsewhere. Nor can he of his own motion acquire a new domicile, since he is not a person *sui juris*.[3] But his domicile may be changed by his father, if he has one; otherwise, according to the best modern authorities, by the surviving mother until her re-marriage; and perhaps, even by the guardian himself, although not a relative, provided he act in good faith.[4] The intent of the parent or guardian in such cases is always material; but this intent is to be determined by facts.

[1] Clarke *v.* Cordis, 4 Allen, 466. See Hope *v.* Hope, 27 E. L. & Eq. 249.

[2] Ware *v.* Coleman, 6 J. J. Marsh. 198; Sears *v.* Terry, 26 Conn. 273; Dorman *v.* Ogbourne, 16 Ala. 759; Munson *v.* Munson, 9 Tex. 109; Lacy *v.* Williams, 27 Mis. 280.

[3] Macphers. Inf. 579; Brown *v.* Lynch, 2 Bradf. 214; Story Confl. Laws, § 46.

[4] Potinger *v.* Wightman, 3 Merivale, 67; 2 Kent Com. 227, 430; 1 Burge Col. & For. Laws, 39; Brown *v.* Lynch, 2 Bradf. 214.

The original domicile of an infant is that of his parents at the time of his birth. The infant's place of residence at the time when a guardian is to be appointed determines the jurisdiction of the court. Hence, the court which appointed the first guardian of a ward may not always appoint his successor.[1]

The court of chancery exercises a large discretion. Its authority over the persons and estates of infants, idiots, and lunatics cannot be questioned elsewhere. No tribunal short of the legislature can interpose a check upon its powers. But it is different with probate courts. Their jurisdiction is founded upon local statutes, maintained in derogation of the common law, made subject to supervision of supreme tribunals, and confined to the exercise of special powers sparingly conferred. From the fact that the English equity courts are unfettered in their authority, chancery courts in this country incline to the same direction; hence, they construe strictly the powers of the probate courts while maintaining their own: a matter of little difficulty, since the supreme authority is in their hands, whether in matters of probate, equity, or common law. With especial strictness are the powers of probate tribunals scrutinized in matters which do not grow out of the settlement of estates of deceased persons.[2]

It may devolve on chancery to appoint guardians where testamentary guardians decline or are disqualified to act. So where there are two or more testamentary guardians and they fail to agree.[3] And it is the English rule that testamentary guardianship does not go over upon the guardian's death, no successor having been indicated in the will; but chancery must supply the vacancy.[4] The same may be said of the courts in this country with probate jurisdiction.[5]

[1] Brown *v.* Lynch, 2 Bradf. 214.

[2] See, for instance, as to insane persons and spendthrifts, Holden *v.* Scanlin, 30 Vt. 177; Sears *v.* Terry, 26 Conn. 273; Strong *v.* Birchard, 5 Conn. 357; Cooper *v.* Summers, 1 Sneed, 453; Hovey *v.* Harmon, 49 Me. 269.

[3] Macphers. Inf. 113; ib. 104.

[4] Bac. Abr. Guardian & Ward, A.

[5] See The People *v.* Kearney, 31 Barb. 430; Judge of Probate *v.* Hinds, 4 N. H. 464.

In selecting the proper person as guardian, the judge is allowed to exercise a liberal discretion, and his decision will not be disturbed on appeal except for good and sufficient cause. Such is the rule both in England and America.[1] But this discretion is not an arbitrary one; it must be exercised in conformity with certain fixed principles. And if the judge appoint without giving reasonable notice, so that parties interested have not a fair opportunity to be heard upon the petition, his appointment may be set aside on appeal.[2]

Where the father of an infant is living, courts have ever been unwilling to assume jurisdiction. Chancery, according to the old rule, as we understand Blackstone to mean,[3] could not appoint a guardian except for fatherless children. But the correctness of this principle was afterwards doubted; and when the rule became settled, in Lord Thurlow's time, that the father could not give a valid receipt for his child's legacy, the necessity of appointing a guardian to collect and hold personal property was apparent.[4] And since the substitution of chancery and probate wards in practice for socage wards, guardianship of the minor in the father's lifetime has frequently been sought in the courts.[5]

But the English chancery reluctantly interferes with the father's rights in such cases. Lord-Chancellor Hart in 1828 refused to bestow the chancery guardianship of a minor upon a third person, on the ground that the father is guardian of his own children by paramount title and common right. And while he admitted that the court should in all cases assume the superintendence of the child's fortunes, he added, that during the father's life no other could be placed over the child, except under very peculiar circumstances, and even then rather as a

[1] *In re* Kaye, 1 Law Rep. Ch. 387; Battle *v.* Vick, 4 Dev. 294; White *v.* Pomeroy, 7 Barb. 640; Sadler *v.* Rose, 18 Ark. 600.

[2] Underhill *v.* Dennis, 9 Paige, 202.

[3] 3 Bl. Com. 427.

[4] Cooper *v.* Thornton, 3 Br. C. C. 96; Dagley *v.* Tolferry, 1 P. Wms. 285; 2 Kent Com. 220, and cases cited; Lang *v.* Pettus, 11 Ala. 37.

[5] See *Ex parte* Bond, 8 L. J. 252, Ch.

curator than a guardian.[1] And the later decisions are to the same effect; as, for instance, *Fynn's Case*, where Vice-Chancellor Bruce refused to make the mother a chancery guardian of her children against the father's wishes, though satisfied that the latter was unable to maintain them, and was such a person as would not have been selected for the guardianship of another person's children.[2]

The great difficulty which arises in the English chancery practice, where guardianship is sought by a stranger, namely, that a father's custody of his own children is thereby disturbed, has been frequently obviated in this country by statute. And in many States, while the father is living, probate guardians are appointed, whose powers, being limited to the infant's estate, do not come in conflict with the parental right to the ward's person.[3] Yet in other States the probate courts can only grant guardianship to orphans, that is, to fatherless children;[4] and where this is the case, chancery might assume jurisdiction in an extreme case, though the father were living.

Most frequently the court's discretion is to be exercised, whether in chancery or probate appointments, in cases where the child is fatherless, and moreover too young to nominate for himself. Who, then, shall be selected? The mother, if living and competent for the trust, would appear to be the most suitable person, unless re-married, and so in fact is she considered in this country. But in English chancery practice it is said that no great importance is attached to her rights; though undoubtedly she and the next of kin have together the first claim.[5] And it is improper to appoint the mother without some information as to the father's family.[6] On the other hand, the court

[1] Barry *v.* Barry, 1 Moll. 210.

[2] 12 Jur. 713. And see Spence's Case, 2 Ph. 247; Ball *v.* Ball, 2 Sim. 35.

[3] Mass. Gen. Stats. ch. 109, § 4; Clark *v.* Montgomery, 23 Barb. 464.

[4] Poston *v.* Young, 7 J. J. Marsh. 501; Hall *v.* Lay, 2 Ala. 529.

[5] Macphers. Inf. 112.

[6] Cooke's Case, 6 E. L. & Eq. 47.

refuses to select guardians for infants residing with their mother until she has indicated her own wishes.[1]

In this country, probate guardians are appointed with more exclusive reference to the mother's choice, and the next of kin are less favorably regarded. And it is not uncommon to find guiding principles indicated by statute for all cases. The American rule is clearly stated in a recent New Jersey case; namely, that the mother, and, after the mother, the next of kin, of an infant under fourteen is entitled to preference, and that such claim cannot be disregarded unless for some satisfactory reason.[2]

It is further stated, in this case, that a greater latitude is allowed to the court, as between relatives having no legal claim to the services of the child and the natural guardian; and reasons which might be deemed insufficient to bar the mother's rights might decide as between other relations.[3]

The leading consideration for the court should be the interest and welfare of the child; and this, which becomes almost the only rule of choice between distant kindred, may control even the selection of the father himself.[4] Hence, in a case where children had been left with their grandparents for many years with the consent of the father, who was a widower and a seafaring man, guardianship was refused to their uncle, though he had been designated by the father on his death-bed.[5] If the child is fatherless, and the mother's manner of life would be likely to exercise an unfavorable influence, she will not be appointed, nor will her wishes have much weight.[6] Nor is the appointment of an executor or administrator desirable, if a conflict of interests is thereby created.[7] Nor the selection of a

[1] Lockwood *v.* Fenton, 17 E. L. & Eq. 90; *In re* Thomas, 21 E. L. & Eq. 524. As to other relatives, see Macphers. Inf. 112.

[2] Albert *v.* Perry, 1 McCart. 540. And see Read *v.* Drake, 1 Green Ch. 78; Allen *v.* Peete, 25 Miss. 29; People *v.* Wilcox, 22 Barb. 178.

[3] Albert *v.* Perry, ib.

[4] Bennett *v.* Byrne, 2 Barb. Ch. 216; Compton *v.* Compton, 2 Gill, 241.

[5] Foster *v.* Mott, 3 Bradf. 409.

[6] Albert *v.* Perry, 1 McCart. 540.

[7] Crutchfield's Case, 3 Yerg. 336; Isaacs *v.* Taylor, 3 Dana, 600; Massingale *v.* Tate, 4 Hayw. 30; Parker *v.* Lincoln, 12 Mass. 17.

stranger, when the next of kin can be had, unless the parent expressly desires it.[1] Nor of one who holds adverse religious opinions, though there is at this day far more toleration than formerly on this point.[2] And the objection that a particular appointment will subject the ward's estate to extraordinary expense ought to be considered.[3] In general, it is the duty of the court to regard the general character of the person who applies for letters of guardianship; the influence he is likely to exert, and, if the estate be difficult to manage, his business qualifications.

On the other hand, no fanciful reasons should be allowed to determine the selection of the court between distant relations. The circumstance that the infant inherited the principal part of his property through one line of the family is not to prejudice his next of kin in the other.[4] But the fact that he has always been in the charge of his relatives on one side is entitled to weight.[5] If children are already in a good home, this is a reason why they should not be disturbed. But the mother's consent to relinquish them to a certain relative is of little avail, for it might have been extorted from her under pressure of poverty.[6] Although the prudent choice of a minor arrived at fourteen may be almost conclusive, as we have already seen, yet it would seem that while under that age his preferences are entitled to no consideration.

The father's testament constitutes a guardian; but when the appointment is too informal to take effect under the statute, as constituting testamentary guardianship, a chancery or probate guardian must be appointed. In such case, the choice thus informally indicated carries great weight with the court.[7] And

1 See Sullivans' Case, 1 Moll. 225; Morehouse *v.* Cooke, Hopk. 226; Lady Teynham *v.* Lennard, cited 2 Atk. 315; Spaun *v.* Collins, 10 S. & M. 624.

2 Underhill *v.* Dennis, 9 Paige, 202; Macphers. Inf. 113; *Ex parte* Whitfield, 2 Atk. 315.

3 Bennett *v.* Byrne, 2 Barb. Ch. 216.

4 Underhill *v.* Dennis, 9 Paige, 202; Albert *v.* Perry, 1 McCart. 540.

5 Albert *v.* Perry, 1 McCart. 540.

6 Ib.

7 Hall *v.* Storer, 1 Yo. & C. 556.

on general principle the death-bed wishes of the father are considered by the court; so those of the mother, in States where the mother's choice is favored at all.[1] Such wishes, however, are not conclusive upon the court.

As concerns the right of a married woman to be appointed guardian, there is doubt and uncertainty. The *dicta* are apt to go one way and the decisions another; doubtless out of judicial deference to the sex. Some hold that married women are at common law capable of becoming guardians; but they draw their conclusions rather from the analogies of administration, than from positive authority in their favor. When it is considered that chancery and probate guardians are a modern creation, the ancient cases, from such species of guardianship as are now extinct, are hardly worth looking after. It is true there are several cases which sustain the acts of married women while acting as guardians, or rather *quasi* guardians; at the same time clear precedents for their actual appointment are wanting.[2] In spite of the liberal tendency of the age, we conclude that while such guardianship would not be deemed absolutely void, public policy is decidedly against the appointment. Not the least important objection is the inability of married women to furnish proper recognizance, and to manage trust property without constantly encountering legal obstacles. Hence, the English rule has been on the marriage of a female guardian to choose another in her stead, on the ground that she is no longer *sui juris*, and has become liable to the control of her husband; though she is said to be still at liberty to go before the master to propose herself as her own successor.[3]

[1] Knott *v.* Cottee, 2 Ph. 192; Kaye's Case, 1 Law Rep. Ch. 387; Lady Teynham *v.* Lennard, 4 Br. P. C. 302; s. c. cited 2 Atk. 315; Bennett *v.* Byrne, 2 Barb. Ch. 216; Cozine *v.* Horne, 1 Bradf. 143.

[2] Wallis *v.* Campbell, 13 Ves. 517. This was the case of an illegitimate child. As cited in Macphers. Inf. 111, it might be considered authority for the appointment of married women as guardians.

[3] Macphers. Inf. 111; Anon. 8 Sim. 346; Gornall's Case, 1 Beav. 347. A married woman is unfit to be chancery guardian. Kaye's Case, 1 Law Rep. Ch. 387. See further Jarrett *v.* State, 5 Gill & Johns. 27; Palmer *v.* Oakley, 2 Doug.

Persons residing out of the jurisdiction will not usually be appointed guardians, although one who was out of the State might yet control from a distance; for, it is said, there must be some one answerable to the court.[1] But if the sureties on the guardian's bond reside within the jurisdiction and are pecuniarily responsible, is not some one answerable to the court? The cases, however, are rare where such an appointment would be advantageous to the ward for business reasons; and hence, others are usually chosen, both in chancery and probate. In some of the United States, the appointment of non-residents is prohibited by statute; and even without such prohibition the court is justified in withholding letters of guardianship, where the petitioner is beyond the reach of State process.[2] But the person selected need not reside within the jurisdiction of the county court making the appointment. Where infants are domiciled abroad, some one at home will be appointed, if a guardian is required, even though the father wishes it otherwise.[3] Exceptions to this rule have been made in strong cases, and a non-resident guardian appointed.[4]

The usual practice in chancery, is for the court, as soon as the petition is presented, to make an order for a reference to a master to approve of a proper person for the guardianship. For this purpose, the master is attended by all proper parties; and, after a full hearing, he makes his report, in which he mentions the infant's age and fortune, the evidence and legal grounds on which his approval of the guardian is based, and the maintenance proper for the child. The Vice Chancellor confirms or varies the report at his discretion, and then makes the appointment. From his decision appeal lies to the full court.[5]

433; Farrer *v.* Clark, 29 Miss. 195; Holley *v.* Chamberlain, 1 Redf. 333; Kettletas *v.* Gardner, 1 Paige, 488; *Ex parte* Maxwell, 19 Ind. 88.

1 Logan *v* Fairlee, Jacob, 193.

2 Finney *v.* State, 9 Mis. 227.

3 Stephens *v.* James, 1 M. & K. 627; Lethem *v.* Hall, 7 Sim. 141.

4 Daniel *v.* Newton, 8 Beav. 485; *In re* Thomas, 21 E. L. & Eq. 524.

5 Macphers. Inf. 106, 107, and cases cited; 2 Kent Com. 227.

The guardian thus appointed, if guardian of the person and estate, is required to enter into recognizance, with sufficient sureties, to account regularly or whenever called upon, by the court. But, according to the modern English practice, guardians of the person and not of the estate are exempted from this requirement.[1]

In some cases, guardians are appointed by the court without reference to a master. Thus, as where the father applies, or the infant above fourteen makes a selection, the court acts without reference, out of regard for their special privilege.[2] And where the property of the infant is very small, the same favor has been granted, in order to save legal expense to the estate.[3] The child should usually be present at the hearing; but, in a recent Irish case, the court dispensed with the requirement, on evidence that the child was less than a month old and of delicate health.[4]

Our usual practice in the appointment of probate guardians is more simple. Petition is presented by the person desiring the appointment, whereupon a citation is issued, for all parties interested to appear on a certain court day. The judge, upon the day specified, after a summary hearing, appoints the guardian, and issues letters of guardianship upon filing bond with proper security. Appeal may be taken within a limited time by any person aggrieved, and the tribunal of last resort then hears the parties, determines the choice, and makes a final decree, — to which the lower court conforms and issues letters of guardianship accordingly. The infant, if under fourteen, is rarely produced in court nor does the judge make an order of reference.[5]

The appointment of a chancery guardian is of itself an act exercised by the court of highest authority, in such matters.

[1] Macphers. Inf. 107, 108; 2 Kent Com. 227.

[2] *Supra*, pp. 409, 415; Macphers. Inf. 7 8,109

[3] Bond *ex parte*, 11 Jur. 114.

[4] Stutely *v.* Harrison, 1 Ir. Eq. 256; 13 Jur. 800. And see Benison *v.* Worsley, 15 E. L. & Eq. 317.

[5] For practice in particular States, see local statutes; also Smith's (Mass.) Prob. Practice; Comst. Dig.; Reese (Ga.) Manual; Willard N. Y. Sur.

The appointment cannot be impeached elsewhere, nor set aside by a common-law tribunal. The court which creates the guardian superintends his acts and removes him if necessary. Such is the nature of chancery jurisdiction wherever it exists.[1] But the effect of appointments made by probate authority is not the same. In general, the same principles apply as in grants of administration; probate jurisdiction being much the same whether over the estates of deceased persons or of infants. For fraud or excess of jurisdiction, letters of probate guardianship may be attacked collaterally; though not otherwise. And a person sued in the common-law courts cannot defend on the ground that the guardian is unsuitable for his trust. The letters of guardianship sufficiently disprove it. They are the guardian's credentials of authority everywhere, and, if improperly issued, should be revoked by the court which can issue them.[2]

The decree of the court appointing a guardian is *prima facie* evidence of the ward's disability;[3] and is even held conclusive in some cases. For it is unreasonable to compel the guardian of an insane person or spendthrift to furnish proof of his ward's condition in every collateral suit on his behalf, and to encounter new investigations of facts already established, concerning which men's minds greatly differ. But the *prima facie* evidence of infancy is generally simple and easily obtained. The authority of his guardian turns upon a simple question of fact: the date of birth. And while we apprehend that the recitals contained in letters of guardianship afford *prima facie* proof on this point, in all contests involving the guardian's authority, the pre-

[1] Macphers. Inf. 119.

[2] Speight *v.* Knight, 11 Ala. 461; Kimball *v.* Fisk, 39 N. H. 110; Warner *v.* Wilson, 4 Cal. 310. As to the effect of defective notice in probate appointments, see Davison *v.* Johonnot, 7 Met. 388; Breed *v.* Pratt, 18 Pick. 115; Conkey *v.* Kingman, 24 Pick. 115; Cleveland *v.* Hopkins, 2 Aik. 394; Chase *v.* Hathaway, 14 Mass. 222; The People *v.* Wilcox, 22 Barb. 178; Palmer *v.* Oakley, 2 Doug. 433; Sears *v.* Terry, 26 Conn. 273; Gronfier *v.* Puymirol, 19 Cal. 629. As to other informalities, see State *v.* Hyde, 29 Conn. 564; Lee *v.* Ice, 22 Ind. 384.

[3] White *v.* Palmer, 4 Mass. 147.

sumption thus raised must be very slight, since it is common to issue letters of probate guardianship upon the mere allegation of infancy in the petition and without special proof.[1]

One who has been appointed guardian and acted as such, cannot deny the jurisdiction of the court which appointed him in a collateral suit.[2] If he ascertains that his appointment was without jurisdiction, he should surrender his letters at once and cease to act.

The principles of the civil law, as later adopted in Holland, France, and Spain, with reference to the jurisdiction and method of appointing guardians, differs not greatly from ours. The jurisdiction competent to make the selection was that of the domicile of the minor, or in which his property was situated. Under the French code, a family council is called together at the instance of the parties interested, and nominates a suitable person or persons to take the trust, where the children are orphans and not otherwise provided for; and these persons, when they are approved by the judge, take an oath well and faithfully to discharge their trust and complete the necessary qualifications. In Louisiana, the selection is made by the family council in the same manner.[3]

1 Leonard *v.* Leonard, 14 Pick. 280. See 2 Greenl. Evid. §§ 363–368.

2 Thurston *v.* Holbrook's Estate, 31 Vt. 354; Hines *v.* Mullins, 25 Geo. 696.

3 3 Burge Col. & For. Laws, 938–943; 2 Kent Com. 231.

CHAPTER III.

TERMINATION OF THE GUARDIAN'S AUTHORITY.

GUARDIANSHIP lasts until the end of the period for which it was instituted. But it may be sooner terminated by the death or marriage of the ward, or by the death, resignation, removal, or supersedure of the guardian himself; or, if the guardian be a female, by her marriage. These topics will be considered in order.

As the relation of guardian and ward usually exists for merely temporary purposes, it is plain that when those purposes are fulfilled, the trust must terminate. The object of guardianship, in the case of infants, is fulfilled when the infant becomes of age, for he is then free and competent under the law to transact his own business and control his own person. No guardian therefore, of an infant, whether a socage, natural, testamentary, chancery, or probate guardian, can act after the ward is twenty-one years old.[1]

But the natural limitation of the guardian's authority may be even sooner, if derived from testamentary appointment. For the testator may designate a shorter period or some particular event which shall determine the relation. Thus, if he appoints his wife to be guardian until her re-marriage, her trust terminates on marrying again.[2] And if no successor was indicated in the will, a chancery or probate appointment must supply the vacancy.[3]

[1] 1 Bl. Com. 461, 462, Harg. *n.*; 2 Kent Com. 221–227.

[2] Selby *v.* Selby, 2 Eq. Ca. Ab. 488; Holmes *v.* Field, 12 Ill 424; Corrigan *v.* Kiernan, 1 Bradf. 208.

[3] Macphers. Inf. 104, and cases cited; *supra*, pp. 397, 408, 413.

The legal authority of guardians in socage also terminated, strictly speaking, when the infant became fourteen.[1] So did that of guardians for nurture, as distinguished from those by nature.[2] This was because the ward was recognized as partially qualified to act for himself, having passed through the period of nurture. He was then allowed to elect a guardian.[3] Still the guardianship continued effectual during minority in both cases, unless a new choice was made by the ward.[4] But no guardians in socage, for nurture, testamentary, or by judicial appointment were ever rendered devoid of power, by the mere fact that the infant had passed the period of nurture. An anomalous exception is found in Ohio, where it has been held that probate guardianship wholly ceases when the ward reaches twelve, if a female, or fourteen, if a male, and that a new appointment must then be made.[5] This rule is, however, one of statutory construction.

No more precise limit can be assigned to the authority of guardians over insane persons and spendthrifts, than that of the ward's necessities. When he becomes restored to reason or is otherwise fit to control his own person and estate, this guardianship ceases; for the purposes of the trust are felt no longer. But a period so difficult to fix should be judicially determined, for which cause a formal discharge from guardianship is to be sought and obtained, and meantime the guardian's authority will continue.[6]

Death of the ward necessarily terminates guardianship. And after the ward's death the guardian's only duty is to settle up his

[1] 1 Bl. Com. 461, Harg. *n.*; 2 Kent Com. 222.

[2] Ib.

[3] 1 Bl. Com. 462, Harg. *n.*; and see ch. 1, *supra*.

[4] Rex *v.* Pierson, Andr. 313; Mendes *v.* Mendes, 3 Atk. 624. And see Macphers. Inf. 41, 65; Byrne *v.* Van Hoesen, 5 Johns. 66.

[5] Perry *v.* Brainard, 11 Ohio, 442; Maxsom *v.* Sawyer, 12 Ohio, 195. See Dibble *v.* Dibble, 8 Ind. 307; Matter of Dyer, 5 Paige, 534.

[6] Dyce Sombre's Case, 1 Phil. Ch. 437; Hovey *v.* Harmon, 49 Maine, 269; Wendell's Case, 1 Johns. Ch. 600; Kimball *v.* Fiske, 39 N. H. 110; Chase *v.* Hathaway, 14 Mass. 222.

accounts and pay the balance in his hands to the ward's personal representatives, whereupon his trust is completely fulfilled.

The lawful marriage of any ward, whether male or female, must necessarily affect the rights of the guardian. So far as the ward's person is concerned, there can be no question that the guardianship ends. Marriage is paramount to all other relations, and its proper continuance being inconsistent with guardianship of the person, the latter yields to it, whatever may be the sex of the ward. But as to the estate the rule, in view of late married women's statutes, is not so clear. If however a male ward marries a female, whether she be minor or adult, his guardian retains power over his estate, as before, until he becomes of age.[1]

Hence arises a difficulty where a male and female ward marry, both being minors and having estates in the hands of their respective guardians. Does the husband, though under age, take all the rights of an adult husband? Or does the wife's estate remain in keeping of her guardian until the husband is old enough to control it in person? The better opinion is that it goes to the husband, whatever his age. The inevitable consequence is that the husband's guardian must take it from the wife's guardian, and hold both estates during minority. This seems an awkward arrangement, but it is nevertheless the lawful one. More troublesome would be a case under the recent statutes in this country relative to married women, concerning which we do not find a judicial decision. But it seems the technical rule applies, as before, to the detriment of the female ward's interests. It might be well to declare by statute that the wife's guardian shall continue to manage her estate during her minority.[2]

The marriage of the female ward, it is said, does not, *ipso facto*, determine the authority of her guardian over her estate.

[1] Reeve Dom. Rel. 328; 2 Kent Com. 226; Bac. Abr. Guardian (E.); Eyre *v.* Countess of Shaftesbury, 2 P Wms. 103; Mendes *v.* Mendes, 3 Atk. 619; ib. 1 Ves. 89; Jones *v.* Ward, 10 Yerg. 160.

[2] See Reeve Dom. Rel. 328; 2 Kent Com. 226. See Anon., 8 Sim. 346.

Hence an order of court, transferring the custody of the property to the husband, is first necessary; though the husband will be entitled to such order upon motion. Such is the rule declared in New York.[1] But while in England the Court of Chancery never appoints a guardian for a female infant after marriage, neither does it discharge an order for a guardian because of marriage; because, as Mr. Macpherson thinks, the marriage of a female, if valid, supersedes guardianship, of its own force.[2] Probate wards in this country are frequently married, and their guardians settle their accounts without order of court or revocation of letters, on the supposition that the marriage *ipso facto* puts an end to their authority.

Guardianship is terminated by the death of the guardian. But the ward does not thereby necessarily become free, for a successor in the trust continues to control him. The executor or administrator of the guardian, as such, has no authority; for guardianship is a personal trust and not transmissible. But he should close the accounts of the deceased guardian in court and pass the balance over to the successor. This successor is the person next indicated in the will appointing testamentary guardians, or the survivor of joint guardians, or some one appointed in chancery or probate to fill the vacancy, as the case may be.[3]

The office of a guardian was regarded as something so honorable at the common law that it could not be easily refused, much less resigned. Natural guardians, of necessity, could not resign. We have seen, in another connection, how far the natural guardian may practically surrender his children's custody, by allowing others to adopt them, by placing them in a charitable institution, and the like; which is the only sense in which this guardianship may be considered as voluntarily transferred. So guardians in socage, being designated

[1] Whitaker's Case, 4 Johns. Ch. 378. But see *contra* Jones *v.* Ward, 10 Yerg. 160; Nicholson *v.* Wilborn, 13 Geo. 467; Anon., 8 Sim. 346; Armstrong *v.* Walkup, 12 Gratt. 608.

[2] Macphers. Inf. 113, citing Roach *v.* Garvan, 1 Ves. 160; 8 Sim. 336.

[3] Co. Litt. 89; Bac. Abr. Guardian (E).

by the law, could not in strictness resign; if they could shift their authority at all, it must have been by assignment. There is reason to believe that, before the Statute of Marlbridge,[1] they could assign, but only to the extent of placing the ward's body in custody of another. In later times, no assignment whatever has been permitted. For, as Lord Commissioner Gilbert observed, guardianship in socage is an interest, not of profit, but of honor, committed to the next of kin, inherent in the blood; and therefore not assignable.[2]

The resignation of a testamentary guardian is not, as a rule, permitted. In 1752, the guardians of the young Earl of Spencer, who was then in his eighteenth year, petitioned the Court of Chancery that they might be discharged from their trust, as he was then going abroad on his travels, and would not be under their care. Lord Hardwicke (as the reporter says) refused it with some warmth, as a thing which had never been done at the request of the guardians themselves; and added that, if they would not continue to act in the trust, as they had accepted it, he should compel them. But afterwards, at the importunity of counsel, finding that the mother and the infant also acceded to the request, he yielded so far as to allow a petition to be filed on behalf of the infant, upon which he made an order that the care and direction of the infant's education and person should be committed to two near relatives until further order, and that the allowance for his maintenance and education should be paid to them. But in doing so the Lord Chancellor declared that while the special circumstances of this case justified his action, he would not in general comply with such petitions, nor should this case be drawn into precedent. The court, he added, must take care of the infant, even though it did not punish the guardian for not doing so.[3]

Though this was a case of testamentary guardianship, we

[1] 52 Hen. 3, ch. 17.

[2] Gilb. Eq. Rep. 175. For full discussion, see Macphers. Inf. 25–27; Co. Litt 88 *b*, Harg. *n*. 13, and authorities cited.

[3] Spencer *v*. Earl of Chesterfield, Amb. 146.

presume the rule equally strict, or nearly so, in case of a chancery guardian. In either instance the court can make an order, as deemed best for the infant's interests. There need be no summary removal. Chancellor Kent, in *Ex parte* Crumb, claimed that chancery could doubtless discharge or charge a guardian, even if appointed by a surrogate; but that in the case of a testamentary guardian there should be very special reasons for interference. He refused here, however, to make any change, there being no special cause shown.[1]

It is now frequently provided by statute that probate guardians and other trust officers may, in the discretion of the court, be allowed to resign. But in absence of such legislation, it would appear that no such guardian can resign as a matter of right; nor can the probate court legally accept his resignation and appoint a successor. Yet it is held in Illinois that, under a statute which permits the judge "to remove guardians for good and sufficient cause," he may consider resignation a sufficient cause, and thereupon discharge the guardian.[2] There is something harsh and offensive in the removal of a guardian from office. Moreover, numerous unforeseen emergencies may arise, so as to render the continuance of the trust improper; as if the guardian should become a confirmed invalid, or make himself obnoxious to the ward and his relations, or display a want of prudence in managing the estate not inconsistent with good intentions. He might be fully aware of the advantage of a change to all parties concerned, and might desire to be relieved, provided he could withdraw with honor, and without submitting to a humiliating investigation of petty and insufficient grounds of complaint. This opportunity is afforded in allowing him to resign. And further, as Mr. Macpherson has observed of testamentary appointees, "it can never be for the infant's benefit to continue him in the care of a negligent or reluctant guardian." [3]

1 *Ex parte* Crumb, 2 Johns. Ch. 439. See 2 Kent Com. 227.

2 Young *v.* Lorain, 11 Ill. 624. See Pepper *v.* Stone, 10 Vt. 427.

3 Macphers. Inf. 128, commenting upon Spencer *v.* Earl of Chesterfield, *supra.*

The chancery court may undoubtedly remove all guardians of its own appointment and substitute others at discretion for proper cause. This rule extends still further: for, according to American authority, chancery may remove all guardians, whether appointed by the court itself, by probate tribunals, by testament, or even by express act of the legislature, whenever the guardian abuses his trust or the interests of the ward require it.[1] This statement is somewhat too sweeping, so far as the English courts are concerned. So, too, probate tribunals are authorized in most if not all of the States to remove guardians of their own appointment on good and sufficient cause.

And as two persons, or sets of persons, cannot at the same time hold the same trust, it follows that one guardian must be removed, or a vacancy otherwise created, before the court can make a new appointment. This principle, apparently simple, has sometimes been overlooked; when, for instance, a court has issued new letters without revoking the old, or seeks to supersede a testamentary by a probate guardian. The appointment of a new guardian does not of itself terminate the authority of one previously chosen. It is an act without jurisdiction, and void. But natural guardians need not be formally removed, nor guardians in socage. The rule applies only to guardians testamentary and guardians by judicial appointment, who hold by a higher authority than either of these.[2]

If a guardian does not behave to the satisfaction of the Court of Chancery, orders regulating his conduct are frequently made upon him; and if any such steps be taken as to induce suspicion that the infant will suffer by the conduct of the guardians, the court will interpose.[3] This is the English rule as to guardians in general. But in this country, probate guardian-

[1] Cowls *v.* Cowls, 3 Gilm. 435. See *Ex parte* Crumb, 2 Johns. Ch. 439; Disbrow *v.* Henshaw, 8 Cow. 349.

[2] Bledsoe *v.* Britt, 6 Yerg. 458; Grant *v.* Whitaker, 1 Murph. 231; Robinson *v.* Zollinger, 9 Watts, 169; Fay *v.* Hurd, 8 Pick. 528; Thomas *v.* Burrus, 23 Miss. 550; 2 Ch. Cas. 237; Morgan *v.* Dillon, 9 Mod. 141; Copp *v.* Copp, 20 N. H. 284.

[3] Roach *v.* Garvan, 1 Ves. 160; Duke of Beaufort *v.* Berty, 1 P. Wms. 705.

ship is usually determined for misconduct by a summary removal.

There can be no removal of a probate guardian without cause shown.[1] Courts of chancery are equally bound to observe this principle; but their discretion is absolute. A mere stranger cannot apply to have a guardian removed; it must be a party in interest.[2] Nor can one who has been properly removed, though the mother herself, claim any right of recommending a successor.[3]

Among the causes which have been deemed sufficient for the removal of a guardian are these: Appointment to the trust without proper notice to other parties interested.[4] Gross and confirmed habits of intoxication.[5] Any breach of official duties amounting to misconduct.[6] Abandonment of the trust.[7] Ignorance or imprudence on the part of the guardian, whereby the ward's interests suffer.[8] But not insolvency alone; though otherwise where one has been adjudged a bankrupt, or is guilty of fraud.[9] Nor is intermeddling with the estate before qualification as guardian a ground for removal, if in good faith and by advice of counsel.[10] Nor in Indiana, as the statute provides, can one be displaced except for unfaithful performance of the trust or insufficient security.[11] But guardians may in general be removed wherever it will be for the ward's interest.[12] And it appears that there may be a combination of circumstances to justify the removal.[13]

1 Whitney *v.* Whitney, 7 S. & M. 740.

2 Colton *v.* Goodson, 1 How. (Miss.) 295.

3 Hamilton *v.* Moore, 32 Miss. 205.

4 Morehouse *v.* Cooke, Hopk. 226.

5 Kettletas *v.* Gardner, 1 Paige Ch. 488.

6 Barnes *v.* Powers, 12 Ind. 341; Sweet *v.* Sweet, Speers Eq. 309.

7 Lefever *v.* Lefever, 6 Md. 472.

8 Nicholson's Appeal, 20 Penn. St. 50.

9 Chew's Estate, 4 Md. Ch. 60; Cooper's Case, 2 Paige Ch. 34. See Lord Thurlow in Smith *v.* Bate, Dick. 631.

10 Stone *v.* Dorrett, 18 Tex. 700.

11 Morgan *v.* Anderson, 5 Blackf. 503.

12 *Ex parte* Crutchfield, 3 Yerg. 336.

13 Windsor *v.* McAtee, 2 Met. (Ky.) 430.

Religious opinions were formerly made a test of the guardian's capacity to act. Such conflicts seldom arise at the present day. It was held in a Pennsylvania case, a few years ago, that difference of belief on religious subjects constitutes no cause for a guardian's removal, if no harsh or unfair means have been used to erase the impressions left by the parents on the child's mind.[1]

For the same reason that non-residents are held incompetent for appointment, guardians must surrender their authority when they move out of the jurisdiction, or the court will take it from them. The rule is not uniform in all the States. Under the statutes in Indiana, Alabama, and some other States, removal from the State constitutes *per se* ground for displacement from office.[2] But since, as we have seen, non-residents may sometimes be appointed guardians, the more reasonable rule is to make them liable to displacement whenever, as non-residents, they would not have been appointed in the first instance.[3]

As in making appointments, the court is allowed a liberal discretion over removals, and its decision will not be reversed on appeal unless palpable injustice has been done.[4] But the guardian is a trustee; and although he may in contemplation of law have no beneficial interest, yet he has such an interest as the law recognizes and will protect.[5]

The guardian is entitled to notice before removal, that he may appear in defence; and, if removed without such notice, unless he has waived it by his voluntary appearance in court, he has good ground for appeal; and it is doubtful whether a new appointment under such circumstances has any validity whatever.[6] The authorities are clear in requiring notice

[1] Nicholson's Appeal, 20 Penn. St. 50.

[2] Nettleton *v.* State, 13 Ind. 159; Cockrell *v.* Cockrell, 36 Ala. 673.

[3] See Speight *v.* Knight, 11 Ala. 461; also *supra*, p. 419.

[4] Nicholson's Appeal, 20 Penn. St. 50; Young *v.* Young, 5 Ind. 513.

[5] Isaacs *v.* Taylor, 3 Dana, 600.

[6] Hart *v.* Gray, 3 Sumn. 339; Gwin *v.* Vanzant, 7 Yerg. 143; Myers *v.* Pearsoll, 17 Ind. 405; Croft *v.* Terrell, 15 Ala. 652.

wherever proceedings for removal involve the guardian's personal character; but where the discharge is sought on other grounds, and the ward's rights are deemed of paramount importance, as when one under guardianship for insanity is restored to reason, or a ward arrived at fourteen wishes to exercise the privilege of nominating a successor, removals without notice are sometimes sustained;[1] still the better opinion is in favor of notice in all cases.[2]

It is held in Vermont that when a guardian who has been removed from office appeals, and in the mean time another has been appointed in his place and given bonds, the powers of the old guardian cease, and the new one takes control, until he is restored.[3]

We have seen that chancery courts in this country claim the right of removing testamentary guardians. In England, the rule is not laid down so strongly. Testamentary guardians are not removed, but superseded in their functions: a refinement adopted, it is said, out of deference to the act of parliament.[4] In this sense are to be understood certain expressions of Lord Hardwicke and Lord Redesdale, which would seem to extend the authority of the court to actual removal from office.[5] Lord Nottingham, in *Foster* v. *Denny*, said that he could not remove a guardian constituted by act of parliament.[6] This is still the doctrine of the English chancery; but it exercises full jurisdiction in ordering infants to be made wards of court, with suitable directions for their maintenance and education; and it will restrain the testamentary guardian from interference with the person and estate of wards thus taken under its protection.[7]

1 Hovey *v.* Harmon, 49 Maine, 269; *supra*, ch. 2.

2 Montgomery *v.* Smith, 3 Dana, 599; 1 N. H. 448; Copp *v.* Copp, 20 N. H. 284; Lee *v.* Ice, 22 Ind. 384. But see Cooke *v.* Beale, 11 Ired. 36.

3 The State *v.* McKown, 21 Vt. 503.

4 Macphers. Inf. 128.

5 Lord Hardwicke in Roach *v.* Garvan, 1 Ves. 160; Lord Redesdale in O'Keefe *v.* Casey, 1 Sch. & Lef. 106.

6 2 Ch. Cas. 237.

7 Smith *v.* Bate, Dick. 631; Ingham *v.* Bickerdike, 6 Mad. 275. See also M'Cullochs *in re*, 1 Dru. 276; 12 Jur. 100.

By the common law, certain persons, as idiots, lunatics, deaf and dumb persons, persons under outlawry or attainder, and lepers removed by writ of leprosy, were passed over in the guardianship. And where a guardian became incapable of acting, the office devolved upon the next person to whom the inheritance could not descend.[1] Such guardians do not appear to have been removed from office.

The marriage of a female guardian may terminate her authority; though that of a male guardian never does. The old rule of the common law appears to have been, that when a female guardian in socage married, her husband became guardian in right of his wife; but that on her death guardianship ceased on his part, and went to the infant's next relation.[2] Testamentatary guardianship in England, seems to be left to the operation of the will in such cases: chancery refusing to interfere with the testator's own directions.[3] But it is customary for the father to designate successors in the event of marriage. What has already been said on the subject of appointing married women guardians applies, likewise, in this connection.[4] Certainly, if marriage does not absolutely put an end to the guardian's authority, it has the effect of joining her husband in the trust. In Louisiana, the mother, by the advice of a family meeting, may be retained in the tutorship of her minor children, notwithstanding her re-marriage.[5]

There are some other cases in which it is said, that a new guardian may be appointed, as though guardianship had already determined. Thus, where a testamentary guardian has not acted, and declines to act, chancery may appoint a successor.[6] So in other cases where the guardian renounces his appointment.[7] Filing a bond, with proper security, is

[1] Co. Litt. 88, 89; Macphers. Inf. 24, 25.

[2] Co. Litt. 89 *a*; Bac. Abr. Guardian & Ward (E). See 7 Vt. 372.

[3] Macphers. Inf. 129; Morgan *v.* Dillon, 9 Mod. 135; Dillon *v.* Lady Mount Cashell, 4 Br. P. C. 306. See Corbet *v.* Tottenham, 1 Ba. & Be. 59.

[4] See last chapter.

[5] Gaudet *v.* Gaudet, 14 La. An. 112.

[6] *Ex parte* Champney, 1 Dick. 350; O'Keefe *v.* Casey, 1 Sch. & Lef. 106.

[7] McAlister *v.* Olmstead, 1 Humph. 210; Lefever *v.* Lefever, 6 Md. 472.

sometimes regarded as the condition precedent to a probate appointment, and it is thought that letters need not be revoked in such a case. But this is by no means settled.[1]

Outlawry and attainder of treason — or what is known as civil death — did not put an end to guardianship in socage; because, it was said the guardian had nothing to his own use, but to the use of the heir.[2] The same principle, doubtless, applies to other guardians. But a guardian might be properly removed on such grounds.

[1] Russell *v.* Coffin, 8 Pick. 143; Fay *v.* Hurd, ib. 528; Barns *v.* Branch, 3 McCord, 19; Clarke *v.* Darnell, 8 Gill & Johns. 111.

[2] Co. Litt. 88 *b*; Macphers. Inf. 25.

CHAPTER IV.

NATURE OF THE GUARDIAN'S OFFICE.

THE powers and duties of a guardian relate either to the person of the ward, or to the ward's estate, or to both person and estate. As guardian of the person, he is entitled to the custody of the ward; is bound to maintain him in a style suitable to the latter's means and condition in life; and, if the ward be a minor, he superintends his education, directs him in the choice of a pursuit; in general, he supplies the place of a judicious parent. As guardian of the estate, he manages the ward's property, both real and personal, with faithfulness and care, changes investments whenever necessary, with permission of the court, pays the just debts of the ward, collects his dues, puts out his money on interest, keeps regular accounts, and is, in effect, the ward's trustee.[1] Whether the guardianship be in socage, testamentary, or by chancery or probate appointment, these powers and duties are essentially the same; although, as we have seen, socage guardianship was created with special reference to the ward's real estate.[2] Moreover, as will fully appear in the succeeding chapters, chancery and probate guardians are brought more closely under judicial control and supervision than either guardians in socage or testamentary guardians.

But while guardianship of the person resembles the relation of parent and child, it is not altogether like it. The parent must support his child from his own means; and in return the child's labor and services belong to him. But the guardian is not bound to supply the wants of his ward, except from

[1] 2 Kent Com. 230-233. [2] *Supra*, ch. 1.

the ward's own estate in his hands and the liberality of others, though it were to keep the child from starving. On the other hand, the guardian has no more right to the labor and services of his ward than any stranger. Nor are guardians of the estate vested with an interest precisely like that of trustees; for while the latter may sue and be sued in their official capacity, suits by and against infants are brought in the name of the ward and not the guardian.[1]

Guardians in socage acquired authority as guardians of the ward's estate; and guardianship of the estate drew after it, in such case, guardianship of the person; so that they were guardians of both person and estate.[2] Testamentary guardians under the statute of Charles II. acquire authority through the father's devise to them of the "custody and tuition" of his children; and this devise of the person carries with it as incident a devise of the estate; so that they too are guardians of both person and estate.[3] But chancery guardians are not always invested with such powers; for the court will make such orders as are needful in all cases. The court sometimes appoints a guardian of the person only, for a special and temporary purpose.[4] Where a suit is pending, and it becomes necessary to appoint a guardian, chancery appoints a guardian of the person only, the estate being under the direction of the court. But where no suit is pending, and proceedings are commenced by petition, the guardian is appointed for both person and estate.[5] Probate guardianship is subject, in great part, to local legislation; but it may be safely asserted, as a general principle, that all probate guardians are guardians of both person and estate, and that the court cannot commit guardianship of the person to one and guardianship of the property to another.[6]

[1] See Infancy, last chapter, *infra*.

[2] But see Bedell *v.* Constable, Vaugh. 185, cited *supra*.

[3] Stat. 12 Car. 2, ch. 24, §§ 8, 9; Vaugh. 178.

[4] Macphers. Inf. 114; *Ex parte* Becher, 1 Br. C. C. 556; *Ex parte* Woolscombe, 1 Mad. 213.

[5] Macphers. Inf. 105; 2 Kent Com. 229.

[6] See Tenbrook *v.* M'Colm, 7 Halst. 97.

The guardian is not always entitled to the custody of the infant's person; but chancery will exercise its discretion for the benefit of the latter, as to delivering him up to the guardian or permitting him to remain elsewhere, and as to the persons who are to have access to him, and the circumstances attending such access, and generally as to his education.[1] And it is the policy of our legislation to leave the child's person in his parents' keeping so far as possible. But the guardian may be a "guardian of the person and estate" notwithstanding.

In discussing the rights and duties of a guardian, this question meets us at the outset: What is the nature of the guardian's office? This will be best seen by examining the different kinds of guardians, as they respectively arose.

Guardianship in socage arose very early at common law, and is the first in order. These guardians were considered as trustees. According to the old authorities, the guardian in socage had not a bare authority, but an actual estate and interest in the land, though not to his own use.[2] Hence he might elect whether to let the estate or occupy it for the ward's benefit. He was considered as entitled to the possession of the ward's property, and incapable of being removed from it by any person. In other words, this guardian had the legal, but not the beneficial, interest.

Not long after the statute of Charles II. chancery was called upon to determine the nature of testamentary guardianship. Lord Macclesfield, in the case of *Duke of Beaufort* v. *Berty*,[3] stated that testamentary guardians were but trustees; that the statute merely empowered the father to appoint a different person as guardian and to continue the relation beyond the age of fourteen and until the ward became twenty-one; and that both socage and testamentary guardians were equally trustees. And in the important case of *Eyre* v. *Countess of Shaftesbury*,[4]

[1] Macphers. Inf. 119; Anon., 2 Ves. Sen. 374.

[2] Co. Litt. 90 *a*; Plowd. ch. 23. See Macphers. Inf. 28.

[3] 1 P. Wms. 703.

[4] 2 P. Wms. 102.

this principle, though with another admitted difference as to succession, was again affirmed. This general rule has received judicial sanction in England quite recently.[1]

Chancery guardianship, of still later origin, resembles in its nature testamentary guardianship. The same principles are constantly asserted in regard to both. In either case, the guardian has a vested interest in his ward's estate, may bring actions relative thereto, and make leases during the minority of the infant. He has in all respects the dominion *pro tempore* of the infant's estate and possesses more than a naked authority.[2]

The same may be said of probate guardianship in this country, which, under statute modification, has become, if any thing, more like trusteeship than the other kinds.[3] And in *Thompson* v. *Boardman*[4] the analogies of the old law have been extended to the case of a spendthrift's guardian.

It is often difficult to say what in strictness is a trustee, since every trust is limited by the instrument which creates it. And the powers of a guardian differ greatly from those of an executor or administrator. But so far as guardianship of the estate is concerned a guardian is in fact a trustee; for he holds the legal estate to the benefit of another. To apply the term *agent* to the guardian's office seems therefore harsh and unnatural, whatever may be the ward's position.[5]

Where there are two or more testamentary guardians, and one of them dies or is removed, the survivor or survivors shall continue. The very nature of the trust demands it.[6] In England, it is otherwise with joint guardians by chancery appointment; for if one dies the office determines.[7] But the survivors

1 Gilbert *v.* Schwenck, 14 M. & W. 488; s. c. 9 Jur. 693.

2 People *v.* Byron, 3 Johns. Cas. 53.

3 See Truss *v.* Old, 6 Rand. 556; Isaacs *v.* Taylor, 3 Dana, 600; Alexander *v.* Alexander, 8 Ala. 796; Pepper *v.* Stone, 10 Vt. 427.

4 1 Vt. 370.

5 But see *dictum* of Shaw C. J. in Manson *v.* Felton, 13 Pick. 206. See Thompson *v.* Boardman, 1 Vt. 370.

6 See Bac. Abr. Guardian (A).

7 Bradshaw *v.* Bradshaw, 1 Russ. 528.

will be appointed without a reference,[1] so that after all the rule is only formal. In this country, the more reasonable doctrine prevails, as to both chancery and probate guardianship, that the survivors shall continue the trust, like co-executors, and on the same principle. This was declared to be the rule as to joint chancery guardians in a leading New York case.[2] And a Vermont court applies it likewise to probate guardians.[3] The statutes enacted in many of the States remove all further doubt on the subject.

Of two or more persons appointed joint guardians under a will, one may qualify without the other.[4] But while a joint guardian who has once declined the trust has no further right to be appointed, he may yet be selected in preference to others to fill a vacancy. Thus it has been held that where three testamentary guardians, one of whom was the mother, were named by the father in his will, and the mother became sole guardian, by the refusal of the others to act with her, they were properly selected by the court, after the mother's death, on their own application, in preference to the person nominated in her will.[5]

On the principle that guardians are trustees, it is held that joint guardians may sue together on account of any joint transaction founded on their relation to the ward, even after the relation ceases.[6] Also that the receipt of one is the receipt of all.[7] Also that one can maintain trespass against the other for forcibly removing the child against his wishes; for one of two joint trustees cannot act in defiance of the other.[8] And where one guardian consents to his co-guardian's misapplication of funds, he is liable.[9] Guardians, like other trustees,

1 Hall *v.* Jones, 2 Sim. 41.
2 People *v.* Byron, 3 Johns. Cas. 53.

3 Pepper *v.* Stone, 10 Vt. 427. See also remarks of Chancellor Sanford in Kirby *v.* Turner, Hopk. 309, as to the nature of joint guardianship.

4 Kevan *v.* Waller, 11 Leigh, 414.

5 Johnston's Case, 2 Jones & La T. 222.

6 Shearman *v.* Akins, 4 Pick. 283.

7 Alston *v.* Munford, 1 Brock. 266.

8 Gilbert *v.* Schwenck, 14 M. & W. 488.

9 Pim *v.* Downing, 11 S. & R. 66. See Clark's Appeal, 18 Penn. St. 175.

— executors and administrators excepted, — may portion out the management of the property to suit their respective tastes and qualifications, while neither parts irrevocably with the control of the whole; and in such case each is chargeable with no more than what he received, unless unwarrantable negligence in superintending the other's acts can be shown.[1] And the discharge of one who has received no part of the estate relieves him from liability.[2] On the other hand, it is presumed that the survivor of joint guardians received the whole estate, in absence of proof to the contrary.[3]

In English practice, the court of chancery holds the ward's property within its grasp with a tightness unknown to American tribunals. The regular course is to get in all the money due the infant, and to invest it in the public funds. A receiver is, if necessary, appointed to facilitate collections, and generally the same person is made a permanent receiver of the ward's real estate, to collect all rents. Where there is an executor he will not be interfered with, except under strong circumstances of suspicion, but an administrator is treated with less consideration.[4] Even executors who are also testamentary guardians, must bring their funds into court after settling up the estate of their testator.[5] Chancery, thus managing actively the ward's property, makes its own scheme for maintenance, and allows the guardian a certain fixed income accordingly.[6]

Probate guardianship in this country is quite different. Schemes of maintenance are seldom heard of. Nor are receivers appointed. The guardian usually collects his ward's dues, whether from the executor of the parent or others, and manages the property on his own responsibility, with little judicial interference. He regulates at discretion the sum

[1] Jones's Appeal, 8 Watts & S. 143.
[2] Hocker *v.* Woods, 33 Penn. St. 466.
[3] Graham *v.* Davidson, 2 Dev. & Bat. Eq. 155.
[4] Macphers. Inf. 268, and cases cited.
[5] Ib. 118; Blake *v.* Blake, 2 Sch. & Lef. 26.
[6] Macphers. Inf. 213, *et seq.*

proper for annual expenditure, and changes the rate when expedient. Of course, he is held accountable, on legal principles much the same as those of the English chancery; but he seldom applies to the court for directions, unless some perplexity arises, or it becomes expedient to sell real estate, or when the ward cannot be supported without breaking in upon the principal fund.

The same person is frequently executor under the parent's will, and also guardian of the minor children. Hence the question will sometimes arise whether he holds the fund in the one or the other capacity. It is clear that where one is both guardian and executor, he cannot be sued in both capacities, nor are both sets of sureties liable.[1] He is in the first instance liable as executor; and in general, to render him liable as guardian, there should be some distinct act of transfer. His plain duty is to keep the trusts distinct and not blend them. In the former case, his accounts rendered will show the transfer of the legacy or distributive share from his account as executor to his account as guardian; and thereby his liability as guardian will become fixed.[2] But in the latter case, or if no clear evidence appears elsewhere of an actual transfer, can it be presumed? The better opinion is that, after the time limited by law for the settlement of the estate has elapsed, and there is no evidence of intent to hold longer as executor, he shall be presumed a guardian; on the principle that what the law enjoins upon him to do shall be considered as done.[3] And certainly very slight evidence would confirm any possible doubt; such as the division of the parent's estate among other heirs, the payment of legacies, or where he has placed some of the chattels on the ward's farm.[4] But the rule may be otherwise

[1] Wren *v.* Gayden, 1 How. (Miss.) 365.

[2] Alston *v.* Munford, 1 Brock. 266; Burton *v.* Tunnell, 4 Harring. (Del.) 424; *contra*, Conkey *v.* Dickinson, 13 Met. 51; Stillman *v.* Young, 16 Ill. 318; Foteaux *v.* Lepage, 6 Clarke (Iowa), 123; Scott's Case, 36 Vt. 297.

[3] Watkins *v.* State, 4 Gill & Johns. 220; Karr *v.* Karr, 6 Dana, 3.

[4] Johnson *v.* Johnson, 2 Hill Ch. 277; Drane *v.* Bayliss, 1 Humph. 174.

with joint executors,[1] and we need hardly add, that this doctrine applies in strictness only to personal assets which pass through administration; since real estate, ordinarily, goes at once to the heir.

A guardian cannot blend distinct trusts of guardianship by appointment. Thus where a person was appointed guardian of an infant who became insane shortly before reaching his majority, and the same guardian continued to act, styling himself guardian of "A. B., an idiot," it was held that his trust properly expired with the infancy of the minor.[2] Nor does it matter that the probate court recognizes a continuation of the trust by passing his accounts; for an actual appointment, after the regular form, is always essential to a guardian's authority.

Where the person designated as executor of a will is under age it becomes necessary to appoint an administrator during minority, which was at common law denominated *durante minore ætate*.[3] So when the next of kin is under age, the English practice in such cases is to appoint the infant's guardian, unless there is some other next of kin competent to act; though the rule is not invariable.[4] And in the English case of *John* v. *Bradbury*, decided as late as 1866, it is affirmed that the guardian of an infant sole next of kin shall not only administer in preference to creditors, but shall be exempted from security, except in very strong cases, notwithstanding the creditors request it.[5] So he is preferred to the husband of a married woman who died after a judicial separation.[6] But in this country while there are statutes in some States favoring similar doctrines, in others the court has full discretion in selecting a substitute for the child.[7] Such administrator has for the time

1 Watkins *v.* State, 4 Gill & Johns. 220. See Clancy *v.* Dickey, 2 Hawks. 497.

2 Coon *v.* Cook, 6 Ind. 268.

3 1 Wms. Ex'rs, 419, 420; 2 Redf. Wills, 92, 93.

4 Ib.

5 John *v.* Bradbury, Law Rep. 1 P. & D. 245.

6 Goods of Stephenson, Law Rep. 1 P. & D. 287. But the husband usually administers. See *supra*, Husband and Wife.

7 1 Wms. Ex'rs, 419; 2 Redf. Wills, 94, and cases cited; Mass. Gen. Stats. ch. 94.

being all the powers of a general administrator, but his term of office is restricted to the infant's minority.[1]

A *quasi* guardianship often arises at law where there has been no regular appointment. The general principle thus recognized is that any person who takes possession of an infant's property takes it in trust for the infant. Hence courts of equity will always protect the helpless in such cases by holding the person who acts as guardian strictly accountable. The father may thus be a *quasi* guardian.[2] So may a step-father.[3] Or one whose appointment as guardian was irregular.[4] But not an executor or administrator in rightful possession of the infant's property; for he holds in a different capacity.[5] Chancery has full jurisdiction over the transactions of all persons standing *in loco parentis*.[6]

On the same principle, one regularly appointed guardian of an infant is held responsible for acts committed before qualifying as such by giving bonds.[7] And although his authority ceases when the ward attains majority, he continues personally responsible so long as his possession of the property continues.[8]

The guardian's authority is limited to the jurisdiction which appoints him, and does not extend to foreign countries, unless permitted by foreign laws. Every nation is sovereign within its own borders, but powerless beyond them. The rights of foreign guardians have been, to some extent, admitted however on the principle of comity.[9] These rights may be considered, first, as to the person of the ward; second, as to his estate.

First, as to the ward's person. Many writers on public law

[1] 1 Wms. Ex'rs, 428, and notes; 2 Redf. Wills, 94, 95.

[2] Pennington *v.* Fowler, 3 Halst. Ch. 343; Alston *v.* Alston, 34 Ala, 15.

[3] Espay *v.* Luke, 15 E. L. & Eq. 579.

[4] Crooks *v.* Turpin, 1 B. Monr. 185.

[5] Bibb *v.* McKinley, 9 Port. 636; Minfee *v.* Ball, 2 Eng. 520.

[6] Espay *v.* Luke, 15 E. L. & Eq. 579.

[7] Magruder *v.* Darnall, 6 Gill, 269.

[8] Mellish *v.* Mellish, 1 Sim. & Stu. 138; Armstrong *v.* Walkup, 12 Gratt. 608.

[9] See Story Confl. Laws, §§ 492–529.

claim that the guardian's authority extends everywhere. Others again deny that it extends beyond the jurisdiction which appoints.[1] In England, the paternal authority is recognized, even in aliens; but if an infant has a guardian appointed by any other authority out of the jurisdiction, the appointment fails as soon as the infant comes to England, and the court of chancery will thereupon appoint a guardian on petition.[2] But in a very recent case liberal favor was shown toward the foreign guardian of wards domiciled abroad. He had sent them to England to be educated, and wished to remove them to their own country in order to complete their education. The court refused to interfere with their removal, and allowed the exclusive custody to the foreign guardian; at the same time however refusing to discharge an order appointing English guardians.[3]

In this country, the rights and powers of guardians over the ward's person are considered strictly local, even as between different States,[4] though the paternal right would probably be recognized as in England.[5] But in Massachusetts, a few years ago, the custody of a child was awarded to a foreign guardian, in preference to one appointed within the jurisdiction, the court observing that while the former had no absolute right to the child, his office would be deemed an important element in determining to whom custody should be given.[6]

Second, as to the ward's property. A distinction has been made between movables and immovables. As to immovable property, such as real estate, it is almost universally admitted that the law *rei sitæ* shall govern.[7] But writers do not agree as to movable property, such as goods and personal chattels, whether the law of the domicile shall prevail over that of the

1 See Story Confl. Laws, §§ 495–497, and authorities cited.

2 Macphers. Inf. 577; *Ex parte* Watkins, 2 Ves. 470.

3 Nugent *v.* Vetzera, Law Rep. 2 Eq. 704. See 27 E. L. & Eq. 451.

4 Story Confl. Laws, § 499; Morrell *v.* Dickey, 1 Johns. Ch. 153; Kraft *v.* Wickey, 4 Gill & Johns. 332; Burnet *v.* Burnet, 12 B. Monr. 323.

5 See Townsend *v.* Kendall, 4 Min. 412.

6 Woodworth *v.* Spring, 4 Allen, 321.

7 Story Confl. Laws, §§ 500–502.

situation. Mr. Story considered the weight of foreign authority in this respect, in favor of admitting the guardian's rights to prevail everywhere to the same extent as they are acknowledged by the law of the domicile.[1] And this seems to be the Scotch doctrine.[2] But according to the doctrine of the common law, now fully established both in England and America, the rights of a guardian over all property whatsoever are strictly territorial, and are recognized as having no influence upon such property in other countries where different systems of jurisprudence are established. No foreign guardian can, *virtute officii*, exercise his functions in another country or State, without taking out other letters of guardianship or otherwise conforming to the local law. Such is the rule in both countries.[3]

But the rigor of this rule is sometimes abated. In England, personal property will, under certain circumstances, be paid to an owner who, if domiciled and resident in that country, would not be allowed to receive it.[4] So administration *durante minore ætate* has been granted to a foreign guardian.[5] In this country, there are local statutes which permit non-resident guardians to sue on compliance with certain formalities, or even without them.[6] But otherwise they cannot bring actions of any sort.[7] And this seems to be the English rule likewise.[8] While courts of equity will permit property to pass to the foreign guardian, in pursuance of law, it seems that they will generally exercise

[1] Story Confl. Laws, § 500.

[2] Ib. § 503; Fraser Parent & Child, 604.

[3] Story Confl. Laws, § 504.

[4] Macphers. Inf. 577; Goods of Countess Da Cunha, 1 Hag. 237.

[5] Goods of Sartoris, 1 Curteis, 910.

[6] *Ex parte* Heard, 2 Hill Ch. 54; Hines *v.* State, 10 S. & M. 529. Sims *v.* Renwick, 25 Geo. 58; Grist *v.* Forehand, 36 Miss. 69; Martin *v.* McDonald, 14 B. Monr. 544; Carlisle *v.* Tuttle, 30 Ala. 613; Warren *v.* Hofer, 13 Ind. 167.

[7] Morrell *v.* Dickey, 1 Johns. Ch. 153; Kraft *v.* Wickey, 4 Gill & Johns. 322; Rogers *v.* McLean, 31 Barb. 304. This is the rule in Louisiana. Succession of Shaw, 13 La. An. 265.

[8] Story considers it doubtful. Beattie *v.* Johnston, 1 Phillips Ch. 17; 10 Cl. & Fin. 42; *contra*, Morrison's Case, cited in 4 T. R. 140, and 1 H. Bl. 677, 682. See Woodworth *v.* Spring, 4 Allen, 321, 325.

discretion, and in some cases require good security,[1] in others, direct the payment of a regular allowance,[2] and in others, refuse payment altogether;[3] the welfare of the infant being always considered in such cases.

The principles applicable to non-resident guardians in this country are similar to those in case of foreign executors and administrators.[4]

As each legislature in this country derives its authority from a written constitution, questions sometimes arise in our courts as to the validity of certain statutes, which in Great Britain are of no importance, since there an act of Parliament is the supreme law. Thus it is not uncommon for our legislatures to authorize or confirm the sale of lands held by guardians and other trustees, by special statutes; and such statutes have been attacked either as an interference with the property rights of infants and their heirs, or as an usurpation of judicial functions.[5] Such acts are, however, constitutional, according to the best authorities.[6] But in a New Jersey case, it was intimated by the Chancellor that, if fraud or sinister motives on the guardian's part were shown, the special act might be judicially avoided.[7] It is held that the legislature may enable a foreign guardian to sell lands within the State.[8] So a general law may be enacted for enabling guardians and other trustees to enter into agreements as to the disposition of property held by them, consistently with constitutional provisions which pro-

1 Case of Andrews' Heirs, 3 Humph. 592; Martin *v.* McDonald, 14 B. Monr. 544.

2 McNeely *v.* Jamison, 2 Jones Eq. 186. And see *Ex parte* Dawson, 3 Bradf. 130; M'Liskey *v.* Reid, 4 Bradf. 334.

3 See 2 Story Eq. Jur. § 1354 *b*; Stephens *v.* James, 1 M. & K. 627.

4 Commonwealth *v.* Rhoads, 37 Penn. St. 60. And see Pratt *v.* Wright, 13 Gratt. 175.

5 See Davison *v.* Johonnot, 7 Met. 388, for a full discussion of the question.

6 Clarke *v.* Van Surlay, 15 Wend. 436; Cochran *v.* Van Surlay, 20 Wend. 365; Davison *v.* Johonnot, 7 Met. 388; Snowhill *v.* Snowhill, 2 Green Ch. 20; *contra*, Opinion of Justices cited in 4 N. H. 572; Jones *v.* Perry, 10 Yerg. 59.

7 Snowhill *v.* Snowhill, 2 Green Ch. 20.

8 Boon *v.* Bowers, 30 Miss. 246; Nelson *v.* Lee, 10 B. Monr. 495.

tect the rights of individuals; notwithstanding the rights of persons remotely interested in the estate, who are either not in existence or only contingently concerned, may be thereby compromised without their assent.[1]

[1] Clarke *v.* Cordis, 4 Allen, 466.

CHAPTER V.

RIGHTS AND DUTIES OF GUARDIANS CONCERNING THE WARD'S PERSON.

As the guardian of a minor stands in the place of a parent, his rights and duties, so far as concerns the person of his ward, are in general those of a parent. His rights relate chiefly to the ward's personal custody. His duties are those of protection, education, and maintenance. These rights and duties will be considered at length in the present chapter.

Guardianship, generally, carries with it the custody of the ward's person. This is especially true where the ward's parents are both dead or incompetent to act. Some one must then exercise the right of custody; and who is more suitable than the officer invested by law with the responsibility of paying for the child's education and maintenance? Hence the guardian's title is, in this respect, higher than that of relatives and friends; and he may insist upon taking the child from the control of a step-mother or grandmother, or from any person to whom the father has informally committed the care.[1] For such considerations, however material in determining the selection of a guardian, become superseded by the actual appointment. And it has been said that the decision of the court as to the guardian's appointment is a final decision as to the care and custody of the ward.[2]

But the custody of infants, as we have seen, is a subject within the free discretion of courts of equity; and where the interests of the ward require it, the care of his person will be

[1] Coltman *v.* Hall, 31 Me. 196; Bounell *v.* Berryhill, 2 Cart. 613.

[2] Senseman's Appeal, 21 Penn. St. 331.

committed to others.[1] Chancery jurisdiction applies in this respect to testamentary and chancery guardianship. The good of the child is superior to all other considerations. Of this the court will judge in each case by the circumstances, and make orders accordingly, both as to actual custody and as to the persons who may have access to the child. In determining where the infant shall reside, the infant's inclination will have considerable weight, if he be of sufficient age; but not, it would appear, during the period of nurture.[2]

The right of chancery courts to regulate the personal custody of infants subject to probate guardianship has also been asserted in this country. This principle determined the decision of the court in the New York case of *The People* v. *Wilcox*.[3] Here it appeared that the parents had separated, the father being a man of intemperate habits. The child, by the father's permission, was subsequently brought up at the house of his paternal grandparents. Upon the father's death, the grandparents secured letters of guardianship, without notice to the mother, who was resident elsewhere. She afterwards came forward and claimed control of her child, then only nine years old. It appeared that the child was happy and well provided for at the home of his grandparents. But it also appeared that the mother was a person of good character, and that no sufficient reason existed for depriving her of her natural offspring. The child was therefore taken from the legal guardian and his custody awarded to the mother.

But, whatever might have been the language of the court in this case, it is apparent that the circumstances were of a peculiar character. This decision turned not merely upon chancery powers. It recognized the deeper principle of natural law, that

[1] Roach *v.* Garvan, 1 Ves. 160; Macphers. Inf. 119; Story Eq. Juris. § 1341; Ward *v.* Roper, 7 Humph. 111.

[2] Anon., 2 Ves. Sen. 374; Regina *v.* Clark, 40 E. L. & Eq. 109; People *v.* Wilcox, 22 Barb. 178; Bounell *v.* Berryhill, 2 Cart. 613; Rex *v.* Greenhill, 4 Ad. & El. 642. See Parent & Child, *supra*, as to custody.

[3] 22 Barb. 178.

the relation of parent and child shall not be roughly severed. Hence we find probate guardianship in this country frequently limited by positive enactment, so as to reserve to the parents the natural control of their own children and the right to educate, when alive and competent to transact business.[1]

As to probate guardians, it is to be added that the more natural course, so far, at least, as strangers and distant relatives are concerned, is to apply for the removal of the guardian already appointed, and for the appointment of another competent to take actual control of the ward's person.

The English cases are numerous where the mother's claim has been postponed to that of the testamentary or chancery guardian.[2] And where the mother clandestinely removes her child, the court will order him to be delivered up to the guardian.[3] So where she procures his marriage in violation of the statute.[4] And in a conflict between the mother and the infant's paternal relatives, pending the appointment of a chancery guardian, the court has given the *interim* custody to strangers.[5] But the court interferes with reluctance as against the mother, where no misconduct on her part appears, especially if the infant is of tender years or delicate constitution, and requires maternal care and nourishment. And Lord Eldon observed, in a case where the mother's rights came in conflict with those of the testamentary guardian, that though the effect of the appointment of a guardian is to commit the custody of the guardianship, the court looks with great anxiety to the execution of the duty belonging to the guardian, and the attention expected to be paid to the reasonable wishes of the natural parent.[6]

Testamentary guardians cannot be controlled in their rights by expressions in other parts of the will appointing them which

[1] See Smith's Prob. Pract. 82, 87.

[2] See Macphers. Inf. 119–121.

[3] Wright *v.* Naylor, 5 Mad. 77.

[4] Eyre *v.* Countess of Shaftesbury, 2 P. Wms. 103; Gilb. Eq. 172.

[5] *In re* North, 11 Jur. 7. See Anderton *v.* Yates, 15 E. L. & Eq. 151.

[6] Earl of Ilchester's Case, 7 Ves. 380.

amount to a mere recommendation. A case of this sort came before Lord-Chancellor Cottenham in 1847. The testator had appointed testamentary guardians over his children in due form, but had further expressed the wish that in case of his wife's death during their minority they should be placed under the care of certain female relatives. The wife having died, the female relatives desired to assume full control. The Lord Chancellor refused to accede to this extent; but, upon his suggestion, an arrangement was effected, satisfactory to all parties, so as to give the immediate custody to the relatives, while preserving to the testamentary guardian that general control and superintendence which it was his duty to exercise under the will.[1]

Chancery will grant access in certain cases while awarding the custody of the infant to other persons. Not only have orders of access been made in the mother's favor, but, after her death, access has been allowed to her representatives.[2] And where Lord Hardwicke appointed a grandmother guardian in preference to the father's executor, he ordered that the latter should have free access to the infants.[3] So in a Georgia case the court, while confirming the guardian's right of custody, allowed access to a near relative on her request.[4]

Proceedings on a writ of *habeas corpus* may determine the question of legal custody. But a child in the personal keeping of his guardian is in legal custody; nor can unlawful imprisonment or restraint be imputed from the guardian's refusal to surrender such child to the parent.[5] On the other hand, the court cannot entertain *habeas corpus* to restore to the guardian a child forcibly removed by the parent, unless the child is actually restrained of liberty.[6] Besides the writ of *habeas*

[1] Knott *v.* Cotter, 2 Ph. 192.

[2] Ord *v.* Blackett, 9 Mod. 116; Machphers. Inf. 120.

[3] Hunter *v.* Macrae, 17 Oct. 1738; 5 Hill Mss. 46; Macphers. Inf. 121.

[4] *Ex parte* Ralston, 1 R. M. Charlt. 119.

[5] People *v.* Wilcox, 22 Barb. 178; Townsend *v.* Kendall, 4 Min. 412.

[6] Foster *v.* Alston, 6 How. (Miss.) 406.

corpus, there is a remedy by petition to the court of chancery.[1]

The question whether the guardian may change the ward's domicile from one country or State to another, has given rise to much discussion. In England, it was decided in the early part of this century that the surviving parent, being also the guardian, was competent to do so.[2] The case came before Sir William Grant, and was argued by counsel with great learning and ability. It was here shown that the best continental jurists supported these views; among them, Voet, Rodenburgh, Bynkershoek, and Pothier. This is the leading case on the subject, and its authority has been fully recognized in the United States.[3] The great objection to a change of the infant's domicile is that the right of succession to personal property may be thereby affected; and it seems probable that, if the change is made with fraudulent intent, to the ward's injury or the custodian's private advantage, it will not be sustained. Moreover as the case above referred to was that of a parent, it has been doubted whether a guardian, as such, not being a parent, has the right to change his ward's domicile. In Pennsylvania, the guardian's authority has been denied, and the power confined to the parents.[4] But Chancellor Kent expresses dissatisfaction with such a doctrine, and considers the objection against the guardian's power too refined and speculative.[5] The other American authorities sustain this view, though in general assuming the principle, rather than asserting it. The question does not seem to have been raised in England: With the facilities of modern travel and the liberal intercourse of nations the tendency increases in favor of the guardian's power to change in good faith his ward's domicile, even though not endowed

[1] Story Eq. Jur. § 1340, and cases cited; Parent & Child, *supra.*

[2] Potinger *v.* Wightman, 3 Mer. 67. And see preceding chapter.

[3] Holyoke *v.* Haskins, 5 Pick. 20; 2 Kent Com. 227 *n.*

[4] School Directors *v.* James, 2 Watts & Serg. 568; and see Story Confl. Laws, §§ 494, 504.

[5] 2 Kent Com. 227, *n.* (c.) where this subject is fully discussed.

with parental authority. This principle is readily admitted, so far as different counties in the same State are concerned.[1] And it would be unwise for American courts to apply, as between States united under one general government, the same rigidly exclusive doctrines which foreign countries differing in religion, customs and civil institutions, may see fit to adopt in their intecourse with one another.

The English Chancery Court reluctantly permits its wards to be carried out of the jurisdiction. The Chancellor in *De Manneville* v. *De Manneville* restrained a father, himself an alien, from removing his child to a foreign country.[2] In other cases, permission has been granted under stipulations for the benefit of the child; the guardian being required to transmit regular returns to the court with vouchers, and to bring back the ward within a specified time.[3] Similar orders in chancery have been made in this country, though rarely.[4] Lord-Chancellor Cottenham has observed, on this subject, that while circumstances may occur, such as the ill-health of the ward, so as to render his removal necessary, the general rule ought to be against permitting an infant ward to be taken out of the jurisdiction. He further declared his regret that this rule had not been more strictly adhered to, and his conviction that a permanent residence abroad was injurious to the future prospects of English children, inasmuch as they were thus deprived of their religious opportunities, separated from their natural connections, estranged from the members of their own families, withdrawn from those courses of education which their contemporaries were pursuing, and accustomed to habits and manners which were not those of their own country, and were consequently becoming from day to day less and less adapted to the position

[1] *Ex parte* Bartlett, 4 Bradf. 221.

[2] 10 Ves. 52. See Dawson *v.* Jay, 27 E. L. & Eq. 451.

[3] Jeffreys *v.* Vanteswartsworth, Barn. 141; Jackson *v.* Hankey, Jac. 265, *n.*; Stephens *v.* James, 1 M. & K. 627; Lethem *v.* Hall, 7 Sim. 141; Talbot *v.* Earl of Shrewsbury, 18 L. J. 125. See Macphers. Inf. 129–132.

[4] *Ex parte* Martin, 2 Hill Eq. 71.

which they should afterwards occupy in their native land.[1] If it be said that such a sentiment favors national pride to the detriment of liberal education, we may reply that the tree is best judged by its fruits, and that foreign travel is of little benefit when those who might have added to the renown of their own country grow into idle pleasure-seekers and loiter their lives away as citizens of the world.

Insane persons and spendthrifts cannot manifestly be subjected to the same personal restraint and custody as infants. But the fact that such ward occupies his own house affords him no special immunity against his guardian. Accordingly, it has been held that the guardian of a spendthrift may enter the dwelling-house of the latter, in the performance of official duties, without his permission and against his will.[2]

The guardian has not the same right as a father to the personal services of the infant. For as his duty to educate and maintain is limited by law to the ward's resources, and is not like the responsibility of a parent, absolute, so his rights are those of a representative, who should seek to add to the trust fund in his hands and not to his own private emolument.[3]

By the common law, the guardian could maintain an action of trespass and recover damages for his ward; and the statute of Westminster II., ch. 32, gave a writ of ravishment by means of which he could recover the body of the heir as well as damages.[4] The equity of this statute extends to testamentary, chancery, and probate guardians, as well as to guardians in socage. On this principle, it has been held that the guardian may sue and recover damages for the seduction of his female ward.[5]

The guardian, acting *in loco parentis*, may bind out his ward as an apprentice whenever the father could do so. This, however, is a matter almost exclusively of statute regulation. And, while the father is usually held liable in damages for his

[1] Campbell *v.* Mackay, 2 M. & C. 31.
[2] State *v.* Hyde, 29 Conn. 564.
[3] See 4 Port. 390; Bouv. Dict. "Guardian."
[4] Bac. Abr. Guardian F.
[5] Fernslee *v.* Moyer, 3 Watts & Serg. 416.

son's breach of contract, it would seem that the guardian is not personally responsible for his ward unless the statute makes him so.[1]

As the guardian is bound to promote the moral welfare of the person entrusted to his care, he may warn off from the ward's premises any persons improper for him to associate with, and if necessary, expel them forcibly. This right is to be reasonably construed; and in the use of means and the amount of force necessary to effect his object, he is allowed a liberal discretion, such as a parent might exercise under like circumstances.[2] And in many other respects the rights of a guardian resemble closely those of a parent.

The guardian's duties as to the ward's person are those of protection, education, and maintenance. In exercising them, he is bound to regard the ward's best interests. Guardians, as we have seen, are seldom appointed where there is not some property. But even though the ward is penniless, we are not to suppose that one vested with the full right of custody can neglect with impunity those offices of tenderness which common charity as well as parental affection suggest. For to the orphan he stands in the place of a parent, and supplies that watchfulness, care, and discipline which are essential to the young in the formation of their habits, and of which being deprived altogether, they would better die than live.

It is, however, to be always borne in mind that while the father is bound to educate and maintain his children absolutely and from his own means, no such pecuniary responsibility is imposed upon the guardian. The latter need only use for that purpose the ward's fortunes. Hence, in supplying the wants of his ward, he is to consider, not the style of life to which they have been accustomed, so much as the income of their estate at his disposal. Whatever their social rank may have been, he may, provided they are left destitute, place them to work, or if they are too young or feeble, surrender them to some chari-

1 Velde *v.* Levering, 2 Rawle, 269.

2 Wood *v.* Gale, 10 N. H. 247.

table institution. He should, however, act with delicacy and prudence; and he may properly consider in this connection the habits and tastes of the children, and the wishes of their relatives; and he can relieve himself of responsibility by asking judicial guidance. The court show a liberal disposition to protect the guardian from personal liability on account of his ward. And if he has permitted the ward, at his own cost, to remain in the care and custody of another, without express contract as to the period of time, he may, whenever he pleases, terminate his personal liability by giving notice. Nor does it affect the case that his ward is then too sick to be removed.[1]

On the other hand, the guardian may make himself liable for his ward whenever he chooses to do so. And if a guardian contracts with another to support his ward, he may become personally bound by his failure to limit the right for indemnity to the estate in his hands. On this principle, a case in Vermont was decided a few years ago.[2] The guardian had contracted for the board of his ward, at a dollar and a half a week, fixing no limitation as to time. The person furnishing the board afterwards notified him that he should raise the price to two dollars a week, and that if this was not satisfactory the ward must be taken away. The guardian did not take the ward away, nor on the other hand did he expressly accede to the new contract. But the court inferred from the circumstances that he had made himself personally liable for the increased rate. It was observed in this case that the guardian has the possession and control of the ward's estate, for his support and maintenance, and has the power of indemnifying himself for any contracts he may make; that it is his business to know the amount and situation of the estate, and that he is not obliged to incur any liability beyond it. If he do so it is his own fault, for which others, who cannot be so well possessed of this knowledge ought not to suffer. But the court also held that

[1] Spring *v.* Woodworth, 4 Allen, 326; Overton *v.* Beavers, 19 Ark. 623; Bredin *v.* Dwen, 2 Watts, 95; Hussey *v.* Roundtree, Busb. 110.

[2] Hutchinson *v.* Hutchinson, 19 Vt. 437.

under the above contract the guardian was not personally liable for extra charges against the ward, such as repairs on clothing, washing, care and medical attendance while sick, and burial expenses.

It is held that the guardian appointed in one State may sue a foreign guardian for the support and education of wards left with the former by consent of the latter guardian.[1] So wherever a town is liable for the support of a ward as a pauper, his guardian may claim reimbursement for necessary expenses incurred after the ward's property has been exhausted.[2]

The doctrine has been repeatedly declared that no guardian can expend more than the income of his ward's estate without proper judicial sanction. This is the settled rule in chancery, and it is universally applicable in the United States.[3] And a similar principle prevails under the civil law.[4] But to what extent the guardian renders himself personally liable, by exceeding the income without previous sanction of the court, is not quite clear. The English rule is undoubtedly strict. But as to probate guardians, and in modern practice, legal formalities have been considerably relaxed. In most of the United States the guardian is, doubtless, justified in breaking the principal fund, under strong circumstances of necessity, for the benefit of his ward, and he may leave his conduct to the subsequent approval of the court when he presents his accounts. In cases of risk and uncertainty, however, the proper course is to obtain a previous order.[5]

The order in which the ward's property should be expended for his support is as follows: first, the income of the property;

1 Spring *v.* Woodworth, 2 Allen, 206.

2 Fiske *v.* Lincoln, 19 Pick. 473. See Preble *v.* Longfellow, 48 Me. 279.

3 *In re* Bostwick, 4 Johns. Ch. 100; Myers *v.* Wade, 6 Rand. 444; 2 J. J. Marsh. 403; Villard *v.* Chovin, 2 Strobh. Eq. 40; State *v.* Clark, 16 Ind. 97.

4 Payne *v.* Scott, 14 La. An. 760.

5 Story Eq. Jur. § 1355; Chapline *v.* Moore, 7 Monr. 150; Davis *v.* Harkness, 1 Gilm. 173; Davis *v.* Roberts, 1 Sm. & M. Ch. 543; Royston *v.* Royston, 29 Geo. 82; Foteaux *v.* Lepage, 6 Clarke (Iowa). 123; Gilbert *v.* McEachen, 38 Miss. 469; Phillips *v.* Davis, 2 Sneed, 520; Cummins *v.* Cummins, 29 Ill. 452.

next, if that proves insufficient, the principal of personal property; lastly, if both are inadequate, the ward's real estate, or so much of it as may be necessary. The ward's real estate can never be sold, except under a previous order of court. Nor can a guardian use in maintaining his ward the proceeds of real estate, sold for the purpose of reinvestment only, any more than he could have used the real estate itself. He should ask to sell for the purpose of maintenance.[1]

In some cases, it becomes both reasonable and necessary to exceed the ward's income. Thus courts of chancery authorize the capital to be broken upon, where the property is small and the income inadequate for support.[2] As where the ward's education is nearly completed, especially if he will thereby be fitted for a profession. Or where the ward is mentally or physically unfit to be bound out as an apprentice.[3] So, too, in case of extreme sickness, or other emergency, where an unusual outlay becomes necessary.[4] And the guardian can anticipate the income of one year in supplying the casual deficiency of another.[5] And he may treat an increase of value in his ward's property as income.[6] And he may use the accumulated profits of previous years where necessary. In short, the guardian is allowed a liberal discretion in expenditures for maintenance and education so long as he refrains from encroaching upon the ward's capital.[7] And it is held that he is limited in his disbursements, not to the income of the ward's estate actually in his hands, but to the income of the ward's estate wherever situated.[8]

As the father is bound to support his own children, he cannot,

1 Strong *v.* Moe, 8 Allen, 125.

2 McDowell *v.* Caldwell, 2 McC. Ch. 43; Farrance *v.* Viley, 9 E. L. & Eq. 219.

3 Johnston *v.* Coleman, 3 Jones Eq. 290.

4 Long *v.* Norcom, 2 Ired. Eq. 354; Clarke *in re*, 17 E. L. & Eq. 599.

5 Carmichael *v.* Wilson, 3 Moll. 87; Bybee *v.* Tharp, 4 B. Monr. 313.

6 Long *v.* Norcom, 2 Ired. Eq. 354; Macphers. Inf. 337, 338.

7 Brown *v.* Mullins, 24 Miss. 204.

8 Foreman *v.* Murray, 7 Leigh, 412; Maclin *v.* Smith, 2 Ired. Eq. 371. And see Coe's Trust *in re*, 4 K. & J. 199.

when guardian, claim the right to use the income of their property for that purpose; much less to disturb the principal. But, as we have seen, a father is allowed, when his means are small, to claim assistance from their fortunes, to bring them up in becoming style. And where the father, when acting as guardian for his own children, might have reimbursed himself, any other person, as guardian, may help him.[1]

A guardian is presumed to furnish all necessaries for his infant ward, and a stranger who furnishes them must, in general, contract with the guardian himself.[2] But where the guardian makes purchases, the party furnishing the goods is not bound to see that payment is made from the ward's income. This risk must be run by the guardian himself, for the facts are within his own peculiar knowledge.[3]

The allowance of money for the maintenance and education of infants constitutes an important branch of the English chancery jurisprudence. Generally speaking, whenever application is made for the appointment of a chancery guardian, maintenance is also applied for; and the guardian receives no more than the annual sum fixed by the court. The ward's whole fortune is held at the disposal of the court, whether the infant was made a ward by suit or otherwise. If a suit be pending, the guardian receives his allowance through the receiver or some other officer of the court. If there be no suit pending, the executor or trustee pays the annual sum fixed by the court; and, if the whole proceeds of real estate be ordered for maintenance, the tenants are safe in attorning to the guardian. But parties making payment are discharged only to the extent of the allowance decreed.[4]

Testamentary guardians are, however, frequently authorized by the testator to apply at discretion from the income of the

[1] Macphers. Inf. 219; Clark *v.* Montgomery, 23 Barb. 464; Myers *v.* Wade, 6 Rand. 444; Walker *v.* Crowder, 2 Ired. Eq. 478. See Parent & Child, *supra.*

[2] State *v.* Cook, 12 Ired. 67; Royston *v.* Royston, 29 Geo. 82.

[3] Broadus *v.* Rosson, 3 Leigh, 12; Hutchinson *v.* Hutchinson, 19 Vt. 437.

[4] Macphers. Inf. 106; *Ex parte* Starkie, 3 Sim. 339.

infant's fund, or from the capital, for his support; and such discretion will not be controlled so long as the guardian acts in good faith. But trustees and guardians frequently procure an order of maintenance, notwithstanding, in order to relieve themselves of all responsibility.[1] Doubts were formerly entertained of the power of chancery to interfere in these and other cases where the infant had not been made a ward of chancery by suit. No such doubts now exist, however; and the court will, on petition, and without formal proceedings by bill, settle a due maintenance.[2]

Courts of chancery treat the guardian as the proper judge of the place where his ward shall be educated, and will, if necessary, issue orders to compel obedience. But if guardians disagree as to the mode of their ward's education, the court will exercise its own discretion and will not consider itself bound by the wishes of the majority.[3] Parol evidence of the deceased father's wishes is admissible, and the court will pay attention to such wishes, although informally expressed, in judging of the mode of education of children as well as in the appointing of a guardian.[4]

1 Macphers. Inf. 213; Livesey *v.* Harding, Taml, 460; French *v.* Davidson, 3 Mad. 396; Collins *v.* Vining, 1 C. P. Cooper, 472.

2 Story Eq. Jur. § 1354 and cases cited. And see Kettletas *v.* Gardner, 1 Paige, 488.

3 Story Eq. Jur. § 1340; Macphers. Inf. 121; Tremaine's Case, Strange, 168; Hall *v.* Hall, 3 Atk. 721.

4 Anon., 2 Ves. Sen. 56; Campbell *v.* Mackay, 2 M. &. C. 34; *contra,* Storke *v.* Storke, 3 P. Wms. 51. See Parent and Child, *supra.*

CHAPTER VI.

RIGHTS AND DUTIES OF THE GUARDIAN AS TO THE WARD'S ESTATE.

WE have seen that chancery guardians have only a limited authority over the estates of their wards, inasmuch as the court makes a fixed allowance, to be consumed in maintenance and education, leaving the bulk of the infant's estate in the hands of executors, trustees, or its own officers. In this country, guardians almost invariably assume the full management of their ward's fortunes, unless restrained by the will of the testator; and, whenever they do so, they are bound by the principles which regulate the general conduct of all trustees.

The leading principle recognized by chancery in supervising the guardian's conduct is, that the ward's interests are of paramount consideration. Hence, two observations are to be made at the outset of this chapter. The first is, that unauthorized acts of the guardian may be sanctioned if they redound to the ward's benefit; while, on the other hand, for unauthorized acts by which the ward's estate suffers, the guardian must pay the penalty of his imprudence.[1] The second is, that the guardian's trust is one of obligation and duty, and not of speculation and profit; and he is, therefore, not permitted to reap any personal benefit from the use of the ward's money.[2] We shall have occasion to apply these observations as we proceed.

Among the most obvious powers and duties of the guardian in the management of his ward's property are these: To collect

[1] Milner *v.* Lord Harewood, 18 Ves. Jr. 259; Capehart *v.* Huey, 1 Hill Ch. 405.

[2] 2 Kent Com. 229.

all dues and give receipts for the same. To procure such legacies and distributive shares from testators or others as may have accrued. To take and hold all property settled upon the ward by way of gift or purchase, unless some other trustee is interposed. To collect dividends and interest, and the income of personal property in general. To receive and receipt for the rents and profits of real estate. To receive moneys due the ward on bond and mortgage. To pay the necessary expenses of the ward's personal protection, education, and support. To invest and re-invest all balances in his hands. To sell the capital of the ward's property, change the character of investments when needful, convert real into personal and personal into real estate, in a suitable exigency; but not without judicial direction. To account to the ward or his legal representatives at the expiration of his trust. And, in general, to exercise the same prudence and foresight which a good business man would use in the management of his own fortunes, though under more guarded restraints.[1]

The right to collect a debt implies the right to sue. Hence, the guardian may, in the exercise of good discretion, and acting under competent legal advice, institute suits to recover the ward's property.[2] And this right extends to property fraudulently obtained from the ward before the guardian's appointment.[3] But he must sue in general in the name of his ward, and not in his own name.[4] And if he institutes groundless and speculative suits, and is unsuccessful, he must bear the loss.[5] So, too, whenever his conduct shows fraud or heedless imprudence. Otherwise, he is entitled to his costs and legal expenses out of the ward's estate.[6]

[1] Genet *v.* Tallmadge, 1 Johns. Ch. 3; Jackson *v.* Sears, 10 Johns. 435; Eichelberger's Appeal, 4 Watts, 84; Swan *v.* Dent, 2 Md. Ch. 111; Crenshaw *v.* Crenshaw, 4 Rich. Eq. 14.

[2] Smith *v.* Bean, 8 N. H. 15; Shepherd *v.* Evans, 9 Ind. 260.

[3] Somes *v.* Skinner, 16 Mass. 348.

[4] Longstreet *v.* Tilton, Coxe, 38; Sillings *v.* Bumgardner, 9 Gratt. 273.

[5] Brown *v.* Brown, 5 E. L. & Eq. 567; Savage *v.* Dickson, 16 Ala. 257.

[6] Taylor *v.* Kilgore, 33 Ala. 214; 1 Foster (N. H.) 204. Among the cases in

A guardian is now generally permitted to submit to arbitration questions and controversies respecting the property and interests of his ward, and the award made in pursuance thereof is binding on all parties.[1] So he may compromise when acting in good faith and sound discretion for the benefit of his ward.

which the guardian may sue in his own name are the following: For non-payment of rent. Pond *v.* Curtiss, 7 Wend. 45. For trespass on his ward's lands. Truss *v.* Old, 6 Rand. 556; Bacon *v.* Taylor, Kirby, 368. For intermeddling with the issues and profits thereof. Beecher *v.* Crouse, 19 Wend. 306. For an injury to any property of the ward in his actual possession. Fuqua *v.* Hunt, 1 Ala. 197. Or where he has the right of possession. Sutherland *v.* Goff, 5 Porter, 508; Field *v.* Lucas, 21 Geo. 447. Or on a note payable to himself, as guardian, though given for a debt due to the ward. Jolliffe *v.* Higgins, 6 Munf. 3; Baker *v.* Ormsby, 4 Scam. 325; Thacher *v.* Dinsmore, 5 Mass. 299.

But debts and demands of the wards should in general be prosecuted in their name. And the guardian cannot sue in his own name, after his female ward's marriage, for a debt due her before such marriage. Barnet *v.* Commonwealth, 4 J. J. Marsh. 389. Nor on a promise to the guardians of the minor children of A. B., for this is a promise to the wards. Carskadden *v.* McGhee, 7 Watts & Serg. 140. Nor on an award, although he had submitted to arbitration. Hutchins *v.* Johnson, 12 Conn. 376. Nor where a statute authorizes guardians to "demand, sue for, and receive all debts due" their wards. Hutchins *v.* Dresser, 26 Me. 76. And see Hoare *v.* Harris, 11 Ill. 24. He cannot act on a petition for partition. Stratton's Case, 1 Johns. 509; Totten's Appeal, 46 Penn. St. 301. Nor subscribe a libel for divorce. Winslow *v.* Winslow, 7 Mass. 96. He is sometimes authorized by statute, however, to sue in his own name for the use of the ward. Fuqua *v.* Hunt, 1 Ala. 197. And see Anderson *v.* Watson, 3 Met. (Ky.) 509; Hines *v.* Mullins, 25 Geo. 696.

A guardian is to be sued in person upon notes executed by him in his official capacity. See 1 Pars. Bills & Notes, 89, 90; Thacher *v.* Dinsmore, *supra*.

A guardian is not liable in assumpsit for necessaries; the remedy, if any, being on his probate bond. Cole *v.* Eaton, 8 Cush. 587. But he may be sued upon his own contract touching his ward's estate. Stevenson *v.* Bruce, 10 Ind. 397. And judgment should then be against him personally, and not against the ward. Clark *v.* Casler, 1 Cart. Ind. 243. Where the judgment is to bind the ward's property, suit should be against the ward. Otherwise, the property of the guardian must be levied upon, who will look to the infant's estate for his own reimbursement. Tobin *v.* Addison, 2 Strobh. 3; Clark *v.* Casler, 1 Smith, Ind. 150. And see Raymond *v.* Sawyer, 37 Maine, 406. As to conclusiveness of judgments, see Morris *v.* Garrison, 27 Penn. St. 226. Judgment against a person "as guardian," is a judgment against him personally, the additional words being descriptive merely. No action lies against a guardian upon the ward's contract; but suit should be against the ward who may defend by guardian. Brown *v.* Chase, 4 Mass. 439.

[1] Weed *v.* Ellis, 3 Caines, 253; Weston *v.* Stewart, 11 Maine, 326; Hutchins *v.* Johnson, 12 Conn. 376; Goleman *v.* Turner, 14 S. & M. 118; Strong *v.* Beroujon, 18 Ala. 168.

But the guardian's compromise of a baseless and unjust claim, would not be upheld in equity as against the ward, nor, as it would seem, against the guardian himself, no blame attaching to the latter.[1] An infant cannot, in any event, be bound by the fraudulent compromise of his guardian.[2] On the same general principles, and with like limitations, the guardian may release a debt due his ward. The same rule as to compounding and releasing debts appears to prevail in England as in this country; and it applies to all trustees alike.[3] The original doctrine seems to be this: that he cannot bind his ward by arbitration unless the court shall previously authorize him to do so, or subsequently approve, on the ground that it was for the ward's benefit.

A guardian, it is said, cannot by his general contracts bind the person or estate of his ward.[4] Nor can he avoid a beneficial contract made by his infant ward.[5] Nor waive a benefit to which the ward is entitled by decree.[6] For any thing which he does injurious to the infant is a violation of duty. And the insertion in a contract of words importing the title "guardian" will not shield the guardian from personal liability. In the language of Chief-Justice Parsons: "As an administrator cannot by his promise bind the estate of the intestate, so neither can the guardian by his contract bind the person or estate of his ward."[7] But the rule is, after all, a technical one; for the insertion of words showing representative capacity imports that the contract was made as a trustee. And on all such contracts, fairly made, the guardian is entitled to reimbursement from his ward's estate. It is simply meant that the person with whom the guardian contracts on behalf of his ward may presume a sufficiency of assets. For if one acting in a trust capacity

1 Underwood *v.* Brockman, 4 Dana, 309.
2 Lunday *v.* Thomas, 26 Geo. 537.
3 Blue *v.* Marshall, 3 P. W. 381.
4 Jones *v.* Brewer, 1 Pick. 317; Tenney *v.* Evans, 14 N. H. 343.
5 Oliver *v.* Houdlet, 13 Mass. 237. And see Bac. Abr. Guardian G.
6 Hite *v.* Hite, 2 Rand. 409.
7 Forster *v.* Fuller, 6 Mass. 58.

could claim exemption from all personal liability, on the ground that there was none of the ward's property left in his hands for payment, he might abuse his privileges. His knowledge of the exact state of the trust fund and his power of management would give him an immense advantage over the other contracting party. Hence the propriety of the rule that guardians are personally bound on their contracts, in dealing with others on the ward's behalf; while in turn they bind the estate by charging their expenses to the ward's account, to be passed upon by the court. The insertion of words implying a trust become therefore essential in determining whether a contract was intentionally made by the guardian on his own or his ward's account.

If the guardian contracts a debt for his ward's benefit, he becomes, in this sense, personally liable; and this even though the debt be for necessaries.[1] But the goods, in such case, must have been supplied by the guardian's order and on his credit. The guardian has the same right to judge as to what are necessaries, according to the estate and social position of his ward, that a parent would have for his own child.[2] He is of course entitled to reimbursement for necessaries supplied by himself. So where he advances money to the ward for the education of the latter.[3] On the ward's own contract for necessaries, the guardian is not personally liable. And it would appear that an express contract must in all cases be shown, to charge the guardian personally; and that his knowledge of the ward's contract, and failure to dissent, will not suffice. But he may ratify any contract of the ward by words or acts.[4]

The title to promissory notes made payable to the guardian is *prima facie* in him. And this is true, though his authority has ceased. Hence he may maintain suit, unless the defendant

1 Simms *v.* Norris, 5 Ala. 42.

2 Nicholson *v.* Spencer, 11 Geo. 607; Kraker *v.* Byrum, 13 Rich. 163.

3 Smith's Appeal, 30 Penn. St. 397.

4 Tucker *v.* M'Kee, 1 Bailey, 344; Hargrove *v.* Webb, 27 Geo. 172; Oliver *v.* Houdlet, 13 Mass. 237. And see Mason *v.* Caldwell, 5 Gilman, 196.

can show that it has been transferred to the successor, or otherwise disprove title.[1] The guardian may, however, indorse over such note on the cessation of his authority; in which case the person in lawful possession should sue. So too the guardian may, after his ward's death, transfer a note for the ward's money, payable to the ward or bearer, to a third person for collection.[2]

The promise of a guardian to pay his ward's debts is not collateral, within the Statute of Frauds; and therefore it need not be expressed in writing.[3] And where a guardian, on surrendering his trust, transfers to his successor a debt due the ward, this is sufficient consideration to support the promise of the latter to pay the former guardian's debt.[4]

Conversions, that is to say, changes made in the character of trust property, from personal into real or real into personal estate, are never favored. The previous sanction of chancery should always be sought; and this is only given under strong circumstances of propriety. The same may be said of exchanges of the ward's property. Courts are reluctant to disturb the property of those who are only temporarily disabled from assuming full control. Sales of real estate are in general only partial, and for necessary purposes. But sales and exchanges of personal estate are very common. And the guardian may sell personal estate for the purposes of the trust without a previous order of court, provided he acts fairly and with good judgment; though his safer course is to obtain permission. But sales of the real estate of the ward would be extremely perilous, if not absolutely void, unless previous authority had been obtained. Undoubtedly, they could not bind the ward under such circumstances. Nor is the guardian permitted to sell first and obtain judicial sanction afterwards. So the guar-

[1] Chambless *v.* Vick, 34 Miss. 109.
[2] Fletcher *v.* Fletcher, 29 Vt. 98.
[3] Roche *v.* Chaplin, 1 Bailey, 419.
[4] French *v.* Thompson, 6 Vt. 54.

dian must not buy land with the infant's money without the direction of chancery.[1]

But a practical conversion takes place where the guardian uses the trust money in paying off the ward's mortgage debts. He is bound to apply rents and profits in keeping down the interest on such encumbrances; nor can he, in general, invest personal estate more judiciously than in freeing the land from debt altogether.[2] An order of court is not necessary in such cases, nor for judgment debts, but it would be required for discharging other than direct encumbrances.[3] So, too, a guardian may redeem his ward's estate from foreclosure.[4] The statutes of most American States have greatly altered the law on the subject of conversions, so as not only to facilitate the sale of real estate belonging to *cestuis que trust*, but to enable their fiduciaries, under judicial authority, to make specific performance of contracts and to release vested and contingent interests.

Where, at the time the court orders the sale or purchase of real estate by the guardian, the conversion was beneficial to the ward, it would appear that the guardian is not made liable, if such conversion afterwards turns out injurious.[5] But whether an order of court would protect conduct notoriously imprudent, as if there should be a sudden and marked decline in the value of the land from some cause not within the consideration of the court at the time of issuing the order, and such as would have been sufficient for its revocation, and the guardian, nevertheless, goes on and makes the sale at a sacrifice, may well be doubted.

1 Macphers. Inf. 278 *et seq.*; 2 Kent Com. 228–230 and notes; Story Eq. Jur. § 1357; Witter *v.* Witter, 3 P. Wms. 101; *Ex parte* Phillips, 19 Ves. 122; Ware *v.* Polhill, 11 Ves. 278; Royer's Appeal, 11 Penn. St. 36; *Ex parte* Crutchfield, 3 Yerg. 336; Dorr, Petitioner, Walker Eq. 145; Kendall *v.* Miller, 9 Cal. 591; Matter of Mason, Hook. 122. See Harris *v.* Harris, 6 Gill & Johns. 111.

2 Macphers. Inf. 285; March *v.* Bennett, 1 Vern. 428; Jennings *v.* Looks, 2 P. Wms. 278.

3 Palmes *v.* Danby, Prec. in Ch. 137; s. c. 1 Eq. Ab. 261; Waters *v.* Ebral, 2 Vern. 606.

4 Botham *v.* M'Intier, 19 Pick. 346; Marvin *v.* Schilling, 12 Mich. 356.

5 Bonsall's Case, 1 Rawle, 266.

Where a guardian purchases, on behalf of his ward, a house and lot expressly subject to a mortgage, he becomes personally liable for the amount of the unpaid debt; even though he had been authorized by the court to make the purchase. But the court will afford him relief from the ward's estate.[1] In an English case, where a guardian borrowed money to pay off encumbrances on the ward's estate and promised to give the lender security, but died before doing so, the court refused to decree specific performance; though the lender's money had been duly applied for that purpose.[2] Here, however, there had been no written contract.

It is a general principle that acts done by a guardian without authority will be protected, and will bind the infant, if they turn out eventually beneficial to the latter; but the guardian does such acts at his own peril. The transaction will perhaps avail as between the guardian and third parties; but the infant, on arriving at majority, may usually disaffirm it altogether, and require the guardian to place him *in statu quo*.[3] This risk is restricted to unauthorized acts; for no guardian can be an infallible judge of what is beneficial to his ward; and to make him liable in ordinary cases, beyond the limits of good faith and a sound discretion, would be intolerable. Hence, as judicial control becomes relaxed, the guardian's unauthorized acts may fairly be considered as lessening in number and importance.

It is to be observed, however, that chancery not only punishes corruption, but treats with suspicion all acts and circumstances evincing a disposition on the guardian's part to derive undue advantage from his position. This rule is applicable to trustees in general. The trust should be managed exclusively in the interest of the *cestui que trust;* or, in case of guardianship, for the ward's benefit. The guardian cannot reap any benefit from the use of the ward's money. He cannot act for his own benefit in any contract or purchase or sale as to the subject of

[1] Woodward's Appeal, 38 Penn. St. 322. See Harding *v.* Larned, 4 Allen, 426.

[2] Hooper *v.* Eyles, 2 Vern. 480.

[3] Macphers. Inf. 339.

the trust. If he settles a debt upon beneficial terms, or purchases it at a discount, the advantage is to accrue entirely to the ward's estate.[1] He cannot be permitted to place himself in an attitude of hostility to his ward, or derive any benefit from the latter's loss.[2] Wherever he abuses the confidence reposed in him, he will be held to a strict accountability.

Where the guardian purchases for himself at sales of his ward's property, his conduct will be closely scrutinized. But where no fraud appears, and the sale appears beneficial to the ward, the more reasonable doctrine is that the transaction is sustainable in equity, subject to the ward's subsequent election, on reaching majority, to disaffirm the sale. The guardian, meanwhile, takes the legal title; more especially, if the sale was conducted through a third party, who afterwards conveyed to him.[3]

The guardian is not to apply property exempt from attachment or execution in satisfaction of his ward's debts.[4] He must not mingle his own funds with those of his ward. Where there are several wards he must allot to each his due share of expenses and profits. And, if he becomes insolvent, and gives the bulk of the property received by him to one, and little or nothing to the others, equity will still treat the property as belonging to the wards in their proper shares.[5]

So far as the guardian acts within the scope of his powers he is bound only to the observance of fidelity, and such diligence and prudence as men display in the ordinary affairs of

1 White *v.* Parker, 8 Barb. 48; 2 Kent Com. 229; Dietterich *v.* Heft, 5 Barr, 87; Clowes *v.* Van Antwerp, 4 Barb. 416; Lefevre *v.* Laraway, 22 Barb. 168; Kennaird *v.* Adams, 11 B. Monr. 102; Sparhawk *v.* Allen, 1 Foster (N. H.) 9; Heard *v.* Daniel, 26 Miss. 451; Jennings *v.* Kee, 5 Ind. 257.

2 Mann *v.* McDonald, 10 Humph. 275.

3 *Ex parte* Lacey, 6 Ves. 625; Lefevre *v.* Laraway, 22 Barb. 168; Chorpenning's Appeal, 32 Penn. St. 315; Hoskins *v.* Wilson, 4 Dev. & Batt. 243; Blackmore *v.* Shelby, 8 Humph. 439; Hudson *v.* Helmes, 23 Ala. 585. See *infra.* In Missouri, under the Spanish laws, the guardian might purchase lands of his ward by the court's permission. M'Nair *v.* Hunt, 5 Mis. 300.

4 Fuller *v.* Wing, 5 Shep. 222.

5 Case of Hampton, 17 S. &. R. 144.

life. And in absence of misconduct his acts are liberally regarded. He is not liable for investments carefully made, which afterwards prove worthless. Nor is he responsible for funds of which he was robbed without his fault.[1] But for any fraudulent transaction to which he lends himself he must suffer the consequences.[2] And if by his negligence the estate has suffered loss, he must make good the deficiency.[3] What acts amount to fraud or culpable negligence will depend upon circumstances. Ignorance of duty is equivalent to misconduct, where the ward's interests suffer by it.[4]

The guardian's responsibility extends only to such property of his ward as is accessible to him. But having once come into possession, or gained knowledge of his right of possession, it is his duty to account for the property; for the law then imposes upon him a *prima facie* liability.[5] And the fact that money was collected in another State beyond his jurisdiction, cannot affect his obligation to account.

Courts of equity follow the ward's property whenever wrongfully disposed of; and any person in whose hands it is found will be held as trustee, if it can be shown that it came into his possession with notice of the trust.[6] And legacies charged on land and payable to the ward on reaching majority, though paid meanwhile to his guardian, remain a lien on the land until actually received by the ward.[7] Innocent third parties are not affected by the guardian's fraud. But where they neglect to make reasonable inquiries as to facts which ought to have raised suspicion in their minds, they may have to suffer for their imprudence.[8]

[1] Furman *v.* Coe, 1 Caines' Cas. 96.

[2] McCahan's Appeal, 7 Barr, 56.

[3] 2 Kent Com. 230; Glover *v.* Glover, 1 McMull. 153; Royer's Appeal, 11 Penn. St. 36; Wynn *v.* Benbury, 4 Jones Eq. 395.

[4] Nicholson's Appeal, 20 Penn. St. 50.

[5] Bethune *v.* Green, 27 Geo. 56; Howell *v.* Williamson, 14 Ala. 419; Martin *v.* Stevens, 30 Miss. 159.

[6] Carpenter *v.* McBride, 3 Fla. 292.

[7] Cato *v.* Gentry, 28 Geo. 327.

[8] Gale *v.* Wells, 12 Barb. 84; Hunter *v.* Lawrence, 11 Gratt. 111.

The guardian has the management and control of his ward's real estate so long as his general authority lasts. It is his duty to collect the rents for the benefit of his ward. He may avow for damage *feasant*, sue for non-payment of rent, and bring trespass and ejectment in his own name. This was the common-law rule as to guardians in socage, and it still applies to testamentary, chancery, and probate guardians. The recognized principle is that such guardians have an authority coupled with an interest, and not a bare authority.[1] A guardian makes himself personally liable where he negligently permits others to collect the rents, or occupies the premises himself, or suffers them to remain unoccupied.[2]

The guardian may also lease his ward's lands. But his demise cannot last for a longer period than the law allows for the continuance of his trust. And it will determine upon the ward's death in any event. A lease made by a guardian, extending beyond the minority of his ward, was once considered void; but the modern rule treats such leases as void only for the excess at the election of the ward.[3] The same principles apply to guardians of insane persons and spendthrifts. And the rule embraces assignments of the ward's leases.[4] The father, as natural guardian, cannot lease the land of his child; nor can the mother; nor can any mere custodian of the person.[5] So, too, guardians may take premises on lease. And though the words "A. and B., guardians" of certain minors, are used in a lease, the guardians are personally bound to the lessor to pay the rent.[6]

[1] Shaw *v.* Shaw, Vern. & Scriv. 607; Bacon *v.* Taylor, Kirby, 368; 2 Kent Com. 228; Pond *v.* Curtiss, 7 Wend. 45; Huff *v.* Walker, 1 Cart. 193. And see O'Hara *v.* Shepherd, 3 Md. Ch. 306.

[2] Wills's Appeal, 22 Penn. St. 325; Clark *v.* Burnside, 15 Ill. 62.

[3] Bac. Abr. Leases I.; 2 Kent Com. 228; 1 Washb. Real Prop. 307; Rex *v.* Oakley, 10 East, 494; Putnam *v.* Ritchie, 6 Paige, 390; Field *v.* Schieffelin, 7 Johns. Ch. 150; Hedges *v.* Riker, 5 Johns. Ch. 163.

[4] Ross *v.* Gill, 4 Call, 250.

[5] Anderson *v.* Darby, 1 N. & McC. 369; Magruder *v.* Peter, 4 Gill & Johns. 323; Ross *v.* Cobb, 9 Yerg. 463. See Drury *v.* Conner, 1 Har. & G. 220.

[6] Hannen *v.* Ewalt, 18 Penn. St. 9. See Snook *v.* Sutton, 5 Halst. 133.

The guardian may grant an easement in his ward's lands; but it is of no avail beyond the limit of his guardianship.[1] He may authorize the cutting of standing timber, and allow others to carry it away.[2] But his license should be given in all cases for his ward's benefit. And if trees are cut and carried away by his permission, so that trespass cannot be maintained, he must make compensation to the ward.[3]

Guardians may assign dower. And it seems that the guardian's assignment will bind the heir, although Blackstone and Fitzherbert state the law otherwise.[4] The deed of a married woman, guardian of infants, in such capacity, does not convey her right of dower.[5] Guardians may also institute proceedings for partition. Such proceedings, in England, should be by bill in equity.[6] In this country, the subject is commonly regulated by statute. A guardian may purchase for his ward, who is one of the heirs, such portion of an estate as the other heirs refused to take on partition, and the court ordered to be sold.[7]

From what has been already said, it appears clear that the guardian may execute all the deeds and other writings necessary to the fulfillment of his trust. But such instruments should be signed in the name of his ward.[8] On the same principle that agents and trustees are personally bound when they exceed their authority, a guardian makes himself personally liable for stipulations which he has no right to insert in a deed, and for authorized covenants, so badly worded that they fail to bind the ward's estate.[9] Where a married woman has executed

[1] Watkins *v.* Peck, 13 N. H. 360; Johnson *v.* Carter, 16 Mass. 443.

[2] Fonbl. Eq. Tr. 82 *n.*; Thompson *v.* Boardman, 1 Vt. 367.

[3] Truss *v.* Old, 6 Rand. 556.

[4] 2 Bl. Com. 136; Fitzh. N. B. 348; 1 Washb. Real Prop. 226; Jones *v.* Brewer, 1 Pick. 314; Young *v.* Tarbell, 37 Me. 509; Curtis *v.* Hobart, 41 Me. 230; Boyers *v.* Newbanks, 2 Ind. 388; Clark *v.* Burnside, 15 Ill. 62.

[5] Jones *v.* Hollopeter, 10 S. & R. 326.

[6] Macphers. Inf. 340.

[7] Bowman's Appeal, 3 Watts, 369.

[8] Hunter *v.* Dashwood, 2 Edw. Ch. 415.

[9] Whiting *v.* Dewey, 15 Pick. 428.

a deed as guardian, it would seem, on principle, that the joinder of her husband is unnecessary.[1]

It is the guardian's duty to keep the ward's premises in repair, and he may use cash in his hands for that purpose within reasonable limits. But he cannot build or make expensive permanent improvements without a previous order from a court of equity, which is to be construed strictly.[2] And where he advances money for such purposes, without first obtaining an order, it would appear that he is without a remedy.[3] But the court will sometimes protect such expenditures, on the ground that the ward has received a benefit thereby.[4] And this seems the more reasonable doctrine, though not clearly recognized in this country. Authority granted to expend a certain sum for this purpose, is no authority to exceed that sum, though it should prove inadequate.[5] Nor has the builder any lien upon the ward's real estate for such excess.[6]

Stock and farming utensils on the ward's farm are, *prima facie*, the ward's property, as against a guardian who has carried on the farm in person.[7] But this does not exempt from attachment property of the guardian which he purchases and places upon the ward's lands; for the question of title is always open to proof.[8]

As to personal estate, one of the first duties of all trustees is to place the property in a state of security. Guardians in this respect are treated on the same footing as other trustees. *Choses in action* should be reduced to possession without unnecessary delay.[9] Money temporarily in the guardian's hands

1 Palmer *v.* Oakley, 2 Doug. 433.

2 Payne *v.* Stone, 7 S. & M. 367; Miller's Estate, 1 Penn. St. 326. And see Powell *v.* North, 3 Ind. 392.

3 Hassard *v.* Rowe, 11 Barb. 22; Bellinger *v.* Shafer, 2 Sandf. Ch. 293.

4 See Macphers. Inf. 295; 1 Atk. 489; Hood *v.* Bridport, 11 E. L. & Eq. 271; Jackson *v.* Jackson, 1 Gratt. 143.

5 Snodgrass's Appeal, 37 Penn. St. 377.

6 Guy *v.* DuUprey, 16 Cal. 195.

7 Tenney *v.* Evans, 11 N. H. 346.

8 Ib. 14 N. H. 343.

9 See Hill Trustees, 447, and cases cited; Caffrey *v.* Darby, 6 Ves. 488;

should be deposited in some responsible bank. But wherever placed and however invested, the trust funds should be separated, by distinguishing marks, from his private property. Otherwise, he would be personally liable for loss. Hence, if a guardian deposits money in a bank to his own account, and the bank afterwards fails, he must suffer the consequences.[1] So if he purchases stock or takes a promissory note in his own name it will be treated as his own.[2] And it would appear that he is not permitted in such cases to show by other evidence an intent to charge his ward; for the act itself is conclusive against him.[3]

In collecting outstanding debts a reasonable time is to be allowed the guardian. Ordinary prudence and diligence is the rule; and for culpable negligence he may make himself personally liable, even though the demand be against a person residing in another State.[4] He is not to sue in all cases where ordinary modes of collection fail; for the expenses of litigation are to be weighed against the chances of realizing a benefit. What is a reasonable time will depend upon circumstances. It is his duty to contest all improper claims, though presented by the surviving parent.[5] Nor can he with safety permit the administrator of the estate of his ward's father to control property of which he is the legal custodian. And he must hold an administrator to account in all cases.[6] But he is not personally liable, in every case, on a note received by him with other assets, which turns out afterwards to be worthless, on

Powell *v.* Evans, 5 Ves. 839; Lewson *v.* Copeland, 2 Br. C. C. 156; Tebbs *v.* Carpenter, 1 Mad. 298; Caney *v.* Bond, 6 Beav. 486.

[1] Wren *v.* Kirton, 11 Ves. 377; Fletcher *v.* Walker, 3 Mad. 73; McDonnell *v.* Harding, 7 Sim. 178; Routh *v.* Howell, 3 Ves. 565; Matthews *v.* Brise, 6 Beav. 239.

[2] Jenkins *v.* Walter, 8 Gill & Johns. 218; White *v.* Parker, 8 Barb. 48; Knowlton *v.* Bradley, 17 N. H. 458. But see Brown *v.* Dunham, 11 Gray, 42.

[3] Brisbane *v.* The Bank, 4 Watts, 92; Stanley's Appeal, 8 Barr, 431.

[4] Potter *v.* Hiscox, 30 Conn. 508.

[5] *Ex parte* Guernsey, 21 Ill. 443.

[6] Wills's Appeal, 22 Penn. St. 325.

the ground that it might have been collected when transferred to him; for a guardian's liability has its reasonable limits.[1] And money paid to a guardian by mistake cannot be recovered again, if he has paid it out before receiving notice of the mistake.[2]

Like all other trustees, the guardian is bound to make his ward's funds productive. He should see that the capital which comes to his hands is well secured; procure a change of securities whenever necessary; and invest surplus moneys where they may draw interest. For funds accruing during the continuance of his trust he is allowed a reasonable time for making his investment, usually limited to six months, though in some cases a year is allowed, and in others only three months; and he cannot suffer the ward's money to remain longer idle.[3] But he may keep a suitable surplus on hand for current and contingent expenses; also sums too small to be wisely invested.[4] And family relics and ornaments, household furniture and farm stock, are generally exempted from the rule of investment.

The investment of the trust funds is therefore one of the most important duties of a guardian, both as respects the interests of his ward and his own security. Testamentary guardians, like trustees under deeds of trust, should follow the direction of the testator in making investments; and for losses arising from such course they are not responsible. But their powers are to be construed strictly; and where the will is silent or the directions are in general terms, or manifestly improper, chancery rules of investment must prevail.[5]

In England, the estates of infants and persons of unsound

[1] Stem's Appeal, 5 Whart. 472; Waring *v.* Darnall, 10 Gill & Johns. 127.

[2] Massey *v.* Massey, 2 Hill Ch. 492.

[3] Worrell's Appeal, 23 Penn. St. 44; White *v.* Parker, 8 Barb. 48; Karr *v.* Karr, 6 Dana, 3; Pettus *v.* Sutton, 10 Rich. Eq. 356.

[4] Baker *v.* Richards, 8 S. & R. 12; Knowlton *v.* Bradley, 17 N. H. 458.

[5] Macphers. Inf. 266. And see Hill Trustees, 368–384, and Wharton's notes.

mind under chancery guardianship are usually controlled by the court. The general practice is to get in all the money due the ward and invest it in the public funds. For this purpose a receiver is appointed, if necessary. The court will not allow the ward's money to be left out on personal security, without reference to a master as to the sufficiency of the security; nor upon judgment security; but, where advantageously invested on the security of real estate, in Great Britain, the court will not disturb the investment. The statute of 4 and 5 William IV. ch. 29, authorizes investments on real security in Ireland, under the direction of the English court of chancery.[1]

In this country, the management of the personal estate of infants and others is usually left to their guardian, subject to recognized principles of law which he is bound to follow. There are statutes in many States which authorize the investment by fiduciaries in particular stocks. In others, it is provided that investments may be made in any manner for the interest of all concerned.[2] It is the general rule that either public securities or real securities are to be preferred.[3] Investments in stock of the United States, or of the State having jurisdiction of the ward, are doubtless proper; so, mortgage investments on first-class property within the State, and city and town securities are frequently designated as suitable investments. But navigation and other incorporated companies, whose stability is uncertain, are unsuitable.[4] For small sums of money savings banks of good repute may be found convenient. United States Bank stock has been considered a proper investment.[5] And while in some States, fiduciary officers are strictly limited in their power of investments; in others, as Massachusetts, there is no favored stock, and they are only

[1] Macphers. Inf. 266; Hill Trustees, 395; Norbury *v.* Norbury, 4 Mad. 191.

[2] Gary *v.* Cannon, 3 Ired. Eq. 64.

[3] Gray *v.* Fox, Saxt. 259; Worrell's Appeal, 9 Barr, 508.

[4] Worrell's Appeal, 23 Penn. St. 44.

[5] Boggs *v.* Adger, 4 Rich. Eq. 408; *contra,* Smith *v.* Smith, 7 J. J. Marsh. 238. And see Watson *v.* Stone, 40 Ala. 451.

bound to exercise reasonable prudence and sound faith.[1] But for losses which are without the protection of this rule, the guardian or other trustee is always personally responsible. And loans on the credit of a single individual, or a single firm, without other security, are not sustained.[2] Nor investments in indorsed notes of parties of bad or doubtful standing;[3] though the rule would be otherwise if their credit is good. Loans to individuals with good collateral security are upheld.[4] Speculative investments may be made by prudent men in their own business, but not by fiduciaries with their trust funds. If a loan by the guardian be sanctioned by the court he is not liable for loss, unless it arises from his subsequent neglect.[5] But the assent of the court must be in writing and of record; not given by parol.

Negligence and unreasonable delay in the investment of trust funds is a breach of official duty for which the trustee is held answerable. And where the guardian suffers cash balances to remain idle in his hands, or mingles the ward's money with his own, he is chargeable with interest, and in case of misconduct with compound interest.[6] It remains a disputed question whether the guardian should be charged with compound interest for mere delinquency; but it seems that he should not. In some cases a trustee has been so charged, because the trusts under which he acted required him to place the fund where more than simple interest would have accumulated. In others, the principle seems to have been to exact it as a penalty for his misconduct in deriving, or seeking to derive some pecuniary

[1] Konigmacher's Appeal, 1 Penn. 207; Lovell *v.* Minot, 20 Pick. 116.

[2] Smith *v.* Smith, 4 Johns. Ch. 281; Clay *v.* Clay, 3 Met. (Ky.) 548; Boyett *v.* Hurst, 1 Jones Eq. 166; Clark *v.* Garfield, 8 Allen, 427.

[3] Harding *v.* Larned, 4 Allen, 426; Fletcher *v.* Fletcher, 29 Vt. 98.

[4] Lovell *v.* Minot, 20 Pick. 116.

[5] O'Hara *v.* Shepherd, 3 Md. Ch. 306; Bryant *v.* Craig, 12 Ala. 354; Carlysle *v.* Carlysle, 10 Md. 440.

[6] Barney *v.* Saunders, 16 How. 535; Swindall *v.* Swindall, 8 Ired. Eq. 285; Knott *v.* Cottee, 13 E. L. & Eq. 304; Stark *v.* Gamble, 43 N. H. 465; Clay *v.* Clay, 3 Met. (Ky.) 548. But see Reynolds *v.* Walker, 29 Miss. 250.

advantage from the trust money. In all cases courts of chancery have exercised a liberal discretion, according to the circumstances.[1] The rule announced by Chancellor Kent cannot, therefore, be considered quite accurate.[2]

Where a guardian speculates with his ward's funds, or employs them in trade, he must account for the profits. As this is a clear breach of trust, compound interest is properly chargeable. It would seem to be the true rule in equity, where large profits, which ought to have gone to the credit of the *cestui que trust*, are appropriated by his trustee, to require them to be turned in on account; and to impose compound interest instead as a penalty only when there are practical difficulties in the way of enforcing such a rule. It is obvious that in this country a guardian can frequently afford to pay compound interest for the use of his ward's money, if he is suffered to retain the full profits of the speculation for himself.[3] Where he loans his ward's money on usury, and thereby forfeits the whole debt, he is liable for principal and interest.[4] But this need not prevent him from investing at more than the ordinary or "legal" rate, if it be in reality lawful; and, in some States he is bound to do so.[5] It has been held that where a guardian employs his ward's money in a business which he allows his son to manage, with a portion of the profits as his compensation, and the transaction is free from fraud, he is not chargeable with his son's share of the profits.[6]

Where the trust property is already invested on securities which would not be sanctioned by the court, the question some-

[1] See language of the Master of the Rolls in Jones *v.* Foxhall, 13 E. L. & Eq. 140; Roche *v.* Hart, 11 Ves. 58.

[2] 2 Kent Com. 231, and note ib. with citation of authorities. And see Roche *v.* Hart, 11 Ves. 58; Robinson *v.* Robinson, 9 E. L. & Eq. 70; Light's Appeal, 24 Penn. St. 180; Kenan *v.* Hall, 8 Geo. 417; Greening *v.* Fox, 12 B. Monr. 187; Bentley *v.* Shreve, 2 Md. Ch. 215; Pettus *v.* Clauson, 4 Rich. Eq. 92.

[3] Spear *v.* Spear, 9 Rich. Eq. 184.

[4] Draper *v.* Joiner, 9 Humph. 612.

[5] Foteaux *v.* Le Page, 6 Iowa, 123; Frost *v.* Winston, 32 Mis. 489.

[6] Kyle *v.* Barnett, 17 Ala. 306.

times arises how far it is the guardian's duty to call them in and invest in other securities. In this, and in matters of re-investment, the same principles would be held to apply as to general trustees. And since such questions have arisen almost always under testamentary trusts, and not as between guardian and ward, the reader is referred to works on that subject, for a full exposition of the law. We will simply add that much is to be left to a guardian's discretion, in this and all other respects, where he manages the property of his ward on the footing of a trustee; and that he will not be held to strict account for losses occasioned in the exercise of his authority, where he has acted *bona fide*, and according to the best of his judgment, though not with all the promptitude and skill which the exigencies of the ward's situation demanded.[1]

[1] See Hill Trustees, and Wharton's notes, 379–384.

CHAPTER VII.

SALES OF THE WARD'S REAL ESTATE.

Courts of chancery have no inherent original jurisdiction to direct the sale of lands belonging to infants. The legislative power of a State may take the property of its citizens in the exercise of the right of eminent domain. But a judicial tribunal properly hesitates to assume such functions. The common law, which recognized fully the right of individuals to the enjoyment of their possessions, and particularly of real estate, without disturbance, appears to have treated lands belonging to infants as property which should be preserved intact until the owner became of sufficient age to dispose of it according to his own pleasure. Timber might be felled, and mineral ore dug out and carried away; but though such acts constituted a technical conversion of real estate, they were in effect but a mode of enjoyment of the rents and profits, and the guardian was obliged to account for these products of the soil to the infant owner. Sales of the ward's lands were authorized in certain cases, as where there were debts to be paid, encumbrances to be discharged, judgments to be satisfied, and necessary repairs to be made upon the premises. But in such cases the court of chancery violated no rights of ownership; since it is the universal doctrine that property can only be held subordinate to the obligation of paying one's debts. Courts of chancery went no further, except when authorized by statutes. They preferred that the infant's property should remain, while guardianship lasted, impressed with its original character. Not even purchases of real estate were favorably regarded. And when a sale became necessary, the real estate was not resorted to until other means of raising money had failed; nor was a general sale of the lands ordered whenever a partial sale would suffice.

On this subject Lord Hardwicke observed as follows, in *Taylor* v. *Philips*[1]; "There is no instance of this court's binding the inheritance of an infant by any discretionary act of the court. As to personal things, as in the composition of debts, it has been done, but never as to the inheritance; for that would be taking on the court a legislative authority, doing that which is properly the subject of a private bill." This language received the subsequent approval of Lord-Chancellor Hart.[2] It has also been quoted as the recognized law in this country.[3]

Hence, too, whenever the court of chancery has permitted purchases of lands, the infant's right to affirm or disaffirm on reaching majority has been reserved. Lord Eldon lays down with great caution the power of the court in changing the infant's property, so as not to affect the infant's power over it when he comes of age.[4] One objection to conversions of property, namely that the laws of inheritance are not the same in real and personal estate, became obviated in equity by treating the proceeds throughout as impressed with the character of the original fund.[5] Another objection, upon which English writers have dwelt at length, arose under the law of testamentary dispositions, which allowed infants to give and bequeath personal estate, males at the age of fourteen, and females at twelve, while real estate could not be devised under twenty-one. Here again chancery decreed, whenever a conversion was authorized, that the right of testamentary disposition should not be thereby

1 2 Ves. 23.

2 Russel *v.* Russel, 1 Moll. 525.

3 Rogers *v.* Dill, 6 Hill, 415. See also the learned and elaborate opinion of the court, with citation of English authorities, in Williams' Case, 3 Bland, 186; Jewett *Ex parte,* 16 Ala. 409; Thompson *v.* Brown, 4 Johns. Ch. 619.

4 Ware *v.* Polhill, 11 Ves. 278; *Ex parte* Phillips, 19 Ves. 122.

5 Wheldale *v.* Partridge, 5 Ves. 396; Macphers. Inf. 284; Story Eq. Juris. §§ 790–793, and authorities cited; 2 Kent Com. 230 and *n.*; Forman *v.* Marsh, 1 Kern, 544; March *v.* Berrier, 6 Ired. Eq. 524; Huger *v.* Huger, 3 Desaus. 18.

changed. The wills act of 1 Vict. ch. 26, dispenses with this distinction in testamentary dispositions altogether.[1] And this latter objection never could have arisen in the courts of some of the United States.

The nature of personal property, its convertibility into cash, and the necessity frequently arising for changes of investment in order to make it sufficiently productive, have brought about a more flexible rule so far as its purchase and sale is concerned, and no actual conversion takes place. Hence, courts of chancery at the present day assume considerable latitude in directing changes from one species of personal estate to another. Especially liberal must be the rule in those States where the trustee is free to invest in any securities deemed proper, provided he observes prudence and good faith. Hence, too, the guardian himself may sell and re-invest his ward's personal estate, and make purchases, without a previous order of court. But this is to be considered rather the American than the English rule ; since, as we have already seen, a guardian's discretion is strictly limited in England, and the practice of the chancery courts in such matters is to control the property.[2]

Legislative authority may intervene to direct the absolute sale of an infant's lands. And since the ownership of real estate in this country is vested with comparatively little of that sanctity and importance which the ancient laws of primogeniture and feudal tenure threw about it, and inasmuch as purchases and sales of land are fast becoming matters of every day occurrence, the legislatures of most of the United States have seen fit to enact laws for facilitating the sales of real estate by fiduciary officers.

They are comparatively recent, and not altogether uniform, in their provisions. But in most essential features they are alike. They constitute a permanent system. As cases are constantly arising under these laws, we shall here briefly

[1] Macphers. Inf. 278, and cases cited. See Hill on Trustees, 396 *n.*

[2] See last chapter.

notice some of the principles which have a special bearing upon the sales of real estate, so far as guardians are concerned.

The American statutes relative to the sale of lands belonging to infants have the following points in common: *First*, an application to the court on the infant's behalf upon which the order of sale issues. *Second*, a special bond to be filed by the guardian. *Third*, the formal sale of the land. *Fourth*, the execution of the deed to the purchaser. *Fifth*, a proper disposition of the proceeds of the sale. The judicial order of sale is frequently termed a license. The exact method of procedure is indicated in the statutes themselves.

As to the disposition of the proceeds, the guardian's conduct is to be regulated by the terms of his license. If he was permitted to sell for the purpose of maintenance and support, the moneys obtained must be so appropriated; if for the payment of certain debts, those debts must be paid; if for investment in other securities, he must invest therein; and, unless the court leaves the investment to his own discretion, he is bound to invest as it orders. Any other course of conduct will subject him to penalties for breach of his special bond. He is not justified in appropriating the proceeds of the sale for the above objects generally, however reasonable it might be to do so on other considerations; but for the particular object contemplated by the court in granting the license.[1] Not even the ward's assent to his disposition of the proceeds can exonerate the guardian from responsibility to the parties immediately interested, for such losses as occur by reason of his disregard of this rule.[2] Nor is his special bond discharged by the fact that he produced the proceeds of the sale in court, and was then ordered to withdraw them; for the guardian and not the court is the proper custodian of the fund.[3] Any person not the guardian, authorized to sell in such cases, is held to account in like manner.[4]

[1] Strong *v.* Moe, 8 Allen, 125.
[2] Harding *v.* Larned, 4 Allen, 426.
[3] State *v.* Steele, 21 Ind. 207.
[4] Pope *v.* Jackson, 11 Pick. 113.

The most difficult question which arises under the statutes relating to sales of the infant's lands, is that of the essentials of the purchaser's title. In what cases may the guardian's sale be set aside? What statute provisions shall be regarded as imperative, and what as merely directory? How far will irregularities avoid the guardian's acts, and who is at liberty to impeach them? One proposition may be laid down at the outset. It is that inasmuch as the authority of the guardian to make, and of the court to permit, an absolute sale of the infant's lands, is limited to the grant of powers conferred by the legislature, the terms of such grant should be carefully followed. Sales made in utter disregard of the precautions wisely interposed by law are absolutely worthless.[1]

On the other hand, it must be admitted that there is always a hardship imposed upon a *bona fide* purchaser, whose rights once apparently vested, are afterwards pronounced null. If the purchaser took the child's lands by collusion and fraud, or, being the guardian himself, abused his trust to secure his own profit, equity may justly suffer the transaction to be set aside altogether. But a stranger who pays his purchase-money honestly and fairly ought not to be compelled to suffer for mere irregularities under the law. For such fraudulent acts of the guardian as necessarily follow the consummation of a bargain — as the misapplication of the purchase-money — it is clear that the purchaser is not liable.[2] As to those which precede such consummation the purchaser is put on his guard, unless from the very nature of the case, they could not have come to his observation. Irregularities or omissions to comply with statute formalities seem to range themselves in three classes: those which are immaterial; those which will render a sale voidable by certain parties interested; those which go to the foundation of the sale and render it void altogether. And, according to

[1] *Ex parte* Guernsey, 21 Ill. 443; Barrett *v.* Churchill, 18 B. Monr. 387; Patton *v.* Thompson, 2 Jones Eq. 411; Mason *v.* Wait, 4 Scam. 127.

[2] Fitzgibbon *v.* Lake, 29 Ill. 165.

the judicial construction of such irregularities and omissions, will the purchaser's title be determined.

Where the sole authority of the guardian is derived from the statute, courts will reluctantly declare any part of that statute immaterial, except in the sense that the responsibility for non-compliance is thrown upon the guardian or the court, and not upon the purchaser. Informalities in the recitals of a *bona fide* deed, defective notices, the insertion of irrelevant or superfluous matter in the order of sale, errors of the guardian in his allegations or of the court in issuing process, have been in this sense ruled as immaterial. But such cases are generally not so much of statutory direction as of judicial rule and common-law analogies in supplying the intention of the legislature where the statute was silent. The general principle prevails, that it is wise policy to sustain judicial sales, and that they should not be declared void or voidable for slight defects.[1]

As to irregularities or omissions which will render a sale voidable, either the infant heir or some other person in interest has been unfairly dealt with. Here the privilege is accorded, to the party or parties wronged, of having the sale set aside on appeal or by direct proceedings instituted for that purpose; but not in a collateral manner. We need not speak of the infant's right of election in certain cases on attaining majority. Where in general the guardian obtained his license without duly notifying a person in interest, such person is allowed to have the sale set aside. The purchaser's title is, however, good in the mean time. Nor can any one take advantage of the defective proceedings but those whose interests were injuriously affected. And a special limit is frequently set by law to proceedings of this kind, for the sake of quieting titles; otherwise, the ordinary Statute of Limitations seems to apply.[2]

1 Fitzgibbon *v.* Lake, 29 Ill. 165; Cooper *v.* Sunderland, 3 Iowa, 114; Thornton *v.* McGrath, 1 Duvall, 349; Ackley *v.* Dygert, 33 Barb. 176.

2 Kimball *v.* Fisk, 39 N. H. 110; Bryan *v.* Manning, 6 Jones, 334; Field *v.* Goldsby, 28 Ala. 218; Dutcher *v.* Hill, 29 Mis. 271; Gilmore *v.* Rodgers, 41 Penn. St. 120; Marvin *v.* Schilling, 12 Mich. 356; Kenniston *v.* Leighton, 43 N. H. 309.

But as to irregularities or omissions which render the sale void altogether, there is some confusion of authority. The principle itself is a clear one, but in the application there is much difficulty. Doubtless the license of a court without competent jurisdiction would be void. But where the court has jurisdiction, it is material to inquire what provisions of the statute are positive and what are declaratory. In some cases, a very strict rule seems to have been pursued; in others, the construction has been liberal in favor of the purchaser's rights. The execution of the statute bond would seem to be an essential; so, too, a formal sale; the filing of the requisite oath; the offer of such land as the license designates and none other; the delivery of a deed to the purchaser and receipt of the purchase-money. And yet the guardian's failure to comply with certain of these formalities in some States does not affect the purchaser's title. The difficulty is set at rest in Massachusetts by a statute provision as to the essential particulars which a *bona fide* purchaser is bound to notice.[1] We can only add that, in States where the legislature supplies no such provision, a purchaser cannot feel safe in disregarding any forms of procedure indicated in so many words; and that, the more explicit the language of the statute, the more careful he should be in insisting on the prescribed course, especially as to the sale and the method of conducting it.[2]

The purchaser may sometimes maintain a bill in equity for rescinding the sale on account of illegality. But he must offer to surrender possession and to account for the use and occupation of the premises.[3] And it seems that he may, by his laches, forfeit his right of objection to the sale.[4]

Where a non-resident guardian applied for the sale of real estate in Maine belonging to his ward, also a non-resident, the

[1] Gen. Stats. Mass. ch. 102, §§ 37–48.

[2] Williams *v.* Morton, 38 Me. 47; Owens *v.* Cowan, 7 B. Monr. 152; Palmer *v.* Oakley, 2 Doug. 433; Stall *v.* Macalester, 9 Ham. 19; Frazier *v.* Steenrod, 7 Iowa, 339. See Gibson *v.* Roll, 27 Ill. 88.

[3] Shipp *v.* Wheeless, 33 Miss. 646; Loyd *v.* Malone, 23 Ill. 43.

[4] Cooper *v.* Hepburn, 15 Gratt. 551.

person authorized in that State to make the sale was ordered to transmit the proceeds to such non-resident guardian.[1] Statutes have been frequently enacted by which non-resident guardians may sell their wards' lands, on petition to the court having jurisdiction, with an authenticated copy of the letters of guardianship, and compliance with the ordinary formalities of such sales.

It is held in New York that the statutes of that State provide for judicial sales only in cases where the legal title is in the infants; and that, independently of such statutes, the Court of Chancery may order a sale of the equitable estate. On this principle a chancery sale was sustained, as against the infants, where the trust-estate of infants in lands had been transferred by a contract made between the guardian and purchaser with the approval of the court.[2] Other sales of this kind have been allowed where the legal estate was in the infant.[3] The course of procedure in that State is somewhat peculiar, and English chancery precedents are strongly favored. It is held that the part-owner of lands in which an infant is interested ought not to be allowed to make the sale.[4] So too the sale of a court, contrary to the provisions of a devise, is utterly void.[5] Both of these principles are doubtless of general application in this country.

[1] Johnson *v.* Avery, 2 Fairf. 99.

[2] Woods *v.* Mather, 38 Barb. 473.

[3] *In re* Hazard, 9 Paige, 365.

[4] *In re* Tillotsons, 2 Edw. Ch. 113.

[5] Rogers *v.* Dill, 6 Hill, 415. See also Matter of Ellison, 5 Johns. Ch. 261; Sutphen *v.* Fowler, 9 Paige, 280.

CHAPTER VIII.

THE GUARDIAN'S BOND, INVENTORY, AND ACCOUNTS.

It is the practice of the English Court of Chancery to require chancery guardians appointed on petition without suit to enter into recognizance to account. When reference is made to a master on the original petition for guardianship, he is directed to make a report approving of the security offered as well as of the person desiring the appointment. On this report the court proceed to act. A recognizance with sureties is usually taken; but the court uses its discretion; and sometimes the personal recognizance of the guardian is deemed sufficient. This recognizance is vacated when the infant comes of age. No recognizance in modern practice is required from the guardian of the person who is appointed where the infant has been made a ward of chancery during the pendency of a suit. Nor is it given by guardians selected by the court for special purposes; as, for instance, to give formal consent to an infant's marriage under Lord Hardwicke's Act. In a word, the chancery rule appears to be that guardians of the estate give security for the performance of their trust, but guardians of the person none. Special circumstances may, however, arise for requiring recognizance from the latter.[1]

Since the active management of the infant's estate is frequently entrusted to a receiver, selected as an officer of the court, the latter is also bound to account annually and pay his balances into court. For performance of these duties he gives proper security. He is allowed a salary for his services.[2]

[1] Macphers. Inf. 108, 348, 553; 2 Kent Com. 227.

[2] Macphers. Inf. 266. As to chancery practice in New York, see *In re* Morrell, 4 Paige, 44; Minor *v.* Betts, 7 Paige, 596.

In this country, as we have seen, most guardians of the estate are what may be termed probate guardians, deriving their authority under the appointment of courts which most resemble the old ecclesiastical courts of England. The practice which has grown up in most of the States, as well as our statute law, places guardians, therefore, in many respects, on the same footing as executors and administrators. Like such officers, they give bonds, file inventories, and render regular accounts to the court; and the same principles which apply to the one class, in these respects, apply also to the other.

A probate guardian, before receiving from the court his letters of appointment, is obliged to give bond, with good security, for the faithful performance of his trust. As such guardian is entrusted with both the person and estate of his ward, the language of his bond should be framed accordingly. In some States the statute prescribes the terms, substantially as follows: To make a true inventory of the ward's estate which shall come to his possession or knowledge; to manage the property according to law and the best interests of the ward; and to discharge his trust faithfully in relation thereto; to render regular accounts to the court; and, finally, to make due settlement with the ward or other person lawfully entitled at the expiration of his trust. The bond, in case of an infant, stipulates for a faithful discharge of duties as to custody, education, and maintenance; but, where the ward is an insane person or spendthrift, for custody and maintenance only.[1]

The penal amount of the guardian's bond, as in other cases, is usually fixed at double the amount of the estate to be accounted for. The sureties are to be approved by the court. When such sureties are insolvent or the penal sum named in the bond is insufficient, or from any other cause the bond becomes unsatisfactory, a new bond may be ordered with such security as the court deems proper. This bond is made payable to the judge or his successors in office and is kept on file, to be sued in behalf of

[1] Smith's Prob. Pract. 88, 89. See Thomas *v.* Williams, 9 Fla. 289.

the ward or any other person who may be injured by the misconduct of the guardian while in office.[1]

A probate bond may be good, though inartificially drawn, if substantially in compliance with the statute.[2] And if it contains more than the law requires, it is nevertheless good for such portion as is lawful.[3] But, perhaps not, if it contains less. A bond is not to be avoided for slight defects committed through carelessness or error. In some instances, defective bonds have been cured in equity, so as to hold both principal and sureties, and made enforceable, even though void at law.[4] A bond is not vitiated which contains a proper recital of the ward's name, although there is a discrepancy in names between the bond and letters of guardianship.[5] The true principle which distinguishes such cases seems to be that the identity of the parties should sufficiently appear.

Where there are several wards, one probate bond is sufficient for all.[6] But separate bonds for each ward would not be improper, and, in some instances, might be even preferable. The names of all the wards should be embraced in the bond, where only one is furnished.

Natural guardians are not required to give bond. Nor were guardians in socage. Nor, in England, are testamentary guardians to furnish security to the court. The reason is that these guardians were not judicially appointed nor answerable in general to the court. The same law prevails in many parts of this country.[7] But in some States testamentary guardians are treated like executors, in respect to their appointment; that is to say, the will which names them must be admitted to probate and letters issued; and the testator's appointment is made sub-

[1] See Mass. Gen. Stats. ch. 101; ib. ch. 109; 2 Barb. Ch. 216.

[2] Probate Court *v.* Strong, 27 Vt. 202; Alston *v.* Alston, 34 Ala. 15.

[3] Pratt *v.* Wright, 13 Gratt. 175.

[4] Wiser *v.* Blachly, 1 Johns. Ch. 607; Sikes *v.* Truitt, 4 Jones Eq. 361; Bumpas *v.* Dotson, 7 Humph. 310.

[5] Shuster *v.* Perkins, 1 Jones, 325.

[6] Cranston *v.* Sprague, 3 R. I. 205.

[7] See *supra*, ch. 1, 2.

ject to judicial approval. In such cases, the testamentary guardian, like the executor, is required to give security; but he may be exempted from doing so, provided the testator requested such exemption, and the court deems it safe to grant the request.[1]

The bond of a probate guardian renders him and his sureties liable for all estate of the ward which shall come to his possession or knowledge. This includes money due from the guardian to the ward at the time of his appointment and the rent of real estate occupied by the guardian before that time.[2] Property received from persons resident in another State is covered by the bond as much as property originally within the jurisdiction.[3] But while the property is beyond his reach and cannot be obtained without a foreign appointment, the liability of his bondsmen would not seem to extend beyond a general dereliction of duty on his part in neglecting the proper means of obtaining it. The bond of guardians of foreign wards, appointed for recovering estate situated in their own State, binds them to account only for such property, nor can they be held liable for the custody of the wards while the latter remain non-residents. A legacy due from the executor of the ward's father, proceeds of real estate sold by him, and other estate lawfully payable to the guardian by the executor, must all be accounted for, and the guardian's sureties are doubtless liable. But for property unlawfully received by the guardian, although he may be compelled to account for it on his personal responsibility, his sureties are not liable, since it does not come to his hands as guardian.[4]

The liability of sureties lasts while the responsibilities of the guardianship continue, and it does not terminate by the resignation or death of the guardian.[5] Not even the statutory limita-

[1] See Mass. Gen. Stats. ch. 109.

[2] Mattoon *v.* Cowing, 13 Gray, 387; Neill *v.* Neill, 31 Miss. 36; Williams *v.* Morton, 38 Maine, 47.

[3] McDonald *v.* Meadows, 1 Met. (Ky.) 507.

[4] Livermore *v.* Bemis, 2 Allen, 394; Allen *v.* Crosland, 2 Rich. Eq. 68; Ballard *v.* Brummitt, 4 Strobh. Eq. 171.

[5] Moore *v.* Wallis, 18 Ala. 458.

tion to suits against executors and administrators operates to relieve such sureties for the default of their deceased principal.[1] They are liable so long as the official bond can be sued at all. But a surety may be discharged at any time upon his petition and after due notice to all parties interested, and thereupon the court will order the guardian to furnish new security, and, upon his failure to do so, may remove him. But such surety remains liable until the new bond is approved.[2] The personal representative of a deceased surety, it would appear, may compel the guardian to furnish new security in like manner.[3] The approval of a new bond and the discharge of a former surety terminate *ipso facto* the liability of such surety, so far as new acts of the guardian are concerned, notwithstanding the security substituted may prove insufficient, or the instrument fatally defective.[4] One surety cannot be discharged from his liability without the other, unless the latter consents to remain solely responsible.[5]

Where the guardian has filed an additional bond, as in case of a large accession to the original estate, both bonds remain valid and the sureties are all deemed co-sureties, and liable as such.[6] And a bond voluntarily offered by the guardian and approved in the ordinary form is as binding as though it had been ordered by the court.[7] Where the sureties of an old bond are released and a new bond is substituted, the proper rule is that the old sureties and the new are liable together as co-sureties for the defaults of the guardian, previous to filing the new bond, and that the new sureties alone bear the responsibility of his subsequent misconduct.[8] Contribution is in proportion to the penal sum named in the respective bonds.

1 Chapin *v.* Livermore, 13 Gray, 561.

2 Jamison *v.* Cosby, 11 Humph. 273; Mass. Gen. Stats. ch. 101; Bellune *v.* Wallace, 2 Rich. 80.

3 Moore *v.* Wallis, 18 Ala. 458.

4 Hamner *v.* Mason, 24 Ala. 480. See Kendrick *v.* Wilkinson, 18 Ind. 206.

5 See Newcomer's Appeal, 43 Penn. St. 43; Sebastian *v.* Bryan, 21 Ark. 447; Frederick *v.* Moore, 13 B. Monr. 470.

6 Loring *v.* Bacon, 3 Cush. 465; Commonwealth *v.* Cox, 36 Penn. St. 442.

7 Potter *v.* State, 23 Ind. 550.

8 Loring *v.* Bacon, 3 Cush. 465; Bell *v.* Jasper, 2 Ired. Eq. 597; Hutchcraft

Many of the decisions in regard to administration bonds apply on principle to those of guardians. Thus, a bond which is not signed by the guardian, is not binding even upon his sureties.[1] And if altered, after being signed by two sureties, with the consent of the principal only, and then signed by two other sureties, ignorant of the alteration, it is not binding upon any of the sureties; not upon the two first, because altered without their consent; not upon the other two, because they were not informed of the release of the two former.[2] So joint guardians who wish to limit their respective liabilities must furnish separate bonds; since both are responsible for all the acts of each other during the continuance of the joint guardianship where they execute a joint bond.[3]

Where real estate has been sold by a guardian and the proceeds remain unaccounted for at the expiration of his trust, it is a question whether the sureties on his general bond shall be held responsible, or those on the special bond given for sale of the real estate. The best authority is in favor of charging the latter and not the former sureties for the guardian's misapplication of such moneys.[4] The present rule in Massachusetts, where a guardian who has been licensed to sell real estate for the purpose of investment, fails to invest, and charges himself instead, in his accounts, with the proceeds and interests from year to year, is to hold him responsible for the proceeds of the sale upon his special bond, but for the interest upon his general bond.[5] The omission to give a special bond for the sale of real estate is, on the foregoing principles, no breach of the guardian's general bond.

v. Shrout, 1 Monr. 206; Jones *v.* Blanton, 6 Ired. Eq. 115; Ammons *v.* The People, 11 Ill. 6.

[1] Wood *v.* Washburn, 2 Pick. 24.

[2] Howe *v.* Peabody, 2 Gray, 556.

[3] Brazier *v.* Clark, 5 Pick. 96; Sparhawk *v.* Buell's Adm'r, 9 Vt. 41; Boyd *v.* Boyd, 1 Watts, 365. But see Williams *v.* Harrison, 19 Ala. 277.

[4] Williams *v.* Morton, 38 Maine, 47; Brooks *v.* Brooks, 11 Cush. 22; Potter *v.* State, 23 Ind. 607; *contra*, Fay *v.* Taylor, 11 Met. 529; Withers *v.* Hickman, 6 B. Monr. 292. See Andrews Heirs' Case, 3 Humph. 592.

[5] Mattoon *v.* Cowing, 13 Gray, 387. See Pratt *v.* McJunkin, 4 Rich. 5.

One of the probate guardian's first duties after his appointment is to file an inventory of the ward's effects. This is a schedule, prepared by discreet and disinterested persons, and verified by their oath, wherein the amount of the ward's estate, both real and personal, together with the separate items, are duly entered at a just valuation. The inventory serves as the basis of the guardian's accounts and primarily fixes his liability. Here again, the statute relative to infants borrows from the long established practice of the English ecclesiastical courts, with regard to executors and administrators. But one inventory is in general necessary; and, if subsequent effects come to the guardian's hands, he will place them in his accounts to the ward's credit. It is to be observed that though probate inventories are *prima facie* evidence of the existence of assets and their true valuation, they are by no means conclusive. And the guardian may show in rendering his accounts that he was not chargeable with certain items which therein appeared, or that the sale of property realized less than its appraised worth; and he will be credited accordingly. On the other hand, property omitted from the inventory which comes within the guardian's reach in any manner, should be accounted for, as well as all gains realized over and above the appraisers' valuation. During the long period for which a guardian's authority frequently lasts, the inventory may become of little practical consequence, except as furnishing for himself the starting-point in his system of accounts, and determining, for the convenience of others interested, the fact and extent of his original liability. If two or more persons under guardianship are interested in different property, or have unequal interests in the same property, separate schedules should be rendered for each.[1]

The accounts of guardians are in England subject to the

[1] Matter of Seaman, 2 Paige, 409; Hooker *v.* Bancroft, 4 Pick. 50; Mass. Gen. Stats. ch. 100, 109; State *v.* Stewart, 36 Miss. 652; Clark *v.* Whitaker, 18 Conn. 543; Fuller *v.* Wing, 5 Shep. 222; Green *v.* Johnson, 3 Gill & Johns. 388. And see as to inventories generally, 1 Wms. Ex'rs, 878–883; 2 Redf. Wills, 200–205.

direction of the Court of Chancery. Guardians and receivers who have entered into recognizance as officers of the court are compelled to present their accounts on application made by any person interested. Such proceedings are by petition, or on motion filed. Receivers are expected to pass their accounts regularly, and a guardian is compelled to account by enforcing his recognizance. The common rules as to executors and trustees apply to guardians. But unless there is misconduct shown, the guardian need not show specifically how he has used the sum allowed as maintenance. A receiver's accounts are sometimes examined on application of strangers. Mr. Macpherson says that there is scarcely a modern instance to be found where an account has been taken from a guardian without suit.[1] In like manner, equity treats as guardians all persons who take possession of an infant's estate, whether duly authorized to act or not, and obliges such persons to account, on application made by the infant himself, or on his behalf.[2] Courts of equity in this country are doubtless authorized to entertain like proceedings against all *quasi* guardians.[3] But under our statutes probate guardians, duly appointed, are invariably made liable to account, in the first instance, to the local court issuing letters of guardianship, which thus becomes, in fact, the general depository of accounts relative to the estates of deceased persons and wards.

An important distinction is observable in the accounts of probate guardians, between the final account and those rendered from time to time pending the minority of the ward. The rule is that these intermediate accounts, although judicially approved and passed, are by no means conclusive. They serve to show the guardian's liability and to keep the court informed of the general condition of the trust funds, to determine when the guardian's bond should be increased, and to ascertain as to

1 Macphers. Inf. 108 ; ib. 259, 348.

2 Macphers. Inf. 259 ; Story Eq. Jur. § 1195 ; Morgan *v.* Morgan, 1 Atk. 489.

3 Chaney *v.* Smallwood, 1 Gill, 367.

the propriety of sales and investments. Such accounts remain *prima facie* evidence of the sum of the guardian's indebtedness to his ward, but nothing more. The privilege remains to the ward, as we shall notice in the next chapter, of disputing their accuracy when he comes of age. But on the final account of the guardian, which is to be rendered at the expiration of his trust, the question comes before the court as to the general fairness of his management, and items allowed in former accounts may then be stricken out as improper. The reason of this is that the *cestui que trust* had no earlier opportunity of judging as to the correctness of the trustee's accounts, and ascertaining that final balance, which is, after all, the estate in controversy. But the final account, once examined and approved by the court, and not reversed on appeal, the ward's period of objecting to the same having also expired by limitation, such account, together with all which preceded, concludes all parties interested, and cannot be re-opened in any court; certainly not unless for fraud, or manifest error: perhaps in most states not at all.[1]

With probate guardians it is the usual practice to present accounts with vouchers annually, or as otherwise directed by the court, the parties in interest other than the ward having been first cited, unless their approval appears indorsed upon the account. The account is considered by the court and passed after due examination upon the oath of the guardian. The vouchers are retained by the guardian, but the account is recorded and filed in the court. The accounts of wards having different interests in property should be rendered separately.[2] Guardians sometimes make settlement out of court, rendering no returns, but

[1] Boynton *v.* Dyer, 18 Pick. 1; Diaper *v.* Anderson, 37 Barb. 168; Manning *v.* Baker, 8 Md. 44; 3 Md. Ch. 234; 5 Harring. 221; Allman *v.* Owen, 31 Ala. 167; Reynolds *v.* Walker, 29 Miss. 250; State *v.* Strange, 1 Cart. 538; Stevenson's Appeal, 32 Penn. St. 318; Brent *v.* Grace's Adm'r, 30 Mis. 253; Seaman *v.* Duryea, 10 Barb. 523; Seaman *v.* Duryea, 1 Kern. 324; Yeager's Appeal, 34 Penn. St. 173.

[2] Armstrong *v.* Walkup, 9 Gratt. 372.

this practice is not common where the infant's estate is large; nor is it safe, since the failure to account is a breach of the guardianship bond, and renders the sureties liable. Any party in interest may compel the guardian to present his accounts years after the guardianship is at an end, notwithstanding he has a receipt in full from the ward; for no mere lapse of time can be set up against a trust, although the usual limitation to suits on specialties might determine the remedies of parties aggrieved as against the guardian and his sureties.[1] But lapse of time taken in connection with other circumstances, showing a due execution of the trust, will be favorably regarded; and the guardian's account need not then be so strictly made up and proved, as would be otherwise necessary.[2] Where no effects have come to the guardian's possession or knowledge, he need not file either inventory or account; but so soon as there is property his liability becomes fixed; and he cannot be exempted from account on the ground that the ward's estate does not more than balance his own outlays and expenses. The final account is not allowed by the court, until the ward has had the opportunity of examining it. But on the termination of a guardian's trust, pending the infancy of the ward, a final account has been allowed after examination by a suitable guardian *ad litem* on the ward's behalf.[4]

Where the same person is both executor of the parent's estate and guardian of the infant heir, he should first settle his executor's account, and then transfer the balance by way of distributive share to the account of guardianship.[5] Accounts of joint guardians may generally be rendered on the oath of one

[1] Clarke *v.* Clay, 11 Fost. 393; Bard *v.* Wood, 3 Met. 74; Crain *v.* Barnes, 1 Md. Ch. 151; Wade *v.* Lobdell, 4 Cush. 510; Gilbert *v.* Guptill, 34 Ill. 112.

[2] Gregg *v.* Gregg, 15 N. H. 190; Pierce *v.* Irish, 31 Maine, 254.

[3] Woodbury *v.* Hammond, 54 Maine, 332; Whitney *v.* Whitney, 7 S. & M. 740.

[4] See Smith Prob. Pract. 182.

[5] Conkey *v.* Dickinson, 13 Met. 51; Mattoon *v.* Cowing, 13 Gray, 387; O'Hara *v.* Shepherd, 3 Md. Ch. 306; Crenshaw *v.* Crenshaw, 4 Rich. Eq. 14; State *v.* Tunnell, 5 Harring. 94; Runkle *v.* Gale, 3 Halst. Ch. 101; 9 Rich. Eq. 408.

of them.[1] Where a guardian dies, resigns, or is removed, his final account must be presented, and it is the successor's duty to see that the former guardian is held to a strict compliance with his bond; otherwise, he may make himself liable to the ward. The final account of a deceased guardian is properly presented by his personal representative who may be cited into court for that purpose; but for a deficit beyond the actual assets in their hands, the sureties must answer.[2] Hence the administrator of a deceased surety has been sometimes permitted to supply the missing final account.[3] Where a guardian absents himself and has left an attorney in charge of the estate, such attorney may, in Pennsylvania, be summoned by the court.[4] It would appear that a guardian cannot be cited to account before the ward's majority, unless his trust has been first determined; and that his balances should, in such case, be paid to a successor and not to the court.[5]

The decree of the court allowing a partial account, wherein an item is omitted or improperly stated, does not relieve the guardian from liability for the error on his subsequent accounts. He must make the necessary correction as soon as possible. If notes are inventoried and the guardian's accounts do not charge him therein with the interest thereon, or credit him with their loss as worthless, the presumption is that he has embezzled the property or else neglected to make collections; and in either case he is chargeable for the full amount.[6] The accounts should include only transactions between guardian and ward, and should terminate with the expiration of the trust; since the relation is in other respects as between debtor and creditor.[7]

1 See Mass. Gen. Stats. ch. 101.

2 Gregg *v.* Gregg, 15 N. H. 190; Royston *v.* Royston, 29 Geo. 82; Peck *v.* Braman, 2 Blackf. 141; Waterman *v.* Wright, 36 Vt. 164; Farnsworth *v.* Oliphant, 19 Barb 30; State *v.* Grace, 26 Mis. 87.

3 Curtis *v.* Bailey, 1 Pick. 198.

4 Petition of Getts, 2 Ashm. 441.

5 Hughes *v.* Ringstaff, 11 Ala. 564.

6 Starrett *v.* Jameson, 29 Me. 504.

7 Cunningham *v.* Cunningham, 4 Gratt. 43; Crowell's Appeal, 2 Watts, 295.

Valuations should be reduced to the lawful standard of currency.[1] All items are not necessarily proved by vouchers; small charges may be allowed on the guardian's oath; and oral proof is frequently admissible as in the settlement of other probate accounts.

We have anticipated in former chapters the general principles on which guardians are considered liable in the settlement of their accounts: as for instance the payment of interest on sums not invested, losses of money and failure to collect debts, the proper allowance for maintenance and education of infants, and other matters which come before our courts of probate jurisdiction when the accounts are presented for allowance. As the guardian is allowed his costs and expenses in suits on the ward's behalf, so he may charge bills of professional counsel properly paid; but he cannot make the estate pay for advice and services rendered on his own account under any colorable pretext.[2] Interest has been allowed on sums of money necessarily advanced by him to his ward; and this seems reasonable.[3] And wherever the father's circumstances are such as justify the allowance of maintenance from the property of his children, their guardian can pay the money over and charge it in his accounts.[4] As to the guardian's own charges, there can be no question that he is neither obliged to maintain his wards at his own expense, nor justified in appropriating their earnings to himself. But as the services of children and the cost of their board are always mutual offsets, the courts are reluctant to allow charges of this sort, for or against a guardian who brings up his ward in his own family; more especially where the claim seems to have been made up from after-thought and without previous stipulation. In this sense, we understand certain *dicta* of the courts to the effect that a guardian cannot

1 See McFarlane *v.* Randle, 41 Miss. 411; Neilson *v.* Cook, 40 Ala. 498.

2 McElhenny's Appeal, 46 Penn. St. 347; Alexander *v.* Alexander, 8 Ala. 796.

3 Hayward *v.* Ellis, 13 Pick. 272. But see Evarts *v.* Nason, 11 Vt. 122.

4 Clark *v.* Montgomery, 23 Barb. 464. See Spedden *v.* State, 3 Har. &. J. 251.

charge for board where he has offered to bring up the ward at his home free of expense; for it is to be supposed that there is mutuality in all contracts, and that reasonable notice may terminate any liability which has no fixed limit.[1] Like principles are applicable to demands against the guardian for his ward's services, which courts in different States have frequently had occasion to consider.[2]

One rule has always prevailed in England as to the compensation of executors, guardians, and other trustees; namely, that the services rendered should be treated as honorary and gratuitous. Chancery makes no allowance of any sort beyond a reimbursement for necessary expenses actually incurred. However much the honor of being trusted may be deemed a fair equivalent for the guardian's time, trouble, and responsibility, it is not found to suffice for receivers and other officers of the Court of Chancery, whose fees in some measure tend sensibly to diminish the ward's sense of gratitude to the custodians of his fortune. It is found necessary to allow compensation to trustees in some of the British colonies in order to induce suitable men to accept office; and even in the English courts at the present day there is a strong inclination to multiply exceptions to the general rule. Considerations of policy are alleged in support of the established doctrine of chancery; but the arguments seem not unanswerable. In this country compensation is allowed the guardian, while the probate court fees are usually trifling in comparison. And it does not appear that the English rule as to trust officers generally was ever adopted in a single State.[3]

1 Manning *v.* Baker, 8 Md. 44; Armstrong *v.* Walkup, 9 Gratt. 372; Hayden *v.* Stone, 1 Duvall, 396; Hendry *v.* Hurst, 22 Geo. 312; 2 McC. Ch. 43; Cunningham *v.* Pool, 9 Ala. 615.

2 Phillips *v.* Davis, 2 Sneed, 520; Bass *v.* Cook, 4 Porter, 390; Armstrong *v.* Walkup, 12 Gratt. 608. Among the miscellaneous items which have been allowed a guardian in his accounts may be mentioned that of *bona fide* expenses incurred in removing the ward to another State. Cummins *v.* Cummins, 29 Ill. 452.

3 See Story Eq. Juris. § 1268 and *n.*; and § 1268 *a.*; 2 Redf. Wills, 890–892; 2 Wms. Exrs. 1682–1685, and cases cited. In some parts of this country, custom

For the default and misconduct of the guardian the proper remedy is by suit on the probate bond. And such suits are brought in the name of the judge, or the State, according to the requirements of statute, for the benefit of the person or

or the local law has established a commission as the guardian's compensation. In others, the statute allows what the court may deem just and reasonable. The commission allowed the guardian has varied, according to different decisions and under special circumstances, all the way from one to ten per cent, which last may be considered the maximum. Holcombe *v.* Holcombe, 2 Beas. 415; *In re* Harland's Accounts, 5 Rawle, 323; Walton *v.* Erwin, 1 Ired. Eq. 136; Armstrong *v.* Walkup, 12 Gratt. 608. In New York, the rule established for trustees is five per cent on sums not exceeding one thousand dollars; half that amount upon all sums between that and five thousand dollars; and one per cent on all sums exceeding that amount. Matter of Roberts, 3 Johns. Ch. 43. And this rule practically obtains in many other States. One-half the commission is reckoned for sums received, and one-half for sums disbursed. They are to be computed by a guardian at the foot of partial accounts or about the time of actual receipt and disbursement, and not when they are brought forward upon his final account. Huffer's Appeal, 2 Grant, 341; Vanderheyden *v.* Vanderheyden, 2 Paige, 287. Where commissions, at the court's discretion, are allowed, special services performed by the guardian may be considered in fixing the rate of commission, but not as an additional charge. And it is justly observed in a Pennsylvania case, that since the guardian is a trustee for custody and management, and not, like an executor, merely for distribution, what is allowable to the one may not always suffice for the other. McElhenny's Appeal, 46 Penn. St. 347. Even in New York the unfairness of an inflexible rule, applicable to all who hold trust moneys, has led to the assertion of a doctrine in a recent case, which threatens to disturb the chancery rule, formerly considered as well settled; namely, that services of a professional or personal character, rendered the ward, may be allowed to the guardian, besides the usual commission, on the ground that they were rendered not as guardian but as an individual. Morgan *v.* Morgan, 39 Barb. 20. In Maine, Massachusetts, and other States where the court allows what is reasonable, the guardian may charge specific sums for special services, instead of or in addition to a commission, provided the whole does not exceed a fair rate of compensation. Longley *v.* Hall, 11 Pick. 120; Rathbun *v.* Colton, 15 Pick. 471; Emerson, Appellant, 32 Maine, 159; Dixon *v.* Homer, 2 Met. 420; Evarts *v.* Nason, 11 Vt. 122. The ordinary commission is sometimes refused for disbursement of the guardian's final balance to the ward, and receipt of the original fund; nor is it allowable on the principal in mere reinvestments. Commissions may be forfeited by the guardian's misconduct; but not, in some States, for the mere omission to account until cited in. Clerk-hire is properly charged as an expense to the estate, in cases of magnitude and difficulty, where such assistance is required. Vanderheyden *v.* Vanderheyden, 2 Paige, 287; Knowlton *v.* Bradley, 17 N. H. 458; 34 Ala. 442; 29 Maine, 504; Royston *v.* Royston, 29 Geo. 82; Magruder *v.* Darnall, 6 Gill, 269; 7 Monr. 150; Clowes *v.* Van Antwerp, 4 Barb. 416.

persons injured.[1] This is the remedy for creditors as well as the ward himself and his next of kin. Thus, in Massachusetts, suit on the probate bond for neglect to furnish necessaries is the only course left open to one who has supplied the ward, in order to reach the guardian.[2] In most States, the guardian's bond cannot be sued until he has been summoned before the court to account; nor until leave of the court has been first obtained; except in certain cases of debts which appear of record.[3] The reason is that the balances due from the guardian and the extent of his liability cannot be properly ascertained until the accounts are presented. So, too, while the guardian may sue his ward, after the latter attains majority, when it appears that the final indebtedness is in his own favor, he must wait until the court has ascertained and decreed its amount.[4] As to sureties, it is said that they may be sued without a previous suit against the principal; the common-law rule that an executor must first be found guilty of *devastavit* being held inapplicable to guardians.[5] To all suits on guardian's bonds there is a limitation prescribed by law. Thus in Massachusetts the period is four years from the time the guardianship terminates, whether by death, removal, or resignation of the guardian, or the arrival of the infant ward at full age; and the same rule applies to general and special bonds.[6] In some other States the period is five years.[7] In Indiana, it is three

[1] Davis *v.* Dickson, 2 Stew. 370; 27 Mis. 399; Potter *v.* State, 23 Ind. 607; Pearson *v.* McMillan, 37 Miss. 588.

[2] Cole *v.* Eaton, 8 Cush. 587. See also Conant *v.* Kendall, 21 Pick. 36.

[3] Stillwell *v.* Miles, 19 Johns. 304; Bailey *v.* Rogers, 1 Greenl. 186; Salisbury *v.* Van Hoesen, 3 Hill, 77; Anderson *v.* Maddox, 3 McCord, 237; Jarrett *v.* State, 5 Gill & Johns. 27; Hunt *v.* White, 1 Cart. 105; Foteaux *v.* Le Page, 6 Iowa, 123; Ammons *v.* People, 11 Ill. 6; Pratt *v.* McJunkin, 4 Rich. 5. But see Justices *v.* Willis, 3 Yerg. 461.

[4] Smith *v.* Philbrick, 2 N. H. 395; Shollenberger's Appeal, 21 Penn. St. 337.

[5] State *v.* Strange, 1 Smith, Ind. 367; Call *v.* Ruffin, 1 Call, 333; 1 Met. (Ky.) 22. And see Horton *v.* Horton, 4 Ired. Eq. 54; Moore *v.* Hood, 9 Rich. Eq. 311; Potter *v.* Hiscox, 30 Conn. 508; Clark *v.* Montgomery, 23 Barb. 464.

[6] Loring *v.* Alline, 9 Cush. 68.

[7] Johnson *v.* Chandler, 15 B. Monr. 584.

years.[1] Where no special period is fixed by law, the ordinary limitation to suits on sealed instruments must be held to apply.[2]

Sureties, as well as the guardian, are estopped by the recitals in the guardianship bond.[3] They are also concluded by the amount adjudged due from the guardian on settlement of his accounts.[4] They cannot become parties to the accounting of their principal either in the original proceedings or on revision.[5] Where sureties are compelled to respond in damages for the default of their guardian, they may seek indemnity from his property. Equity also allows them to enforce contribution as among themselves. Thus, if co-sureties on one bond pay the whole amount of a deficiency they may use the other bond to obtain a proportional reimbursement.[6] So where there are three co-sureties, and one proves insolvent, the surety who has responded in damages to the full extent may compel his solvent co-surety to pay him one-half of the amount.[7] A surety may always take security from his principal for his own indemnity. But it stands to reason that the surety of a guardian cannot secure himself by any pledge of the ward's property; for this would be permitting fraud in order to prevent fraud, and the infant's pretended security would be to him no security at all.[8]

1 State *v.* Hughes, 15 Ind. 104.

2 Ragland *v.* Justices, 10 Geo. 65.

3 Sasscer *v.* Walker, 5 Gill & Johns. 102.

4 Commonwealth *v.* Rhoads, 37 Penn. St. 60.

5 *In re* Scott's Account, 36 Vt. 297. But see Curtis *v.* Bailey, 1 Pick. 198.

6 Commonwealth *v.* Cox, 36 Penn. St. 442.

7 Waller *v.* Campbell, 25 Ala. 544; See State *v.* Paul's Ex'or, 21 Mis. 51; Jamison *v.* Cosby, 11 Humph. 273; Hocker *v.* Wood, 33 Penn. St. 466.

8 Poultney *v.* Randall, 9 Bosw. 232; Foster *v.* Bisland, 23 Miss. 296.

CHAPTER IX.

RIGHTS AND LIABILITIES OF THE WARD.

HAVING treated at length of the rights and liabilities of guardians, their appointment and removal, and the settlement of their accounts, it only remains for us to consider the powers and duties of the ward himself. Some of these have been already noticed incidentally; others, so far as minor wards are concerned, fall within the general scope of Infancy; but, a few legal principles remain for discussion under the present head, to which we shall now direct the reader's attention.

There is a distinction to be drawn between infant wards, and insane persons or spendthrifts under guardianship. As to the former, the law recognizes a growing responsibility, as it were, on their part; a postponement of many rights and duties to the period of maturity, but not utter and total suspension or loss. Hence, sales made and contracts performed while an infant ward's disabilities last are frequently held subjected to his future approval, being treated as neither absolute nor yet void in the mean time. Hence, is that principle of election so constantly asserted at law on his behalf; hence, too, the right he exercises when of age of passing in review accounts old and almost forgotten, to ascertain the balance justly due him. But as to insane persons and spendthrifts, their responsibilities are for the time blotted out; the disability may be temporary or it may be permanent; but while it lasts it is complete; and it may be essential that transactions on their behalf should stand or fall, irrespective of their choice, and beyond the possibility of future interference. This suggestion is thrown out simply by way of caution; for while the same principles are constantly applied to all wards alike, it is unsafe to draw broad conclusions or argue with confidence from mere analogies.[1]

Thus it is asked whether an insane person under guardianship can make a will, if in fact *compos mentis*. Clearly, questions of mental capacity and undue influence may arise whenever a will is presented for probate. And *prima facie* an insane person, if not a spendthrift, under guardianship, is *non compos mentis*, and his testamentary capacity may well be doubted. It is settled, however, in the State of Massachusetts that a valid will may be executed by a person under such guardianship, notwithstanding the circumstances of his situation; the fact of testamentary capacity at the date of execution being open to proof.[2]

For assault and battery, a ward, like all other persons, is entitled to damages. But where his guardian is the offender, there are technical difficulties in the way of maintaining a suit. Many authorities allow an infant to sue his guardian by next friend; but a spendthrift, it is said, cannot do so. His remedy may be found in getting the guardian removed for misconduct and securing the appointment of a successor, or perhaps obtaining his discharge from guardianship altogether. An action can then be brought by himself or the new guardian, as the case may be. The guardian may in all cases be held criminally responsible for the injury committed.[3]

A guardian may be restrained by injunction from committing waste. So he is responsible for damages thus occasioned; and it has been held that a judgment against sureties on the guardian's bond for waste committed by the guardian will not before satisfaction bar a suit by the ward against one who participated in the waste.[4] The ward may also sue for use and

[1] Thus, in Vermont, it is held that a spendthrift may be compelled to give security to the town of his settlement against loss by his becoming chargeable afterwards as a pauper, as a condition for his release from guardianship. Williston *v.* White, 11 Vt. 40.

[2] Breed *v.* Pratt, 18 Pick. 115.

[3] Mason *v.* Mason, 19 Pick. 506.

[4] Powell *v.* Jones, 1 Ired. Eq. 337. See Bank of Virginia *v.* Craig, 6 Leigh, 399; Hill. Injunctions, 412.

occupation, although he has a general guardian.[1] Where one assumes to be guardian or agent of a guardian, and enters an infant's lands, the latter may elect to treat him as a wrong-doer, and bring trespass, or charge him as a guardian.[2] So where a guardian wrongfully holds over. But the ward cannot sue his guardian for money had and received. His proper course, at least in this country, is to institute proceedings for the latter's removal, and then to sue on the official bond.[3]

Whenever guardianship has been terminated, an action of account lies in favor of the ward. And this action is brought by the new guardian, or by next friend, or by the ward himself, if the period of his legal disability has expired. While his guardianship continues, chancery permits the ward by next friend to file his bill against the guardian for account. But this seems to apply rather to chancery than probate guardians; since direct proceedings for account in the court which issued letters of guardianship, followed by removal of the guardian, if unfaithful, and suit on his probate bond, afford the infant under such guardianship an ample and expeditious remedy. But for chancery guardians, purely testamentary guardians, and *quasi* guardians, the more complicated process of a bill in equity becomes the necessary resort. And this in England is still the usual course of procedure.[4]

The ward's right to call his guardian to account may be barred by limitation. In Pennsylvania, it is said that the same principle applies as in other legal proceedings; and eighteen years' delay after the ward attains majority has been held fatal to a suit.[5] But in Illinois the rule is differently stated, and the guardian's liability to account is there considered to last as

[1] Porter *v.* Bleiler, 17 Barb. 149. See Senseman's Appeal, 21 Penn. St. 331; Sawyer *v.* Knowles, 33 Maine, 208. And see Chilton *v.* Cabiness, 14 Ala. 447.

[2] Sherman *v.* Ballou, 8 Cow. 304; Blomfield *v.* Eyre, 8 Beav. 250.

[3] Brooks *v.* Brooks, 11 Cush. 18.

[4] Monell *v.* Monell, 5 Johns. Ch. 283; Reeve Dom. Rel. 335; Linton *v.* Walker 8 Fla. 144; Swan *v.* Dent, 2 Md. Ch. 111; Lemon *v.* Hansbarger, 6 Gratt. 301; Macphers. Inf. 259, 348.

[5] Bones's Appeal, 27 Penn. St. 492. See Magruder *v.* Goodwin, P. & H. 561.

long as the bond continues in force; the citation to account before the probate court being merely a means to ascertain delinquency as the foundation of a suit, and not of itself a suit at law or in equity.[1] The former may be regarded as the true doctrine for chancery guardianship; the latter for probate guardianship. The guardian's administrator in either case should close up the trust accounts, if not already settled, before he makes distribution; since he may otherwise remain liable for many years.[2] But in most States the general subject of limitation in all trusts is regulated by statute.

Courts of chancery will always aid the ward in recovering property embezzled, concealed, or conveyed away in fraud of his rights. The proper mode of procedure is by bill in equity. And while a probate guardian suspected of fraud should be cited to account, it has been held that his estate being insolvent and his sureties irresponsible, it is not necessary for the ward to sue them before he can file a bill to recover such property as he can trace.[3] A summary process in the nature of an inquisition is provided by statute in some States, for ascertaining the whereabouts of stolen and missing property belonging to wards, by means of which all suspected persons, including the guardian himself, can be summoned before the probate court to answer lawful inquiries under oath.[4]

Fraudulent transactions cannot stand as against the ward. Equity will go to the substance rather than the form, in order to ascertain the real motives of one who professes to turn over trust property to third parties, and will do equity if possible. Where a guardian, for instance, transfers a note with words importing trust to his private creditors as security for his own debt, the ward can follow it into their hands, or against other parties, and stop payment, whether sufficient consideration was

1 Gilbert *v.* Guptill, 34 Ill. 112.

2 Musser *v.* Oliver, 21 Penn. St. 362. See Felton *v.* Long, 8 Ired. Eq. 224; Mitchell *v.* Williams, 27 Mis. 399; Pearson *v.* McMillan, 37 Miss. 588.

3 Hill *v.* McIntire, 39 N. H. 410.

4 Mass. Gen. Stats. ch. 109; Sherman *v.* Brewer, 11 Gray, 210.

paid by the holder or not.[1] But in all cases of this sort, third parties should have some notice, actual or constructive, of the existence of a trust; otherwise, they cannot be made to suffer loss further than the usual rules of stolen property apply.[2] Rights of wards to real estate are frequently protected on these principles. Thus, where a mother interested in certain lands with her children, obtained partition after being appointed their guardian, bought in the premises, and, without paying the full purchase-money, gave a mortgage, taking an assignment to herself as guardian, the claim of the mortgagee with notice was postponed to the children's share.[3] So where a guardian who held a mortgage in his own right agreed with the mortgagor to substitute the ward's money for his own, letting the securities remain as before, this was held to be an equitable investment of the ward's money, and good against any subsequent disposition which the guardian might make while in failing circumstances, to secure his own creditor.[4]

But fraud is a question of evidence. And the payment of a debt to a guardian before it is due is not sufficient in itself to establish an unfair purpose. Hence it was decided in a North Carolina case, that where one, owing a bond to a guardian in failing circumstances, the bond being in behalf of the ward, and not yet due, held also a note against the guardian himself, which he gave to an attorney to collect, with explicit instructions not to make an exchange, but to collect the note given him, and with the proceeds to take up the bond due the guardian, and such attorney received a bank check from the guardian, and believing the money to be in bank, and that the check was as good as money, returned the note to the guardian, and took up the bond in his hands, these acts having been per-

[1] Lockhart *v.* Philips, 1 Ired. Eq. 342.

[2] Hill *v.* Johnston, 3 Ired. Eq. 432.

[3] Messervey *v.* Barelli, 2 Hill Ch. 567.

[4] Evertson *v.* Evertson, 5 Paige, 644. In this case, the creditor had not even notice of the ward's rights.

formed in good faith, the ward could not pursue his former debtor.[1]

Although the proceeds of real estate sold by a guardian under the order of court may still be treated in equity as real estate, this is not necessarily the case at law. And in any event such proceeds lose their original character, and become personalty on the first transmission, though to an infant.[2]

We have seen that the transactions of a guardian on behalf of his infant ward are valid, if within the scope of his general powers, or authorized by the courts of equity; sustainable, though neither within the scope of his powers, nor previously authorized, if the court afterwards deems them prudent or beneficial to the ward; in other cases, subject to the ward's own disaffirmance on reaching majority. Herein consists the infant's right of election. Few acts of the guardian can be pronounced valid, except in the sense that they are authorized, either generally or specially, by the court which exercises supervision; and few of his transactions can be so utterly without authority as to be absolutely void *per se*. The general rule of election recognizes, then, two principles: first, the privilege of the infant ward, on attaining full age, to avoid his guardian's transaction; second, the right of courts of equity to control this privilege by interposing to pronounce the transaction good. The whole doctrine, therefore, seems in strict accordance with that more general rule, that the accounts of the guardian are open to the inspection of the ward at majority, and may be disputed down to the smallest item. And where, as in the case of probate guardians, settlements out of court do not dispense with final returns for preservation and public record, the tendency of the decisions must be in favor of bringing the question of affirmance or disaffirmance of the guardian's

[1] Wynne *v.* Benbury, 4 Jones Eq. 395; and see, as to fraud generally, Story Eq. Jur. §§ 317–320; Harrison *v.* Bradley, 5 Ired. Eq. 136; Dawson *v.* Massey, 1 Ba. & Be. 329; Henry *v.* Pennington, 11 B. Monr. 55.

[2] Dyer *v.* Cornell, 4 Barr, 359. And see State *v.* Satterfeld, 9 Ired. 358.

transaction before the court, instead of leaving it to acts of the late ward *en pais*. These principles suffice for general application to compromises, submissions to arbitration, investments and reinvestments of personal property, and similar transactions, undertaken by the guardian on the strength of a previous order of court, or at the risk of its subsequent approval.[1] Yet, statutes sometimes interpose to render such transactions complete on permission of the court absolutely.

But as to transactions which involve the purchase or sale of real estate, on the infant ward's behalf, the rule is very strict.[2] A defective sale of real estate under the statute may therefore be set aside on a bill in equity filed by the infant against the guardian and the purchasers. And where the guardian contracts to buy real estate for the ward's benefit, the ward, on reaching majority, may either complete the contract or reject it, and look to the guardian for payment.[3] But he cannot, in absence of fraud, compel the vendor to refund the money paid down as a bonus.[4] Nor can he, having once renounced, seek to be relieved against such renunciation.[5] The right of election goes to the ward's personal representatives if he dies under age.[6]

All advantageous bargains which a guardian makes with the ward's funds are also considered subject to the ward's election, either to repudiate or to uphold the contract and take the profits. This applies, in general, to improper acts; as where the guardian speculates with the trust funds, or invests them in his own business. The ward may either take the investment as he finds it, with all the profits, or demand the original fund, with interest; though he cannot avoid a transaction in

1 Barnaby *v.* Barnaby, 1 Pick. 221. See *supra*, ch. 6, 8.

2 2 Kent Com. 230; Eckford *v.* De Kay, 8 Paige, 89; Westbrook *v.* Comstock, Walker Ch. 314. See *supra*, ch. 7.

3 Loyd *v.* Malone, 23 Ill. 43; Hopk. 337.

4 Yerger *v.* Jones, 16 How. 30.

5 Floyd *v.* Johnson, 2 Litt. 109.

6 Singleton *v.* Love, 1 Head, 357. See further Infants, *post.*

part and ratify in part.[1] For it is right that the ward should enjoy all the advantages which have accrued from the use of his own money; and it is also right that the guardian should not derive gain at the ward's loss. The old rule of chancery in this respect has been gradually relaxed; so that acts of a trustee, which might once have been considered fraudulent and void, are now voidable only.[2]

Thus it is that the rule may now be considered well settled, that the guardian who buys at the sale of his ward's lands or other property is secure in his purchase, and retains all the benefits arising therefrom, unless the ward chooses to set it aside and claims to be reinstated in his own possession. This rule is laid down, however, with great caution in the courts; and it is frequently said that the transaction is treated all the same, whether the guardian bought the property outright or there was a colorable purchase by means of third parties; moreover, that such sales, in order to stand at all, must have been conducted fairly and in good faith.[3] Where the circumstances show fraud and collusion, courts of equity hesitate little in setting the transaction aside.[4] And a material question for consideration in such sales is whether a fair price was paid. Parties affected with notice of the circumstances cannot complain if their title to real estate becomes thereby impaired; but it is hard that purchasers without notice should suffer. On this latter principle, and for the security of title, rests a recent decision in Massachusetts, to the effect that the guardian's purchase of his ward's real estate is voidable by the ward only as against the guardian, or a purchaser claiming under him with knowledge of the circumstances; and not as against a subse-

[1] 2 Kent Com. 230; Docker *v.* Somes, 2 M. & K. 664; Kyle *v.* Barnett, 17 Ala. 306; Singleton *v.* Love, 1 Head, 357; White *v.* Parker, 8 Barb. 48.

[2] See Hill on Trustees, 159, 536.

[3] 2 Kent Com. 230; Scott *v.* Freeland, 7 S. & M. 409; Elrod *v.* Lancaster, 2 Head, 571; Patton *v.* Thompson, 2 Jones Eq. 285; Chorpenning's Appeal, 32 Penn. St. 315. And see *supra*, ch. 6, 7.

[4] Hayward *v.* Ellis, 13 Pick. 272.

quent grantee or mortgagee without notice.[1] Here that constructive notice which the public records furnish is probably to be deemed unavailing.[2]

This brings us to the general subject of transactions between the guardian and ward, from which the former derives a benefit. Here, as in the guardian's purchases, equity is not disposed to favor him. "In this class of cases," says Judge Story, "there is often to be found some intermixture of deceit, imposition, overreaching, unconscionable advantage, or other mark of direct and positive fraud."[3] Equity will relieve against such transactions, on the general principle of utility, although there may not have been actual imposition; but if an improper advantage has been taken, the ground for relief is still stronger. And it is noticeable that a more stringent rule has been laid down as to guardians than applies to transactions between parent and child; for a guardian is not supposed to be influenced by that affection for his ward which parents entertain towards their own offspring, and therefore has no such powerful check upon his selfish feelings.[4]

Such questions generally arise at and about the time the ward attains majority, and pending the final settlement of the guardian's accounts. The English rule is very strict, and courts are extremely watchful to prevent all undue advantage at this critical period. Therefore, gifts and conveyances of the ward's property, in consideration of the guardian's services, on a final adjustment may be set aside afterward in equity, even after the ward's death. "Where the connection is not dissolved, the accounts not settled, every thing remaining pressing upon the mind of the party under the care of the guardian," observes Lord Eldon, "it is almost impossible that the trans-

1 Wyman *v.* Hooper, 2 Gray, 141.

2 As to the English doctrine, see Morse *v.* Royal, 12 Ves. 372; Cary *v.* Cary, 2 Sch. & Lef. 173; Naylor *v.* Winch, 1 S. & St. 567.

3 Story Eq. Jur. § 307.

4 Pierce *v.* Waring, cited 1 Ves. 380, 2 Ves. 548; Hylton *v.* Hylton, 2 Ves. 547; Hatch *v.* Hatch, 9 Ves. 296. See Hill on Trustees, 157–160.

action should stand."[1] Nor are the circumstances under which the gift was made considered of much account; for the guardian's superior age and knowledge of the world, and the fact that he holds the property in his hands, place him at a decided advantage, whether he chooses to adopt a threatening tone or to impose upon the ward's mind by excessive kindness. These general principles apply, though not always in the same degree, to all others sustaining fiduciary relations; including receivers and agents who manage the property of a *cestui que trust*. And unfair advantages of every sort, which the guardian aims to secure on a final adjustment of his accounts,—whether it be in the shape of compensation or the waiver of indebtedness incurred by his misconduct,—follow one invariable rule: that equity will relieve the ward against the consequences of his one-sided bargain.[2]

In this country the rule is somewhat different; for certain circumstances, such as the recognition that compensation is justly due a trustee for his services, contribute to relax the rule in the guardian's favor. Settlements and bargains between the guardian and ward out of court are, however, frequently set aside for corrupt influence. So are gifts and conveyances, in consideration of the guardian's services; more especially when undue influence is shown from special circumstances.[3] In Pennsylvania, it is said that settlements will not stand unless full deliberation and good faith are manifest; but that a settlement made in good faith, especially if wise and prudent, cannot be impeached, after the ward's death, by his representa-

1 Hatch *v.* Hatch, 9 Ves. 296.

2 Hylton *v.* Hylton, 2 Ves. 547; Wood *v.* Downes, 18 Ves. 120; Mulhallen *v.* Marum, 3 Dr. & W. 317; Aylward *v.* Kearney, 2 Ba. & B. 463; Hunter *v.* Atkins, 3 M. & K. 135; Macphers. Inf. 260–264; Revett *v.* Harvey, 1 Sim. & Stu. 502; Duke of Hamilton *v.* Lord Mohun, 1 P. Wms. 118. But see Cray *v.* Mansfield, 1 Ves. Sen. 379, where gift to an agent was supported.

3 Hall *v.* Cone, 5 Day, 543; Waller *v.* Armistead, 2 Leigh, 11; Sullivan *v.* Blackwell, 28 Miss. 737; Clowes *v.* Van Antwerp, 4 Barb. 416; Briers *v.* Hackney, 6 Geo. 419; Fridge *v.* State, 3 Gill & Johns. 103; Richardson *v.* Linney, 7 B. Monr. 571.

tives.[1] This is doubtless the rule elsewhere. And the mere fact that a settlement has been made between guardian and ward, with allowances in the guardian's favor, is not conclusive of fraud, though every intendment is still to be construed on the ward's behalf.[2]

The fact that settlements out of court are not generally regarded in this country as conclusive, inasmuch as the probate guardian must still file his accounts and submit his transactions to the court, is a great safeguard against fraud. So, too, a fixed rule is established for the final adjustment of all matters in controversy between guardian and ward. The chancery practice is to allow the ward a reasonable time, after attaining majority, usually one year, to reopen all accounts between himself and his guardian.[3] Hence a receipt in full, or a formal release, has been set aside as inconclusive. And where the ward makes a partial inspection only, without examining the vouchers, so much the greater is his equity to relief.[4] But in probate guardianship, settlements out of court give way to settlements in court. And if the ward makes no objection to the guardian's final account as presented, and it is thereupon approved and recorded, no necessity for application of the chancery rule, of reopening the account, seems to exist, except upon very strong proof of fraud or error.[5]

[1] Hawkins's Appeal, 32 Penn. St. 263.

[2] Kirby *v.* Taylor, 6 Johns. Ch. 242; McClellan *v.* Kennedy, 8 Md. 230; Spalding *v.* Brent, 3 Md. Ch. 411; Meek *v.* Perry, 36 Miss. 190; Myer *v.* Rives, 11 Ala. 760.

[3] Matter of Van Horne, 7 Paige, 46.

[4] Revett *v.* Harvey, 1 Sim. & Stu. 502; Wych *v.* Packington, 3 Br. P. C. 46; Rapalje *v.* Norsworthy, 1 Sandf. Ch. 399; Johnson *v.* Johnson, 2 Hill Ch. 277.

[5] Kittredge *v.* Betton, 14 N. H. 401; Musser *v.* Oliver, 21 Penn. St. 362; Pierce *v.* Irish, 31 Maine, 254; Boynton *v.* Dyer, 18 Pick. 1; Hickman's Appeal, 7 Barr, 464; Southall *v.* Clark, 3 Stew. & Port. 338; Bybee *v.* Tharp, 4 B. Monr. 313. Among the decisions which apply to transactions between the guardian the following may be noticed. If a guardian makes a gratuity to the ward, he cannot afterwards charge the amount to him. Pratt *v.* McJunkin, 4 Rich. 5. Where he advances money on his ward's account, he may have an assignment of the security. Kelchner *v.* Forney, 29 Penn. St. 47. He is not necessarily bound to pay over cash on settlement; but securities taken in the performance

Transactions after the period of guardianship, between parties lately holding the relation of guardian and ward, especially if the ward still remains under the influence of a former guardian, may be set aside upon the same principle of constructive fraud. It is true that bargains between them are good whenever the influence is fully removed; even to gifts and conveyances in consideration of past services, the accounts having been finally closed, the property duly transferred, and the late parties to the fiduciary relation standing toward one another as man and man. Under these circumstances, the late guardian may purchase property of his late ward.[1] But such transactions are always to be regarded with suspicion. And where the influence still continues, as if the ward be a female, or a person of weak understanding, and the guardian continues to control the property or to furnish a home, the court is strongly disposed to set aside the bargain altogether.[2] Thus where a guardian procures the late ward's indorsement of his own notes without consideration, the parties who take such notes with knowledge of the fiduciary relationship, have been enjoined

of his official duty, are transferable at a just valuation, the same as any specific chattels, and the ward must take them in this form. Goodson *v.* Goodson, 6 Ired. Eq. 238. But the guardian's note or bond for the balance of money adjudged due on a final settlement is no payment to the ward, nor does it discharge the guardian's sureties. It is a mere postponement of final payment, and affords evidence of an admitted liability on his part. Wardlaw *v.* Gray, 2 Hill Ch. 644; Hamlin *v.* Atkinson, 6 Rand. 574. The guardian cannot buy up an equitable encumbrance, and enforce it against the ward who is ready to refund. Taylor *v.* Taylor, 6 B. Monr. 559. The ward may release to one of joint guardians and not to the others, and thus hold the sureties. Kirby *v.* Taylor, 6 Johns. Ch. 242; though this may be effected by general rules as to probate bonds. A receipt in full discharges only for the amount actually received by the wards, and binds only such wards as were authorized to give it; and its validity and effect, though under seal, may be considered in court. Witman's Appeal, 28 Penn. St. 376; Barnes *v.* Compton, 8 Gill, 391; Felton *v.* Long, 8 Ired. Eq. 224; Magruder *v.* Goodwyn, 2 P. & H. 561; Stark *v.* Gamble, 43 N. H. 465; Wade *v.* Lobdell, 4 Cush. 510.

[1] Oldin *v.* Samborne, 2 Atk. 15.

[2] See Macphers. Inf. 260; Huguenin *v.* Baseley, 14 Ves. 273; Dent *v.* Bennett, 4 M. & C. 269; Mellish *v.* Mellish, 1 Sim. & Stu. 138; Dawson *v.* Massey, 1 Ba. & B. 219.

from enforcing them against the indorser.[1] And if the guardian purchase rights of the late ward in his father's property for a grossly inadequate consideration, it will be set aside.[2] The circumstance that the guardian had better opportunities of acquaintance with the actual condition and value of the property than the ward himself is properly to be considered on the latter's behalf. Purchases of the guardian's property by the late ward are to be closely scrutinized in like manner.[3]

This principle applies to *quasi* guardians, even to parents. Not many years since a young lady, who had been living for thirteen years with her mother and step-father, joined the latter within twelve months after she became of age, at his request and under his influence, in a promissory note for which she received no consideration. The payee some years later obtained judgment at common law, and was about to take out execution, when the court of chancery interfered on motion, restrained the payee from enforcing his execution, and ordered the money paid into court.[4]

The ward may be barred by the lapse of time or by his own acts from disaffirming his own transactions or his guardian's unauthorized acts. But such lapse of time is to be computed from the time he becomes competent to act. And, to be barred by his own acts, it should appear that he acted after termination of his disability, with deliberation and on full knowledge of the essential facts.[5]

It is a rule of the English Court of Chancery that no one can marry a ward of the court without its express sanction. And

1 Gale *v.* Wells, 12 Barb. 84.

2 Wright *v.* Arnold, 14 B. Monr. 638; Williams *v.* Powell, 1 Ired. Eq. 460.

3 Sherry *v.* Sansberry, 3 Ind. 320.

4 Espey *v.* Luke, 15 E. L. & Eq. 579. And see Maitland *v.* Backhouse, 16 Sim. 58.

5 Fish *v.* Miller, 1 Hoff. Ch. 267; Binion *v* Miller, 27 Geo. 78; Scott *v.* Freeland, 7 S. & M. 409; Hume *v.* Hume, 3 Barr, 144; Worrell's Appeal, 23 Penn. St. 44; Sherry *v.* Sansbery, 3 Ind. 320; Penn *v.* Heisey, 19 Ill. 295; Singleton *v.* Love, 1 Head, 357; Macphers. Inf. 538–543; Lee *v.* Brown, 4 Ves. 361; Cory *v.* Gertcken, 2 Mad. 40; Allfrey *v.* Allfrey, 11 Jur. 981.

wherever a guardian is appointed he must give a recognizance that the infant shall not marry without its leave.[1] If a man should marry a female ward without the approbation of the court, he, and all others concerned, will be treated as guilty of a contempt of court, and punished accordingly. So where there is reason to suspect an improper marriage of its wards, the court will interfere, by injunction, to prevent the marriage, to forbid all intercourse between the lovers, and even to take the ward from the custody of the guardian or any other person who is supposed guilty of connivance with the match. When an offer of marriage is made, the court refers it to a master to ascertain and report whether the match is suitable, and also what settlement should be made upon the ward. Where a marriage has been celebrated without leave, the court will interfere to protect the female ward against the consequences of her indiscretion, and will compel the husband to make a suitable settlement upon her.[2] This whole subject is peculiar to the laws of England, and has no application whatever to courts of chancery in this country; unless it be that orders might issue in some cases of improvident marriage to compel the settlement of a suitable portion upon the female ward. Yet authority is wanting for the exercise of chancery jurisdiction even to this extent: so repugnant does it appear to the whole tenor of our legislation. But where property of a ward is under the control of a court of equity, and the husband needs its assistance, a suitable provision might be compelled; for this would be in accordance with the general rule as between husband and wife.[2]

[1] Story Eq. Juris. §§ 1358–1361; Macphers. Inf. 191–209; Eyre *v.* Countess of Shaftesbury, 2 P. Wms. 111; Smith *v.* Smith, 3 Atk. 305; Stackpole *v.* Beaumont, 3 Ves. 98; Stevens *v.* Savage, 1 Ves. Jr. 154.

[2] Kenny *v.* Udall, 5 Johns. Ch. 464, 473; s. c. 3 Cow. 591; Van Epps *v.* Van Deusen, 4 Paige, 64; Van Duzer *v.* Van Duzer, 6 Paige, 366. See also Redfield's note to Story Eq. Juris. § 1361; Chambers *v.* Perry, 17 Ala. 726.

PART V.

INFANCY.

CHAPTER I.

THE GENERAL DISABILITIES OF INFANTS.

ALL persons are infants, in legal contemplation, until they have arrived at majority. The period of majority differs in different States and countries; but this general principle remains the same.

By the civil law, full majority was not attained until the person had completed his twenty-fourth year; he was then said to be *perfectæ ætatis — ætatis legitimæ.*[1] This period was likewise adopted in France (though it was afterwards changed), and it prevails still in Spain, Holland, and some parts of Germany.[2] By the French civil code, the age of full capacity is twenty-one years, except that twenty-five years is the majority for contracting marriage without paternal consent, by the male, and twenty-one by the female.[3] The law of Scotland adopts the age of twenty-one.[4] Among the Greeks and early Romans, women were never of age, but subject to perpetual guardianship, except as wives; this gradually changed, and the civil law, as it stood in the time of Justinian, permitted females as well as males to attain their majority at twenty-five.[5]

1 1 Burge Col. & For. Laws, 113.
2 Ib. 114.
3 Code Civil, § 145, 488; 2 Kent Com. 233.
4 Ersk. Inst. B. 1, tit. vii.; 1 Bl. Com. 464.
5 Inst. 1, 23, 1; 1 Bl. Com. 464.

The common law of England, from the remotest times, fixed twenty-one as the period of absolute majority for both sexes; or, to be more exact, an infant attains full age on the beginning of the day next preceding the twenty-first anniversary of his birth.[1] The same rule is applied in most parts of the United States, though, in some of the States, females have an enlarged capacity to act at eighteen.[2] Under the statutes of Vermont, Ohio, and Illinois, and some other Western States, females are deemed of age at eighteen.[3] The code of Louisiana follows common-law, not civil-law, principles, and adopts twenty-one as the limitation for both sexes.[4] Thus arbitrary is the law which fixes the period of majority, nature assigning no precise and uniform period at which the disability of infancy shall cease, though clearly indicating that there must be some such period.

A man born the first day of February, 1600, after eleven o'clock at night, was adjudged in England to be of full age after one o'clock on the morning of the last day of January, 1621.[5] This is because the common law makes no allowance for fractions of a day. But the civil law, in order to secure to the person the full protection afforded on account of his minority, did not hold the commencement of the day to be its completion, if injurious to his interests.[6] In some instances, the civil law permitted the State or Sovereign to grant *venia ætatis* to full-grown persons who stood in need of it, and thus to place them constructively on the footing of infants; but nothing of the sort is recognized at common law.[7]

[1] 2 Kent Com. 233; 1 Bl. Com. 463; 1 Salk. 44; Ld. Raym. 480, 1096; 3 Wils. 274; Hamlin *v.* Stevenson, 4 Dana, 597; State *v.* Clarke, 3 Harring. 557; Wells *v.* Wells, 6 Ind. 447.

[2] 2 Kent Com. 233. See Crapster *v.* Griffith, 2 Bland Ch. 5.

[3] Sparhawk *v.* Buel, 9 Vt. 41; Stephenson *v.* Westfall, 18 Ill. 209.

[4] Louisiana Code, arts. 41, 93. This was the long-settled rule likewise in Texas. Means *v.* Robinson, 7 Tex. 502.

[5] Fitzhue *v.* Dennington, 6 Mod. 259; 1 Salk. 44, and citations in last section. And see 1 Jarm. Wills, Eng. ed. 1861, 39; Met. Contr. 38. Judge Redfield dissents from this rule. See 1 Redf. Wills, 18–20.

[6] J. Voet, lib. 4, tit. 4, n. 1.

[7] See 1 Burge Col. & For. Laws, 116, 117.

The principle of an enlarged capacity in infants has been incidentally noticed. It is reasonable to suppose that they who are constantly growing, become naturally competent for certain purposes long before they attain complete majority, and that young men and women may well be allowed the exercise of more discretion than babes. Hence, we find that infants of suitable age are allowed to contract a valid marriage; that males of the age of fourteen and upwards, and females at the age of twelve, could once dispose of personal estate by will, and at fourteen may still choose or nominate their own guardians; that children of discretion have a voice in determining the right of custody and control. But not until attaining majority could a person at the common law convey, lease, or make contracts in general which would bind him; and the foregoing must then be considered as among the exceptions to the rule that persons are legally incapable so long as they are minors.[1]

Legislative emancipation has existed in Louisiana. In the case of an emancipated minor under such statutes, by which he is relieved from the time prescribed by law for attaining the age of majority, he is invested with all the capacities in relation to his property and obligations, which he would have, had he actually arrived at the age of twenty-one years. And he may be appointed administrator of an estate.[2] But the right of legislative emancipation seems never to have been distinctly admitted at the common law in any such sense.

Supposing a conflict of laws should arise over the contract of an infant by reason of the period of majority being differently assigned by the law of the domicile of his origin and that of his actual domicile, or of the situation of real property, or of the place where he has entered into a contract. The rules for such cases are these: *First*, that the actual domicile will be preferred to the domicile of birth. *Secondly*, that the law of situation of real

[1] Co. Litt. 78 *b*, 89 *b*, and Harg. note. As to the privilege of wills, see stat. 1 Vict. ch. 26, § 7 *infra* p. 24.

[2] Succession of Lyne, 12 La. An. 155.

property must prevail over that of domicile. *Thirdly*, that the law of the place where a contract is made must prevail over that of domicile.[1]

Next as to the infant's right of holding office. There are numerous old cases to be found in the books where an infant has been adjudged capable of holding offices that involve no pecuniary or public trust, and require only moderate skill and diligence: such as the office of park-keeper, forester, sheriff, and jailer; though on the ground apparently that such offices formerly were capable of grant, and the grantees had the power to act by deputy.[2] But the modern doctrine seems to be clear that no office of pecuniary and public responsibility can be conferred upon an infant; not so much because of mental incapacity on his part, as for the very good reason that a person who is not legally responsible for the duties of his office cannot be, in point of law, a proper person to execute them. A public office, which requires the personal receipt and disbursement of money, is not then to be filled by an infant.[3] Nor can an infant act as administrator, executor, or trustee; or by his concurrence (in the absence of fraud on his part) sanction a breach of trust.[4] He cannot be a guardian, an attorney under a power (except to receive seisin), a bailiff, a factor, or a receiver.[5]

The service of a notice of replevy by an infant is, in England, illegal and void; and it would appear that he cannot be sheriff's officer.[6] But in New Hampshire, it is held that an infant may be deputed to serve and return a particular writ; on the ground

[1] Male *v.* Roberts, 3 Esp. 163; 1 Burge Col. & For. Laws, 118 *et seq.*; Story Confl. Laws, §§ 75, 82, 332; Thompson *v.* Ketcham, 8 Johns. 189; Hierstand *v.* Kuns, 8 Blackf. 345; Saul *v.* His Creditors, 17 Martin, 597; 2 Kent Com. 233 *n.*; Huey's Appeal, 1 Grant (Penn.), 51.

[2] Bac. Abr. Infancy and Age, E; 3 Mod. 222; Young *v.* Fowler, Cro. Car. 555; Macphers. Inf. 448.

[3] Claridge *v.* Evelyn, 5 B. & Ald. 81. See Crosbie *v.* Hurley, 1 Alcock & Napier, 431.

[4] Macphers. Inf. 449; Wilkinson *v.* Parry, 4 Russ. 272. But though wrongly appointed, he will be liable to account for money received by him after reaching majority. Carow *v.* Mowatt, 2 Edw. Ch. 57.

[5] Macphers. Inf. 448, 449; Co. Litt. 3 *b*, 172.

[6] Cuckson *v.* Winter, 2 M. & Ry. 306.

that while offices where judgment, discretion, and experience are essentially necessary to the proper discharge of the duties they impose, are not to be entrusted to infants, offices may be held which are merely ministerial, and require nothing more than skill and diligence.[1] But a distinction is properly taken between the case of officers of justice ordinarily liable for false return, misfeasance, and the like, and those who have no such liability; and for this reason, while in Vermont, an infant may serve a particular writ, he cannot be specially authorized to serve mesne process by the magistrate.[2]

In ancient times, minors appear to have frequently sat in the British Parliament. Thus it is related that a son of the Duke of Albemarle took part in debate when only of the age of fourteen; and history states that about the 10th James I. there were forty members not above twenty years of age, and some not above sixteen.[3] But by statute it is now provided that an infant cannot sit in the House of Lords, or vote at an election for a member of the lower house, or be elected.[4]

There are provisions in the Constitution of the United States and of the different States, adopted undoubtedly because it was considered contrary to sound public policy to commit any offices requiring considerable skill and prudence, not to say pecuniary and public responsibility, to the young and immature. By the Constitution of the United States, no person can be President who has not attained the age of thirty-five years; nor a senator, who is under the age of thirty years; nor a representative in congress who is not twenty-five years of age. Corresponding laws abound in the different States as to the eligibility of local officers. So is the disqualification to vote universally applied by our laws to minors, and restrictions upon the right of suffrage may extend even further.[5]

1 Moore *v.* Graves, 3 N. H. 408. But see Tyler *v.* Tyler, 2 Root, 519.

2 Barrett *v.* Seward, 22 Vt. 176; Harvey *v.* Hall, ib. 211.

3 See Macphers. Inf. 449 *n.*; 1 Parl. Deb. 420, notes.

4 7 & 8 Wm. 3, ch. 25.

5 The officer who usually administers the oath of office cannot refuse to do so on such grounds. People *v.* Dean, 3 Wend. 438.

The true principle to be extracted from the authorities seems therefore to be that the court will inquire whether an infant, as such, is by law capable of discharging suitably, faithfully, and efficiently the duties of a particular office, and so as to leave open all the usual remedies to others; and this is a proper rule of guidance, the statutes being silent, rather than ancient precedents laid down as to particular offices in times when they were transmissible in families and mere sinecures.[1]

There are, undoubtedly, certain offices which an infant may properly hold. And the legislature is competent to establish an earlier or later period at which persons shall be deemed of full age for certain purposes. Hence in Massachusetts, under a law fixing eighteen years as the age for military duty, and empowering an infant at that age to enlist of his own accord, and without the parent's assent, in the militia, it is held that he may be elected company clerk, or even, as it would appear, a commissioned officer of the company.[2]

Infants who have arrived at sufficient maturity in years and understanding are capable of committing crimes; and it is said that they cannot plead in justification the restraint of a parent, as married women can that of the husband. The period of life at which a capacity of crime exists is determined by law to a certain extent; for a child under seven is conclusively incapable of crime, one between seven and fourteen only *prima facie* so, and one over fourteen *prima facie* capable like any other.[3]

An exception to this rule is usually stated in certain cases of physical impotence; for it is argued that a boy under fourteen years of age is physically undeveloped, and therefore

[1] As to some of the old decisions as to what offices an infant might or might not hold, see Bac. Abr. Infancy and Age, E; also Moore *v.* Graves, 3 N. H. 408, *passim.*

[2] Dewey, Petitioner, 11 Pick. 265. See Hands *v.* Slaney, 8 T. R. 578.

[3] 1 Bish. Crim. Law, § 460; 1 Russ. Crimes, Grea. ed. 2. The text-writers have said that an infant can never plead constraint of the parent, but this may be doubted. See Humphrey *v.* Douglass, 10 Vt. 71.

cannot be legally guilty of rape or similar crimes.[1] Incapacity for a crime might properly be considered in connection with incapacity of criminal intent; and yet the later rule of Ohio and some other States seems the more correct one, which is to reject the doctrine of conclusive presumption of incapacity, and allow evidence to be furnished.[2] But investigations on this point might be held *contra bonos mores.*

Where a statute creates an offence infants under the age of legal capacity are not presumed to have been included; yet where an act is denounced as a crime, even felony or treason, it extends as well to infants if above fourteen years, as to others.[3]

An infant may be indicted for obtaining goods by false pretences.[4] He is liable to bastardy process.[5] And following the general principle already announced, children less than fourteen have been convicted for arson and murder, the *prima facie* presumption of incapacity being overcome.[6] But in this country a child less than seven cannot be indicted for nuisance though owner of the land.[7] And it is reasonable to add that the evidence of malice which is to supply age ought to be strong and clear, beyond all doubt and contradiction.[8]

An infant, it is held in Tennessee, may make a criminal complaint, and be what is known as the prosecutor.[9]

The age at which persons may dispose of their property, real or personal, by last will and testament, is now determined by statute in England, and in most parts of the United States. In England, the modern statute 1 Vict. ch. 26, § 7, provides that

[1] 1 Bish. Crim. Law, §§ 466, 672, and cases cited; State *v.* Handy, 4 Harring. 566; Reg. *v.* Phillips, 8 Car. & P. 736.

[2] Williams *v.* The State, 14 Ohio, 222; People *v.* Randolph, 2 Parker, 174; Commonwealth *v.* Green, 2 Pick. 380.

[3] 1 Hawk. 1; 4 Bl. Com. 23; 1 Bish. Crim. Law, § 462.

[4] People *v.* Kendall, 25 Wend. 399.

[5] Chandler *v.* Commonwealth, 4 Met. (Ky.) 66.

[6] See 4 Bl. Com. 23, 24; 1 Bish. Crim. Law, § 464, and cases cited.

[7] People *v.* Townsend, 3 Hill, 479.

[8] See 4 Bl. Com. 24.

[9] State *v.* Dillon, 1 Head, 389.

no will made by any person under the age of twenty-one years shall be valid. This went into effect in 1838.[1] And the provisions of this statute have been substantially enacted either before or since in most of the American States; so that the policy of the present day may be said to exclude the testamentary capacity of all infants.[2] Nor is this unjust; for the law itself draws up as good a will for children as they are likely to make.

But the ancient rule was otherwise: namely, to the effect that males at fourteen and females at twelve might make wills of their personal property, thus conforming to the older rule of the civil and canon law.[3] And such, as we have seen, was the age when a testamentary guardian could be appointed. But though no objection was admissible to the probate of wills in the ecclesiastical courts, merely for want of age, yet if it could be shown that the testator was not of sufficient discretion, whether of the age of fourteen, or four and twenty, that would overthrow the testament.[4] This always operated to discourage such wills from being made. Yet the objection was not insuperable; for there is a clear instance on record where an infant sixteen years of age made a testament in favor of his guardian and schoolmaster, which was established by evidence of the child's capacity and free will.[5]

The English text-writers, with reference to the old law, have laid it down that express approval of a former will after the infant had accomplished the years of fourteen or twelve, would make it strong and effectual.[6] But as concerns the later statutes, if not as a general principle for modern times, it appears

[1] See also 20 & 21 Vict. ch. 77.

[2] 1 Redf. Wills, 15–18; 4 Kent Com. 506, 507.

[3] 1 Wms. Ex's, 15; 1 Redf. Wills, 15–17. But there are some irreconcilable opinions on the subject to be found in the old books. See Co. Litt. 89 *b*, Hargrave's note.

[4] 2 Bl. Com. 497; 1 Wms. Ex'rs, 15.

[5] Arnold *v.* Earle, 2 Cas. tem. Lee, 529.

[6] 1 Wms. Ex'rs, 16; Swinb. pt. 2, § 2, pl. 7; Bac. Abr. Wills, B.

pretty clear that where a will is required to be in writing, and executed before witnesses, in order to be valid, and is thus executed before the testator arrives at the required age, it cannot be rendered valid after the testator arrives at such age, except by republication with all the usual formalities.[1] And even the old books admit that the mere circumstance of an infant having lived some time after the age when he became capable of making a will cannot alone give validity to one made during his incapacity.[2]

The maxims of the older law on this subject adhere somewhat to American jurisprudence; for we find that in many States a distinction is still made between personal and real estate.[3]

Infants may be admitted to testify in the courts, if of sufficient understanding. There is no precise age at which the law excludes them on the conclusion that they are mentally and morally incompetent. By the common-law rule, every person over the age of fourteen is presumed to have common discretion and understanding until the contrary appears; but under that age it is not so presumed; and the court will, therefore, make inquiry as to the degree of understanding which the child offered as a witness may possess. But this preliminary examination, which is made by the judge at discretion, is to be

[1] 1 Redf. Wills, 19.

[2] Herbert *v.* Torball, 1 Sid. 162; Swinb. pt. 2, § 2, pl. 5; 1 Wms. Ex'rs, 16.

[3] Thus in Rhode Island, Virginia, Arkansas, and Missouri, the age for making wills of real estate is fixed at twenty-one, and for disposing of personalty in the same manner at eighteen; and in Connecticut at twenty-one for real estate, and seventeen for personalty. Among the States where the right to dispose of estate, both real and personal, is now limited to persons of full age, are Massachusetts, Vermont, New Hampshire, Maine, Ohio, Indiana, New Jersey, Kentucky, Virginia, Pennsylvania, Delaware, and Michigan. In some States, a distinction is made between males and females as to testamentary capacity, and the latter may make wills, as in Vermont and Maryland, at eighteen. In New York and Illinois, the principle is to discriminate between real and personal estate, and between males and females; and while as young as sixteen a female in the former State may make a valid will of personalty. See 1 Redf. Wills, 18 *n.*; 4 Kent Com. 506, 507; Williams *v.* Heirs, Busbee, 271; Davis *v.* Baugh, 1 Sneed, 477; Moore *v.* Moore, 23 Tex. 637; Posey *v.* Posey, 3 Strobh. 167; Corrie's Case, 2 Bland Ch. 488.

directed to the point whether the witness comprehends the solemn obligation of an oath; and if the child appears to have sufficient natural intelligence to distinguish between good and evil, and to comprehend the nature and effect of an oath, he is an admissible witness.[1] In Indiana, a statute provides that all children over the age of ten shall be presumed to be competent. And a child under ten years of age was deemed competent to testify, whose answers when she was examined by the court disclosed that, though she was ignorant of the nature of the punishment for false swearing, yet, she comprehended the obligations of an oath, and believed that any deviation from the truth, while under oath, would be followed by appropriate punishment.[2] Of the capacity of such witnesses for comprehending the matter as to which they testify, of the strength of the memory, and in general as to the weight which may be attached to their testimony in any particular state of facts, a jury should make their estimate carefully.

Children have been admitted to testify at the early age of seven, and even of five; but the dying declarations of a child only four years old were once ruled out,[3] for the reason that, however precocious the child's mind, she could not have had that idea of a future state which is necessary to make such declarations admissible.[4] Different systems of religious education render the judicial test in this respect far from precise; for while there are cases where the court has put off a trial, in order to specially instruct an infant witness as to the nature and solemnity of an oath, this practice is not of late years strongly countenanced; the opinion gaining ground that the effect of the oath upon the conscience should arise from reli-

[1] 1 Greenl. Evid. § 367; 2 Russ. Crimes, 590; Rex *v.* Brazier, 1 East P. C. 443; State *v.* Whittier, 21 Me. 341.

[2] Blackwell *v.* State, 11 Ind. 196.

[3] Rex *v.* Pike, 3 Car. & P. 598; Rex *v.* Brashier, 1 East P. C. 443.

[4] Rex *v.* Pike, 3 Car. & P. 598. And see Rex *v.* Brashier, 1 East P. C. 443; 1 Greenl. Evid. § 367; Commonwealth *v.* Hutchinson, 10 Mass. 225.

gious feelings of a permanent nature and gradual growth.[1] But in cases where the intellect is sufficiently matured, but the education only has been neglected, it appears that a postponement of the trial might properly be asked.[2]

On the principle that chancery is bound to see that an infant litigant's rights and interests are protected, not only is an unwilling infant not compellable to testify in his suit, but his deposition, though given freely on his part, may be suppressed, at the discretion of the court, as containing admissions unfavorable to his cause.[3]

With respect to the marriage settlements of infants, there was formerly considerable controversy. For, on the one hand, it was urged that infants were in general incapable of entering into valid contracts with respect to their property; on the other, that since infants might make a valid contract of marriage, they ought to be able to arrange the preliminaries. At an early period the opinion prevailed in England, that the mar-

[1] Rex *v.* White, 2 Leach C. C. 48*n.*; 1 Greenl. Evid. § 367; Rex *v.* Williams, 7 Car. & P. 320; Regina *v.* Nicholas, 2 Car. & K. 246.

[2] Per Pollock C. B., Regina *v.* Nicholas, ib. With regard to the weight and effect of the testimony of children, Blackstone observes, that when the evidence of children is admitted, "it is much to be wished, in order to render the evidence credible, that there should be some concurrent testimony of time, place, and circumstances, in order to make out the fact; and that a conviction should not be grounded on the unsupported accusation of an infant under years of discretion." 4 Bl. Com. 214. To this Mr. Phillips replies that in many cases, undoubtedly, the statements of children are to be received with great caution; yet that a prisoner may be convicted upon such testimony alone and unsupported; and that the extent of corroboration necessary is a question exclusively for a jury. It may be observed that the preliminary inquiry as to the competency is not always of the most satisfactory description, and is such that a child might upon slight practising of the memory appear well qualified. The severest test appears in the examination which follows; and as Mr. Phillips well concludes, "Independently of the sanction of an oath, the testimony of children, after they have been subjected to cross-examination, is often entitled to as much credit as that of grown persons; what is wanted in the perfection of the intellectual faculties is sometimes more than compensated by the absence of motives to deceive." 1 Phil. Evid. 9th ed. 6, 7.

[3] Serle *v.* St. Eloy, 2 P. Wms. 386; Napier *v.* Effingham, 2 P. Wms. 403; Moore *v.* Moore, 4 Sandf. Ch. 37. But see Walker *v.* Thomas, 2 Dick. 781; Bennett *v.* Welder, 15 Ind. 332.

riage consideration communicated to the contracts of infants, respecting their estate, an efficacy similar to that which the law stamps upon marriage itself; and Lords Hardwicke and Macclesfield contributed to strengthen it, by maintaining that the real estate of an infant would be bound by a marriage settlement.[1] Lord Northington later held to a different opinion; and Lord Thurlow overturned the doctrine altogether, boldly declaring that the contracts of male and female infants do not bind their estates, and that consequently a female infant cannot be bound by any articles entered into during minority, as to her real estate; but may refuse to be bound, and abide by the interest the law casts upon her, which nothing but her own act after the period of majority can fetter or affect.[2] Other distinguished equity jurists, including Lord Eldon, subsequently expressed their approval of Lord Thurlow's decision.[3] And the rule became settled within the last forty years, that the real estate of a female infant was not bound by the settlement on her marriage, because her real estate does not become by the marriage the absolute property of the husband, although by the marriage he takes a limited interest in it.[4] So was it decided that neither the approbation of the parents or guardians, nor even of the court of chancery, independently of positive statute, would make the infant's settlements binding.[5]

The inconvenience of such a state of things called for statute remedy; and in 1855 an act was passed which enabled male

[1] Harvy *v.* Ashley, 3 Atk. 607; Cannel *v.* Buckle, 2 P. Wms. 243; Peachey Mar. Settl. 25 *et seq.*

[2] Drury *v.* Drury, 2 Eden, 58; Durnford *v.* Lane, 1 Bro. C. C. 115; Clough *v.* Clough, 5 Ves. 716.

[3] See Peachey Mar. Settl. 28; Milner *v.* Lord Harewood, 18 Ves. 275; Caruthers *v.* Caruthers, 4 Bro. C. C. 509.

[4] Simson *v.* Jones, 2 Russ. & M. 376; Campbell *v.* Ingilby, 21 Beav. 567; 25 L. J. Eq. 760. For summary of the English chancery doctrine, see Peachey Mar. Settl. 37.

[5] Peachey Mar. Settl. 53, 54; ib. 29–43 and cases cited *passim; In re* Waring, 21 L. J. Eq. 784; Simson *v.* Jones, 2 Russ. & M. 365; Borton *v.* Borton, 16 Sim. 552; Field *v.* Moore, 25 L. J. Eq. 69; 25 E. L. & Eq. 498.

infants not under twenty, and female infants not under seventeen, with the approbation of the Court of Chancery, to make valid settlements of all their property, real or personal, and whether in possession, reversion, remainder, or expectancy.[1] The statute has already received some interpretation in the courts; and so much in favor was it, that almost immediately upon its passage it was acted upon in chancery.

This subject has received little attention in the United States. But in New York some decisions have been made, of a like tenor with those in the English chancery. Thus, in 1831, that a legal jointure settled upon an infant would bar her dower; and, by analogy to the statute, a competent and certain provision settled upon the infant in bar of dower, to which there is no objection but its mere equitable quality.[2] And in 1843, that a female infant was not bound by agreement to settle her real estate upon marriage.[3] So, in Maryland, a female infant cannot bind her real estate by her marriage settlement.[4]

An objection to the validity of a marriage settlement, on the ground that the parties to it were infants, can only be made by the parties themselves. A trustee acting under it has no such power.[5] But since privies in blood can avoid an infant's voidable conveyance, it is held that if the infant dies after making a settlement of real estate and without having attained majority, her privies in blood may avoid the settlement.[6]

Marriage articles are not of themselves binding upon the infant or her privies; but they are binding upon the adult hus-

[1] 18 & 19 Vict. ch. 43. See Peachey Mar. Settl. 45. For construction of this statute see *In re* Dalton, 39 E. L. & Eq. 145; s. c. 6 De Gex, Mac. & G. 201. But see *Re* Catherine Strong, 2 Jur. N. S. 1241; 5 W. R. 107.

[2] M'Cartee *v.* Teller, 2 Paige, 511.

[3] Temple *v.* Hawley, 2 Sandf. Ch. 153.

[4] Levering *v.* Levering, 3 Md. Ch. 365. See Burr *v.* Wilson, 18 Tex. 367.

[5] Jones *v.* Butler, 30 Barb. 641.

[6] Levering *v.* Levering, 3 Md. Ch. 365. See Whitingham's Case, 8 Rep. 42; Macphers. Inf. 465; Brown *v.* Brown, Law Rep. 2 Eq. 481.

band.[1] Yet if the infant dies under age, her privies cannot take the benefits of the proposed settlement and of the inheritance likewise; they may have the more beneficial, and that is all.[2]

[1] Brown *v.* Brown, Law Rep. 2 Eq. 481; Whichcote *v.* Lyle's Exrs. 28 Penn. St. 73.

[2] Brown *v.* Brown, ib.

CHAPTER II.

ACTS VOID AND VOIDABLE.

ONE leading principle runs through all cases which relate to infants. It is that such persons are favorites of the law, which extends its protection over them so as to preserve their true interests against their own improvidence, if need be, or the designs of others. This principle is found constantly in chancery practice. We have traced it already in cases of custody, control, and guardianship, — particularly in such as come before the American courts. It appears again in matters of legal emancipation and the minor's right to his own wages. It generally determines the result of transactions between an infant and his parent or guardian, where fraud and undue influence are suspected. It is applied when a guardian presents his accounts for allowance. We are now to see this same principle at work in the general contracts of infants, controlling and regulating them in great measure, and serving better than any other to explain the shifting and contradictory decisions of the English and American courts on this vexed subject.

Infancy is a personal privilege, allowed for protection against imposition. The general rule of the present day is that an infant shall be bound by no act which is not beneficial to him. And most contracts of infants are divided into the two classes of void and voidable.[1]

There is much confusion in the older books on the subject of void and voidable contracts.[2] The keenness with which such

[1] Smith Contr. 225; Met. Contr. 38, 39; 2 Kent Com. 234.

[2] See Shep. Touch. 232; Bac. Abr. Infancy and Age, I, and cases cited in Zouch *v.* Parsons, 3 Burr. 1794.

a distinction must always cut is an objection to its practical use at the present day; yet writers have sought to adapt the weapon to the infant's wants. They have searched for some infallible test between void and voidable. Thus Mr. Bingham, after a review of the English cases, years ago, concluded that the only safe criterion was, that "acts which are capable of being legally ratified are voidable only; and acts which are incapable of being legally ratified are absolutely void." [1] But this was only to shift the uncertainty, and replace one difficulty by another. What acts can be legally ratified and what cannot? As Kent properly observes, such a criterion does not appear to free the question from its embarrassment or afford a clear and definite test.[2] Again, a Massachusetts judge of repute declared, many years ago, that the books agree in one result; that whenever the act done *may be* for the infant's benefit it shall not be considered void, but he shall have his election, when he comes of age, to affirm or avoid it; and this, he adds, is the only clear and definite proposition which can be extracted from the authorities.[3] Even this rule, though much better, is found difficult of application, and has been pronounced unsatisfactory in some of the later cases.[4] Besides, it is lacking in comprehensiveness and scope. A more precise and intelligible test than either was that applied in one of the earlier English cases by Ch. J. Eyre, and cited since with approval by Judge Story and Chancellor Kent:[5] namely, that where the court can pronounce that the contract is for the benefit of the infant, as for instance for necessaries, then it shall bind him; where it can pronounce it to be to his prejudice, it is void; and that where it is of an uncertain nature, as to benefit or prejudice, it is voidable only, and it is

[1] Bing. Inf. 234.

[2] 2 Kent Com. 234.

[3] Per Ch. J. Parker, Whitney *v.* Dutch, 14 Mass. 457. See 2 Kent Com. 234; Met. Contr. 39.

[4] Met. Contr. 40; 1 Am. Lead. Cas. 4th ed. 242.

[5] See United States *v.* Bainbridge, 1 Mason, 82; 2 Kent Com. 236; McGan *v.* Marshall, 7 Humph. 121.

in the election of the infant to affirm it or not.[1] The doctrine seems hardly capable of a closer analysis; though this is by no means clear and conclusive.

The equitable doctrine differs not from the legal as to the contracts of infants. In general, when a contract *may* be for the benefit or to the prejudice of an infant, he may avoid it, as well in equity as at law. Where it can never be for his benefit, it is utterly void. Infants are favored in all things which are for their benefit, and are saved from being prejudiced by any thing to their disadvantage. For infants are by law generally treated as having no capacity to bind themselves, from the want of sufficient reason and discernment of understanding. In regard to their acts, some are voidable and some are void; so in regard to their contracts, some are voidable and some are void.[2] The liberality and freedom exercised in common-law courts at the present day, in shaping general doctrines with reference to infants and their contracts, must be ascribed in a large degree to the influence of the equity tribunals and their decisions.

"In short," as Judge Story observes, "the disabilities of an infant are intended by law for his own protection, and not for the protection of the rights of third persons; and his acts may therefore, in many cases, be binding upon him, although the persons under whose guardianship, natural or positive, he then is, do not assent to them." [3]

The privilege, too, of avoiding his acts or contracts, where these are voidable, is a privilege personal to the infant, and which no one can exercise for him, except his heirs and legal representatives.[4] Hence, the other contracting party remains bound though the infant is not; for being an indulgence which the law allows infants, to secure them from the fraud and imposition of others, it can only be intended for their benefit, and

[1] Keane *v.* Boycott, 2 H. Bl. 511.
[2] 1 Story Eq. Jur. §§ 240, 241; 1 Fonbl. Eq. B. 1, ch. 2, § 4.
[3] United States *v.* Bainbridge, 1 Mason, 83.
[4] Ib.; Keane *v.* Boycott, 2 H. Bl. 511; Met. Contr. 38; Smith Contr. 231.

is not to be extended to persons of the years of discretion, who are presumed to act with sufficient caution and security.[1] And were it otherwise, this privilege, instead of being an advantage to the infant, would in many cases turn out greatly to his detriment.

Thus, where a person of full age promises to marry a minor and afterwards breaks off the match, he may be sued by the minor upon this contract; though he would have had no corresponding remedy against the minor for breach of promise.[2] So a third person, not a party to the contract, cannot take advantage of the infancy of the parties. Thus, in an action for seducing a servant from his master's service, the defendant cannot justify on the ground that the servant was an infant, and therefore not by law bound to perform his contract for service made with the master.[3] On the same principle (connected with others), the acceptor of a bill of exchange, or the maker of a promissory note, cannot resist payment in a suit by an indorsee, though the indorser be an infant.[4] Nor can the purchaser at a sale under an execution set up infancy to defeat prior transactions of the judgment debtor.[5] Nor can the vendor avoid the infant's purchase on such a ground.[6] Nor is a stranger permitted to impeach the conveyance of an infant.[7]

So, too, it seems to be the settled doctrine that infancy does not protect the indorsers or sureties of an infant; or those who have jointly entered into his voidable undertakings. They,

[1] Bac. Abr. Inf. I, 4; 1 Pars. Contr. 275; Johnson *v.* Rockwell, 12 Ind. 76; Hartness *v.* Thompson, 5 Johns. 160; Brown *v.* Caldwell, 10 S. &. R. 114.

[2] Holt *v.* Ward, 2 Str. 937; Harvey *v.* Ashley, 3 Atk. 610; Hunt *v.* Peake, 5 Cow. 475; Willard *v.* Stone, 7 ib. 22; Warwick *v.* Cooper, 5 Sneed, 659; Cannon *v.* Alsbury, 1 Marsh. 78.

[3] Keane *v.* Boycott, 2 H. Bl. 511.

[4] Met. Contr. 39; Taylor *v.* Croker, 4 Esp. 187; Nightingale *v.* Withington, 15 Mass. 273; Hardy *v.* Waters, 38 Me. 450; Frazier *v.* Massey, 14 Ind. 382.

[5] Alsworth *v.* Cordtz, 31 Miss. 32.

[6] Oliver *v.* Houdlet, 13 Mass. 237.

[7] Dominick *v.* Michael, 4 Sandf. 374.

if of full age, may be made liable though the infant himself escapes responsibility.[1]

But third persons should be allowed to protect themselves against undue liabilities on an infant's behalf. Thus, an officer selling property at public auction is not bound to accept the bid of an infant.[2]

And although infancy is a personal privilege, yet the administrator of the estate of an infant may avail himself of the infancy of his intestate, to avoid a transaction to which the latter was a party during his life, and which remained voidable at his death.[3] And as a rule the right of avoidance passes to privies in blood or estate.[4]

The strong tendency of the modern cases is to regard all contracts of infants as voidable only; and thus almost to obliterate the ancient distinction of void and voidable contracts altogether.[5] And the *dicta* are of frequent occurrence at the present day that deeds and contracts of an infant are not absolutely void, but voidable only, unless manifestly to the infant's prejudice; and that beneficial contracts are voidable only at most.[6]

Yet there are cases where a contract may still be pronounced absolutely void. In *Regina* v. *Lord*, an English case, the question arose on the conviction of a servant for unlawfully absenting himself from his master's employment. Denman C. J., in delivering the judgment of the court, observed: "Among many objections, one appears to us clearly fatal. He

[1] Motteux *v.* St. Aubin, 2 Black, 1133; Jaffray *v.* Fretain, 5 Esp. 47; Hartness *v.* Thompson, 5 Johns. 160; Parker *v.* Baker, 1 Clarke Ch. (N. Y.) 136.

[2] Kinney *v.* Showdy, 1 Hill, 544.

[3] Counts *v.* Bates, Harp. 464; Parsons *v.* Hill, 8 Mis. 135.

[4] Dominick *v.* Michael, 4 Sandf. 374; Beeler *v.* Bullett, 3 A. K. Marsh. 281; Nelson *v.* Eaton, 1 Redf. (N. Y.) Sur. 498; Jefford *v.* Ringgold, 6 Ala. 544. And see *supra*, p. 530.

[5] See Met. Contr. 40; Shaw C. J. in Reed *v.* Batchelder, 1 Met. 559.

[6] See Ridgely *v.* Crandall, 4 Md. 435; N. H. M. Fire Ins. Co. *v.* Noyes, 32 N. H. 345; Jenkins *v.* Jenkins, 12 Iowa, 195; Scott *v.* Buchanan, 11 Humph. 468; Babcock *v.* Doe, 8 Ind. 110.

was an infant at the time of entering into the agreement which authorizes the master to stop his wages when the steam-engine is stopped working for any cause. An agreement to serve for wages may be for the infant's benefit; but an agreement which compels him to serve at all times during the term, but leaves the master free to stop his work and his wages whenever he chooses to do so, cannot be considered as beneficial to the servant. It is inequitable, and wholly void."[1]

So an infant's bond with penalty and for the payment of interest is held to be void on the ground that it cannot possibly be for his benefit.[2] And a bond executed by a minor as surety is void.[3] So the mortgage of a minor's property to secure her husband's debt.[4] The infant's promissory note as surety is void.[5] And so is said to be a release by a minor to his guardian, which affords the latter more protection than a receipt.[6] But, in Vermont, it was decided that there is no general rule exempting an infant from paying interest as necessarily injurious to him.[7] An infant's release of his legacy or distributive share is held to be void in Tennessee.[8] In such cases, an infant is called upon to become the party to some undertaking substantially for the benefit of another, and not for his own profit.

Now it is admitted that the decisions are frequently contradictory and uncertain; yet, these cases of void contracts almost invariably proceed upon the doctrine that the infant's act was prejudicial to his interest; and certainly if any contract can be so pronounced on mere inspection, it is a contract whereby an infant becomes bound upon another's debt. The technical form of the transaction is of less importance. There

[1] Regina *v.* Lord, 12 Q. B. 757.

[2] Baylis *v.* Dineley, 3 M. & S. 477; Fisher *v.* Mowbray, 8 East, 330.

[3] Allen *v.* Minor, 2 Call, 70; Met. Contr. 40; Carnahan *v.* Allderdice, 4 Harring. 99.

[4] Chandler *v.* McKinney, 6 Mich. 217; Cronise *v.* Clark, 4 Md. Ch. 403. See Colcock *v.* Ferguson, 3 Desaus. 482.

[5] Maples *v.* Wightman, 4 Conn. 376; Curtin *v.* Patton, 11 S. & R. 305; Nightingale *v.* Withington, 15 Mass. 272.

[6] Fridge *v.* The State, 3 Gill & Johns. 115.

[7] Bradley *v.* Pratt, 23 Vt. 378.

[8] Langford *v.* Frey, 8 Humph. 443.

are many cases where an infant's bonds, mortgages, and promissory notes have been held not void, but under the circumstances of the case voidable only, as where given in ordinary transactions which may prove beneficial with relation to the minor's property.[1] And reference to the later cases will show that the modern rule is broadly announced in many States, that an infant's promissory note, his statutory recognizance and his mortgage, whether of real estate or chattels, are all voidable and not void.[2] This we conceive to be the reasonable view of the subject.

It is true, however, that the decisions are not invariably placed by the court upon this ground. The rule of Perkins, which was adopted by the Court of King's Bench in the celebrated case of *Zouch* v. *Parsons*, is that all deeds of an infant which do not take effect by delivery of his hand are merely void, and all such as do take effect by delivery of his hand are voidable. In the one case an interest is conveyed, in another a mere power.[3] This case has come down as authority for all future times; and the rule has frequently been cited with approval, in support of mortgages, bonds, and deeds; but we question the propriety of its modern application as a principle, however useful in describing an incident. So manual delivery, it was said, must accompany the sale of an infant's personal property to render it valid.[4] The real reason of such a rule might have been that solemn instruments and transactions of grave importance ought not to be lightly entered upon; but it is clear that

[1] State *v.* Plaisted, 43 N. H. 413; Roberts *v.* Wiggin, 1 N. H. 73; Richardson *v.* Boright, 9 Vt. 368; Palmer *v.* Miller, 25 Barb. 399; Reed *v.* Batchelder, 1 Met. 559; Patchkin *v.* Cromack, 13 Vt. 330; Conroe *v.* Birdsall, 1 Johns. Cas. 127; Everson *v.* Carpenter, 17 Wend. 419; Dubose *v.* Wheddon, 4 M'Cord, 221; Little *v.* Duncan, 9 Rich. 55. See Adams *v.* Ross, 1 Vroom (N. J.), 505; See Garin *v.* Burton, 8 Ind. 69. But see M'Minn *v.* Richmond, 6 Yerg. 9; Beeler *v.* Young, 1 Bibb, 519.

[2] See *e. g.* Goodsell *v.* Myers, 3 Wend. 479; Reed *v.* Batchelder, 1 Met. 559; Patchkin *v.* Cromack, 13 Vt. 330; State *v.* Plaisted, 43 N. H. 413, and cases cited; Palmer *v.* Miller, 25 Barl. 399; Mustard *v.* Wohlford, 15 Gratt. 329.

[3] Perkins, § 12; Zouch *v.* Parsons, 3 Burr. 1804; Boot *v.* Mix, 17 Wend. 131; 2 Kent Com. 236, 237 *n.*; State *v.* Plaisted, 43 N. H. 413; Conroe *v.* Birdsall, 1 Johns. Cas. 127.

[4] Fonda *v.* Van Horne, 15 Wend. 631.

ere the present day much of the ancient veneration for parchment deeds under seal has disappeared; while the tendency is to place real and personal estate transactions on much the same footing, distinguishing rather by the value than the nature of the property.

It is held that an infant may make a voidable purchase of land; for, says Lord Coke, striking the legal principle with wonderful clearness for that day, "*it is intended for his benefit*, and at his full age he may either agree thereunto and perfect it, or without any cause to be alleged, waive or disagree to the purchase."[1] For this reason, rather than the technical one referred to, it may be said in general that the conveyance of land by a minor is also voidable and not void; though here again the courts have been prone to cite the rule of Perkins.[2] But the decided cases usually presume that a valuable consideration has passed to the infant, or at least that there is nothing *prima facie* prejudicial to him. Lord-Chancellor Sugden, in 1842, in *Allen* v. *Allen*, took occasion to review Lord Mansfield's decision in *Zouch* v. *Parsons*, and commended it as sound law in respect that a deed which takes effect by delivery, and is executed by an infant, is voidable only; though he intimated that his own decision might equally well be referred to the benefit arising to the infant from the deed; which, indeed, was one of the grounds on which Lord Mansfield had decided that celebrated case.[3]

So leases to infants are not absolutely void; but voidable only.[4] And an exchange of property made by an infant is

[1] Co. Lit. 2 *b*; Met. Contr. 40; Bac. Abr. Inf. 6; Ferguson *v.* Bell, 17 Mis. 347.

[2] Kendall *v.* Lawrence, 22 Pick. 540; Gillet *v.* Stanley, 1 Hill, 121; Bool *v.* Mix, 17 Wend. 119; Wheaton *v.* East, 5 Yerg. 41; Phillips *v.* Green, 5 Monr. 344; Eagle Fire Ins. Co. *v.* Lent, 6 Paige, 635; Pitcher *v.* Laycock, 7 Ind. 398. See Welborn *v.* Rogers, 24 Geo. 558.

[3] Allen *v.* Allen, 3 Dru. & War. 340. See Co. Litt. 51 *b.*, *n.* by Hargrave.

[4] Zouch *v.* Parsons, 3 Burr. 1806; Hudson *v.* Jones, 3 Mod. 310; Taylor Landlord & Tenant and cases cited; Griffith *v.* Schwenderman, 27 Mis. 412.

voidable.[1] And it is held that the infant's bond for title to real estate is voidable and not void.[2] So a power of attorney to authorize another to receive seisin of land for an infant, in order to complete his title to an estate conveyed to him by feoffment is voidable only; it being an authority to do an act for his benefit.[3]

Where a minor agrees, as the consideration of the conveyance of land, to pay certain debts of the grantor, and afterwards does in fact pay them, it is held that the agreement constitutes a valuable consideration for such conveyance, and will support it against the grantor's creditors.[4]

But letters of attorney from an infant conveying no present interest are held to be absolutely null. This point was discussed in *Zouch* v. *Parsons*, and on the distinction of Perkins's rule, it was maintained that writings "which take effect" cannot include letters of attorney or deeds, which delegate a mere power and convey no interest. Whatever might be thought of this explanation the conclusion follows: "that powers of attorney are an exception to the general rule, that the deeds of infants are only voidable; and a power to receive seisin is an exception to that. The end of the privilege is to protect infants; and to that object all the rules and their exceptions must be directed."[5] And the English courts have uniformly held the infant's warrant of attorney void, even though executed jointly with others.[6] In this country, there are decisions in some States to the same effect;[7] in others, again, the rule is deemed somewhat doubtful.[8]

[1] Co. Lit. 51 *b*; Williams *v.* Brown, 34 Me. 594.

[2] Weaver *v.* Jones, 24 Ala. 420.

[3] Met. Contr. 41; 1 Rol. Ab. 730; Zouch *v.* Parsons, *supra.*

[4] Washband *v.* Washband, 27 Conn. 424.

[5] Per Lord Mansfield, in Zouch *v.* Parsons, 3 Burr. 1804. And see Cummings *v.* Powell, 8 Tex. 88.

[6] Saunderson *v.* Marr, 1 H. Bl. 75; Ashlin *v.* Langton, 4 Moore & S. 719, and cases cited.

[7] Lawrence *v.* M'Arter, 10 Ohio, 37; Waples *v.* Hastings, 3 Harring. 403; Bennett *v.* Davis, 6 Cow. 393; Semple *v.* Morrison, 7 Monr. 298; Pyle *v.* Cravens, 4 Litt. 17; Knox *v.* Flack, 22 Penn. St. 337.

[8] Pickler *v.* State, 18 Ind. 266. But see Trueblood *v.* Trueblood, 8 Ind. 195.

A power of attorney from an infant to sell a note is lately held voidable, not void, in California.[1] In Massachusetts an instrument of assignment, not under seal, which appoints the assignee attorney to receive the fund to his own use is not void.[2] And in Maine the act of an infant in transferring a negotiable note, though his name be written by another under parol authority, is voidable only.[3] The good sense of the rule seems to be, as a recent writer observes, that an authority delegated by an infant for a purpose which may be beneficial to him, or which the court cannot pronounce to be to his prejudice, should be considered as rendering the contract made, or act done by virtue of it, as voidable only, in the same manner as his personal acts and contracts are considered.[4] And, we may add, the English and most of the American decisions do not seem to carry the rule beyond cases of the technical "warrant of attorney" to appear in court and bind the infant, as in confessing judgment. What we call "powers of attorney" are less likely to be to the infant's prejudice.

So an infant cannot bind himself by cognovit.[5] "We come to this conclusion," said Lord Abinger, "on three grounds, each of which is fatal to the validity of the cognovit. First, it is bad because it falls within the principle which prevents an infant from appointing and appearing in court by attorney; he can appear by guardian only. Secondly, by this means the minor is made to state an account, which the law will not allow him to do, so as to bind himself; if an action be brought against him, the jury are to determine the reasonableness of the demand made. Thirdly, the general principle of law is,

See Whitney *v.* Dutch, 14 Mass. 457; Met. Contr. 41; Cummings *v.* Powell, 8 Tex. 88; 1 Am. Lead. Cas. 4th ed. 242 *et seq.*

[1] Hastings *v.* Dollarhide, 24 Cal. 195.

[2] McCarty *v.* Murray, 3 Gray, 578.

[3] Hardy *v.* Walters, 38 Me. 450.

[4] Met. Contr. 42. And see Powell *v.* Gott, 13 Mis. 458.

[5] Oliver *v.* Woodroffe, 4 M. & W. 653 (1839). But the second of these grounds is not now tenable. See Williams *v.* Moor, 11 M. & W. 256.

that a minor is not to be allowed to do any thing to prejudice himself or his rights."

A sale to an infant is a valid transfer of the property out of the vendor; even though the infant be not bound afterwards to pay the stipulated price.[1] But the courts are very reluctant to allow the infant to use his privilege as a means of defrauding others. And where an infant purchased and took possession of property and afterwards delivered, under his agreement with the vendor, certain other property in satisfaction of the purchase, it was held that he could not recover what he had delivered in an action of trover.[2] So if one receives rents while an infant, he cannot demand them over again upon reaching majority.[3] But it is held that receiving an order in payment does not prevent an infant from afterwards avoiding his own sale.[4]

An infant may in some States avoid his usurious contracts, and recover the money so lent under the count for money had and received.[5] But the policy of usury is becoming abandoned in many parts of the country.

An infant may avoid his release of damages for an injury or an award upon a submission entered into by him. But, if upon trial, the jury shall find such damages to have been satisfied by an adequate compensation the infant shall recover nominal damages only.[6] The rule is general that an infant is not bound by his agreement to refer a dispute to arbitration; nor by an award, though in his own favor; though this is usually voidable only.[7]

Among the acts of the infants which are in the later cases regarded as voidable and not void are the following. His deed

1 Crymes *v.* Day, 1 Bail. 320.

2 Farr *v.* Sumner, 12 Vt. 28.

3 Parker *v.* Elder, 11 Humph. 546.

4 Abell *v.* Warren, 4 Vt. 149. And see further, ch. 5, *post.*

5 Millard *v.* Hewlett, 19 Wend. 301.

6 Baker *v.* Lovett, 6 Mass. 78.

7 Watson on Awards, ch. 3, § 1; Smith Contr. 280; Britton *v.* Williams, 6 Munf. 453; Barnaby *v.* Barnaby, 1 Pick. 221. See Guardian & Ward, *supra.*

of gift to a trustee.[1] His appeal from a justice's decision.[2] Judgments against him.[3] His covenant to carry and deliver money.[4] His indorsement of a note.[5] And in short, deeds and instruments under seal, with perhaps the exception of powers of attorney; though it is otherwise, perhaps, if the instrument should manifestly appear on the face of it to be fraudulent or otherwise to the prejudice of the infant; "and this," says Judge Story, "upon the nature and solemnity, as well as the operation, of the instrument."[6] In Massachusetts, a contract of charter to an infant, though by parol, is voidable and not void.[7]

It has been repeatedly decided in England, that where an infant becomes the holder of shares by his own contract and subscription he is *prima facie* liable to pay calls or assessments; but he may repudiate that contract and subscription; and if he does so while an infant, although he may on arriving at full age affirm his repudiation, or receive the profits, it is for those who insist on this liability to make out the facts.[8]

An absolute gift of articles of personal property made by an infant can be revoked or avoided by him.[9] And the executed contract of an infant follows the same rule as an executory one; he may rescind the one as well as the other.[10] But if before rescission the adult make a *bona fide* sale of property purchased of the minor, trover will not lie against him.[11]

1 Slaughter *v.* Cunningham, 24 Ala. 260.

2 Robbins *v.* Cutler, 6 Fost. 173.

3 Trapmall *v.* State Bank, 18 Ark. 53; Kemp *v.* Cook, 18 Md. 130.

4 West *v.* Penny, 16 Ala. 186.

5 Hardy *v.* Waters, 38 Me. 450.

6 Per Story J., Tucker *v.* Moreland, 10 Pet. 71; 2 Kent Com. 236, 11th ed. *n.* and cases cited. And see Regina *v.* Lord, 12 Q. B. 757.

7 Thompson *v.* Hamilton, 12 Pick. 425.

8 Smith Contr. 285; Newry & Enniskillen R. R. Co. *v.* Coombe, 3 Exch. 565; London & Northwestern R. R. Co. *v.* M'Michael, 5 Exch. 114.1

9 Person *v.* Chase, 37 Vt. 647.

10 Hill *v.* Anderson, 5 S. & M. 216.

11 Carr *v.* Clough, 6 Fost. 280.

The rule is a general one that an infant cannot trade, and consequently cannot bind himself by any contract having relation to trade. "We know, by constant experience," says Mr. Smith, "that infants *do*, in fact, trade, and trade sometimes very extensively. However, there exists a conclusive presumption of law that no infant under the age of twenty-one has discretion enough for that purpose."[1] In *Dilk* v. *Keighley*, the infant was a glazier, and the person who sued him sought to make out that the goods furnished were in the nature of necessaries, to enable the infant to earn a livelihood; but this plea did not avail.[2] And an infant, rescinding a trading contract with another, may recover back in an action for money had and received a sum which he had paid towards the purchase of a share in the defendant's trade, if without consideration, and he had actually derived no benefit or profit from the business.[3] So, too, as an infant cannot trade, he cannot become a bankrupt, and a fiat against him is void.[4]

Yet, even in trading contracts it must not be forgotten that the current of modern decisions is to make the transactions of an infant voidable and not void. The English case of *Goode* v. *Harrison* is exactly in point; where a person was held liable for goods supplied him as one of a partnership, on the ground that the contract was voidable, not void, and that when the infant became of age he had substantially ratified his former act. "It is clear," says Justice Bayley, "that an infant may be in partnership. It is true that he is not liable for contracts entered into during his infancy; but still he may be a partner. If he is in point of fact, a partner during his infancy, he may, when he comes of age, elect whether he will continue

[1] Smith Contr. 278. See Whywall *v.* Champion, 2 Stra. 1083; Dilk *v.* Keighley, 2 Esp. 480.

[2] Dilk *v.* Keighley, 2 Esp. 480.

[3] Corpe *v.* Overton, 10 Bing. 252; Holmes *v.* Blogg, 8 Taunt. 508. See next chapter.

[4] Smith Contr. 282, and cases cited; Belton *v.* Hodges, 9 Bing. 365.

that partnership or not. If he continue the partnership he will then be liable as a partner."[1] Nor is another principle to be lost sight of in trading contracts; namely, that fraudulent representations and acts, though made by an infant, may sometimes make his contract binding upon him; but of this hereafter.

In this country, it is likewise admitted that, in point of fact, infants do sometimes trade;[2] but that, nevertheless, their trading contracts do not absolutely bind them, being voidable at their option.[3] And it is held in Massachusetts, that an infant cannot be compelled to pay for grain furnished for horses owned by a firm of which he was a member, though the horses were employed in the usual business of the firm, and though he was emancipated by his father.[4] But we understand the principle of that decision to accord with the English doctrine; which doctrine does not appear too far extended in South Carolina, where it was once expressly decided that a person's express or implied ratification upon reaching majority makes him liable for a debt of the firm contracted during his infancy, although he was ignorant of the existence of the debt at the time of such ratification, and had, on being informed of it, refused to pay for it.[4] For the principle indicated is, that to affirm a partnership contract, is to affirm it with its usual inseparable incidents. Certainly, the infant member of a firm cannot be permitted to derive undue advantages over his partner.[5]

What, then, is the difference between the void and the voidable contracts of an infant? Simply this: that the void contract is a mere nullity, of which any one can take advantage, and which is, in legal estimation, incapable of being ratified;

[1] 5 B. & Ald. 147. See Smith Contr. 283.

[2] Whitney *v.* Dutch, 14 Mass. 457; Houston *v.* Cooper, Penning. 865; Kitchen *v.* Lee, 11 Paige, 107.

[3] Mason *v.* Wright, 13 Met. 306.

[4] Miller *v.* Sims, 2 Hill (S. C.), 479.

[5] See Kitchen *v.* Lee, 11 Paige, 107.

while a voidable contract becomes at the option of the infant, though not otherwise, binding upon himself, and all concerned with him.[1] Acts or circumstances, then, which amount to a legal ratification serve to make the voidable contract of an infant completely binding and perpetually effectual; and this period of ratification is to be usually referred to the date when the disability of infancy ceases, and he becomes of full age,—though not always. What amounts to a legal ratification, under such circumstances, we shall show in a subsequent chapter. On the other hand, acts or circumstances which at the proper time amount to disaffirmance will render the infant's voidable contract of no effect.

An infant's voidable conveyance of land, which is a solemn instrument, and perhaps his deeds generally, cannot be avoided or confirmed during his minority.[2] This is in accordance with the rule last laid down. But as to many other transactions it is different, particularly where the contract relates to personal property. And the American cases seem to establish clearly the doctrine that an infant's sale or exchange of personal property, or contract for such sale or exchange, may be rescinded by him at any time during minority; and when the transaction is thus avoided, the title to the property revests in the infant.[3] So may the infant put an end to his contract for labor.[4]

[1] See Met. Contr. 41; Story Eq. Jur. § 241.

[2] Zouch *v.* Parsons, 3 Burr. 1794; McCormie *v.* Leggett, 8 Jones, 425; Bool *v.* Mix, 17 Wend. 119; Emmons *v.* Murray, 16 N. H. 385; Cummings *v.* Powell, 8 Tex. 80; Phillips *v.* Green, A. K. Marsh. 87.

[3] Grace *v.* Hale, 2 Humph. 27; Shipman *v.* Horton, 17 Conn. 481; Kitchen *v.* Lee, 11 Paige, 107; Willis *v.* Twombly, 13 Mass. 204; Carr *v.* Clough, 6 Fost. 280.

[4] Abell *v.* Warren, 4 Vt. 149; Francis *v.* Felmet, 4 Dev. & Bat. 498. See Tillinghast *v.* Holbrook, 7 R. I. 230.

CHAPTER III.

ACTS BINDING UPON THE INFANT.

We have seen that the general contracts of infants are either void or voidable, and that the tendency at this day is to treat them as voidable only. But keeping in view the principle that an infant's beneficial interests are to be judicially protected, we shall find that there are some contracts which he ought to be able for his own good to make; some contracts of which it may be said, that the privilege of standing upon a clear footing is worth more to him than the privilege of repudiation. Some such contracts there are, recognized as exceptions to the general rule; these are neither void nor voidable, but are obligatory *ab initio*, and thus neither require nor admit of ratification on the infant's part.[1]

The most important of this class of contracts are those for necessaries; which in fact are so important, that they are often mentioned as the only exception to the rule of void and voidable contracts. The general signification of the word necessaries has already been discussed with reference to married women; but it is readily perceived that what are necessaries for a wife may not be equally necessaries for a child, and what are necessaries for young children may not be equally necessaries for those who have nearly reached majority. The leading principles of the doctrine of necessaries being made clear, and a rule of legal classification judicially announced, any man of ordinary intelligence knows how to apply it; though juries will not and can not always agree in their conclusions on this point, every one having some preconceived notions of his own on topics so con-

[1] See Met. Contr. 64; Smith Contr. 268 *et seq.*

stantly occurring in our every-day life, and involving individual tastes and preferences.

Plainly, it is wrong to prevent an infant from attaining objects not only not detrimental, but of the utmost advantage, to him, "since," as it has been observed, "otherwise he might be unable to obtain food, clothes, or education, though certain to possess at no very distant period the means of amply paying for them all." [1]

Food, lodging, clothes, medical attendance, and education, to use concise words, constitute the five leading elements in the doctrine of the infant's necessaries. But, to apply a practical legal test, we must construe these five words in a very liberal sense, and somewhat according to the social position, fortune, prospects, age, circumstances, and general situation of the infant himself. "It is well established by the decisions," says one writer, "that under the denomination *necessaries* fall not only the food, clothes, and lodging necessary to the actual support of life, but likewise means of education suitable to the infant's degree; and all those accommodations, conveniences, and even matters of taste, which the usages of society for the time being render proper and conformable to a person in the rank in which the infant moves." [2] Says another: "The word *necessaries* is a relative term, and not confined to such things as are positively required for mere personal support." [3] The language of a Massachusetts judge is this: "It would be difficult to lay down any general rule upon this subject, and to say what would or would not be necessaries. It is a flexible, and not an absolute term." [4]

Articles of mere ornament are not necessaries. The true rule is taken to be that all such articles as are purely ornamental are not necessary, and are to be rejected, because they cannot be requisite for any one; and for such matters therefore an

[1] Smith Contr. 269.

[2] Ib. 269.

[3] Met. Contr. 69. And see Peters *v.* Fleming, 6 M. & W. 42.

[4] Breed *v.* Judd, 1 Gray, 458, per Thomas J.

infant cannot be made responsible. But if they were not of this description, then the question arises whether they were bought for the necessary use of the party, in order to support himself properly in the degree, state, and station of life in which he moved; if they were, for such articles the infant may be made responsible.[1] The result of the cases on both sides of the Atlantic seems to be that unless the articles are, both as to quality and quantity, such as must be necessaries to any one, the burden of proof lies on the plaintiff to show such a condition of life of the defendant as might raise to the rank of necessaries things which would otherwise be considered luxuries.[2]

In England, a pair of solitaires (or shirt fasteners) worth £25, are not, it would appear, necessaries for any infant.[3] But it seems that presents to a bride, when she becomes the defendant's wife, may be necessaries.[4] Betting books are not necessaries.[5] Horses, saddles, harness and carriages may be necessaries under some circumstances; but not ordinarily; and this is the better doctrine, English and American.[6] Wedding garments for an infant who marries, are within reasonable limits, necessaries.[7] But not the treats of an undergraduate at college.[8] Nor, in Arkansas, as it appears, kid gloves, cologne, silk cravats, and walking canes.[9] The uniform of an officer's servant is adjudged a necessary; but not cockades for his company.[10] An insurance contract is not a necessary.[11] Those

[1] Per Parke B., Peters *v.* Fleming, 6 M. & W. 42.

[2] Smith Contr. 272, 5th Am. ed., Rawle's *n.*, and cases cited; Harrison *v.* Fane, 1 Man. & Gr. 550; Wharton *v.* McKenzie, 5 Q. B. 606; Rundel *v.* Keeler, 7 Watts, 239; Bent *v.* Manning, 10 Vt. 225; Merriam *v.* Cunningham, 11 Cush. 40.

[3] Ryder *v.* Wombwell, Law Rep. 4 Exch. 32.

[4] Genner *v.* Walker, 19 Law Times (N. S.), 398; 3 Am. Law Rev. 590.

[5] Ib.

[6] Harrison *v.* Fane, 1 Man. & Gr. 550; Grace *v.* Hale, 2 Humph. 67; Aaron *v.* Harley, 6 Rich. 26; Merriam *v.* Cunningham, 11 Cush. 40; Beeler *v.* Young, 1 Bibb, 519; Owens *v.* Walker, 2 Strobh. Eq. 289.

[7] Sams *v.* Stockton, 14 B. Monr. 232.

[8] Wharton *v.* McKenzie, 5 Q. B. 606; Brooker *v.* Scott, 11 M. & W. 67.

[9] Lefils *v.* Sugg, 15 Ark. 137.

[10] Hands *v.* Slaney, 8 T. R. 578; Coates *v.* Wilson, 5 Esp. 52.

[11] New Hampshire Ins. Co. *v.* Noyes, 32 N. H. 345. See Harrison *v.* Fane, 1 Man.

who incline to pursue the subject still further will find some interesting decisions as to balls, serenades, suits of satin and velvet, and doublets of fustian, among the ancient cases which have survived the fashions they describe.[1]

It is usual to leave the question of necessaries in each case to the jury, without very positive directions. But the dividing line between court and jury is not in this respect clearly marked, as the latest English cases teach us. *Ryder* v. *Wombwell* lays it down that the question whether articles are necessaries is one of fact, but, like other questions of fact, should not be left to the jury unless there is evidence on which they could reasonably find that they were.[2] The immediate object of this decision was to set aside a verdict deemed improper; as to the fitness of such a rule in its broader application there is considerable doubt.[3] But it has frequently been said, that in a very clear case a judge would be warranted in directing a jury authoritatively that some articles, like diamonds and race-horses, would not be necessaries for any minor.[4]

The propriety of classing education as among the necessaries of an infant rests rather upon respectable *dicta* than precedents. Lord Coke includes among necessaries for which an infant may bind himself by contract, "good teaching and instruction, whereby he may profit himself afterwards;" and the doctrine within strict limits is undoubtedly correct.[5] In Vermont, it is

& Gr. 550; Davis *v.* Caldwell, 12 Cush. 512; Bent *v.* Manning, 10 Vt. 225; Stanton *v.* Willson, 3 Day, 37; Glover *v.* Ott, 1 M'Cord, 572; Rundel *v.* Keeler, 7 Watts, 239.

[1] See cases cited Met. Contr. 69, 70; Cro. Eliz. 583.

[2] Ryder *v.* Wombwell, Law Rep. 4 Exch. 32.

[3] Of this rule says Cockburn C. J., of the Queen's Bench, still later: "I really cannot understand it, unless it means that it is to be a question of law for the judge to determine whether the articles disputed are, or are not, necessaries. If that is to be taken to be law, of course I must act upon it; but I should certainly have preferred the law as it was previously understood to be, that it was for the jury to say what articles were reasonably necessary with reference to the position of the defendant, the infant." Genner *v.* Walker, 19 Law Times (N. S.), 398; 3 Am. Law Rev. 590.

[4] See Harrison *v.* Fane, Davis *v.* Caldwell, and other cases, *supra*.

[5] Co. Litt. 172; 1 Sid. 112; Met. Contr. 69 *n.*; Smith Contr. 269, 273.

decided that a collegiate education is not to be ranked among those necessaries for which an infant can render himself absolutely liable.[1] But the court seems to make this but a *prima facie* rule, and to admit that extraneous circumstances might be shown to make even this a necessary; while a good common-school education is strongly pronounced to be such. And the judge adds: "I would not be understood as making any allusion to professional studies, or to the education and training which is requisite to the knowledge and practice of mechanic arts. These partake of the nature of apprenticeships, and stand on peculiar grounds of reason and policy. I speak only of the regular and full course of collegiate study."[2]

An infant is not liable, at common law, for the expense of repairing his dwelling-house, on a contract made by him for that purpose; although such repairs were necessary for the prevention of immediate and serious injury to the house.[3] So timber furnished to an infant for building on his own land is not a necessary.[4] The law is extremely reluctant to permit an infant's real estate to be encumbered in any possible way. And it is ruled that the services and expenses of counsel in a suit brought to protect the infant's title to his real estate cannot for similar reasons be charged against the infant on his own contract.[5]

But the doctrine that legal expenses cannot be charged as necessaries for an infant appears not to prevail longer in Connecticut; and the more liberal rule is asserted, that in cases where, under peculiar circumstances, a civil suit is the only means by which an infant can procure the absolute necessaries which he requires, power cannot be denied him to make the necessary contracts for its commencement and prosecution;

[1] Middlebury College *v.* Chandler, 16 Vt. 683.
[2] Per Royce J., ib.
[3] Tupper *v.* Caldwell, 12 Met. 559; West *v.* Gregg, 1 Grant (Penn.), 53.
[4] Freeman *v.* Bridger, 4 Jones Law, 1.
[5] Phelps *v.* Worcester, 11 N. H. 51.

for it would be a reproach to the law to hold otherwise.[1] In this particular case, the circumstances justifying relief were very strong. Moreover, the English cases long ago established that money advanced to an infant to procure him liberation from arrest, where he was in execution, or taken in custody on a debt for necessaries, could be recovered as necessaries.[2] And we have already seen that legal expenses may be sometimes classed as necessaries for married women.[3]

The doctrine of necessaries is manifestly not to be extended to an infant's trading contracts. Thus the board of four horses for six months, the principal use of which was in the business of a hackman, is not within the class of necessaries for which an infant is liable, although the horses are occasionally used to carry his family out to ride.[4]

But the question in all such cases is one of mixed law and fact. And articles *prima facie* to be classed as luxuries, such as wines, fruits, and the use of a horse and carriage, might under some circumstances, become necessaries; as if, for instance, medically prescribed, for an infant's health; though this salutary rule is not designed to support a quibble.[5] The infant's clothes may be fine or coarse, according to his rank; his education may vary according to the station he is to fill, and the extent of his probable means when of age; and as to servants, attendance, and the like, this will depend on his social position.[6] And upon such issues, quantity may be as much for the consideration of the jury as quality.[7]

If one furnish an infant necessaries, and also other articles not necessary under his circumstances and condition, he is not on that account precluded from recovering for the necessaries;

[1] Munson *v.* Washband, 31 Conn. 303.
[2] Clarke *v.* Leslie, 5 Esp. 28; 2 Eden, 72.
[3] *Supra*, p. 78.
[4] Merriam *v.* Cunningham, 11 Cush. 40.
[5] See Wharton *v.* Mackenzie, 5 Q. B. 606.
[6] See Alderson B., Chapple *v.* Cooper, 13 M. & W. 258.
[7] Burghart *v.* Angerstein, 6 Car. & P. 690.

though, as to the balance of his claim, he may be without a remedy.[1]

The board of an infant is included among the necessaries for which he may pledge his credit.[2] But here, too, we must keep within our principle. Thus where an infant took a house to carry on the business of a barber; the house containing five rooms, two on the ground floor, one of which he occupied as a shop, the other to reside in, and three above which he underlet; he was held not to be liable for the rent.[3] An infant may contract for his necessary lodging, but he cannot bind himself for more.

An infant is not liable for necessaries when he lives under the roof of his father, who provides every thing which seems proper. And so when he is supplied by a guardian or widowed mother. The parent or the legal protector having the means, and being willing to furnish all that is actually necessary, the infant can make no binding contract for any article without such protector's consent. *Prima facie*, where the child resides at home, proper maintenance is furnished him: and the tradesman who furnishes goods to an infant does so at his peril; it is incumbent upon him to show the necessity of a supply.[4] But an infant, when absent from home, and not under the care of his parent or guardian, is usually liable for his own necessaries.[5] And the law will imply a promise on the part of an infant, having no legal protector to make payment.[6]

[1] Turberville *v.* Whitehouse, 12 Price, 692; Bent *v.* Manning, 10 Vt. 225. And see Johnson *v.* Lines, 6 W. & S. 80; Wilhelm *v.* Hardman, 13 Md. 140.

[2] Bradley *v.* Pratt, 23 Vt. 378.

[3] Lowe *v.* Griffith, 1 Scott, 458.

[4] Bainbridge *v.* Pickering, 2 Blacks. 1325; Story *v.* Pery, 4 Car. & P. 526; Angel *v.* M'Lellan, 16 Mass. 28; Wailing *v.* Toll, 9 Johns. 141; Johnson *v.* Lines, 6 W. & S. 80; Kline *v.* L'Amoreux, 2 Paige, 419; Perrin *v.* Wilson, 10 Mis. 451; Freeman *v.* Bridger, 4 Jones Law, 1; Smith *v.* Young, 2 Dev. & Bat. 26; Connolly *v.* Hull, 3 M'Cord, 6; Elrod *v.* Myers, 2 Head, 33; Kraker *v.* Byram, 13 Rich. 163; Tilton *v.* Russell, 11 Ala. 497; Hussee *v.* Roundtree, Busbee Law, 110.

[5] Angel *v.* M'Lellan, 16 Mass. 28; Hunt *v.* Thompson, 3 Scam. 179.

[6] Hyman *v.* Cain, 3 Jones Law, 111.

There is no inflexible rule of law, however, which makes it incumbent on the tradesman who supplies an infant, to inquire as to his situation and resources before giving him credit for necessaries; though it would be prudent always for him to do so.[1] And the parent may sanction by words or conduct the child's purchase, so as to make it obligatory. As in a case where the infant daughter, living with her mother at a hotel, drove to the plaintiff's store in a carriage, accompanied by her mother, who waited in the carriage while her daughter purchased the goods, some of which she took home in the carriage, while others were delivered at the hotel; here it might be reasonably inferred, as the court decided, that the whole had come under the mother's inspection, so as to make her liable for the purchase.[2]

The English cases seem to lay especial stress upon the question whether articles are or are not of themselves necessaries. And it is held not only that an infant may enter into a contract for necessaries for ready money, but that he may be bound by any reasonable contract for necessaries on a credit, though he has an income of his own, and an allowance amply sufficient for his support.[3] In South Carolina, a contrary doctrine is maintained; namely, that an infant who is furnished with necessaries, or the means in cash of procuring them, by his parent or guardian, or from any other source, is *prima facie* not liable for necessaries furnished him on credit.[4] This is, likewise, the rule in some other States.[5]

Claims against an infant for necessaries being perfectly valid at law, the creditor cannot sue in equity.[6] And while it is true that an infant cannot bind himself when he has a parent or guardian who supplies his wants, he may be bound by the purchase

[1] Brayshaw *v.* Eaton, 7 Scott, 183.
[2] Dalton *v.* Gib, 5 Bing. N. C. 198.
[3] Burghart *v.* Hall, 4 M. & W. 727; Smith Contr. 273.
[4] Rivers *v.* Gregg, 5 Rich. Eq. 274. And see Mortara *v.* Hall, 6 Sim. 465.
[5] Nicholson *v.* Wilborn, 13 Geo. 467.
[6] Oliver *v.* McDuffie, 28 Geo. 522.

of necessaries under the express or implied authority of his guardian.[1] But not for any thing absurd or improper in quantity or quality.[2] And where credit is given to a parent, the infant's estate is not answerable.[3]

The rule as to necessaries in general is, that it is the province of the court to determine whether the articles sued for are within the class of necessaries, and, if so, it is the proper duty of the jury to pass upon the questions of quantity, quality, and their adaptation to the condition and wants of the infant.[4] But as the reader is already apprised, this rule is neither stated nor applied with invariable precision in all cases. Generally, the question is one of fact for the jury; and the two principal circumstances are, whether the articles are suitable to the minor's estate and condition, and whether he is, or is not, without other means of supply.[5] An infant will be held to pay for necessaries what they are reasonably worth, but not what he may foolishly have agreed to pay for them.[6] Nor can the court be precluded, by the form of the contract, from inquiring into their real value.[7]

An infant is liable to an action at the suit of a person advancing money to a third party to pay for necessaries furnished to the infant.[8] But it is thought otherwise as to money supplied directly to the infant, to be by him thus expended, though the money be actually laid out for necessaries.[9] The reason for this distinction is said to be that in the latter case the contract arises upon the lending, and that the law will not support contracts which are to depend for their validity upon a subsequent

1 Watson *v.* Hensel, 7 Watts, 344.

2 Johnson *v.* Lines, 6 W. & S. 80.

3 Sinklear *v.* Emert, 18 Ill. 63.

4 Peters *v.* Fleming, 6 M. & W. 42; Harrison *v.* Fane, 1 Man. & Gr. 550; Phelps *v.* Worcester, 11 N. H. 51; Merriam *v.* Cunningham, 11 Cush. 40; Beeler *v.* Young, 1 Bibb, 519.

5 Per Shaw C. J., Davis *v.* Caldwell, 12 Cush. 512.

6 Locke *v.* Smith, 41 N. H. 346.

7 See 10 Mod. 85; Met. Contr. 73; 2 Kent Com. 240.

8 Swift *v.* Bennett, 10 Cush. 436; Randall *v.* Sweet, 1 Denio, 460.

9 Macphers. Inf. 505, 506; Ellis *v.* Ellis, 5 Mod. 368; 12 Mod. 197; Earle *v.* Peele, 1 Salk. 386; Clark *v.* Leslie, 5 Esp. 28.

contingency.[1] One writer admits that according to some reports of a leading case, the court held that if the money were actually expended for necessaries the infant would be chargeable;[2] but adds that the weight of authority is, that the infant is not liable at law for money thus lent and appropriated.[3] What this weight of authority may be, is not apparent. The equity rule is, that if money is lent to an infant to pay for necessaries, and it is so applied, the infant becomes liable in equity; for the lender stands in place of the payee.[4] And this is the New York doctrine, whether legal or equitable.[5] Nor should circuity of action be favored at this late day, especially when the object is after all to enforce a moral obligation in small transactions.

The old books say that an infant may bind himself by his deed to pay for necessaries.[6] Yet, it is clearly settled that he cannot do so by a bond in a penal sum; for it cannot be to his advantage to become subject to a penalty.[7] But on the question whether an infant is bound by a note not negotiable given for necessaries, there is an irreconcilable difference of opinion in the authorities; though Story considers the weight of modern English and American authorities greatly in favor of holding promissory notes given or indorsed by an infant voidable only, and therefore capable of being ratified after the party comes of age.[8]

The mischief of holding an infant's promissory note for

[1] See Swift *v.* Bennett, ib.

[2] Ellis *v.* Ellis, 12 Mod. 197.

[3] Met. Contr. 72. The learned writer quotes a *dictum* from 10 Mod. 67, to controvert that of 12 Mod. 197, which last held that money might be sometimes properly charged upon the infant. But the context only contemplates the "great difference between lending an infant money to buy necessaries, *and actually seeing the money so laid out.*" Besides, it is not clear which of the two is the better *dictum.*

[4] Marlow *v.* Pitfeild, 1 P. Wms. 558.

[5] Smith *v.* Oliphant, 2 Sandf. 306. And see Randall *v.* Sweet, 1 Denio, 460, per Bronson C. J.

[6] Com. Dig. Infant. But see next page.

[7] Ayliff *v.* Archdale, Cro. Eliz. 920; Corpe *v.* Overton, 10 Bing. 252; Smith Contr. 281; Met. Contr. 75.

[8] Story Notes, 6th ed. § 78, and cases cited. And see 2 Kent Com. 11th ed. 257; Bayley Bills, ch. 2, pp. 45, 46, 5th ed. See last chapter.

necessaries to be worthless, is the same as in loans of money for the same purpose; namely, that an infant is thereby allowed to get his supplies without paying for them. Equity influences the later cases; that somewhat novel and yet manifestly just principle gaining ground that one who receives advantages is liable on an implied contract to furnish a suitable recompense. Reeve and others state the law thus: that an infant is not bound by any express contract for necessaries to the extent of such contract, but is bound only on an implied contract to pay the amount of their value to him. That when the instrument given by him as security for payment is such that, by the rules of law, the consideration cannot be inquired into, it is void and not merely voidable. That whenever the instrument is such that the consideration may be inquired into, he is liable thereon for the true value of the articles for which it was given.[1] This excellent statement could hardly be improved upon; and, for a topic so entirely unsettled, is as well entitled to be called good law as any thing else. And, what is more, it has justice in it. The doctrine has received substantial encouragement in Massachusetts.[2] And the same practical result seems to be reached in New Hampshire, and other States, so as further to give the infant's indorser or surety a remedy against him.[3]

In a late Vermont case, this later rule received a striking illustration. An infant boarded in a country town for some twenty weeks at a reasonable price. The person to whom he was indebted owed his own adult son money, and for the convenience of the parties drew an order upon the infant, authorizing him to pay the amount of the board to his son; which order was duly received, and the infant agreed to pay it. Soon after, by consent of the parties, this order was surrendered, and

[1] Reeve Dom. Rel. 229, 230; 2 Dane Abr. 364, 365; Met. Contr. 75.

[2] Stone *v.* Dennis, 13 Pick. 6, 7, per Shaw C. J.; Earle *v.* Reed, 10 Met. 387.

[3] M'Crillis *v.* How, 3 N. H. 348; Conn *v.* Coburn, 7 N. H. 368; Dubose *v.* Wheddon, 4 M'Cord, 221; Haine *v.* Tarrant, 2 Hill (S. C.), 400; McMinn *v.* Richmonds, 6 Yerg. 9. See *contra*, Swasey *v.* Vanderheyden, 10 Johns. 33.

the infant substituted in its place his promissory note. This note was negotiable, but never was negotiated; and the holder, the adult son of the person furnishing board, brought a suit thereon. The evidence showed that the defendant's board constituted the sole consideration of the note. It was held that the consideration of the note was open to inquiry, and that, upon the facts found, the defendant was liable to the plaintiff for the full amount of the note; and, as the court also decided, with interest.[1]

Infancy of the maker of a note does not excuse the want of a demand on him by the holder in order to charge the indorsee.[2]

There are other contracts besides necessaries which are excepted from the general rule, and are made obligatory upon the infant; being neither void nor voidable.

Thus contracts of marriage are binding, if executed; they cannot be avoided on the ground of infancy. These have been considered in another connection.[3] So, too, the general rights and liabilities of a husband as to custody, maintenance, and the like, incidental to the marriage relation, apply to infants as to adults.[4] So is a contract for the burial of a spouse held beneficial and binding upon an infant.[5]

1 Bradley *v.* Pratt, 23 Vt. 378. Says the learned judge who gave the opinion in this case, after a full examination of the conflicting authorities, as to the infant's liability on his promissory note for necessaries: "We may then, we think, regard the question as still *in dubio*, and justifying the court in treating it as still an open question. And being so, we should desire to put it upon safe and consistent ground. We are led, then, to inquire what is the true principle lying at the foundation of all these inquiries. We think it is, that the infant should be enabled to pledge his credit for necessaries to any extent consistent with his perfect safety. All the cases and all the elementary writers expressly hold that it is for the benefit of the infant that he should be able to contract for necessaries; and we see no reason why he may not be allowed to contract in the ordinary modes of contracting, so far as his perfect safety is maintained always." See Thing *v.* Libbey, 16 Me. 55.

2 Wyman *v.* Adams, 12 Cush. 210.

3 See Husband & Wife, ch. 1.

4 Bac. Abr. Infancy and Age, B; 3 Burr. 1802; Met. Contr. 66.

5 Chapple *v.* Cooper, 13 M. & W. 259.

The acts of an infant that do not touch his interest, but which take effect from an authority which he is by law trusted to exercise are binding; as if an infant executor receives and acquits debts to the testator, or an infant officer of a corporation joins in corporate acts, or any other infant does the duties of an office which he may legally hold.[1] This seems to arise from the consideration which the law pays to the rights of others besides the infant; or, to put it differently, the doctrine may rest upon this fact, that the infant in such cases does not act *quasi* infant. So the acts of the king cannot be avoided on the ground of infancy; partly for the same reasons, partly as one of the attributes of his sovereignty.[2] This attribute of sovereignty may enter as an element into the public acts of infants in this country who are improperly chosen to civil offices, yet whose official acts should be sustained.

It is held that infants and married women, owning proprietary rights in townships, are not by reason of legal incapacity prevented from being bound by the acts of proprietors at legal meetings.[3] And the same is doubtless true of infant shareholders in corporations generally. Their incapacity would, otherwise, block the wheels of business altogether in matters where property and not persons are usually represented.

An infant defendant is as much bound by a decree in equity as a person of full age; therefore, if there be an absolute decree made against a defendant, who is under age, he will not be permitted to dispute it unless upon the same grounds as an adult might have disputed it; such as fraud, collusion, or error.[4] As to the binding force of judgments at law, the rule does not seem to be equally strong.

It is an old and well settled doctrine that an infant will be

[1] Met. Contr. 66. See Butler *v.* Breck, 7 Met. 164; Roach *v.* Quick, 9 Wend. 238.

[2] See ib.

[3] Townsend *v.* Downer, 32 Vt. 183.

[4] 1 Dan. Ch. Practice, 205; Ralston *v.* Lahee, 8 Clarke (Iowa), 17. But see Tibbs *v* Allen, 27 Ill. 119; Driver *v.* Driver, 6 Ind. 286.

bound by any act which the law would have compelled him to perform; as if the infant make equal partition of lands, or assign dower, or release an estate mortgaged on satisfaction of the debt.[1] But it is held that this rule does not apply to the case of a voluntary distribution; for the law, though it would have coerced a distribution, might not have made just such a one as was made by the parties.[2]

Enlistments are binding contracts under the public statutes.[3] Whenever a statute authorizes a contract which from its nature or objects is manifestly intended to be performed by infants, such a contract must, in point of law, be deemed for their benefit and for the public benefit; so that when *bona fide* made it is neither void nor voidable, but is strictly obligatory upon them. Yet if there be fraud, circumvention, or undue advantage taken of the infant's age or situation by the public agents, the contract could not, in reason or justice, be enforced.[4]

On like principles, a minor may be bound by his indentures of apprenticeship, executed in strict conformity to statute; this being likewise deemed for his benefit. By the custom of London, and under the laws of some States, the covenants of the minor apprentice are obligatory upon him. But it is otherwise by the common law of England, and also under the statutes of Elizabeth, and in New York, Massachusetts, and other States. Still, although the infant is not liable for breach of his covenants, he cannot dissolve the indenture.[5] The English doctrine is that indentures are so far binding, that the master may enforce his rights under them; and the legal incidents of service

[1] Co. Lit. 38 *a*, 172 *a*; 3 Burr. 1801, Met. Contr. 67; Jones *v.* Brewer, 1 Pick. 314; Bavington *v.* Clarke, 2 Penn. 115.

[2] Kilcrease *v.* Shelby, 23 Miss. 161.

[3] King *v.* Rotherfield Greys, 1 B. & C. 345; Commonwealth *v.* Gamble, 11 S. & R. 93; United States *v.* Bainbridge, 1 Mason, 83, before Story J.

[4] Per Story J., ib. And see Franklin *v.* Mooney, 2 Tex. 452.

[5] Met. Contr. 66. See Woodruff *v.* Logan, 1 Eng. 276; Stokes *v.* Hatcher, 1 South, 84; M'Dowles' Case, 8 Johns. 331; Blunt *v.* Melcher, 2 Mass. 228; Rex *v.* Inhabitants of Wigston, 3 B. & C. 484.

as apprentice attach to this relation; unless the master by his own misconduct deprives the infant of the benefits of the contract, in which case the law will release the latter from his bargain.[1]

In this country, the cases are very common where a minor is said to be emancipated and entitled to contract for and receive his own wages. But the significance of the word emancipation is not exact; and, certainly, the legal obligation of the infant's contract for work is by no means commensurate with his right to the fruits of his own toil. His legal capacity to do acts necessarily binding does not seem to be enlarged by the circumstance that his father has given him his time; and the general rule, independent of apprentice acts, is that an infant who contracts to perform labor for a fixed time at a definite rate, may put an end to it whenever he chooses, and claim compensation *pro rata* for his services.[2] Infants, or rather their older advisers, have sometimes the effrontery, after rescinding a contract beneficial to themselves, to demand wages from their employers, without the allowance of reasonable offsets; but the courts are not so foolish as to indulge them in this respect; hence, in numerous instances, it is decided that where an infant puts an end to his contract of service, his demand for proportional wages is subject to the reasonable deduction of his employer for part-payments, board, and necessaries furnished him during the same period, even to the entire extinction of his own claim.[3] And the injury sustained by his employer will be

[1] 5 Dowl. & Ry. 339; 6 T. R. 558; Cro. Jac. 494; Cro. Car. 179; Met. Contr. 66; Rex *v.* Mountsorrel, 3 M. & S. 497.

[2] Person *v.* Chase, 37 Vt. 647; Van Pelt *v.* Corwine, 6 Ind. 363; Dallas *v.* Hollingsworth, 3 Ind. 537; Davies *v.* Turton, 13 Wis. 185; Moses *v.* Stevens, 2 Pick. 332; Mason *v.* Wright, 13 Met. 306; Lufkin *v.* Mayall, 5 Fost. 82; Francis *v.* Felmet, 4 Dev. & Bat. 498; Judkins *v.* Walker, 17 Me. 38. But see Weeks *v.* Leighton, 5 N. H. 343; Harney *v.* Owen, 4 Blackf. 336; Wilhelm *v.* Hardman, 13 Md. 140; M'Coy *v.* Huffman, 8 Cow. 84; Medbury *v.* Watrous, 7 Hill, 110.

[3] Thomas *v.* Dike, 11 Vt. 273; Hoxie *v.* Lincoln, 25 Vt. 206; Lowe *v.* Sinklear, 27 Mis. 308; Stone *v.* Dennison, 13 Pick. 1; Squier *v.* Hydliff, 9 Mich. 274; Wilhelm *v.* Hardman, 13 Md. 140.

taken into account.[1] But the infant cannot be sued for breach of his agreement of service.[2] And of course he may set off his own labor against the employer's demand for necessaries.[3]

A case occurred in Massachusetts a few years ago, where an infant, in consideration of an outfit to enable him to go to California, agreed, with his father's assent, to give the party furnishing the outfit one-third of all the avails of his labor during his absence, which he afterwards sent accordingly. The jury having found that the agreement was fairly made, and for a reasonable consideration, and beneficial to the infant, it was held that he could not rescind the agreement and recover the amount sent, deducting the cost of the outfit, and any other money expended for him under the agreement.[4] This offer, the court observed, would not place the parties in *statu quo*, for the defendants took the risk of the life, health, and good fortune of the plaintiff. Under all the circumstances of the case, the sum advanced was a reasonable consideration for a third part of the proceeds of the plaintiff's labor.

It is a well known principle that when a contract is dissolved by mutual consent, *pro rata* wages may be recovered without express agreement. This applies to infants as well as adults. But a father is so far bound by his son's contract that his own claim for compensation depends upon his son's proper performance.[5] The employer, on the other hand, cannot make a new contract with the minor, so as to supersede the first one, without the assent of the father, or other person with whom the original contract was made.[6]

1 Thomas *v.* Dike, 11 Vt. 273; Hoxie *v.* Lincoln, 25 Vt. 206; Lowe *v.* Sinklear, 27 Mis. 308; Moses *v.* Stevens, 2 Pick. 336. *Contra,* Meeker *v.* Hurd, 31 Vt. 639.

2 Frazier *v.* Rowan, 2 Brev. 47.

3 Francis *v.* Felmet, 4 Dev. & Bat. 498.

4 Breed *v.* Judd, 1 Gray, 455.

5 Rogers *v.* Steele, 24 Vt. 513. See Thomas *v.* Williams, 1 Ad. & E. 685.

6 McDonald *v.* Montague, 30 Vt. 357. And see Gates *v.* Davenport, 29 Barb. 160. See also Parent & Child, *supra.*

CHAPTER IV.

THE INJURIES AND FRAUDS OF INFANTS.

In this chapter we shall treat, first, of injuries and frauds committed by an infant; secondly, of injuries and frauds suffered by an infant.

First, as to injuries and frauds committed by an infant. It is a general principle that infancy shall not be permitted to protect wrongful acts. To use the forcible expression of Lord Mansfield, the privilege of infancy is given as a shield and not a sword.[1] And minors are liable, not only for their criminal acts, but for their torts; and must respond in damages in all cases arising *ex delicto* to the extent of their pecuniary means, irrespective of the form of action which the law prescribes for redress of the wrong.[2]

An infant is then as fully liable as an adult in an action for damages occasioned by injury to the person or property of another by his wrongful act.[3] True, it has been observed, that where infants are the actors, that might probably be considered an unavoidable accident, which would not be so where the actors are adults.[4] But, says Reeve, where the minor commits a tort with force, he is liable at any age; for in case of civil injuries with force, the intention is not regarded.[5]

1 Zouch *v.* Parsons, 3 Burr. 1802.

2 Met. Contr. 49; 1 Addison Torts, 731; 8 T. R. 335; 2 Kent Com. 240, 241; School District *v.* Bragdon, 3 Fost. 507; Bullock *v.* Babcock, 3 Wend. 391; Oliver *v.* McClellan, 21 Ala. 675.

3 Conklin *v.* Thompson, 29 Barb. 218.

4 Bullock *v.* Babcock, 3 Wend. 391.

5 Reeve Dom. Rel. 258. See Neal *v.* Gillett, 23 Conn. 437.

It follows from what we have said, that for an injury occasioned by an infant's negligence, he may be held civilly answerable. As where, in sport, he discharges an arrow in a school-room where there are a number of boys assembled, and thereby disables another.[1] And even though under seven years of age, a child is liable in trespass for breaking down the shrubbery and flowers of a neighbor's garden.[2] But not for turning horses which were trespassing on his father's land into the highway, for this does not constitute a tort.[3] All the cases agree that trespass lies against an infant. And minors are chargeable in trespass for having procured others to commit assault and battery.[4]

But, supposing the trespass to have been committed by the express command of the father; is the infant then liable? So it was thought in a Vermont case, where the decision nevertheless rested on a different ground.[5] "An infant, acting under the command of his father, as a wife in the presence of her husband, might be excused from a prosecution for crime, if it should appear that the intent was wanting, or that he was acting under constraint; yet he is answerable *civiliter* for injuries he does to another." [6] And more recently this question is plainly decided in Maine, in the affirmative.[7]

An infant in the actual occupation of land is responsible for nuisances and injuries to his neighbor, arising from the negligent use and management of the property.[8] And ejectment may be maintained against an infant for disseisin, that being a tort.

The cases on the subject of an infant's torts do not seem quite consistent, so far as decisions upon the facts are concerned; but the principle which runs through them all seems to harmonize the apparent contradictions. This is the principle: that the

[1] Bullock *v.* Babcock, 3 Wend. 391.

[2] Huchting *v.* Engel, 17 Wis. 231.

[3] Humphrey *v.* Douglass, 10 Vt. 71.

[4] Sikes *v.* Johnson, 16 Mass. 389; Tift *v.* Tift, 4 Denio, 177; Scott *v.* Watson, 46 Me. 362.

[5] Humphrey *v.* Douglass, 10 Vt. 71.

[6] Per Williams C. J., ib.

[7] Scott *v.* Watson, 46 Me. 362.

[8] 1 Addis. Torts, 731; McCoon *v.* Smith, 3 Hill, 147.

courts will hold an infant liable for what are substantially his torts, but not for mere violations of a contract, though attended with tortious results, and though the party ordinarily has the right to declare in tort or contract at his election. It must be remembered that, for his contracts, the infant is not ordinarily liable; for his torts he is. And this distinction is at the root of the legal difficulty. The plaintiff cannot convert any thing that arises out of a contract into a tort and then seek to enforce the contract through an action of tort. Therefore was it held that where a boy hired a horse and injured it by immoderate driving, this was only a breach of contract for which he was not liable.[1] And where in an exchange of horses the infant had falsely and fraudulently warranted his mare to be sound, he was protected from the consequences on the same principle.[2] The English cases, decided many years ago, exhibit a strong disposition to rule in favor of an infant's exemption. And the language of the court in *Manby* v. *Scott*, with reference to the delivery of goods to an infant, and suit afterwards for trover and conversion, was that the latter shall not be chargeable: "for by that means all infants in England would be ruined."[3] Says a judge, deciding a case on the same general principle, "the judgment will stay for ever, else the whole foundation of the common law will be shaken."[4]

But a more equitable principle pervades the later cases. And in Vermont an infant was held answerable, not many years ago, where he hired a horse to go to a certain place and return the same day, then doubled the distance by a circuitous route, stopped at a house on the way, left the horse all night without food or shelter, and by such overdriving and exposure caused the death of the horse.[5] This is the Massachusetts doctrine

[1] Jennings *v.* Rundall, 8 T. R. 335.

[2] Green *v.* Greenbank, 2 Marsh, 485; Howlett *v.* Haswell, 4 Campb. 118; Morrill *v.* Aden, 19 Vt. 505.

[3] 1 Sid. 129, quoted with approbation in Jennings *v.* Rundall, *supra.*

[4] Johnson *v.* Pye, 1 Keb. 905. See *n.* to Howlett *v.* Haswell, *supra.*

[5] Towne *v.* Wiley, 23 Vt. 355.

likewise.[1] The distinction relied upon is, that when property is bailed to an infant, his infancy protects him so long as he keeps within the terms of the bailment; but when he goes beyond it, there is a conversion of the property, and he is liable just as much as though the original taking was tortious.[2]

Chief-Justice Marshall pronounces infancy to be no complete bar to an action of trover, although the goods converted be in the infant's possession, in virtue of a previous contract. "The conversion is still in its nature a tort; it is not an act of omission but of commission, and is within that class of offences for which infancy cannot afford protection."[3] This doctrine is approved in New York.[4] And in Maine.[5] So, in England, detinue will lie against an infant, where goods were delivered for a special purpose not accomplished.[6] And the general rule seems to be now well established that an infant is liable for goods entrusted to his care, and unlawfully converted by him; though, as to what constitutes such conversion, the authorities are not agreed.[7]

It is held that while a ship-owner cannot sue his infant supercargo for breach of instructions, he may bring trover for the goods.[8] And an infant, prevailing on the plea of infancy in an action on a promissory note given by him for a chattel which he had obtained by fraud and refused to deliver on demand, has been still held liable to an action of tort for the conversion of the chattel: the original tort not having been superseded by a completed contract.[9] And replevin will lie for the goods even where a suit for damages might fail.[10] But for breaking

1 Homer v. Thwing, 3 Pick. 492.

2 Towne v. Wiley, *supra*, per Redfield J. The rule is otherwise in Pennsylvania. Penrose v. Curren, 3 Rawle, 351.

3 Vasse v. Smith, 6 Cranch, 226.

4 Campbell v. Stakes, 2 Wend. 137.

5 Lewis v. Littlefield, 15 Me. 233.

6 Mills v. Graham, 4 B. & P. 140.

7 See Story Bailments, § 50; 2 Kent Com. 241; Baxter v. Bush, 29 Vt. 465.

8 Vasse v. Smith, 6 Cranch, 226.

9 Walker v. Davis, 1 Gray, 506. And see Fitts v. Hall, 9 N. H. 441.

10 Badger v. Phinney, 15 Mass. 359.

a borrowed carriage an infant is held not liable.[1] And the conversion of specific goods by an infant should be carefully distinguished from what is in substance a breach of his contract to sell and account for profits.[2]

Where an action for money had and received was brought against an infant to recover money which he had embezzled, Lord Kenyon said that infancy was no defence to the action; that infants were liable to actions *ex delicto* though not *ex contractu*, and though the action was in form an action of the latter description, yet it was in point of substance *ex delicto*.[3] For embezzlement of funds, therefore, an infant may be considered liable.[4] And in New York, and some other States, an infant is held responsible in tort for obtaining goods on credit, intending not to pay.[5]

In New Hampshire, the general rule is stated to be, that if false representations are made by an infant at the time of his contract, he may set up infancy in defence; but if the tort is subsequent to the contract, and not a mere breach of it, but a distinct, wilful, and positive wrong of itself; then, although it may be connected with a contract, the infant is liable.[6]

The plea of infancy has been long considered, both in England and this country, a good defence to an action for fraudulent representation and deceit. Thus, the rule is, that an infant who falsely affirms goods to be his own, and that he had a right to sell them, and thereby induces the plaintiff to purchase them, is not responsible.[7] Still more frequently has it been held that for a false and fraudulent representation that he was of full age, there is no remedy against the infant; whether

1 Schenck *v.* Strong, 1 South, 87.

2 See Munger *v.* Hess, 28 Barb. 75. And see Burns *v.* Hill, 19 Geo. 22.

3 Bristow *v.* Eastman, 1 Esp. 172.

4 Elwell *v.* Martin, 32 Vt. 217.

5 Wallace *v.* Morse, 5 Hill, 391, and cases cited. But the rule appears otherwise in Indiana. Root *v.* Stevenson's Adm'r, 24 Ind. 115.

6 Fitts *v.* Hall, 9 N. H. 441; Prescott *v.* Norris, 32 N. H. 101.

7 Grove *v.* Nevill, 1 Keb. 778; 1 Addis. Torts, 661; Prescott *v.* Norris, 32 N. H. 101; Morrill *v.* Aden, 29 Vt. 465. But see Word *v.* Vance, 1 Nott & M'-Cord, 197.

money were advanced or goods entrusted to him on the strength of such representation.[1] The reader must reconcile these rules with some of the foregoing cases as best he may.

If any thing be needed to show the inadequacy of common-law remedies for frauds and wilful misrepresentations, it is just such maxims as these, which have been perpetuated from the old books. Chancery, handling its weapons with more freedom, is accomplishing results in this respect more widely useful. The doctrine of the English equity courts appears to have been, for years, that where payment is made to one falsely representing himself as an infant, this is a discharge for the sum paid; but where there was no such misrepresentation the trustee still remains liable; the mere belief that one was of age affording no ground of justification.[2] But an English bankruptcy case of recent date carries the principle farther; far enough to startle those who have reposed upon the assurance that the ancient judgments "will stay for ever." A young man, who from his appearance might well have been taken to be more than twenty-one years of age, engaged in trade, and wished to borrow or to obtain credit, and for the purpose of doing so represented himself to the petitioner as of the age of twenty-two, expressly and distinctly. It was held that, whatever the liability or non-liability of the infant at law, he had made himself liable in equity to pay that debt.[3]

In a somewhat later case, it was held that an infant's settlement upon his wife might be avoided by him on arriving at majority, notwithstanding there was some evidence that he fraudulently misstated his age to her solicitor; the fact being, however, that she, a widow of thirty-two, knew perfectly well

[1] Johnson *v.* Pye, 1 Sid. 258; Price *v.* Hewett, 8 Exch. 146; s. c. 18 E. L. & Eq. 522; Burley *v.* Russell, 10 N. H. 184; Conroe *v.* Birdsall, 1 Johns. Cas. 127; Merriam *v.* Cunningham, 11 Cush. 40; Brown *v.* McCune, 5 Sandf. 224.

[2] Overton *v.* Banister, 3 Hare, 503; Stikeman *v.* Dawson, 1 De G. & S. 90.

[3] Unity & Banking Association, *in re*, 3 De G. & J. 63 (1858). Lord Justices Bruce and Turner concurred in this opinion, both expressing some reluctance in giving the judgment. See also frauds of married women, *supra*.

that he was under age, and was not misled by his representation.[1] Lord-Justice Turner, commenting upon the case, said: "There can be no doubt that it is morally wrong in an infant of competent age, as it is in any other person, to make any false representation whatever; but the observance of obligations or duties which rest only upon moral grounds cannot be enforced in chancery. Some wrong or injury to the party complaining must be shown." He further observes: "The privilege of infancy is a legal privilege. On the one hand, it cannot be used by infants for the purposes of fraud. On the other hand, it cannot, I think, be allowed to be infringed upon by persons who, knowing of the infancy, must be taken also to know of the legal consequences which attach to it." [2]

The result of these late English decisions is to re-open in that country the whole subject of an infant's liability on his fraudulent misrepresentations; and considerable uncertainty appears to pervade the latest common-law decisions in that country, which incidentally bear upon the subject.[3] Whether the new or the old doctrine is in the end to prevail, it is too early yet to say; but a collision has come, towards which equity and the common law were fast tending.[2]

The civil-law doctrine is clearly that if a minor represents himself of age, *and from his person he appears to be so*, any contract made with him will be valid; and the law protects those who are defrauded, not those who commit fraud.[4] Such was the Spanish law as formerly prevalent in our South-western States.[5] In a Maryland case, too, we find the suggestion that if an infant forms a partnership with an adult he holds himself

[1] Nelson *v.* Stocker, 4 De G. & J. 458 (1859).

[2] Ib. p. 465.

[3] See De Roo *v.* Foster, 12 C. B. N. S. 272 (1862); Wright *v.* Leonard, 11 C. B. N. S. 258.

[4] 1 St. Dom. pt. 1, B. 4, Tit. 6, § 2.

[5] See able discussion of this subject by Hemphill, C. J., Kilgore *v.* Jordan, 17 Tex. 341. There is not another American case to be found where this subject is so fully discussed, in its civil law, common law, and English equity bearings.

out fraudulently to the world.[1] In Texas, the fraudulent representations of an infant are binding upon him.[2] Intimations are sometimes found in the courts as to gross frauds which might bind an infant.[3] Beyond this there seems no authority for asserting that the American doctrine on this subject is unsettled, or that it is likely to feel the change now going on in the English courts. In fact, an equity court in North Carolina refused, not many years since, to compel specific performance of an infant's contract on the alleged ground of fraudulent misrepresentation of his father and himself, that he was of full age; following the old common-law rule instead of opposing it.[4]

But our statutes sometimes quicken the infant's sense of honor. Thus, in Iowa, it is enacted that one who, in selling real estate represents himself to be of full age, and induces the grantee to buy on the strength of that representation cannot afterwards disaffirm his contract on the ground of infancy.[5]

Secondly. As to injuries and frauds suffered by infants.

Infants have a right to sue, by guardian or next friend, to recover damages for injuries done to person or property by the tortious acts of another; and the ordinary principles of law, in this respect, apply to them as to adults.[6] But by reason of their tender years, their rights and remedies receive a somewhat peculiar treatment in the courts, as we proceed to show.

Thus it is held that a child eight years old may sue one who sells and delivers to him a dangerously explosive substance, such as gunpowder, though upon his own request.[7] Such

1 Kemp *v.* Cook, 18 Md. 130. The remark is quoted as that of Lord Mansfield in Gibbs *v.* Merrill, 3 Taunt. 307, but this must be an error, as no such language appears in the case referred to, while the decision went upon a totally different ground.

2 Kilgore *v.* Jordan, 17 Tex. 341.

3 Stoolfos *v.* Jenkins, 12 S. & R. 399; 2 Kent Com. 241. And see Sterling *v.* Adams, 3 Day, 411; Davies J., in Henry *v.* Root, 23 N. Y. 544.

4 Dibble *v.* Jones, 5 Jones Eq. 389.

5 Proutz *v.* Edgar, 6 Iowa, 353.

6 1 Addis. Torts, 712.

7 Carter *v.* Towne, 98 Mass. 567.

actions are grounded upon the ignorance of the child and the negligence of those who fail to regard it. The principle involved is precisely that of the case where a man delivers a cup of poison to an idiot or puts a razor into the hand of an infant. The child uses that ordinary care of which he is presumed capable; and though this may amount, logically, to actual carelessness, his right of action is not thereby forfeited. Whoever, then, would avoid a suit like this, must regulate his own discretion to suit the party with whom he deals, and act at all times with befitting prudence.

But there are cases where the child himself may have no right of action for injuries received. As if he be technically a trespasser, and meddling with property which does not belong to him. Of this rule a recent English case affords an example, where a boy, four years old, coming from school, saw a machine exposed for sale in a public place, and by direction of his brother, seven years old, placed his fingers within the machine whilst another turned the crank and thereby crushed his fingers.[1] The court held that no action would lie. But if the trespass of the infant does not substantially contribute to produce the injury, it would appear that no defence can be legally interposed on this ground.[2]

Another and the more common class of exceptions consists of cases where the parents or other persons having charge of the child have been guilty of negligence. The rule of New York, Massachusetts, and Illinois is, that a child too young to have discretion for himself cannot recover if his protector fails to exercise ordinary care, but that he may if he uses such care as is usual with children of the same age, and the protector exercises ordinary care besides.[3] The English rule, as formerly

[1] Mangan *v.* Atterton, 1 Exch. 239. And see Hughes *v.* McFie, 2 H. & C. 744; 33 L. J. (Ex.) 177.

[2] See Daley *v.* Norwich & Worcester R. R. Co., 26 Conn. 591.

[3] Wright *v.* Malden & Melrose R. R. Co., 4 Allen, 283; Hartfield *v.* Roper, 21 Wend. 617; Kreig *v.* Wells, 1 E. D. Smith, 74; Munn *v.* Reed, 4 Allen, 431; Lehman *v.* Brooklyn, 29 Barb. 236; City of Chicago *v.* Starr, 42 Ill. 174.

understood, does not take into consideration the circumstance of the protector's negligence at all.[1] And in Vermont, Connecticut, and Pennsylvania the child's exercise of ordinary care is alone regarded.[2]

The latest English cases, however, lean toward the doctrine first above stated. Thus when the child, at the time of injury, was in the care of his grandmother, at a railroad station, where she had purchased tickets for both, it was held that the plaintiff was so identified with his grandmother that, by reason of her negligence, no suit was maintainable against the company.[3]

To take common illustrations of this principle. Allowing a child seventeen months old to be in the public street without a suitable attendant is want of ordinary care on the parents' part, and if the child be run over there is no remedy.[4] But suffering a boy eight or ten years old to play on the street after dark is not necessarily so.[5] And even as to children, four years of age or thereabouts, it is not expected that parents who have to labor for themselves and cannot hire nurses are to be without remedy for themselves or their children every time the child steps into the street unattended.[6] No child capable of running about can be kept tied up in the house and subjected to constant watch. This rule is reasonably and beneficially applied; and the circumstances are in general for the jury.

The same principle may be further illustrated by a late Illinois case. A heavy counter, some eighteen feet long and three feet high, which had been placed across the sidewalk in one of the principal thoroughfares of Chicago, remained so for two or three weeks, when some children were climbing upon it and

[1] Lynch *v.* Nurdin, 1 Q. B. 29. Doubted, however, in Lygo *v.* Newbold, 9 Exch. 302.

[2] Robinson *v.* Cone, 22 Vt. 213; Daley *v.* Norwich & Worcester R. R. Co., 26 Conn. 591.

[3] Waite *v.* North-Eastern R. R. Co., 5 Jur. (N. S.) 936.

[4] Kreig *v.* Wells, 1 E. D. Smith, 74.

[5] Lovett *v.* Salem, &c. R. R. Co., 9 Allen, 557.

[6] City of Chicago *v.* Major, 18 Ill. 360.

thereby caused it to fall over. One of the children, six years old, was killed, and the parents sued the city, under statute, for damages. The court held, upon the state of facts before them, that the action would not lie because there was negligence shown on both sides, — on the part of the city in allowing the counter to remain in that situation, and on the part of the parents in permitting the child, at his age, to roam the crowded thoroughfares of the city at a great distance from his home. The negligence on the part of the city was less than that attributable to the child's parents, and therefore there could be no recovery.[1]

Causa proxima non remota spectatur is the maxim usually applied in cases of torts, whether the plaintiff be infant or adult. But where the tort is occasioned by the negligence of one person, the infant is not debarred of his right to sue the other party who shared in it. As where a child too young to take care of himself — there being, we shall suppose, no negligence on the part of the parent — is in danger of being run over by a steam-engine, and some stranger catches him up, meaning to save his life, and imprudently rushes over the track and falls with the child. An accident so occasioned might, under some such circumstances, give a right of action against either the stranger or the railroad company, or against them jointly.[2]

While an infant is liable for torts, it does not follow that his contracts in compensation for torts are binding. In fact, his submission to an award, and notes given or money paid in pur-

[1] City of Chicago *v.* Starr, 42 Ill. 174. In this case it was further suggested that the degree of carelessness is not to be judged from a single fatal accident; but that the question is rather what would have been the course of a prudent person prior to the accident. And the habitual carelessness of the parents in allowing the child to go about unattended was considered material. Ibid.

[2] See North Penn. R. R. Co. *v.* Mahoney, 57 Penn. St. 187. The views expressed in this case may not meet, in all respects, the concurrence of other courts; but the principle extracted in the text seems to the writer a correct one.

suance thereof, follow the principle of void and voidable contracts.[1] So, on the other hand, where he releases or compromises for any injury himself has sustained, the same rule applies.[2] Since the parent cannot sue, as such, for the child's injuries, neither can he make a binding compromise, except as to his own demand upon the defendant.[3]

[1] Hanks *v.* Deal, 3 McCord, 257; Pitcher *v.* Turin Plank Road Co., 10 Barb. 436; Ware *v.* Cartledge, 24 Ala. 622.

[2] Baker *v.* Lovett, 6 Mass. 78.

[3] See Loomis *v.* Cline, 4 Barb. 453. But see Merritt *v.* Williams, 1 Harp. Ch. 306.

CHAPTER V.

RATIFICATION AND AVOIDANCE OF CONTRACTS.

THAT indulgence which the law allows infants, to secure them from the fraud and imposition of others, can only be intended for their benefit, and therefore persons of riper years cannot take advantage of such transactions. The infant may rescind his own deed or contract; but the adult with whom he deals is held bound meantime, unless the transaction be void, and not voidable.[1]

But the infant may confirm his voidable contract on arriving at full age; and if he does so by such writings, words, or acts as amount to a legal ratification, he will become liable then and thereafter. But what is in law a sufficient ratification remains to be considered.

Much of the discussion on this point is now dispensed with in England, by a short statute to the effect that "no action shall be maintained whereby to charge any person upon any promise made after full age to pay any debt contracted during infancy, or upon any ratification, after full age of any promise or simple contract made during infancy, unless such promise or ratification shall be made by some writing, signed by the party to be charged therewith."[2] This statute is known as Lord Tenterden's Act. Here is a clear, precise, and definite rule; and any apparent want of equity is compensated by the certainty with which a very troublesome subject is managed, one which has so constantly led to unprofitable litigation. The

[1] Smith *v.* Bowen, 1 Mod. 25; 2 Kent Com. 236; Warwick *v.* Bruce, 2 M. & S. 205; Brown *v.* Caldwell, 10 S. & R. 114; *supra*, ch. 2.

[2] Stat. 9 Geo. 4, ch. 14, § 5 (1828).

same, or similar provisions, are to be found in the laws of some of our States.[1]

But even statutes will raise legal difficulties. And the difficulty which arises under this particular act is to distinguish ratification from a new promise. What is meant by a *ratification* in the words of this statute? The Court of Exchequer, not many years since, admitting, in the course of argument, that the statute made a distinction between ratification and new promises, gave it as their opinion that any act or declaration which recognizes the existence of a promise as binding, is a ratification of it; and that the statute "ratification" goes so far as to comprehend such a ratification as would make a person liable as principal for an act done by another in his name.[2] And hence certain letters written by the defendant in reference to payment of his debt out of his money in the hands of a third party were held binding. More lately this definition of ratification was reconsidered by the same court in another case, where the correspondence was over a dishonored bill of exchange, and another person, not the infant, was to be primarily liable; and the judges were divided in opinion. But the disposition seemed to be to define ratification anew, as a willing admission that the party is *liable and bound* to pay the debt arising from a contract which he made when an infant.[3]

Still later a man, being of age, signed the following statement at the foot of an account of the items and prices of goods furnished to him while an infant by the plaintiff: "Particulars of account to the end of 1867, amounting to £162 11*s*. 6*d*. I certify to be correct and satisfactory." It was held that this was not a sufficient ratification under the statute, because these

[1] See Thurlow *v*. Gilmore, 40 Me. 378.

[2] Harris *v*. Wall, 1 Exch. 122.

[3] Mawson *v*. Blane, 10 Exch. 206; 26 E. L. & Eq. 560. See, further, Smith Contr. 287. Lord Ellenborough considered it more correct to say in general, that the infant makes a new promise after he comes of age. Cohen *v*. Armstrong, 1 M. & S. 724. As to what is a sufficient compliance with the statute, see Hartley *v*. Wharton, 11 Ad. & El. 934; Hyde *v*. Johnson, 2 Bing. N. C. 778; Hunt *v*. Massey, 5 B. & Ad. 902.

words did not really admit the debt to be a debt existing and binding upon the defendant.[1]

Independently of all statutes, however, the question has been asked again and again, what language and what conduct on the part of the infant attaining to majority will suffice to give binding force to his acts originally voidable. The American cases on this point are very numerous. And it must be confessed that the more this subject has been discussed, the less it appears to be understood. Two principles are evidently in conflict: the one, that an infant should be protected against his own imprudence; the other, that *bona fide* creditors ought not to be cheated. Some cases have given more prominence to the first principle, others to the second.

There cannot be much doubt that at the time Lord Tenterden's Act was passed, the English rule was, that an infant may by his general conduct, independently of a precise promise or new contract, on his part, render himself liable for his contracts made while an infant.[2] The statute was passed to change this rule. On that point we need not dwell. This does not bind American courts, it is true, for they had adopted in many instances, another rule of the common law to which they were at liberty to adhere, in spite of the later English decisions; since it was the rule our ancestors brought over with them.

Now, what is the American doctrine? We take a case decided within a few years in Massachusetts, where an infant had made a promissory note, and after majority admitted several times that he owed the debt, and said he would pay it when he could. Says the court: "It has long been settled that a direct promise, when of age, is necessary to establish a contract made during minority, and that a mere acknowledgment will not have that effect."[3] We take still another decided in New York about the same time. Says a judge of the Court

[1] Rowe *v.* Hopwood, Law Rep. 4 Q. B. 1.

[2] See Goode *v.* Harrison, 5 B. & Ald. 147; Smith Contr. 283, 284.

[3] Proctor *v.* Sears, 4 Allen, 95 (1862), per Metcalf J.

of Appeals, after a most exhaustive review of the cases: "I think that the course of decision in this State authorizes us to assume that the narrow and stringent rule, formerly enunciated, that to establish the contract, when made in infancy, there must be a precise and positive promise to pay the particular debt, after attaining majority, is not sustained by the more modern decisions."[1] Time has not with us lessened the force of Kent's observation, many years ago, that "the books appear to leave the question in some obscurity, when and to what extent a positive act on the part of the infant is requisite."[2]

It may be remarked that a great change was gradually developed in the law of infancy, by making contracts voidable which before were deemed void.[3] This might reasonably be deemed to have introduced a new element into the consideration of such cases; the result tending towards freedom in the courts, and enabling them to repudiate artificial refinements and do substantial justice. It certainly throws upon the modern courts a greater responsibility than formerly in ruling between complete and incomplete ratification; or (if legal precision requires another expression), in determining whether a new promise has passed from the person after attaining full age. But this change has not always been kept in view.

In New York the modern doctrine is that ratification or confirmation of the contract made in infancy will bind the party if it take place after his coming of age; that a new promise, positive and precise, equivalent to a new contract, is not now essential; but a ratification or confirmation of what was done during the minority is sufficient to make the contract obligatory.[4] And it is well observed that the words "ratify and confirm" necessarily import that there was something in existence to which the ratification or confirmation could attach, entirely ignoring therefore the notion that an infant's obligations or contracts were extinguished by the state of infancy.[5]

1 Per Davies J., Henry *v.* Root, 33 N. Y. 545 (1865).
2 2 Kent Com. 237.
3 See ch. 2, *supra*.
4 Henry *v.* Root, 33 N. Y. 526.
5 Ib.

It is settled that silence for an unreasonable time taken in connection with other facts, such as using the property purchased, retaining possession of it, selling or mortgaging it, or in any way converting it to the infant purchaser's own use, would be sufficient ratification to bind the infant after reaching manhood.[1] As where a minor bought a yoke of oxen, for which he gave his note, and after arriving at full age converted the oxen to his own use and received the avails.[2] Mere lapse of time, it is true, will not usually amount to confirmation. But a brief lapse of time in connection with other circumstances may amount to confirmation.[3] And cases are not wanting to establish the position that ratification will be inferred from tacit assent under circumstances where silence is not excusable.

Yet that the cases are somewhat conflicting and difficult to be reconciled, will appear from the citation of a few. In Alabama, an infant ten days before majority purchased a note and drew an order upon a third person in payment, and received notice of non-payment. It was held in a suit several years after that his failure to renew the note and disaffirm, warranted the conclusion that he intended to abide by it.[4] Still more rigidly was the same doctrine enforced in an earlier New York case.[5] Part-payment, or even promise of part-payment, may operate as confirmation.[6] So may authority given to an agent to pay, though the agent does nothing.[7] Submitting the question of liability after coming of age to arbitration does not amount to ratification.[8] But letters indicating intent to

[1] See note Am. editor in 16 E. L. & Eq. 558; Lawson *v.* Lovejoy, 8 Me. 405; Boyden *v.* Boyden, 9 Met. 519; Cheshire *v.* Barrett, 4 McCord, 241; Boody *v.* McKenney, 23 Me. 517.

[2] Lawson *v.* Lovejoy, 8 Me. 405. And see Alexander *v.* Heriot, 1 Bail. Ch. 223; Deason *v.* Boyd, 1 Dana, 45; Vandevort's Appeal, 43 Penn. St. 462; Stern *v.* Freeman, 4 Met. (Ky.) 309; Belton *v.* Briggs, 4 Desaus. 465.

[3] Cresinger *v.* Welch, 15 Ohio, 156.

[4] Thomasson *v.* Boyd, 13 Ala. 419.

[5] Delano *v.* Blake, 11 Wend. 85.

[6] Little *v.* Duncan, 9 Rich. Law, 55; Stokes *v.* Brown, 4 Chand. (Wis.) 39.

[7] Orvis *v.* Kimball, 3 N. H. 314.

[8] Benham *v.* Bishop, 9 Conn. 330.

abide by a former award may; as well as the enjoyment of its benefits.[1] A promise to settle by note against a third party is held sufficient.[2] So is a promise to settle by work.[3] Nor do the recent cases seem to require that a promise to settle should be very precisely expressed. The mere retention of consideration money appears to amount to ratification in California.[4] But this is not the general rule elsewhere.[5] Keeping and using an article purchased during infancy, with equivocal expressions of intention, may bind the infant so that he cannot return it afterwards to the vendor. A verbal promise is sufficient to bind.[6] A contract to work is ratified by continuance in the employer's service for a month after attaining full age.[7] Plea of the execution of a note, in defence of a suit in assumpsit, is held to be confirmation of the note itself.[8] Slight words importing recognition and confirmation of the promise, have been treated as sufficient; or, at least, as sufficient for a jury to consider.[9]

On the other hand are numerous decisions which seem to bear against the creditor. Says a Massachusetts judge in an early case: "By the authorities a mere acknowledgment of the debt, such as would take a case out of the statute of limitations, is not a ratification of a contract made during minority."[10] Yet the much-quoted distinction there taken between "acknowledgment" that a debt is due, and verbal "ratification and confirmation" is either exceedingly subtle, or at the present day frequently misapplied. The distinction further developed leads, as we find, to the conclusion that where one says he

1 Barnaby *v.* Barnaby, 1 Pick. 221; Jones *v.* Phenix Bank, 4 Seld. 228.

2 Taft *v.* Sergeant, 18 Barb. 320.

3 Edgerly *v.* Shaw, 5 Fost. 514.

4 Hastings *v.* Dollarhide, 24 Cal. 195.

5 Benham *v.* Bishop, 9 Conn. 330.

6 West *v.* Penny, 16 Ala. 186; Martin *v.* Mayo, 10 Mass. 137.

7 Forsyth *v.* Hastings, 27 Vt. 646.

8 Best *v.* Givens, 3 B. Monr. 72.

9 Hoit *v.* Underhill, 9 N. H. 436; Bay *v* Gunn, 1 Denio, 108; Whitney *v.* Dutch, 14 Mass. 457.

10 Whitney *v.* Dutch, 14 Mass, 460, per Parker C. J.

owes the debt and has not the means of payment, but will pay as soon as able, or words to this effect, this is only an acknowledgment, and not binding.[1] Such decisions do not always support the explanation sometimes given, that the American cases proceed upon the ground of *intention* to ratify, though there are cases which support so reasonable a view.[2]

What is it that suffices to take a case out of the statute of limitations? "Either an express promise to pay, or an unqualified acknowledgment of *present* indebtedness; in which latter case *the law will imply a promise to pay*."[3] What is ratification of a contract? So far as a definition may be hazarded, it is a voluntary admission that one is *liable and bound* by the terms of an existing though inchoate or imperfect contract. A debt is, of course, created by contract, express or implied. But some say that there must always be a new contract made by the minor on reaching majority. To hold that a new contract for payment is essential, differs certainly from ruling that ratification and confirmation of an existing contract binds one who was lately an infant. But once again such contracts of an infant are called voidable. Does not the term *voidable* imply something still different? something which binds until expressly repudiated? And if so, how doubly inconsistent to exact a specific promise to pay, over and above an admission of present indebtedness. In truth, the law is here overburdened with its own definitions; judicial terms, inconsistent and varied, bewilder the judicial mind; and thankless, indeed, must be the task of refining upon distinctions which rest upon no rational basis of difference.[4]

[1] See Proctor *v.* Sears, 4 Allen, 95; Thompson *v.* Lay, 4 Pick. 48; Ford *v.* Phillips, 1 Pick. 203; Hall *v.* Gerrish, 8 N. H. 374; Goodsell *v.* Myers, 3 Wend, 479; Wilcox *v.* Roath, 12 Conn. 550; Chandler *v.* Glover, 32 Penn. St. 509.

[2] See Thing *v.* Libbey, 16 Me. 55; Dana *v.* Stearns, 3 Cush. 372; Smith *v.* Kelly, 13 Met. 309. And see note to 16 E. L. & Eq. 558.

[3] See Gailey *v.* Crane, 21 Pick. 523; Wakeman *v.* Sherman, 5 Seld. 91; Marshall C. J., in Clemenstine *v.* Williamson, 8 Cranch, 72; Story J., in Bell *v.* Morrison, 1 Pet. 351.

[4] See *supra.* Lord Kenyon seems responsible for the doctrine that the

The writer makes no attempt to reconcile the numerous *dicta* of the courts on this important subject. They are irreconcilable. If American decisions themselves may be regarded as pointing out a general rule, it seems to be this: that the mere acknowledgment that a certain transaction constitutes a debt is insufficient to bind him lately an infant; but that an acknowledgment to the extent that he justly owes that debt, with equivocal expressions as to some future payment, may or may not be considered sufficient, though the better opinion is in favor of their sufficiency; that acts or omissions on his part, which are prejudicial to the adult party's interests, or evince his own intention to retain the advantages of a contract made during infancy may be, especially when reasonable time has elapsed, construed into a ratification, — the presumption of honorable motives being fair and reasonable under such circumstances; and finally, that a distinct, unequivocal promise, verbal or written, made after attaining majority, is always sufficient, this apparently superseding the former promise altogether.[1]

Some cases go even farther, and require an express repudiation on the infant's part. Such is the principle which seems

case of infancy differs in essence from that under the statute of limitations. He says: "In the case of an infant, I shall hold an acknowledgment not to be sufficient, and require proof of an *express promise* to pay, made by the infant, after he had attained that age when the law presumes that he has discretion." Thrupp *v.* Fielder, 2 Esp. 628. But the learned judge probably had not reflected that the law implies a promise to pay in every case under the statute of limitations where none is expressed. And if mere acts and circumstances may raise an implied promise at law, so as to bind the infant, it would be reasonable to suppose that the terms of an acknowledgment of present indebtedness might be strong enough to do the same. The intent to be *bound* by a contract made during infancy would seem more material than the intent to provide definitely for its adjustment.

[1] See American cases collected in Am. editor's note to 16 E. L. & Eq. 558; Bobo *v.* Hansell, 2 Bail. 114; Ackerman *v.* Bunyon, 1 Hilt. (N.Y.), 58; Vaughan *v.* Parr, 20 Ark. 600; Richardson *v.* Boright, 9 Vt. 368; Hodges *v.* Hunt, 22 Barb. 150; State *v.* Plaisted, 43 N. H. 413; Wright *v.* Steele, 2 N. H. 51; Conklin *v.* Ogborn, 7 Ind. 553; Merriam *v.* Wilkins, 6 N. H. 413; Jones *v.* Butler, 30 Barb. 641; Curtis *v.* Patton, 11 S. & R. 305; Norris *v.* Vance, 3 Rich. 164. See Oswald *v.* Broderick, 1 Clarke (Iowa), 380.

to support the partnership cases already noticed,[1] and it comports with the theory that such contracts are voidable. And in several recent instances the English courts have held that an infant shareholder is *prima facie* liable to pay calls or assessments, and must repudiate within a reasonable time after attaining manhood, or remain bound.[2] But stock and partnership transactions stand upon a footing somewhat peculiar, and we are not justified in deducing therefrom a general principle that express repudiation is necessary in all voidable contracts of an infant; for the decisions certainly do not go to this length, whatever the *dicta*.[3]

Express acts of disaffirmance leave no doubt of intention on this point; and they, of course, suffice to avoid the contract made during infancy. As in a sale where one gives notice that he considers the bargain void, and offers to return the consideration.[4] There are many other ways in which one may disavow his intention of carrying into effect the contract made during infancy, as by leaving the service of the person to whom he was engaged and going into the service of another, entering lands once conveyed and conveying them anew; but he should lose no time after reaching majority in averring his intent and pursuing his remedies.

It is not essential to a valid ratification that the person lately an infant should know that he was not legally liable on his contract made during infancy.[5] Ignorance of the law excuses no one. But there is a *dictum* of Lord Alvanley to the contrary, which has been frequently repeated in American

1 See Goode *v.* Harrison, 5 B. & Ald. 147; *supra*, ch. 2.

2 Dublin & Wicklow R. R. Co. *v.* Black, 8 Exch. 181; 16 E. L. & Eq. 556; Smith Contracts, 285, and cases cited.

3 See Holmes *v.* Blogg, 8 Taunt. 39; Richardson *v.* Boright, 9 Vt. 368; Kline *v.* Beebe, 6 Conn. 494; Hoit *v.* Underhill, 9 N. H. 439.

4 See Willis *v.* Twambly, 13 Mass. 204; Aldrich *v.* Grimes, 10 N. H. 194; Williams *v.* Norris, 2 Litt. 157; Hill *v.* Anderson, 5 S. & M. 216; M'Gill *v.* Woodward, 3 Brev. 401.

5 Morse *v.* Wheeler, 4 Allen, 570; Met. Contr. 59.

courts, and once constituted the basis of a decision in Pennsylvania.[1]

A conditional promise when of age to perform a contract made during minority will not sustain an action thereon without proof that the condition has been fulfilled.[2]

If an infant makes a lease of his land (which is binding if for his benefit, but not otherwise), and accepts rent after attaining full age, and by other slight acts affirms the contract, this is a ratification, and he cannot afterwards disaffirm.[3] And where a minor mortgages his land, and on coming of age conveys it to another person in fee, subject to the mortgage, which he recognized in the second deed, it is held to be a ratification of the mortgage.[4] Ratification of a conveyance is ratification of the mortgage made to secure payment; he cannot repudiate the one and not the other.[5] So slight acts of assent on the infant's part are held sufficient to confirm leases made by a guardian beyond the term of his authority.[6]

As to the infant's mortgage, it may be further remarked that a minor cannot avoid a mortgage given to secure either real or personal property purchased by him without avoiding the sale also.[7] The purchase and mortgage back constitute one transaction. And an assignment of the mortgage will carry to the assignee all the mortgagee's rights, whether the infant affirms or disaffirms.[8] The subsequent ratification of a mortgage, as of other deeds, relates back to the first delivery, so as to affect

1 Harmer *v.* Killing, 5 Esp. 103; Hinely *v.* Margaritz, 3 Barr, 428. See Curtis *v.* Patton, 11 S. & R. 305; Reed *v.* Boshears, 4 Sneed, 118; Norris *v.* Vance, 3 Rich. 164.

2 Proctor *v.* Sears, 4 Allen, 95; Everson *v.* Carpenter, 17 Wend. 419; Chandler *v.* Glover, 32 Penn. St. 509.

3 Ashfield *v.* Ashfield, W. Jones, 157; Wimberley *v.* Jones, 1 Geo. Dec. 91.

4 Boston Bank *v.* Chamberlin, 15 Mass. 220; Story *v.* Johnson, 2 Yo. & Coll. Exch. 607; Phillips *v.* Green, 5 Monr. 355; Lynde *v.* Budd, 2 Paige, 191.

5 Young *v.* McKee, 13 Mich. 552; Bigelow *v.* Kinney, 3 Vt. 353; Robbins *v.* Eaton, 10 N. H. 561.

6 See Smith *v.* Low, 1 Atk. 489.

7 Heath *v.* West, 8 Fost. 101; Dana *v.* Coombs, 6 Greenl. 89.

8 Ottman *v.* Moak, 3 Sandf. Ch. 431.

all intermediate persons, except purchasers for a valuable consideration.[1] And where a loan of money was made to an infant for which he executed a bond and mortgage, and in a will made after he became of age directed the payment of "all his just debts" and died; it was held that the will sufficiently confirmed the mortgage.[2] Even notes given for the purchase-money of land, not secured by mortgage, have been equitably enforced; and the court has refused to permit the notes to be disaffirmed and the land reclaimed.[3]

It would seem that the infant is not precluded from disaffirming his conveyance of real estate by the mere lapse of time. Laches is not imputable to an infant.[4] Where land has been sold by an infant it was said in a Connecticut case, years ago, the period of acquiescence being thirty-five years, that the infant ought to declare his disaffirmance within a reasonable time; and similar *dicta* may be found in other courts; but there seems to be no doubt upon the decided cases, that mere acquiescence is no confirmation of a sale of lands unless it has been prolonged for the statutory period of limitation; and that an avoidance may be made any time before the statute has barred an entry.[5]

Yet lapse of time, together with slight circumstances, have in many instances sufficed to sustain an infant's deed. A Missouri case, indeed, holds that mere declarations or a promise upon contingency will not ratify and confirm.[6] But the authorities generally manifest extreme repugnance at setting

[1] Palmer *v.* Miller, 25 Barb. 399.

[2] Merchants' Fire Ins. Co. *v.* Grant, 2 Edw. Ch. 544.

[3] Weed *v.* Beebe, 21 Vt. 495.

[4] Smith *v.* Sackett, 5 Gilm. 534.

[5] 1 Am. Lead. Cas. 4th ed. 256; Met. Contr. 60, 61 and cases cited; Tucker *v.* Moreland, 10 Pet. 58; Boody *v.* McKenney, 23 Me. 517; Drake *v.* Ramsay, 5 Ohio, 251; Jackson *v.* Burchin, 14 Johns. 124; Urban *v.* Grimes, 2 Grant, 96; Vaughan *v.* Parr, 20 Ark. 600; Voorhies *v.* Voorhies, 24 Barb. 150; Ware *v.* Brush, 1 McLean, 533; Moore *v.* Abernethy, 7 Blackf. 442; Cole *v.* Pennoyer, 14 Ill. 158.

[6] Clamorgan *v.* Lane, 9 Mis. 446.

aside a solemn conveyance of land and re-opening beneficial transactions, merely to suit the caprice or dishonorable intent of infants.[1] This may explain another *dictum* to the effect that an infant's deed will be confirmed by any deliberate act after he comes of age, by which he takes benefit under it or recognizes its validity;[2] which is not without precedents for support. Thus, in some instances where the infant after coming of age saw the purchaser make valuable improvements and incur considerable expense, and said nothing for years, he was held bound.[3] So, too, it would seem, where one knowing his title, permits another to purchase without giving notice of his claim.[4] While mere lapse of time less than the statute period will not suffice, yet the lapse of a less period in connection with such circumstances may. A tribunal of justice may properly decline to become the instrument of a knave. So, in Illinois, the statute makes conveyances of a minor binding, unless disaffirmed and repudiated within three years after reaching majority.[5]

The purchaser of an infant's lands succeeds to all the infant's rights in relation to it, although those rights grow out of his infancy.[6]

Whether it is necessary that an entry upon the land to regain seisin be made to perfect the title of the person intending to disaffirm his conveyance as infant, does not clearly appear from the authorities. The old rule was that in order to avoid a feoffment this was necessary. But conveyance by feoffment has been superseded by other methods of transferring

[1] See cases cited in last section.

[2] McCormic *v.* Leggett, 8 Jones, 425.

[3] Wheaton *v.* East, 5 Yerg. 41; Wallace *v.* Lewis, 4 Harring. 75; Jones *v.* Phenix Bank, 4 Seld. 235.

[4] Hall *v.* Simmons, 2 Rich. Eq. 120; Alsworth *v.* Cordtz, 31 Miss. 32; Belton *v.* Briggs, 4 Desaus. 465; Cresinger *v.* Welch, 15 Ohio, 156; Emmons *v.* Murray, 16 N. H. 385.

[5] Blankenship *v.* Stout, 25 Ill. 132. And see Ferguson *v.* Bell, 17 Mis. 347; Bostwick *v.* Atkins, 3 Comst. 53; Pursley *v.* Hays, 17 Iowa, 311; Sheldon *v.* Newton, 3 Ohio N. S. 494; Rainsford *v.* Rainsford, Spears Ch. 385.

[6] Thompson *v.* Gaillard, 3 Rich. 418. See Jackson *v.* Todd, 6 Johns. 257; Hall *v.* Jones, 21 Md. 439.

real property in England, and it is not in use here. In some of the earlier New York cases, where an infant had sold wild lands to other persons, and had after coming of age conveyed by similar deed the same lands to another, it was held that the first conveyance had been legally avoided, and the last purchaser was entitled to the property.[1] A case before the Supreme Court in the United States is supposed to sustain the same view; only *arguendo*, however, for in point of fact the person making the second conveyance remained in possession all the time; and, as the court observed, "could not enter upon himself."[2] Following the indication of these three important cases, several of the State courts have since held that a conveyance by an infant of the same land to another person, after he comes of age, effectually avoids a deed of bargain and sale made in infancy; and this without entry on his part.[3] But the New York courts have latterly been disposed to retrace their steps; reluctance to do injury to others, doubtless, contributing to increase the strictness of requirements on the infant's part. Their present rule appears to be that, unless the lands were wholly vacant, or the infant remained in possession, he must make an entry or do some other act of equal notoriety before he can pass title by a second conveyance.[4] There is no authority in the New England States to oppose this later doctrine; nor do we find any in the other Middle States.[5] But doubt is removed by statutes, in Maine, Massachusetts, and some other States, which permit parties to recover land by writ of entry without making actual entry. And it is held in

[1] Jackson *v.* Carpenter, 11 Johns. 539; Jackson *v.* Burchin, 14 Johns. 124. See Met. Contr. 44, 45, where this subject is discussed.

[2] Tucker *v.* Moreland, 10 Pet. 58, per Story J.

[3] Hoyle *v.* Stowe, 2 Dev. & Bat. 320; Pitcher *v.* Laycock, 7 Ind. 398; McGan *v.* Marshall, 7 Humph. 121; Hughes *v.* Watson, 10 Ohio, 127; Peterson *v.* Laik, 24 Mis. 541.

[4] Dominick *v.* Michael, 4 Sandf. 421; Bool *v.* Mix, 17 Wend. 133; Voorhies *v.* Voorhies, 24 Barb. 150.

[5] See Roberts *v.* Wiggin, 1 N. H. 75; Worcester *v.* Eaton, 13 Mass. 375. See also Harrison *v.* Adcock, 8 Geo. 68; Moore *v.* Abernathy, 7 Blackf. 442.

Maine, that such a writ dispenses with entry and amounts to disaffirmance.[1]

If an infant contract to sell real estate he cannot be held to the agreement after attaining majority upon refusal to sanction it.[2] But it is held that acquiescing in the settlement of boundaries after coming of age binds the infant.[3]

The same reasoning which applies to property transferred by the infant applies to his purchases. If an infant, for instance, takes a conveyance of land during minority and retains possession after coming to majority, circumstances may make that a binding transaction. So if an infant lessee remains in possession of the house or land demised, and pays rent after majority, he cannot repudiate the lease afterwards.[4]

When an infant purchases property, and continues to enjoy the use of the same, and then sells it or any part of it, and receives the money for it, he must be considered as having elected to affirm the contract, and he cannot afterwards avoid payment of the consideration.[5] Some authorities would confine the affirmation of a purchase of land to an actual subsequent sale, but this is quite unreasonable, and contrary to the general doctrine; for there may be many other acts which constitute just as full and undoubted evidence of a design on the infant's part to affirm such contract as an actual sale of the land. Thus continuous occupation of premises, improvements, and offers to sell, have been deemed sufficient.[6] And Chief-Justice Shaw observes that if an infant, after coming of age, retains landed property purchased by him during minority for his own

[1] Chadbourne *v.* Rackliff, 30 Me. 354. And see Cole *v.* Pennoyer, 14 Ill. 158. Mr. Metcalf appears to doubt the correctness of the rule in Jackson *v.* Carpenter, even as to cases of wild lands. See Met. Contr. 45, 46 and cases cited.

[2] Walker *v.* Ellis, 12 Ill. 470. Still less if fraud be practised upon him. Griffis *v.* Younger, 6 Ired. Eq. 520.

[3] George *v.* Thomas, 16 Tex. 74.

[4] Holmes *v.* Blogg, 8 Taunt. 35; Smith Contr. 284; Bac. Abr. tit. Infant, K. 612; Baxter *v.* Bush, 29 Vt. 465; Armfield *v.* Tate, 7 Ired. 258.

[5] Boody *v.* McKenney, 10 Shep. 517; Hubbard *v.* Cummings, 1 Me. 11; Boyden *v.* Boyden, 9 Met. 519; Robbins *v.* Eaton, 10 N. H. 561.

[6] See Robbins *v.* Eaton, 10 N. H. 561.

use, or sells or otherwise disposes of it, such acts being only conscientiously done with intent to ratify or affirm, affirmation or ratification may be inferred.[1] The same principle has been declared in other cases, even to the extent of holding that mere continuance in possession is an affirmance.[2] It will be observed that such latter conduct involves two elements: lapse of time and the exercise of acts of ownership.

This rule was applied in a recent well-considered New York case, upon a full examination of the authorities. An infant had given his note for certain real estate; and, very foolishly, or very dishonorably, endeavored to avoid payment upon majority, while holding to the benefits of his purchase. It was held that by his acts he had ratified the contract of purchase.[3]

Since a married woman conveys her lands, by force of statute provisions, perplexing questions may arise as to the effect of a conveyance executed in conformity with late acts, yet ineffectual because of her infancy.[4] It would appear from some late American cases, that the wife still continuing covert after becoming of age, acts which might constitute ratification in ordinary cases may not always be set up against her.[5]

To render a subsequent conveyance an act of dissent to the prior conveyance of an infant, it must be inconsistent therewith, so that the two cannot stand together.[6] And it is held that where land was conveyed by a person under age in exchange for other lands, and he after coming of age sells and conveys the lands so received, the last deed amounts to a confirmation of the first.[7]

By a well-known rule of equity, the proceeds of lands sold

[1] See Boyden *v.* Boyden, *supra.*

[2] Dana *v.* Coombs, 6 Greenl. 89; Cheshire *v.* Barrett, 4 McCord, 241; Lynde *v.* Budd, 2 Paige, 191.

[3] Henry *v.* Root, 33 N. Y. 526.

[4] Harbman *v.* Kendall, 4 Ind. 403.

[5] Matherson *v.* Davis, 2 Cold. 443; Miles *v.* Lingerman, 24 Ind. 385. This subject appears to have received little attention as yet; but the equity doctrine, to argue from the case of marriage settlements, appears to be that the wife may by acts give validity to such deeds, after attaining full age and notwithstanding her coverture. See *supra*, ch. 1.

[6] Leitensdorfer *v.* Hempstead, 18 Mis. 269; McGan *v.* Marshall, 7 Humph. 121.

[7] Williams *v.* Mabee, 3 Halst. Ch. 500.

during minority retain the character of real estate. And such property remains real and not personal, even after the infant attains majority, so long as there is no act or intent on his part to change its character;[1] but the character ceases when he attains majority, and obtains possession of the proceeds.[2]

Where a new promise is requisite on reaching majority, it must be made to the party with whom the infant contracted, or to his agent or attorney; not to a stranger.[3] But a promise to an agent authorized to present the claim and receive payment and give discharge, binds him lately an infant.[4] And where a writing addressed to another than the plaintiff is relied on, not as constituting a ratification or containing a promise, but as evidence of a ratification previously made by the defendant, it is held admissible in the plaintiff's favor.[5] Nor is it necessary that the agent should have disclosed his authority before the defendant made his admission.[6]

So, too, while an infant, or one in priority with him, may object to a contract on the ground that it was not for his benefit, a third person, a stranger, has no right to say that the infant may not make or assume what contract he pleases.[7]

An act of the infant, clearly showing his intention not to be bound by a mortgage, is a sufficient avoidance of it.[8] A prompt declaration of intention to disaffirm, and conveyance to another, will answer.[9] So a contract of sale.[10] But no express ratification is necessary to confirm his conveyance. Acts and omissions may be construed by a jury as amounting to confirmation.[11] And a party in possession under the deed of an infant cannot be regarded as a trespasser before it is avoided.[12]

1 Foreman *v.* Foreman, 7 Barb. 215.

2 Forman *v.* Marsh, 1 Kern. 544.

3 Bigelow *v.* Grannis, 2 Hill, 120; Goodsell *v.* Myers, 3 Wend. 479.

4 Mayer *v.* McLure, 36 Miss. 389.

5 Stern *v.* Freeman, 4 Met. (Ky.) 309.

6 Hoit *v.* Underhill, 10 N. H. 220. And see Tate *v.* Tate, 1 Dev. & Bat. 22.

7 See Douglas *v.* Watson, 34 E. L. & Eq. 447.

8 State *v.* Plaisted, 43 N. H. 413.

9 White *v.* Flora, 2 Overton, 426; Hoyle *v.* Stowe, 2 Dev. & Bat. 320.

10 Mustard *v.* Wohlford, 15 Gratt. 329. And see Cook *v.* Toumbs, 36 Miss. 685.

11 Phillips *v.* Green, 5 Monr. 344; Scott *v.* Buchanan, 11 Humph. 468; Houser *v.* Reynolds, 1 Hayw. 143.

12 Wallace *v.* Lewis, 4 Harring. 75.

An infant upon reaching majority, who chooses to disaffirm his sale of real estate, may do so, without first refunding, or offering to refund, the purchase-money. This is declared in several cases.[1] But the principle is firmly established by the courts that he cannot on attaining full age hold to the purchase, and thus affirm that, while pleading his infancy to avoid the payment of the purchase-money.[2] He must, sooner or later, place the original purchaser in *statu quo;* this common honesty, as well as the law, demands. For this purpose the purchaser may bring suit. And the same principle applies alike to property, real or personal.

So if an infant sell goods and receive the money for them, he cannot recover back the goods without returning the money.[3] Nor damage property he has received, and then demand the full price, on offering to restore it.[4] Nor recover partnership property after rescinding the partnership agreement, while liabilities of the firm are outstanding.[5] If the former vendee be sued for use and occupation of land, it is held that he may recoup for valuable improvements.[6] And the plea of false warranty may sometimes be set up against the infant's attempt by affirmance to enforce a hard bargain.[7] To multiply these illustrations is unnecessary; the cardinal principle is to do substantial justice between the two parties to a contract.

1 Pitcher *v.* Laycock, 7 Ind. 398; Cresinger *v.* Welch, 15 Ohio, 156; Miles *v.* Lingerman, 24 Ind. 385. But see Stuart *v.* Baker, 17 Tex. 417.

2 Kline *v.* Beall, 6 Conn. 494; Bailey *v.* Barnberger, 11 B. Monr. 113; Strain *v.* Wright, 7 Geo. 568; Hillyer *v.* Bennett, 3 Edw. Ch. 222; Lowry *v.* Drake, 1 Dana, 46; Kitchen *v.* Lee, 11 Paige, 107; Tipton *v.* Tipton, 3 Jones, 552; Womack *v.* Womack, 8 Tex. 397; Smith *v.* Evans, 5 Humph. 70; Manning *v.* Johnson, 26 Ala. 446.

3 Badger *v.* Phinney, 15 Mass. 359; Bartholemew *v.* Finnemore, 17 Barb. 428.

4 Carr *v.* Clough, 6 Fost. 280; Bartholemew *v.* Finnemore, *supra.*

5 Furlong *v.* Bartlett, 21 Pick. 401; Sadler *v.* Robinson, 2 Stew. 520.

6 Weaver *v.* Jones, 24 Ala. 420.

7 Morrill *v.* Aden, 19 Vt. 505. And see Heath *v.* West, 8 Fost. 101; Shipman *v.* Horton, 17 Conn. 481; Edgarton *v.* Wolf, 6 Gray, 453.

CHAPTER VI.

ACTIONS BY AND AGAINST INFANTS.

It is a fundamental principle that the rights of property shall vest in infants, notwithstanding their tender years; and incidentally thereto they have the right of action. Yet, it is clear that if the infant is unfit to make a contract he is unfit to sue on his own behalf. Hence is the rule that while process is sued out in the infant's own name, it is in his name by another; that is to say, some person of full age must conduct the suit for him. The same principle applies to all civil actions, whether founded on a contract or not.

At common law, infants could neither sue nor defend, except by guardian. They were authorized, by Stat. Westm. 1, to sue by *prochein ami* (or next friend) against the guardian in chivalry, who had aliened any portion of the infant's inheritance.[1] Stat. Westm. 2, ch. 15, extended this privilege to all other cases where they could not sue formally. Lord Coke lays down that, since these statutes, the infant shall sue by *prochein ami* and defend by guardian.[2] And Fitzherbert is to the same effect.[3] But Mr. Hargrave thinks it probable that Fitzherbert and Lord Coke did not mean to exclude the election of suing either by *prochein ami* or by guardian.[4] And whether they did or not, guardianship at the present day, so unlike guardianship as they understood it, justifies the modern practice; which is to appoint a special person as *prochein ami* only in case of necessity, where an infant is to sue his guardian, or the

[1] Macphers. Inf. 13, 352.

[2] 2 Inst. 261, 390; Co. Litt. 135 *b*; 3 Robinson's Pract. 229.

[3] F. N. B. [27] H.

[4] Harg. *n.* Co Litt. 135 *b*.

guardian will not sue for him, or it is improper that the guardian should be the *prochein ami.* In other cases, the rule is to sue by guardian or *prochein ami.*[1] But an infant may sue by his next friend though he has a guardian, if the guardian does not dissent.[2] And in some States the choice allowed the infant is still more liberal.[3]

An infant cannot prosecute an action either in person or by attorney. This is well settled.[4] But advantage must be taken by plea in abatement of the infant's suing by attorney, or by application to a judge, or the court, for it is not error after judgment either on verdict or by default.[5] Where infancy of the plaintiff is pleaded in abatement to a suit brought by a minor in his own name without any guardian or next friend, the court may allow the infant to amend by inserting in his writ that he sues by A., his next friend.[6] Nor does this rule deprive the infant of the professional services of an attorney; it relates to the parties to the suit.[7]

Generally speaking, when an action is brought by an infant, he sues in his own name by a certain person as next friend. A *prochein ami*, commencing his authority with the writ and declaration, can only maintain the suit for such causes of action as may be prosecuted without special demand; as for personal injuries done to the infant, or for sums of money where the writ itself is considered as the demand.[8] In England, it was once considered that the special admission of a guardian for an

[1] Claridge *v.* Crawford, 1 Dowl. & Ry. 13; 3 Robinson's Pract. 230; Younge *v.* Younge, Cro. Car. 86; Goodwin *v.* Moore, Cro. Car. 161; Apthorp *v.* Backus, Kirby, 407; M'Giffin *v.* Stout, Coxe, 92.

[2] Thomas *v.* Dike, 11 Vt. 273; Robson *v.* Osborn, 13 Tex. 298.

[3] Hooks *v.* Smith, 18 Ala. 338.

[4] Cro. Eliz. 424; Cro. Jac. 5; 1 Co. Lit. 135 *b*· Harg. *n.* 220; Miles *v.* Boyden, 3 Pick. 213; Clark *v.* Turner, 1 Root, 200; Mockey *v.* Grey, 2 Johns. 192; Timmons *v.* Timmons, 6 Ind. 8; Nicholson *v.* Wilborn, 13 Geo. 467.

[5] 2 Saund. Pleading, 207; Bird *v.* Pegg, 5 B. & Ald. 418; Finley *v.* Jowle, 13 East, 6; Apthorp *v.* Backus, Kirby, 407. But as to the infant himself, see Bird *v.* Pegg; Jones *v.* Steele, 36 Mis. 324.

[6] Blood *v.* Harrington, 8 Pick. 552.

[7] People *v.* New York C.P., 11 Wend. 164.

[8] Miles *v.* Boyden, 3 Pick. 219.

infant to appear in one case would serve for others.[1] But the modern rule is that the special admission of *prochein ami* or guardian, to prosecute or defend for an infant, shall not be deemed an authority to prosecute or defend in any but the particular action specified.[2] Sometimes there would be an advantage in suing by guardian if this can legally be done.[3]

The guardian, like the *prochein ami*, is, in English practice, appointed by the court before the plaintiff can proceed in the action, and no legal right of parentage or of guardianship will enable any one to act for the infant without such appointment.[4] But where the infant's father, being a necessary witness, could not properly be *prochein ami* in a certain suit, the court, on motion, appointed a friend of the family with the father's concurrence.[5] No authority from the infant to the guardian or *prochein ami* to sue is necessary, though the infant be on the very eve of majority; though it is intimated that the court might interfere if fraud was shown.[6] As the *prochein ami* is an officer of the court, if the infant wishes him removed he must apply to the court for that purpose, and an entry of the change should be made of record.[7] But on the plaintiff coming of age, he may, it seems, remove the *prochein ami* of his own authority, and appear thereafter by his own attorney.[8]

But while, in theory, the *prochein ami* is still legally appointed by the court, in practice, such formalities are now very generally waived. In Connecticut, Massachusetts, Virginia, and other States, no entry of record is requisite admitting a person to sue as guardian or next friend, the recital in the writ and count being deemed sufficient evidence of admission unless seasonably challenged by the opposite party, when the order may be

[1] Archer *v.* Frowde, 1 Stra. 304.
[2] 2 Saund. Plead. 207; Macphers. Inf. 353.
[3] 3 Robinson's Pract. 229.
[4] Macphers. Inf. 353.
[5] Claridge *v.* Crawford, 1 Dowl. & Ry. 13.
[6] Morgan *v.* Thorne, 9 Dowl. 228.
[7] Davies *v.* Locket, 4 Taunt. 765; Morgan *v.* Thorne, ib.
[8] See Bac. Abr. Infant, K. 2.

supplied.[1] In New York, on the other hand, a *prochein ami* must be appointed for the infant plaintiff before process is sued out; and such is the practice in some other parts of this country.[2]

So, too, in this country, more deference seems to be shown to the infant's wishes than in England. Thus, in Massachusetts, the court on the personal petition of a minor, twenty years of age, withdrew the authority of the *prochein ami*, and ordered all further proceedings in the suit postponed until the minor should attain full years.[3] In the choice of a guardian and *prochein ami*, a minor above fourteen has much latitude of discretion; and when he attains full age he may enter the fact upon record, and without further formality proceed to conduct the suit for himself.[4]

Where an infant has brought an action by his next friend, and has recovered damages which have been received by the attorney, the money is the money of the infant, and he may sue the attorney for it.[5]

A *prochein ami* is liable for costs, and the remedy is against him for attachment, which should be absolute in the first instance.[6] This is the English practice. It would appear that execution cannot issue against the infant himself; and this from the very circumstance that the next friend is, in theory, one who comes forward to assume all such liabilities.[7] But in conformity with statutes in Massachusetts, it is held that a

[1] See Guild *v.* Cranston, 8 Cush. 506; Burwell *v.* Corbin, 1 Rand. 151; 3 Robinson's Pract. 230; Trask *v.* Stone, 7 Mass. 241; Judson *v.* Blanchard, 3 Conn. 579. And see Stumps *v.* Kelley, 22 Ill. 140.

[2] Wilder *v.* Ember, 12 Wend. 191; Haines *v.* Oatman, 2 Doug. 430.

[3] Guild *v.* Cranston, 8 Cush. 506.

[4] Clark *v.* Watson, 2 Ind. 399; Shuttlesworth *v.* Hughey, 6 Rich. 329.

[5] Collins *v.* Brook, 4 Hurl. & Nor. 276. And see Smith *v.* Redus, 9 Ala. 99.

[6] Newton *v.* London, Brighton, &c. R. R. Co., 7 Dow. & L. 328 (1849); Dow *v.* Clark, 2 Dowl. 302. See Price *v.* Duggan, 4 Man. & Gr. 225.

[7] Ib.; Stephenson *v.* Stephenson, 3 Hey. 123; Perryman *v.* Burgster, 6 Port. (Ala.) 199; Sproule *v.* Botts, 5 J. J. Marsh. 162. But see Proudfoot *v.* Poile, 3 Dow. & L. 524; Macphers. Inf. 356, 357, and cases cited.

prochein ami, as such, is not liable for costs;[1] nor does he seem to be always strictly considered in our courts a party to the suit.[2] And the infant plaintiff is made liable for his own costs.[3]

An infant can appear and defend in civil suits by guardian only, and not by attorney, or in person.[4] The process is the same against an infant as in ordinary cases; but he needs some one to conduct his defence, and hence every court, wherein an infant is sued, has power to appoint a guardian *ad litem*, for the special purposes of the suit, since otherwise he might be without assistance.[5]

A guardian *ad litem* is one appointed for the infant to defend in the particular action brought against him, and is therefore to be distinguished from guardians of the person and estate.[6] If there be a general chancery, probate, or testamentary guardian, already appointed, it is his place to defend the infant from all suits, so long as his authority over the infant's property continues; though this is a matter usually regulated in this country by statute.

What has been observed of the appointment of *prochein ami* may be said, in general, of that of the guardian *ad litem*. The two correspond, and the principles of law applicable to the one are in general to be applied to the other.[7] In a criminal case no guardian *ad litem* is appointed.

The writ and declaration in actions at law against infants are to be made out as in ordinary cases. In English practice, where the defendant neglects to appear, or appears otherwise

1 Crandall *v.* Slaid, 11 Met. 288.

2 Brown *v.* Hull, 16 Vt. 673.

3 Howett *v.* Alexander, 1 Dev. 431; Smith *v.* Floyd, 1 Pick. 275.

4 Co. Litt. 88 *b n.* 16; 135 *b*; 2 Stra. 784; Macphers. Inf. 358; Alderman *v.* Tirrell, 8 Johns. 418; Knapp *v.* Crosby, 1 Mass. 479; Miles *v.* Boyden, 3 Pick. 213; Bedell *v.* Lewis, 4 J. J. Marsh. 562; Starbird *v.* Moore, 21 Vt. 529.

5 Bac. Abr. Guardian, B. 4.

6 Larkin *v.* Mann, 2 Paige, 27; Roberts *v.* Stanton, 2 Munf. 129; Bac. Abr. Guardian *supra*, cases cited by Bouvier.

7 See Macphers. Inf. 358.

than by guardian, the plaintiff may apply for and obtain a summons, calling on him to appear by guardian within a given time; otherwise the plaintiff may be at liberty to proceed as in other cases, having had a nominal guardian assigned to the infant.[1] A like rule prevails in New York and other States.[2] Courts will go so far to protect an infant as to see that process is properly served, a guardian *ad litem* appointed for him, and the formal answer filed.[3]

Infancy may be specially pleaded in bar.[4] The plaintiff replies either that the defendant was of age or that the goods were necessaries, or that he confirmed the contract when he came of age. If there be several defendants, the party who is a minor should plead his infancy separately. Infancy is an issuable plea; and it may be pleaded with other pleas without leave of court.[5] Where there are several issues, one of which is upon the plea of infancy, that being found for the infant, the whole case is disposed of.[6] In New York, infancy may be given in evidence under the general issue.[7]

An infant defendant is liable to costs in the same manner as any other defendant, notwithstanding he has a guardian.[8] Macpherson says that the guardian of an infant defendant is subject to the same liability for costs as the *prochein ami*, or the guardian of an infant plaintiff.[9] No authority is given for this statement, and it seems that the guardian of an infant defendant is not liable.[10]

If an infant comes of age pending the suit, he can assert his

1 See Macphers. Inf. 359.

2 Van Deusen *v.* Brower, 6 Cow. 50; Judson *v.* Storer, 2 South. 544; Clarke *v.* Gilmanton, 12 N. H. 515.

3 Alexander *v.* Frary, 9 Ind. 481.

4 Clemson *v.* Bush, 3 Binn. 413; Hillegass *v.* Hillegass, 5 Barr, 97.

5 15 & 16 Vict. ch. 76, § 84. See Delafield *v.* Tanner, 5 Taunt. 856; Dublin & Wicklow R. R. Co. *v.* Black, 8 Exch. 181.

6 Rohrer *v.* Morningstar, 18 Ohio, 579.

7 Wailing *v.* Toll, 9 Johns. 141.

8 Anderson *v.* Warde, Dyer, 104; Gardiner *v.* Holt, Stra. 1217.

9 Macphers. Inf. 361.

10 See Perryman *v.* Burgster, 6 Port. (Ala.) 199.

rights at once for himself, and if he does not he cannot generally complain of the acts of his guardian *ad litem*.[1]

The same leading principles noticeable in suits at law are to be recognized in equity proceedings, by or against infants ; and the doctrines of next friend and guardian *ad litem* receive ample discussion in the chancery courts.[2]

Among the miscellaneous matters of chancery practice relating to infants, may be mentioned proceedings in partition, orders for maintenance and education, the management of trust funds by guardians and other trustees, and the award of custody. These subjects have already been incidentally considered in the course of this treatise.

1 Mitchell *v.* Berry, 1 Met. (Ky.) 602. And see Marshall *v.* Wing, 50 Me. 62.

2 See 1 Daniell Ch. Pl. 3d Am. ed. 66 *et seq.*; ib. 150 *et seq.*, where the English and American authorities are very fully cited.

PART VI.

MASTER AND SERVANT.

CHAPTER I.

NATURE OF THE RELATION; HOW CREATED AND HOW TERMINATED.

A MASTER is one who has legal authority over another; and the person over whom such authority may be rightfully exercised is his servant.[1] The relation of master and servant presupposes two parties who stand on an unequal footing in their mutual dealings; yet not naturally so, as in other domestic relations, nor necessarily because the subordinate is wanting in either years or discretion. This relation is, in theory, hostile to the genius of free institutions. It bears the marks of social caste. Hence it may be pronounced as a relation of more general importance in ancient than in modern times, and better applicable at this day to English than American society.

Master and servant has, nevertheless, uniformly been regarded as one of the domestic relations. In lands where human slavery is lawfully recognized, it is pre-eminently so; and thus were its foundations deeply laid in the civil law. In the early days of the common law, it formed a distinct part of the English household jurisprudence; and in a state of society where landed proprietors are few and wealthy, where rank and titles are maintained with ostentatious display, where the humble born are taught to obey, rather than aspire, this must so

[1] See Reeve Dom. Rel. 339.

continue. Not only cooks, butlers, and house-maids are thus brought within the scope of this relation, but farm-hands, plantation laborers, stewards, bailiffs, factors, family chaplains, and legal advisers.

Thus is explained what at first may seem an anomaly, that the common law, under the head of master and servant, discusses principles which, in this day, belong more justly to the relation of principal and agent; and that we constantly find an offensive term used in court to denote duties and obligations, which rest upon the pure contract of hiring. Clerks, salaried officers, brokers, commission merchants, all are designated as servants; and our topic in this broad sense is not, if words mean any thing, within the influence of the domestic law at all. Nor is it possible to extend the lines so as to include these persons without abandoning consistency of purpose, and yielding up the vital principle of legal classification.

Were the writer then untrammelled by authority, his treatment of this topic, as one of the domestic relations, would be confined to what are denominated at common law menial servants, so called from being *intra mœnia*, or rather to domestic servants, extending the definition to all such as are employed in and about a family in carrying on the household concerns, whether their occupations be within or without of doors, so long as they constitute part of the family. In this restricted sense, the law of master and servant is manifestly of little importance to-day. But as the reader may have perceived, on perusal of the topic of guardian and ward, legal precision must sometimes be sacrificed to legal usage; and as terms have been carried in both instances beyond their original signification, for the sake of analogy, we are bound to follow, even though it be into logical confusion.

How much the law of master and servant is understood to mean, may be gathered from the books. Blackstone comprehends under this head slaves, menial servants, apprentices, hired laborers, and servants *pro tempore*, such as stewards, factors, and bailiffs, and he thereupon proceeds to discuss principles applicable to all such classes alike.[1] Reeve carries the discussion still further, as to factors, brokers, attorneys, and agents generally.[2] Kent, writing for later readers, with a clearer appreciation of his limits, classifies into slaves, hired servants, and apprentices, and confines his discussion more carefully to what might subserve the wants of the domestic law; yet, not with exactness.[3] None of these writers erred in their general views; the principles of the law had already spread out with the growth of society in such a manner that they were obliged to follow the authorities. For the same reason the present writer, keeping in view the natural boundaries of his subject, will, nevertheless, take a somewhat comprehensive and desultory range; thereby meeting better the practical wants of the lawyer, and satisfying a reasonable expectation.

Slavery, for obvious reasons, need no longer be treated as a branch of the law of master and servant. We come first, then, to hired servants, or servants proper; and as to these the contract between them and their masters arises upon the hiring; the servant being bound to render the service, and the master to pay the stipulated consideration.[4] The next class is that of apprentices: fairly distinguishable, as comprising such, usually minors, as are bound out under public statutes, and over whom, by reason of their tender years, and in accordance with the spirit of such statutes, the master stands somewhat in the stead of a parent. Yet, apprentices might be bound out merely to learn a trade, and as part of the education furnished by their judicious parents; and Blackstone mentions that very large sums were sometimes given with them for their instruction at his day.[5] Thirdly, persons commonly known in popular

[1] 1 Bl. Com. Ch. 14.
[2] Reeve Dom. Rel. 339 *et seq.*
[3] 2 Kent Com. Lec. 32.
[4] 1 Bl. Com. 425; 2 Kent Com. 258.
[5] See 1 Bl. Com. 426; 2 Kent Com. 263, 264.

speech as workmen or *employés*, who are brought within the principles of one or both of the two preceding classes, and to whom the relation of master and servant may well be said to apply. In this class are included day-laborers, factory operatives, miners, colliers, and numerous others, of whom nothing more definite can be said than that they are hired to perform services of a somewhat unambitious character. If to these be added all other occupations to which the same rules are from time to time applied in court, it is gratifying to reflect that the servant is frequently the social equal, or even the superior, of his master.

The rights of workmen or *employés* furnish a fruitful topic for legislation. And so widely do the English and American systems differ in these and kindred matters, that judicial precedents may not always be safely interchanged between the two nations. Further is it to be remarked that apprentices and workmen are very generally affected by the same statutes.

Prior to 1824, English industrial legislation leaned decidedly in favor of the master. Trade monopolies, of which Sir Edward Coke complained so justly, were indeed greatly restricted in the time of James I.;[1] yet their influence was felt down to a much later period; and certain corporations and guilds enjoyed exclusive privileges, which obstructed almost entirely the enterprise of individuals. Attempts were made from time to time to better the condition of the working classes, and to regulate the payment of their wages; but while fines and imprisonment were the punishment of the employed, the employer suffered rarely for his own misconduct beyond rescission of the contract.[2] To exercise a trade in any town without having previously served an apprenticeship of seven years, was a penal offence.[3] So, to entice or seduce artisans to settle abroad and

1 3 Inst. 181. See 4 Bl. Com. 159.

2 See Acts 20 Geo. 2, ch. 19, 6 Geo. 3, ch. 25; Macdonald Handybook, 70, &c.; 1 Bl. Com. 426, 427.

3 4 Bl. Com. 160

communicate their knowledge, to engage in the export of machinery, all this was criminal, and punished with severity, the object proposed by such legislation being to prevent the destruction of home manufactures.[1] An important act, passed in May, 1823, was calculated to ameliorate the condition of workmen, by enlarging the powers of magistrates on behalf of apprentices; yet, English petty magistrates were always inclined to obsequiousness, and their tribunals had not the confidence of the working classes, as remains the fact to this day.

Public sentiment of later years, however, has undergone a great change, and class legislation has fallen into comparative disrepute. No principle so beneficial to workmen has been introduced as that of arbitration. This doctrine of arbitration appears distinctly set out in the Act 5 Geo. IV. ch. 96, of 1824, a consolidating statute which gets rid of former inequalities, and marks the latest era in English industrial legislation. Yet the arbitration provisions of this act are said not to have worked well in practice, partly, as a writer suggests, because of the requisite intervention of a justice of the peace, partly from its lack of simplicity.[2] But a very recent act establishes "equitable councils of conciliation" to adjust differences between masters and workmen, upon a plan much resembling the French courts of *Prud'hommes*.[3] The plan is, that masters and workmen shall each elect their own delegates to a board or council, which is empowered to fix upon the rate of wages between employer and employed, and otherwise adjust disputes peculiarly appertaining to such service.[4]

1 4 Bl. Com. 160.

2 Macdonald Handybook, 137, — a small and convenient compendium recently published (1868).

3 30 & 31 Vict. ch. 105 (1867).

4 This experiment had been tried in the English manufacturing districts for some years previous to the passage of the act, and with marked success. A celebrated strike at Nottingham, in 1860, led to its first practical application; and though there was then no statute countenancing such a court, manufacturers

There is comparatively little legislation of this sort to be found in our States. Trade is less fettered in America than it was in England; and disputes between master and servant have been generally adjusted between themselves or by the ordinary legal methods. The fluctuation of society in America, the variety of pursuits always open to active competitors, the opportunities freely afforded for social elevation, together with the fact of a wider distribution of our manufacturing population than in England, contribute to the difference. The *employé* of to-day becomes the employer of to-morrow. Yet humane laws are frequently enacted, and still more frequently called for. In Connecticut, Pennsylvania, and other States, children are specially protected from laborious toil unsuited to their years, and the hours of work in the mills are reduced to a proper limit.[1] And young children are to be taught the necessary branches of a common education, notwithstanding their employment.[2]

The relation of apprentice was, in its original spirit and policy, as Kent has observed, calculated to give the apprentice a thorough trade education, and to advance the mechanic arts.[3] To some extent, it has that significance still. The English system, beyond what has just been noticed of working men generally has, however, referred more especially to the poor or parish apprentices, who, under a late act, may be bound out to the sea service as well as a trade.[4] In many American States there appear to exist no provisions for binding out others than poor children and orphans. Again, in other States,

elsewhere were soon led to adopt the system from its manifest convenience. To introduce such a court into England is said to have been a favorite speculation of the late Lord Brougham. See Macdonald Handybook, 274.

[1] See 2 Kent Com. 11th ed. 266, and notes, referring to statutes of Pennsylvania, Maine, New Hampshire, Connecticut, and New Jersey.

[2] There are similar acts in England lately passed. See Factory Acts, 7 Vict. ch. 15; 10 Vict. ch. 29; 16 & 17 Vict. ch. 104; 24 & 25 Vict. ch. 117; 30 & 31 Vict. ch. 103.

[3] 2 Kent Com. 266.

[4] 1 Bl. Com. 426, notes by Chitty and others.

as New York, Massachusetts, and Pennsylvania, the provisions are more general.[1] The principle of such statutes is to permit those having custody to assign to strangers a certain authority over their children, until the latter reach majority; and town authorities, or overseers of the poor, may, in many instances, supply the want of natural protectors. But, inasmuch as the infant's own assent is now made essential to such instruments, so far as binding him beyond the age of discretion is concerned, as courts do not hesitate to disregard them, if at all inequitable, or even if drawn up not in strict conformity to statute, while, as we have seen, the child's freedom to dispose of his time in general when left to earn his living, is very favorably regarded, it cannot be said that apprenticeship by indenture is thought as desirable as formerly. Public authorities may resort to it with advantage for securing good homes to the homeless; parents not equally so; though the poor may often thus secure a trade education for their children without cost to themselves. There can certainly be nothing unreasonable in permitting one of suitable discretion to make any fair contract of service, whether verbal or in writing, and the advantages may often constitute an adequate compensation for his labor. If he be very discreet he will not, however, make a contract to last without possible modification for any great length of time.[2]

[1] See 2 Kent Com. 262, *passim*, 11th ed., and *n.*

[2] There are many English and American decisions as to the mutual rights and duties of master and apprentice, most of which are of local or limited application. The English cases will be found in Macdonald Handybook, 76, 216. Prospective damages cannot be recovered by the master where the apprentice unlawfully quits the service. Lewis *v.* Peachey, 1 H. & C. 518. To make the master liable on his covenant to teach a trade it must appear that the apprentice was ready and willing to be taught. Raymond *v.* Minton, 1 Law Rep. Exch. 244. Such indentures are strictly construed and must be executed according to statute. St. Nicholas *v.* St. Bodolph, 12 C. B. N. S. 645. Questions relating to the conviction of apprentices or workmen for misconduct constantly arise under the English statutes; also as to the parish settlement of pauper apprentices. See Macdonald, 76; ib. 218. Boast *v.* Firth, Law Rep. 4 C. P. 1. In this country, it would appear to be the rule, that contracts of apprenticeship, not executed in strict accordance with statute are invalid; or, rather, are voidable by the parties concerned. Maltby *v.* Harwood, 12 Barb.

To come, then, to the strictly legal relation of master and servant. This contract arises purely upon the hiring. If the

473; Bolton *v.* Miller, 6 Ind. 262. But see Brewer *v.* Harris, 5 Grat. 285. See Page *v.* Marsh, 36 N. H. 305. Yet the relation of master and servant may be inferred, notwithstanding, from the acts and conduct of the parties. Maltby *v.* Harwood, ib.; Page *v.* Marsh, 36 N. H. 305. And see Westlake *v.* Adams, 5 C. B. N. S. 248. In many instances, the courts exercise a supervisory influence; and they will insist upon the provisions being reasonable; in some cases, requiring the insertion of fair covenants on the master's part, such as instruction of the apprentice in some particular trade; and they will even cancel improper indentures. Commonwealth *v.* St. Germans, 1 Brown (Penn.), 24; Owens *v.* Chaplain, 3 Jones (Law), 323; Finch *v.* Gore, 2 Swan, 326; Bakers *v.* Winfrey, 15 B. Monr. 499; Lammoth *v.* Maulsby, 8 Md. 5; Bell *v.* Herrington, 3 Jones (Law), 320. See People *v.* Pillow, 1 Sandf. Sup. 672. Both in this country and in England, the apprentice on reaching full age may abandon the contract, though the rule of avoidance is not expressed with uniformity. Drew *v.* Peckwell, 1 E. D. Smith, 408; Walker *v.* Chambers, 5 Harring. 311; Forsyth *v.* Hastings, 27 Vt. 646; Wray *v.* West, 15 L. T. N. S. 180, Q. B. It is held that overseers of the poor, in binding out paupers as apprentices, act as public officers and not as the agents of their towns. Glidden *v.* Unity, 10 Fost. 104. The master's right of custody as against an unwilling apprentice, who wishes to return to his parents, appears in this country to be quite doubtful, though the indentures be well drawn; the wishes of the child being apparently regarded as paramount. People *v.* Pillow, 1 Sandf. Sup. 672. In several instances, where imperfect indentures had been terminated, the master was held not liable for the apprentice's services on a *quantum meruit*, their original engagement contemplating nothing of the kind. Maltby *v.* Harwood, 12 Barb. 473; Page *v.* Marsh, 36 N. H. 305. And see Van Dorn *v.* Young, 13 Barb. 286. The assignment of apprenticeship is in some States pronounced void, the trust being personal; and in general it is voidable by the infant himself. Tucker *v.* Magee, 18 Ala. 99; Huffman *v.* Rout, 2 Met. (Ky.) 50; Allison *v.* Norwood, Busbee, 414; Commonwealth *v.* Van Lear, 1 S. & R. 248; Phelps *v.* Culver, 6 Vt. 430. Yet the infant's renewed assent may give force to it. See Williams *v.* Finch, 2 Barb. 208; Nickerson *v.* Howard, 19 Johns. 113. And statutes may be found to regulate this subject. In some States, and perhaps in all, infancy is a good plea to action of covenant on such indentures. M'Knight *v.* Hogg, 1 Const. 117. See Phillips *v.* Clift, 4 Hurl. & Nor. 168; Brock *v.* Parker, 5 Ind. 538. As to the construction and method of execution of such indentures, see also Whitmore *v.* Whitcomb, 43 Me. 458; Van Dorn *v.* Young, 13 Barb. 286; Glidden *v.* Unity, 10 Fost. 104; Wright *v.* Brown, 5 Md. 37. For enticement of an apprentice, the master has the usual remedies against third persons. Holliday *v.* Gamble, 18 Ill. 35; Hooks *v.* Perkins, Busbee, 21. Though this seems to be because of the relation of servant rather than apprentice. Cox *v.* Muncey, 6 C. B. N. S. 375. And a father who executes such indenture is bound to exercise his paternal authority to aid in its enforcement. Van Dorn *v.* Young, 13 Barb. 286. See, as to enticement, ch. 4 *infra*. A settlement between master and apprentice made soon after the expiration of the term will be viewed with great jealousy. McGunigal *v.* Mong, hiring be general, without any particular time limited, the old law construes it into a year's hiring.[1] But the equity of this rule applied only to such employment as the change of seasons affected; as where the servant lived with his master or worked at agriculture. By custom, such contracts have become determinable in the case of domestic servants, upon a month's notice, or, what is an equivalent, payment of a month's wages.[2] Laborers are hired frequently by the day, and to hire by the week is not unusual.[3] Yet, as to hiring in general, the rule still is that if a master engage without mentioning the time, it is a general hiring, and in point of law a hiring for a year.[4] Custom modifies this principle, and the date and frequency of periodical payments are material circumstances in each case. The principle of yearly hiring is applicable to all contracts of hiring and service, whether written or unwritten, whether express or implied, and whatever the nature of the service; its modifications arise whenever the contract contains stipulations inconsistent with its application, or where, from some well known custom upon the subject, the parties may be considered to have contracted with sole reference to such custom.[5]

The rule as to hiring does not apply to cases where there has been a service, but no contract of hiring and no circumstances from which a contract can be inferred. And a contract of hiring cannot be presumed where the circumstances tend to rebut such a presumption, as where paupers have been taken

5 Barr, 269. As a rule, except in cases of paupers, both the English and American statutes require that the infant shall execute the deed, if of fourteen, as well as his parents, and the policy of the law is against binding out one of discreet years, unless he is made a party to the instrument. See Reeve Dom. Rel. 3d ed. 342, Editor's notes; 2 Kent Com. 11th ed. 263, 264 and notes; Stats. Vermont, New York, Maine, &c. The infant's informal assent will not bind him. Commonwealth *v.* Moore, 1 Ashm. 123; Squire *v.* Whipple, 1 Vt. 69. It must be distinctly expressed in the indenture. Harper *v.* Gilbert, 5 Cush. 417.

[1] Co. Litt. 42; 1 Bl. Com. 425.

[2] Nowlan *v.* Ablett, 2 Cr., M. & R. 54; Fawcett *v.* Cash, 5 B. & Ad 904; Fewings *v.* Tisdal, 1 Exch. 295.

[3] R. *v.* Pucklechurch, 5 East, 382.

[4] Fawcett *v.* Cash, 5 B. & Ad. 904; See Lilley *v.* Elwin, 11 Q. B. 742.

[5] Smith Mast. & Serv. 41, 42; Rex *v.* Worfield, 5 T. R. 506; Baxter *v.* Nurse, 1 Carr. & K. 10; Hathaway *v.* Bennett, 10 N. Y. 108.

to live with their relatives out of charity,[1] or where the agreement was for cohabitation and not for service.[2]

Where either party is at liberty to determine the service at any time without notice, the hiring cannot be considered a yearly contract.[3] Or if the hiring be expressly for less than a year; although done purposely to avoid the consequences of a yearly hiring.[4] Or if the agreement be to do work by the piece or job.[5] Or if certain portions of the year are specially excepted.[6] Or if the master has not entire control, and the servant is at liberty when not engaged for his master to work for others; though this rule is to be cautiously applied.[7] The same principle holds good where the hours of working are limited by contract.[8]

We find at the outset, then, a distinction made in practice between servants, menial or domestic, and other servants; which distinction is founded upon a custom of dissolving the relation, not at the end of a year, but at any time upon giving the other a month's wages. An English writer says that no general rule can be laid down as to who do and who do not come within the category of menial servants; every case must stand upon its own circumstances.[9] But in a late case, where the subject was fully discussed, the disposition manifested was to extend the word "domestic" beyond the signification "menial;" and a family huntsman was brought within the above rule.[10] The reason is apparently that contracts for servi-

1 Rex *v.* Sow, 1 B. & Ald. 178; Smith Mast. & Serv. 42.

2 Rex *v.* Northwingfield, 1 B. & Ad. 912.

3 Smith Mast. & Serv. 43, 44 and cases cited; Rex *v.* Great Bowden, 9 B. & C. 249, and cases cited.

4 Rex *v.* Standon Massey, 10 East, 576; Dunsford *v.* Ridgwick, 2 Salk. 535; Rex *v.* Coggeshall, 6 M. & S. 264.

5 Rex *v.* Woodhurst, 1 B. & Ald. 325.

6 Rex *v.* St. Helen's, 4 B. & Ad. 726.

7 Rex *v.* Killingholme, 10 B. & C. 802. See Reg. *v.* Ravenstonedale, 12 Ad. & El. 73.

8 Reg. *v.* Preston, 4 Q. B. 597.

9 Smith Mast. & Serv. 2d ed. 52.

10 Nicoll *v.* Greaves, 17 C. B. N. S. 27. The dictionaries furnish little aid on this point.

ces which bring the parties into such close proximity and frequency of intercourse, that they are valuable only when mutually agreeable and otherwise intolerably annoying, should be readily terminated at the option of either party.[1]

A governess engaged at a yearly salary, though residing in the house, is, however, held not to be within the class of menial or domestic servants: regard being paid by the court to the dignity of her position.[2] But the head gardener is, though living not in the master's house, but in his own cottage in the domain.[3]

At the common law, a servant might be hired either by deed or by a parol contract, but when hired or retained by deed he could only be discharged by an equally formal instrument; when hired by parol he might be discharged by parol.[4] But since the enactment of the Statute of Frauds, contracts of hiring must be frequently expressed in writing, in order to be legally effectual. Under this statute, the contract of service may be verbally made and proved if it is capable of performance within a year; otherwise, it must be in writing. Hence, a verbal agreement to hire for a year, commencing at a future day, is insufficient.[5] In short, a contract for personal service which is not to go into operation for a year, or is to continue in force and hold the parties together for a longer period, must be in writing.[6] Yet it seems that a contract made on a certain day to serve for a year from the following day is not within the Statute of Frauds.[7]

Restraint of trade sometimes enters as an element into agreements between master and servant. If professional men,

1 Per Erle C. J. ib. See further, Nowlan *v.* Ablett, 2 C., M. & R. 54; Johnson *v.* Blenkensopp, 5 Jur. 807; Crocker *v.* Molyneux, 3 Car. & P. 470.

2 Todd *v.* Kerrich, 8 Exch. 151; 14 E. L. & Eq. 433.

3 Nowlan *v.* Ablett, 2 C., M. & R. 54.

4 Smith Mast. & Serv. 16; Dalt. Just. cap. 58.

5 Bracegirdle *v.* Heald, 1 B. & Ald. 722; Giraud *v.* Richmond, 2 C. B. 835.

6 See 1 Smith Lead. Cas. 432, and American notes, where this subject is thoroughly examined.

7 Cawthorn *v.* Cordrey, 32 L. J. N. S. C. P. 152.

manufacturers, or tradesmen take clerks, apprentices, or workmen into their employ, and require them to agree that they will not carry on a like profession, manufacture, or trade within certain limits; this for the purpose of securing themselves against competition; the contract, being in restraint of trade, is illegal and void.[1] The general rule is that, in order to render such a contract valid at law, the restraint must be *first*, partial only; *secondly*, upon an adequate, or as the law now seems to stand, not a mere colorable restriction; *thirdly*, reasonable and not oppressive.[2] Even then equity would be loth to enforce it specifically if it be at all hard or even complex;[3] though in many cases it will do so.[4]

To the same head as contracts in restraint of trade belong contracts by which the services of individuals are secured for a specified time, or for life, to a particular master. Contracts for life are not illegal at common law; but they are very strongly objectionable; and, in this country, it is doubtful whether they would ever be enforced, so contrary are they to our public policy.[5] But some writers commend such contracts, and in England agreements whereby, in substance, workmen engaged to serve, for a term of seven years, certain persons or their firm, and on others, at a certain scale of wages subject to determine in the event of sickness or incapacity of the men, or cessation of business by the employer, were considered valid and unobjectionable.[6]

But, in Massachusetts, a contract made by an adult with

[1] Com. Dig. "Trade," D. 3; Mitchel *v.* Reynolds, 1 P. Wms. 181; S. C. 1 Smith Lead. Cas. 508, Am. ed. notes; Lange *v.* Werk, 2 Ohio N. S. 520; Lawrence *v.* Kidder, 10 Barb. 641; Gilman *v.* Dwight, 13 Gray, 356; Duffey *v.* Shockey, 11 Ind. 71.

[2] 1 Smith Lead. Cas. ib.

[3] Kemble *v.* Kean, 6 Sim. 335.

[4] Kemble *v.* Kean, 6 Sim. 335; Benwell *v.* Inns, 24 Beav. 307. And see Smith Mast. & Serv. 51 *et seq.*; Mallan *v.* May, 11 M. & W. 653; Mumford *v.* Gething, 7 C. B. N. S. 305.

[5] See Wallis *v.* Day, 2 M. & W. 277; 1 Smith Lead. Cas. 521.

[6] Pilkington *v.* Scott, 15 M. & W. 657; Hartley *v.* Cummings, 5 C. B. 247. See 1 Smith Lead. Cas. ib.

a citizen of the United States to serve him, "his executors and assigns," for five years, without fixing the nature and extent of the services, or the place of their performance, in consideration of ten dollars, and of being fed, clothed, and lodged, and at the expiration of the contract being paid "the customary freedom dues," is pronounced illegal and void, even if valid where made.[1] "Such a contract, it is scarcely necessary to say, is against the policy of our institutions and laws," was the language of the court.

As a general rule, every person of full age, free from all other incompatible engagements, may become either a master or servant; and the service need not be performed under a legally binding contract, for the service may be constituted *de facto*.[2] The usual law of contracts applies to all who enter the relation. And arrangements for remunerating a servant by a portion of the profits may, under some circumstances, constitute him as partner rather than a mere servant.[3]

The relation of master and servant is created, so far as may affect the rights of third persons, when one suffers another to proceed in a service in which the latter engaged only as a volunteer.[4] Yet one cannot by merely rendering services voluntarily, without request or assent, compel the other to become his debtor.[5]

A municipal or other corporation may sustain the *quasi* relation of master and servant with those in its employ, so as to be liable for the negligence of the person employed.[6] Such a relation between railroad companies and those in their employ, is constantly recognized in the courts.

The two terms, "master and servant" and "principal and

1 Parsons *v.* Trask, 7 Gray, 473. And see Mary Clark's Case, 1 Blackf. (Ind.) 122.

2 Smith Mast. & Serv. 1.

3 Ib. 29.

4 Hill *v.* Morey, 26 Vt. 178.

5 Webb *v.* Cole, 20 N. H. 490; Alton *v.* Mulledy, 21 Ill. 76.

6 See Scott *v.* Mayor of Manchester, 37 E. L. & Eq. 495.

agent," are frequently interchanged as though identical in meaning, and, indeed, one is usually quite as exact as the other. In Ohio, the distinguishing feature of the relation of service has been said to be that the employer keeps control over the mode and manner of work, and this applies to contractor, agent, or servant; independent contracts, however, not falling within the rule.[1] But, in Illinois, contractors building a railroad appear to be treated as servants of the company in a more liberal sense.[2] In Connecticut, it is said, that the manner of paying for work constitutes no criterion, nor the existence of actual present control and supervision on the part of the employer; but that these are both circumstances to be weighed in each case.[3] Where one is neither employed, paid, nor controlled by another, he is not his servant in the legal sense.[4] We have seen that adult children remaining in a family may be *de facto* servants, so as to lay the foundation of certain suits.

We are now to inquire in what manner the relation of master and servant may be terminated. The causes which justify discharge by the master are various, and the rule depends somewhat upon the nature of the particular employment in question. But most decisions are reducible to three leading classes: *First*, wilful disobedience of a lawful order; *second*, gross moral misconduct; *third*, habitual negligence in business, or other serious detriment to the master's interests.[5]

An instance of the first class came before Lord Ellenborough, where a farmer's servant was ordered to go with the horses a mile off just as dinner was ready, and he said he would not go until he had had his dinner.[6] And another, more recent, is where a farm servant refused to work during harvest without

1 Cincinnati *v.* Stone, 5 Ohio N. S. 38.

2 Chicago, &c. R. R. Co. *v.* McCarthy, 20 Ill. 385. There is much difficulty in applying the rule as to railroad contractors. See 1 Redf. Railways, 506.

3 Corbin *v.* American Mills, 27 Conn. 274.

4 McGuire *v.* Grant, 1 Dutch. 356.

5 Smith Mast. & Serv. 70; 2 Kent Com. 259.

6 Spain *v.* Arnott, 2 Stark. 256.

beer.[1] In a carefully considered English case, the court went even so far as to justify dismissal of a house-maid who persisted in leaving the house without permission to visit a sick and dying mother.[2] In these cases, and especially the last, the authority of the master is very strongly upheld; more so, perhaps, than American policy would concede. Where the misconduct is slight, and a first offence, where the reasons for disobedience are extreme, and where the servant's general conduct is exemplary, this, it seems, ought to go strongly in his own justification, for the mutuality of contracts is always properly considered. An obstinate refusal to do an unlawful act is clearly no ground for dismissal.[3]

Instances of the second class are not uncommon. Immorality is sufficient cause for dismissal;[4] even the pregnancy of a maid-servant, according to Lord Mansfield.[5] Embezzlement is a good ground, though the sum embezzled be less than the arrears of wages.[6] The same is true of robbery.[7] Habitual drunkenness is doubtless a good ground, if it seriously interferes with the due performance of the particular service.[8] Acts and conduct which pointedly indicate fraudulent misbehavior towards the master may, and should, justify prompt dismissal.[9]

The third class furnishes many examples; though the rule here is to be laid down with much caution, for a practical application is difficult. There are some English cases where conduct, which might ordinarily seem justifiable on a servant's part, has been punished by dismissal, the court carrying out the prevailing policy against teaching the secrets of trade to

1 Lilley *v.* Elwin, 11 Q. B. 742.

2 Turner *v.* Mason, 14 M. & W. 112. And see Smith Mast. & Serv. 71.

3 See Jacquot *v.* Bourra, 7 Dowl. 348.

4 Atkin *v.* Acton, 4 Car. & P. 208.

5 Cald. 11; ib. 57.

6 Brown *v.* Croft, 6 Car. & P. 16 *n.*; Spotswood *v.* Barrow, 5 Exch. 110.

7 Libhart *v.* Wood, 1 W. & S. 265; Trotman *v.* Dunn, 4 Camp. 211; Smith Mast. & Serv. 72.

8 Gonsolis *v.* Gearhart, 31 Mis. 585. See Lord Denman in Wise *v.* Wilson, 1 Car. & K. 662.

9 See Horton *v.* McMurtry, 5 Hurl. & Nor. 667; Singer *v.* McCormick, 4 W. & S. 266.

strangers or foreigners.[1] So have many decisions seemed to sustain the master, where the servant lacked in blind devotion to his selfish interests, or asserted a generous independence of opinion a little too boldly.[2] But at the present day, certainly in America, more might be claimed for the servant and less for the master. Yet the legal principle is correct that for habitual negligence, or for such conduct as prevents a mutual agreement from being carried out to the reasonable satisfaction of the employer, the person employed may be dismissed; nor would it seem to matter much whether it be through wantonness or palpable inefficiency amounting to a breach of implied undertaking.[3] A servant betraying his master's confidence may, it seems, be discharged.[4] But the relation continues though the master obtains a commitment of the servant to prison.[5] So, where absence is warrantable, or where the absence is temporary for no bad purpose, and the master has suffered no serious loss thereby.[6] Where serious danger, though perhaps not actual damage, is occasioned to the master's business by his servant's conduct, he is justified in dismissing the servant on that account; as if an apothecary's assistant should frequently employ an ignorant shop-boy to make up prescriptions to save himself work.[7] Herein the servant's negligence amounts to a breach of his implied undertaking.

The public profession of an art is a representation and undertaking to all the world that the person professing has the requisite skill and ability. Hence where one is employed as a scene painter, and proves an incompetent person, he cannot sue because of dismissal on this account.[8]

1 Turner *v.* Robinson, 5 B. & Ad. 789.

2 See Lacy *v.* Osbaldiston, 8 Car. & P. 80; Ridgway *v.* Hungerford Market Co., 3 Ad. & El. 171; Amor *v.* Fearon, 9 Ad. & El. 548.

3 See Callo *v.* Brouncker, 4 Car. & P. 518, cited Smith Mast. & Serv. 73.

4 Beeston *v.* Collyer, 2 Car. & P. 609.

5 Rex *v.* Barton, 2 M. & S. 329.

6 Filleul *v.* Armstrong, 7 Ad. & El. 557.

7 Wise *v.* Wilson, 1 Car. & K. 662. Though here the relation was admitted to be not strictly that of servant or apprentice.

8 Harover *v.* Cornelius, 5 C. B. N. S. 236. And see Stanton *v.* Bell, 2 Hawks, 145.

If good ground of discharge exists, and is known to the master at the time of dismissal, it is sufficient to justify the discharge, although he chose to allege some other cause.[1] But it would seem that if the master, at the time he discharged the servant, did not know of any act of misconduct on the servant's part which would justify dismissal, the mere existence of such misconduct would not afterwards avail in his own justification.[2]

A contract of service, like all other contracts, may be dissolved by mutual consent, or by the death of either party, or by the completion of the term of service.[3]

A servant who occupies premises belonging to his master is not presumed to occupy as tenant, but by virtue of the relation of service; and, if such be the case, he acquires no estate therein by the performance of his duties, even though he be also allowed to use the premises for carrying on an independent business of his own.[4] If properly dismissed from the service, therefore, he has no right to remain until ejected upon notice as a tenant; but the termination of his service is likewise the termination of his right to the premises.

[1] Smith Mast. & Serv. 76, and cases cited; Baillie *v.* Kell, 4 Bing. N. C. 638; Ridgway *v.* Hungerford Market Co., 3 Ad. & El. 171; Mercer *v.* Whall, 5 Q. B. 447.

[2] Cussons *v.* Skinner, 11 M. & W. 161. But see Spotswood *v.* Barrow, 5 Exch 110.

[3] See Thomas *v.* Williams, 1 Ad. & El. 685.

[4] White *v.* Bayley, 10 C. B. N. S. 227; Smith Mast. & Serv. 40, 41.

CHAPTER II.

MUTUAL OBLIGATIONS OF MASTER AND SERVANT.

SOME obligations arising from the relation of service rest more especially upon the master; others again more especially upon the servant.

A moral obligation, resting upon every master whose connection with his servant is a very close one, the latter being manifestly on an inferior footing, is to exert a good influence, to regard the servant's mental and spiritual well-being. Positive law enjoins the same duty in a variety of instances with regard to apprentices and workmen under age, by requiring their masters to teach them to read, write, and cipher, to see that they attend public worship, and, in general, to take due care of their morals.[1]

From such view of a master's obligation comes, doubtless, a rule which some deduce from the old books, that a master has the common-law right to chastise his servant or apprentice moderately; but, on principle, the limitation must be to those servants or apprentices under age, who, by positive law, are committed somewhat as children to their master's keeping.[2] The right is denied as to ordinary servants in this country.[3] "The only civil remedies," says an English writer, "a master has for idleness, disobedience, or other dereliction of duty, or breach of contract on the part of a servant, are, either to bring an action against him, or, as Puffendorf expresses it, 'to expel

[1] See Stats. N. Y., Conn., &c., 2 Kent Com. 262 and *n.*

[2] See Bac. Abr. Tit. Master and Servant, N.; 1 Bl. Com. 428; 2 Kent Com. 260.

[3] Commonwealth *v.* Baird, 1 Ashm. 267.

the lazy drone from his family, and leave him to his own beggarly condition.'"[1]

As to necessaries, Kent pronounces the better opinion to be that the master is not bound to provide even a menial servant with medical attendance and medicines during sickness.[2] And so far as special medical attendance furnished an adult servant capable of taking care of himself, is concerned, the rule is so settled;[3] though Lord Kenyon, and perhaps Lord Eldon, once thought otherwise.[4] Yet a master is legally bound to provide medicines for his apprentice.[5] And reference to the authorities will show that, as to domestic servants, courts are not indisposed to infer authority from the master's own conduct.[6] The duty of a master to provide food and other necessaries rests upon contract, express or implied; and it was the English doctrine, as expressed in 1802, that neglect to furnish sufficient food, clothing, or lodging to any infant of tender years unable to provide for and take care of himself, whether child, apprentice, or servant, so as thereby to injure his health, was an indictable offence; which principle a later English statute has extended even further, wherever there is the legal liability to provide necessaries.[7]

How far the master is bound to find work for his servant has sometimes been considered in the courts. The legal principle is that of substantial justice. A master may hire a servant for a certain period, and, paying the wages or salary agreed upon, may keep him in sufficient work or not; but he cannot deprive the servant of his full compensation through

1 Smith Mast. & Serv. 69; Puff. Law Nature, b. 6, ch. 3, § 4.

2 2 Kent Com. 261.

3 Smith Mast. & Serv. 118-120; Wennall *v.* Adney, 3 Bos. & Pull. 247; Sweetwater Co. *v.* Glover, 29 Geo. 399; Clark *v.* Waterman, 7 Vt. 76.

4 Scarman *v.* Castell, 1 Esp. 270; Simmons *v.* Wilmott, 3 Esp. 93.

5 Reg. *v.* Smith, 8 Car. & P. 153.

6 Cooper *v.* Phillips, 4 Car. & P. 581; Sellen *v.* Norman, 4 Car. & P. 80; Friend's Case, Russ. & Ry. C. C. 22. As to indicting the husband rather than the wife, see Rex *v.* Saunders, 7 Car. & P. 277.

7 14 & 15 Vict. ch. 11. See Smith Mast. & Serv. 117.

discontinuance of his own business, or from other like cause.[1] But where the contract of hiring merely contains an undertaking to pay certain stipulated wages in proportion to the work done, there is no implied obligation on the master's part to find work; though the disposition is to construe contracts of doubtful significance into an agreement on the master's part to enable the servant to earn regular and reasonable wages.[2]

It is the duty of every master to indemnify his servant from the consequences of lawful acts, done in pursuance of orders, which the servant was bound to obey. And as to an act not *malum in se*, but which might have been either lawful or unlawful, and which the servant was induced by the conduct of his master to believe to be lawful, the rule of indemnity likewise applies.[3] But it would appear that for an act *malum in se*, or which the servant knew to be unlawful, although done by him in obedience to his master's orders, the master is not bound to indemnify his servant; for the servant should have refused obedience.[4]

It is likewise the duty of the master to receive into his service a person already engaged, and if he fails to do so, he is liable in damages; though here a legally binding contract would have to be shown by the plaintiff.[5] Nor will courts of chancery grant injunction to compel specific performance, except perhaps in cases where the relation exists only by remote analogy and the connection between master and servant is not close; the remedy must otherwise be left to the common-law courts.[6] "Consider," said Lord-Chancellor Truro, "what the effect would be; how is it possible for an employer or an agent to go on in the intimate connection which such a contract is

[1] Aspdin *v.* Austin, 5 Q. B. 671; Elderton *v.* Emmens, 6 C. B. 160; Smith Mast. & Serv. 49, 50.

[2] See Pilkington *v.* Scott, 15 M. & W. 657; Hartley *v.* Cummings, 5 C. B. 247; Smith, ib. 48, 50; Sykes *v.* Dixon, 9 Ad. & El. 693.

[3] Collins *v.* Evans, 5 Q. B. 830; Rawlings *v.* Bell, 1 C. B. 951; Cro. Jac. 468; Story Agency, § 339; Smith Mast. & Serv. 121.

[4] Smith, ib.

[5] Bracegirdle *v.* Heald, 1 B. & Ald. 722; Blogg *v.* Kent, 6 Bing. 614.

[6] Stocker *v.* Brockelbank, 20 L. J. Ch. N. S. 408. See Willis *v.* Childe, 13 Beav. 117.

calculated to create?"[1] So, too, has injunction been lately refused to enforce a contract of apprenticeship, as a proceeding without precedent.[2]

Two remedies, both at common law, are open to every servant who has been wrongfully discharged from his master's employ: one, to treat the contract as a continuing one, and sue in damages for breach thereof; the other to consider it as rescinded, and sue his master on a *quantum meruit* for the services he has actually rendered.[3] Formerly, it was thought that he had a third remedy, namely, to wait till the termination of the period of service, and then sue for his whole wages in *assumpsit*, relying on the doctrine of constructive service;[4] but it would appear that this course cannot now be adopted; for the discharged servant is bound to make the best use of his time.[5]

The first is the remedy usually adopted. To sustain this action, the servant must have been ready and willing to serve; but he need not offer to do so. The amount of damages which he should recover must depend upon the nature of the contract and the wages agreed upon; the jury may exercise a large discretion; and, where no specific wages have been agreed upon, the measure is fixed by considering what is the usual rate of wages for the employment contracted for, and what time would be lost before another situation could be obtained.[6]

The second form of action treats the contract of service and hiring as rescinded; and the ground on which the servant sues is one applicable to contracts in general; namely, that when one party to a contract has absolutely refused to perform some-

[1] Stocker *v.* Brockelbank, ib.

[2] Webb *v.* England, 29 Beav. 44.

[3] Lilley *v.* Elwin, 11 Q. B. 755; Planche *v.* Colburn, 8 Bing. 14; Colburn *v.* Woodworth, 31 Barb. 381.

[4] Gandall *v.* Pontigny, 1 Stark. 157; Collins *v.* Price, 5 Bing. 132; 2 Smith Lead. Cas. 17, *n.* to Cutter *v.* Powell.

[5] Smith Mast. & Serv. 94 *n.*, and cases cited; Fewings *v.* Tisdal, 1 Exch. 295; Beckham *v.* Drake, 2 Ho. Lords Cas. 606; Sherman *v.* Champlain Trans. Co., 31 Vt. 162; Goodman *v.* Pocock, 15 Q. B. 576.

[6] See Beckham *v.* Drake, 2 Ho. Lords Cas. 606; Fewings *v.* Tisdal, 1 Exch. 295; Smith *v.* Thompson, 8 C. B. 44; Given *v.* Charron, 15 Md. 502; Nations *v.* Cudd, 22 Tex. 550; Sherman *v.* Champlain Trans. Co., 31 Vt. 162.

thing essential on his side of the contract, the other party is at liberty to terminate it, and sue for services rendered under a *quantum meruit*.[1] Where this remedy is elected the servant can only recover wages for the period during which he actually served.[2]

But while the servant may elect either of the two remedies he cannot pursue them together; and if he sues on both counts in his action he must take the verdict upon one only.[3]

Wages are due in general for work performed; and although the amount of wages is left to the master, a reasonable remuneration must be given.[4] But the mere existence of a valid contract of hiring and service does not necessarily imply a contract to pay wages; for board, lodging, clothes, or the opportunity of learning business, might be sufficient compensation; particularly in case of the young.[5]

So any employer has a right to judge for himself how he will carry on his own business, and workmen, having knowledge of the circumstances, must judge for themselves whether they will enter his service.[6]

The master is not bound to pay increased wages for increased labor, unless he has contracted to do so.[7] Nor under an ordinary contract of hiring by the day is the person hired bound to prolong his services in order to complete any particular piece of work on which he may happen to be employed.[8] Nor is there any new implied contract to pay wages on simple

[1] 2 Smith Lead. Cas. 17, *n.* to Cutter *v.* Powell, and authorities cited; Smith Mast. & Serv. 99. See Goodman *v.* Pocock, 15 Q. B. 576.

[2] Fewings *v.* Tisdal, 1 Exch. 295.

[3] Goodman *v.* Pocock, 15 Q. B. 576; Colburn *v.* Woodworth, 31 Barb. 381.

[4] Bryant *v.* Flight, 5 M. & W. 114; Peacock *v.* Peacock, 2 Camp. 45; Lawson *v.* Perry, Wright, 242. But see Taylor *v.* Brewer, 1. M. & S. 290. See Goodman *v.* Pocock, 15 Q. B. 576; Costigan *v.* Mohawk R. R. Co., 2 Denio, 609.

[5] Smith Mast. & Serv. 100*n.*; Rex *v.* Shinfield, 14 East, 541; Davies *v.* Davies, 9 Car. & P. 87; Maltby *v.* Harwood, 12 Barb. 473.

[6] Hayden *v.* Smithville, &c. Co., 29 Conn. 548.

[7] Bell *v.* Drummond, Peake, 45.

[8] Wyngert *v.* Norton, 4 Mich. 286.

dissolution of a special contract.[1] The action for wages should, of course, be brought against the person by or for whom the plaintiff was hired; and to ascertain this is not always easy.[2]

The master cannot set off against the servant's claim for wages, money paid by him to his own medical attendant, unless the servant so stipulated.[3] Nor, in an action for an infant's wages money advanced for articles not necessaries; or coach fare for her mother.[4] Nor can he set off against wages a claim for articles lost or broken by carelessness; he should sue in a cross-action.[5] But, in an action of compensation for services, the employer may show, by way of recoupment of damages, loss sustained through the negligence of the person employed.[6]

Modern bankruptcy acts frequently provide that servants or clerks shall be preferred to general creditors in the distribution of assets.[7] It would appear that the bankruptcy of the master does not, *per se*, dissolve a contract of hiring; yet, the assignees cannot let out personal services for him.[8]

The death of the master discharges his servant; and, according to the strict rule of law, it would appear that where the contract is entire for a year's service, and neither custom nor statute intervenes, the death of the master in the middle of the year utterly deprives the servant of compensation for the broken period.[9] A contract of apprenticeship, in so far as it was a personal contract, is also terminated by the master's

1 Lamburn *v.* Cruden, 2 Man. & Gr. 253.

2 See Smith Mast. & Serv. 104, 105, and cases cited.

3 Sellen *v.* Norman, 4 Car. & P. 80.

4 Hedgeley *v.* Holt, 4 Car. & P. 104.

5 Le Loir *v.* Bristow, 4 Camp. 134.

6 Still *v.* Hall, 20 Wend. 51; Pixler *v.* Nichols, 8 Iowa, 106; English *v.* Wilson, 34 Ala. 201. See as to an infant, Meeker *v.* Hurd, 31 Vt. 639. And see Stoddard *v.* Treadwell, 26 Cal. 294.

7 See 12 & 13 Vict. ch. 106; also United States Bankruptcy Acts.

8 See Thomas *v.* Williams, 1 Ad. & El. 685; Williams *v.* Chambers, 10 Q. B. 337.

9 Wms. Ex'rs, 644; Smith Mast. & Serv. 111. But see Jackson *v.* Bridge, 12 Mod. 650.

death.[1] But the rule of apportionment is now so much favored that it is apprehended to be unlikely that a construction so inequitable would in this day be permitted to apply to contracts which left the intention of the parties in doubt on this point. And custom is applicable, in the case of domestic servants at least, so as to give them wages for the whole time served, though they do not continue in service for a year.[2] The executors or administrators of the master, are the persons to whom a servant must look for such arrears; not an intermeddler with the estate, nor kindred.[3] In some States, wages of domestic servants and laborers are made preferred debts; independently of statute, it is not probable that they are so entitled.[4] Legacies, if actually bequeathed to servants, are sometimes held to extinguish claims against the master's estate for wages.[5] On legal principle, moreover, when a servant dies in the middle of the term for which engaged, his representatives can, it seems, claim nothing; but here again might custom apply the rule of apportionment.[6] So where the servant leaves wrongfully, or is dismissed by his master for rightful cause, the periodical pay-day not having come round, he can claim nothing *pro rata*.[7] Yet, with regard to the common case of a hired servant, though the hiring be in a general way, the understanding is common that the servant shall be entitled to his

[1] Bac. Abr. Tit. Master and Servant, G. But statutes are not always to this effect. Phœbe *v.* Jay, 1 Bre. 268.

[2] Cutter *v.* Powell, 6 T. R. 320; Smith Mast. & Serv. 112.

[3] 2 Wms. Ex'rs, 822 *n.*, 3d ed.; Welchman *v.* Sturgis, 13 Q. B. 522.

[4] 2 Wms. Ex'rs, ib. But see 2 Bl. Com. 511.

[5] See Booth *v.* Dean, 1 Myl. & K. 560; Smith Mast. & Serv. 343 *et seq.* But when work is rendered in consideration of a future legacy, and the legacy is not left, the servant may sue on a *quantum meruit.* See Nimmo *v.* Walker, 14 La. An. 581.

[6] Smith Mast. & Serv. 115; Cutter *v.* Powell, 6 T. R. 320.

[7] 2 Smith Lead. Cas. 17, *n.* to Cutter *v.* Powell; Dalt. Just. Ch. 58, p. 129; Spain *v.* Arnott, 2 Stark. 236; Turner *v.* Robinson, 6 Car. & P. 15; Ridgway *v.* Hungerford Market Co., 3 Ad. & El. 171; Lane *v.* Phillips, 6 Jones (Law), 455; Whitley *v.* Murray, 34 Ala. 155; Marsh *v.* Rulesson, 1 Wend. 514.

wages for the time he serves.[1] Unless some such rule could be enforced, the stronger party would be constantly tempted to make dismissal a pretext for refusing to pay to the weaker the little pittance which was justly due.

Where the performance of a condition is prevented by the act of God it is excused.[2] And where one performs services under a contract, and is, before the expiration of the full period, disabled by sickness or inevitable accident from completing his contract, he is entitled to recover as upon a *quantum meruit* for the period of such disability.[3] Yet it seems that where illness or other cause renders one permanently incompetent to perform his contract this is a sufficient cause of dismissal, if the employer choose to so regard it.[4]

Where the agreement provides that either party may terminate it at any time, the servant may quit at any time on his own motion, and recover on the contract for services rendered.[5] But if the servant agrees to work for a given time, with the privilege of leaving if dissatisfied, he cannot recover if he leaves without alleging dissatisfaction, but merely to attend to other business.[6]

If the contract, though for a certain period, be terminated by mutual consent, recovery may be had on a *quantum meruit* for the services actually performed.[7] And work accepted by the employer, though not done according to the terms of the contract, must be paid for at its fair value, not exceeding the stipulated price.[8] So a person employed on a particular service

1 See remarks in Cutter *v.* Powell, *supra;* Smith Mast. & Serv. 116. And see Kessee *v.* Mayfield, 14 La. An. 90; Gates *v.* Davenport, 29 Barb. 160; Massey *v.* Taylor, 5 Cold. 447; Costigan *v.* Mohawk R. R. Co., 2 Denio, 609.

2 Cruise Dig. Condition, 41, 43.

3 Wolfe *v.* Howes, 20 N. Y. 197; Cuckson *v.* Stones, 1 El. & El. 248; Fenton *v.* Clark, 11 Vt. 557; Seaver *v.* Morse, 20 Vt. 620.

4 See Harmer *v.* Cornelius, 5 C. B. N. S. 236; Cuckson *v.* Stones, *supra;* Seaver *v.* Morse, 20 Vt. 620.

5 Evans *v.* Bennett, 7 Wis. 404.

6 Monell *v.* Burns, 4 Denio, 121.

7 Given *v.* Charron, 15 Md. 502.

8 English *v.* Wilson, 34 Ala. 201; Dermott *v.* Jones, 23 How. (U. S.) 220.

by the month or year, may have a right to compensation for services rendered on request, out of the range of such employment, even without express contract as to the terms of payment.[1] Conditions precedent, such as submission of work to inspectors, performance according to the estimate of third parties, special stipulations and the like, may enter into such contracts.[2] And where the agreement was that the value of labor and services should be applied in payment of land for the purchase of which no written contract had been made out, it was held that an action for the value of the labor and services would not lie.[3]

But if I sell land to another to be paid for in work which he presently performs, and I then refuse to convey, he may recover pay for his work.[4] So it was held where the defendant had contracted to sell the plaintiff a house, which the plaintiff, with the defendant's knowledge and without objection from him, put in repair, and also performed labor in part-payment; and where afterwards he was prevented from completing his contract by the fault of the defendant; that he might recover for both the labor performed and the value of the improvements.[5]

Where a person engaged the services of a thatcher for a certain period at weekly wages for the purpose of hiring him out to do thatching work for his profit; and the thatcher during the period of employment thatched some stacks for the employer, for which work he received and claimed special compensation; it was held that the thatcher was responsible to his employer for injury to the wheat occasioned by the negligent manner in which he performed the work.[6]

[1] Cincinnati, &c. R. R. Co. *v.* Clarkson, 7 Ind. 595.

[2] See Baason *v.* Baehr, 7 Wis. 516; Butler *v.* Tucker, 24 Wend. 447.

[3] Congdon *v.* Perry, 13 Gray, 3.

[4] Leach *v.* Rogers, 28 Geo. 247.

[5] Wright *v.* Haskell, 45 Me. 489.

[6] Holmes *v.* Onion, 2 C. B. N. S. 790; Pixler *v.* Nichols, 8 Iowa, 106; English *v.* Wilson, 34 Ala. 201. But as to an infant servant, see Meeker *v.* Hurd, 31 Vt. 639.

Mr. Starkie observes that the giving a character of a servant is one of the most ordinary communications which a member of society is called on to make, but it is a duty of great importance to the interests of the public; and in respect of that duty a party offends grievously against the interests of the community in giving a good character where it is not deserved, or against justice and humanity in either injuriously refusing to give a character, or in designedly misrepresenting one to the detriment of the individual.[1] But, as Mr. Smith remarks, "In the absence of any specific agreement to that effect, there is no *legal* obligation binding a person who has retained another as a servant, to give that person any character at all on dismissal; and no action will lie against him for refusing to do so.[2] And the decisions on this subject fully establish the principle that representations of a servant's character, oral or written, are on the footing of privileged communications; and that wilful misrepresentation must appear on the master's part to render him liable; not merely wrong and unfair statements made in good faith and without malicious intent.[3]

Of the mutual liabilities of master and servant, some are to be discussed with more especial reference to the latter than the former. Thus the servant, once engaged by a valid contract to enter his employer's service, cannot refuse or neglect to do so without becoming liable in damages; though whether the master may care to pursue his remedy is another matter.[4] The same may be said of one who, without sufficient cause, leaves his employment before the legal termination of the period agreed upon.[5] That the service is unpleasant or the labor severe would not alone justify his departure.[6]

1 1 Stark. Slander, 293.

2 Smith Mast. & Serv. 222; Carrol *v.* Bird. 3 Esp. 201.

3 Ib. 223–250, and cases cited; Fountain *v.* Boodle, 3 Q. B. 12; Hodgson *v.* Scarlett, 1 B. & Ald. 240; 2 Stark. Slander, 58.

4 See Richards *v.* Hayward, 2 Man. & Gr. 574; Smith Mast. & Serv. 64.

5 Bird *v.* Randall, 3 Burr. 1345; Lees *v.* Whitcomb, 5 Bing. 34.

6 Angle *v.* Hanna, 22 Ill. 429.

While performing service under his contract the servant is bound to regard the interests of his master. He cannot, it would appear, solicit his master's customers into his own business, so long as his engagement lasts, without rendering himself liable to action; but it is held that he can do so when the service is at an end, and he sets up for himself.[1] He must account to his employer, like all other agents, for money or other goods received in the line of duty; and except in certain cases, cannot set up the *jus tertii* in opposition to the latter's interests.[2] So is the servant liable for gross negligence in the care of his master's property entrusted to him; though not for ordinary accidents.[3]

Servants are also liable for fraud and misfeasance, as in cases of simple bailment generally. Suits of this sort, strictly applicable to servants, are extremely rare; but there are instances to be found in the old books. Thus it is said that if a man deliver a horse to his servant to go to market, or a bag of money to carry to London, which he neglects to do, the master may have an action of account or detinue against him.[4] So is the servant liable in a suit brought by his master to indemnify the latter from the consequences of his negligence or misconduct.[5]

The old writers say that the servant may justify a battery in the necessary defence of his master; and the master, as the

[1] Nichol *v.* Martyn, 2 Esp. 732. Yet we presume that this action would lie, if the servant had availed himself, to his master's injury and his own profit, of certain peculiar facilities derived under the contract of employment, though he waited till the engagement ended before making use of them.

[2] See Story Agency, § 217, and note; Dixon *v.* Hamond, 2 B. & Ald. 310; Smith Mast. & Serv. 67, and cases cited; Murray *v.* Mann, 2 Exch. 538; Cheesman *v.* Exall, 6 Exch. 341.

[3] Savage *v.* Walthew, 11 Mod. 135; Bac. Abr. Tit. "Master and Servant," M. I.; Smith Mast. & Serv. 65.

[4] Bac. Abr. Tit. "Master and Servant," M.

[5] Green *v.* New River Co., 4 T. R. 589; Pritchard *v.* Hitchcock, 6 Man. & Gr. 165; Smith Mast. & Serv. 66. But see Colburn *v.* Patmore, 1 Cr., M. & R. 73.

weight of argument goes, may do the same on his servant's behalf.[1]

A mere agent or servant is a competent witness for his principal or master, from public convenience or necessity.[2]

[1] See 2 Kent Com. 261; 1 Bl. Com. 429; Hawk. P. C. 61, ch. 60, §§ 23, 24.

[2] Wainwright *v.* Straw, 15 Vt. 215; Stringfellow *v.* Mariot, 1 Ala. 573; Doe *v.* Himelick, 4 Blackf. 494; 1 Greenl. Evid. § 416; 1 Phill. Evid. 10th ed. 507 *et seq.*

CHAPTER III.

RIGHTS AND LIABILITIES OF THE SERVANT AS TO THIRD PERSONS.

As a general rule, servants are not liable personally on contracts entered into by them on behalf of their masters. Such a principle would be inconsistent with the very relation. But, like any other agent, a servant may make himself liable, provided he contract on his own and not his master's behalf.[1] Questions of this sort turn upon circumstances; as to whom for instance the credit was given. But if there be a wrong or omission of right on the servant's part; if, for instance, he transcends his powers, or acts without authority, like all other agents, he becomes personally liable to the person with whom he deals in his master's name.[2] For, in respect to such contract, he is no servant at all, but one who wilfully or innocently misrepresents himself as such.

Instances of this principle occur in the every-day transactions of life. A broker who puts his own name to a bill of exchange, without words to imply an agency, renders himself personally liable to a stranger.[3] The receipt of a servant is the receipt of his master, for money rightfully paid him in the course of business.[4] A sheriff's deputy is not liable to a judgment creditor for money collected by him under an execution in the creditor's favor.[5]

1 Smith Mast. & Serv. 194; Story Agency, § 261; Owen *v.* Gooch, 2 Esp. 567; Thomson *v.* Davenport, 9 B. & C. 88.

2 Smout *v.* Ilberry, 10 M. & W. 1; Paterson *v.* Gandasequi, 15 East, 62; s. c. 2 Smith Lead. Cas. 358.

3 Leadbitter *v.* Farrow, 5 M. & S. 345; Jones *v.* Littledale, 6 Ad. & El. 486.

4 Bamford *v.* Shuttleworth, 11 Ad. & El. 926.

5 Colvin *v.* Holbrook, 2 N. Y. 126.

The reason of the general rule of exemption is, that the principal or master, not the agent or servant, shall answer for the consequences of the latter's contract. The servant is directly responsible to his master, not then to strangers.[1]

But, as Lord Kenyon has observed, the principle does not apply to cases where there is corruption in the foundation of the contract, or it is bottomed in oppression or immorality.[2] Where money is obtained by means of trespass or tort; where a servant misappropriates a fund entrusted to him to be paid to others; in these and similar cases it has been held that the servant is suable by third persons.[3]

If, for instance, a debtor sends by his own servant money which he owes his creditor, and the servant refuses to deliver it, and retains it, an action for the money may be maintained by the creditor against the servant. But it is otherwise if the debtor countermanded his orders and received the money back from the servant.[4]

In cases of tort, the rule is general that all persons concerned in the wrong are chargeable as principals. For a misfeasance, therefore, or positive wrong, which affects the person or property of another, the servant cannot shield himself by the excuse that he acted merely in obedience to his master's orders, or for his master's benefit.[5] It is said that in such a case he is sued, not as a deputy or servant, but as a wrongdoer.[6]

But a distinction is taken between misfeasance and nonfeasance. For mere negligence, or nonfeasance, the servant

[1] See Shearm. & Redf. Negligence, 128; Smith Mast. & Serv. 194 *et seq.*

[2] Miller *v.* Aris, 3 Esp. 232; Smith Mast. & Serv. 204.

[3] Buller *v.* Harrison, Cowp. 565; Tugman *v.* Hopkin, 4 Man. & Gr. 389; Howell *v.* Batt, 5 B. & Ad. 504.

[4] Lewis *v.* Sawyer, 44 Me. 332.

[5] Sands *v.* Child, 3 Lev. 352; Lane *v.* Cotton, 12 Mod. 488; Perkins *v.* Smith, 1 Wils. 328; Smith Mast. & Serv. 213, 214; Richardson *v.* Kimball, 28 Me. 463; Bennett *v.* Ives, 30 Conn. 329; Johnson *v.* Barber, 5 Gilm. 425. See Hill *v.* Caverly, 7 N. H. 215.

[6] See Lane *v.* Cotton *supra*, per Lord Holt.

is not liable to a stranger.[1] Thus where a banker is employed to collect a note, which he puts into the hands of another banker, through whose negligence the debt is lost, the creditor cannot sue the latter banker, though he was the one actually in fault.[2] This same principle is applied in Massachusetts, to protect one servant from the injurious consequences of his own wrongful acts to a fellow-servant whenever such acts amount to nothing more than mere negligence or carelessness.[3] So the servant of a carrier is not generally responsible for the loss of a parcel, to the owner, who should look to the master.[4]

Government is not liable for the torts and frauds of its agents. Nor are public officers in general liable for the misdeeds of their subordinates. Thus the Postmaster-General cannot be sued for the loss of letters in the post-office through the fault of his agents.[5] Public policy furnishes, perhaps, the strongest reason for this doctrine. "As to an action lying against the party really offending," Lord Mansfield, however, observed, "there can be no doubt of it; for whoever does an act by which another person receives an injury, is liable in an action for the injury sustained."[6] And in several instances have deputy postmasters been sued in damages for their own torts.[7] So are certain public officers, as sheriffs, and others, acting in a purely ministerial capacity, frequently held to answer the consequences of their misconduct.[8]

1 See Lane *v.* Cotton *supra*, per Lord Holt.

2 Montgomery Bank *v.* Albany Bank, 7 N. Y. 459.

3 Albro *v.* Jaquith, 4 Gray, 99. And see Brown *v.* Lent, 20 Vt. 529. But see Phelps *v.* Wait, 30 N. Y. 78.

4 Williams *v.* Cranstoun, 2 Stark. 82. See Smith Mast. & Serv. 213 *et seq.*

5 Whitfield *v.* Lord Le Despencer, Cowp. 765. Nor should he be, since he is but the servant of government; the common employer of both superior and subordinate officials. See 4 Am. Law Rev. 1–17.

6 Ib. And see Smith Mast. & Serv. 219.

7 See 5 Burr. 2709, 2711, 2715.

8 Bac. Abr. Tit. "Sheriff."

CHAPTER IV.

RIGHTS AND LIABILITIES OF THE MASTER AS TO THIRD PERSONS.

In this chapter we shall discuss, *first*, the rights, *second*, the liabilities, of the master as concerns third persons.

First, as to his rights. The right of action to the master for personal injuries sustained by his servant is recognized in several instances.[1] This right grows out of the loss of service sustained by the master, and the same principle has been noticed with reference to parents. A service *de facto* is sufficient in all such cases.[2]

Again, the action for seduction depends upon the existence of the relationship of master and servant; and the loss of service gives the right of action. This action is usually brought by the parent, or one standing in the stead of a parent; though legal remedy is not perhaps confined to such persons.[3]

For enticing away or harboring one's servant the common law also gives the right of action against the offending party; and where a person, *after notice*, continues to employ another man's servant, that other, it is said, may maintain an action against him, although at the time he hired him the second master did not know that he was hiring another man's servant; whence it follows that one who did not entice may yet be liable for harboring.[4] The mere attempt to entice a servant away,

[1] See Duel *v.* Harding, Str. 595; Hall *v.* Hollander, 4 B. & C. 660; Hodsoll *v.* Stallebrass, 11 Ad. & El. 301; Dixon *v.* Bell, 1 Stark. 287.

[2] Smith Mast. & Serv. 83–85 and cases cited; Bac. Abr. Tit. "Mast. & Serv." O.

[3] See Parent and Child *supra*; Smith Mast. & Serv. 85 *et seq.*

[4] Fawcet *v.* Beavres, 2 Lev. 63; Smith Mast. & Serv. 79; Blake *v.* Lanyon, 6 T. R. 221; Bird *v.* Randall, 3 Burr. 1352; Reg. *v.* Daniel, 6 Mod. 99, 182. And see Lumley *v.* Gye, 2 Ell. & Bl. 216, where the question is fully discussed. But laches may be imputable to the master. Demyer *v.* Souzer, 6 Wend. 436.

no damage following, would not entitle the master to maintain an action.[1] Nor will the action lie after the master has recovered from the servant a stipulated penalty for leaving the service;[2] nor for inducing a servant to leave at the expiration of the time for which he was hired, though he had no previous intention of leaving.[3]

A binding contract between the servant and his first master must, of course, be shown.[4] Nor can the injured party of two, socially equal, who occupy a relation of constructive service, rely with certainty upon the force of language to help him through his suit against a stranger. In a late English case, some doubts were expressed whether this remedy was to be extended beyond the case of menial servants and laborers; whether, in fact, the higher classes could claim its benefit at all in matters growing out of their mutual contracts.[5] The general rule of the law is certainly to confine its remedies by action to the contracting parties, and to damages directly and proximately consequent on the part of him who is sued; the case of master and servant is exceptional.[6] The right of action in cases, founded upon the pure relation of service, is not greatly favored in this country.[7]

The old rule was that a master deprived of the services of an apprentice or servant by the enticement or harboring of another, might sometimes waive the tort, and sue for the wages due from the second master: the maxim being, that the acquisition of the servant was the acquisition of the master; but, as

1 Bird *v.* Randall, 3 Burr, 1352.

2 Ibid.

3 Nichol *v.* Martyn, 2 Esp. 734; Boston Glass Manufactory *v.* Binney, 4 Pick. 425.

4 See Smith Mast. & Serv. 79 and cases cited. Sykes *v.* Dixon, 9 Ad. & El. 693; Campbell *v.* Cooper, 34 N. H. 49.

5 Lumley *v.* Gye, 2 Ell. & Bl. 216. This suit was with reference to the enticement of Wagner, the vocalist, from one theatre to another. The majority of the court (Coleridge J. dissenting) thought the action would lie, even though the parties were not strictly master and servant.

6 See Coleridge J. ib. And see Ashley *v.* Harrison, 1 Esp. 48.

7 See Scidmore *v.* Smith, 13 Johns. 322; Peters *v.* Lord, 18 Conn. 337.

Mr. Smith has observed, this rule applied more strictly during the existence of villenage.[1] Most of the cases to sustain this principle relate to apprentices in a seafaring way; but it is thought to extend to servants in general.[2]

What a servant may acquire during the relation of service entirely without the legitimate consideration of such service, does not belong to the master. This rule must be reasonably and beneficially applied according to circumstances. One may become bound by a contract for hiring, but, if not an absolute slave, he may generally gain something for himself otherwise if he choose. Thus, if one in the service of another, not employed to invent, make an invention, the patent-right is his, and not his master's.[3]

It is held in New Hampshire, that if a servant, having his master's money for a specific purpose, make use of it in performing a service which he, without his master's privity, has undertaken for another, the master cannot, by afterwards adopting the servant's act as his own, charge that other party upon the contract made by him with the servant.[4]

Second. As to the master's liabilities. A master is liable for the act of his servant, done in the course of his employment about his master's business.[5] Supposing I have a servant, and that servant is in the habit of purchasing the family supplies, in the course of his usual employment; his contracts for such purchases will bind me. But is that simply because he is my servant? If his usual employment be upon the farm, and I never gave him authority to make purchases, he cannot bind me by going to the store merely because he happens to be my servant. So I can authorize others to purchase family supplies: it may be my wife, or my child, or any friend. In all

[1] See Smith Mast. & Serv. 80, 81.

[2] Co. Litt. 117 *a*, *n.*; Smith *supra* and cases cited; Lightly *v.* Clouston, 1 Taunt. 112.

[3] Bloxam *v.* Elsee, 1 Car. & P. 558. But see Smith Mast. & Serv. 82.

[4] Webb *v.* Cole, 20 N. H. 490.

[5] Helyear *v.* Hawke, 5 Esp. 72.

such cases, then, I am bound because, as is commonly said, I have constituted another my agent, not strictly because I have a servant.

No power, therefore, can be inferred from the relation of master and servant, it is said, by which the latter can bind the former.[1] Mr. Smith states the principle more correctly, when he says that the power which a servant possesses of binding his master by contracts is founded upon, *or rather is the basis of*, the general law of principal and agent.[2] For in truth, it would seem that the relation of master and servant is the older at the law. However this may be, the rule is properly stated, at the present day, to be that the servant can only bind his master as his agent; and this on the principle, common to both branches of the law, that the act of the servant or agent is, in fact, the act of his master or principal: the maxim being, *Qui facit per alium facit per se.*[3]

The well-known rules of agency need not, then, be set out here at any length. We only observe that the contract of a servant, in order to bind the master, must be within the scope of his authority; that this authority may be expressly conferred or may be implied from the master's conduct; that subsequent ratification of the servant's acts is as binding as a previous authority; that the authority of a servant is coextensive with his usual employment, and the scope of his authority to be measured by the extent of his employment.[4] All these principles the reader will find much more fully illustrated in any treatise upon agency than in one which professes to take up simply the law of the domestic relations. There may be servants for a variety of purposes; there may be agents for a variety of purposes; and between servant and agent is as yet

[1] Moore *v.* Tickle, 3 Dev. 244.

[2] Smith Mast. & Serv. 122. See Bac. Abr. tit. "Master & Servant," K.

[3] Ib. And see Co. Litt. 52 *a*; Story Agency, §§ 7, 8.

[4] See Story Agency, §§ 74, 75; ib. § 239, *et seq.*; Bird *v.* Brown, 4 Exch. 798; Smith Mast. & Serv. 123–126; Co. Litt. 207 *a*; Bac. Abr. tit. "Authority," B; 2 Kent Com. 612 *et seq.*

no strict line of legal demarcation. In general, a master is not liable on the contract of his servant, unless the servant, at the time he entered into it, assumed to act as his agent.[1] But this principle is not artificially applied, the question of actual intent prevailing.[2]

Where a servant is employed to transact business, and has no particular orders with reference to the manner in which that business is to be transacted, he is considered as invested with all the authority necessary for transacting the business entrusted to him and which is usually entrusted to agents employed in similar matters. In every case, such authority embraces the appropriate means to accomplish the desired end.[3] Thus, a servant sent, without money, to buy goods, has implied authority to pledge his master's credit.[4] And in numerous instances the master has been considered bound by his servant's warranty, that being usual in effecting certain sales; though not where the warranty is subsequent to the sale and not part of the same transaction;[5] for the rule is general that acts and admissions by the servant out of the course of his employment will not bind the master.[6]

There is an important legal distinction between general agents and special agents; hence comes the rule that wherever a master has held out his servant as his general agent, whether in all kinds of business, or in transacting business of a particular kind, the master will be bound by the servant's act, if within the scope of his usual employment, notwithstanding

[1] Wilson *v.* Tumman, 6 M. & G. 236; 4 Inst. 317; Walker *v.* Hunter, 2 C. & B. 334.

[2] See Trueman *v.* Loder, 11 Ad. & El. 594, 595; Smith Mast. & Serv. 132.

[3] Story Agency, §§ 60, 85; Smith Mast. & Serv. 128; Cox *v.* Midland Counties R.R. Co., 3 Exch. 278; Howard *v.* Baillie, 2 H. Bl. 618.

[4] Tobin *v.* Crawford, 9 M. & W. 718. And see Weisger *v.* Graham, 3 Bibb, 313.

[5] See Murray *v.* Mann, 2 Exch. 538; Alexander *v.* Gibson, 2 Campb. 555; Helyear *v.* Hawke, 5 Esp. 72; Woodin *v.* Burford, 2 Cr. & M. 391; Saunderson *v.* Bell, 2 Cr. & M. 304; and other cases cited in Smith Mast. & Serv. 129, 130.

[6] Fairlie *v.* Hastings, 10 Ves. 128; Story Agency, § 136; Garth *v.* Howard, 8 Bing. 451.

the servant has acted contrary to his master's orders.[1] This is a principle of frequent application.[2] But where a servant is employed by his master to act for him in a single transaction, he must be regarded as the special agent of his master; and in such case it is incumbent upon every one dealing with him, who wishes to charge his master upon his contracts, to inquire into the extent of his authority, as, should he exceed it, his master will not be bound.[3]

Since the nature of the usual employment of a servant is the measure of his implied authority, it follows that this authority can neither be limited by the private instructions of the master nor controlled by any secret agreement between him and his servant. "If this could be done," says a recent writer, "in what a perilous predicament would the world stand in respect of their dealings with persons who may have secret communications with their principal. There would be an end of all dealing but with the master."[4] But if a third party knows of private agreements or instructions, he cannot, of course, charge the master upon any inconsistent contract; for it enters an element into his own dealings with that servant.[5]

Hitherto we have spoken of the master's liability on his servant's contracts; now we come to his civil liability for the servant's torts. This subject receives at the present day more attention in the courts than any other topic of the so-called law of master and servant; perhaps more than all the other topics together. Here we find not only the maxim *qui facit per alium facit per se* cited (so well applied to the law of agency), but that other, more strictly appropriate to the present relation, *respondeat superior*. The universal rule is that whether

1 Smith Mast. & Serv. 132–135; Story Agency, §§ 126, 127.

2 See Nickson *v.* Brohan, 10 Mod. 109; Rimell *v.* Sampayo, 1 Car. & P. 255. See Jordan *v.* Norton, 4 M. & W. 155.

3 Smith Mast. & Serv. 137; Ward *v.* Evans, 2 Ld. Raym. 928; Waters *v.* Brogden, 1 Y. & J. 457.

4 Smith Mast. & Serv. 133; 10 Mod. 110.

5 Howard *v.* Braithwaite, 1 Ves. & B. 209.

the act of the servant be of omission or commission, whether his negligence, fraud, deceit, or even wilful misconduct, occasion the injury, so long as it be done in the course of his employment, his master is responsible in damages to third persons.[1] And it makes no difference that the master did not authorize, or even know, of the servant's act or neglect; for even if he disapproved or forbade it, if the act be done in the course of the servant's employment, he is none the less liable.[2]

So far is this doctrine carried that a master is even held liable for an injury occasioned by the wanton and violent conduct of his servant in the performance of an act within the scope of his employment. Thus where the conductor of an omnibus, in removing therefrom a passenger whom he deemed to be intoxicated, forcibly dragged him out and threw him upon the ground, so that he was seriously injured, it was held that the proprietor was liable.[3]

Whether an act amounts to negligence, misfeasance, and the like, is to be determined in each case by its own circumstances.[4] But among the many instances which have been considered as falling within the rule are these: Negligent driving by a servant.[5] The negligent kindling of a fire.[6] Piling up wood improperly.[7] Mismanagement of a boat whereby another is injured.[8] Fraud committed in the course of the servant's employment.[9] And it is to be observed that the master's responsibility is not confined to those who work under his

1 Story Agency, § 452; Smith Mast. & Serv. 151, 152; Shear. & Redf. Negligence, 65.

2 Smith ib.

3 Seymour *v.* Greenwood, 7 Hurl. & Nor. 355.

4 See Crofts *v.* Waterhouse, 3 Bing. 319.

5 Michael *v.* Alestree, 2 Lev. 172; Jones *v.* Hart, 2 Salk. 441.

6 Filliter *v.* Phippard, 11 Q. B. 347. This principle is frequently applied to fires caused by locomotive engines. See Smith Mast. & Serv. 153, *n.*

7 Harlow *v.* Humiston, 6 Cow. 189.

8 Page *v.* Defries, 7 Best & S. 137; Huzzey *v.* Field, 2 C., M. & R. 432.

9 Story Agency, § 264; Southern *v.* How, Cro. Jac. 471.

immediate supervision, but extends to all others whom he selects to do any work or superintend any business for him.[1]

A master is liable, though the act of the servant was not necessary for the proper performance of his master's orders, or was even contrary thereto; so long as the servant is acting in execution of his master's orders.[2] Perhaps this may not readily be understood. But take the common instance of negligent driving; where, we shall suppose, a coachman injudiciously, but not wantonly, turns his horses so as to run down another's carriage.[3] Unless the rule of liability were carried to such an extent, we should find masters constantly escaping the consequences of their servants' behavior.

But a master is not responsible for any act or omission of his servants which is not connected with the business in which they serve him and does not happen in the course of their employment.[4] Beyond the scope of his authority, the servant is as much a stranger as any other person. Thus, where a servant is employed only to harrow one field and watch a fire in another, and he undertakes besides to burn a pile of rubbish.[5] So, where one who is authorized to distrain cattle trespassing on his master's land, drives the horses of a neighbor on to the land and then distrains them.[6] It should be remembered that, to render one person liable for another's wrongs, the relation of master and servant, or principal and agent, must exist between them.[7]

1 Rex *v.* Hoseason, 14 East, 605; Laugher *v.* Pointer, 5 B. & C. 554; Wayland *v.* Elkins, 1 Stark. 272. As if he should employ a baliff, steward, or superintendent. How far this principle might be extended, it is useless to speculate.

2 Smith Mast. & Serv. 157.

3 Croft *v.* Alison, 4 B. & Ald. 590; Joel *v.* Morison, 6 Car. & P. 501; Sleath *v.* Wilson, 9 Car. & P. 607. And see Illidge *v.* Goodwin, 5 Car. & P. 190.

4 Smith Mast. & Serv. 160; Shaw *v.* Reed, 9 W. & S. 72; Harriss *v.* Mabry, 1 Ired. 240; Lowell *v.* Boston & Lowell R.R. Co., 23 Pick. 24; Shearman & Redf. Negligence, 69; Foster *v.* Essex Bank, 17 Mass. 500; Brown *v.* Purviance, 2 Har. & Gill, 316.

5 Wilson *v.* Peverly, 2 N. H. 548. And see Oxford *v.* Peter, 28 Ill. 434.

6 Lyons *v.* Martin, 8 Ad. & El. 512; Goodman *v.* Kennell, 3 Car. & P. 167; Lamb *v.* Lady Palk, 9 Car. & P. 629; M'Kenzie *v.* McLeod, 10 Bing. 385.

7 Stevens *v.* Armstrong, 6 N. Y. 435.

Some cases might lead to the belief that a master is liable for the careless driving of his servant, because he entrusts him with the carriage.[1] This is not correct. The true principle is that, while a master is liable where the servant is in the line of his employment at the time of committing an injury, though he may go out of the way, and do his work in an improper and roundabout manner, yet this liability does not extend further. Take, for example, a late case, where the master sent his carman and clerk to deliver some wine and bring back some empty bottles, and on their return, when about a quarter of a mile from the office, the carman, instead of doing as he was bidden, and putting up the horses, was induced by the clerk to drive in quite another direction on business of the clerk's, and thus injured a person in the street; the master was held not to be liable.[2] The distinction in such cases is not always clear, as examination will show.

It has been held that a servant could have no implied authority to do that which it would not be lawful, under any circumstances, for either him or his employer to do.[3] Nor does presumption of authority arise from the fact of the act being done for the master's benefit, or from his silence with regard to it.[4] Nor, on general principles, is the master liable if the person injured was not in the exercise of ordinary care at the time of the injury.[5] Many decisions indicate the doctrine that for wilful acts of the servant the master is not responsible; but this exemption usually seems to rest in reality upon the

[1] Sleath *v.* Wilson, 9 Car. & P. 607.

[2] Storey *v.* Ashton, Law Rep. 4 Q. B. 476. And see Mitchell *v.* Crassweller, 13 C. B. 237; 16 E. L. & Eq. 448; Whatman *v.* Pearson, Law Rep. 3 C. P. 422; Limpus *v.* London, &c. Co., 1 Hurl. & Colt. 526; Patten *v.* Rea, 2 C. B. N. S. 606; 40 E. L. & Eq. 329; Bard *v.* Yohn, 26 Penn. St. 482; Crockett *v.* Calvert, 8 Ind. 127; Wright *v.* Wilcox, 19 Wend. 343.

[3] Poulton *v.* Southwestern R. R. Co., Law Rep. 2 Q. B. 534. See Russell *v.* Irby, 13 Ala. 131.

[4] Church *v.* Mansfield, 20 Conn. 284.

[5] Smith Mast. & Serv. 161; Butterfield *v.* Forrester, 11 East, 60.

ground that the acts complained of were not done in the course of the servant's employment.[1]

We find, however, many cases where a distinction is maintained at the common law between actions on the case for negligence, unskilfulness, and carelessness, and actions for trespass, so far as concerns the master's liability to third parties. In the latter class of cases, the principle of master and servant is considered not to apply; for the master is not responsible unless he command the act or concur in it; while, again, a man may be liable in trespass for the act of one not strictly his servant.[2] Thus, if the command be express, the master is liable; so if trespass be the necessary consequence of obeying his orders;[3] so if he be present and does not prevent the injury;[4] but not where there is no exercise of volition, either express or implied, on his part.[5] Says Parke B., "The result of the authorities is, that if a servant, in the course of his master's employ, drives over any person, and does a wilful injury, the servant, and not the master, is liable in trespass; if the servant by his negligent driving causes an injury, the master is liable in case; if the master himself is driving, he is either liable in case for his negligence, or in trespass, because the act was wilful."[6] The American cases are also very numerous where the master has been excused from the consequences of the wilful and wanton trespass of his servant; though the disposition seems not strong to maintain any such technical distinction between different kinds of injuries. Thus if the engineer of a train purposely run over an animal on the

1 See Shearm. & Redf. Negligence, 73; Harris *v.* Nicholas, 5 Munf. 483; Moore *v.* Sanborne, 2 Mich. 519; Wright *v.* Wilcox, 19 Wend. 343.

2 Smith Mast. & Serv. 172–177, and cases cited.

3 Gregory *v.* Piper, 9 B. & C. 591; Lyons *v.* Martin, 8 Ad. & El. 512. See Eastern Counties R. R. Co. *v.* Broom, 6 Exch. 314.

4 Chandler *v.* Broughton, 1 C. & M. 29.

5 McManus *v.* Crickett, 1 East, 106, per Kenyon C. J.; Sharrod *v.* London & Northwestern R. R. Co., 4 Exch. 580.

6 Gordon *v.* Rolt, 4 Exch. 365.

track, or if the driver of a wagon wantonly injure a boy who asked a ride with him, the master is held not liable, though the servant be at the time occupied about his employer's business.[1]

But to apply the foregoing principle in all its strictness is not easy. Thus there are instances when railway companies have been held liable for apparently wanton and wilful acts of their conductors.[2] After all, the principle of scope of the servant's employment seems best to explain the extent of the master's liability; and the American cases appear to have applied it, whatever the nature of the injury.[3]

The rule as to real and personal estate is, in this respect, substantially the same. Thus, where one agreed to convey land to another, and the second party agreed to build a house thereon, and pay for the land; and while the agreement was in force, the workmen of the second party undermined the wall of an adjoining house, it was held that the first party was not answerable for the injury, though the title to the land still remained in him.[4] The general principle to be extracted from the cases, in regard to the use of real property, is, that the owner of real estate, either absolutely, or for the time being; he who has the management and control, and takes the benefit and profit of the estate; he at whose expense and on whose account the business is conducted; shall be responsible to third persons for the carelessness, negligence, or want of skill, of those who are carrying on and conducting the business by which they are damnified.[5]

1 Illinois Central R. R. Co. *v.* Downey, 18 Ill. 259; Vanderbilt *v.* Richmond Turnpike Co., 2 N. Y. 479; Shearm. & Redf. Negligence, 72; Wright *v.* Wilcox, 19 Wend. 343; Moore *v.* Sanborne, 2 Mich. 519; Harris *v.* Nicholas, 5 Munf. 483; Johnson *v.* Barber, 5 Gilm. 425.

2 Weed *v.* Panama R. R. Co., 17 N. Y. 362; Milwaukee & Miss. R. R. Co. *v.* Finney, 10 Wis. 388. And see Seymour *v.* Greenwood, 7 Hurl. & Nor. 355.

3 See Shearm. & Redf. Negligence, 72.

4 Earle *v.* Hall, 2 Met. 353.

5 Per Shaw C. J., ib. See Benedict *v.* Martin, 36 Barb. 288; Luttrell *v.* Hazen, 3 Sneed, 20; Elder *v.* Bemis, 2 Met. 599; Simons *v.* Monier, 29 Barb. 419. The single case of nuisance may be excepted, ib.; Hilliard *v.* Richardson, 3 Gray, 349; Harlow *v.* Humiston, 6 Cow. 189.

But for a nuisance on land by which injury is occasioned, the owner or occupant may be liable to others, through his own contributory negligence. Thus where an excavation in front of a building was left open and unguarded, and although this was done by a contractor for the work, yet it continued for some time after the owner of the premises had knowledge of its condition, and had been notified by the authorities of the danger, the owner was held liable for an injury occasioned by falling into the hole.[1]

An exception to the master's responsibility for the tortious acts of his servant is found in the rule, now well settled in England and America, that a master is not responsible to his own servant for any injury which the latter may sustain through the negligence or wrongful act of a fellow-servant, unless the master has been negligent in his selection of the servant at fault.[2]

The application of this rule is usually to railway companies; but all who occupy the relation of master and servant come within its scope. A late case in the English House of Lords, decided on appeal, to the effect that the employers of a manufacturing establishment are not responsible for injuries to their *employés* under these circumstances, places the much-contested doctrine on settled foundations, so far as concerns that country.[3] The Lord Chancellor, in delivering his opinion in this case, referred with approval to the usual argument urged in favor of the rule; namely, that the workman who contracts to do work of any particular sort, knows, or ought to know, to what risks he is exposing himself, and should make his contract accordingly.[4]

1 Chicago *v.* Robbins, 2 Black, 418. See Clark *v.* Fry, 8 Ohio St. 358; Brackett *v.* Lubke, 4 Allen, 138.

2 Smith Mast. & Serv. 187; Priestley *v.* Fowler, 3 M. & W. 1; Hutchinson *v.* York, &c. R. R. Co., 5 Exch. 343; Farwell *v.* Boston & Worcester R. R. Co., 4 Met. 49; Bartonshill Coal Co. *v.* Reid, 3 Macq. H. L. 266; Abrah m *v.* Reynolds 5 Hurl. & Nor. 143; Shearm. & Redf. Negligence, 101, and cases cited; Sherman *v.* Rochester R. R. Co., 17 N. Y. 153.

3 Wilson *v.* Merry, Law Rep. 1 Sc. App. 326.

4 Ib.

So it is held on like grounds that a master is not liable to his servant for any defects in the materials furnished to the latter for use in the master's service, unless he was negligent in providing such materials or in pointing out their defects.[1] In short, ordinary care and diligence on his part will protect the master from liability to his own servants; and ordinary care is usually presumed to exist, in absence of proof to the contrary.[2] But for his own negligence a master is liable to his own servants as to any one else.[2] And it is incumbent upon him to use ordinary care in the selection of servants,[3] and in the procurement of materials.[4]

The principle of a master's liability for his own negligence as respects his servant is well illustrated by the curious case of *Marshall* v. *Stewart.* Here, a miner who was employed in the defendant's mine, went down as usual to his day's work, but he and the other miners, after working a short time, held a meeting amongst themselves to discuss their supposed wrongs; and they resolved to go up from the pit at noon, the usual hour of their return being five o'clock in the afternoon, and represent their grievances together to the manager. While so coming up, this miner was killed by a stone which fell from the top of the shaft. In the lower court, it was ruled that his legal representatives had no cause of action, inasmuch as he was leaving his work without proper cause and for a purpose of his own, and thus received the injury. It appeared in evidence that the planking at the mouth of the pit was in an unsafe state, and therefore the stone fell. When the case came

[1] Shearm. & Redf. Negligence, 103, and cases cited.

[2] Shearm. & Redf. 104; Roberts *v.* Smith, 2 Hurl. & Nor. 213; Brydon *v.* Stewart, 2 Macq. H. L. 30; Cayzer *v.* Taylor, 10 Gray, 274; Ashworth *v.* Stanwix, 3 El. & El. 701.

[3] Gilman *v.* Eastern R. R. Co., 10 Allen, 233; Faulkner *v.* Erie R. R. Co., 49 Barb. 324. The English statement of the rule is that "Negligence cannot exist if the master does his best to employ competent persons; he cannot warrant the competency of his servants." Tarrant *v.* Webb, 25 Law J. N. S. Com. Pl. 263.

[4] Ryan *v.* Fowler, 24 N. Y. 410; Williams *v.* Clough, 3 Hurl. & Nor. 258.

before the House of Lords, the ruling of the lower court was reversed, on the principle that, whether the miner was leaving his work properly or not, still the master was liable, being bound to take him up just as safely as he let him down. Lord-Chancellor Cranworth urged that while the master's liability for accidents occasioned by his neglect towards those whom he employs, extends only to the time of their actual employment, great latitude must be given to the phrase "engaged in his employment." Whatever the servant does in the course of his employment according to the fair interpretation of the words, *eundo, morando, et reduendo*, for all that the master is responsible.[1]

The rule that a master is not responsible to one servant for the negligence of another, applies to the case of a person who is injured while voluntarily assisting the servant.[2] A guest, a friend, a relative, any one engaged in the same common work, comes within the principle. So, too, where an owner gave general directions to his servant to throw the snow and ice from his roof, and a friend of the servant voluntarily assisted him in the work, the owner was held liable for an injury caused by ice and snow thrown by the one as well as the other.[3]

But where the servant of a certain firm, who was employed by the defendants to carry cotton from a warehouse, was receiving the cotton upon his dray, and, in consequence of the negligence of the defendants' porters, in lowering the bales from above, a bale fell upon him, it was held that he was not deprived of the right of action.[4] For though in some respects they were both performing work for the same master; yet they were not under the same control, or forming part of the same establishment, or employed in one common object.

To determine who do and who do not occupy the legal rela-

[1] Marshall *v.* Stewart, 2 Macq. Ho. Lords, 30; 33 E. L. & Eq. 1. But see Paterson *v.* Wallace, 28 E. L. & Eq. 48.

[2] Degg *v.* Midland R. R. Co., 40 E. L. & Eq. 376; Potter *v.* Faulkner, 1 Best & Smith, 800.

[3] Althorf *v.* Wolfe, 22 N. Y. 355.

[4] Abraham *v.* Reynolds, 5 Hurl. & Nor 143.

tion of master and servant, so as to lay the foundation of an action for negligence is then a matter of considerable difficulty. Who is the actual master; and who is the actual servant? Many such controversies arise where railroads are in the hands of contractors and in process of construction.[1] So a police officer, or a fireman, is not necessarily a servant of the city, so as to take away his right of action for an injury; and the same may be said of other public officers.[2] But an express agent, lawfully travelling, may be a servant of the company, where employed by the superintendent of the road to act as brakeman during one trip.[3] It is essential that the relation *de facto* should have existed at the time of the injury complained of; for while, on the one hand, a mere volunteer may then be a servant, in legal contemplation, a general servant who has completed his particular employment may be constructively out of the service when the accident occurs.[4]

A "fellow-servant," within the meaning of the rule of a master's exemption from liability, is usually understood to be any one serving the same master, and under his control, whether equal, inferior, or superior to the injured person in his grade or standing.[5] Of course, the mere fact that two persons are engaged in ministering to the wants of one individual, does not necessarily make them fellow-servants; thus, one may have clerks in his office business, and domestics at his home; they are not engaged in a common employment.

Yet should this distinction, though often exceedingly difficult of application in the perplexed and complicated relations of

[1] 1 Redf. Railw. 3d ed. 506–509.

[2] Kimball *v.* Boston, 1 Allen, 417; Palmer *v.* Portsmouth, 43 N. H. 265.

[3] Chamberlain *v.* Milwaukee R. R. Co., 11 Wis. 238. And see Stone *v.* Codman, 15 Pick. 297; Flint *v.* Gloucester Gas-Light Co., 9 Allen, 552.

[4] See Brown *v.* Purviance, 2 Har. & Gill, 316.

[5] Faulkner *v.* Erie R. R. Co., 49 Barb. 324; Shearm. & Redf. Negligence, 115; Feltham *v.* England, Law Rep. 2 Q. B. 33; Wigmore *v.* Jay, 5 Exch. 354. But in some of the Western States this rule appears to be relaxed somewhat for the injured servant's benefit. Louisville & Nashville R. R. Co. *v.* Collins, 2 Duv. 114; Little Miami R. R. Co. *v.* Stevens, 20 Ohio, 415.

modern business, be reasonably enforced. The latest English doctrine is certainly in favor of the master's exemption in cases of doubt: for, the Lord Chancellor observes in *Wilson* v. *Merry*, "I do not think the liability, or non-liability, of the master to his workmen can depend upon the question whether the author of the accident is not, or is, in any technical sense, the fellow-workman, or *collaborateur* of the sufferer. In the majority of cases in which accidents have occurred, the negligence has, no doubt, been the negligence of a fellow-workman; but the case of the fellow-workman appears to me to be an example of the rule, and not the rule itself. The rule, as I think, must stand upon higher and broader grounds."[1] The expressions "fellow-workmen," "*collaborateur*," "foreman," "manager," and the like, when used in a strict or limited sense, are, it may be added, calculated to mislead; especially when used in connection with railroad, mining, and manufacturing corporations; hence, some apparent confusion arises. We must always look at the functions the party discharges, and his position in the organism of the force employed, and of which he forms a constituent part.[2]

As a general rule, the master is not criminally liable for the acts of his servants, unless he expressly command or personally co-operate in them. Each offender against public justice must answer for himself.[3] Where one, however, procures innocent agents to do acts amounting to a felony, the employer and not the innocent agent, is held accountable; for this is his own act.[4] As to penalties, the rule in this country is sometimes understood to be the same.[5] Yet, penal actions in general have more the character of civil suits than of criminal proceedings;

1 Wilson *v.* Merry, Law Rep. 1 Sc. App. 326, *supra.* Lord Cranworth and the others concurred in this opinion, and their remarks are to the same purport.

2 See remarks of Lord Colonsay in Wilson *v.* Merry, *supra.*

3 Smith Mast. & Serv. 143; Story Agency, § 452; Rex *v.* Huggins, 2 Ld. Raym. 1574.

4 Reg. *v.* Bleasdale, 2 Car. & K. 166.

5 Deerfield *v.* Delano, 1 Pick. 465; Goodhue *v.* Dix, 2 Gray, 181; Shearm. & Redf. Negligence, 78.

and, under the revenue laws, penalties are frequently imposed upon the master.[1] So again are masters indicted for public nuisances committed by their servants.[2] This is the English rule. Some of the proceedings authorized by statute against corporations in this country for damages caused by the negligence of their servants will be found to contain a like principle.

The foregoing brief statement of principles may suffice for the present treatise in its limited space and scope. To enter upon the law further, or to attempt an analysis of the numerous and conflicting cases which constantly arise at the present day under what might be called the analogies of master and servant would be at present impossible. We trust in time to see the topic of master and servant confined to its legitimate and proper limits, as one of the domestic relations, and some new and more comprehensive title applied to such decisions as clearly affect mankind in the external concerns of life.

[1] See Smith Mast. & Serv. 145–147; Attorney General *v.* Siddon, 1 Cr. & J. 220; Atcheson *v.* Everitt, Cowp. 391.

[2] 1 Bl. Com. 431, 432; Turberville *v.* Stampe, 1 Ld. Raym. 264.

INDEX.

A.

B.

C.

E.

M.

R.

W.

Cambridge: Press of John Wilson & Son.